MW01071230

FUNDRAISING

SAGE was founded in 1965 by Sara Miller McCune to support the dissemination of usable knowledge by publishing innovative and high-quality research and teaching content. Today, we publish more than 850 journals, including those of more than 300 learned societies, more than 800 new books per year, and a growing range of library products including archives, data, case studies, reports, and video. SAGE remains majority-owned by our founder, and after Sara's lifetime will become owned by a charitable trust that secures our continued independence.

Los Angeles | London | New Delhi | Singapore | Washington DC

FUNDRAISING
PRINCIPLES AND PRACTICE

MICHAEL J. WORTH
The George Washington University

Los Angeles | London | New Delhi
Singapore | Washington DC

Los Angeles | London | New Delhi
Singapore | Washington DC

FOR INFORMATION:

SAGE Publications, Inc.
2455 Teller Road
Thousand Oaks, California 91320
E-mail: order@sagepub.com

SAGE Publications Ltd.
1 Oliver's Yard
55 City Road
London, EC1Y 1SP
United Kingdom

SAGE Publications India Pvt. Ltd.
B 1/I 1 Mohan Cooperative Industrial Area
Mathura Road, New Delhi 110 044
India

SAGE Publications Asia-Pacific Pte. Ltd.
3 Church Street
#10-04 Samsung Hub
Singapore 048763

Acquisitions Editor: Maggie Stanley
eLearning Editor: Robert Higgins
Editorial Assistant: Nicole Mangona
Production Editor: Jane Haenel
Copy Editor: Mark Bast
Typesetter: Hurix Systems Pvt. Ltd
Proofreader: Laura Webb
Indexer: Terri Corry
Cover Designer: Janet Kiesel
Marketing Manager: Liz Thornton

Copyright © 2016 by SAGE Publications, Inc.

All rights reserved. No part of this book may be reproduced or utilized in any form or by any means, electronic or mechanical, including photocopying, recording, or by any information storage and retrieval system, without permission in writing from the publisher.

Printed in the United States of America

Library of Congress Cataloging-in-Publication Data

Worth, Michael J.

Fundraising : principles and practice / Michael J. Worth.

pages cm
Includes bibliographical references and index.

ISBN 978-1-4833-1952-0 (pbk. : alk. paper)

1. Fund raising. 2. Nonprofit organizations. 3. Charities. I. Title.

HV41.2.W67 2016
658.15'224—dc23   2015011366

This book is printed on acid-free paper.

SUSTAINABLE FORESTRY INITIATIVE
Certified Chain of Custody
Promoting Sustainable Forestry
www.sfiprogram.org
SFI-01268
SFI label applies to text stock

15 16 17 18 19 10 9 8 7 6 5 4 3 2 1

Contents

Detailed Contents

2 Understanding the Nonprofit Sector and Nonprofit Organizations

3 Understanding Donors

6 Annual-Giving Programs   147

7 Major-Gifts Programs 175

10 Foundation Support

11 Campaigns   299

12 Managing Fundraising Programs

13 Organizing and Managing Fundraising Staff

14 Legal and Ethical Considerations   381

15 International Fundraising and Philanthropy   411

Preface

This book is intended to serve as a core text in courses related to fundraising offered by colleges and universities. Many of these courses are offered as part of the curriculum in degree programs and certificate programs related to the broader fields of nonprofit management, social work, education, museum studies, and others. Many also are offered in schools of professional studies or continuing education that prepare students for careers in the nonprofit sector. It is not intended as a text for courses that take a theoretical approach to the nonprofit sector or philanthropic studies. It is not intended to provide a foundation for the academic study of fundraising or philanthropy but for students who are preparing for careers as nonprofit professionals. But it also is not a how-to manual specifically intended for use in short-term training programs, although instructors in such programs who wish a more academic approach may find it useful. Most students enrolled in courses using this text are likely either to have no experience in fundraising or to be early in their fundraising careers, but ideally some experienced practitioners may find that it adds perspectives on some points. While this book includes a chapter on international fundraising, its focus is on fundraising for nonprofit organizations and institutions in the United States, in which most students studying with this text are likely to pursue their careers.

BLEND OF THEORY AND PRACTICE

The book assumes that students are preparing for positions of *leadership* in the nonprofit sector and thus seek both an understanding of relevant theory and research *as well as* insights on practical applications. Its purpose is to define central terms and concepts of fundraising but also to engage students in thinking critically about issues in philanthropy and fundraising practice. It reflects the author's view that an effective fundraising professional needs a broad understanding of the nonprofit sector and organizations and the concerns of donors and funders as well as fundraising skills. Accordingly, this book emphasizes principles and concepts; it provides references to both academic works and more hands-on material, available in print and on the web, for students who may wish to explore more in either direction. It may be of interest to students studying outside the United States, where organized fundraising is a growing activity, but it is based on the U.S. system and the cases generally relate to American organizations and institutions.

This text provides a comprehensive *overview* of topics related to fundraising, but it is *selective* in the discussion of each. There are entire books devoted to each of the topics represented by individual chapters in this text, and students are encouraged to pursue additional reading. This text thus serves as a *menu*, on which students may "click" to delve more deeply into any of the topics discussed.

Consistent with its purpose and intended audience, this text takes a balanced approach, encompassing principles described in the extensive practitioner literature, produced by organizational fundraisers and consultants over the past century, as well as the growing, but still relatively limited, body of academic work specifically focused on fundraising, including dissertations, books, and articles in peer-reviewed journals. It includes insights from some of the pioneers of fundraising who wrote decades ago, as well as new ideas related to contemporary and emerging practices. The author recognizes that this approach runs the risk that some pragmatic readers may find it too academic and that some academics may find it insufficiently grounded. But this balanced approach is intentional, in order to provide a comprehensive and useful overview of a field that is still developing and that remains a mix of art and science.

Case studies and discussion questions are included with every chapter to enable the application of principles to real-world situations and to encourage students' analytical thinking. Examples and cases in this text are drawn from various nonprofit subsectors. Differences among types of organizations are highlighted and discussed in terms of how they may affect the application of principles and practices in those environments.

OVERVIEW OF CHAPTERS

The topics covered in this text closely follow those in my graduate course in the Trachtenberg School of Public Policy and Public Administration at The George Washington University, Managing Fundraising and Philanthropy, which I have offered for more than thirteen years. Indeed, I have tried to adopt a conversational, somewhat informal tone in this text, similar to how I might address students in the classroom.

The Introduction includes my reflections on changes in the fundraising profession over the decades encompassed by my own career. The Conclusion likewise includes some of my views on the role of fundraising professionals in their organizations, now and in the future. Both may be considered optional reading for students.

Chapters 1 through 5 establish an important foundation for the balance of the book. The first chapter provides an introduction to fundraising and philanthropy as those activities have developed historically in the United States. The second chapter offers an overview of the nonprofit sector and nonprofit organizations, including a summary of theories that explain the sector and the behavior of organizations. This chapter, as well as some other sections of the book, draws on material included in my earlier textbook, *Nonprofit Management: Principles and Practice* (Worth, 2014). Students who have previously taken a course on general nonprofit management may find this chapter useful as a refresher or may decide to skim it. However, it is essential reading for students who have no such previous experience, since fundraising practice is fundamentally related to the unique non-profit environment. Chapter 3 provides a survey of the literature regarding donor behavior and motivations, including practitioner wisdom and the findings of research. It also considers the implications for giving of increasing diversity and a multicultural nation. Chapter 4 introduces fundamental fundraising principles, many of which are elaborated on in later chapters where they are most relevant. Chapter 5 discusses organizational preconditions for successful fundraising and actions that organizations take to establish them.

Chapters 6 through 11 are focused on specific fundraising programs, methods, and strategies, including annual giving, major gifts, planned giving, foundation and corporate support, and campaigns. Much of the material in these chapters is drawn from the practitioner literature, but in keeping with the overall approach of the book, academic research and theories are cited as they may apply, either to confirm or challenge the assumptions of conventional practice.

Additional chapters discuss the management of fundraising programs and development staff and consider significant legal and ethical principles. These topics are considered later in the book, not because I regard them as unimportant but because I think many students can best understand their implications after establishing a foundation of knowledge in the field. The concluding chapter is focused on international and global fundraising and philanthropy and may be optional reading for students who have an interest in that broader perspective. Excluding optional material, the book provides one chapter per week for a fourteen-week course; of course, reading also can be accelerated to fit a different course calendar.

This book is for any student who desires an understanding of fundraising. Not all of them will be planning to pursue careers as fundraising professionals. Some may be considering careers in general nonprofit management or expect to engage with nonprofit organizations in other roles. But there is some emphasis on the role of fundraising professionals, that is, development officers. It is my hope that some students who start this book not planning on a fundraising career may be considering one upon its completion.

The overall philosophy of the book is that fundraising is an honorable and important specialization within the field of nonprofit management, providing the opportunity of fulfilling careers and advancing the vital missions of the important organizations and institutions that philanthropy supports.

INSTRUCTOR TEACHING SITE

A password-protected site, available at study.sagepub.com/worthfundraising, features resources designed to help instructors plan and teach their course. These resources include exam questions, chapter-specific PowerPoint presentations, an instructor guide, and videos.

Acknowledgments

I am grateful to SAGE Publications for undertaking this book, which is the second of my titles that SAGE has published. In particular, I express thanks to my editor, Maggie Stanley, for her support and encouragement.

I thank the reviewers whose comments have been helpful as this book evolved. They include the following:

Rick J. Arrowood, Northeastern University

T. Gregory Barrett, University of Arkansas at Little Rock

Rosemary Bonacci, Utica College

Patricia H. Deyton, Simmons College School of Management

Michael J. Goff, Independent Sector

Ann Haugland, University of Iowa

Patrick A. Kelsey, Savannah College of Art and Design

I offer special thanks to John Kendrick, assistant vice president at The George Washington University, for his review and comment on Chapter 8 (Planned Giving).

My work on this project has been ably supported by my graduate assistants at The George Washington University, including Molly Callaghan (2012–2013), Brittney Seiler (2013–2014), and Gretchen Wieland (2014–2015).

Finally, I am grateful for the many lessons I have learned from the talented fundraising professionals who have been my colleagues over the years, as well as the insights that academic researchers have added to our body of knowledge. Fundraising is a noble profession, practiced by people whose efforts make the world a better place.

Michael J. Worth
Professor of Nonprofit Management
The George Washington University
Washington, DC

About the Author

Michael J. Worth is professor of nonprofit management in the Trachtenberg School of Public Policy and Public Administration at The George Washington University in Washington, DC. He was vice president for development and alumni affairs at George Washington for eighteen years, where he planned and directed two comprehensive campaigns. He previously served as director of development at the University of Maryland College Park. Earlier in his career, he was assistant to the president at Wilkes University and director of development at DeSales University.

Dr. Worth has served as a member of the Commission on Philanthropy of the Council for Advancement and Support of Education (CASE) and as editor of the *CASE International Journal of Educational Advancement*. He has written academic and practitioner-oriented books related to fundraising, governing boards, and nonprofit management. Works include *Leading the Campaign* (2010) and the textbook *Nonprofit Management: Principles and Practice* (3rd ed., 2014).

Dr. Worth provides fundraising and management advice to educational institutions, national associations and institutions, and nonprofit organizations. He holds a BA in economics from Wilkes College, an MA in economics from The American University, and a PhD in higher education from the University of Maryland.

Introduction

From Chance to Choice

In June 1972, Hurricane Agnes moved north over the East Coast of the United States, delivering record-breaking rains. Eventually downgraded to a tropical storm, it remained stationary over upstate New York for days, continuing to dump rain and swelling the Susquehanna River to a record level. The Susquehanna runs from New York State through Pennsylvania and Maryland and into the Chesapeake Bay and had always been prone to flooding. But Agnes was unprecedented and the river rose to a historic height, threatening to erode and exceed the levees built to protect the city of Wilkes-Barre, Pennsylvania, then a community of some 50,000 people and the heart of a metropolitan area that included a few hundred thousand.

I was at the time employed at Wilkes College (now Wilkes University), with its campus located along the banks of the Susquehanna near downtown Wilkes-Barre. I had graduated from Wilkes just a few years earlier, pursued a graduate degree, and then returned for the attractive opportunity to teach introductory economics and work part of my time as assistant to the president. I knew little about how the college obtained its resources and essentially nothing about fundraising.

When the levees gave way, a wall of water over forty feet high crashed into the city and the surrounding area. It destroyed a cemetery, disinterring the remains of many people. It carried vehicles along like surfboards, depositing them in jumbled piles. It destroyed many homes and commercial buildings close to the river and severely damaged others, covering many to their rooftops. That included the fifty-eight buildings on the campus of Wilkes College.

When I eventually was able to make my way back to the campus many days later, after passing through checkpoints the National Guard maintained to limit access and provide security to the stricken area, the devastation was shocking. Bulldozers were pushing books out from the bottom floor of the library, where they had sunk into a mush. Cranes were lifting waterlogged grand pianos from the performing arts center through holes that had been cut in the roof. There was a pervasive stench from the mud that covered everything. I ran into the college's president, Francis J. Michelini, known to everyone as "Dr. Mike," as he walked across the campus in boots, surveying the damage and directing some crews that had already begun the task of restoration. I asked if there was anything I could do to help, given that the president's office was full of debris and lacked electricity, making it problematic for me to immediately resume my usual administrative duties. And it was summer, so I was not teaching.

"Here's our situation," he explained. "We have less than three months to rebuild this campus or we're out of business. If we don't open for classes in September, the students

1

will go elsewhere and we will not have the revenue to pay the faculty, so they will leave, too. It is going to cost about $20 million [1972 dollars] to restore this campus and I have signed contracts totaling that amount. But it is money we just don't have."

The college's director of development, Tom Kelly, who was responsible for fundraising, had been in his job only a brief time and his office was essentially a one-person operation. "Here's what you can do," the president suggested. "Go over and work with Tom and see how much money you guys can raise between now and September." And so Tom and I set up shop on the top floor of the administration building, powered by a generator, provided with a temporary phone line, and armed with a copy of the *Foundation Directory* and a list of alumni. Our charge was to raise the money for what Dr. Michelini had named "Operation Snapback," the effort to save the college from which we both had graduated just a few years before.

Throughout the summer, we feverishly wrote letters, made phone calls, and visited corporations, foundations, and individuals, carrying photographs of the devastation and asking for their help. Many were moved and responded generously, although there were also some who expressed reservations. What if we were not successful? What if we could not raise the money and the college was forced to close? What would happen to their money then? We provided assurance that we would not fail and were sustained by Dr. Michelini's unfailing optimism and determination. By early September we had raised, by my recollection, several million dollars, a considerable amount for that time but not enough to pay the $20 million bill coming due. Then, in the second week of September—the nick of time—President Richard Nixon arrived on campus to personally deliver a federal grant to cover the balance of the cost. It had proven quite helpful that our local congressman was a senior member of the House of Representatives Committee on Appropriations. His name, ironically, was Daniel J. Flood. The college survived and does today.

Many people lost their homes and all their possessions in the 1972 Agnes disaster. Lives were forever changed. I was fortunate not to have suffered substantial tangible losses, although some members of my family did. But my life was changed as well. I learned about the rewards that come from working for a cause with the goal of sustaining an important institution. I experienced the satisfaction that comes from interacting with a wide variety of interesting and accomplished people, who generously share their personal resources to support a cause. I decided to pursue a fundraising career.

Eventually I moved on, serving as director of development and public relations at Allentown College (now DeSales University), director of development at the University of Maryland College Park, and vice president for development and alumni affairs at The George Washington University, a position I held for more than eighteen years. I was also professor of education while serving as vice president and taught part-time. In 2001, I joined the full-time faculty of the Trachtenberg School of Public Policy and Public Administration as professor of nonprofit management and began to consult on fundraising with educational institutions and nonprofit organizations of various types, broadening my experience and perspective beyond higher education to the larger nonprofit sector.

The beginning of my fundraising career surely was under highly unusual circumstances. But, in another way, it was typical of the time. In comparison with now, there were few people who held professional positions in fundraising, and almost all of them had discovered the field as I did, more or less by accident. Many had transitioned from another profession. I knew some who were former members of the clergy, or former professors, or people who had been in volunteer roles that evolved into paid positions. Few, if any, had selected fundraising as their career goal—they came to the field by *chance*. Indeed, that was also true of careers in nonprofit management more generally.

Unlike my fundraising colleagues of decades ago—and unlike me—many of the students who enroll in my graduate courses at The George Washington University today have come to the field by *choice*, having made a decision to pursue careers in nonprofit management, as fundraising professionals or in general leadership roles.

When I began my fundraising career, there were few professional conferences or training programs available. The largest professional association in the field today, the Association of Fundraising Professionals (AFP; originally known as the National Society of Fund Raisers), had been founded in 1960 but was floundering and in debt by the early 1970s (AFP website). The Association for Healthcare Philanthropy (AHP; originally the National Association for Hospital Development), had existed only since 1967 (AHP website). And the Council for Advancement and Support (CASE), which encompasses professionals who work in fundraising and related fields in education, would not exist in its current form until 1974 (CASE website), although its predecessor organizations, the American Alumni Council (AAC) and the American College Public Relations Association (ACPRA), had roots going back to 1913 and 1917, respectively (CASE website).

The Fund Raising School, which offers professional training programs, also was created in 1974 as a for-profit business, which later became a nonprofit and is now operated by the Lilly Family School of Philanthropy at Indiana University (Kelly, 1998). College level courses related to fundraising were almost nonexistent in the early 1970s; the first research program to study the nonprofit sector was established in 1978, at Yale University (Program on NonProfit Organizations at Yale website).

The landscape is different today. By 2012, AFP included 28,588 members in 230 chapters (AFP 2012 Annual Report). CASE's membership encompassed 3,600 institutional members and about 70,000 individuals (CASE website), and AHP reported about 5,000 members, employed at 2,200 health care institutions (AHP website). Opportunities for formal education and training have increased dramatically over the past forty years. In addition to the extensive training programs offered by professional associations like AFP, AHP, and CASE, fundraising has found its place in the curriculum of colleges and universities. The nation's first school dedicated to the study of philanthropy (the Lilly Family School of Philanthropy at Indiana University) was established in 2013. By 2014 more than a dozen institutions nationally were offering a master's degree in fundraising, attracting both American and international students (Gose, 2014a).

Fundraising remains a blend of art and science and a field in which experience is still more valued than formal credentials. But it continues to evolve in the direction of increased professionalism. Doug White, a veteran fundraiser who now teaches fundraising at Columbia University, predicts that "the fundraiser of the future will have an academic background to supplement his or her more personal skills," adding, "today, it's a good idea. Tomorrow, it's going to be essential" (Gose, 2014a).

In addition to the increased number of staff members specifically dedicated to fundraising as a primary responsibility, fundraising has become an essential component of the job for chief executive officers—presidents and executive directors—at educational institutions and nonprofit organizations, who spend a substantial portion of their time and effort on this activity. Applied knowledge and skills in fundraising are essential for those who hold executive leadership positions in the nonprofit sector today. Equally important is a broad and grounded understanding of the nonprofit sector, fundraising, and philanthropy, necessary to providing informed and effective leadership that has a positive impact on society.

Overview of Fundraising and Philanthropy

If we were to stop people at random and ask them to explain the differences among the sciences of biology, chemistry, and physics, most would probably offer relatively accurate responses. Likewise, if we asked them to define architecture and psychology, almost everyone would say that architecture deals with buildings and psychology with human behavior. Asked to name some historic figures in any of these fields, many would identify names like Isaac Newton, Albert Einstein, Madame Curie, Frank Lloyd Wright, and Sigmund Freud. If we asked what doctors and lawyers do, almost everyone would know the answer. Most universities have departments of schools bearing the names of these disciplines and professions, which also appear on the diplomas of many graduates. If we were to ask people to explain the difference between philanthropy and fundraising, to name historic figures related to either, to express an opinion on where either subject should be studied within a university, or to define what fundraisers do, many might pause before providing an uncertain response. This is understandable. Like traditional academic disciplines and honored professions, philanthropy and fundraising have been pursued in one form or another for centuries. But they remain ill-defined for many people, and their place in the academic firmament remains unclear, even a matter of debate. To be sure that we have a common understanding as a foundation for the balance of the text, let's begin our discussion by clarifying some vocabulary and concepts that are mentioned throughout the book, reviewing some history, and considering the place of fundraising as a professional field today.

FUNDRAISING, DEVELOPMENT, AND ADVANCEMENT

The Association of Fundraising Professionals (AFP) defines **fundraising** simply as "the raising of assets and resources from various sources for the support of an organization or a specific project" (AFP Fundraising Dictionary Online). This is somewhat broad in that it does not necessarily restrict the resources to gifts and grants or the sources to the private sector. Lindahl (2010) offers a more specific definition: "the management of relationships between a nonprofit organization and its various donors for the purpose of increasing gift revenue to the organization" (p. 4). Three important dimensions of Lindahl's definition are that fundraising involves relationships, those relationships have a purpose, and that the purpose is gifts—that is, financial resources voluntarily bestowed without any expectation of a quid pro quo. Lindahl's definition captures the essential meaning of fundraising as the term is used in this book.

But the definition may be somewhat broader in practice. For example, corporations make gifts to nonprofit organizations, but they also provide support through various partnerships that benefit both sides. These are quid pro quo transactions, and the payments generally are **earned income** of the nonprofit, not gift revenue. By Lindahl's definition, the pursuit of these partnerships is not fundraising. However, fundraising professionals within nonprofit organizations are sometimes responsible for establishing relationships with corporate partners as well as donors, and many comprehensive relationships between corporations and nonprofits entail both gifts and earned income that are not easily disentangled. Indeed, in 2004, AFP amended its code of professional ethics, which had long required that fundraisers not accept compensation based on a percentage of gifts, to include a similar prohibition with regard to the solicitation of corporate partnership arrangements (Hall, 2005). For those reasons, nonprofit-corporate partnerships are discussed in this book. Lindahl's definition also does not specifically address **grants**, but grants from private sources (generally corporations or foundations) are gift-like; that is, they are "philanthropic in nature," so the pursuit of them is considered fundraising (CASE, 2009, p. 68). Grants are different from **contracts**, which involve payments for specific goods or services that the organization provides and are thus earned income. The pursuit of contracts might be called new-business development or something similar, but it is not fundraising. By definition in this book, fundraising involves only private-sector sources of support, not government, and so the pursuit of government grants is not considered.

The organizations with which this book is primarily concerned are those classified as **charitable nonprofits** within the meaning of U.S. tax law. The pursuit of gifts to these organizations is sometimes called **charitable fundraising** or **philanthropic fundraising**, to distinguish the activity from fundraising for political campaigns or for other noncharitable purposes. Other terms that are sometimes used instead of fundraising include **fund development** and **resource development**. However, again, this book just uses the term *fundraising*.

Two other terms are sometimes used as synonyms for fundraising, although their precise definitions are distinct. One of those is **development**. Depending on which historical account one accepts, the term *development* was introduced at Northwestern University or at the University of Chicago in the 1920s (Kelly, 1998). At that time, universities typically conducted intensive fundraising campaigns episodically, in order to secure support for specific projects, usually new buildings. However, in thinking about its future growth and development, the university determined that it would be desirable to establish an ongoing structure for cultivating relationships with donors, rather than proceeding in fits and starts as individual projects required. The purpose was to look beyond just one project at a time and make fundraising a strategy for continuous institutional development, for which the term *development* became an abbreviation. A new office was created at the university to manage this ongoing effort, called the "department of development" (Kelly, 1998, p. 150).

Originally, development was a broad concept. It encompassed building acceptance for the institution among its constituencies, recruiting students, and securing financial support. Although the term is often used interchangeably with fundraising today, development relates to longer-term goals. As I explain in a previous book, with reference to higher education:

> In [the broader] concept of development, fund raising is but one aspect of a complex process involving the institution, its hopes and goals, and the aspirations of its benefactors. Fund raising is episodic; development is continuous. Fund raising is focused on a particular objective or set of goals; development is a generic and long-term commitment to the financial and physical growth of the institution. Successful fund raising requires a specific set of inter-personal and communicative skills; development requires a broader understanding of the institution and its mission as well as patience, judgment, and sensitivity in building relationships over the long haul. A "fund raiser" is an individual skillful in soliciting gifts; a "development officer" may be a fund raiser, but he or she is also a strategist and manager of the entire development process. (Worth, 2002, pp. 8–9)

By the late 1950s, the professional staff at colleges and universities had come to include individuals dedicated to fundraising (development) and others who worked in alumni relations, communications, public relations, and other specialties that also involved external constituencies. These functions often had no organizational relationship within the institution, and indeed, staff members belonged to two different professional associations. The American Alumni Council (AAC) encompassed primarily individuals working in alumni relations, while public relations and communications professionals belonged to the American College Public Relations Association (ACPRA). Both AAC and ACPRA included some staff members who were engaged in fundraising, creating an overlap that sometimes led to rivalry. In 1958, representatives of the two organizations met at the Greenbrier Hotel in West Virginia and developed a report that would influence the future of higher education. The report called for integrating the various functions under one campus executive, in order to gain greater coordination and lighten the burden on presidents. The movement initiated at Greenbrier culminated in 1974 with the merger of AAC and ACPRA to create CASE, the Council for Advancement and Support of Education (Worth, 2002). Despite its historically broader meaning, the term *development* had become identified with fundraising and was not an acceptable umbrella to encompass the diverse work of those who would be members of the new, consolidated association. The term **institutional advancement** was adopted as the common rubric, encompassing fundraising, alumni relations, public relations, communications and marketing, and in some cases, government relations and enrollment management. In ensuing years, the term *institutional advancement*, or just **advancement**, has come to be widely adopted in higher education, although not all campuses actually practice the organizational model implied. The term *advancement* also has been adopted by some nonprofit organizations and institutions outside of higher education, and its use does not necessarily imply that any particular management structure exists. Like *development* before, *advancement* has come to be used as a synonym for fundraising by some people. Thus, it is not uncommon to meet someone who works in an office of institutional advancement whose title is director of development and who, when asked what he or she does, may reply "fundraising."

This book follows common practice and uses the terms *fundraising* and *development* interchangeably. It uses *advancement* or *institutional advancement* when those terms are in direct quotes from other authors or to describe specific situations in which fundraising and other externally focused activities are indeed linked in the organization's management structure. Whether *development* or *fundraising* is used in this book, what is implied is a process similar to that described with regard to development, rather than the narrowest meaning of fundraising as the solicitation of gifts.

PHILANTHROPY AND CHARITY

Like *fundraising* and *development*, the terms **philanthropy** and **charity** are often used interchangeably. *Philanthropy* is commonly used as the umbrella, encompassing all giving, and that practice is followed in this book, except where the distinction may be relevant. But there is a difference between the two concepts.

Charity is often defined as giving intended to meet current human needs, for example, to feed the hungry or to aid the victims of a natural disaster. It is emotionally driven and often impulsive, as evidenced by the outpouring of gifts made within days of the terrorist attacks of September 11, 2001, the Haitian earthquake in 2010, Hurricane Sandy in 2012, and Typhoon Haiyan in the Philippines in 2013. Frumkin (2006) offers a succinct definition: "It [charity] can best be understood as the uncomplicated and unconditional transfer of money or assistance to those in need with the intent of helping" (p. 5).

Philanthropy is investment in the infrastructure of society. It is often undertaken with a long-term view and is more rational than charity. In Payton's (1988) words, it is "the 'prudent sister' of charity" (p. 2). Typical examples of philanthropy might include gifts made to construct new hospitals, endow universities, or sustain museums. Frumkin (2006) offers another way to distinguish philanthropy from charity. He relates it to the old teaching about providing a hungry person a fish, which would be charity, versus teaching that person how to fish, which would be philanthropy. So for example, the goals of both charity and philanthropy might be to improve the lives of poor children. Charity would provide them with shelter, while philanthropy would build them a school.

The terms are sometimes used in ways that can lead to confusion. For example, the Internal Revenue Code provides tax deductions for gifts to charitable nonprofits, which include many hospitals, universities, museums, and others that most people do not think of as charities and that are often recipients of support more consistent with the definition of philanthropy. And the deduction is called a **charitable deduction**, regardless of whether the nature of the gift meets the stricter definitions of philanthropy or charity.

Some authors give philanthropy a broad definition. For example, Payton (1988) calls it "voluntary action for the public good" in the subtitle of his seminal book *Philanthropy* and includes both the giving of money and the giving of time and effort by volunteers. But it is also reasonable to differentiate volunteerism from philanthropy, since a volunteer is actively involved with the organization and/or its beneficiaries, whereas someone who gives financial resources—a philanthropist—may do so without any significant commitment of his or her time. In this book, *philanthropy* refers to the giving of financial resources, not to dispute the broader meaning but just to simplify and focus the discussion.

Sometimes public policy debates relate to the concepts of charity and philanthropy. For example, some argue that only gifts that directly assist people in urgent need should be eligible for a tax deduction, since, as explained later in this book, the deduction represents a form of subsidy from taxpayers. Those who hold that view might say that giving to universities, symphony orchestras, and similar institutions primarily benefits affluent, highly educated people rather than those in economic need and thus should not receive such a subsidy (Eisenberg, 2014). But these arguments may not fully recognize the role of philanthropy as, in Lohmann's (1992) words, an "investment in civilization" (p. 163). The goal of both charity and philanthropy is to improve the human condition. If the goals of philanthropists were ultimately achieved, that is, were there strong institutions to meet human needs as they arise, then perhaps the need for charity would be reduced or eliminated. As I observed in a previous work, "In the imperfect world of the present, both types of giving are important and complementary in their impacts" (Worth, 2014, p. 20).

FUNDRAISING AND PHILANTHROPY

Fundraising and philanthropy are intertwined, and both are discussed in this text. Although the analogy is not perfect, the relationship between fundraising and philanthropy is somewhat like the relationship between teaching and learning. In both cases, the purpose of the former is to engender the latter. But there is no guarantee that the activity will produce the intended result, which may occur for reasons unrelated to the activity. In other words, students may not learn from their teachers or may learn on their own. Fundraising may not produce gifts, and some people may offer gifts spontaneously without prompting. But, surely, to be an effective teacher or fundraiser one needs an understanding of how learning occurs or what motivates donors to give. This book is primarily concerned with the practice of fundraising and management of the fundraising function in nonprofit organizations and institutions. But theories and research related to philanthropy are also discussed because such understanding is essential to the effective practice of fundraising.

FUNDRAISING PROFESSION AND FUNDRAISING PROFESSIONALS

Whether fundraising is a "profession" or just an "occupation" is a question that has generated discussion and debate. Most people think it is an occupation, since it does not meet all of the criteria that usually define a profession, like law or medicine. However, in this book, the terms *fundraising profession* and *fundraising professional* are used to describe the field and individuals who are employed in it, respectively. That is just common usage and implies no position on the academic debate about the status of the field. When the term *fundraiser* is used in this book, it refers to those who are paid staff members involved in fundraising, but not to volunteers (for example, members of governing boards) who may be engaged in fundraising without compensation. They will usually be referred to as fundraising volunteers, volunteer leaders, or by similar terms. In this book, the term **development officer** is a synonym for *fundraiser*, which again, is common usage. The fundraising professional who has overall responsibility for an organization's fundraising program is called the chief development officer, although the individual holding that position is commonly titled director of development. In this book, nonprofit chief executive officers, often titled president or executive director, are called CEOs. They are not fundraising professionals, although much of their time may in fact be dedicated to fundraising. Fundraising professionals include both staff members and consultants, who are not employed by one nonprofit organization. This definition of fundraising professionals is consistent with the membership of AFP, which encompasses staff members and consultants but is open to others only through an associate member category (AFP website).

Now that we have established common vocabulary and clarified some basic concepts and terms, let's look at the history of philanthropy and fundraising, so that we can understand the balance of our discussion in a broad context.

HISTORY OF AMERICAN PHILANTHROPY

Virtually all cultures and religions throughout history have included an emphasis on the importance of helping others, both through giving and service. Robbins (2006) identifies the roots of modern philanthropy in the Greco-Roman tradition of community, citizenry, and social responsibility and the Judeo-Christian ethic of helping others, especially those less fortunate. The legal foundations of nonprofit organizations and philanthropy in the United States are derived from English common law, notably the Statute of Charitable Uses and the Poor Law, both passed in 1601. These laws clarified the relationship between the English government and the Church of England and defined the legitimate activities to be supported by charity (Anheier and Salamon, 2006). They are still reflected in American legal principles. But despite their ancient roots, the traditions of voluntarism and philanthropy have reached their fullest expression in the United States.

America's Early Centuries

As early as 1835, the Frenchman Alexis de Tocqueville visited America and wrote about his observations in his well-known book, *Democracy in America*. He noted the unique propensity of Americans to establish "voluntary associations" to address social needs that in other parts of the world were more commonly provided by government. Of course, the United States was founded in rebellion against the English monarchy, and some distrust of government has been a part of its culture from the beginning, supporting a preference for private, voluntary initiatives. In addition, its early citizens lived with limited resources on a continent physically distant from established civilizations of Europe, so self-reliance was a necessity. Voluntary action built institutions and infrastructure in the young American colonies, including churches, schools, and even roads. However, government also played an important role, and the separation of church and state that we accept as a fundamental principle today was less established. Indeed, in colonial America, government supported churches. And churches sponsored many of the institutions that served community needs, providing services that today might be considered a responsibility of government.

Emergence of Large-Scale Philanthropy

American philanthropy in the nation's first centuries was small in scale, usually related to religion, to the poor, and to local community needs. Large-scale philanthropy did not arise until the late nineteenth century and early twentieth century, with the growth of large personal fortunes as a result of the industrial revolution. This was the era of John D. Rockefeller, Andrew Carnegie, and other business leaders who constructed and endowed universities, libraries, and other institutions across the country. Rockefeller founded the University of Chicago, Rockefeller University, the Rockefeller Foundation, and other important institutions. In addition to libraries, for which he is best known, Carnegie created more than twenty unaffiliated institutions, including Carnegie Hall, Carnegie Institute of Technology (now Carnegie-Mellon University), the Carnegie Endowment for International Peace, the Carnegie Corporation of New York, and the Carnegie Institution for Science (Carnegie Institution for Science website).

Although Rockefeller and Carnegie are perhaps the best-known philanthropists of the early twentieth century, others of that era also made substantial contributions. For example, Julius Rosenwald, an early leader of Sears, Roebuck & Company (sadly for Mr. Roebuck, known now just as "Sears"), dedicated his fortune to building thousands of elementary schools for African Americans in the South during the early twentieth century (Zunz, 2012). And, although the industrialists of that era were primarily male, women also had an impact on philanthropy at that time. For example, Madam C. J. Walker built a successful cosmetics business, selling products to African American women. She used her wealth to make gifts to the Tuskegee Institution, the YMCA, the NAACP, and other organizations that advanced the status of African American women (Frumkin, 2006).

Carnegie's famous essay "The Gospel of Wealth" was published in 1889 and became the definitive statement of the philosophy behind large-scale philanthropy by the wealthy. Carnegie expressed the obligation of those who have accumulated wealth to give back to the society that enabled them to succeed, saying, "The man who dies thus rich dies disgraced" (p. 664). This philosophy became a part of American culture and a hallmark of American capitalism. An economy characterized by relatively free markets enables individuals to amass substantial wealth, but it comes with the expectation that they will share their bounty with others, either during their lifetimes or at death. The continuing influence of Carnegie's philosophy is illustrated by the Giving Pledge, initiated by a new generation of wealthy entrepreneurs and investors in the twenty-first century. Led by Bill and Melinda Gates and Warren Buffet, the Giving Pledge is a movement to encourage billionaires around the world to publicly commit to dedicating at least one-half of their wealth to philanthropy either during their lives or at death. By 2011, some sixty-nine individuals or couples had made the commitment and had begun to meet together periodically to learn from each other's experience (Di Mento, 2011). However, as discussed later in this chapter, large-scale philanthropy also has critics, who question the influence it enables the wealthy to achieve.

Emergence of Mass Philanthropy

While the large-scale philanthropy of Carnegie, Rockefeller, and other titans of the industrial revolution had national impact, the early twentieth century also marked the beginning of mass philanthropy, a uniquely American phenomenon. As Zunz (2012) observes, "Turning large fortunes into public assets for the good of [humankind] was a huge project. But what gave philanthropy even more of a central place in modern American life was the simultaneous creation of a people's philanthropy—or mass philanthropy—that engaged the large American middle and working classes in their own welfare" (p. 44).

Mass philanthropy began in the field of public health. One of the great scourges of the early twentieth century was tuberculosis, which afflicted one-quarter of New York City children in 1908 (Zunz, 2012). The National Association for the Study and Prevention of Tuberculosis was founded that same year and introduced the idea of selling Christmas seals that people could affix to their holiday card envelopes in addition to postage stamps. The 1908 seals campaign raised $135,000 and "marked a turning point in the acceptance of mass philanthropy by the American population" (Zunz, 2012, p. 48). Other national charities also trace their beginnings to this period, including the Boy Scouts, Girl Scouts, American Cancer Society, and NAACP.

A priest, two ministers, and a rabbi established the first cooperative, or federated, fundraising effort, in Denver in 1887 (Sargeant, Shang et al., 2010). United Jewish Charities were established in various cities beginning in 1895 (Zunz, 2012). But the idea gained momentum in 1913 with the founding of the Federation for Charity and Philanthropy in Cleveland. The Federation became the model for community chests established across the country, which eventually evolved into local chapters of United Way. It was also in Cleveland, in 1914, where local banker Frederick Harris Goff created the first community foundation, intended to receive and manage funds from average citizens to meet longer-term needs of the community. As Zunz (2012) observes, "The two projects sprang from a common idea of pooling resources in an enlarged community. Both promoted an original synthesis between charity and philanthropy, between volunteers and professionals, between lodge and town, between rich and average Americans, based on a vision of a metropolitan society" (p. 53). The federal income tax was introduced in 1913, and Congress approved the granting of tax deductions for gifts to certain nonprofits in 1917, giving further encouragement to the growth in giving.

Mass philanthropy was given impetus by the compelling national needs that emerged during World War I, the Great Depression, and World War II. Although local community needs remained important, Americans gained a broader sense of national identity and gave to meet needs of their fellow citizens across the country as well as people abroad who were suffering as a result of the wars. Philanthropy flourished in the post–World War II era, amid an expanding U.S. economy, and became an ever more central component of American life. As Zunz (2012) describes, "By the 1950s, mass philanthropy was so well integrated into everyday life in the United States that one could identify the season by the door-to-door collection in progress—winter and spring for health agencies and the Red

Cross, fall for community chests. A large part of the American population understood that their small gifts cumulatively enhanced the life of the nation and in turn their own" (p. 3).

The combination of elite philanthropy and mass philanthropy continues to characterize giving in the United States today. As discussed in chapters ahead, it is reflected in the fundraising programs of nonprofit organizations and institutions, which include both programs of broad-based solicitation to secure a large number of small gifts and efforts to secure major gifts from the most affluent donors.

The New Philanthropists

The closing decade of the twentieth century was a time of economic prosperity, based on the rapid adoption of information technology and the growth of technology companies. Substantial wealth was created among a new generation of entrepreneurs and investors, rivaling and even exceeding the fortunes of Rockefeller, Carnegie, and other giants of the industrial revolution a century before. Like the earlier industrialists, many of these individuals sought to apply their wealth to philanthropy, but they adopted new ideas and new methods and came to be identified as "the new philanthropists" (Greenfeld, 2000).

The late 1990s brought criticisms of traditional philanthropy that influenced the new generation of donors. Particularly influential was a widely read article published in the *Harvard Business Review*, written by Christine Letts, William Ryan, and Allen Grossman (1999). Titled "Virtuous Capital: What Foundations Can Learn From Venture Capitalists," the article was an indictment of traditional foundations' grant-making practices. The authors argued that the short-term grants made by foundations to support nonprofits' programs were in fact diverting the time and attention of nonprofit executives toward fundraising rather than building the capacity of organizations themselves, thus limiting their impact. Or, to use the terms of Collins and Porras (1994), nonprofit leaders were forced to be "time tellers" rather than "clock builders," with the result that organizations could not gain the scale needed to effect major social change.

Letts et al. (1999) advocated an approach to philanthropy that would parallel the approach of venture capitalists to investing in companies, including a more sustained financial commitment, high engagement by the philanthropist in developing the organization's strategies, and perhaps most significantly, the requirement that organizations meet agreed-on performance standards. For entrepreneurs who had sold their companies in the late 1990s and become venture capitalists themselves, the concept had particular appeal. The article became the manifesto of a new approach to giving known as **venture philanthropy**. New philanthropic organizations, called **venture philanthropy funds**, were created to practice this approach. Some tenets of venture philanthropy came to be reflected in giving by some traditional foundations, with at least a portion of their grants, under the rubric of **high-engagement grant making**.

Other new terms and concepts entered the philanthropic vocabulary during the 2000s, including **strategic philanthropy**, **catalytic philanthropy**, and **outcome-oriented philanthropy**. Each has a somewhat different definition—and various authors define them differently—but the common element is encompassed by the latter term; it refers to philanthropy in which "donors seek to achieve clearly defined goals; where they and [the organizations they support] pursue evidence-based strategies for achieving those goals;

and where both parties monitor progress toward outcomes and assess their success in achieving them" (Brest, 2012, p. 42).

New philanthropists do support existing institutions and organizations, but some are primarily **entrepreneurial donors**, who are more committed to a cause or a theory of change than to any specific organization. They are donors with ideas in search of organizations that will implement them. They may support existing organizations that are willing to adopt their approach and grant them an engaged role, but others prefer to create a new organization over which they can exercise more control. They can present a challenge for fundraisers working for traditional institutions and organizations.

Principles of the new philanthropy gained adherents and visibility over the first decade of the twenty-first century. New journals and research centers were launched, new books were written, many conferences were held, and new organizations and companies were created to advise philanthropists desiring to follow an outcome-oriented approach. Online **charity watchdogs** and rating services, for example, Charity Navigator and the Better Business Bureau Wise Giving Alliance, were developed to provide individual donors with the information needed to make more rational giving decisions. The extent to which individual donors are indeed influenced by such data or take a primarily rational approach to their giving is a subject of research and debate. This text comes back to that question and its implication for fundraising in a later chapter.

In today's environment, the traditional distinction between charity and philanthropy discussed earlier in this chapter may no longer be adequate to fully capture the array of types of giving. Stannard-Stockton (2011) proposes definitions for "three core approaches" that could provide more clarity, perhaps avoiding some of the misunderstanding evident in some discussions about giving. As Box 1.1 portrays, the definition of *charity* remains similar to the classic one discussed earlier—giving to meet current human needs. Philanthropy is divided into two subtypes. The first, which Stannard-Stockton (2011) calls **philanthropic investment**, is similar to the traditional definition of philanthropy, that is, building institutions and organizations that will meet human and social needs over the long term. The second type of philanthropy, strategic philanthropy, is somewhere between charity and philanthropic investment. Its purpose is to bring about social change, according to a theory of change held by the philanthropist, in order to improve the condition of society and human lives. For example, to go back to the example of poor children mentioned earlier in this chapter, charity would provide them with shelter, philanthropic investment would

BOX 1.1 Three Core Approaches to Giving		
Approach	**Donor's Goal**	**Donor's Criteria for Success**
Charity	Meet current human needs	Impact for the money spent, for example, number of people served
Philanthropic investment	Build organizations and institutions for the long run	Longer-term improvement in programs, strength of the organization
Strategic philanthropy	Social change, application of a theory of change	Program outcomes that demonstrate the validity of the theory of change

Source: Based on Stannard-Stockton (2011).

build them a school, and strategic philanthropy would support development of a new educational program intended to lift the children out of poverty.

PHILANTHROPY'S SCALE AND IMPACT

Cutlip's (1965/1990) book *Fund Raising in the United States: Its Role in American Philanthropy* remains the most comprehensive discussion of fundraising's early history in the United States. In that book, he describes American philanthropy as having achieved "fabulous dimensions" in the post–World War II era, increasing from $1.25 billion in 1940 to over $10 billion in 1963 (p. 477). Growth continued over the next five decades, with total giving exceeding $335 billion in 2013. Giving in current dollars—that is, ignoring the effects of inflation—roughly doubled every ten years over the period from 1972 to 2012, with the exception of the period from 2002 to 2012. The latter encompassed the Great Recession and modest declines in giving in 2008 and 2009. If the totals are portrayed in inflation-adjusted dollars, which may provide a better measure of philanthropy's impact, the growth is somewhat less dramatic. On average, giving has remained relatively constant in relationship to gross domestic product (GDP), at about 2 percent (Giving USA, 2014a). Accordingly, it tends to increase in periods of economic expansion and to flatten or decline in recessions. There is also a strong correlation between total philanthropy and the level of the U.S. stock market. That reflects the fact that some gifts from individuals are paid with appreciated securities and giving by foundations is constrained by the value of their investments. Giving by individuals is also influenced in part by what economists call the **wealth effect**, that is, the psychological impact of fluctuations in household wealth, including stocks, on their willingness to spend and make gifts.

As shown in Figure 1.1, the largest source of philanthropy is living individuals, who accounted for 72 percent of the total in 2013. Bequests, gifts made by individuals that

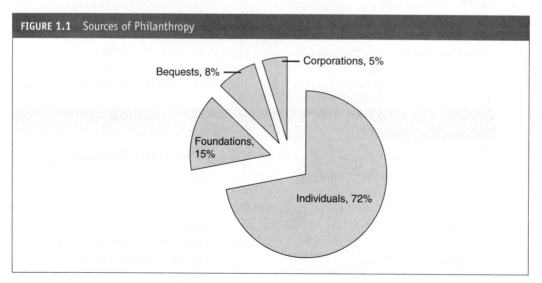

FIGURE 1.1 Sources of Philanthropy

Corporations, 5%
Bequests, 8%
Foundations, 15%
Individuals, 72%

Source: Based on Giving USA. (2014). *Highlights*. Chicago, IL: Giving USA Foundation.

become effective at the time of their deaths, accounted for an additional 8 percent. Thus, in total, 80 percent of gifts came from private individuals. While some people may think about corporations and foundations as the most visible sources of philanthropy, they accounted for 5 percent and 15 percent, respectively, of philanthropy in 2013 (Giving USA, 2014b). And, since many foundations were established with original gifts from individuals, the impact of individual donors is even greater than the percentages portray. Given this reality, this book emphasizes fundraising from individual donors, with one chapter each devoted to raising funds from corporations and foundations.

As shown in Figure 1.2, the largest recipient of philanthropy—accounting for almost one-third—is religion, followed by education at 16 percent. It may surprise some people to learn that organizations in the fields of human services; arts, culture, and humanities; and environment and animals together account for only 20 percent of the total, although they represent a substantial portion of the total number of nonprofit organizations.

While philanthropy has had a demonstrable impact on the advancement of many institutions and causes, it is not without critics. Some criticisms are directed at particular approaches to giving. For example, the high engagement of new philanthropists has raised concerns that donors will encroach on the autonomy of nonprofit organizations and institutions and substitute donors' judgments for the expertise of professionals who

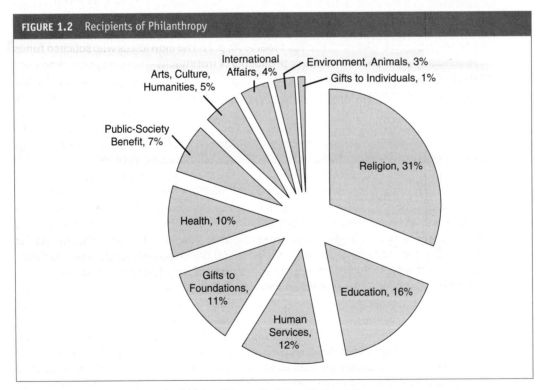

FIGURE 1.2   Recipients of Philanthropy

Source: Based on Giving USA. (2014). *Highlights.* Chicago, IL: Giving USA Foundation.

have more experience with the issues those organizations address. Other critics fear that the new philanthropists' emphasis on performance will discourage nonprofits from taking bold actions and to focus instead on more short-term results, which may be measureable but not bring about significant social change (Brest, 2012).

Some criticisms of philanthropy are more fundamental, going beyond any particular approach, and some have a long history extending back to the days of Carnegie. For example, some argue that philanthropy ameliorates the impact of social problems and thus stands in the way of more fundamental change, perpetuating control by wealthy elites. Others say that philanthropy enables the wealthy to drive social policy in directions that should be determined through more democratic means. For example, some have charged that substantial funding from the Bill and Melinda Gates Foundation has had an outsized influence on education policy in the United States, which should be determined by public entities under political control rather than the views of a few wealthy donors (Sievers, 2010).

EVOLUTION OF FUNDRAISING AS A PROFESSIONAL FIELD

Like large-scale philanthropy, organized fundraising began in the twentieth century. In America's earlier centuries, the methods for soliciting gifts were generally personal and primitive, consisting primarily of "passing the church plate, of staging church suppers or bazaars, and of writing 'begging letters'" (Cutlip, 1965/1990, p. 7). The individuals who solicited funds were generally principals—trustees or presidents of institutions—or paid agents, who were often given a percentage of the funds raised. Solicitations, even by paid agents, often reflected a religious commitment that was extended to other causes, including education. There were no individuals who could be called fundraising professionals comparable to those who are employed today. Most philanthropy was provided by a small number of wealthy individuals, and there were few organized fundraising efforts (Cutlip, 1965/1990). But there were inklings of a more systematic approach and the seeds of modern fundraising methods.

In 1641, William Hibbens, Hugh Peter, and Thomas Weld sailed from Boston to London on a fundraising mission for a struggling young Harvard College. The men requested printed material and were sent "New England's First Fruits," the first reported example of a fundraising brochure. Weld remained in England and never returned to America. So, too, did Peter, who was hanged in England for crimes committed under British law. Hibbens was the only one to return to America, a year later, with 500 British pounds for Harvard. As Cutlip (1965/1990) observes, "Such were the diverse rewards of early fund raisers!" (p. 4).

In 1829, Matthew Carey, a paid solicitor in Philadelphia, introduced new concepts, including rated prospect lists and advance promotion of the fundraising appeal. Unfortunately, his effort was unsuccessful. He wrote, "This experiment was tried for twenty days and a half. The last four days there were but twelve dollars received and on the last day there was but a single dollar collected, which was not sufficient to pay the collector. . . . [It is] surely time to abandon the plan as hopeless" (Cutlip, 1965/1990, p. 8). However, the techniques that Carey introduced were, in Cutlip's words, "in embryo, the elements of modern fund raising" (p. 8).

Benjamin Franklin demonstrated insight on the fundraising process when he provided advice to Gilbert Thomas on how to raise funds for the Presbyterian Church in Philadelphia. In its essence, the process he proposed is still employed:

In the first place I advise you to apply to all those whom you know will give something; next to those whom you are uncertain whether they will give anything or not, and show them the list of those who have given; and lastly, do not neglect those whom you are sure will give nothing, for in some of them you may be mistaken. (Cutlip, 1965/1990, p. 6)

But despite these early roots, fundraising before the twentieth century was "generally amateur and personal, a transaction between two individuals, with no role for organization, strategy, or professional managers" (Worth, 2002, p. 25).

Beginning of a Profession

A significant innovation in fundraising came in the first decade of the twentieth century. YMCA executive Lyman L. Pierce had begun in 1902 a fundraising campaign to secure $300,000 toward construction of a new YMCA in Washington, DC. His campaign had come within $80,000 of its goal, but by 1905 it had stalled. Pierce called for help from Charles Sumner Ward, a fellow YMCA executive from Chicago, who had become known for his fundraising skills. Ward came to Washington to help Pierce complete the floundering campaign. As Cutlip (1965/1990) describes:

The collaboration of Ward and Pierce produced the first modern fund-raising campaign techniques: careful organization, picked leaders spurred on by team competition, prestige leaders, powerful publicity, a large gift to be matched, . . . careful records, report meetings, and a definite time limit. (p. 44)

Ward followed a process similar to Benjamin Franklin's advice from more than a century earlier. He introduced the campaign clock or thermometer as a graphic device to show progress toward attaining the campaign's goal, in order to create urgency and excitement. The campaign's ultimate success was announced at a press conference at the Willard Hotel in Washington on May 2, 1905. As Cutlip (1965/1990) describes, "The jubilation was echoed outside the hotel by the loud honking of horns on the new cars" (pp. 46–47).

Although Ward and Pierce collaborated on the campaign, the method developed became known as the "Ward method" and was widely adopted in campaigns that followed, continuing until the present (Cutlip, 1965/1990). But Ward's contribution went beyond the introduction of a new fundraising method. First, the very idea that there was a method to fundraising was itself innovative and a departure from earlier practice, which had relied on the personal charisma and social connections of individuals. Second, Ward himself represented something new—a fundraising *professional*, who developed strategy and managed the process but who was not himself a solicitor of gifts, unlike the paid agents who had raised funds for early colleges and other institutions. Indeed, Ward was personally quite different from the charismatic personalities who were associated with fundraising in earlier times. One of his contemporaries, Carlton Ketchum, described him as "an austere and reserved man, very far indeed from any of the campaign types which we all know." Ward's role, said Ketchum, "was that of the originator of a sane and practical method and the firmness to insist on its thorough application . . . rather than any personal magnetism" (Cutlip, 1965/1990, p. 86). By creating a new role of fundraising strategist and manager who was not a solicitor of gifts, Ward established a distinction between fundraising as a process, rather than the narrower activity of just asking for money, and represented a model for the emergence of fundraising professionals in the decades ahead.

The decade following Ward's innovative YMCA campaign in Washington saw the expansion of national charities and the emergence of national fund drives, which accelerated during World War I. The American Red Cross War Council was created by President Woodrow Wilson to centralize wartime relief efforts. Ward and Pierce were hired, on loan from the YMCA, to direct its fundraising, and they secured more than $690 million. Five national drives for Liberty Loans raised $14 billion, under the direction of John Price Jones, a former journalist and advertising executive, who was loaned to the wartime effort by his firm (Kelly, 1998).

Era of Consultants

Following the end of World War I, Ward and Pierce, Jones, and others founded consulting firms to take their methods to a broad array of institutions and organizations. Ward and Pierce, as partners, and Jones founded their firms in 1919, beginning what Kelly (1998) calls the "era of fundraising consultants," which she dates from 1919 to 1949 (p. 145). Over the next decade, the number of consulting firms expanded, many founded by individuals who had been trained either by Ward and Pierce or by Jones. These two schools came to define two different philosophies. Those who followed Ward and Pierce became known as the "Y school" and were characterized by their religious orientation and a view of fundraising as a calling, even though their firms were operated for a profit. Jones and his followers saw fundraising as a business and mocked the Y school as "the Christers" (Cutlip, 1965/1990, p. 43). Followers of Ward and Pierce returned the fire, nicknaming Jones "High Price Jones," with reference to his business orientation (Zunz, 2012, p. 67). Consultants dominated fundraising during the period between the world wars. The largest firms founded the American Association of Fundraising Counsel (AAFRC) in 1935 and established standards for best and ethical practices. AAFRC is today known as the Giving Institute. In addition to maintaining Standards of Practice and Professional Code of Ethics for consultants, it publishes the most comprehensive annual report on philanthropy, Giving USA (Giving Institute website).

Even today, there continues to be a subtle tension between the perception of fundraising as a noble undertaking related to charitable mission and the perception that it is a business, oriented to a bottom line without any particular attachment to the mission. It is reflected in the sometimes complicated relationships that fundraising professionals have with colleagues within their own organizations, some of whom may view fundraisers as outsiders not fully invested in the values of the organization.

There always have been, and continue to be, individuals and firms who work as professional solicitors, that is, as paid agents. Today they include firms that conduct direct mail or telephone solicitations. Some may even accept a percentage of the funds raised as their compensation, although that practice is almost universally regarded an unethical now. Some paid solicitors may indeed call themselves "consultants," but they are not. Consultants do not solicit or receive gifts; rather, they advise and direct others who do, including the organization's volunteer and executive leaders and fundraising professional staff. Their compensation is based on time and effort expended or a fixed fee determined in advance and based on the scope of the assignment, rather than a percentage of funds raised. Again, the latter is considered unethical and is not a practice followed by firms that are members of the Giving Institute or by other reputable consultants.

The distinction between professional solicitors and consultants is recognized in the laws of many states. Most states and the District of Columbia require that nonprofit organizations soliciting their citizens register and pay a fee before commencing their fundraising activity, with most exempting religious organizations. In addition, many states require that professional solicitors and fundraising consultants working with organizations soliciting within their boundaries also register. (State laws often refer to fundraising consultants as "fundraising counsel," although they are not providing legal advice.) Although requirements vary from state to state, many require that professional solicitors meet higher requirements than fundraising counsel, often obtaining a bond and meeting additional reporting requirements that do not apply to consultants who just provide advice (Fishman, 2012).

In the days before World War II, it was common for consulting firms to assign a **resident manager** to an institution conducting a campaign. The resident manager would work at the institution for a period of months or years to direct the effort and advise the volunteers and executive leaders, who would conduct the actual solicitations. The resident manager remained an employee of the consulting firm, not the institution, and would move on to another location and another assignment at the end of each campaign.

The model obviously produced episodic rather than continuous fundraising efforts by nonprofit organizations and institutions. After World War II, the economy was growing, the needs of nonprofit organizations and institutions were increasing, and episodic fundraising was no longer sufficient. Some institutions and organizations began to hire fundraising professionals as full-time employees. The resident manager model still exists, but most consultants today assist organizations by conducting studies and providing advice, with ongoing programs and campaigns being managed by in-house fundraising professionals.

Growth of the Fundraising Profession

The transition to what Kelly (1998) calls the "era of staff fund raisers" was gradual over the period from about 1949 to 1965 (p. 151). Kelly's research in the libraries of NSFRE (now AFP) and CASE identified no full-time staff fundraisers before the late 1940s. But by 1965 the numbers had become more substantial, growing first in independent colleges and universities. Full-time staff fundraisers began to appear at public colleges and universities in the mid-1970s. Similar positions began to increase in nonprofit institutions and organizations outside of higher education during the 1970s, 1980s, and beyond (Kelly, 1998). By 2013, membership in the three largest professional associations—AFP, AHP, and CASE—was approximately 100,000, although CASE's membership included some who worked primarily in advancement fields other than fundraising.

In many organizations, fundraisers now are senior officers, serving as a part of the management team, often with the title of vice president. And as the profession has grown, it has developed subspecialties, and new associations have been created to provide information, training, and other services to individuals working in these areas. For example, the Partnership on Philanthropic Planning (PPP) was founded in 1988 as the National Committee on Planned Giving and serves professionals working in that field (PPP website). The Association of Advancement Services Professionals (AASP) supports individuals concerned with database management and reporting; gift and biographic records management; donor relations, including donor recognition and stewardship; and prospect development, including prospect research and prospect management (AASP website). Professionals in prospect research have their own association, known as APRA, founded in 1987 as the American Prospect Research Association (APRA website). We will learn more about the work of these specialized fields later in this text.

Despite the growth of the fundraising profession and its increasing stature within many organizations, there are also significant challenges faced by those who work as professionals in the field, especially in smaller nonprofit organizations rather than larger institutions, such as universities. A study by the consulting firm CompassPoint and the Evelyn and Walter Haas, Jr. Fund, released in 2013, found a high rate of turnover in fundraising positions, with some remaining vacant for significant periods of time. It also uncovered underlying issues that contribute to this instability, including inadequate fundraising systems and a lack of commitment to fundraising by some nonprofit CEOs and governing boards. It noted an absence of fundraising culture in some organizations, unrealistic goals, and a need for investment and reform of the director of development position. The authors recommend a substantial effort by the nonprofit sector to improve these conditions (Bell and Cornelius, 2013).

STATE OF THE ART

This is a textbook intended for use in courses on fundraising, not a hands-on manual for fundraising professionals or nonprofit executives. But neither is its purpose to offer an entirely academic discussion of fundraising. Fundraising developed in the real world of practice, and throughout most of its history the bulk of its literature has consisted of the observations and reflections of practitioners. It was considered an art, like blacksmithing, to be handed down from one generation to the next through the telling of stories and supervised experience. The effort to establish a systematic body of knowledge and theory, to make fundraising more of a science, is recent and remains a work in progress.

Writing in 1998, Kelly describes the "relatively dismal state of research and theory on fund raising" (p. 106). More than a decade later, in 2010, Sargeant, Shang, et al. cite "the emerging contribution of fundraising science" but suggest that it is still inadequate. They state that establishing and drawing "on its own academic base" still remains "the next step" for the fundraising profession (p. 41). Relevant theory and research exist on some topics, but on other points practitioner wisdom is still the predominant source. In other words, fundraising as a professional field continues to evolve. It is no longer sufficient to base a discussion of fundraising entirely on the reflections of practitioners. But an effort to explain it entirely in terms of theory also would not be useful.

Although research directly related to fundraising practice remains limited, some research in related areas is informative. The relevant research can be placed in four general categories.

1. *Research on the nonprofit sector and nonprofit organizations.* Theories have been developed to describe and explain the nonprofit sector in the United States and the behavior of nonprofit organizations, and the body of research is considerable. It does not necessarily address fundraising directly, but it establishes the arena in which fundraising occurs and helps to explain the role of fundraising professionals within their organizations and society. Some prominent theories in this area are reviewed in Chapter 2.

2. *Research related to philanthropy.* A substantial body of research relates to philanthropy. As discussed, philanthropy is intertwined with, but not synonymous with, fundraising— they are, in a sense, two sides of the coin. This research includes studies that consider the role and impact of philanthropy on society and studies that concern the motivations and behavior of donors. The latter are, of course, particularly relevant to fundraising, and selected theories and research are reviewed in Chapter 3.

3. *Research in related professional fields* (for example, public relations, marketing, and communications). As discussed in the next section of this chapter, some authors think that fundraising is an element of marketing. Indeed, there are marketing theories and research that can be applied to some aspects of fundraising, which are described at relevant points in later chapters of this book.

4. *Research specifically related to fundraising practice.* Research specifically related to fundraising has been encouraged by the leading professional organizations. AFP established its Research Council in 1991 "to identify . . . research priorities, recognize and promote research, publish research results, and seek support for research on philanthropy and fundraising" (AFP website). Both AFP and CASE present awards to recognize research contributions, in published works as well as dissertations, although many of the winning studies have been about donors rather than fundraising.

Most of the research related to fundraising is of an applied nature, concerning management of the fundraising function and models for planning, controlling, and evaluating programs. Other studies have focused on the fundraising process, the roles and characteristics of fundraisers, and fundraising for specific types of organizations. Some scholars have tested fundraising practices in field experiments, although the findings also could be viewed as relating primarily to donor behavior. This research is cited in relevant sections throughout this text. However, despite a growing emphasis on research-based fundraising practice, most principles of fundraising remain those derived from the experiences and reflections of fundraising professionals.

FUNDRAISING AND OTHER PROFESSIONAL FIELDS

One of the reasons that fundraising research is still limited is that fundraising remains ill-defined, both as a professional field and a field of study. Some studies have been completed by scholars in the social sciences, communications, public relations, marketing, nonprofit management, and other fields. Many of the doctoral dissertations on fundraising topics have been written by graduate students in education and focus on higher education institutions.

Some authors have sought to define fundraising as a subspecialty within other, more established fields; two contenders are public relations and marketing, with marketing drawing the broadest support. Both are professional fields as well as fields of study. Both have homes in academic units at universities, which have generated a research literature.

In *Effective Fund-Raising Management*, the first fundraising textbook and a monumental work, Kelly (1998) argues that fundraising is a specialization of public relations. She advances a theory of fundraising practice based on models developed by public relations scholars. But the view that fundraising is marketing has the support of multiple scholars and, perhaps, the majority of fundraising practitioners (Lindahl, 2010).

Lindahl makes the case for fundraising as marketing in his 2010 book:

> The field of marketing models fundraising in several ways. [Both] involve relationships. Marketing is more than just promotion or sales, just as donor relationships with a nonprofit organization involve more than just asking. Marketing seeks to understand the customer and develop products to meet the customer's needs and wants. Fundraisers help guide and direct donors' philanthropic impulses. They discuss the impact of a major gift on the organization, and they report back on the use of the funds for charitable purposes. (p. 2)

Lindahl (2010) also offers an example of how a marketing approach might apply in a given case:

> Perhaps an organization is interested in a new health clinic program that doesn't include dental care. A major donor may have an interest in dental care. The organization adds the dental clinic program into the health clinic; and the donor funds the additional cost. Without the agreement to add the dental care, the donor may not have given at all or at a different level. (p. 3)

But, Lindahl cautions, "This concept shouldn't be taken too far . . . if the donor had suggested setting up an art museum within the health clinic, the organization may not have wanted to modify [its] 'product'" (p. 3).

A thorough description of marketing is beyond the scope of our discussion here, but it is useful to clarify one essential point—it is more than just communication.

Marketing intends to influence people to *do* something, to result in *action*. As Andreasen and Kotler (2008) explain,

> Marketing's objectives are not *ultimately* to educate or change values or attitudes. It may seek to do so as a *means* of influencing behavior. . . . If someone has a final goal of imparting information or knowledge, that person is in the education profession, not marketing. Further, if someone has a final goal of changing attitudes or values, that person may be described as a propagandist or lobbyist, or perhaps an artist, but not a marketer. While marketing may use the tools of the educator or the propagandist, its critical distinguishing feature is that its ultimate goal is to influence behavior. (p. 36, italics original)

Marketing's emphasis on influencing behavior makes it attractive as a framework for understanding fundraising, but there are also ways in which the fit seems less than perfect. For one thing, marketing is concerned with consumers, but in nonprofits donors and consumers may not be the same people. For example, donors may give to support a homeless shelter, but the benefits of the shelter's services go to others who do not pay. In addition, marketing begins with the needs and wants of customers, and a company designs its products to address them. But fundraising is different because it starts with the needs of the nonprofit organization and its programs, some of which cannot be changed to meet donors' desires because they are central to the organization's mission (Kelly, 1998).

Paton addresses the fundraising-as-marketing question in a thoughtful essay, first written in 1995 and edited and adapted for a 2007 publication (Paton, 2007). He argues that the relevance of marketing techniques varies among components of a fundraising program. It is highly relevant in "'mass fundraising,' . . . [which] uses the media to interest and appeal to large, remote, and distributed audiences" (p. 31). But it is less relevant in "participative fundraising," which includes more personalized approaches to individuals and may involve volunteers as well as fundraising professionals (p. 31). It is also less relevant to fundraising from institutional donors, for example, foundations and corporations.

According to Paton (2007), the relevance of marketing to fundraising also varies depending on donor motivations. We look at Paton's model again in Chapter 3, where we consider donor motivations in greater detail, but in summary, he proposes that motivations range across a continuum, from pure gifts to pure exchange with mixed motives in the middle. Paton argues that marketing may provide a useful framework for fundraising when the transaction is a pure exchange but that its relevance decreases as one moves across the spectrum toward mixed motives and, eventually, pure gifts, where marketing may not be very useful or appropriate at all.

Second, Paton observes that in a for-profit business, marketing professionals are involved in determining what products will be offered, based on their knowledge of consumers' needs and wants. But, as mentioned previously, in a nonprofit, donors and clients (consumers) may be different people. Fundraisers are engaged in meeting donor needs, but decisions about how to meet the needs of clients are made by program staff. Paton calls this disconnect "the real difficulty with the fundraising-as-marketing view" (p. 34). But similar to Lindahl's (2010) caution, Paton offers a nuanced conclusion: "fundraising can usefully be seen in marketing terms—but this does not mean the unthinking use of commercial practices" (p. 36).

The theoretical debate about whether fundraising is marketing or a distinctive activity is of practical relevance. It is sometimes reflected in issues concerning the management of the two functions within organizations. Indeed, in some organizations, "the marketing/communications/public relations department and the fundraising/development department are at odds with each other. Members of each department have different priorities and at times even have adversarial relationships" (Blackbaud, n.d.). One difference is that the development office has one very specific goal, raising more money, while communications and marketing programs are aimed at more than securing gifts. Those programs are focused on the overall organization, including goals such as attracting new clients and securing a positive public image (Blackbaud, n.d.). Marketing goals are often immediate, for example, generating clients or attendance at an event. Fundraising, when understood as the ongoing process of development, is focused on building and sustaining relationships and on creating an infrastructure of volunteers and programs that may produce results only over the long term (Blackbaud, n.d.). In some organizations, "online equals marketing, offline equals development" (Sullivan, 2013). In other words, the marketing department handles mass communication and fundraising for smaller gifts that are transactional, while the development office engages in one-on-one contacts to build relationships with major donors and prospects (Sullivan, 2013).

These differences and tensions lead some to question the effectiveness of a management structure in which a single individual is responsible for both functions, that is, the institutional advancement model discussed previously in this chapter (Blackbaud, n.d.). But other observers predict a convergence of fundraising and marketing, as the growing capabilities of social media enable more personalized communication with donors at all levels (Sullivan, 2013).

It is important to note that while marketing and public relations include activities in which businesses, nonprofits, and government agencies all engage, fundraising is an organizational function that is *exclusive to nonprofit organizations*. Thus, perhaps it may best be understood as a specialty within **nonprofit management**. Nonprofit management also draws on the principles of other disciplines, but it has emerged as distinctive, both as a profession and an academic field of study. Because fundraising is an activity exclusive to nonprofits and is inherently connected to mission, its effective practice requires a deep understanding of the nonprofit sector, nonprofit organizations, and broader principles of nonprofit management. Those topics are explored in the next chapter of this text.

PROCEEDING WITH PRIDE

This book is premised on the view that fundraising is a noble and important activity, central to the advancement of important organizations and institutions that play critical roles in our society. Some nonprofit CEOs, and even some fundraising professionals, sometimes may view fundraising as an unpleasant requirement of their jobs, rather than as a central part of their service. But as Rosso (2011a) emphasizes, "Fundraising is the servant of philanthropy" (p. 5). Fundraising is not about extracting resources from reluctant donors but rather extending to those who have the capacity to advance a nonprofit's mission the privilege of doing so and of having a positive impact on society and the future. For that reason, "the person seeking the gift should never demean the asking by clothing it in apology" (Rosso, 2011a, p. 8). Rather, fundraising is an honorable endeavor that should be undertaken with pride.

CHAPTER SUMMARY

Fundraising as a professional field is less understood by the public than fields like science, medicine, or law. Fundraising involves gifts, but some fundraisers also are responsible for partnerships with corporations, which produce earned income. Some people use the term *resource development* to encompass the pursuit of nonphilanthropic support as well as gifts. *Development* is a term commonly used as a synonym for fundraising, while *institutional advancement* is used primarily in higher education to describe the coordinated management of fundraising and other functions. Fundraising is a process that involves relationships and is more than the solicitation of gifts.

Charity is giving that addresses current human needs. *Philanthropy* is giving to build the infrastructure of society, for example, universities and hospitals, in order to meet human needs over the long run. The terms are often used interchangeably, and *philanthropy* is used as the umbrella encompassing both. Acknowledging the new approach of some philanthropists today, it may be more accurate to define *charity*, *philanthropic investment*, and *strategic philanthropy* as three related but distinct concepts.

The roots of American philanthropy go back to the nation's early centuries, but large-scale philanthropy started in the first decades of the twentieth century with people like Andrew Carnegie and John D. Rockefeller, who had made fortunes in the industrial revolution and gave to establish libraries, foundations, and other institutions. Mass philanthropy also began in the early twentieth century and engaged average Americans in giving. In the late 1990s and early 2000s, a new generation of entrepreneurs and investors, who had acquired wealth in the technology boom, defined new concepts in philanthropy that emphasized the results accomplished. By 2013, total philanthropy had grown to $335 billion, most of which was given by individual donors.

Despite early roots, organized fundraising in the United States began in the early twentieth century. One significant innovation was the intensive campaign, introduced by YMCA executives Charles Sumner Ward and Lyman L. Pierce. Ward and Pierce managed fundraising for the American Red Cross in World War I and, along with other well-known figures, founded consulting firms beginning in 1919. Consulting firms dominated the field until the 1950s, when organizations began to appoint full-time fundraisers to their staffs. Until that time, consulting firms often assigned a resident manager to an organization to direct its fundraising for a period of time, but that model is now uncommon. Such consultants advised and managed organizational staff and volunteers but did not solicit gifts. There always have been paid agents who solicit gifts, but consultants only conduct studies and provide advice. Reputable consultants are paid a fixed fee and do not accept a percentage of the funds raised.

The number of fundraisers employed by nonprofit institutions and organizations has grown throughout the post–World War II period, and many now serve as senior executives of their organizations. The field has become specialized, with professional associations focused on subfields. But there is still high turnover in development positions, due in part to the inadequacy of fundraising systems and culture in some nonprofit organizations.

Much of the literature of fundraising has been developed by practitioners and consultants, but the development of research and theory has increased. Some research relates to the nonprofit sector and nonprofit organizations; some is focused on philanthropy and the motivations of donors; some is in other fields related to fundraising, for example, marketing; and some addresses fundraising practice and the management of programs. Most principles of fundraising still are drawn from the practitioner literature; some have been confirmed and others challenged by research.

Some authors define fundraising as a specialization of other fields, including public relations and marketing. Fundraising draws on the knowledge and methods of such fields, but it is an organizational function exclusive to nonprofit organizations. Managing fundraising is a specialization of nonprofit management, which itself is a distinctive profession and field of study. Fundraising is "the servant of philanthropy" (Rosso, 2011a, p. 5) and should be undertaken with pride, not apology.

Key Terms and Concepts

Catalytic philanthropy
Charitable deduction
Charitable fundraising
Charitable nonprofits
Charity
Charity watchdogs
Contracts
Development
Development officer
Earned income
Entrepreneurial
  donors
Fund development

Fundraising
Grants
High-engagement
  grant making
Institutional
  advancement
  (advancement)
Nonprofit
  management
Outcome-oriented
  philanthropy
Philanthropic
  fundraising

Philanthropic
  investment
Philanthropy
Resident manager
Resource
  development
Strategic
  philanthropy
Venture
  philanthropy
Venture philanthropy
  funds
Wealth effect

Case 1.1: The Meth Project

In the 1990s, Tom Siebel founded software company Siebel Systems and built it into a firm employing 8,000 people and generating $2 billion in annual revenue. He sold the company to Oracle for $5.9 billion in 2006 and turned his attention to philanthropy (Verini, 2009).

When Siebel bought a ranch in Montana, he was appalled at what he learned. Montana had the nation's fifth worst rate of abuse of crystal methamphetamine, commonly known simply as meth. It was destroying lives, leading to violence, and accounting for one-half of all imprisonments in the state (Kramer, 2009). Siebel decided to do something about it. Rather than work through an existing nonprofit organization, he created the Meth Project, with the goal of educating young people about the drug's dangers. Using $26 million of his own funds, he hired an advertising agency and renowned film producers to develop hard-hitting messages that would come to blanket the state's media. The Meth Project would become the largest purchaser of advertising in Montana. Siebel also traveled the state to advocate against the use of meth and developed other outreach programs. Explaining his hands-on approach, Siebel states, "If you look at the great philanthropic institutions in the nation, it's just baffling to me how they mismanage their resources. . . . They could be changing the world" (Verini, 2009).

Within the first two years of the Meth Project's beginning, Montana's ranking for meth use dropped from fifth to thirty-ninth among the states, dropping 45 percent among young people and 72 percent among adults (Kramer, 2009). The State of Montana now pays for the project, using state and federal funds, and the Meth Project's approach was adopted by seven other states, which experienced similar declines in meth use (Verini, 2009).

Some critics argue that the positive trends may not be entirely attributable to the Meth Project. Some question the Meth Project's research methodologies and data regarding its results, while others cite alternative explanations for the decline in meth use. They include increased law enforcement by state and federal governments and laws restricting access to pseudoephedrine, an over-the-counter medication used to produce meth (Verini, 2009). Moreover, a 2010 study conducted at the University of Washington found that the use of meth was already declining when the Meth Project was initiated and concluded that the project "had no discernable impact on meth use" (Anderson, 2010, p. 732). Responding to critics, Siebel states, "The Meth Project is saving lives, pure and simple. It was an outrageous exercise in prevention. It has proven to date incredibly successful" (Verini, 2009).

In 2013, the Meth Project became a part of a larger nonprofit organization, the Partnership at Drugfree.org (Goldberg, 2013), which sought to expand its impact by organizing the first Meth Awareness Week (Besson, 2013).

Case 1.2: New York City Parks

Designed in the nineteenth century and encompassing 843 acres in the center of New York City, Central Park is described as "a masterpiece of landscape architecture . . . and the nation's first public park" (Central Park website). But by the 1970s, the park was in a state of decay. "Meadows had become barren dustbowls; benches, lights, and playground equipment were broken, and the one-hundred-year-old infrastructure was crumbling. Socially, the Park bred a careless, even abusive attitude . . . evidenced by unchecked amounts of garbage, graffiti, and vandalism. Positive use had increasingly been displaced by illicit and illegal activity" (Central Park website).

In the 1970s, philanthropists George Soros and Richard Gilder supported a study of the park. Its recommendations led eventually to the creation of the Central Park Conservancy, a nonprofit organization intended to raise private funds for restoration of the park and an endowment to support its maintenance. Over the following decades, the Conservancy conducted three capital campaigns toward park projects and to raise operating funds, resulting in a dramatic improvement in the park's physical condition. Intricate stone bridges and historic structures were restored, lawns were resodded, and fountains were refurbished and again became gathering places for large numbers of people (Foderaro, 2012).

Under continuing budgetary pressure, New York City reduced its funding of the park; by 1998, public funds covered only one-third of the park's budget. In that year, the city signed over management of the park to the Conservancy under a long-term contract (Sparks, 2012). By 2014, the Conservancy had raised $700 million to support the park, and philanthropy was providing 75 percent of the annual operating budget (Central Park website). The largest gift to the Conservancy came in 2012 from hedge fund manager John A. Paulson, who committed $100 million. "The cycles of decline and restoration that this park has suffered for so long will be broken forever," said Doug Blonsky, president of the Conservancy (Foderaro, 2012). By all accounts, Central Park had never looked as good or been as popular. It was once again a treasured asset of New York City (Foderaro, 2012).

But some expressed concern that the impact of the Central Park Conservancy, and a similar organization that supported Prospect Park in Brooklyn, was limited to wealthier parts of the city. While applauding the improvements that philanthropy had brought to Central Park and Prospect Park, Daniel Squadron, a state senator representing parts of Brooklyn and Manhattan, raised questions: "What about the kids who depend on St. Mary's Park, in the Mott Haven section of the South Bronx, where the baseball bleachers don't have seats and the cracked tennis court has no net? Or what about the thousands of people who depend on Flushing Meadows-Corona Park, in Queens, the former home of the World's Fair, now marred by graffiti, broken drainage and pervasive litter?" (Squadron, 2013). He advocated creating a new Neighborhood Parks Alliance that would receive contributions from the wealthier conservancies, equivalent to 20 percent of their annual operating budgets, to be dedicated to supporting parks in less affluent parts of the city. Squadron proposed that these gifts from "contributing parks" to "member parks" be required by law. "New playgrounds in Central Park are good," he argued, "New playgrounds in Central Park and newly functioning parks in the South Bronx and beyond are even better" (Squadron, 2013).

Squadron's proposal was not met with universal approval. Some philanthropists argued that if the proposal became law, it would have a chilling effect on giving to the park conservancies (Soskis, 2013). One critic wrote, "That the government might have a say in how private donors direct their charitable contributions is a sharp, even stunning, departure from the American tradition of independent philanthropy" (Soskis, 2013).

The ensuing debate evoked arguments going back to the days of Andrew Carnegie regarding the role of philanthropy in a democratic society and the responsibility of philanthropists to the less fortunate. Some argued that having flagship parks dependent on private funds rather than government "would sanction the erosion of public stewardship, leading to a two-tiered system in which certain green spaces flourish while the majority of the city's nearly two thousand parks languish" (Soskis, 2013). Some extended the argument to philanthropic support for public schools, saying that it could increase inequality between schools in wealthy areas and those that remain totally dependent on government support.

Large-scale philanthropy can occur only if there is accumulation of substantial private fortunes. But that also may occur at times of growing wealth inequality. Debate about whether and how wealthy philanthropists should use their resources to address the social conditions that accompany it is not new. Making the connection between the present-day controversies about New York City parks to the age of Carnegie, Soskis (2013) concludes, "If we are now inhabiting a Second Gilded Age, witnessing a widening gulf between the wealthiest and the rest, as well as an efflorescence of large-scale philanthropic giving, we are also seeing a heightened sensitivity to the intimate connection between these two developments, a concern that marked that earlier age as well."

Questions for Discussion

1. In Case 1.1, in what ways does Tom Siebel's approach to philanthropy reflect the new philanthropists discussed in this chapter?

2. In Case 1.1, is Tom Siebel's approach best described as charity, philanthropic investment, or strategic philanthropy?

3. In Case 1.2, do you think the law should require that gifts made to the Central Park Conservancy be shared with organizations that would help parks in low-income parts of New York City, or do you think that philanthropists should be able to direct their private resources as they see fit?

4. What should be the responsibility, if any, of wealthy philanthropists to address social issues such as income and wealth inequality? How does your answer relate to the concepts of charity and philanthropy?

5. Reflecting on issues raised by the case of New York City parks, should the tax deduction provided for charitable gifts be greater for those that specifically have an impact on low-income communities and people? Or should all philanthropy be treated equally under the tax law?

Suggestions for Further Reading

Books

Cutlip, S. M. (1990). *Fund raising in the United States: Its role in America's philanthropy*. New Brunswick, NJ: Transaction Publishers. (Note: Cutlip's classic 1965 book was republished in 1990 with a new preface by Cutlip and an introduction by John J. Schwartz. The 1990 edition is more readily available than the original 1965 edition. Cutlip's book remains the most complete discussion of the early years of organized fundraising in the United States and is a classic that remains an important resource for individuals interested in that topic.)

Frumkin, P. (2006). *Strategic giving*. Chicago: University of Chicago Press.

Zunz, O. (2012). *Philanthropy in America: A history*. Princeton, NJ: Princeton University Press.

Articles

Brest, P. (Spring 2012). A decade of outcome-oriented philanthropy. *Stanford Social Innovation Review, 10*(2), 42–47.

Sievers, B. R. (2010). Philanthropy's role in liberal democracy. *The Journal of Speculative Philosophy, 24*(4), 380–398.

Websites

Association of Fundraising Professionals: www.afpnet.org

Association for Healthcare Philanthropy: www.ahp.org

Council for Advancement and Support of Education: www.case.org

Giving Institute: http://givinginstitute.org

Venture Philanthropy Partners: www.vppartners.org

Understanding the Nonprofit Sector and Nonprofit Organizations

America's nonprofit sector is large, diverse, and complex. It includes an estimated 2.3 million organizations, of which 1.6 million are registered with the Internal Revenue Service (IRS) (Roeger, Blackwood, & Pettijohn, 2012). They range in size from those that employ hundreds, even thousands of people to others that are managed entirely by volunteers. Their activities touch every aspect of our lives, from nurturing our souls and spirits to educating our minds and protecting our health. The sector and its organizations also are complex. Some nonprofits may not seem like nonprofits at all, and some organizations that sound like nonprofits are not. Indeed, some organizations are hybrids that include for-profit components or that work closely with government. We could experience a good sample of this universe by taking an imaginary walk around my home town of Washington, DC, starting out from my office on the campus of The George Washington University, located in the neighborhood of Foggy Bottom, near the White House. Some of the organizations we would see are unique to Washington because it is the nation's capital, but a similarly diverse array may be found in any major American city.

Leaving my building, we might walk a couple of blocks west, passing The George Washington University Hospital, and then head south toward the Vietnam Veterans Memorial. Along the way we would pass Western Presbyterian Church, where we might see people waiting to have breakfast or dinner at Miriam's Kitchen. Although independent of Western Presbyterian, Miriam's is located in the basement of the church and provides food and other services to the homeless. Taking another turn we would pass the national headquarters of the American Red Cross and the National Park Service. Continuing on, past the Washington Monument and heading up the National Mall toward the Capitol, we would see the buildings of the Smithsonian Institution and, perhaps, catch sight of the National Archives, just a block off the Mall. Depending on our route back to the university, we might walk past the National Geographic Society, the Cato Institute, and the Brookings Institution. Taking a slightly different route, we would see the AFL-CIO, a federation of labor unions, and the U.S. Chamber of Commerce, which represents the interests of the business community. They are located about a block apart from each other, near the White House.

Returning to the campus, we would likely need to stop at a Starbucks, since it would have been a long walk and we would be tired! While drinking some coffee, we might reflect on the many sites we have seen and how they represent America's nonprofit sector.

We would surely identify Miriam's Kitchen as a nonprofit; indeed, its mission of serving the homeless is probably what most people think about when the term *nonprofit* is used. In addition, it is almost totally supported by gifts and a large portion of its workforce is volunteers, both conditions that would fit common perceptions of a nonprofit. We might not think about Western Presbyterian Church as a nonprofit, although it is, and we might assume that The George Washington Hospital is a nonprofit, although it is not. Indeed, the hospital is a for-profit business owned jointly by The George Washington University, a nonprofit, and Universal Health Services, a Fortune 500 corporation. This combination of nonprofit and for-profit entities might seem unusual, but we would have seen other examples on our walk. For example, both the National Geographic Society and the Smithsonian are nonprofit organizations that have for-profit subsidiaries to manage business aspects of their operations. The Smithsonian is, of course, especially complex, since it is a nonprofit with a for-profit arm that is also our national museum and receives substantial government support.

Most people would readily recognize the American Red Cross as one of the nation's largest nonprofit organizations, although like a government agency, it has a mandate to provide services to the U.S. military and to the nation in times of disaster. The Vietnam Veterans Memorial, the National Mall, and the Washington Monument are, of course, property of the federal government, but all are also beneficiaries of philanthropy. For example, when the Washington Monument was damaged by an earthquake in 2011, the needed repairs cost $15 million. One-half of the cost was covered by the federal government and the other half by a gift to the nonprofit Trust for the National Mall, which partners with the National Park Service, from investor David Rubenstein. And this was not Mr. Rubenstein's only gift to support a national institution. He purchased an original copy of the Magna Carta for $23 million at auction and gave it to the National Archives. And he gave $4.5 million to build a new home for the pandas at the National Zoo, which is part of the Smithsonian (Heath, 2013).

Finally, we might wonder what to make of the Cato Institute and the Brookings Institution, both nonprofit think tanks that often reflect different perspectives on public policy questions, or the AFL-CIO and the Chamber of Commerce, which often lobby on opposite sides of public policy debates. How can all of these organizations be nonprofits, and what do they have in common? These are questions I explore in an earlier work (Worth, 2014), from which some of the following sections have been condensed.

CHARACTERISTICS OF NONPROFITS

As Salamon (1999) explains, all nonprofit organizations have certain characteristics in common. They are **organized entities**, most incorporated under state law, and they are rooted in the **tradition of volunteerism**, even if they have paid staff members. They are private and **self-governing**, with the autonomy to determine how they will pursue revenues, what programs they will operate, and who will benefit from their activities. They may receive government funding in the form of grants or contracts that require them to provide specific services, but they also have the freedom to eschew government funds and operate entirely with revenue from private sources, including earned income and philanthropy.

Although various terms are used to label the nonprofit sector, including the independent sector, third sector, voluntary sector, and social sector, the term most commonly used—*nonprofit sector*—really refers to something that such organizations do *not* do. Nonprofit organizations do not distribute their profits; in other words, they face a **nondistribution constraint**. Nonprofit organizations can earn a profit and many do. But that profit must be reinvested in their programs and cannot be used to personally benefit owners or investors. They may pay their employees reasonable compensation for the services they provide, but they may not reward them beyond what those services are worth, as if they were owners of the enterprise. In exchange for these limitations, nonprofits are exempt from taxation by the federal government, a privilege that is also extended with regard to most state taxes.[1] But this exemption applies only to revenue directly related to nonprofits' **tax-exempt** purposes. To the extent that a nonprofit generates income from business activities not related to its charitable purposes, those revenues could be subject to the **unrelated business income tax (UBIT)**, although the overall organization could remain exempt. For example, if a museum operates a parking garage that is used only by staff and visitors, that would be related to its purpose as a museum, and the revenue would not be taxable. But if the museum's garage was open to the general public, the revenue might be considered unrelated and would be taxed; in other words, the IRS would consider the museum to be in the parking business, which is not related to the mission of a museum. Nonprofits are careful to clarify the relationship between earned-income activities and charitable mission where one exists.

Finally, a nonprofit's activities are of **public benefit**. The public benefit is probably obvious when the mission is to feed the hungry, preserve important national treasures, or prevent drug abuse and addiction. But what about organizations that may advocate or even lobby for opposing points of view, like the U.S. Chamber of Commerce and the AFL-CIO? In our society, the encouragement of open debate on all sides of an issue is considered to be a public benefit because it advances the policy dialogue essential to democracy. That explains why tax exemption is granted to organizations that advocate competing views, so long as they follow requirements of the law.

A nonprofit's broad purposes are stated in its charter and elaborated upon in its mission statement. Nonprofits are **mission-driven**. Mission is the guiding star and the bottom line; it guides planning, major decisions, and standards by which the organization's effectiveness is evaluated. As James Phills (2005) explains,

> Mission is the psychological and emotional logic that drives an organization. It is the reason why people get up in the morning and go to work in a nonprofit. . . . Mission [defines] the social value that the organization creates. The key feature of social value—whether it is spiritual, moral, societal, aesthetic, intellectual, or environmental—is that it transcends economic value. Thus, it is inextricably linked to fundamental human values, which are the basis for intrinsic worth or importance. (p. 22)

CLASSIFICATIONS OF NONPROFITS

With such a large and diverse nonprofit sector, we need to place organizations into categories that can be more easily analyzed. Various frameworks are used, including the **National Taxonomy of Exempt Entities (NTEE)**, which places nonprofits into twenty-six major groups under ten broad categories, based on their purpose, activities, and programs. NTEE classifications are similar to industry classification codes used to group for-profit companies. But since our focus here is on fundraising and philanthropy, the classifications most relevant to us—and probably the best known—are those used by the IRS, reflecting the basis for organizations' exemption from the federal corporate income tax.

Figure 2.1 provides an illustration of the nonprofit sector based on IRS classifications. The IRS places nonprofits in thirty different categories, but many are not relevant to our discussion about fundraising, so Figure 2.1 is simplified. It shows the organizations of the most interest to us in this text—charitable nonprofits—in the center. We'll come back to them—let's look first at the other categories.

On the left side of Figure 2.1 are nonprofits exempt from taxation under section 501(c)(4) of the tax code, which the IRS calls **social welfare organizations** but many people call **advocacy organizations**. Two examples are the Sierra Club and the NRA. As the term *advocacy* suggests, these are organizations that seek to influence public attitudes and advocate positions on public policy issues. They also may engage in lobbying for legislation without any specific limitation.[2] They are themselves exempt from taxation, but a gift to

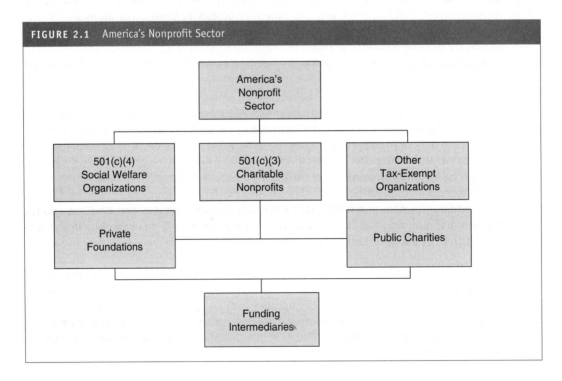

FIGURE 2.1   America's Nonprofit Sector

one of them is *not* tax deductible for the donor—that is the tradeoff for the right to lobby without limitation.

Some 501(c)(4) organizations work closely with affiliated 501(c)(3) charitable organizations. For example, the Sierra Club is an advocacy organization, but the Sierra Club Foundation is a separate entity that provides education and other programs that qualify as charitable under the tax law. An individual can pay dues to belong to the Sierra Club, which would not be deductible, and also make a gift to the Sierra Club Foundation, which would be. Many professional and industry associations also maintain two related entities, one an advocacy organization and the other a 501(c)(3) that supports educational programs and research. Two related organizations working in this way obviously need to be careful to assure that the activities of each are clearly delineated in order to comply with the requirements of their respective tax statuses.

On the right side of Figure 2.1 are all other tax-exempt organizations, which are classified under various sections of the Internal Revenue Code (IRC). They include, for example, labor unions, chambers of commerce, and fraternities and sororities, among many others. They are exempt from tax, but gifts to them are generally not deductible. Many play important roles in the nation and in local communities, but again, our emphasis here is on the charitable nonprofits shown in the middle of Figure 2.1, which account for 63 percent of organizations in the sector (Roeger et al., 2012).

To be a charitable nonprofit, an organization must meet three tests. First, it must be organized and operated for one or more of eight purposes: charitable, religious, educational, scientific, literary, testing for public safety, fostering national or international amateur sports competitions, and prevention of cruelty to children or animals. The IRC does not specially mention health, although health care institutions are one of the largest components of the nonprofit sector as measured by revenue and employment. *Charitable* is a broad term, but the IRS (2014a) offers some examples of what is encompassed, including the following:

> relief of the poor, the distressed, or the underprivileged; advancement of religion; advancement of education or science; erecting or maintaining public buildings, monuments, or works; lessening the burdens of government; lessening neighborhood tensions; eliminating prejudice and discrimination; defending human and civil rights secured by law; and combating community deterioration and juvenile delinquency.

In addition to demonstrating that its primary purpose fits into one of these criteria, a charitable nonprofit also must meet three additional tests. It must show that it is supported by the public rather than one or a few donors, a point explained further in the next section of this chapter. It must meet the nondistribution test. And it must limit its political activities. The latter requires that it not support candidates for public office and that its expenditures on lobbying fall within limits defined by tax law (IRS, 2015). The tradeoff for accepting these limitations and requirements is that charitable nonprofits are both exempt from taxation *and* eligible to receive gifts that are **tax deductible** to donors. The latter provides a considerable benefit to donors and an advantage to charitable nonprofits in their fundraising.

For example, suppose a donor is in the 25 percent tax bracket and makes a $100 gift to a charitable organization. He or she can deduct that $100 from his or her income before calculating the tax due. At 25 percent, that produces a tax saving of $25; in other words, the donor's tax bill will be $25 less than it would have been without the deduction. The effect of the deduction is to reduce the actual out-of-pocket cost of that gift from $100 to $75, since the additional $25 would otherwise have been paid in taxes. Some view the tax savings as a form of subsidy from taxpayers, and some economists refer to the government's loss of revenue as a **tax expenditure**. And since states also provide deductions for charitable gifts, the donor may gain additional tax benefits. It is important to understand that these benefits are not tax loopholes, and taking advantage of them is not unethical. Rather, they have been placed in the law intentionally in order to encourage charitable gifts and the activities they support.

Religious congregations are charitable nonprofits that are tax exempt under section 501(c)(3). But they are also unique in that they are protected by the constitutional provision of religious freedom. For that reason, they are not required to register with the IRS, although some do so voluntarily (Blackwood, Roeger, & Pettijohn, 2012).

PUBLIC CHARITIES AND PRIVATE FOUNDATIONS

As Figure 2.1 depicts, there are two types of charitable nonprofits—**public charities** and **private foundations**. Both are important to our discussion of fundraising and philanthropy. There are technical definitions of both categories, but it is sufficient to understand that public charities receive funding from multiple sources, including donors and government; that is, they are supported by the public. Most offer programs directly to clients—they are **operating public charities**—and they include many of the organizations most of us know best, including universities, hospitals, arts institutions, museums, research institutes, and those that provide human and social services. In contrast, private foundations are funded by one or a few donors, which may include a corporation, an individual, or members of a family. Some of the best known examples are the Bill and Melinda Gates Foundation, established with gifts from Bill and Melinda Gates; the Ford Foundation, created by Henry Ford with his personal wealth; and the Walmart Foundation, a corporate foundation created by Walmart. Some foundations do operate their own programs and are known as **operating foundations**, but most are **grant-making foundations** that provide support to other nonprofit organizations and institutions. Most but not all foundations are intended to exist in perpetuity. The gifts made to create them are invested and only the annual investment earnings are spent to support programs, while the principal remains preserved.

One big difference between public charities and private foundations is that donors who make gifts to public charities can deduct those gifts up to 50 percent of income, whereas gifts to a private foundation can be deducted only up to 30 percent of income in a given year. In addition, private foundations also must pay a modest tax on their investment earnings and are required to spend a minimum of 5 percent of their assets each year, conditions that do not apply to public charities. For those reasons, public charities are usually careful to assure that they maintain a sufficient base of public support to avoid reclassification as a private foundation.

At the bottom of Figure 2.1 are a group of charitable nonprofits called **funding inter-mediaries**. These are organizations that receive money from one or more sources and, as the term *intermediary* implies, then pass that money along to other organizations. Grant-making private foundations are by definition funding intermediaries, but so are some public charities, which are sometimes called **supporting public charities**. The United Way and Jewish federations are public charities that are funding intermediaries. So are charitable gift funds operated by commercial wealth management companies, for example, the Fidelity Charitable Gift Fund. It may be confusing that some funding intermediaries that are public charities use the word *foundation* in their names, although they are not classified as private foundations. For example, **community foundations** are public charities and so are **institutionally related foundations** that raise funds to support a single related entity—for example, the National Park Foundation, which supports the National Park Service, and the University of Florida Foundation, which raises and manages funds for the exclusive benefit of the public institution it serves. The various types of foundations and their characteristics are discussed in more detail in Chapter 10 of this book.

NONPROFIT REVENUE SOURCES

Many people may think nonprofit organizations receive most or all of their revenue from gifts, but indeed, that is far from the case for the sector overall. Sources of revenue vary among the various nonprofit subsectors, so we need to dig down a little deeper to understand the full picture. With our focus on fundraising, one of the most important differences is the extent to which different types of organizations depend on philanthropy.

The largest source of revenue for the nonprofit sector overall is fees for services and goods paid by clients or customers, accounting for 50 percent. This includes, for example, tuition paid by students, tickets purchased by concertgoers, and hospital bills paid by private individuals or their private insurance companies. Another 24 percent of revenue comes from fees for services and goods paid to nonprofits by government, for example, payments Medicare and Medicaid make to hospitals to cover medical care for people they insure. These government payments are distinct from government grants, which often have restrictions on their use but are not payment for specific services or goods. Government grants account for another 8 percent of nonprofit sector revenue. Looking at the charitable nonprofit sector overall, gifts account for only 13 percent of total revenue, but this percentage is greatly affected by the inclusion of hospitals and universities, which—as students will readily understand—generate substantial revenues from fees for service! Excluding hospitals and universities, gifts account for 24 percent of the revenue of the remaining organizations overall (Roeger et al., 2012).

As Figure 2.2 portrays, revenue derived from gifts varies considerably among charitable subsectors, comprising 69 percent in international affairs; 57 percent in arts, culture, and humanities; 49 percent in environment and animals; 20 percent in human services; 17 percent in education; and less than 5 percent in health. The differences are largely explained by the role of fees for service and government support, which account for high percentages in education and health but lower percentages in organizations concerned with animals and the environment and those in international and foreign affairs. Organizations

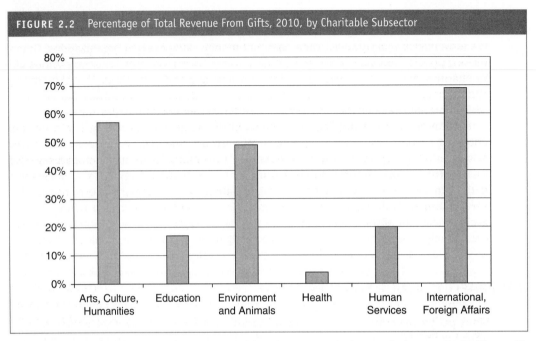

FIGURE 2.2 Percentage of Total Revenue From Gifts, 2010, by Charitable Subsector

Source: Based on data from Roeger, K. L., Blackwood, A. S., & Pettijohn, S. J. (2012). *The nonprofit almanac, 2012.* Washington, DC: Urban Institute Press, pp. 178–189.

in human services also receive substantial government support, including payments for services they provide to individuals who qualify for government benefit programs, explaining why gifts are a lower percentage of their overall revenues. And remember that the percentages do not tell the story in terms of absolute impact; as we saw in Figure 1.2, except for religion, education and human services receive the largest percentages of overall philanthropic dollars (16 percent and 12 percent, respectively), even though gifts are a relatively small percentage of revenue for organizations in those fields.

In addition, these figures do not reflect the differing utility of various types of revenue. For example, fees for services may be offset by the costs of providing those services, whereas gifts may provide unrestricted or flexible revenue that can be used to build the organization or to undertake new innovative programs. Thus, even where gifts may comprise a relatively small percentage of total revenue, they may be critical to achieving an organization's goals and be highly desired by its leaders. The relative importance of various sources of revenue has implications for how organizations are structured and behave, as discussed further soon.

NONPROFIT FINANCIAL CONCEPTS

The subject of nonprofit financial management is a large one, beyond the scope of this text. But a basic understanding of a few terms is essential and will be important to have later in the text when we discuss different types of gifts and how they must be managed. Students already familiar with nonprofit accounting may skim or skip this section; those who wish to know more will find suggested additional reading at the end of this chapter.

Nonprofit finances are different from those of individuals and for-profit businesses. For one thing, a nonprofit receives gifts and grants, some of which have been designated by the donor to be used for a specific purpose (Bowman, 2011). This requires that a nonprofit maintain a variety of funds, each subject to different conditions.

A nonprofit's **operating funds** are much like those each of us manages in his or her checking account. In general, payments received are intended to be spent within the same period to pay current bills. A nonprofit's operating funds may be **unrestricted** or **restricted**. Fees nonprofits receive for services provided to customers or clients and gifts from donors who do not designate a specific use are generally unrestricted, which means they may be used to meet any expense. Nonprofits also receive payments that are restricted to particular purposes, and they are required to ensure that they are spent accordingly. For example, if a donor makes a grant to a school and specifies that it be used to purchase art supplies, the school would not be able to use it for sports equipment. The flexibility that comes with unrestricted gifts makes them highly valued by nonprofit organizations. However, many donors, especially when larger gifts are involved, prefer to place some restrictions on their use. The organization has a legal obligation to comply with such restrictions, and, of course, doing so may be essential to receiving further support from the donor.

Funds may be **temporarily restricted** or **permanently restricted**. Funds that are temporarily restricted might result from an advance payment on a gift or grant to cover some activity that has not yet occurred. In the earlier example, the grant to purchase art supplies is temporarily restricted until the supplies are purchased. As the term implies, funds that are permanently restricted can *never* be used for anything other than the intended purpose. That would be the case with most **endowment funds** created by donors. The investment income that endowment funds generate may be unrestricted or restricted, depending on the stipulations of the donor, but if the donor directs that principal be preserved *in perpetuity*, then the organization can never expend it. Some donors may direct that principal remain invested for a term of years, after which it may be expended; funds resulting from such an arrangement are called **term endowments**.

There are two basic categories of endowment funds that an organization might hold: **board-designated endowment** (also called **quasi-endowment**) and **permanent endowment** (also called **pure endowment**). As the term suggests, a board-designated endowment includes funds that the organization's board has decided to invest for the long term, using only the investment earnings. For example, the organization may have accumulated reserves that exceed what it really needs to have; the board may decide that those funds should be invested, in order to enhance long-term stability. Since it was the board's decision to place the funds in the endowment, the board has the authority to withdraw the funds from the endowment if it determines that to be necessary or desirable. But a board would be reluctant to draw down quasi-endowment funds except in relatively dire circumstances.

With a permanent or pure endowment, the board has limited or no flexibility. The board does not have the legal authority to invade the original principal of the gift or to use the income for purposes not consistent with the donor's direction without first obtaining the donor's approval or, with strong justification, permission from a court of law.

It may be a common perception that endowment is an asset held only by relatively few major institutions, such as universities, foundations, and museums. And those types of organizations do have the largest endowments. But recent years have seen efforts to raise endowment funds by a larger and more diverse group of organizations. Some of them view endowment as a way to develop a stream of revenue than might offset fluctuations in other sources over the long term. In 2013, the largest endowments were those of the Gates Foundation, valued at $36 billion, and Harvard University, worth almost $31 billion. But some other nonprofit endowments include those of the Salvation Army ($1.9 billion), the American Red Cross ($828 million), the World Wildlife Fund ($195 million), and City Year ($9 million) ("Facts and Figures," 2013).

One additional principle of nonprofit accounting is especially relevant to our focus on fundraising, the distinction between the **cash basis** of accounting and the **accrual basis** of accounting. Using the cash basis, financial transactions are recorded only when money changes hands, that is, when a payment is received or a bill is paid. But that may present a misleading picture of the actual financial situation, since it does not reflect **accounts payable**, that is, obligations the organization has undertaken but not yet fulfilled, or **accounts receivable**, for example, **pledges**—promises to give that donors have made.

Pledges are counted as revenue when a donor has signed a written commitment. In that case, the transaction would not be recorded as revenue when the pledge is paid—that would be double counting. So, signed pledges are revenue, although the funds are not available to the organization until the pledge is paid (Bowman, 2011). As discussed later in this text, it is not uncommon for an organization to complete a successful campaign, having reached its goal but without much cash on hand as a result. Pledges will have been recorded as revenue, but it may be years before the organization has the cash.

EXPLAINING THE NONPROFIT SECTOR

Now that we have an understanding of the types of organizations that comprise the nonprofit sector, sources of nonprofit revenue, and some key principles of nonprofit financial management, there remains a fundamental question: why does this sector exist? Theories that address this question have been proposed by economists, sociologists, historians, political scientists, psychologists, social psychologists, anthropologists, and scholars in other disciplines. Some of the most prominent theories are summarized in Box 2.1.

Historians explain the existence of the nonprofit sector in terms of historical forces and events. They describe the nation's early tradition of voluntary action and the role of urbanization, industrialization, and immigration in shaping society and creating the need for the services nonprofits provide. The freedoms of speech, religion, assembly, and petition, enshrined in the First Amendment to the U.S. Constitution, have provided an environment that supported voluntary action throughout American history. And public policy, notably tax exemption and the deductibility of gifts, has supported the nonprofit sector's growth (Hall, 2006). Sociologists study relationships between and among people in groups

BOX 2.1	Some Prominent Theories Explaining the Nonprofit Sector
History	The nonprofit sector reflects voluntary traditions of early America, changing social needs arising from various historical movements, and the tax structure as it has evolved throughout U.S. history.
Sociology	Involvement in nonprofits helps socialize individuals, reinforce norms and values, and develop social capital. Nonprofits are mediating structures that help people interact with large bureaucracies, such as government and business.
Political science	Nonprofits exist to accommodate diversity, undertake social experimentation, provide freedom from bureaucracy, and address minority needs.
Economics	Nonprofit organizations fill gaps left by market failure and government failure. Some nonprofits arise because of action on the supply side, that is, social entrepreneurs or donors motivated to solve a problem or promote a cause.
Interdisciplinary	Lohmann's theory of the commons defines common goods as a separate category, distinct from private and public goods. At least some nonprofits exist to provide common goods to groups of individuals who share an interest in them.

Source: Worth, M. J. (2014). *Nonprofit management: Principles and practice* (3rd ed.). Thousand Oaks, CA: Sage, p. 55.

and explain how nonprofits help to socialize individuals, reinforce common norms and values, build social capital, and provide mediating structures between individuals and large organizations in the governmental and business sectors (O'Neill, 2002). Political scientists look at the role of nonprofits in supporting democratic traditions and how they affect power relationships within society. They describe how nonprofits accommodate diversity, undertake social experimentation, provide freedom from bureaucracy, and address minority needs (Clemens, 2006). Economists have developed the best-known theories to explain the nonprofit sector, although their theories are sometimes controversial.

Failure Theories

One set of influential theories advanced by economists to explain the existence of the nonprofit sector is called **failure theories**. Economists analyze the world in terms of exchanges that occur in markets. People give up something, usually money, and get something in return. Economists use the term *goods* to mean everything that comes in return, including services or even intangible benefits, like psychological peace or warm feelings.

Through the forces of supply and demand, markets are effective in determining the production and consumption of what are called **private goods**, that is, goods we consume as individuals without any positive or negative effect on others. So, for example, the clothing we wear, the food we eat, and haircuts we receive are private goods; we capture the full benefit of using them with little, if any, impact on others. If we buy them, they will be provided, and if we don't, they will cease to be produced; the market is a relatively effective mechanism for determining how society's resources are allocated to the production of private goods.

But some goods have **externalities**. In other words, your consumption of them affects others, either negatively or positively. To use a positive example, if you were personally to hire a contractor to pave your street, that would provide you with the benefit of a smoother ride, but your neighbors also would enjoy that ride at no cost to them. In this example, they would be what are called **free riders**, who enjoy the positive externalities you have created but cannot capture entirely for yourself. There is no way you could prevent neighbors from gaining this benefit at your expense, so you probably would be disinclined to pay for paving of the street alone. For goods like this, the market does not do a very good job of allocating resources, so we define them as **public goods**, assigning their production to government and paying for them through our taxes. We all benefit and we all pay for public goods, like fire and police protection, military defense, and for the most part, paved roads. This theory helps to further explain the points made by Kelly (1998) and Paton (2007) discussed in Chapter 1. Giving is unlike a commercial exchange because the benefits created may go to people other than those who paid. Those who benefit may be, in the context of failure theories, like free riders, but the benefits they receive are, indeed, intended by the donors. That intention distinguishes a gift from a purchase and perhaps fundraising from marketing.

But let's get back to the question at hand: why is there a nonprofit sector? In part, because of **market failure** (Hansmann, 1987). Markets are inherently ineffective in providing public goods because of the free rider problem. But government may fail as well—there may be **government failure** (Weisbrod, 1975, 1988). This does not mean that government is necessarily inept but rather that it may be constrained in what it can do. For example, there may not be political support for addressing the needs of minority groups or consensus about the best way to address emerging problems like climate change. The solution to a problem may not be clear, and it would simply be too risky for government to commit public funds to an untested strategy. Or government may be too large and too bureaucratic to fully recognize and respond to local needs. In cases where neither the market nor government can provide a needed good, economists theorize, nonprofits step in to fill the gap. Sometimes they do this by providing goods directly, and at other times they mobilize public opinion and build consensus until government is able to act. Think here about Case 1.1 in Chapter 1, which describes the initiative undertaken by Tom Siebel to reduce drug abuse in Montana. There was no way for the market to address the problem, and government may have been constrained by uncertainty about what efforts could be effective. But after the Meth Project presented evidence of results from a new approach, the State of Montana was able to step in and take action itself. Nonprofit action filled a gap until the government could provide the good.

Although failure theories have gained wide acceptance, some economists offer a different approach to explaining the nonprofit sector. Various **supply-side theories** attribute the existence of the nonprofit sector to the initiatives of individuals who have created organizations, often motivated by religious faith or social conscience rather than any economic incentives (James, 1987; Rose-Ackerman, 1996; Young, 1983). Thus, theories of **social entrepreneurship** and **altruism** offer a counterpoint to the failure theories. To apply the example from Case 1.1, supply-side theorists would explain the Meth Project in terms of Tom Siebel's motivations, rather than failure of the market or the government in Montana.

Theory of the Commons

In his 1992 book *The Commons*, sociologist Roger Lohmann introduced the **theory of the commons**, which differed from the failure theories. According to Lohmann (1992), the commons are "an economic, political, and social space outside the market, households, and state in which associative communities create and reproduce social worlds" (p. 59). Rejecting the dichotomy of public and private goods, Lohmann defines a third kind of good— **common goods**. As he explains,

> One of the most powerful criticisms of the application of the public goods orientation to nonprofit or voluntary action is that most commons fail to fit the description of a public good. [For example,] church services, lodge meetings, food pantries, scientific meetings, amateur athletic events, and most other commons are available to some people (members and participants) without being available to all. Thus, they fail to meet the criterion of indivisibility, which is one of two defining characteristics of public goods.
>
> Yet many of the desired or preferred ends or objectives of common action are clearly not private goods either. They cannot be fully alienated and controlled exclusively by particular individuals without ceasing to be what they are. There is an undeniably other-oriented quality to any religious ritual, scientific finding, or artistic expression, for example. (p. 171)

Thus, whereas private goods benefit only the individual who consumes them and public goods benefit everyone, common goods are of benefit to (or of interest to) only the members of a particular commons. Lohmann (1992) acknowledges that failure theories may explain nonprofits that derive much of their revenue from earned income, for example "through ticket sales or fees charged for services, such as orchestras, opera companies, hospitals, nursing homes, and various types of social service agencies." But, he argues, "Contemporary economists have largely ignored large portions of the commons" (p. 175).

What Lohmann adds to understanding of fundraising and philanthropy is insight on the behavior of donors. I may make a gift to the annual fund of my alma mater, but probably not to yours. I may support research to find a cure for a disease that afflicts members of my family, but you may support research related to another one that afflicts your family more. I may give to an organization that promotes the study of nonprofit management, but probably not to one that promotes farming. In other words, for any organization, not every person is a prospect for a gift. Only members of a particular commons are.

EXPLAINING NONPROFIT ORGANIZATIONS

Now that we have examined some macro theories that explain the nonprofit sector, let's turn to some micro theories, that is, theories that explain the behavior of individual nonprofit organizations. The field of organizational theory is large, and recent years have produced a considerable body of work specifically addressing the distinctive features of nonprofit organizations. Thus, our discussion must be selective and focus on a few theories that have particular relevance for fundraising and philanthropy.

Nonprofits as Systems

One of the early organizational theorists, Max Weber, who wrote in the early twentieth century, defined the concept of the **bureaucracy** as an ideal model for an organization. To Weber, bureaucracies characterized by formal hierarchy and rules could become machine-like in their efficiency and effectiveness. It was a model that seemed to fit well with the emerging industrial age in which Weber wrote, and it may still describe how many people think about organizations today, especially large ones. Weber's view of organizations as machines—and people as cogs—eventually was overtaken by theorists of the "human relations school," who emphasized human needs, motivations, and incentives in the workplace (Rainey, 2003). But all of these theories addressed the *internal* dynamics of organizations and the behavior of individuals within them and did not consider how organizations might interact with or adapt to the environment around them.

Thinking shifted in the 1960s, when theorists began to look at organizations as **systems** and analyze how they interact with and adapt to the *external* environment that surrounds them. A landmark book by Daniel Katz and Robert Kahn published in 1966, *The Social Psychology of Organizations*, introduced the concept of organizations as **open systems**, and their work has influenced the thinking and writing of numerous other scholars since. Because systems theory describes how a nonprofit organization interacts with and adapts to its environment, it provides a fundamental framework for understanding fundraising and an organization's relationships with donors.

A simple system is one that receives inputs, processes those inputs in some way, and produces outputs. It also receives feedback from its environment and is able to adapt in light of the information it receives, that is, to learn. For that reason, systems theorists see organizations more like living organisms than machines, always evolving in order to survive in a constantly changing environment around them.

Organizations may be **closed systems** or open systems, although most are on a continuum between those two extremes. A closed system is one that is relatively self-sufficient and does not need to respond much or at all to influences from the external environment. It is difficult to think of an organization that is totally closed, but some governmental agencies that provide essential services may be somewhat so, since they are likely to receive sufficient appropriations and have relative autonomy in determining their own policies and procedures. Some nonprofit institutions that have large endowments may be relatively closed. If they are able to mostly operate on their investment earnings and are not overly reliant on client payments or gifts, they may be relatively free to chart their own courses without paying too much attention to outside pressures. Some people argue that endowed foundations demonstrate these qualities, and as a result, their grant making is often less responsive to society's needs than it should be.

Most nonprofit organizations are relatively open systems. They have missions defined in terms of social benefit. They are reliant on financial support that comes from outside, either from donors, clients, or government. They are chartered and regulated by government, and their tax exemption is viewed as a public subsidy. Because they enjoy tax benefits and serve public purposes, they are often the subject of scrutiny from charity watchdogs and the media. With these characteristics, it would be difficult for them to remain totally closed, oblivious to the circumstances and pressures of the world around them.

In addition, many organizations rely on volunteers at various levels. In some nonprofits, volunteers—called **service volunteers**—directly provide its programs, for example, tutoring children or providing food to victims of disaster. In most nonprofits, the governing board also is composed of volunteers, some of whom may have begun their involvement with the organization as service volunteers and thus have knowledge and opinions about its programs. Of course, volunteers *choose* to be associated with a nonprofit organization; they receive no tangible compensation. They are free to come or go as they may prefer and also to hold and express opinions. Volunteers may work directly with clients and alongside staff. Some of them may also be donors, and some of them may serve on the governing board. Information and opinion often flow freely up, down, and around the organization, crossing the boundaries that define it.

Boundary-Spanning Roles

In an open-systems environment, the boundaries between what is *inside* and what is *outside* are often permeable. That makes the role of **boundary spanners**—who provide linkages between internal and external—especially important (Grønbjerg, 1993). Nonprofit CEOs and other staff members may sometimes function in a boundary-spanning role, for example, when they are involved in fundraising or advocacy. But much of their work also will be confined to internal matters, including the management of budgets, staff, and programs. On the other hand, the organization's governing board and fundraising professionals generally will have little responsibility for day-to-day management of the organization's programs. They are, by definition and design, the organization's principal boundary spanners.

Governing Boards as Boundary Spanners

Members of the governing board of a nonprofit include individuals drawn from the organization's community, however that community may be defined, depending on the nature and scale of activities. In organizations that have members, boards are often elected by the membership. In other organizations, the board may be self-perpetuating; new members are elected by the current members of the board. Some boards may have members who are appointed by another organization, for example, a sponsoring religious congregation. And some nonprofits have hybrid boards, with members chosen through a combination of these methods.

Sometimes the organization's CEO serves as a member of the governing board, other times not. But most board members are not employees of the organization. They may be donors, clients or former clients, local community leaders, business leaders, and members of other groups. Most are unlikely to have the same professional expertise of individuals on the nonprofit's staff. For example, an organization offering services to children may have a CEO who is a trained social worker or psychologist and knows more about the needs of young children than laypeople serving on the board who have only their personal experiences to inform their views. But it would not be desirable or appropriate to simply defer to the professional judgment of the CEO in all matters concerning management of the organization and its programs. The organization's mission is to address needs of its community, and it is supported by that community. Since it is tax exempt, it receives a public subsidy for providing service to the community. The community thus has a stake in how it manages its resources and what activities it undertakes. So, one of the governing board's responsibilities is to act as a watchdog, representing the interests of the community and assuring that the CEO and other staff members act in its interests. It is the board's responsibility to assure that the nonprofit's resources are properly applied, that its programs are aligned with community needs, and that it is accountable for accomplishing the purposes for which it has been chartered. Indeed, the governing board has fiduciary responsibilities that are defined in law.

In a landmark case in 1974 (formally *Stern v. Lucy Webb Hayes National Training School for Deaconesses and Missionaries* but generally known simply as the Sibley Hospital case) the judge articulated the legal responsibilities of nonprofit boards as the duties of **care**, **loyalty**, and **obedience**. In simplest terms, care means that board members must pay sufficient attention and monitor the organization's finances and management. Loyalty requires that they put the organization's interest ahead of their own and avoid conflicts of interest. And obedience requires the board to assure that the organization follows both the law and the dictates of its charitable mission. In extreme cases, board members can even be held personally liable for improper actions by the nonprofit as a result of their failure to meet these responsibilities.

But the board's responsibilities run in two directions. It is responsible to society for what the organization does, but it also has a responsibility to sustain and protect the organization itself. Since board members are often leaders in the community and have particular credibility in their respective fields, they may be the organization's best advocates and champions in the outside world.

Although many governance scholars give only fleeting, if any, attention to the governing board's fundraising role, others see it as central to the board's larger fiduciary responsibility. For example, Grossnickle (2011) describes the board as "a collective moral authority charged with the well-being of the nonprofit organization" and sees the board's involvement in fundraising as an inherent component of exercising that authority (p. 275).

In summary, nonprofit boards are expected to be like Janus, the Roman god of doorways and archways, who was said to have two faces and be able to look inward and outward at the same time. Janus looked inward to keep an eye on the family and maintain order in the household, while also looking outward to protect the family from any external threats. In the open system of a nonprofit organization, the governing board sits at the boundary between inside and outside, with similar dual responsibilities; in other words, the board stands at the doorway in a boundary-spanning role.

Fundraising Professionals as Boundary Spanners

Fundraising professionals are also boundary spanners. They represent their organizations to donors and may be effective to the extent that they understand and can communicate their organization's mission, values, programs, and priorities. But they also communicate and interpret the attitudes of donors to those inside the organization, including the CEO and program staff. Thus, although they are employed by and compensated by their organizations, fundraisers also have responsibilities that run in two directions and must maintain a Janus-like pose. That can be a complex role when there may be some disconnect between the priorities of the organization and those valued by its donors and other constituents. And, as discussed in Chapter 1, fundraising professionals often do not have the power to shape the organization's programs and priorities, which are determined by the governing board and program staff.

Resource Dependency

Building on open-system theory, Pfeffer and Salancik's (1978) **resource dependency theory** explains how the behavior of nonprofits is influenced by their dependence on external constituencies for financial and other resources. How and from where an organization derives its revenues influences not only its behavior in the external world but also much of what goes on internally, including what goals are established, how performance is measured, the relative position and influence of various groups, and the intangible but important quality of culture.

Resource Dependency and Autonomy

A fundamental assumption of resource dependency theory is that nonprofit organizations seek to manage their resource dependencies in order to maximize autonomy, the ability to determine their own goals and activities. One way they do that is by striving to achieve a diverse mix of revenue sources. If the organization is dependent on one or a few sources of revenue, there is the risk of **goal displacement**, whereby the nonprofit alters its goals and programs to fit the demands and desires—explicit or implicit—of its funding source. Or an organization might take on new programs simply because there is funding available, even if those programs are marginally related to its mission. Over time, chasing the money could lead an organization far away from its original purposes, something referred to as **mission drift**. An organization's mission is not immutable, and nonprofits often revise their mission statements as needs evolve. A conscious and deliberate change in mission could be consistent with keeping the organization relevant and effective. But a gradual and unconsidered evolution in the mission that occurs in response to funding opportunities or constraints could result in an organization that becomes unfocused and ineffective.

Sometimes goal displacement may be subtle. For example, in a widely cited article, Froelich (1999) studied public broadcasting stations to see if their need to raise funds from corporations influenced their programming decisions, which of course, the stations strongly denied. She found that "although respondents insisted that program content was not influenced by corporate support, they demonstrated the *opposite* via 'self-censoring behavior' that continually pressures stations to provide programming more readily salable to corporations" (p. 256, italics added).

Resource Dependency and Internal Power

How an organization obtains its resources affects which groups hold power within it. As Pfeffer (2003) explains, "The people, groups, or departments inside organizations that . . . manage important environmental dependencies, and help the organization obtain resources, [hold] more power as a result of their critical role" (p. xiii). Thus, for example, in an organization that relies on gift support, fundraising professionals likely will hold important positions and their departments will be well funded. In an organization that receives most of its revenue from government, fundraisers may be less central; those who manage supported programs and maintain the accounting and reporting systems required to comply with government regulations will be among the most important people in the organization. In a nonprofit that has substantial earned income, those who produce and market its products may hold significant internal power. For example, in many trade and professional associations, the membership office is responsible for most of the revenue, which comes from dues and other fees members pay. Philanthropy is often a small component of revenue. In this environment, fundraisers may find their efforts constrained by the membership office's concern that gift solicitations could negatively affect membership totals.

Efforts to diversify funding will inevitably confront established structures and power relationships within the organization. And a shift in revenue patterns will alter internal structures and roles. I observed these realities at work in three organizations that were considering ways to increase revenue from philanthropy, but there were both concerns about autonomy and the possible consequences of a changed revenue mix.[3]

One was a nonprofit research institution that historically had relied almost entirely on grants from government agencies and foundations to support its work. As the CEO explained, pressure to diversify funding sources was coming from the directors of major research programs. They were the most powerful group within the organization, since they generated almost all of the grants and contracts that supported the work of their departments. They were reporting a more challenging funding environment, with foundations and government cutting back, and were urging the CEO to explore gifts from individual donors as a way to prepare for a more uncertain future. Autonomy was limited in the existing scenario. As the CEO explained, "All of the research we do is driven by the interests of our funders." He added, "It would be desirable if our scholars had more flexibility to explore some topics of their own choosing, and indeed, our program directors are concerned about retaining our most creative staff members in our current model."

The development office was located in the basement and was poorly equipped, lacking the infrastructure of an effective fundraising operation. The director was capable but relatively inexperienced and was placed far down in the organizational chart, without easy access to the CEO or powerful program directors. Given the organization's principal source of revenue, it is not surprising that the chief fundraising officer was not a major player.

Another organization was also a research institution, with some similarities to the first but with a different revenue profile. It was fortunate to have a substantial endowment, which had supported much of its operation throughout most of its history. This permitted great autonomy, and the researchers employed at the institution historically had the freedom to pursue projects of their own design. But the endowment had declined in the recession of 2007–2009, and the CEO saw a need to develop more philanthropy, in order to assure the institution's future viability. The program directors were assembled to consider the CEO's views, and the reception was not entirely positive. The directors were perceptive in recognizing that more philanthropic support, from corporations, foundations and individuals, might result in diminished autonomy. They expressed concern that donors or sponsors might try to influence the outcomes of their research or perhaps influence their priorities in more subtle ways, through their willingness to fund certain projects over others. Their preferred remedies to financial concerns were for the CFO to do a better job of investing the endowment and for the CEO to obtain major gifts from donors who would place no restriction on their use, an unrealistic expectation. The CEO would face challenges in steering the organization in a new direction.

A third organization was primarily dependent on earned income and received very little philanthropy. It produced educational materials that were sold and offered training programs for a fee. In addition, the organization maintained various marketing partnerships with corporations. Concerned about the vicissitudes of the marketplace, the CEO was interested in the possibility that revenue sources might be diversified through philanthropy.

Although it was a nonprofit, the organization operated much like a business, and indeed, the most influential person in the organization after the CEO held a title similar to "director of sales and marketing." There was no director of development, and the director of sales and marketing, perhaps with some implicit understanding of how resource dependency theory might work, was reluctant to see such a position created. She argued that it would take resources away from her budget for marketing and that the amount of gift revenue that might be raised would be more than offset by declining sales of products. The solution, she proposed, was not to undertake fundraising but to expand the inventory of products and enhance her marketing budget.

The first of these organizations was seeking to diversify its sources of revenue in order to gain financial stability and to expand its autonomy. The second was a relatively closed system seeking to increase philanthropic support but with concerns about the reduction in autonomy that becoming a more open system might entail. The third was an open system—it was quite responsive to its customers and corporate sponsors—but it had a commercial market culture that worked against the long-term perspective essential to increasing philanthropic support. While all three are examples of organizations looking to increase philanthropy, similar tensions may arise in organizations that wish to diversify revenues in other ways. For example, a nonprofit that is mostly supported by gifts may be reluctant to accept the limitations and regulations that come with the acceptance of government funds. And those that are primarily supported by government may not have the capacity or culture to undertake new earned-income ventures. Such organizations may have cultures that value accountability and compliance more than innovation or risk taking, which also may not be highly valued in the cultures of organizations that have substantial endowments. Those dependent on earned income or corporate partnerships may exhibit cultures similar to business firms, and those that rely on individual donors may have a more voluntary culture.

Resource Dependency and Organizational Skills

An organization's revenue model will dictate what skills it must possess or obtain. Collins (2005) defines four revenue models (which he calls economic engines), defined by the extent to which organizations are dependent on business (earned) income and on gifts and grants from private sources. Collins suggests that there may be similarities among organizations in any single quadrant, even though their missions and programs may be quite different. Thinking back on our discussion of resource dependency theory, similarities may include the skills that are most valued, which staff experts hold internal power, and the intangible but important element of culture.

As shown in Figure 2.3, organizations in Quadrant I have little gift support or earned income. They are primarily dependent on government funds. They include some non-profits that provide human and social services and that derive most of their revenue from government grants and contracts. Managers of these organizations must possess political skills and the ability to maintain support among the public, whose attitudes will, of course, influence government decision makers. There would not be much of a role for a fundraising professional in such an organization.

Organizations in Quadrant II rely substantially on gifts from individuals and have little business income. They require managers who are effective fundraisers and who can maintain personal relationships with donors. They include, for example, many national charities that raise funds to support research on specific diseases.

Quadrant III organizations generate substantial earned income and also receive substantial philanthropic support; they require *both* business acumen *and* fundraising skills. They include many performing arts centers, independent educational institutions, and even some national nonprofits (for example, Goodwill and the Girl Scouts) that rely on both types of income. Fundraising professionals employed in such organizations have important roles, but staff members who support the earned-income activities do as well.

Finally, organizations in Quadrant IV may receive private gifts and grants, but earned income is their principal source of support; this is the case, for example, with most health care institutions. They may operate much like businesses and may value business skills above others. Fundraisers employed in these settings may find that their efforts account for a relatively small portion of total revenue and that their role within the organization is commensurate.

As the four quadrants in Figure 2.3 suggest, and as the three examples of research institutions discussed earlier illustrate, the challenges of developing additional philanthropic revenue are more complex than simply adding money to the fundraising budget and printing some brochures. As discussed further in Chapter 5 of this text, fundraising is not an activity that can be successfully confined to the periphery of the organization; it cannot be a mere appendage that generates revenue without shaping the organization in more substantial ways. Enhancing fundraising requires that managers of the organization develop new skills or hire people who possess them. Fundraising must be based on mission and vision, which may need to be refocused in order to be a better fit with the

FIGURE 2.3 Nonprofit Revenue Models: Four Quadrants

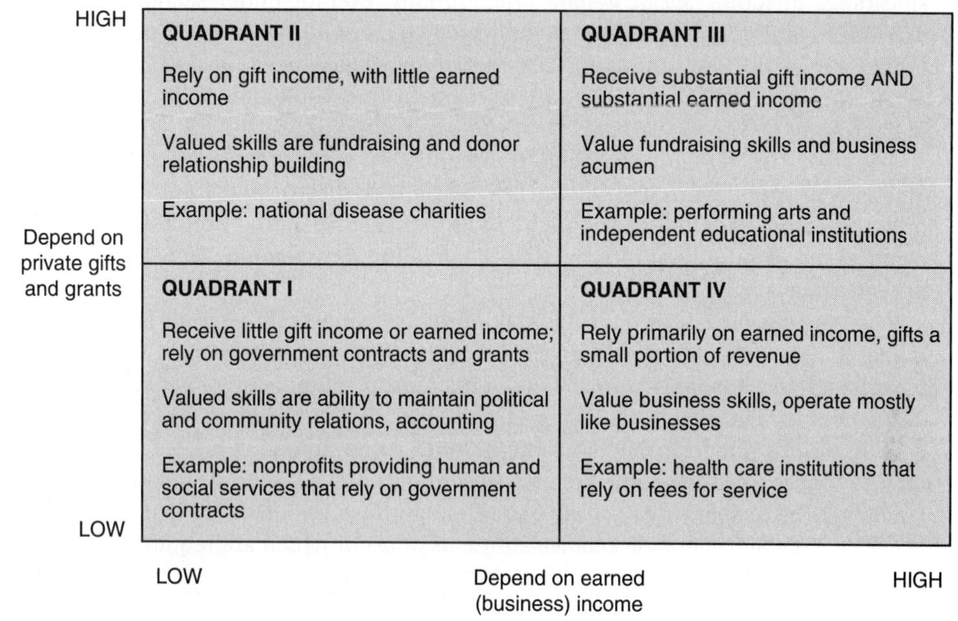

HIGH	**QUADRANT II**	**QUADRANT III**
	Rely on gift income, with little earned income	Receive substantial gift income AND substantial earned income
	Valued skills are fundraising and donor relationship building	Value fundraising skills and business acumen
Depend on private gifts and grants	Example: national disease charities	Example: performing arts and independent educational institutions
	QUADRANT I	**QUADRANT IV**
	Receive little gift income or earned income; rely on government contracts and grants	Rely primarily on earned income, gifts a small portion of revenue
	Valued skills are ability to maintain political and community relations, accounting	Value business skills, operate mostly like businesses
LOW	Example: nonprofits providing human and social services that rely on government contracts	Example: health care institutions that rely on fees for service
	LOW	Depend on earned (business) income HIGH

Source: Adapted from Collins, J.C. (2005). *Good to great and the social sectors: A monograph to accompany Good to Great.* Boulder, CO: author (www.jimcollins.com), p. 21.

priorities of donors. The organization may need to become more open and consider the inevitable tradeoffs between autonomy and external support. Long-established revenue dependencies will have influenced the organization's structure, its internal distribution of power, and its culture, all of which may be deeply entrenched and all of which may be altered in a different revenue model. An organization that seeks to increase philanthropy thus may need to accept fundamental and potentially disruptive change as the price for expanding its financial resources.

CHAPTER SUMMARY

America's nonprofit sector is large, diverse, and complex, including an estimated 2.3 million organizations (Roeger et al., 2012). Nonprofit organizations are *organized entities*, rooted in a tradition of *volunteerism*, that are *private* and *self-governing* and pursue purposes that are of *public benefit*. They are *mission-driven* and face a *nondistribution constraint*, meaning that they cannot distribute profits to owners. They are exempt from the federal corporate income tax and most state taxes.

Nonprofit organizations are classified according to the *National Taxonomy of Exempt Entities (NTEE)* and by the *Internal Revenue Code*. The latter includes many different classifications, including *social welfare organizations*, exempt under section 501(c)(4), and *charitable nonprofits*, which are exempt under section 501(c)(3). Both are tax exempt as organizations, but only the latter can receive gifts that are *tax deductible* to the donor. For that reason, the latter are most relevant to this book's focus on fundraising and philanthropy.

There are two types of charitable nonprofits: *private foundations* and *public charities*. Most private foundations are *funding intermediaries*—they receive funds from individuals or corporations and then distribute them as grants to operating nonprofits. Some public charities are also funding intermediaries, including for example, United Way. The latter are called *supporting public charities*.

The largest source of revenue to the nonprofit sector overall, accounting for 50 percent, is fees for services and goods provided. Philanthropy accounts for 13 percent. But if universities and hospitals are excluded, philanthropy is more significant, accounting for 24 percent of total revenue (Roeger et al., 2012). Since nonprofit organizations receive gifts, nonprofit financial management includes some unique concepts. *Operating funds* may be *unrestricted*, but some are *restricted* to purposes identified by donors or grantors. Funds may be *temporarily restricted*, until the purpose has been fulfilled, or *permanently restricted*. The latter include *endowment funds*, most of which are required to be invested in perpetuity with only investment earnings available to support programs.

Theories to explain the existence of the nonprofit sector have been developed in various social sciences. Among the best known are the *failure theories* of economists, which explain nonprofits in terms of filling gaps left by the market and government. Some economists also have developed *supply-side theories* based on the initiatives of nonprofit founders (Hansmann, 1987; James, 1987; Rose-Ackerman, 1996; Weisbrod, 1975, 1988; Young, 1983). Lohmann's (1992) *theory of the commons* explains nonprofits as providers of *common goods*, which are of interest to particular groups of people who support those organizations.

Most nonprofit organizations are *open systems*, which interact with the environment around them. Because nonprofits obtain funds and other resources from the external community and have voluntary cultures, the boundary between inside and outside is often permeable. That makes *boundary-spanning roles* important. Such roles are played by the governing board and fundraising professionals. The board has a legal fiduciary responsibility to both monitor the organization and serve as its protector and advocate. Both board members and fundraising professionals must look inward as well as outward at the same time to meet their dual responsibilities.

Resource dependency theory describes how nonprofits' sources of revenue may affect their autonomy and also influence internal features, including power relationships and the skills required to manage. One risk is that donor requirements or preferences will result in *goal displacement*. Nonprofits try to maintain autonomy by diversifying revenue sources.

Internal power is held by positions responsible for generating the organization's revenue, and a change in the revenue model will have an impact on internal structure and relationships, which may be disruptive. Nonprofits with similar revenue models may demonstrate similar characteristics, including cultures, even though their missions and programs are quite different.

Fundraising is not an activity that can be successfully confined to the periphery of the organization, and a nonprofit that seeks to increase philanthropy may need to accept fundamental change as the price for expanding its financial resources.

Key Terms and Concepts

Accounts payable
Accounts receivable
Accrual basis
    (of accounting)
Advocacy
    organization
Altruism
    (theories of)
Board-designated
    endowment
Boundary spanners
Bureaucracy
Care (duty of)
Cash basis (of
    accounting)
Closed systems
Common goods
Community
    foundations
Endowment funds
Externalities
Failure theories
Free riders
Funding
    intermediaries
Goal displacement
Government failure
Grant-making
    foundations
Institutionally related
    foundations

Loyalty (duty of)
Market failure
Mission drift
Mission-driven
    (organizations)
National Taxonomy
    of Exempt Entities
    (NTEE)
Nondistribution
    constraint
Obedience
    (duty of)
Open systems
Operating
    foundations
Operating funds
Operating public
    charities
Organized entities
Permanent
    endowment
Permanently
    restricted (funds)
Pledges
Private
    foundations
Private goods
Public benefit
Public charities
Public goods
Pure endowment

Quasi-endowment
Resource dependency
    theory
Restricted (funds)
Self-governing
Service
    volunteers
Social
    entrepreneurship
    (theories of)
Social welfare
    organizations
Supporting public
    charities
Supply-side
    theories
Systems (theory)
Tax deductible
Tax exempt
Tax expenditure
Temporarily restricted
    (funds)
Term endowments
Theory of the
    commons
Tradition of
    volunteerism
Unrelated
    business income
    tax (UBIT)
Unrestricted (funds)

Case 2.1: The Smithsonian Institution and the Catherine B. Reynolds Foundation

The Smithsonian Institution, an educational and research institution in Washington, DC, is best known for its nineteen museums and seven research centers. It is an unusual hybrid of federal government agency and nonprofit institution. It was chartered by Congress as a charitable trust in 1846, in response to a bequest from Englishman James Smithson, who left a gift to the United States of America to establish an institution "for the increase and diffusion of knowledge among men." But the Smithsonian is administered by the federal government, and courts have held that it is legally part of the federal government. More than two-thirds of its workforce are employees of the federal government, while others supported by private funds are known as "trust fund employees." Although significant governance reforms were undertaken in 2007, in 2000 the Smithsonian was governed by a seventeen-member board of regents, including officials of the federal government and private citizens. The secretary of the Smithsonian is the paid chief executive, who is appointed by the board of regents. Throughout most of its history, the Smithsonian relied on ample funding from the U.S. government. But beginning in the 1980s, federal funds failed to keep pace with the Smithsonian's needs. Faced with a change in its environment, the Smithsonian "didn't exactly turn on a dime," and battles over the influence of private donors over the content of exhibits led to subsequent "knockdown, drag-out funding fight[s]," centered in particular on one of the Smithsonian's most prominent components, the National Museum of American History (Thompson, 2002).

By 2000, federal funds were only sufficient to cover the Smithsonian's core budget, including salaries. Private funds needed to be raised for new exhibits, and some standing exhibits had become dated. Deferred maintenance on the Smithsonian's extensive physical facilities had allowed many to deteriorate. Recognizing the need for change, the board of regents reached outside the scientific and museum communities for a new secretary, someone who could bring business methods and private resources to bear on the Smithsonian's mounting problems. Lawrence Small, appointed by the board of regents as the new secretary in 2000, came from a background in banking and finance rather than science or museum management. Small noted the deteriorating condition of the Smithsonian's facilities and the continuing decline in federal funds and committed himself to "a vision that involves two M's: modernization and money," with most of the money to come from more aggressive fundraising in the private sector (Thompson, 2002, p. 22).

Small had met Catherine B. Reynolds, a Washington-area entrepreneur who controlled a large foundation bearing her name. She shared Small's view that the National Museum of American History needed to be updated, and in May 2001, she announced a gift of $38 million from her foundation to support a project on which she and Small had agreed: a 10,000-square-foot "hall of achievement" exhibit, intended to portray the lives of eminent Americans. Small and Reynolds had agreed that the selection of individuals to be portrayed would be determined by a special advisory committee of fifteen people, with ten being appointed by the Reynolds Foundation. The *Washington Post* reported that the contract between the Reynolds Foundation and the Smithsonian provided that if the committee could not agree, the dispute would be resolved not by the curatorial staff but by the secretary himself ("Museums and Money," 2001).

The museum's staff erupted in anger, writing directly to the Smithsonian board of regents saying that the obligations Small had made to the Reynolds Foundation "breach[ed] established standards of museum practice and professional ethics" (Thompson, 2002, p. 26). The story caught the attention of the news media, resulting in a flurry of stories representing the museum curators' views and a *New York Times* editorial asking "what is the curatorial rationale for a permanent exhibit that seems to open the door for commercial and corporate influence at one of the capital's keystone institutions" ("Gifts That Can Warp," 2001). The American Historical Association, including prominent historians among its members, joined the debate in support of the museum staff's views. Museum staff began to post "Dump Small" stickers in elevators, on bulletin boards, and on their own lapels (Sciolino, 2001a). A series of meetings was held between the curators and Ms. Reynolds to try to reach a common understanding, but they did not resolve the differences.

At least two issues were central to the controversy. The first was a difference in philosophy about the meaning of history and the purpose of museums. Historians and museum curators believed that the purpose of museums was to educate and that the study of history should not focus on the personal stories of "great" men and women. Rather, they argued that the teaching of history should focus on broad historical forces and movements, often portrayed in exhibits through their impact on the lives of everyday people. They believed that the purpose of a museum was to encourage people to think critically about history, not to inspire people personally. As one curator expressed it, "We are not a great man/great woman place. . . . This museum is about context, about putting people and events in place within the social fabric" (Thompson, 2002, p. 18). But Ms. Reynolds held a different view of history and the purpose of the museum's exhibits—it should be to inspire young people by portraying the lives of famous Americans and extolling the virtues of entrepreneurship in achieving success. "The foundation was created out of a very entrepreneurial business," Ms. Reynolds said, "and that is the spirit and culture we want to apply to the philanthropic world" (Sciolino, 2001b).

The second, and broader, issue was the question of who should control the content of museum exhibits—professional historians and museum curators or donors. To what degree should private donors have a say in museum exhibits to be developed with the money they are voluntarily giving? One scholar asked, "Will the Smithsonian Institution actually allow private funders to rent space in a public museum for the expression of private and personal views?" (Thompson, 2002, p. 16). Scholars accused Small of "selling" the museum to wealthy donors, with jeopardizing the "integrity and authority" of professional curators, and with having "[preempted] the issue of control" by reaching an agreement with the Reynolds Foundation without adequate consultation with his own staff (Sciolino, 2001b).

Small responded, saying that "government funding cannot do it all" and pointing out that the idea of private donors—who had something to say about how their money would be used—was not exactly new. After all, the Smithsonian Institution had been founded with James Smithson's gift! Small said, "We make no apologies for seeking private support to develop programs or facilities that the public wants and benefits from." He argued, "In all cases, we retain intellectual control while demonstrating to donors that their money can be spent productively and prudently. Does that mean we don't consult them? Of course we do. But the Smithsonian regents and staff control, without limitation or question, the Smithsonian activity" (Small, 2001, p. A25).

In February 2002, Ms. Reynolds canceled the bulk of her foundation's pledge to the Smithsonian, saying merely that she felt the exhibit would not adequately portray "the power of the individual" (Lewis, 2002). But important questions remained, for the Smithsonian and generally for other organizations. Like the Smithsonian, others have long relied on relatively assured sources of revenue, perhaps the government, a single foundation, or some other generous source. But many find themselves now needing to pursue new and more diversified sources of financial support. The questions that need to be addressed clearly go beyond the specific one raised by the Reynolds Foundation's gift to the Smithsonian, that of how history should be portrayed and who should decide. There are more generic questions: What trade-offs are appropriate, realistic, and necessary for institutions and organizations striving to meet their financial needs and develop new sources of revenue while preserving their traditional missions and values? And how can CEOs meet expectations for their leadership in such a time of change?

Source: This case was published in Worth, M. J. (2014). *Nonprofit management: Principles and practice* (3rd ed.). Thousand Oaks, CA: Sage. It is reprinted here with minor revisions.

Additional Sources: Cash (2002); Sciolino (2001c).

Questions for Discussion

1. How do the concepts of closed systems and open systems apply to the case of the Smithsonian and the Catherine B. Reynolds Foundation?

2. How does the theory of resource dependency apply to the case of the Smithsonian and the Catherine B. Reynolds Foundation?

3. How does the concept of boundary spanners apply to the case of the Catherine B. Reynolds Foundation? Who played that role in this case, and were there others who should have been more involved?

4. What does the case of the Smithsonian and the Catherine B. Reynolds Foundation reveal about the culture of the Smithsonian at the time of the events described?

5. Pick a nonprofit organization with which you are personally familiar—maybe one where you have worked or been a volunteer—and examine its Form 990 to determine its sources of revenue. Based on that information, where does the organization lie in the quadrants depicted in Figure 2.3? Does that position coincide with what you may know about which positions hold power within the organization and with its culture?

Suggestions for Further Reading

Books

Bowman, W. (2011). *Finance fundamentals for nonprofits: Building capacity and sustainability*. Hoboken, NJ: John Wiley & Sons.

Salamon, L. (2012). *America's nonprofit sector: A primer* (3rd ed.). New York: Foundation Center.

Worth, M. J. (2014). *Nonprofit management: Principles and Practice*. Thousand Oaks, CA: Sage.

Article

Froelich, K. A. (1999, September). Diversification of revenue strategies: Evolving resource dependence in nonprofit organizations. *Nonprofit and Voluntary Sector Quarterly, 28*(3), 246–268. (Note: This article is dated but still widely cited as a classic.)

Monograph

Collins, J. C. (2005). *Good to great and the social sectors: A monograph to accompany Good to Great*. Boulder, CO: author (www.jimcollins.com).

Website

Internal Revenue Service: http://www.irs.gov/Charities-&-Non-Profits/Charitable-Organizations/Exemption-Requirements-Section-501(c)(3)-Organizations

Notes

1. Technically, although the terms are often used interchangeably, *nonprofit* and *tax exempt* are not exactly the same, since there are some business entities that are tax exempt and there are entities that are taxed but do not distribute profits to owners. In addition, nonprofit is a legal status, since most organizations identified that way are incorporated under state law as nonprofit corporations. Tax exemption is a status conferred by the federal tax code.

2. Section 501(c)(4) organizations also include some large health maintenance organizations.

3. Examples in this section are drawn from the author's experience, but details have been altered to protect confidentiality.

Understanding Donors

Mark Zuckerberg cofounded Facebook out of his dorm room at Harvard. He left college after his sophomore year in 2004 to concentrate on the site. In 2010, Zuckerberg gave $100 million to the Newark, New Jersey, school system. In 2012, he and his wife, Priscilla Chan, gave nearly $500 million to the Silicon Valley Community Foundation, to be used for education and health ("Facebook's Mark Zuckerberg," 2012). In 2013, Zuckerberg and Chan gave another $1 billion to the community foundation, becoming the largest donors under age thirty in history ("Zuckerberg Commits," 2013).

Harvey Ordung was a farmer in Luverne, Minnesota. He never married, had no children, lived simply, and invested his money. People who knew him never thought him to be wealthy. When he died in 2007, he left more than $4.5 million to twelve local nonprofits. Ordung had been a volunteer in his community's Adopt a Grandparent program, where he came to know some children. His bequest included $2.9 million to Luverne Dollars for Scholars, a scholarship program for local young people ("Editorial: A Farmer's Great Legacy," 2009).

In 2009, eighteen colleges and universities—all of them headed by women—received anonymous gifts ranging from $1 million to $10 million. The donor stipulated that the gifts be used for scholarships and general operating expenses, on the condition that the institutions not try to determine from whom the money came ("More Clues Emerge," 2009).

When we read about an exceptional philanthropic gift, we may try to relate it to our own experience. Sometimes the donor is a billionaire, which most of us are not, making it difficult for us to relate on a personal level. Or perhaps the donor is a person of modest means, whose apparent sacrifice exceeds what many of us would consider, so we may also find it difficult to understand on a personal level. Other donors remain anonymous, leaving us admiring but in deep mystery as to their thinking. In Chapter 2, we reviewed some theories that help us to understand the nonprofit sector and the organizations that comprise it. In this chapter, we turn our attention to the other side of the giving transaction, to donors, and consider two fundamental questions: who gives and why? The answers are of obvious practical importance, and our understanding needs to go beyond our own personal experience and intuition.

Our understanding of donors comes from two sources: reflections of practitioners and findings of research. Given the limitations of space, we need to be selective in what we consider from both sources. In this chapter, some insights from early fundraising pioneers are discussed, as well as contemporary ideas that confirm or challenge their opinions.

In addition, some theories and research are related to specific topics considered later in this text, and our discussion of those is deferred until that point.

There are four sources of philanthropic support available to a nonprofit organization: living individuals, estates, corporations, and foundations. In this chapter, we take a brief look at the motivations of corporate and foundation donors, but a separate chapter each is dedicated to corporations and foundations later in the text and they are considered in more detail there. A later chapter also discusses planned giving and provides a more detailed look at gifts from estates. The emphasis in this chapter is on living individual donors, who account for 72 percent of total philanthropy (Giving USA, 2014b).

Some students may wonder where unincorporated companies belong in the taxonomy of donors. Businesses that are not incorporated are privately held by individuals—perhaps one individual, a family, or partners. And privately held businesses are important donors in many communities. They include, for example, many building contractors, real estate firms, restaurants, retailers, and medical and legal practices. Because donors control the company, they are the only ones who benefit from its profits and have the authority to give some of them away as gifts from the company. They are not accountable to public shareholders, so they can follow their own interests in determining what gifts will be made from the funds of the companies they own. There is, of course, a continuum. Larger privately held companies that have many owners may develop systematic giving programs, much like publicly held corporations. But raising funds from closely held private businesses is often much like raising funds from individual donors, and such entities are generally not regarded as a distinct source in terms of the fundraising methods employed.

CORPORATE PHILANTHROPY

Corporations make philanthropic gifts both directly and through foundations that some have established as separate nonprofit entities. Using a foundation offers advantages over direct giving by the corporation, including the ability to add resources to the foundation in highly profitable years and then sustain a relatively even level of giving in years when the business may not be as profitable. Corporations make cash gifts and also give products, known as **gifts-in-kind**. Corporations also engage in a variety of partnerships with nonprofits. As the term *partnership* implies, these relationships bring benefits to both parties. Thus, although they provide a financial benefit to the nonprofit, they are not "philanthropy," since the company often also expects a financial return, either immediately or over the long term as a result of expanded markets, enhanced image, or other advantages. But responsibility for partnerships with corporations is often assigned to fundraising professionals working in nonprofit organizations, so they cannot be ignored in a text on fundraising. Major types of nonprofit–corporate partnerships are discussed in more detail in Chapter 9.

The motivations for corporate philanthropy relate primarily to business goals. That is not to say that individuals who work in corporations are not caring and feeling or that corporations are necessarily cynical in their giving. And some corporate giving may be altruistic, perhaps reflecting the values of senior managers. But the principal responsibility of managers in public corporations is to the shareholders, whose money they are giving away when they make a corporate gift. Corporate philanthropy may reflect **enlightened self-interest**, that is, the idea that companies make gifts that might not have a direct or immediate benefit to the bottom line but that generally help maintain a healthy society in which to do business. But there usually must be a rationale for why the gift is of benefit to the corporation in some manner.

Since the mid-1980s, corporate giving has reflected an approach known as strategic philanthropy—that is, giving according to a plan that relates the corporation's philanthropy to its overall strategic and business goals. Giving is viewed as an investment and is subject to evaluation based on how much return it produces—the extent to which it enhances the corporation's competitiveness. For example, a corporation might target its giving in communities where it plans to develop new facilities or to specific groups of people likely to be customers of its products. Corporate–nonprofit marketing partnerships have evolved from the strategic philanthropy approach. Today, the line between corporate philanthropy and marketing has become blurred as has the line between fundraising and negotiating business relationships.

To understand the motivation for corporate giving, a nonprofit needs to understand the company's business plans and goals, on which its program of philanthropy is likely to be based. Again, this is not to imply that corporations are unethical or greedy. But nonprofits must frame their search for corporate dollars not only in terms of their own needs but with a view to how they also can advance the business interests of the corporation from which they seek support, in other words, how the two organizations can work as partners.

FOUNDATION GIVING

It is not difficult to understand the motivations for giving by foundations. That is what they exist to do; indeed, it is what they are *required* to do as a condition of their tax-exempt status. Foundations are required to expend a minimum of an amount equivalent to 5 percent of the value of their invested assets each year, either for grants or operating expenses.

Foundations are created by corporations, individuals, or families, and their activities generally reflect the interests of the founders. Often those interests are broadly defined, for example, advancing human welfare, improving the environment, or advancing the arts. The donor who established the foundation and/or members of the donor's family may serve on the foundation board and thus have a voice in giving decisions. Where a foundation is controlled or dominated by members of a family it is known as a **family foundation**, and its giving reflects the interests of the family. However, even in that situation, once the family's funds have been given to a foundation, which is a separate legal entity, family members must put on a different hat when they sit at the board table and make decisions as fiduciaries, consistent with the law governing foundations. As they grow and evolve over time, many family foundations become more professionalized in their giving, hiring staff and expanding the board beyond members of the founding family. They become **independent foundations** and become more rational donors, determining grants based on well-articulated priorities and guidelines, which reflect the interest of the founders only broadly. For example, the Bill and Melinda Gates Foundation, although large, is still controlled by the founders, whereas the Ford Foundation, established by Henry Ford, has a broadly representative board not dominated by members of the Ford family.

Raising funds from a family foundation often is similar to raising funds from individuals, since the foundation's grant-making will reflect the motivations of family members. But as foundations become more independent, they become more rational and systematic donors, and securing their support becomes a specialized activity, including written proposals. Chapter 10 discusses foundation fundraising in more detail.

CHARACTERISTICS OF INDIVIDUAL DONORS

Not surprisingly, individual donors present the most complex questions. Let's start with the simpler question of *who* gives, which is a part of what social scientists call donor behavior, then consider the more interesting question of *why* (donor motivation).

A large volume of studies have identified demographic characteristics and attitudes of donors. Some are focused on very narrow circumstances, for example, donors to particular causes and organizations, donors in specific demographic categories, and donors of various types of gifts. But among general findings are the following:

- *Religion.* People who attend religious services are more likely than those who do not to give, both to religious and secular causes (Center on Philanthropy at Indiana University, 2008).

- *Gender.* Female-headed households are more likely to give than male-headed households, and women give more than men at almost every income level, with the exception of households headed by widows or widowers (Center on Philanthropy, 2010a).

- *Age.* The average amount of giving increases as people get older and peaks between ages fifty and sixty-five. Thereafter it declines as people reach retirement age (Havens, O'Herlihy, & Schervish, 2006).

- *Education.* Giving increases with the level of education (Havens et al., 2006).

- *Marital status.* Married people have a higher rate of giving than people who are single, widowed, divorced, or separated (Havens et al., 2006).

- *Income.* The absolute amount of giving increases with income. Although some scholars dispute the point (Havens et al., 2006), most researchers conclude that giving as a percentage of household income follows a U shape; it is higher in the lowest and highest income brackets (Havens et al., 2006; James & Sharpe, 2007).

- *Volunteering.* People who volunteer give more than those who do not (Havens et al., 2006).

- *Employment.* Employed people give a higher average amount, but unemployed people give a higher percentage of their household income (Havens et al., 2006).

- *Citizenship*. U.S.-born people donate more than foreign-born people living in the United States (Havens et al., 2006).

- *Inheritance*. People with earned wealth give more than people with inherited wealth (Havens et al., 2006).

Such data may be of limited usefulness to individual organizations, since they represent societal averages and may not be at all reflective of one organization's constituency. And, of course, the data may lead to misinterpretation. The fact that people of one national origin may give more than those of another may be attributable to differences in income rather than any difference in their inclination to be philanthropic. The fact that unemployed people give a larger percentage of their income than do employed people does not establish that they are more generous. It could reflect in part the fact that both groups deem giving to their religious congregations as essential and maintain it regardless of their employment status. There are many possible explanations for the data on who gives. It describes donor behavior, but it does not tell us much of anything about the why.

Beyond the possibility of misinterpretation, Kelly (1998) identifies another potential issue with the application of such data, which she calls the "theory of magic buttons." This is not a scientific theory but rather a naïve presumption some may hold "that there is a causal link between giving behavior and donor demographics, cognitions, and attitudes, if just the right combination can be found" (pp. 350–351). In other words, some people might think that if we can just identify donors with the right characteristics and send them the right message, giving will automatically result. But reality is somewhat more complicated. Applying this way of thinking to fundraising would be like assuming that a single person of about your own age with some characteristics in common may positively respond to your marriage proposal without the necessity of actually becoming acquainted. That might just lead to an ineffective strategy.

MOTIVATIONS OF INDIVIDUAL DONORS

The motivations of individual donors are interesting to consider, since they involve such fundamental matters as emotions, values, and psychological needs. And, again, since individuals account for the largest component of philanthropy, having information and good theories about why they give is of practical importance.

There has been extensive research on donor motivations. Many studies are based on surveys that obtain data self-reported by donors. Such studies can be informative, but there is always the risk that people will not provide accurate information, perhaps because they do not correctly remember how much they gave or why or perhaps because they are inclined to give what they think are the right answers. For example, if you are asked why you made a gift to help low-income children, you might be reluctant to say that you did so because it made *you* feel good. Other studies are based on interviews conducted by researchers, but researchers may have their own biases, which affect their interpretation of what they hear. Some have involved field experiments; they avoid the potential biases of donors and researchers but may introduce other weaknesses. Many of them are conducted under artificial conditions with small groups of people, so it is not certain that their results can be more generally applied (Bekkers & Wiepking, 2011). This chapter draws on all three types of studies as well as the observations of practitioners.

Altruism or Social Exchange

Traditionally, theories about the motivations of donors have reflected two alternatives: giving is motivated by selfless **altruism**, or giving is a form of **social exchange**. Altruistic donors are those exclusively concerned with the benefits provided to others. In an exchange, donors give something to receive something in return.

Some view philanthropy as a moral and spiritual endeavor and explain it in lofty terms. For example, Schervish (2006) describes how individuals develop a "moral biography" at the "confluence of [their] capacity and moral bearings." He defines philanthropy as "strategic friendship" and strategic friendship as "the foundation of . . . the moral citizenship of care" (p. 485). But some research findings raise questions about the extent of pure altruism in giving. Suppose that a donor gives entirely for altruistic reasons; that is, all he or she cares about are the benefits provided to the clients of a nonprofit organization. In that case, we would expect that donor to reduce his or her gift upon learning that the organization's needs have been met, perhaps through gifts from other donors or through government. This expected effect is called **crowding out**. But various studies have found that crowding out may not occur at all, or if it does, there is often not always a one-to-one reduction in the donor's gift in response to support from other sources. In other words, a donor may continue to give even though the needs he or she cares about already have been addressed. This suggests that the individual is giving for reasons that are not totally altruistic. He or she may be an **impure altruist**, who is receiving some benefit in return, for example, the **joy of giving** (Andreoni, 1989; Bekkers & Wiepking, 2011; Ribar & Wilhelm, 2002). This may explain why some donors continue to give to universities and other institutions that have substantial endowments. It would be difficult to see those institutions as needy, but donors may value the pride of association and enhanced social standing that comes from being known as a donor to, say, Harvard.

In assessing the argument between altruism and self-interest, it is important to recognize that benefits accruing to a donor may be intangible. Rational choice does not exclude feelings or emotions because a gift may meet the donor's emotional and psychological needs. A gift may bring the donor warm feelings, self-esteem, admiration by peers, enhanced social acceptance, or the expectation of reciprocity. Think about the Golden Rule, which encourages us to treat others as we wish to be treated. Most of us would probably accept that as a moral principle and think highly of someone who follows it. But some might argue that we treat others well not only for altruistic reasons but because of our expectation that they will treat us well in return; something called the **norm of reciprocity** may be involved (Gouldner, 1960).

Donors may give because of **empathy** for others in need. We generally respect and like people who are capable of empathy and may think of that as a noble characteristic. But those who subscribe to a theory of giving as rational behavior might consider empathy as a *mechanism* that leads to emotions, some of which will be negative, such as sadness or guilt. Giving motivated by empathy then might still be defined at least in part as self-serving, since it may relieve the donor of the negative emotions that empathy entails (Sargeant, Shang, et al., 2010).

A motivation closely related to empathy is **identification** with the needs of others. Schervish and Havens (2002) call association the "school of identification," arguing that identification with others grows from sharing time and experience with beneficiaries of philanthropy (p. 228). In other words, the needs of strangers may be less compelling than those of people we know and with whom we have established personal relationships, coming to understand their commonalities with ourselves as the basis of identification with them. This principle is implicit in the fundraising strategies of many organizations. Volunteers are often also donors, and organizations sometimes enlist volunteers in various roles, including as members of committees, councils, and boards, with the goal of enhancing their identification through increased association. As discussed in more detail later in this text, involvement and psychological identification are key steps in the process of cultivation for major gifts.

Individual Needs and Social Influences

The benefits that donors might receive can be placed into two broad categories: those related to the individual and those based on social influences (Sargeant, Shang, et al., 2010). The creation of warm feelings or the alleviation of negative feelings relate to the individual's own internal needs. But some motivations derive from social relationships, for example, the desire to be part of a group, the desire to be seen as doing what's right, and the inclination of humans to identify with other individuals and organizations. Various research studies have confirmed that the desire for a good reputation plays a role in some donor decisions (Bekkers & Wiepking, 2010).

The social component of motivation is also emphasized by fundraising practitioners. In his classic 1966 book *Designs for Fund-Raising*, consultant Harold J. "Si" Seymour identifies "two universal aspirations" of human beings, based on his extensive experience with donors. First, he writes, "It is pleasantly easy to say that everyone wants to be loved, admired, respected, remembered favorably, treated fairly, and never played down" (pp. 5–6). The second aspiration that Seymour observes is to be "a worthwhile member of a worthwhile group" (p. 6). Research findings are generally consistent with Seymour's observations. People tend to look for norms of behavior in giving as in other kinds of activities. They will give more if they see, or are told, that others have given more and will respond favorably to suggested gift amounts that establish norms for what is expected. People usually prefer that their gifts be known rather than remain anonymous. They tend to respond to face-to-face solicitations more generously than to impersonal methods, such as the mail. They follow the example of others, especially of those who are members of a group with which they identify or to which they aspire to belong (Bekkers & Wiepking, 2010). Think back here on the advice of Benjamin Franklin, mentioned in Chapter 1, which reflected his understanding of these points.

Recognition of social influences on giving is implicit in many well-established principles of fundraising practice. As discussed in Chapter 7 on major gifts, determination of who will solicit a gift is critical. When volunteer solicitors are involved, they ideally have the right social relationship to the donor and will have given at or above the level of the gift they are requesting, in order to set an example and establish the norm. As Seymour (1966) describes, "The solicitor should be a giver whose own giving standards and whose place in the scheme of things are commensurate with the goals [that solicitor] seeks and the people [that solicitor] sees" (p. 76).

While theories about social influences on giving apply to traditional fundraising strategies, they also can be observed at work in more contemporary strategies. Think about peer-to-peer fundraising that occurs on social media. The desire to be part of a group and to demonstrate support for a friend's efforts motivate others to give, perhaps even to causes that are not a priority for them personally. The ice bucket challenge that raised funds for the ALS Association in 2014 required that individuals post videos of having a bucket of ice dumped on their heads and pledging to give to help eliminate ALS, while challenging others to follow suit. The success of the effort also demonstrates the power of social influences, since few people would be likely to consider such behavior absent urging by their peers.

Social influences also explain why recognition is important to many donors. Economist William Harbaugh (1998) studied this motivation and concludes that "the prestige benefits from public recognition are an important reason why people give." And, he notes, "large anonymous donations are so rare that they are newsworthy events" (p. 277). But it is important to note that the recognition of donors also benefits the organization. The donor may gain recognition for being a generous person, but the nonprofit also gains by identifying that donor as someone who believes in and supports its programs. The donor's reputation helps to validate the nonprofit's worthiness. That is why, as Seymour advises, the status of the person who solicits a gift is important, as is that solicitor's own example of generosity. It may be a common perception that anonymous giving is noble, but most nonprofits would prefer the opportunity to recognize donors by name, in hopes of motivating others to follow their example.

Mixed Motives

Many authors reject the dichotomy between altruism and social exchange as explanations for philanthropy, arguing that donors have **mixed motives** (Kelly, 1998). As Schervish (2009) argues, we do not necessarily need to accept the choice between "either the elegant framework of rational choice theory or the civilized framework of altruism" (p. 36). In other words, a donor may give for a combination of reasons, some principled, some pragmatic. And different combinations of motives may be reflected in different types of gifts.

Think back on the brief description of Paton's (2007) concept in Chapter 1. He argued that there may be a continuum of motivation from pure altruism to pure self-interest, as depicted in Figure 3.1.

On the far left of Figure 3.1, it is possible to imagine a transaction that is entirely altruistic, perhaps an anonymous gift to help people in poverty. But if that gift also creates a warm feeling or reduces the donor's uncomfortable feeling of guilt, then the transaction has

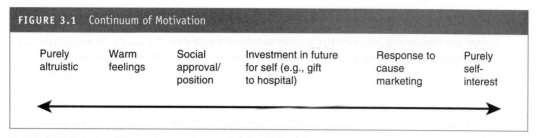

FIGURE 3.1 Continuum of Motivation

| Purely altruistic | Warm feelings | Social approval/ position | Investment in future for self (e.g., gift to hospital) | Response to cause marketing | Purely self-interest |

Source: Based on Paton, R. (2007). Fundraising as marketing: Half a truth is better than nothing. In Mordaunt, J., & Paton, R. (Eds.), *Thoughtful fundraising: Concepts, issues, and perspectives.* New York: Routledge, pp. 29–37.

perhaps just a touch of self-interest as well—it may be slightly to the right of pure altruism on the continuum. A gift that brings you recognition and social approval or acceptance, perhaps a listing in the nonprofit's annual report or your name on a plaque in its building lobby, may be in part altruistic but also in part like a purchase of the benefits that come from enhanced social standing. Your motives might be mixed. Some gifts might be a type of investment in your own future, for example, a gift to a hospital where you think you some-day might be a patient or to support medical research on a disease from which you suffer. The expectation of reciprocity could be high in that transaction; in other words, you might believe that your status as a donor could result in easier access or more effective treatment. If you purchase a product with the understanding that some portion of your payment will go to a charity—that is, you respond to a cause marketing partnership between a corpora-tion and a nonprofit—you may be motivated in part by the benefit to the charity but mostly motivated by a desire to own the product. This is closer to the self-interested end of the spectrum than it is to altruism. On the extreme right side of the continuum are transactions based purely on self-interest, like buying yourself a sandwich. It is hard to imagine a chari-table gift that would be motivated entirely by self-interest, except perhaps, if it is coerced. But that would not be philanthropy; it would be robbery or extortion!

When we look at some specific fundraising methods later in this text, we will see that many of them reflect an assumption of mixed motives, even if implicitly. For example, a nonprofit that rescues animals may present pictures of appealing cats and dogs as a way to highlight the need and elicit your emotions but also promise that your gift will be recog-nized through a listing of your name in its annual report. But organizations need to maintain an appropriate balance between appealing to emotions and offering tangible benefits. There is a risk that by offering benefits that are too tangible and explicit, a nonprofit converts a philanthropic action into a pure exchange, at least in the perception of the donor.

The relevance of this point is illustrated by an organization I observed. It was a mem-bership organization that derived its revenue primarily from member dues and fees but was seeking to increase its revenues by soliciting voluntary gifts from members to support its educational programs.[1] The organization's membership options included tiers at three dollar levels. A basic membership would bring a subscription to the newsletter; the next higher category would include the newsletter and access to online materials; the high-est level of membership included all the benefits of the lower ones and, in addition, the opportunity to attend certain meetings and events. It was a perfectly rational structure that would enable any prospective member to evaluate exactly which package of benefits he or she might wish to *purchase* through membership. And, of course, since dues would indeed represent a purchase, they would not be deductible as a gift.

It is common to offer recognition to donors at various levels as well. But this organization had designed a donor recognition program that closely paralleled its membership structure. Donors at a certain level would receive the newsletter, and donors at higher levels would be entitled to online access and events, just like members. That was by itself somewhat confusing. Moreover, since the organization hoped to obtain gifts far above the range of its membership dues, it had created additional benefits for larger gifts, some of which seemed impractical or unattractive. For example, one might wonder if a donor would be motivated to give $1,000 for the opportunity to have lunch with the organization's executive director, or $2,500 to have lunch with the president, especially considering the fact that donors would be spread out across the country while the executive director and president would usually be having lunch in their home cities. The same question would apply to events held in the organization's headquarters city, where most of its members were not residents. Most donors might see the benefit as something they would be unlikely to experience and thus be disinclined to pay for it. It might be more effective for solicitations to be refocused on the need for gifts to support educational programs and evoke more emotional themes, highlighting the young people who would benefit from those programs and distinguishing philanthropic gifts from membership dues. This would not preclude recognizing donors at various levels, but rather it would represent a tilt toward altruism and away from self-interest with regard to the messages conveyed in gift solicitations. The goal would be to differentiate the philanthropic case from the quid pro quo transaction of membership. This new way of thinking was at first difficult for this organization to accept, but eventually the program was redesigned along the lines just suggested and the results were positive.

Sometimes offering explicit benefits may be effective, but some studies suggest that an emphasis on indirect benefits and values may be more so (Amos, 1982). Based on an extensive review of research on philanthropy, Bekkers and Wiepking (2011) conclude that "there is a danger in offering material benefits for helpfulness. . . . They tend to undermine self-attributions of helpfulness, which reduces the effect of pro-social self-attributions on future helpfulness. Fringe benefits change the decision into an exchange (do I get value for money?)" (p. 935).

Influence of Tax Deductions

One subject that has been the focus of extensive research and discussion is the influence of the charitable deduction on giving. It is common to read statements that seem to imply that the charitable deduction is a loophole or that donors are motivated to give by the opportunity to avoid taxes. But no donor ever gains from making a gift; that is, even considering the subsidy that the charitable deduction provides, a donor would always be better off by keeping the money and paying taxes than by giving it away. Tax planning does indeed influence how much donors are able to give, the timing of their gifts, and the methods by which their gifts are paid; it affects donor *behavior*. Changes in the tax deduction also affect the total charitable giving that occurs. But since no donor is ever financially better off by making a gift, some philanthropic intent is essential and tax avoidance is not by itself a *motivation*.

There have been many analyses related to the impact of taxes on giving, most undertaken by economists. From an economist's perspective, the tax deduction affects the *cost* of a gift. Remember the example in Chapter 2. If a donor in a 25 percent tax bracket gives $100 and receives a deduction for that amount, the tax savings is $25 and the gift thus cost the donor only $75. One point that may seem counterintuitive is that an increase in tax rates actually decreases the cost of giving. For example, consider the donor in our example. If for some reason that person were to move from a 25 percent bracket to a 35 percent bracket, deduction of the $100 gift would produce a tax savings of $35, reducing the cost of that gift to $65, less than the $75 cost in the donor's previous situation. Conversely, a *decrease* in someone's tax bracket, or in general tax rates, would *increase* the cost of a charitable gift, as would any reduction of the allowable tax deduction. Most Americans claim a standard deduction on their income tax returns, so the charitable deduction is not relevant for them. Among those who do itemize, the tax law does favor those with higher incomes, since their higher brackets make the charitable deduction more valuable.

So the question is, in economic terms, how elastic or inelastic is giving? If tax rates change, either increasing or decreasing the cost of giving, to what extent do donors respond by increasing or decreasing their philanthropy? In self-reports by donors, the importance of the charitable deduction is often minimized. For example, in a 2011 study conducted by the Center on Philanthropy at Indiana University (now the Lilly Family School of Philanthropy) and Bank of America, 50 percent of survey respondents indicated that their giving would stay the same even if they received no tax deduction. Fewer than 10 percent indicated that their giving would decrease dramatically if the deduction were eliminated (Center on Philanthropy, 2012). But research tells a somewhat different story. Based on a meta-analysis of studies over forty years, Peloza and Steel (2005) acknowledge a lack of consensus but conclude that "changes in tax deductibility indeed appear to have a marked effect on charitable giving" (p. 269).

The tax deduction makes a difference, since it affects the cost of a gift. Nonprofit organizations should be aware of donors' tax situations and work with them to plan their gifts to maximize tax advantages. That point is emphasized again, in Chapter 8, which concerns planned giving. But since tax deductions are not a primary motivator, it generally does not make sense to put them at the center of fundraising communications. It is likely to be more effective to appeal to donors on the basis of the organization's mission, values, and program impact.

Influence of Accountability and Ratings

Recent years have seen an increased emphasis on the accountability of nonprofit organizations. Form 990s are available online for prospective donors to review, and various charity watchdogs, including the Better Business Bureau Wise Giving Alliance and Charity Navigator, evaluate organizations and publish information to inform donors. Some nonprofits include the Wise Giving Alliance seal of approval or Charity Navigator's rating on their websites. And some promote favorable financial ratios, such as low overhead and low fundraising costs, as evidence of efficiency. How influential are these rankings and ratios with donors?

There is some evidence that donors prefer efficiency—that is, low fundraising costs—and may be turned off by what appear to be expensive fundraising materials (Bekkers & Wiepking, 2011). But the question about the impact of external ratings is less settled. Some studies have found that gifts go up with increased ratings and decline when ratings go down (Gordon, Knock, & Neely, 2009). Donors who do use the websites of charity raters tend to make larger gifts than those who do not (Cnaan, Jones, Dickin, & Salomon, 2011). But this may not reflect the impact of the ratings; rather, it could be that donors of larger amounts are more likely to dedicate the time necessary to review the ratings, whereas smaller donors may not think that effort to be justified by the small risk of a relatively modest gift (Cnaan et al., 2011). One study found that a positive rating increases giving but that a negative rating does not decrease giving, for reasons that are not clear (Sloan, 2009).

Based on the findings of Cnaan et al.'s (2011) analysis, 78 percent of donors do not consult charity ratings when making their gift decisions and 58 percent do not use information from the Internet at all. The authors conclude that "unlike most economic transactions, donating is done with trust, not with scrutiny" (p. 391). And "if the motivation for giving is a personal 'warm glow,' the information provided by third-party watchdogs is extraneous" (pp. 392–393).

The lesson that might be taken from research findings is that charity ratings do not matter very much and that nonprofit organizations should be unconcerned about them. But there are two reasons why such an extreme conclusion might be mistaken. First, studies find that 22 percent of donors do consult the ratings and that those who do give more (Cnaan et al., 2011). Second, it is possible that donor attitudes will change over time as charity ratings gain increased visibility. External ratings cannot be disregarded; however, neither can it be assumed that making positive ratings front-and-center on websites and in fundraising materials will inspire many additional gifts.[2]

WEALTHY DONORS

Wealthy donors are of particular interest to nonprofit organizations and fundraisers, for one obvious reason: they have the financial capability to make larger gifts. And the wealthy, especially members of the social elite, have a well-established tradition of philanthropy (Ostrower, 1995). A significant body of research has focused specifically on the giving behavior and motivations of individuals with high net worth.

Like average people, wealthy (or high-net-worth) donors have mixed motives in giving. And they are, like others, affected by both personal needs and social influences. But, to paraphrase F. Scott Fitzgerald, are they really different from you and me? Do they demonstrate unique behaviors and motivations as donors? A substantial number of studies have focused on this question, and a selected few are reviewed in the following paragraphs.

Paul G. Schervish and John J. Havens, of the Boston College Center on Wealth and Philanthropy, have studied high-net-worth donors and offer insights on their unique motivations.

Having interviewed more than 250 wealthy individuals, Schervish (2008) concludes that "why the wealthy give is a commonplace and a distinctive matter" (p. 165). It is commonplace because wealthy donors are motivated by many of the same forces that influence other donors, including gratitude, family traditions, guilt, and prestige.

But how are the charitable motivations of wealthy people distinctive? Schervish and Havens (2002) argue they are in at least one way, which they call **hyperagency**. Hyperagency is "the enhanced capacity of wealthy individuals to establish or essentially control the conditions under which they and others live" (p. 225). In other words, most of us may be able to make gifts to causes and organizations, and collectively we may have an impact. But holders of significant wealth have the ability "to not just contribute to or support causes, but to relatively single-handedly produce new philanthropic organizations or new directions in existing ones" (Schervish, 2008, p. 65). In other words, wealthy donors have the power to make a difference; they can produce "major outcomes" (Schervish, 2008, p. 178). While most donors respond passively to solicitations from nonprofit organizations, wealthy donors are driven by hyperagency to seek out opportunities to be "a direct producer or architect" (Schervish, 2008, p. 178). Students will recognize similarities in this description to the new philanthropists discussed in Chapter 1.

But if the wealthy have the power of hyperagency, why are they motivated to exercise it? Schervish and Havens (2002) offer an explanation: wealth brings freedom. That freedom includes protection from negative conditions, such as financial worry, but also brings the positive freedom to pursue interests the person finds rewarding. Some individuals live through a phase of accumulation, in which their energy and attention is devoted to business matters, and later find themselves with greater wealth than they need to meet their own and family needs. An individual then may turn his or her attention and financial resources toward "advancing for oneself and leaving for others, a personal legacy of significance" (Schervish & Havens, 2002, p. 230).

One important implication of Schervish and Haven's work is that wealthy people are *inclined* toward philanthropy; that is, they do not need to be pressured to give because it is what they want to do. But, these authors argue, conventional fundraising methods are often intended to "arouse a sense of obligation, offer psychological inducements, and otherwise animate . . . forces . . . to impress upon wealth holders their duty to supply charitable gifts" (p. 223). This **cajoling model** or **scolding model**, as Schervish and Havens (2002) characterize it, is likely to be inappropriate and ineffective in communicating with wealthy donors already inclined to be philanthropic. Use of this model can "fall into assaulting emotions, undercutting liberty, attenuating inspiration, and eliciting only grudging compliance" (p. 224). In the words of one donor whom Schervish and Havens (2002) interviewed, it reduces giving to nothing more than "paying a utility bill" (p. 224). Instead, the authors recommend employing a **discernment approach**, in which fundraisers guide donors through a process of identifying their own values and "decid[ing] how much to allocate to charity as an integral part of making broader financial decisions regarding themselves and their families" (p. 231). This is similar to a marketing approach, since it "provide[s] the opportunity for consumers to do what they are in need of doing," rather than trying to pressure them to do what the organization wants them to do (p. 232). Chapter 7, which considers major gifts, returns to this important point and its implications for fundraising.

TYPOLOGY OF DONORS

In a study of affluent donors in the 1990s, Russ Prince and Karen File identified seven motivational types, which they describe in their book *The Seven Faces of Philanthropy*. Typologies are sometimes helpful as a way to bring order out of chaos, but they have weaknesses as well. They may oversimplify our thinking, especially when the various types overlap. As Prince and File (1994) acknowledge, "donors, like people generally, are more complex than one type." But "donors, like all humans, have attitude and behavior patterns that do form a constellation of effects" (p. xiii). Prince and File's (1994) research has some specific weaknesses, including the fact that donors self-reported their motivations. However, it has resonance with practitioners. Thus, despite its limitations, the seven faces framework adds to our understanding of the motivations of wealthy donors. Let's take a look at the seven types, which are summarized in Box 3.1.

Communitarian. The first of the seven types is the **communitarian**. These individuals are often local business owners who give because "doing good makes sense" (p. 14) and helps to build a prosperous community for their businesses. These are people who often serve on local nonprofit boards and value the relationships they make, which are also generally helpful to their business activity. Donors who have a predominantly communitarian perspective often will be found among those who support nonprofit organizations that serve the local community and federated campaigns, such as United Way.

BOX 3.1 Seven Faces of Philanthropy		
Donor Type	**Characteristics**	**Organizations/Causes Commonly Supported**
Communitarian	Give because it makes sense and helps create a prosperous community in which to do business	Local community organizations and institutions, e.g., United Way
Devout	Giving is an obligation of their faith	Religious organizations
Investor	Interested in tax benefits and the impact of their gifts	Nonprofits that can demonstrate results or that offer financially wise ways of giving, e.g., community foundations
Socialite	Enjoy the social life of fundraising events	Arts organizations and institutions
Altruist	Give for moral reasons	Social causes
Repayer	Give to pay back to society for benefits that they or their families have received	Colleges, universities, schools, medical institutions
Dynast	Give to continue family traditions	Traditional and elite institutions

Source: Based on Prince, R. A., & File, K. M. (1994). *The seven faces of philanthropy: A new approach to cultivating major donors*. San Francisco: Jossey-Bass.

Devout. The second type is the **devout**. As the term implies, these are people motivated by their belief that "doing good is God's will" (p. 15). Although some do support secular organizations and causes, most of their giving goes to religious organizations.

Investor. The **investor** is a third type of donor, who looks at giving as a form of investment and is interested in the costs and benefits. Investors have particular interest in the tax implications of their gifts. "Giving is not a part of their lifestyle, as it is for the Communitarians, not is it an inherent part of how they define themselves, as it is for the Devout. Instead, giving is something personally rewarding that is sanctioned by the IRS, thereby providing financial benefits as well" (p. 47). Investors view giving as a social exchange and do value recognition. And they are concerned with a nonprofit's efficiency and effectiveness, that is, the return on their philanthropic investments. According to Prince and File (1994), this type is common among donors to community foundations.

Socialite. The fourth type is the **socialite**. The term sounds pejorative, but what Prince and File mean are those donors who enjoy fundraising events and whose giving is integral to their social life and standing. They also support education and religious organizations but are especially common among donors to arts organizations, for which events are an important fundraising method.

Altruist. As discussed earlier in this chapter, an **altruist** gives because "it is a moral imperative" (p. 16). Altruists are donors who often do not seek recognition, and some may give anonymously. They are often among donors to organizations that promote social causes.

Repayer. The **repayer** is a donor who sees an obligation to support organizations or institutions from which he or she or family members have benefitted—to give back. Repayers often support colleges, universities, schools, and medical institutions.

Dynast. The **dynast**, part of a relatively small category, is someone who typically has inherited wealth and continues to support organizations that are important to family traditions. Dynasts often support arts organizations, like symphonies and opera companies, and prestigious schools and colleges.

Again, no individual belongs exclusively to one motivational type; in other words, no person should be placed in a simple box. One or another perspective may be predominant, but again, donor motivations are often mixed. But a fundraiser meeting with a donor prospect and listening carefully may find that the individual's statements seem to incline toward one type or another, an insight that may be useful in guiding the conversation. For example, suppose the fundraiser is employed by a health care system, including hospitals. He or she might begin the conversation with the prospect by asking about his or her interest in the health system and listening attentively to the individual's comments. The donor may relate a life story that explains how the health system served a family member, suggesting that this donor may have the perspective of a repayer. The fundraiser might think that this donor would be interested in how to help provide similar opportunities for others and discuss how a gift might increase the quality of medical care. If the donor asks questions about the hospital's finances or about the financial implications of giving, that may suggest an investor mind-set. An investor also may be interested in how the health system affects the local economy and improves the overall business climate. In this case, the fundraiser might emphasize the growth of the health system and other positive trends, suggesting that a gift could bring a good return at a well-managed and effective institution. He or she might also introduce some information about tax incentives and the place of philanthropy in overall financial planning.

If a prospect speaks about his or her involvement in community activities, or if the fundraiser knows the individual is active in organizations like the chamber of commerce, that might reveal a communitarian perspective. It might be helpful to discuss the positive impact of the health system on the community and the large number of patients it serves. If it serves a large number of low-income patients, that fact might also be important to a prospect who presents as an altruist. If the fundraiser can gain a sense of the prospect's predominant type, then he or she can emphasize points that seem to be most relevant to that perspective.

It is, of course, never ethical to provide inaccurate information to a donor or to mislead through intentional omission. But it is just good fundraising practice to emphasize points that resonate with donors' own particular values and to seek the intersection where their support can advance the organization while also providing an expression of their own ideals. The seven faces framework thus provides fundraisers with a useful tool.

WOMEN PHILANTHROPISTS

Women have become a significant force in philanthropy. Giving by women has increased as their economic standing and social roles have changed in recent decades. Nearly 70 percent of American women are in the workforce, and the portion of women holding college degrees tripled between 1970 and 2008. Although income imbalances persist, the gap between men and women has narrowed since the 1970s, and 26 percent of married women earned more than their husbands in 2007 (Center on Philanthropy, 2010a).

In earlier years, it was more common that women did not work outside the home, and those who controlled wealth were often widows who had inherited it from their husbands. Although some had independent charitable interests, many also continued to support organizations that had been favored by their husbands, often with gifts that memorialized their husbands. As Mesch and Pactor (2011) describe, they viewed themselves as "guardians" of the wealth rather than "owners" of the wealth. But the increasing number of women who have achieved their own financial success are pursuing their own independent philanthropic priorities (Mesch & Pactor, 2011). Assuming continued advancement for women, this suggests that women donors are likely to become an even more important resource for nonprofit organizations and institutions and that understanding their philanthropic behavior and motivations is of high practical importance for fundraising. But are women different from men when it comes to giving? Again, studies that address this question are divided between those that examine who gives what and to whom (donor behavior) and those that explore the more complex question of why (motivations).

A study by the Women's Philanthropy Institute at Indiana University's Center on Philanthropy (now the Lilly Family School of Philanthropy) concluded that female-headed households are more likely to give than male-headed households and that women give more than men at almost every income level, with the exception of households headed by widows or widowers (Center on Philanthropy, 2010a). Women also tend to support somewhat different causes and organizations than do men (Center on Philanthropy, 2010b). For example, they are more likely than men to support organizations with an international or community focus or in the areas of religion, health care, youth, and families (Center on Philanthropy, 2010b).

What about motivations? Although findings are not always consistent—and, of course, there are always differences among individuals within any group—the preponderance of studies find that there are gender differences in the motivations to give. In general, researchers have concluded that women are more selfless, empathetic, and generous than men and are motivated by altruism in their giving to a greater extent than men (Mesch, Brown, Moore, & Hayat, 2011). Women are also more motivated by the desire to help others, while men may think more abstractly, for example, about the need for justice (Mesch & Pactor, 2011).

Some research suggests that women are more egalitarian in their giving; that is, they support more organizations while men tend to focus on fewer (Andreoni, Brown, & Rischall, 2003). Some interpret that fact to mean that men are more strategic in their giving (Brown, 2006). But others think that women's philanthropy is becoming more strategic, citing the growth of **giving circles** among women as a manifestation (Hannon, 2013). Through giving circles, groups of donors pool their gifts and collectively decide where to direct them, in order to increase the impact beyond what any one of them might accomplish alone. It is an approach pioneered by women that now has been adopted by various groups (Held, 2014a).

CULTURES OF GIVING

According to the U.S. Census Bureau, by 2020 no single racial or ethnic group will encompass a majority of children under age eighteen. Within three decades, no single group will comprise a majority of Americans (Cooper, 2012). The idea of majority and minority groups is becoming obsolete; instead, a more accurate description of America is a "plurality nation" (Cooper, 2012). The implications for fundraising and philanthropy are profound.

There is literature on the particular giving traditions of various groups of people, including African Americans, Hispanics/Latinos, Asian Americans and Pacific Islanders, Native Americans, Arab Americans, and members of the LGBT community. There also is research on giving by people of various religious faiths. This chapter does not review various groups of people individually but rather considers the implications of increasing diversity for fundraising and philanthropy generally.

Every group of people has a tradition of helping and giving, and every religion includes values that encourage it. For example, recent immigrants often give to family members or organizations in their countries of origin or to organizations in the United States that serve their own communities. Their giving is unlikely to be directed toward secular or traditional organizations. As they are assimilated into American society and gain more wealth, their giving often evolves to support mainstream philanthropic causes and organizations (Osili & Du, 2005). However, this evolution is unlikely to occur among groups that have been excluded or discriminated against; they are likely to continue to focus on giving to benefit their own community, even if they have been in the United States for a long time. Mainstream nonprofits that hope to capture the support of a diverse society thus have a major stake in efforts to achieve greater inclusiveness and bring an end to discrimination.

It is usually risky to generalize about groups of people, since individual differences within each group are likely to be significant. And it is even more risky to generalize about multiple groups that might be placed in some broad category, such as "minorities." Wagner (2011) offers what she appropriately characterizes as "cautious generalizations" about the philanthropy of four groups she reviews: African Americans, Hispanics/Latinos, Asian Americans and Pacific Islanders, and Native Americans (p. 197). (The terms are those used by Wagner, although some people may favor different designations.) Among Wagner's (2011) cautious generalizations are the following:

- Convergence of wealth accumulation, education, career growth, and increased earning capacity allows many to become philanthropists in their own right.

- For many cultures, philanthropy is seen in its broadest sense—gifts of time, talent, and treasure—and revolves around family, church, and education.

- There is direct and informal support to children, the elderly, and community members.

- The level of immediate need is important.

- Planned giving is seldom a priority.

- There is some distrust of traditional nonprofits.

- Most groups are highly influenced by leaders—religious, community, professional, social, and family.

- Diverse populations often express reasons [for their giving] unrelated to tax and economic issues.

- Much philanthropy is focused outside the United States without regard for tax benefits.

- Reciprocity is an accepted concept. Helping those in ways they themselves were helped often motivates giving in diverse populations. (p. 197)

The growing diversity of the nation has significant implications for the fundraising profession. The donors with whom fundraising professionals work will increasingly reflect diverse traditions and values, and developing relationships with those individuals will require understanding of their perspectives. There will be a continuing need for greater diversity within the fundraising profession itself, a need that has been recognized by Association of Fundraising Professionals (AFP) and other professional associations in the field.

GENERATIONS OF DONORS

For the first time in history, four distinct generations are active in philanthropy. The **traditionalists** (also called **matures**) were born before 1946. The **baby boomers** (also called just **boomers**), were born from 1946 to 1964. **Generation X** includes people born from 1965 to 1980. And **Generation Y** (also called **Millennials**) was born from 1980 to 2000 (Davis, 2012). The boomers, a group that includes more than 78 million people, are the largest generation in history. They were born in the period following World War II, during which births were suppressed by wartime economic conditions and the absence of millions of men who served in the military. The boomers are now in the prime of their careers and are prominent among nonprofit executives today. But the Millennials are likely to be especially influential in the future, with their numbers rivaling those of the boomers (Davis, 2012).

Are there generational differences in donor behavior, adjusting for other factors such as race, gender, income, religion, and so forth? One survey, which gained responses from more than 10,000 people, suggests that the answer is not really (Center on Philanthropy, 2008). As we might expect, younger donors are less likely to give and give less than their older counterparts when they do, but their gifts are generally consistent with their income, education level, frequency of religious attendance, and marital status—all variables that have a greater impact on donor behavior. One difference is that younger generations, including Generation X and the Millennials, are less likely to give to religious institutions than are older generations (Center on Philanthropy, 2008).

What about generational differences in donor motivations? Again, adjusting for other differences, Millennials are more likely than other generations to give for the purpose of "making the world a better place." Older generations are more likely than Millennials to report giving motivated by a desire to meet the basic needs of the poor, to give the poor a way to help themselves, to make their community a better place, or because they believe that those with more have a responsibility to help those who are less well off. This may reflect the fact that Millennials are also more globally aware and have a greater interest in supporting organizations that work in the international arena (Center on Philanthropy, 2008).

Generational differences may be most relevant to fundraising with regard to the communication channels through which nonprofits can effectively reach and solicit individuals. Traditionalists grew up with mail as a primary source of communication and are still responsive to direct-mail solicitations. The boomers grew up with television, and nonprofits trying to reach them may do so through television commercials. Generation X grew up with the Internet, and its members are accustomed to receiving information via e-mail and electronic newsletters. Millennials are comfortable with social networks, and nonprofits have sought to engage them with social media campaigns (Davis, 2012). These points are discussed again in subsequent chapters, which consider various fundraising methods.

DONOR-CENTERED APPROACH

This chapter's discussion of donors illustrates two important points. First, it would be naïve and unrealistic to think that fundraisers can *make* donors want to do something they are not already inclined to do. Corporations and foundations have clear objectives for their giving, based on their own goals and priorities. The goals and priorities of individual donors may not be as explicit, but each person has a set of psychological and social needs based on his or her own values and experiences. For the organization seeking their support, these are givens. Fundraisers may be able to help donors discover the connection between their own values and the mission and programs of an organization. But not even the most skillful of communicators is likely to persuade an individual to support a cause toward which he or she is disinclined. The mistaken belief of some nonprofit boards and CEOs that such is possible may explain in part the high turnover among fundraising professionals, who cannot meet such an unrealistic expectation.

Second, successful fundraising is based on a relationship between a nonprofit organization or institution and its donors. As in everyday human interactions, those wishing to develop a relationship may find it best to begin with knowing something about the needs, interests, and values of the other party. We all likely know people who talk incessantly about themselves but who rarely or never show interest in us. Most likely, such people are not our true friends. In recognition of this reality, fundraising has evolved in recent years toward a more **donor-centered** approach, in which "raising money and interacting with donors . . . acknowledges what donors really need and puts those needs first" (Burk, 2003, p. 2). That is not to say that nonprofit organizations can or should design their programs entirely with the goal of satisfying their donors' needs in a manner inconsistent with their missions and carefully considered priorities. But it does imply that developing and maintaining relationships with those who share the organization's goals should be the focus, rather than just the money. As fundraising pioneer Si Seymour (1966) said of people, "Study them and treat them well, for you need them more than money" (p. 16).

CHAPTER SUMMARY

Understanding donors is as essential to successful fundraising as understanding the nonprofit organizations they support. There are three primary sources of support for nonprofit organizations—corporations, foundations, and individuals. The motivations for corporate philanthropy lie primarily in advancing business interests, although some are motivated by *enlightened self-interest*, and people who work in corporations may be altruistic as individuals. Foundations exist to make gifts and are required to do so by law. Individual donors have the most complex motivations.

Much of the research on individual donors describes who gives what and to whom, in other words, *donor behavior*. Data from such studies are useful, but it can be misinterpreted and lead to a "theory of magic buttons" (Kelly, 1998), the erroneous belief that the right messages directed to the right group can automatically produce gifts.

Research and practitioner wisdom explain donor motivations, and there are generally two schools of thought: altruism and self-interest. Altruism is giving with no personal benefit, while self-interested giving brings benefits to the donor; it is a *social exchange.* The benefits a donor receives may be tangible or intangible, such as a warm feeling. Even *empathy* may be explained by the negative feelings it produces, which a donor may seek to reduce by giving. A motivation related to empathy is *identification* with the needs of others. Schervish and Havens (2002) suggest that association with others leads to identification, which is why many nonprofits look to volunteers to become donors.

Many scholars reject the dichotomy between altruism and exchange and say that most donors have *mixed motives.* Paton (2007) proposes a continuum of motivations, ranging from those that are purely altruistic to those that are purely self-interested, with mixed motives in between.

Donors may be influenced by individual needs, for example, to secure positive feelings or to assuage negative feelings such as guilt. Social influences also are important, for example, the desire to be part of a group, for social standing and acceptance, or for recognition. Social influences are implicit in fundraising practices, for example, in the effort to assure that the right person solicits the gift. Research suggests that overemphasizing tangible benefits, such as invitations to events, may risk shifting a donor's mind-set from giving to purchasing and undermine philanthropic intent.

The charitable tax deduction affects the cost of a gift and may influence how much a donor is able to give, but it is not a motivator. A person is always financially better off by not making the gift. Some research suggests that most donors do not consider external ratings by charity watchdogs, although larger donors do consult them, and nonprofit organizations should not ignore such ratings.

Wealthy donors have mixed motives but at least one that is unique: the ability and desire to start new organizations or significantly influence existing ones, called *hyperagency* (Schervish & Havens, 2002). Since wealthy donors are inclined to be philanthropic, fundraisers should avoid a *cajoling model* and adopt a *discernment approach* in their interactions with such donors.

Although typologies can simplify, they are sometimes misleading because the types often overlap and individuals may not fit neatly into one of them. But many practitioners find Prince and File's (1994) seven faces of philanthropy to be a useful framework. Affluent donors are primarily *communitarians, devouts, investors, socialites, altruists, repayers,* or *dynasts,* although most will reflect multiple motivations. Donors sometimes reveal their dominant type in comments made during meetings, and fundraisers can use those cues to guide the conversation toward points that best coincide with the individual's interests.

Women donors demonstrate unique giving behaviors, and research suggests that their philanthropic motivations may differ from those of men. America is becoming a more diverse nation, and nonprofit organizations will need to understand the giving traditions of various groups. The fundraising profession also will need to become more diverse in order to interact effectively with donors of various backgrounds.

There are four distinct generations of donors: the *traditionalists* (also called *matures),* the *baby boomers* (also called just *boomers), Generation X,* and *Generation Y* (also called *Millennials)* (Davis, 2012). Younger donors give less than older donors and are less likely to give to religious institutions. More than older donors, they are motivated to give by the desire to make the world a better place (Davis, 2012). Different generations are accustomed to different communications channels, and nonprofits need to use appropriate methods to communicate with them.

Fundraising practice has in recent years moved toward a more *donor-centered* approach, in which the needs of donors are preeminent.

Key Terms and Concepts

Altruism
Altruist [type]
Baby boomers
   (boomers)
Cajoling model
   (scolding model)
Communitarian [type]
Crowding out
Devout [type]
Discernment
   approach
Donor-centered

Dynast [type]
Empathy
Enlightened
   self-interest
Family foundation
Generation X
Generation Y
   (Millennials)
Gifts-in-kind
Giving circles
Hyperagency
Identification

Investor [type]
Impure altruist
Independent
   foundation
Joy of giving
Mixed motives
Norm of reciprocity
Repayer [type]
Social exchange
Socialite [type]
Traditionalists
   (matures)

Case 3.1: T. Denny Sanford

Denny Sanford was born in St. Paul, Minnesota. His mother died when he was four and his father died when he was twenty. As a teenager, he had some trouble with the law due to drinking and fighting. A judge released him from a juvenile detention center when he promised to go to college. He graduated from the University of Minnesota in 1958 with a major in psychology (Gose, 2007a).

He started his own company two years after college, and in 1982, while still in his forties, he sold it for $10 million. He retired to Florida to play golf. But four years later, he left retirement and purchased United National Bank in Sioux Falls, South Dakota, for $5 million, later renaming it First Premier Bank. First Premier grew into the nation's eleventh largest issuer of Visa and MasterCard credit cards. Mr. Sanford accumulated more than $2.5 billion in personal wealth (Gose, 2007a).

He gave $2 million in 1999 to the Children's Home Society of South Dakota, one of his first large gifts. He explained, "When you see these kids who have been separated from families because of abuse—either sexual or physical—and you see their recoveries and the success that the organization has with these kids, it's absolutely unbelievable" (Gose, 2007a). But Sanford was relatively unknown in the philanthropy world in 2003, when he offered a $35 million gift to the University of Minnesota for a new football stadium, an initiative that ended in widely publicized controversy. The gift was never completed after Sanford and the university could not agree on the cost of the stadium and the control Sanford would have over recognition of his gift in the stadium.

After the controversy with the University of Minnesota, Sanford turned his interest back to South Dakota. In 2004, he gave $16 million to the children's hospital in Sioux Falls, the largest city in the state (Krabbenhoft, 2008). Speaking about his focus on helping children, Sanford once said, "They don't have voices. . . . Give them the right values. Give them the love they need. And give them the health that they so desperately need" (Whelan, 2007). In 2006, Sanford gave $20 million to the University of South Dakota's medical school, which was named in his honor. Not trusting the university governance system, he put the Sioux Valley health system in charge of how the medical school funds would be used (Gose, 2007a). He gave $15 million to the Mayo Clinic, stipulating that the money be used for joint research projects with the children's hospital in Sioux Falls (Gose, 2007b). But his largest gift was yet to come.

On February 3, 2007, Kelby Krabbenhoft, president and CEO of Sioux Valley Hospitals and Health System, announced that Denny Sanford would give $400 million to the organization, which would be renamed Sanford Health. Sanford said at the announcement of his gift, "Now is the time to set things in motion to truly make a difference in people's lives and improve the human condition" (Krabbenhoft, 2008). The gift would be used to expand research and health programs for children. Sanford Children's Clinics would be established across the nation and in other countries. A new Sanford Children's Hospital would be constructed in Sioux Falls.

Krabbenhoft said his goal was to make Sanford as prominent in pediatric medicine as the Mayo Clinic is in geriatric medicine. Mr. Sanford's pledge was completed ahead of schedule, by 2009 ("No. 3: T. Denny Sanford," 2011).

Although Krabbenhoft had solicited Sanford's gift and both described themselves as friends, Sanford emphasized that he would insist on Krabbenhoft producing results. "He still has to perform for me," Sanford said. "He's not a patient man," Krabbenhoft said of Sanford. "He's very kind, generous, and giving—but he is results oriented like any successful CEO is. I get the chance to live up to those expectations" (Gose, 2007b).

In 2007, Mr. Sanford reflected on his life and philanthropy, providing insights on his thinking. "I'm already successful," he said in an interview. "Now I intend to make a difference in the world. . . . It's payback time for me," he said of his giving in South Dakota. "The state has given me the opportunities, and it's time for me to say 'thank you.'" Referring to the early deaths of his parents, he said, "I had an independence forced on me that a lot of people have not. . . . You go with what you have available, and what I had available was me, and no safety net down below." Regarding his approach to philanthropy, he explained, "I am not interested in doing something that isn't a bit unusual. . . . Just to write a big check without a specific mission or project in mind—I have no interest in that." When asked about the views of some people that he exerts too much control over the use of his gifts, he replied, "Everything has some conditions to it" (Gose, 2007a).

T. Denny Sanford's philanthropy did not end with his $400 million gift to Sanford Health. Among many other gifts, in 2011, he gave an additional $100 million to the Sanford

Health Foundation, to be used for research on breast cancer, the cause of his mother's death. And in 2013, he gave $100 million to create a research center that would study human stem cells at the University of California San Diego ("$100 Million Gift," 2013). As Denny Sanford said in 2007, "I want to die broke" (Whelan, 2007).

Case 3.2:   Osceola McCarty

Osceola McCarty was born in Hattiesburg, Mississippi, in 1908. She was conceived when her mother was raped. She was raised by her grandmother and aunt, who cleaned houses, cooked, and did laundry for other people. Ms. McCarty dropped out of school after the sixth grade to care for her ailing aunt and went to work doing laundry, which she did using a scrub board and clothesline, rather than an automatic washer and dryer (Zinsmeister, n.d.).

McCarty was thrifty. She lived all of her life in her family home and spent little. And she saved money, starting as a child. "I never take any of it out," she explained. "I just put it in. . . . It's not the ones that make the big money, but the ones who know how to save who get ahead" (Zinsmeister, n.d.). By the time she retired, at age eighty-six, she had accumulated more than $250,000 (Zinsmeister, n.d.).

Having no close family to advise her, Ms. McCarty visited a local banker to assist her with planning her estate. He handed her ten dimes, each representing 10 percent of her estate, and five slips of paper with the names of beneficiaries she had selected. He asked her to place the dimes by the slips of paper in proportion to how she wanted to allocate the money. She placed one dime on her church, one dime on each of three cousins, and six dimes on the paper labeled "University of Southern Mississippi" (Koten, 2013). The latter added up to $150,000, which would be used to award scholarships to African American students (Bragg, 1995).

McCarty explained, "[It's] more than I could ever use. I wanted to share my wealth with the children. I never minded work, but I was so always busy, busy. Maybe I can make it so the children don't have to work like I did . . . I know it won't be too many years before I pass on and I just figured the money would do them a lot more good than it would me" (Bragg, 1995).

When asked why she chose the University of Southern Mississippi, rather than a historically black institution, she replied, "Because it's here, it's close. . . . My race used to not get to go to that college, but now they can" (Bragg, 1995).

Reflecting on McCarty's gift, the then–executive director of the University of Southern Mississippi Foundation explained that "no one approached her from the university; she approached us. She's seen the poverty, the young people who have struggled, who need an education. She's the most unselfish individual I have ever met" (Bragg, 1995).

Inspired by McCarty's generosity, other people pledged gifts totaling $330,000 so that the university could begin awarding McCarty scholarships immediately (Koten, 2013). When CNN founder Ted Turner announced his gift of $1 billion to the United Nations, he mentioned Osceola McCarty, saying, "If that little woman can give away everything she has, then I can give a billion" (Zinsmeister, n.d.). There was a national outpouring of affection and admiration. McCarty was invited to the White House and was given an honorary degree by Harvard (Koten, 2013).

Osceola McCarty died in 1999 at age ninety-one. Her scholarship fund has continued to grow through investments. By 2013, forty-four students had received scholarships and had gone on to a variety of careers. Today, when a donor informs the University of Southern Mississippi that they have arranged for a bequest, that person is invited to become a member of the McCarty Legacy Society. The society's logo is a tree with six dimes at the end of its branches (Koten, 2013).

Questions for Discussion

1. Was T. Denny Stanford's philanthropy motivated by altruism, self-interest, or mixed motives?

2. Which of the seven donor types described in *The Seven Faces of Philanthropy* seems to best apply to the case of T. Denny Sanford?

3. How does the case of T. Denny Sanford relate to the findings of Schervish and Havens discussed in this chapter?

4. How do the various concepts and theories discussed in this chapter relate to the case of Osceola McCarty? In other words, although it calls for your speculation given the limited information provided in the case, what do you think were her motives?

5. How does the case of Osceola McCarty reflect social influences on giving as discussed in this chapter?

Suggestions for Further Reading

Books

Burk, P. (2003). *Donor-centered fundraising.* Chicago: Cygnus Applied Research.

Davis, E. (2012). *Fundraising and the next generation: Tools for engaging the next generation of philanthropists.* San Francisco: Jossey-Bass.

Oppenheimer, D. M., & Olivola, C. Y. (Eds.). (2011). *The science of giving: Experimental approaches to the study of charity.* New York: Taylor & Francis Group.

Prince, R. A., & File, K. M. (1994). *The seven faces of philanthropy: A new approach to cultivating major donors.* San Francisco: Jossey-Bass.

Articles

Bekkers, R., & Wiepking, P. (2011, October). A literature review of empirical studies of philanthropy: Eight mechanisms that drive charitable giving. *Nonprofit and Voluntary Sector Quarterly, 40*(5), 924–973.

Mesch, D. J., Brown, M. S., Moore, Z. I., & Hayat, A. D. (2011, November). Gender differences in charitable giving. *International Journal of Nonprofit and Voluntary Sector Marketing, 16,* 342–355.

Schervish, P. G., & Havens, J. J. (2002, March). The new physics of philanthropy: The supply side vectors of charitable giving. Part II: The spiritual side of the supply side. *CASE International Journal of Educational Advancement, 2*(3), 221–241.

Website

Lilly Family School of Philanthropy, Women's Philanthropy Institute: http://www
.philanthropy.iupui.edu/womens-philanthropy-institute

Bibliography

Foundation Center. (2008). *Diversity in philanthropy: A comprehensive bibliography of resources related to diversity within the philanthropic and nonprofit sectors.* New York: Foundation Center. (Available for download at http://foundationcenter.org/getstarted/topical/diversity.html)

Notes

1. This example is drawn from the author's experience, but details have been omitted to preserve confidentiality.

2. This section is based in part on research conducted by Leah Weissburg, a graduate student at the Trachtenberg School of Public Policy and Public Administration of The George Washington University, in fall 2013.

CHAPTER 4

Principles of Fundraising

After an introduction to fundraising and philanthropy in Chapter 1, this text now has discussed both parties in philanthropic transactions—nonprofit organizations (in Chapter 2) and donors (in Chapter 3). This chapter begins an exploration of the *process* that brings them together—fundraising—with a discussion of some overarching concepts and principles. Some terms and concepts introduced are explored in more detail in later chapters of this book, so discussion of them here is brief. For example, prospect research is discussed in this chapter as a component of the fundraising process, but Chapter 5 discusses it in greater detail as an aspect of preparing an organization for fundraising. The solicitation programs defined in this chapter—annual giving, major gifts, and corporate and foundation relations—are the focus of subsequent chapters. Planned giving, a strategy for major gifts, also is discussed in a separate chapter later in the book.

While Chapters 2 and 3 draw primarily on the academic literature, this chapter relies much more on the practitioner literature. This is because most of the principles of fundraising have emerged from practice historically, rather than from theory.

TYPES OF GIFTS

As explained earlier, nonprofit organizations receive gifts from three sources—corporations, foundations, and individuals. The gifts can be classified four ways, as summarized in Table 4.1. In reality, the categories overlap, since most gifts can be classified in more than one way.

Defined by Amount

Gifts are defined as **annual gifts**, **leadership annual gifts**, **major gifts**, or **principal gifts** according to the dollar amount (APF fundraising dictionary online; Lowman, 2012; Schubert, 2002). Smaller gifts are called annual gifts, even if they are not necessarily repeated on an annual basis, because they usually are not restricted by the donor and thus can be used by the organization toward its annual operating budget. The definition varies among organizations, but a leadership annual gift is commonly defined as $1,000 or more. These are larger than the average annual gift but smaller than major gifts; for that reason, Lowman (2012) calls them "gap gifts"—possibly too large to be secured through direct

TABLE 4.1   Types of Gifts

Defined by Amount	
Principal gift	Large major gift; sometimes defined as $1 million or more
Major gift	Large gift; sometimes defined as $10,000 or $100,000 or more
Leadership annual gift	Large for an annual gift; sometimes defined as $1,000 or more
Annual gift	Relatively small gift, usually less than $1,000; often repeated on a regular (often annual) basis
Defined by Purpose	
Capital gift	Adds to the organization's physical capital (e.g., buildings) or financial capital (endowment)
Program or project support	Made to support a specific activity (restricted, current operations)
Unrestricted gift	To be used at the discretion of the organization, often used to support the current-year operating budget
Defined by Donor's Perspective	
Ultimate gift	The largest gift of the donor's lifetime; timing based on the donor's circumstances
Special gift	One-time gift made to support a specific purpose, may be repeated periodically but not annually; timing based on the organization's needs
Regular gift	Recurring; timing based on the calendar, usually annually
Defined by Donor's Method	
Planned gift	A gift integrated with the donor's financial and estate planning; may be outright planned gifts, expectancies, or deferred gifts
Pledge	A gift promised now, to be paid in the future, often in installments
Outright gift	A gift the donor completes with one payment, using cash or marketable property

Note: The terms *ultimate gift, special gift,* and *regular gift* introduced by Dunlop (2002).

marketing methods such as mail, e-mail, or phone but not at a level where they would be acquired through a major-gifts program. Similarly, the definition of a major gift varies; for some organizations, it may be $1,000 or $10,000, and for larger nonprofit institutions it may be $100,000 or more. The term *principal gift* is used to refer to large major gifts. *Principal gifts* are defined by dollar level, commonly $1 million or more. Sometimes very large gifts are called "mega gifts," a term introduced by Panas (1984), but the term has no precise definition.

Annual gifts are usually made from the donor's current income. A major gift may be made from the donor's current income, especially if it is paid in installments over a period of years, but it also may be made from the donor's accumulated assets. Principal gifts are almost always made from the donor's assets rather than current income and often from the donor's estate. For this reason, it is understandable that major and principal gifts require greater thought and planning, since they deplete resources that the donor may not be able to replenish (Alexander & Carlson, 2005).

Defined by Purpose

Another way to classify gifts is by their intended purpose, which may or may not be designated by the donor. As the term implies, an unrestricted gift comes with no direction from the donor and can be used by the nonprofit for its general operating purposes. Since such gifts are unrestricted, there is no reason that a nonprofit could not use them to support specific programs or to meet capital needs. But most organizations rely on unrestricted gifts as a line item in their operating budgets and use them for that purpose. As explained, unrestricted gifts are considered annual gifts, both because they are often given on that schedule and because they are generally expended in the year they are received.

Other gifts (or grants) are restricted; they are given for specific purposes, which may be to support a current program or to meet the organization's capital needs.[1] Thinking back on the brief discussion of nonprofit financial management in Chapter 2, there are two kinds of capital—physical capital (buildings and equipment) and financial capital (endowment). Endowment is capital because the principal is usually not available for expenditure but is invested in perpetuity to generate investment returns, which are expendable (Bowman, 2011).

Defined by Donor's Perspective

Dunlop (2002) identified three types of gifts people make based on the donor's perspective. Many people have charities or causes they support with **regular gifts**. They are often made on an annual basis but may be given more frequently, perhaps monthly. The timing is driven by the calendar. For example, a college or university alumna may respond to the first mailing of the year from her alma mater, which typically occurs in the fall, at the beginning of the academic year. Many people make their gifts to charitable organizations near the end of the calendar year, perhaps motivated by the spirit of the holiday season as well as the approaching end of the tax year.

Donors also make **special gifts**, for specific purposes. These gifts are in addition to and usually larger than their regular gifts and are intended to be made one time, although a donor may make multiple special gifts over the years. The timing of special gifts is related to the needs of the organization, rather than the calendar. A nonprofit may undertake a campaign to raise funds for a new building or a major renovation or to purchase a new item of expensive equipment. Or it may seek special gifts to support a one-time program, like a conference or to respond to an emergency. For example, some people may make regular gifts to the Red Cross but then make a special gift to address the extraordinary need for disaster relief following a hurricane. Others may make a special gift in connection with a peer-to-peer fundraising initiative, for example, to sponsor a friend who is participating in a charity walk, run, or ride. Such gifts are usually special gifts because they are tied to one event and are not repeated on a regular basis.

Special gifts are often major gifts, but the terms are not synonymous. Again, a major gift is defined by the dollar amount, and the threshold is established by the organization. From the donor's perspective, the gift is special, because it is in addition to and usually larger than his or her regular gifts (Dunlop, 2002).

Donors who support a nonprofit organization or institution over a long period of time may make regular gifts every year, special gifts from time to time, and eventually what Dunlop calls an **ultimate gift**. An ultimate gift is "an exercise of the giver's full giving capacity. [It] is the largest philanthropic commitment that the giver is capable of making" (Dunlop, 2002, p. 92). The timing of an ultimate gift is driven by the donor's life circumstances rather than the calendar or the needs of the organization. Many ultimate gifts are made using planned giving, for example, as a bequest at the donor's death, but some ultimate gifts also are made during the donor's lifetime.

It is important to distinguish between the terms *principal gift* and *ultimate gift*. A principal gift is defined by amount. An ultimate gift is defined from the donor's perspective; it is the largest gift of which the donor is capable and its timing depends on the donor's circumstances. Think back on the two cases presented in Chapter 3. Osceola McCarty's gift of $150,000 to the University of Southern Mississippi was her ultimate gift, although maybe not defined as a principal gift from the university's perspective. A principal gift is often a donor's ultimate gift, but some wealthy donors may make gifts to various organizations that are exceptional in each case; all of them may be principal gifts from the perspective of those organizations, even though none may be the donor's ultimate gift. For example, T. Denny Sanford's $20 million gift to the University of South Dakota medical school in 2006 was a principal gift from the perspective of that institution, which was renamed in Sanford's honor. But his ultimate gift may have been the $400 million he gave in 2007 to the Sioux Valley Hospitals and Health System, now Sanford Health. That surely was a principal gift from the perspective of Sanford Health, and it seems probable that it was Sanford's ultimate gift, although that cannot be known yet, since he is still living and it is conceivable that he could make an even larger gift at some future time.

Defined by Donor's Method

Gifts also may be classified according to the method the donor uses in making it. An **outright gift** is one completed with a single payment; that is common for annual gifts of modest amounts. But some donors make **pledges**, committing to make a gift that will be paid in the future, perhaps all at once by some date or in installments over some period of time (AFP online). A major gift or a principal gift often is paid over a period of years, but some donors also make a pledge for their annual gifts and plan to pay them in installments, perhaps monthly over the year. Remember from Chapter 2 that a pledge is recorded as revenue by the organization when it is made—it is a receivable—but the subsequent payments are not double counted when they are received.

As the term implies, a **planned gift** is one a donor has included as a part of his or her overall financial and estate planning (AFP online). This is not to imply that other gifts are necessarily unplanned or that they are spontaneous or irrational. But they are likely to be less consequential to the donor's financial situation and so do not require as much careful consideration. A planned gift is not by definition a major or principal gift. For example, a donor could arrange for a bequest of, say, $1,000 to a favorite charity. That would be a planned gift but probably not a major or principal gift from the perspective of the organization receiving it. But many major and principal gifts are, at least in part, planned gifts, since they are likely to have implications for the donor's overall financial situation.

There are three types of planned gifts—**outright planned gifts**, **expectancies**, and **deferred gifts** (Regenovich, 2011). Some outright gifts are planned gifts because they involve complex assets, such as stocks or real estate, and may require the assistance of financial experts to complete. An expectancy is a promise a donor makes to provide a gift to the organization at some future time, generally at death, through a bequest, life insurance, or a retirement plan (Regenovich, 2011). Such promises may be informal or documented in writing. Deferred gifts are gifts the donor makes now but are not available to the organization until some future time, generally after the death of the donor or some other individual. They often involve charitable gift annuities and charitable remainder trusts, the details of which are discussed in Chapter 8.

Prior to the 1970s, *deferred giving* was used as the umbrella term. But the Tax Reform Act of 1969 defined various new forms of giving, and deferred giving was not an accurate description for all of them. The term *planned giving* was introduced as the broader concept, to include the range of gifts described earlier. It has been attributed to Robert F. Sharpe Sr., a prominent consultant in the planned-giving field (Sagrestano & Wahlers, 2012).

SOLICITATION PROGRAMS

Nonprofit organizations raise funds to meet the four types of gifts defined by purpose: unrestricted support for current operations, **restricted gifts** or grants to support current programs and projects, gifts for physical capital, and gifts for financial capital (endowment). Seiler (2011a) calls this the **four-legged stool** of a comprehensive fundraising program. But in practice, an organization's solicitation programs are usually not labeled in exact alignment with these four purposes.[2]

As depicted in Table 4.2, there are three core solicitation programs: annual giving, major gifts, and corporate and foundation support. Some development offices have a distinct program for soliciting principal gifts, but most encompass that within the major-gifts program. Annual gifts and major gifts are, of course, defined by the size of the gift, whereas corporate and foundation support relate to the donor constituency addressed. Corporate and foundation support are pursued through a distinct program because, as discussed in Chapter 3, such donors are distinctive in their motivations, require particular methods to solicit their support, and are most inclined to make certain types of gifts. Some large development offices establish separate programs for corporate support and foundation support, but most place responsibility for both under one program and staff specialist.

Planned giving is not identified here as a core solicitation program, although in common parlance many development offices have a planned-giving "program." But planned giving

TABLE 4.2   Core Solicitation Programs

Solicitation Program	Primary Donor Constituencies (Target Audiences)	Types of Gifts Secured	Common Solicitation Methods
Annual giving	Individuals, local businesses and foundations, corporations (especially sponsorships)	Unrestricted current operating funds (the annual fund)	Mail, phone, electronic communication (e-mail), events, personal solicitation
Major gifts/ principal gifts	Individuals	Physical capital (i.e., buildings, equipment) Financial capital (endowment) Restricted current operating funds (programs or projects) Unrestricted current operating funds (uncommon)	Personal solicitation, written proposals
Corporate and foundation support	Corporations, foundations	Restricted current operating funds (programs or projects) Unrestricted current operating funds (only with a close relationship or in the form of sponsorship) Physical capital (rarely) Financial capital (very rarely)	Written proposals, personal visits

is a method used by some donors, and from the fundraising perspective, it is a *strategy* for the solicitation of major and principal gifts.

It is important to clarify that development offices also have programs that encompass other activities that do not directly involve solicitation. For example, prospect research, donor recognition, communications, and stewardship or donor relations are activities often organized as programs. These are important activities, but they *support* the solicitation programs, which are at the core of fundraising.

In a small development office, some of the solicitation programs may be missing or embryonic, and those that are operational may be managed by one person or a few people. In larger development offices, each program has a dedicated staff of fundraising professionals, and as previously discussed, subspecialties have developed and include individuals working in these areas. That is because each program addresses a somewhat different donor constituency and uses different methods, thus requiring distinct knowledge and skills.

Annual Giving

The **annual giving** program is defined by the size of gifts and the type of gifts it usually emphasizes—unrestricted gifts to support current operations. Most are relatively small in amount, less than whatever the organization defines as a major gift (Lowman, 2012).The funds raised are called the **annual fund**, sometimes called the **sustaining fund** (AFP online).[3]

The terms *annual giving* and *annual fund* have origins in higher education fundraising and refer to the program that solicits regular gifts to meet current operating needs. Colleges and universities have constituencies that are essentially finite. For most, the primary donor constituency is alumni, who remain alumni all of their lives. For that reason, educational institutions traditionally have minimized the risk of donor fatigue by soliciting donors for one annual gift. That is, donors are asked to make one commitment for the year, although it might be paid in installments, and the emphasis is on maximizing the amount of that commitment and increasing it from year to year. Once a donor makes his or her annual fund commitment, that donor traditionally has been omitted from subsequent annual fund solicitations for the balance of the year. This strategy also is followed by other nonprofit organizations that have a finite constituency, including, for example, membership associations.[4]

In contrast, many nonprofit organizations are constantly developing their constituencies and resolicit current donors multiple times a year. For such organizations, the term *annual giving* may not seem to be an exactly accurate description of what occurs. But the term is well-established and widely used throughout the nonprofit sector to identify programs that solicit unrestricted operating support gifts on a regular basis (Weinstein, 2009).

As shown in Table 4.2, individuals are the primary donor constituency for the annual giving program (Rosso, 2011b). Local businesses and foundations also may make unrestricted annual gifts to local nonprofit organizations. Corporations may make unrestricted gifts but usually only if they have a close relationship to the organization. For example, corporations sometimes make annual gifts to organizations at which their employees volunteer or where their executives are board members. Nonprofits that have such connections have a better chance of obtaining an annual corporate gift, as do those that serve communities in which the corporation has a significant presence, either its headquarters or a large number of employees. Corporations also offer **sponsorships**, for example, in connection with a walk, a run, or a benefit dinner. The net proceeds of such an event may be unrestricted and thus might be counted in the annual fund.

Thinking back on our discussion of corporate and foundation motivations in Chapter 3, it is understandable that many prefer to restrict most of their gifts, rather than provide general support. They prefer to have an impact in areas of primary interest or to gain visibility or benefit from the gift, even if indirectly. Even individual donors are often reluctant to make unrestricted gifts of larger amounts. Someone who gives $10 or even $100 may do so merely to support the general purposes of the organization, but if that person gives $10,000 or $100,000, that person likely will prefer that the gift be restricted to some purpose that he or she particularly favors, for the obvious reason that the gift entails a greater sacrifice. Annual giving programs usually obtain relatively modest gifts and rely on volume to accumulate a meaningful total.

Major Gifts

As discussed, major gifts and principal gifts are defined by dollar amount, and the threshold varies among organizations. Corporations and foundations may make gifts or grants that meet the definition by dollar amount, but the *major-gifts program* is focused on individual donors.

Prospects for physical capital projects—for example, new buildings—are primarily individuals, and major gifts are usually required in order to complete such projects. Foundations and corporations may provide support for building projects in some circumstances, again, if there is an established and strong relationship with the nonprofit organization or if there is some direct link between the project and the company's employees, for example, a new hospital in a company town. But most are generally disinclined to give toward brick-and-mortar projects, so the organization has to rely primarily on major gifts from individuals.

Gifts that add to financial capital, that is, endowment, almost always come from individual donors (Newman, 2005). Corporations and foundations, with some exceptions, are unlikely to make such gifts, preferring to have greater short-term impact. Corporations also may be reluctant to give to an endowment fund that may someday be used to support an activity that cannot be foreseen now; they might see such uncertainty as a risk to their reputations down the road. Foundations may argue that they are indeed endowments themselves, investing their assets and generating investment earnings, from which grants are made. Transferring their assets to a nonprofit organization to be used in the same manner might seem like something that defeats their purpose, substituting the judgment of future nonprofit directors for those of the foundation's own future board members. Again, there may be some exceptions. For example, a corporation or foundation may make a gift to an endowment established to honor an individual who is prominent or who is associated with their organization or to support an institution with which it has enjoyed a long and close relationship. But in most cases, these are likely to be relatively modest gifts.

Planned Giving

As discussed, **planned giving** is properly understood as a method used by some donors and as a strategy employed by nonprofit organizations in the context of the major-gifts program. It is common to see references to an organization's planned-giving program, and it is indeed an organized set of activities that sometimes has dedicated staff and resources, but it is not a core solicitation program and thus is not include in Table 4.2.

In smaller development offices, there may not be the need or sufficient potential to justify a staff specialist with expertise in planned giving. In those cases, major-gifts officers may be trained in planned giving so that they are able to discuss the subject with major-gift prospects, but the organization maintains relationships with outside experts—including attorneys, accountants, financial planners, and independent gift planners—who can be consulted when working with a donor whose circumstances require such expertise.

Planned giving is primarily a strategy for securing major and principal gifts, but it is important to note that planned gifts are not defined by dollar amount. Many organizations cast a wide net in promoting them, even to donors who are not the focus of the major-gifts program, for example, to leadership annual fund donors. Even modest bequests, say, for $5,000 or $10,000, are to be encouraged, although many organizations would not define them as major gifts. Prospects for the planned-giving program are identified in part by demographic characteristics they have in common, for example, age and family circumstances, whereas wealth may be the primary criterion in identifying prospects for outright major gifts. Relationships with major-gift prospects are typically managed with the goal of obtaining a commitment on a definite timetable, whereas relationships with planned-giving prospects are often less time sensitive. Closing a planned gift may require a process that extends for as long as seven to ten years or more (Partnership for Philanthropic Planning, 2012). For these reasons, while the planned-giving program supports the major-gifts program and even may be organizationally integrated with that program, it is also distinctive in the ways mentioned earlier, and planned giving is a recognized specialty within the fundraising profession.

The planned-giving program addresses only individual donors, since corporations and foundations are not mortal and thus do not have a need for financial and estate planning. Some planned gifts, especially bequests, may be unrestricted; that is, a donor may simply specify that his or her bequest goes to the organization upon death without any further direction as to how it should be used. In that case, realized bequests could be used to meet current operating needs. However, since it is impossible to predict when bequests will be received, it is generally unwise to rely on them in planning annual operating budgets. Some large institutions with a long history of planned giving and larger **donor constituencies** may be able to project how much is likely to be received each year and include a conservative line item in the budget for that amount, but for most nonprofits this is a risky idea. Similarly, planned gifts usually are not useful for meeting the costs of building projects, since there is no assurance that they will be received within the period of construction or renovation. A planned gift might be designated to support a current program area; for example, a donor might stipulate that a school use her bequest to strengthen its programs in the arts. But bequests usually are not useful for funding specific projects, which, again, require that the timing of support be predictable. Many planned gifts are designated for endowment, which enhances the long-run financial strength of the organization. In that case, the timing of their receipt is not critical to current operations and programs.

Corporate and Foundation Support

As discussed previously, with some exceptions, corporations and foundations are not the most promising prospects for unrestricted gifts or those that address capital needs. Solicitation programs focused on corporations and foundations often focus on specific programs and projects.

Foundations and corporations (excluding family foundations and smaller privately held businesses) usually have formal guidelines defining what they are willing to support and how to apply for a grant (Collins, 2008). Some may issue a **request for proposal**, called an **RFP**, regarding grants they have decided to make in support of established philanthropic priorities. Organizations respond, usually with a formal written proposal, and the foundation or corporation selects grantees that it thinks most capable of advancing their predetermined goals, on a competitive basis. Thus, in these instances, the donor's decision is based more on the capabilities of the nonprofit to advance the donor's priorities than on the organization's own, self-identified needs.

Individuals also make restricted gifts to support special purposes; for example, an individual might make a gift to enable local children to attend the symphony. But individuals are generally less inclined to support something more complicated, like a research project in nanotechnology. Corporations and foundations may employ experts on nanotechnology and would be likely to understand the importance of it, so they would be better prospects for support of such research.

MATCHING PROGRAMS TO NEEDS

As mentioned, a nonprofit organization with a comprehensive fundraising program will maintain a full array of solicitation programs. But, as a practical matter, organizations with limited fundraising capacity may emphasize those programs and donor constituencies most appropriate to meeting their most critical needs. In a classic practitioner book, Broce (1986) explains:

> Institutions should not spend hard-earned dollars on nonproductive [fundraising] programs. . . . An institution with a small endowment but a great need for additional operating support should place its prime emphasis on aggressive annual-gifts programs. It also should be active in corporate-support programs with a continuing interest in planned giving programs, but its primary staff and dollar concentration should be on securing operating funds, which come mostly from individuals. . . . The institution should also be attracting endowment funds, but that should remain a secondary activity. On the other hand, using the same criteria, a research-oriented organization should focus its attention on fund raising from foundations. (p. 20)

Broce's advice is pragmatic and appropriate to some organizations' circumstances. However, as discussed later in this chapter, organizations that intend to increase their capacity and become sustainable need to build comprehensive fundraising programs that address all donor constituencies and secure the range of gifts needed to support the four-legged stool.

MATCHING PROSPECTS TO PROGRAMS

Just as a nonprofit's fundraising programs should reflect its financial needs, its donor prospects are best solicited through the most appropriate program. Prospects can be assigned to one of four quadrants, based on two criteria: their financial capacity for giving and the extent to which they are connected to the organization (Alexander & Carlson, 2005). The latter may mean a formal affiliation, such as a board member, volunteer, or former client would have, or it may mean the individual's "affinity to [the] mission" (Blackbaud, 2010). Both meanings are related, since those who have a connection are the most likely to also have an emotional affinity for the mission of the organization.

As Figure 4.1 portrays, those with modest financial capacity (on the left side of the diagram) are only prospects for annual gifts, since they do not have the resources to make major or principal gifts. Those who have modest financial capacity but a strong connection to the organization (Quadrant I) are "fans" (Blackbaud, 2010). They may upgrade their annual gifts and perhaps even make leadership annual gifts if their income permits. Since they are strongly connected, it is worth asking them to do so.

Those who have modest financial capacity and are not strongly connected (Quadrant II) are "acquaintances" (Blackbaud, 2010). They are at best prospects for annual gifts. They probably will not make leadership annual gifts, both because of their financial limitations and their weak connections. They might be solicited for annual gifts, but the organization would use the most cost-effective methods, since this is not likely to be the most productive segment of the organization's donor constituency (Alexander & Carlson, 2005).

Prospects on the right side of Figure 4.1 have high financial capacity. Those who also are strongly connected to the organization (Quadrant III) are the organization's best donor prospects. Blackbaud (2010) calls them "VIPs," meaning "very important prospects." Relationships with them should be managed as a part of the major-gifts program. What about those who have financial capacity but are not strongly connected (Quadrant IV)? They probably will not provide unrestricted support to the organization, but they might be prospects for specific programs or projects that align with their interests and that arouse their

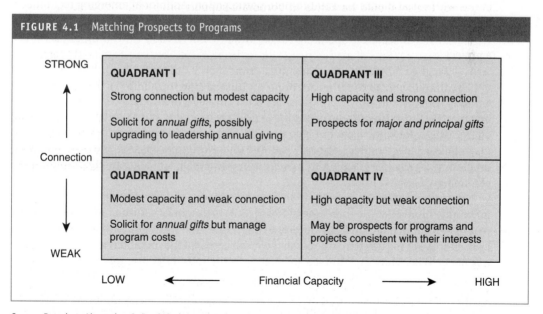

FIGURE 4.1 Matching Prospects to Programs

	STRONG		
	QUADRANT I		**QUADRANT III**
	Strong connection but modest capacity		High capacity and strong connection
Connection	Solicit for *annual gifts*, possibly upgrading to leadership annual giving		Prospects for *major and principal gifts*
	QUADRANT II		**QUADRANT IV**
	Modest capacity and weak connection		High capacity but weak connection
	Solicit for *annual gifts* but manage program costs		May be prospects for programs and projects consistent with their interests
	WEAK		

LOW ⟵———— Financial Capacity ————⟶ HIGH

Source: Based on Alexander, C. D., & Carlson, K. J. (2005). *Essential principles for fundraising success.* San Francisco: Jossey-Bass, p. 17; Blackbaud (https://www.blackbaud.com/files/resource/downloads/Datasheet_BlackbaudGivingScore.pdf).

passions, in a way that the organization by itself does not (Alexander & Carlson, 2005). This might be the case with some entrepreneurial donors, who have their own giving priorities and might consider any organization that has programs or projects consistent with those interests.

SOLICITATION METHODS

Various methods are employed to varying degrees within all solicitation programs, although each emphasizes some over others.[5]

The most common methods include **direct mail**, **phone (telemarketing)**, **electronic communication** (principally **e-mail**), **events**, **personal solicitations**, and **proposal writing**. Mail, phone, and e-mail are collectively called **direct marketing**. Proposal writing is sometimes called **grant writing**, and the skill to do so is called **grantsmanship** (AFP online). But the term *grant writing* is not really accurate, since the organization that writes the proposal really does not *write* the grant; the grant decision is made by a funder.

This chapter provides a brief overview of the most common solicitation methods, which are explored further in later chapters related to programs in which the various methods are most commonly applied. The growth of social media and mobile communications has introduced additional techniques, but the primary method of electronic solicitation is still e-mail. Fundraising using social media and social networks has gained visibility. It includes peer-to-peer fundraising, for example, in which individuals sponsor friends' participation in charity events. From the organization's perspective, the fundraising method is the event, with social media used to promote participation. Additional emerging techniques, for example, crowdfunding, are not discussed in this chapter but are explored in later chapters where they are most relevant, for example, as a strategy for raising funds toward a project.

As Table 4.2 shows, annual giving programs employ the methods of direct marketing but also may include personal solicitation of annual gifts at higher levels, that is, leadership annual gifts (Lowman, 2012). Fundraising events are also a method used by some nonprofit organizations to raise current operating support. Corporate and foundation fundraising often involve personal visits but also usually require written proposals. Fundraising for major gifts usually requires personal visits and often written proposals. The planned-giving program uses personal visits, written proposals, direct mail, and other methods to promote planned-giving opportunities.

The various solicitation methods all have advantages and disadvantages, but some are inherently more effective than others. Rosso (2011b) describes a **ladder of effectiveness** that places various methods on different rungs, from the most effective at the top to the least effective at the bottom. In general, the more personal the method is the more effective it is likely to be. Thus, face-to-face solicitation is the most effective, followed by personal communications using other methods, such as mail, phone, or e-mail. Least effective are impersonal methods, for example, direct mail and phone solicitations using professional callers (Rosso, 2011b). But, of course, there are tradeoffs in cost. Personal solicitation is effective but cannot be conducted in large volume, so it is relatively expensive and needs to be confined to leadership annual gifts, major gifts, and principal gifts. Mail, e-mail, and phone are relatively ineffective compared with personal solicitation, but they are also relatively inexpensive methods that can be used on a broad scale, securing a large number of smaller gifts that may be consequential in total.

THE FUNDRAISING PYRAMID

The **fundraising pyramid** helps to illustrate several principles and provides a useful tool for analyzing an organization's fundraising situation. It reflects some of the same points discussed in previous sections of this chapter but adds further insight. While the pyramid could apply to donors of all categories, including corporations, foundations, and individuals, the giving patterns it implies are mostly relevant to individuals.[6]

The pyramid depicted in Figure 4.2 reflects assumptions about how donors evolve in their giving—it suggests a progression—and it also describes how an organization might go about building its fundraising program from the bottom up.

Pyramid of Donors

Let's start at the bottom of the pyramid. Every nonprofit organization has a fundraising constituency, which forms the base of the pyramid. How that constituency is defined and developed varies, depending on the type of organization, its history, and the circumstances

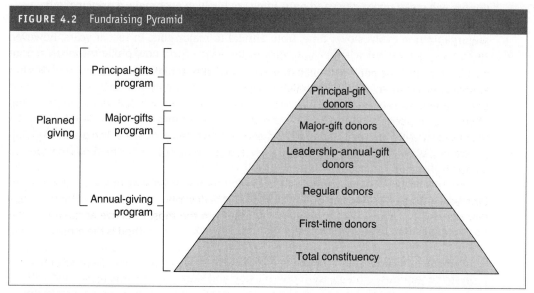

FIGURE 4.2 Fundraising Pyramid

Sources: Alexander & Carlson (2005), p. 17; Ciconte & Jacob (2009), p. 102; Hogan (2008), p. 10; Sargeant et al. (2010), p. 331; Seiler (2011a), p. 45; Williams (2004).

of its location, among other considerations. Chapter 5 discusses this topic in more detail, but a simple way to think about it is that the constituency is the database of donors and potential donors an organization maintains.

An important objective for the annual giving program is the acquisition of first-time donors, that is, moving people up one level from the bottom of the pyramid. Once donors have made a first gift, the program's objective for those donors shifts to retention and upgrading, that is, turning them into **regular donors** and increasing the size of subsequent gifts (Seiler, 2011a). If a donor's annual gift reaches a predetermined level, it is defined as **leadership annual giving (LAG)** (Lowman, 2012). Again, the latter is defined in dollar terms and varies among organizations.

Donors providing annual gifts at the leadership level may be prospects for major gifts, if they have sufficient interest and financial capability. Some donors, usually after a long history of annual giving and periodic major gifts, may become prospects for principal gifts; that is, they may reach the apex of the pyramid in their commitment to the organization and its mission. It is important to note that planned giving does not appear in the fundraising pyramid, again, because it is a strategy for major gifts and is not defined by the amount of the gift. Corporate and foundation support also do not appear in the pyramid because they involve a specific donor constituency rather than the amount of the gift and because corporations and foundations generally do not follow the patterns suggested by the pyramid, which relates primarily to individual donors.

As the narrowing of the fundraising pyramid suggests, the number of individuals encompassed is smaller at each successively higher level. Not all members of the constituency will become first-time donors; not all who do will become regular donors; not all regular donors will become leadership-annual-gift donors; not all leadership-annual-gift donors will make major gifts; and only a few are likely to ever make a principal gift.

Again, the pyramid suggests a progression, in which the donor's giving relationship with the organization evolves over time, from annual to major gifts. In recent years, however, some have questioned whether it applies in the case of the new philanthropists, whom we discussed in Chapter 1, or those motivated by hyperagency, as discussed in Chapter 3 (Schervish, 2008). Such donors may not begin with modest annual gifts and proceed up the pyramid in a predictable manner over a period of years. Indeed, some may provide major gifts or even principal gifts early in their relationships with organizations in which they have decided to invest, especially if that investment comes with their involvement in developing the organization's strategy.

Some also challenge the traditional view that broad-based methods, such as the Internet, are primarily useful at lower levels of the pyramid and see interaction with donors at all levels of the pyramid as more characteristic of a socially networked environment. Dixon and Keyes (2013) argue that the traditional donor pyramid implies a linear progression that no longer accurately portrays how donors are engaged:

> In practice, it turns out, a person's engagement with an organization is generally more continuous—and messy. It doesn't stop and start with discrete levels, and with the broad range of activities available to potential supporters today, it's actually preferable for people to be engaged on multiple levels.

The authors also emphasize the value of the influence individuals may have on the views and participation of others, as a result of their communication via social networks. That influence may give those individuals a high value to the organization, which the traditional pyramid model may not reflect (Dixon & Keyes, 2013).

However, the fundraising pyramid remains a central concept that is commonly applied. It may be most accurate to say that the pyramid describes how practitioners expect most donors to behave over time and provides a snapshot of a fundraising program in terms of the distribution of donor engagement at a given point. As discussed shortly, it also provides a useful tool for planning.

Pyramid of Programs

The solicitation programs discussed are shown on the left side of Figure 4.2. The annual-giving program works at lower levels of the pyramid, the major- and principal-gift programs toward the top. The planned-giving program is focused on prospects for major and principal gifts but also may operate at lower levels of the pyramid, perhaps with less intensity. For example, an organization usually promotes bequests to leadership-annual-fund donors and regular-annual-fund donors, even though they may not yet have made a major gift, especially if they have demographic characteristics that suggest a higher propensity toward planned giving.

The pyramid also suggests how a nonprofit organization might build its fundraising programs over time. A nonprofit just beginning a fundraising program typically would start at the bottom of the pyramid, focusing on development of a constituency and soliciting annual gifts. But if the organization intends to become sustainable and grow, it will need to move up the pyramid, developing regular donors, upgrading their annual gifts, and building a group of leadership-annual-gift donors. It may defer establishing a major-gifts program until it has established a base of prospects for major gifts among its regular- and leadership-annual-gift donors, but as it grows it will be essential to cultivate and solicit such gifts, especially as capital needs arise. As stated earlier, only the most advanced development offices are likely to have a distinctive program focused on principal gifts.

Tool for Planning

A nonprofit with an established fundraising program may find the pyramid to be a useful tool of analysis in understanding the strengths and weaknesses of its program and determining where to allocate its fundraising efforts. The pyramid will have a different shape depending on an organization's constituencies and the array of fundraising programs it has developed (Kihlstedt, 2010).

The pyramid shown in Figure 4.2 is approximately equilateral; that is, its sides are about the same length. It depicts a mature and balanced fundraising program. A nonprofit with a pyramid something like it is operating at all levels, with programs for annual, major, and principal gifts. It is firing on all cylinders, continuously bringing in first-time donors and systematically moving them up the pyramid in order to provide a pipeline of prospects for major and principal gifts. But look at the three pyramids depicted in Figure 4.3.

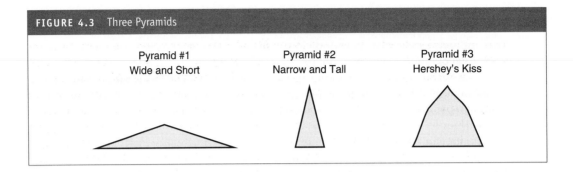

FIGURE 4.3 Three Pyramids

| Pyramid #1 | Pyramid #2 | Pyramid #3 |
| Wide and Short | Narrow and Tall | Hershey's Kiss |

An organization with a pyramid similar to Pyramid 1 (wide and short) has a large base of donors of modest amounts but few at higher levels. It may have done a good job of developing its annual-giving program, but it has few donors at higher levels. Fundraising is probably inefficient, since raising small gifts requires disproportionately high costs. And there are likely to be donors at the bottom of the pyramid who are financially capable of giving more, so the lack of a major-gifts program is likely to leave potential revenue on the table. Facing this scenario, the organization might consider increasing its efforts to develop more leadership-annual-gifts donors and major-gifts donors.

A nonprofit with a donor pyramid similar to Pyramid 2 (narrow and tall) has a small number of major donors and a not very wide base. This could be an unstable situation, since the loss of just a few major donors could result in a substantial loss of revenue, even threaten the organization's ability to survive. This organization should invest in developing a broader base of donors, both to protect itself from the loss of a current major donor and to build a pipeline of new donors who may move up the pyramid in the future.

Pyramid 3 is shaped something like a Hershey's Kiss. It is a healthy pyramid part way up—there is a base of donors at lower levels and in the middle levels, perhaps including leadership annual gifts. But then the pyramid narrows dramatically toward the top, suggesting few donors at the principal-gifts level. That may represent an untapped opportunity for an organization that does have major-gifts donors, some of whom might make principal gifts if the organization dedicates more sustained effort to deepening its relationship with them.

Pareto and the 80/20 Rule

The fundraising pyramid narrows at higher levels because the cells contain *fewer donors* at each successive level. But what if the pyramid were drawn to show the *revenue* generated by each level? It would be inverted, that is, upside down. In other words, in many programs, the higher levels generate more dollars than the lower levels, even though they include fewer donors.

This reality is often described in terms of the **Pareto principle**, named for an early twentieth-century economist who established that 80 percent of the wealth in Italy was controlled by 20 percent of the people (Weinstein, 2009). Although Pareto never stated this fact as any kind of a principle, others have interpreted his finding to mean that 20 percent of the effort in any endeavor accounts for 80 percent of the result. With regard to fundraising, the principle often is expressed as the **80/20 rule**, meaning that "80 percent of the funds raised will come from not more than 20 percent of the donors" (Weinstein, 2009, p. 5). But in recent years some have suggested that it be restated as the **90/10 rule**, reflecting the fact that major and principal gifts have become more important, accounting for a larger percentage of the total amount raised, especially in campaigns (Weinstein, 2009). The data generally support this principle, showing a substantial portion of total support coming from a relatively small number of donors. For example, in 2013, among colleges and universities reporting their fundraising results to the Council for Aid to Education, just twelve gifts on average accounted for 33 percent of all giving (Council for Aid to Education, 2014). And a 2007 study of giving to nonprofits found that 75 percent of "net profit" from fundraising programs was generated by just 10 percent of donors (Sauvé-Rodd, 2007). The underlying reality is that wealth and income have become increasingly concentrated in American society and, indeed, around the world. The capacity of a relatively few large donors may exceed the collective capacity of donors of smaller gifts.

The implications of the 80/20 or 90/10 rule are, again, worth considering, especially for nonprofits that have pyramids shaped something like Pyramid 1 or Pyramid 3. They may see significant increases in revenue from new programs that emphasize major and principal gifts, even with a relatively small volume of gifts at that level.

But the insight can be misapplied. Some nonprofit CEOs, especially in larger organizations that have sources of substantial earned income, sometimes may ask why it is useful to have an annual-giving program at all. The argument goes something like this: if 90 percent of gifts come from the top of the pyramid, why not just concentrate efforts on major and principal gifts rather than dissipate resources on the smaller gifts from annual giving that only account for 10 percent? The problem is, of course, that unless there has been an effective annual-giving program in the past, there are unlikely to be many prospects for major gifts. Even if there are, focusing exclusively on them would be short-sighted. Such a strategy would fail to develop first-time donors who then may become regular and leadership donors and emerge as prospects for major gifts in the future. Governing boards can provide important leadership by establishing goals that reward progress both in producing current gifts and in building the foundation for continuous fundraising success.

Proportionate Giving

The 80/20 or 90/10 rule also is related to another fundamental principle, **proportionate giving**, which was articulated by Seymour (1966). Simply stated, it means that people give in proportion to their financial capacity and that it is unrealistic to assume that donors all will give the same amount. In other words, donors are arrayed in a pyramid, not lined up on the same level.

A common but naïve assumption is that money can be raised using the multiplication table, for example, that a strategy for raising $1 million would be to obtain 1,000 gifts at $1,000 each. This would be unrealistic and undesirable for four reasons. First, obtaining 1,000 gifts at any level might be impossible for an organization with a small constituency.

Second, even if 1,000 gifts could be obtained, it is unlikely that every donor could afford to give as much as $1,000. Third, soliciting a $1,000 gift from someone who is wealthy would leave significant money on the table, since the donor could afford to give much more. Finally, and more subtlety, the strategy would not work because donors have a sense of their fair share and will give proportional to the goal, their own circumstances, and what others are giving. As an example, if I were to ask you to make a gift to my nonprofit organization and told you that the wealthiest family in town already had given $1 million, you might think that your fair and proportional share would be something like $100 or $10, depending on your financial situation. But if I told you that the family had given $100, you might think that your fair share should be something even less, maybe zero. This reality leads to the principle of *sequential fundraising*, a term introduced by consultant George Brakeley Jr. (1980).

The principle of proportionate giving again suggests that a model fundraising program operates at all levels, with principal, major, and leadership annual gifts establishing norms that will have an influence at the successive levels below.

THE FUNDRAISING PROCESS

As noted earlier in this text, fundraising is not synonymous with solicitation. It is a process that begins with the organization or institution itself and includes continuous interactions with donors through a series of planned activities. In her pioneering textbook, Kelly (1998) emphasizes the latter point, writing, "Success is not attributable to happenstance, miracles, or unexplained phenomena; it is the result of planned action—well researched and systematically implemented" (p. 394).

Various authors, spanning decades of fundraising literature, have described the fundraising process in similar ways. For example, Broce (1986) describes the following steps: institutional goals, fundraising goals, prospect identification and evaluation, leadership and prospect involvement, case preparation, organization of the fundraising program, timetable for execution, and solicitation of gifts. Kelly (1998) identifies the steps as research, objectives, programming, evaluation, and stewardship, using the acronym ROPES to summarize them. Lindahl (2010) describes a similar model, including research, planning, cultivation, solicitation, stewardship, and evaluation. Seiler's (2011b) model includes fourteen steps: examine the case, analyze market requirements, prepare needs statement, define objectives, involve volunteers, validate needs statement, evaluate gift markets, select fundraising vehicles, identify potential giving sources, prepare fundraising plan, prepare communications plan, activate volunteer corps, solicit the gift, demonstrate stewardship, and renew the gift. Figure 4.4 provides a simplified illustration of the process, generally consistent with the models described by multiple authors. It does not depict evaluation as a step, on the assumption that evaluation occurs throughout implementation of the process.

The fundraising process is often described as a *cycle*, and indeed, it is with respect to a specific donor or group of donors. Stewardship blends into cultivation for the next solicitation of that donor, and the cycle is repeated throughout the relationship. But from the perspective of the organization managing its program, fundraising is an *ongoing process*, rather than a cycle. The steps may unfold sequentially with regard to a donor or group of donors, but they are all ongoing, concurrent, and overlapping with regard to the nonprofit's overall fundraising efforts. In other words, identification, cultivation, solicitation, acknowledgment, and stewardship activities are always underway with regard to some donors and prospects. For these reasons, the fundraising process is depicted here as somewhat different from the major-gifts fundraising cycle, which is discussed in detail in Chapter 7 of this book.

An additional clarification is important. Figure 4.4 may imply that the fundraising process is linear and unfolds in clear, orderly steps, but that is not the case in practice (Lindahl, 2010). It is iterative and often somewhat messy. For example, prospects are identified and evaluated throughout the process rather than in one step. Gifts may occur before the cultivation process has fully played out. Some solicitations may not receive an immediately positive response but may turn out to be a step in the cultivation process, leading to another solicitation and a gift at a later time. The organization must define its mission, goals, needs, and case at the beginning of the fundraising process, but it also may need to revisit those questions from time to time, as feedback from its philanthropic market may dictate. Remember that fundraising involves people and relationships, which often do not accommodate to rational models.

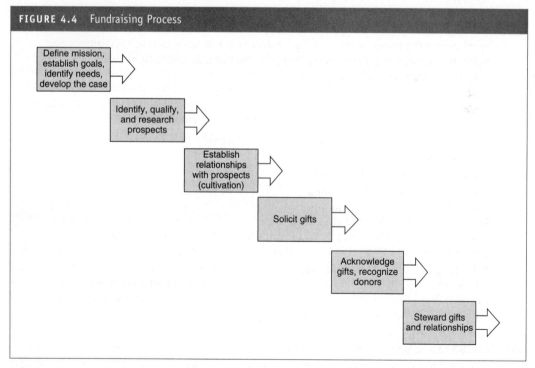

FIGURE 4.4   Fundraising Process

Note: Various authors have described the fundraising process, with similar components (e.g., Broce, 1986; Kelly, 1998; Lindahl, 2010; Seiler, 2011b). This figure includes features common to many other versions but is the author's creation and is not specifically attributable to any other author.

Preparing the Organization

The fundraising process begins with the organization itself. Its mission, goals, and programmatic objectives must be clearly defined, which is often accomplished through strategic planning. And a persuasive case for support must be developed. These activities are discussed in more detail in the next chapter.

Identifying and Researching Prospects

The next step is to identify prospective donors, usually called simply **prospects**. As discussed, the selection of donor constituencies to be emphasized must reflect the organization's resource needs. It is also essential to identify those prospects with the highest potential for the organization, those who are a part of its constituency. Not every corporation, foundation, and individual in the world is a prospect for a given organization. Indeed, proceeding without identifying a **target audience** for a nonprofit's fundraising would be exceedingly inefficient and ineffective; it would be equivalent to walking through town holding a bucket and hoping that money will fall from the sky. In addition to identifying prospects, the process includes undertaking research on those prospects in order to further evaluate their capacity and possible interests, as aligned with the organization's needs. Prospect research and evaluation also are discussed in more detail in the next chapter.

Establishing Relationships (Cultivation)

Once prospects have been identified, the organization establishes and develops relationships with them before proceeding to solicit gifts. That relationship building is called **cultivation**. The term may carry unfortunate overtones of manipulation or cynicism, but cultivation of prospective donors is not a matter of disingenuous schmoozing; rather, it requires substantive and sincere engagement with individuals (Kelly, 1998).

The importance of cultivation varies with the size and purpose of the anticipated gift. If the objective is a major gift, then the cultivation may be intense and prolonged. But if the objective is a modest gift, cultivation may be a small part of the process. For example, think about the last phone call you may have received soliciting a gift. The caller probably did not begin by just saying, "Give me money." More likely, he or she began the conversation by asking, "How are you this evening?" before proceeding to ask for your gift. The caller did devote at least some effort to establishing a relationship, that is, cultivation, although in this case it was necessarily brief. The friendly opening question probably made you feel somewhat more receptive (Simmel & Berger, 2000). But if a nonprofit wanted you to give a larger gift, you might expect that someone would come to see you and stay for a while, perhaps on more than one occasion. Cultivation is at the heart of major-gifts fundraising and is discussed again in more detail in Chapter 7.

Solicitation

Solicitation (asking for the gift) is a pivotal step in the process. As discussed earlier, a variety of methods can be employed, with varied effectiveness, and their selection is related to the overall fundraising strategy. With regard to the fundraising process, the central question about solicitation is timing. Weinstein (2009) defines the "right time" for a solicitation to occur as when the solicitor has developed a "positive relationship" with the prospect (p. 5). Fredericks (2010) likewise places the emphasis on donor readiness, writing that "you must ask when the person is ready to be asked not to fulfill a quota of the number of [solicitations] or to reach a fundraising goal" (p. 18). In other words, cultivation and solicitation need to be in correct proportion, so that the solicitation is not premature but also not deferred indefinitely or past the time when a donor's interest has peaked.

Three Solicitation Strategies

Dunlop (2002), whose writing defined many of the concepts applied in major-gifts fundraising, addresses the question of how cultivation and solicitation should be balanced with regard to three types of gifts—regular gifts, special gifts, and ultimate gifts. Remember that regular gifts are tied to the calendar, special gifts are tied to the needs of the organization, and ultimate gifts are tied to the circumstances of the donor.

Figure 4.5 depicts three solicitation strategies, which Dunlop (2002) calls methods, appropriate to each type of gift. What Dunlop calls **speculative fundraising** is the typical

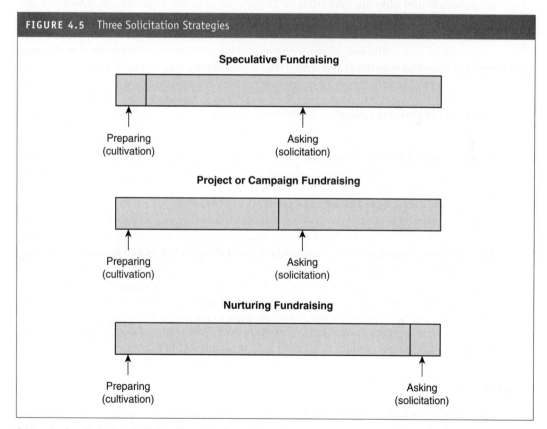

FIGURE 4.5 Three Solicitation Strategies

Source: Dunlop, D. R. (2002). Major gift programs. In Worth, M. J. (Gen. Ed.), *New strategies for educational fund raising*. Westport, CT: American Council on Education and Praeger Publishers, pp. 89–104.

strategy at lower levels of the pyramid; it is characteristic of annual-giving programs. In speculative fundraising, most activity is related to soliciting, receiving, and acknowledging the gift. Little time is devoted to preparing the prospect for solicitation, that is, on cultivation of the relationship. It is exemplified by the telemarketer in the earlier example, who may confine cultivation to the single question of how you are this evening. The brevity is necessary because this strategy requires a high volume of solicitations. It is speculative because the high volume of solicitations is based on the assumption that some percentage of people will respond.

Fundraising for special gifts, which Dunlop (2002) calls **campaign or special project fundraising**, requires committing more time and effort to prepare the donor than that needed in speculative fundraising. The volume of solicitations is lower, and since the gifts are usually larger than the donors' regular gifts, the details of the project need to be discussed in some detail, which requires time. But the solicitation must be made within some reasonable period, since the gift is needed in order to complete the project. Thus, as shown in Figure 4.5, the preparation (or cultivation) phase and the asking (or solicitation) phase of the process may be roughly balanced.

What Dunlop (2002) calls **nurturing fundraising** is an approach most appropriate to the solicitation of ultimate gifts from longtime donors to the organization. The emphasis is on preparing the donor, an activity that may continue for a long time, even many years. Solicitation of an ultimate gift may be a small component of an organization's interaction with a donor over a lifetime of involvement and support. Indeed, it may be that the relationship nurtured is so close and strong that a solicitation may not even be necessary; the donor's gift may simply evolve from his or her overall interactions with the organization.

Sequential Fundraising

The principle of proportionate giving is closely related to a fundamental principle of solicitation: **sequential fundraising**, a term introduced by Brakeley (1980). Sequential fundraising (also sometimes called sequential solicitation) describes the ideal order in which gifts should be solicited from various donors. It is especially important in campaigns, but it can be applied as well in noncampaign solicitation.

Simply stated, sequential fundraising requires that gifts be solicited from the top down and from the inside out. In other words, larger gifts should be solicited before smaller gifts, and those who are closest to the organization should be solicited before those whose connections are less strong.

Why top-down? Think again about my earlier example involving you and the wealthiest family in town. It might be best to solicit that leading family before coming to you, since the size of your gift might be determined at least in part by how much they have given. Gifts in the higher levels have a positive impact on the decisions of donors at lower levels. Of course, you would explain this reality to the wealthiest family when you solicit their gift, since their decision is critical to the success of the overall effort.

Why solicit inside out? Again using the example of the wealthiest family in town, assume that a member of that family is indeed on the board of the organization raising the funds. In that circumstance, if I tell you the family member has given $100, or that he or she has not given at all, you would probably take that as a signal that the person does not think it to be an important cause. You might even be somewhat offended to be asked to support an organization that has a member of a wealthy family on the board when you learn that the family member has not made any gift. You might tell the solicitors to come back when that family has made a financial commitment to support the purposes for which a family member presumably voted as a member of the board. For this reason, the leadership and example of those closest to the organization and those who have the capacity to make gifts in the upper ranges of the pyramid are critical to the success of the overall fundraising effort.

Again, the principle of sequential fundraising has its origins in the observations of practitioners, where it has been long established and firmly advocated. But how can it be explained in terms of theory? Thinking back on the discussion of social influences on giving from Chapter 3, it could make sense. People follow the example of others whom they admire or with whom they wish to be associated (Bekkers & Wiepking, 2011; Seymour, 1966). But for some scholars, the effectiveness of sequential fundraising has presented a logical puzzle (Vesterlund, 2003). If donors are giving to meet public needs, then economic theory predicts that informing them of previous gifts would diminish their responses; they might assume that the needs have been met, so their own gifts are less important. They might not give at all or give less than if they were not told about what others had done. The best fundraising practice then would be to not tell donors what has already been given (Varian, 1994). Some theorists have suggested that announcing donors' gifts provides them with prestige and helps to signal their wealth to others (Silverman, Robertson, Middlebrook, & Drabman, 1984). But that would be true even if all gifts were just announced after the fact. What accounts for the reality fundraisers observe, that gifts are higher if donors are told who has *already given* and how much? Vesterlund (2003) suggests this occurs because the announced gifts of previous donors indicate to other donors that the organization is of high quality and worthy of support; in other words, it validates and legitimizes the organization and the cause. This is especially true if early donors are prestigious individuals (Kumru & Vesterlund, 2010). That accounts for why top-down works, but what about inside out? Assuming that an organization's governing board is the pinnacle of that organization's community (i.e., including a member of the wealthiest family in town) then its members will be among the most prestigious by virtue of their positions on the board and also the most knowledgeable about the merits of the cause. Putting this theory together with practitioners' observations, things make sense. If the board and other insiders have not given, a prospective donor might interpret that as a *negative* indicator of the worthiness of the cause.

Acknowledgment, Recognition, and Stewardship

The fundraising process does not end when the donor makes a gift. Acknowledging the gift promptly and appropriately influences how the donor feels about making it and establishes a foundation for future solicitations. Recalling the norm of reciprocity discussed in Chapter 3, a thoughtful expression of thanks is likely to be the minimum return a donor would expect (Gouldner, 1960). The absence of it could be interpreted as either poor management or ingratitude. The **acknowledgment** includes sending a formal receipt but also expressing thanks in a more personal way, usually by mail, e-mail, or phone or in person. It is what Burk (2003) calls "private affirmation that the donor is appreciated" (p. 98). Although the original source is obscure, it is a common fundraising maxim that a donor should be thanked seven times before a new gift is solicited. The acknowledgments may include written communications, phone calls, online acknowledgment, personal visits, and various types of events ("Donor Acknowledgement," 2014).

Acknowledgement of a gift is the first step in **stewardship**. Stewardship encompasses two components—using the gift for its intended purpose and maintaining continuous communication with the donor in order to sustain and enhance the relationship. Because the cost of acquiring new donors is higher than the cost of renewing the support of previous donors, nonprofits have placed a greater emphasis on stewardship in recent years. As Burk (2003) reports, "About 50 percent of donors do not renew their gifts after making a first contribution and, by the time of the fifth [subsequent solicitation], about 90 percent have stopped giving to the charities that once elicited their support" (p. 19). She observes that "driving home the same messages of 'give, give, give' without satisfying donors' needs for more information on the effectiveness of their giving keeps donor attrition high and prevents not for profits from raising so much more money" (p. 19). Burk's study found evidence of this phenomenon: 46 percent of donors surveyed indicated that they had stopped giving to an organization because they lacked information on how their gifts were used or felt unappreciated, while 93 percent said they would give again if they were provided sufficient information and 74 percent said they would continue giving indefinitely if the organization continued to provide the information they desired (Burk, 2003).

What about donor recognition—what Burk (2003) calls the "public acknowledgement of donors"? (p. 98). How important is it? Specifics of donor recognition are discussed in later chapters, in the context of annual, major, and planned giving, but there is consensus among practitioners that it is generally important. This is reflected in the widespread practice of listing donors by levels and including them as members of giving societies based on the amount of their gifts. Does research support this assumption? Students may remember from Chapter 3 that Harbaugh (1998) found in his studies that recognition does matter. Indeed, he developed an econometric model to predict how donors' needs for prestige might cause them to increase their gifts in order to gain greater recognition. Harbaugh's work thus provides support to the traditional maxims of fundraising practitioners.

The principles discussed in this chapter cut across the various solicitation programs and are revisited in the context of those programs in later chapters. The next chapter focuses on the first steps in the fundraising process: preparing the organization itself and identifying and developing prospects.

CHAPTER SUMMARY

Most principles of fundraising, and central concepts and terms, have been developed in the field of practice rather than through research.

Gifts may be classified four ways: by amount (*annual gifts, leadership annual gifts, major gifts, principal gifts*); by purpose (*unrestricted* support, *restricted* gifts or grants to support current programs and projects, gifts for *physical capital*, and gifts for *financial capital*); by the donor's perspective (*regular gifts, special gifts, ultimate gifts*) (Dunlop, 2002); and by the donor's method in making the gift (*outright, pledge, planned gift*). Planned gifts may be *outright planned gifts, expectancies*, or *deferred gifts* (Regenovich, 2011). Nonprofits raise funds for the four purposes; this is called the "*four-legged stool*" (Seiler, 2011a).

Most development offices maintain three core solicitation programs: annual giving, major gifts, and corporate and foundation support. Some have a distinct program for principal gifts, but most raise them as part of the major-gifts program. Larger development offices may have separate programs for corporate support and for foundation support. Planned giving is a strategy used in major-gifts fundraising, although it may be called a program. Other programs, such as prospect research and stewardship, support the core solicitation programs.

Each solicitation program focuses on particular types of gifts and donor constituencies. Individuals are the primary source of unrestricted gifts, although corporations and foundations also provide such gifts under certain circumstances. Corporations and foundations are more likely to support programs and projects. Individuals are the primary source of gifts for physical capital projects and almost the only source of gifts to endowment. Nonprofit organizations emphasize those programs most relevant to their financial needs but also should develop comprehensive fundraising programs to build capacity and assure sustainability.

Relationships with donor prospects are best managed within one of the programs, depending on prospects' financial capacity and connection with the organization. Those with limited financial capacity are prospects for annual gifts; among those, prospects with a strong connection may become leadership annual donors. Those with high financial capacity and a strong connection are prospects for major and principal gifts. Those with capacity and a weak connection may support programs or projects of interest to them.

The most common methods of solicitation include *direct mail, phone (telemarketing), electronic communication* (primarily e-mail), *events, personal solicitations*, and *proposal writing*. The more personal the method is, the more effective it is likely to be, but costs need to be considered as well.

The *fundraising pyramid* provides a useful tool for analyzing an organization's fundraising situation. Donors begin their relationship with the organization by making a first-time gift. They may rise up the pyramid over time, becoming regular donors, leadership annual donors, major donors, and principal donors. But the pyramid narrows toward the top, since not all donors will increase their giving in the manner implied. Nonprofit organizations usually begin their fundraising with an annual-giving program that operates at lower levels of the pyramid and then build major-gifts programs once a base of donors has been established. The shape of the pyramid of donors can highlight areas of strength and weakness in the organization's fundraising program and help guide efforts to strengthen it. Dixon and Keyes (2013) argue that social media is challenging the linear model portrayed by the pyramid and propose an alternative model of how donors engage with nonprofits today.

Pareto's principle suggests that 80 percent of gifts come from 20 percent of donors toward the top of the pyramid; some people say the ratio is closer to 90/10 today (Weinstein, 2009). But this should not be viewed as justification for not undertaking fundraising programs at lower levels, which helps to build a pipeline of donors for the future. The *90/10* or *80/20 rule* is related to *proportionate giving* (Seymour, 1966), which explains that people give in proportion to their financial ability. For this reason, it is not realistic to think that funds can be raised with equal gifts from many donors, that is, fundraising by the multiplication table.

Fundraising is a process that includes preparing the organization, identifying and researching prospects, developing relationships (cultivation), solicitation, acknowledgment and recognition, and stewardship. Stewardship is cultivation for the next gift. But the steps in the process may not always unfold linearly (Lindahl, 2010).

A central issue is the timing of solicitation and the balance of cultivation and solicitation. Three strategies include *speculative fundraising*, which emphasizes solicitation; *campaign or project fundraising*, in which cultivation and solicitation are balanced; and *nurturing fundraising*, which emphasizes the relationship with the donor (Dunlop, 2002). *Sequential fundraising* requires that gifts be solicited from the top down and inside out, with the largest donors and those who are close to the organization establishing examples that affect the gifts of others (Brakeley, 1980). Some economic theorists believe this is true because the commitment of previous donors, especially if they are prestigious individuals, indicates to others that the cause is worthy.

Stewardship and donor relations have become more important in recent years because 50 percent of first-time donors do not renew their gifts (Burk, 2003). Stewardship includes both the organization's effective use of the gift and continued attention to the relationship with the donor. Both practitioner wisdom and research (e.g., Burk, 2003; Harbaugh, 1998) hold that donor recognition is important.

Key Terms and Concepts

80/20 rule
90/10 rule
Acknowledgment
Annual fund (sustaining fund)
Annual gifts
Annual giving
Campaign or special project fundraising
Cultivation
Deferred gift
Direct mail [as solicitation method]
Direct marketing

Donor constituencies
Electronic communication (e-mail) [as solicitation method]
Events [as solicitation method]
Expectancies
Four-legged stool
Fundraising pyramid
Grant writing
Grantsmanship
Ladder of effectiveness

Leadership annual gifts
Leadership annual giving (LAG)
Major gifts
Nurturing fundraising
Outright gift
Outright planned gift
Pareto principle
Personal solicitations [as solicitation method]
Phone (telemarketing) [as solicitation method]
Planned gift

Planned giving
Pledges
Principal gifts
Proportionate
  giving
Proposal writing
  [as solicitation
  method]
Prospects

Recognition [of
  donors]
Regular donors
Regular gifts
Restricted gift
Request for proposal
  (RFP)
Sequential
  fundraising

Solicitation
Special gifts
Speculative
  fundraising
Sponsorships
Stewardship
Target audience
Ultimate gift
Unrestricted gift

Case 4.1:   United Nations Foundation

Speaking to an audience of dignitaries at a 1997 black-tie dinner in New York, Cable News Network founder Ted Turner made a dramatic announcement. He would give $1 billion over ten years to benefit United Nations programs aiding refugees and children, clearing land mines, and fighting disease (Rohde, 1997). Although the gift would be used for programs, not to support the UN's operating expenses, the amount would be about equivalent to the United Nations' annual budget (Rohde, 1997). Turner's gift was one of the largest in history to that time and has been cited for having inspired later large-scale philanthropy by Bill and Melinda Gates, Warren Buffet, and other wealthy businesspeople (Kristoff, 2012).

Turner's gift was used to create the United Nations Foundation, a nonprofit public charity. In its early years, the foundation operated as a traditional grant maker but subsequently built partnerships to develop new programs directed at keeping girls in school, preventing child marriage, increasing education and access related to reproductive health, providing clean and affordable energy, and reducing or eliminating diseases such as measles, malaria, and polio. The foundation also engaged in advocacy campaigns to promote support for the UN (United Nations Foundation, 2012). Many of the foundation's efforts were undertaken in partnership with corporations and other nonprofit organizations, including the ExxonMobil Foundation, ABC News, Mashable, Johnson and Johnson, the National Basketball Association, the United Methodist Church, the American Red Cross, and the Bill and Melinda Gates Foundation (United Nations Foundation, 2012).

The UN Foundation raised additional funds to supplement Mr. Turner's annual pledge, but the results of these efforts grew slowly, from $67 million in 2008 to $72 million in 2012 (Daniels, 2014). As the final payment on Mr. Turner's initial $1 billion pledge approached, in 2014, the foundation focused on expanding its efforts to develop additional sources of philanthropy in order to secure its future.

One strategy included hiring relationship managers to deepen the foundation's connections with corporations, with the goal of establishing ten "anchor donors" (Daniels, 2014). The foundation also planned to expand online advocacy and fundraising. And, in 2011, it established the Global Entrepreneur's Council to involve younger donors. Members of the council are business leaders from around the world younger than age forty-five. They serve a term of two years, providing the opportunity to continually engage new people. Some members of the council became donors themselves and others helped to secure support from others. For example, one helped to create a Donors Advisors Fund to help reach more wealthy philanthropists, and another used his connections in Hollywood to increase the foundation's visibility among celebrities (McCorvey, 2013).

Richard Parnell, the foundation's chief operating officer in 2014, described the strategy for expanding sources of support, saying, "The dollars are important, but it always goes back to relationships, relationships, relationships" (Daniels 2014).

Case 4.2:   Mitchell Family and the University of South Alabama

Brothers Mayer and Abraham Mitchell founded a real estate business in 1958, in their hometown of Mobile, Alabama. The business was highly successful, and in 1985, the brothers sold the company and focused their efforts on philanthropy. Although they were not alumni, Abraham, Mayer, and Mayer's wife Arlene became interested in the University of South Alabama, located in Mobile (University of South Alabama website).

Gordon Moulton became a professor at the university in 1966 and became president in 1998. Moulton established a close relationship with the Mitchell family. Mayer Mitchell served on the college's board and was succeeded by his wife after his death in 2007. Abraham Mitchell also enjoyed a close relationship with Moulton and sometimes attended board meetings and university events (Blum, 2014).

The Mitchell family was generous in its support of the university over many years. In 1999, they endowed the college of business, which was named for them. That same year, Abraham Mitchell established a scholarship fund that is today the university's largest privately funded scholarship program. The family continued to support various programs and units at South Alabama, including the cancer research institute, a sports arena, and others. By 2011, the family's total giving to the university was approximately $40 million (University of South Alabama website).

In 2011, President Moulton and his chief development officer began to consider another proposal to Abraham Mitchell. Knowing Mitchell's interest in scholarships, in 2012, Moulton sat down for a conversation with him. They discussed the need for scholarships, but no amount was mentioned initially. After subsequent conversations they decided that a fund of $50 million would be required to have the impact both wanted. Mitchell committed to a gift of $25 million to be paid over five years, on the condition that the university matched it with $25 million in gifts from others. Mr. Mitchell subsequently decided to provide for another $25 million in his estate plan. These commitments increased the Mitchell family's total support to the University of South Alabama to $93 million (Blum, 2014).

It was Mitchell's decision to name the scholarship program the Mitchell-Moulton Scholarship Initiative in honor of his long relationship with President Moulton. Addressing Moulton, Mitchell said, "We are grateful for the lives you have touched through your leadership and vision for higher education. I personally appreciate that you have demonstrated to me the value of investing in such a worthy endeavor as the University of South Alabama." President Moulton passed away shortly after, in 2013 ("University of South Alabama Press Release," 2013).

In 2014, the university engaged in fundraising to secure the gifts needed to match Mitchell's pledge, and both the president and chief development officer remained in close touch with him, both informally and by inviting him to meetings on campus to get updates on the scholarship program. Reflecting on his experience in an interview, Mr. Mitchell advises fundraisers to present donors with well-formulated proposals, to provide regular reports on their results, and to stay connected with their donors (Blum, 2014). Bronze statues of Mayer and Abraham Mitchell now stand on the South Alabama campus as a lasting tribute to their support.

Questions for Discussion

1. If you were asked to make a gift, or to provide voluntary service, how important would it be to you to know who has already given or who is already involved as a volunteer? How would you react if you were told that you were the first one to be asked? Why?

2. In Case 4.1, what might have been the shape of the fundraising pyramid at the UN Foundation as it considered new efforts to broaden support after the conclusion of Ted Turner's pledge? How do the efforts described in the case relate to various levels of that pyramid?

3. Given the nature of the UN Foundation's activities described in Case 4.1, if you were planning its fundraising program what emphasis would you place on corporate, foundation, or individual donor prospects? Why?

4. In what ways does Case 4.2 of the Mitchell family and the University of South Alabama reflect the concepts of nurturing fundraising, ultimate gifts, and principal gifts?

5. How is the fundraising process described in this chapter reflected in the relationship between the Mitchell family and the University of South Alabama? Does the process appear to have unfolded linearly?

Suggestions for Further Reading

Books

Alexander, C. D., & Carlson, K. J. (2005). *Essential principles for fundraising success.* San Francisco: Jossey-Bass.

Broce, T. E. (1986). *Fund raising: The guide to raising money from private sources* (2nd ed.). Norman: University of Oklahoma Press. (Note: This book is dated but considered a classic, which is still widely quoted.)

Seymour, H. J. (1966). *Designs for fund-raising.* New York: McGraw-Hill. (Note: This book is dated but considered a classic, which is still widely quoted.)

Weinstein, S. (2009). *The complete guide to fundraising management.* Hoboken, NJ: John Wiley & Sons.

Articles

Dixon, J., & Keyes, D. (2013, Winter). The permanent disruption of social media. *Stanford Social Innovation Review.* Retrieved March 19, 2014, from http://www.ssireview.org/articles/entry/the_permanent_disruption_of_social_media.

Vesterlund, L. (2003, March). The informational value of sequential fundraising. *Journal of Public Economics, 87*(3–4), 627–657.

Website

The AFP Fundraising Dictionary: http://www.afpnet.org/ResourceCenter/ArticleDetail
.cfm?ItemNumber = 3380 (Note: Access requires AFP membership; some cached
versions also may be available on the web.)

Notes

1. For fundraising purposes, the term *unrestricted* has a different meaning from that used for accounting purposes. In fundraising, unrestricted is synonymous with "unspecified" or "undesignated" (CASE,
2009, p. 46).

2. "Fundraising program" is commonly used as an umbrella term to refer to all fundraising-related activities of the organization. For example, Certified Fund Raising Executive (CFRE) International defines it as "an
organization's or institution's strategy, tactics, objectives, case, and needs in their entirety; a campaign that
is loosely defined in terms of time frame and specific funding opportunities; a campaign; a timetable for
a campaign" (http://beta.cfre.org/wp-content/uploads/2013/05/bgloss.pdf). This umbrella use of the term
should not be confused with the *solicitation programs* described in this chapter.

3. Alexander and Carlson (2005) make a distinction between the *annual fund* (the money raised for operating support) and the *annual campaign*, which they say includes, by definition, face-to-face solicitations
involving volunteers. Others (e.g., Williams, 2004, p. 39) use the term *annual giving* as synonymous with
annual campaign. These distinctions are discussed further in Chapter 6.

4. Colleges and universities traditionally have solicited one annual-fund gift each year, but some do solicit
an additional gift or gifts within the same fiscal year.

5. The vocabulary of fundraising is unsettled. That is exemplified by the fact that various authors who
write about fundraising use different terms to identify what this text calls *methods*. Sargeant, Shang, et al.
(2010) use "methods" (p. xxv). Seiler (in Tempel, Seiler, & Aldrich, 2011) uses "vehicles," "strategies," and
"methods" interchangeably (p. 14). Weinstein (2009) calls some methods "strategies" (p. 185). Kelly (1998)
makes a spirited case for "techniques" and criticizes the use of "methods" (p. 41).
This book uses the term *method* to describe mail, phone, and electronic communication; events; and personal solicitations. It uses *techniques* to describe practices that are more technical. For example, CFRE defines
a "telephone-mail campaign" as "a fundraising *technique* that combines mail and telephone solicitation in
a sophisticated manner through the use of paid solicitors and management of the program; a telephone
solicitation supported by a mail component for confirmation of verbal pledges" (italics added; http://beta
.cfre.org/wp-content/uploads/2013/05/bgloss.pdf). That is consistent with the vocabulary used in this book.
Phone and mail are both methods; the way in which they may be combined is a technique.

6. The fundraising pyramid is a concept described and illustrated by many authors (e.g., Alexander &
Carlson, 2005, p. 17; Ciconte & Jacob, 2009, p. 102; Hogan, 2008, p. 10; Sargeant, Shang, et al., 2010, p. 331;
Seiler, 2011a, p. 45; Williams, 2004). The manner in which levels are depicted and labeled varies widely, and
it is impossible to attribute the concept to any one source. The pyramid depicted here is this author's version,
which includes some features found in other versions.

CHAPTER 5

Preparing for Successful Fundraising

The University of Maryland College Park is the flagship campus in the University System of Maryland and by any measure a research university of national stature. It has a sophisticated institutional advancement program and, in 2012, completed a campaign for $1 billion. But when I arrived in College Park in the fall of 1977 to begin my new job as the campus' chief development officer, organized fundraising was a relatively new idea.

Throughout its history, Maryland had relied on state support for most of its budget. In contrast to public universities in the Midwest, which had long histories of private support, fundraising had never been a significant source of revenue for Maryland. This was also true of most public universities in the East at that time. There was a development office located in the university system office that provided some services to the campuses; the athletics department raised funds for scholarships; and a couple of entrepreneurial deans had appointed associate deans who had some responsibility for fundraising, primarily proposal writing to support faculty projects. But there was no central campus development office. The director of development position was newly created, and I was its first incumbent.

The case for support seemed to rely almost entirely on the fact that state support was declining and that some other public universities were securing private funds to make up the difference. There were no clear priorities for fundraising beyond unrestricted gifts. And relatively few people recognized the need to make unrestricted gifts to the university, assuming that it was well supported by the state, which of course, had been true historically. Indeed, some people on campus doubted that private support could or should ever have a significant impact and preferred that the state continue to be almost the exclusive funder. One senior administrator told me in our first meeting that he was among others who had opposed the creation of my position. His argument was that fundraising was unlikely to accomplish much, and in the unlikely event that it did, the state surely would take notice and just reduce the university's public funding accordingly. Moreover, he was concerned that private donors would become another demanding constituency, out to influence the university's policies and programs. The circumstances did not reflect lack of vision on the part of the university's leaders of that time, who recognized the need for change, but rather the culture of the institution as it had developed over many decades. And, again, it was not too different from what was typical at other public institutions in that period and at some even today.

Of course, things have changed dramatically at Maryland, and at other public higher education institutions, in the decades since. As mentioned previously, Maryland completed a campaign for $1 billion in 2012 (UMD Right Now, 2013). But there continue to be other nonprofit organizations and institutions that still have not established the preconditions for successful fundraising. Some have a lack of clear organizational goals, beyond perhaps the vision of a founder or strong executive director. Some desire more unrestricted revenue but have not established a case for how it would advance the organization's mission. Others have a strong desire for more money but are reluctant to invest in fundraising programs that may require time to produce returns. Some have a closed-system culture that keeps donors and potential donors on the outside, without the engagement necessary to build commitment and support. Some have not identified realistic prospective donors and persist in the hope that perhaps Bill and Melinda Gates will somehow just discover them. Others hope that an executive director or fundraising professional can single-handedly bring in additional gift revenue but lack a culture of philanthropy that pervades the organization and makes fundraising a team effort. These organizations must change before they can build a successful fundraising program.

This chapter describes the work an organization must accomplish *before* it is positioned and prepared for fundraising, including clarifying the mission and setting program goals, developing a fundraising strategy and plan, developing a case for support, creating a culture of fundraising, building a fundraising team, and identifying and researching prospects.

STRATEGIC PLANNING TO CLARIFY MISSION AND GOALS

Most nonprofit organizations today, except the youngest and smallest, engage in some form of **strategic planning**, which Bryson (2011) defines as "a deliberate, disciplined approach to producing fundamental decisions and actions that shape and guide what an organization . . . is, what it does, and why" (pp. 7–8). This chapter provides only a brief summary of the strategic planning process, before considering its implications for fundraising. Students who wish a more thorough discussion of strategic planning will find suggested additional reading at the end of the chapter. And examples of strategic plans are readily found on the web.

STRATEGIC PLANNING PROCESS

There are various models for strategic planning. Figure 5.1 depicts a generic process typical of those proposed by various authors, some of whom use somewhat different terminology. The process includes the following steps:

- Prepare for planning, by determining the process to be followed, the participants, and participant roles.

- Clarify the organization's mission, vision, and values.

- Assess the situation by examining the organization's internal *strengths* and *weaknesses* and the *opportunities* and *threats* presented by the external environment (called a **SWOT analysis**).

- Identify the strategic issues or strategic questions that need to be addressed in planning, derived from the mission, vision, values, and the situational analysis.

- Develop goals, which are broad statements of what the organization plans to accomplish and do not need to be quantifiable.

- Develop strategies, describing what the organization will *do* to achieve the goals it has established.

- Develop objectives, which are specific, quantified targets that represent steps toward accomplishing the goals and include deadlines for completion.

- Develop operational/implementation plans.

- Execute the plans and evaluate results. (Worth, 2014)

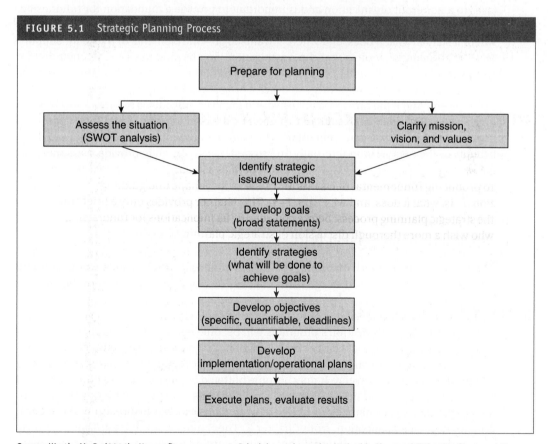

FIGURE 5.1 Strategic Planning Process

Source: Worth, M. J. (2014). *Nonprofit management: Principles and practice* (3rd ed.). Thousand Oaks, CA: Sage, p. 163.

The result of the strategic planning process is a written document—a plan—that provides a roadmap from where the organization is to some new place it wants to be, all in the context of its mission and values and the realities of the environment in which it operates (Worth, 2014).

BENEFITS OF STRATEGIC PLANNING

Although widely practiced by nonprofit organizations, strategic planning has its detractors. One concern is that traditional strategic planning may produce a list of goals but not anything bigger. In other words, it may not produce an overarching **strategy** for the organization's growth and advancement. Other critics point to the amount of time and effort required by the traditional strategic planning model, arguing that it may prove frustrating to the organization's staff and distract them from management of current programs (La Piana, 2008).

But despite its limitations and shortcomings, strategic planning offers significant advantages to a nonprofit organization and is important to provide a foundation for fundraising. It forces the organization to think about its mission and to confront basic questions about where it stands, what it does, and where it wants to go—the elements of a case for support. The SWOT analysis requires that the organization look beyond itself to the environment around it and see itself in the context of broader trends and forces, including the society, economy, and other organizations—in other words, it makes the organization more of an open system. And if the process is inclusive and involves individuals at various levels of the organization, including both staff and volunteer leaders, that may help to build consensus about mission and goals and help establish a culture of philanthropy. In addition to these benefits to the organization internally, the strategic plan also may provide reassurance to donors that the organization is well governed and well managed. Some donors, especially foundations, may consider the existence of a strategic plan an essential sign of sound management.

Goal Displacement and Mission Drift

The alternative to strategic planning would be to undertake fundraising without defining financial needs in terms of the organization's mission and goals—that is, with the purpose of just raising *more*. But that approach has major weaknesses.

If a nonprofit's fundraising is only about money, unrooted from a strategic plan, there is the risk that the organization's programs will become *donor-driven* and that its mission will be jeopardized. Without clarity about missions and goals, an organization has no rationale on which to refuse a gift that might not only detract from its mission but also bring additional costs or controversy. It may become buffeted by the interests of entrepreneurial donors, whose ideas and priorities may pull it in various directions without any coherent focus. For example, think back on the case of the Smithsonian Institution and the Catherine B. Reynolds Foundation, from Chapter 2. The Smithsonian did not have a strategic plan and there was not the internal consensus regarding mission and values that a planning process might have achieved. The secretary's (CEO's) goals were simple: "money and modernization," in other words, just *more*. He was presented with the possibility of a major gift that indeed would have provided both money and modernization of facilities, but in the views of many individuals, the purpose of the gift was not consistent with the institution's mission or values. Not only was the gift not completed, but negative publicity surrounded it, with potentially detrimental effects. If the gift had been completed, some would have argued that goal displacement had occurred.

In reality, of course, even organizations that have strategic plans in place may face situations in which they are offered gifts that do not directly address goals identified in the plan. For example, think back on Lindahl's (2010) example of the health clinic, discussed in Chapter 1. When presented with the offer of a gift to build a dental clinic, which was not part of the original plan, the organization could either refuse or accept it. If it determined that the dental clinic would advance its mission, it might decide to accept the gift and modify its plan accordingly to incorporate this new program. However, it also needs to understand that the gift has not helped to address its needs for health clinic funding, and it must carefully consider the implications of the dental clinic for its overall financial situation. Organizations may remain open to unexpected opportunities presented by the interests and preferences of donors, but opportunism should be bounded by the mission and goals articulated in the strategic plan. In other words, the strategic plan provides a standard against which opportunities may be evaluated. Absent the plan, the organization may be at the mercy of donor priorities and the temptations and pressures that accompany the offer of an unexpected gift.

Motivating Donors

A second reason why fundraising should be based on the mission and priorities described in a strategic plan, rather than on just dollar goals, is simply that the latter are unlikely to inspire significant gifts. Thinking back on our discussion of donor motivations in Chapter 3, it would be unrealistic to expect that many donors would give only to meet some dollar goal disconnected from substantive priorities. As Broce (1986) explains in his classic book, "Donors give gifts to meet objectives, not simply to give money away" (p. 19). Burk (2013) agrees, reporting from her research that "solicitations for unrestricted [gifts] are the weakest, producing the poorest response rates, and sub-par gift values" (p. 72). A striking example is provided by a story about a donor reported in the news media. In 2007, a university solicited a gift from an individual, who had made previous gifts, asking for $25 million to complete its campaign. The individual refused but shortly after gave $50 million to another institution for its medical school. When the first university asked why, he explained, "You asked me to help finish a campaign. They asked me to help cure cancer" (Strout, 2007, p. A21). A strategic plan anchors fundraising in purposes that people care about and thus provides the foundation a compelling case for support. In some form, strategic planning is an essential prerequisite for successful fundraising.

DEVELOPING A FUNDRAISING STRATEGY AND PLAN

Some authors conflate the strategic plan and the **fundraising plan**, but they are different. The strategic plan is about the organization. The strategic plan establishes its mission and programmatic goals and identifies the financial resources necessary to accomplishing those goals. Fundraising may be understood as a *strategy* for accomplishing the organization's goals. The fundraising plan describes how that strategy will be *implemented*.

A **fundraising strategy** defines the overall mix of solicitation programs, methods, techniques, and primary constituencies to be emphasized, in order to meet an organization's financial needs. It is not the same as a **solicitation strategy**, which defines the methods used and the timing of initiatives with regard to a particular prospect or set of prospects, for example, speculative fundraising or nurturing fundraising, as discussed earlier in this book. A fundraising strategy is a broad direction, perhaps no more than an idea or an approach. It may be included in a written plan, but it is not synonymous with a fundraising plan. A fundraising plan defines how the fundraising strategy will be implemented, including what activities will be undertaken, by whom, and on what schedule.

It is important to have both a fundraising strategy and a fundraising plan. As Chait, Holland, and Taylor (2005) note, a plan without a strategy is just wishful thinking. It may produce activity, which may be unproductive. But a strategy without a plan to implement it is also unlikely to produce the best result.

Fundraising Strategies

There are two generic fundraising strategies—**continuous programs** and **campaigns**. Dove (2000) defines the continuous program as the "strategic planning method" (p. 18) or the "continuous lifetime giving program" (2001, p. 32). As the term implies, continuous programs are always underway; the organization is always executing the fundraising process. It is, as Dove (2000) describes, engaged in "perpetual campaigning to satisfy capital and other needs" (p. 18). Unrestricted gifts are solicited on a regular basis, annually or more frequently. Gifts to support programs are pursued as needed. And solicitations for major and planned gifts are solicited when the organization's needs dictate and relationships with donors are at an appropriate stage. The latter is commonly called an **ongoing major-gifts program**.

Of course, within the generic strategy of ongoing programs, an organization may have more specific strategies. For example, think back on the discussion in Chapter 3; the shape of an organization's fundraising pyramid may suggest an emphasis on increasing the donor base or on developing major gifts. The types of resources it needs—unrestricted, program support, capital, or endowment—will define which constituencies should be the principal focus.

Characteristics of the organization's constituency also influence the strategy adopted. As Birkholz (2008) explains, some donors give from current income and others from accumulated assets. An organization with prospects who have income but limited wealth may adopt a **high-volume/low-dollar strategy**, emphasizing broad-based solicitation programs using mail, phone, and the Internet, in order to secure many small and midsized gifts. An organization with a relatively small constituency composed of individuals with significant assets might pursue a **high-dollar/low-volume strategy**, emphasizing major gifts, while minimizing the costs of broad-based solicitation programs. For example, the former is common among national disease organizations, while the latter may be more appropriate to a specialized research organization. Of course, as discussed in Chapter 4, over the long run, most organizations strive to develop programs that are balanced, including both annual and major-gifts programs.

In contrast to an ongoing program, a campaign is, by the best-known definition, "an organized, intensive fundraising effort . . . to secure extraordinary gifts and pledges . . . for a specific purpose or programs . . . during a specified period of time" (Dove, 2000, p. 5). Campaigns are discussed in detail in Chapter 11 of this text.

Fundraising Plan

If the organization is embarking on a campaign, it develops a campaign plan that describes strategies and activities over the period of the campaign, in broad terms. Annual operating plans then are developed for each year of the campaign, which include greater detail. If an organization is not in a campaign—if it is pursuing an ongoing fundraising strategy—the fundraising plan is usually developed on an annual basis. As summarized in Box 5.1, the plan begins with an analysis of current programs and results from the previous year; states goals and objectives for the coming year; provides detailed action plans, including a calendar; and assigns specific responsibility for each activity. Results are continuously monitored so that midcourse corrections can be made as needed, and, of course, year-end evaluation provides the starting point for the next year's planning.

This book does not provide an example of a comprehensive fundraising plan, which can be a lengthy and detailed document. Additional reading is suggested at the end of this chapter. There are also resources, including templates for plans, available on the web.

BOX 5.1 Developing a Fundraising Plan

- Evaluate current development programs and gift data.
- Establish fundraising goals for the upcoming year (e.g., annual fund, planned gifts).
- Set quantifiable objectives that support the goals.
- Design action plans that spell out how those objectives will be met (e.g., direct mail, gift clubs, telemarketing).
- Create a calendar for the entire year that identifies everything that will occur, by when, and who is responsible.
- Monitor the plan's progress throughout the year and make adjustments as needed.
- Evaluate the plan at year's end in light of what was achieved or fell short of expectations.

Source: Adapted from *The operational plan: How to create a yearlong fundraising plan* (2011/2012 edition). Sioux City, IA: Stevenson, Inc.

DEVELOPING THE CASE FOR SUPPORT

As Seiler and Aldrich (2011) define it, "The case is the general argument for why a nonprofit deserves gift support" (p. 27). Although different authors use a somewhat different vocabulary, the terms **case** and **case for support** are often used interchangeably to identify the general argument for giving (Weinstein, 2009). The case is not to be confused with a related term, the **case statement**, which is "a particular expression of the case" (Seiler & Aldrich, 2011, p. 27). The case for support is an *idea*—the essence of why an organization deserves support, ideally capable of expression in no more than a few sentences or paragraphs. It is akin to an "elevator speech," a concise explanation that could be stated in the time it takes to ride an elevator.

The case statement is a document that expresses the case but also includes more comprehensive information. The case statement may be developed in two versions—an **internal case statement** and an **external case statement**. The internal case statement contains detailed information and data that, as the term implies, is primarily useful to individuals working within the organization. It is "an encyclopedic accumulation of information" (Seiler & Aldrich, 2011, p. 27) providing raw material that can be adapted for proposals and various fundraising communications.[1] The external case statement is intended for prospective donors; it is often a brochure or is communicated electronically. It is less detailed than the internal case statement and usually includes more emotional language, photos, and stories related to the organization's work. The internal case statement is a reference document; the external case statement is a sales document.

Characteristics of a Strong Case

In his classic book, *Designs for Fund-Raising*, Seymour (1966) offers a memorable phrase that is still often quoted; he writes that the purpose of a good case is "to catch the eye, warm the heart, and stir the mind" (p. 22). In somewhat more detail, a strong case exhibits the following essential characteristics:

- It starts with a cause larger than the organization itself (Seiler & Aldrich, 2011).

- It establishes the organization's credibility and differentiates it from others (Seiler & Aldrich, 2011).

- It describes achievable program goals.

- It justifies financial needs in terms of program goals and organizational strategy.

- And, as Seymour (1966) established and others have confirmed (Seiler & Aldrich, 2011), it appeals to emotion as well as reason.

People give not because an organization has needs but because it meets needs. For that reason, the case begins with the social or human *problem* that the organization addresses. This could, of course, also be a positive *opportunity* that would bring benefits to people and the community served, but it should be a cause larger than the organization's own financial needs. More bluntly, the case is not about you, it's about what you do!

The case should explain, even if succinctly, why the particular organization is a sound vehicle for donors who care about the social or human problem it addresses; that is, it should establish the organization's credibility and capability. And it should describe program goals that are likely to be seen as achievable. Some cases describe lofty goals that are noble but simply do not ring true because the goals seem out of proportion to the capacity of the organization or the fundraising goal to which they relate. For example, eliminating hunger in the world is a worthy goal. But donors may not see it as one achievable by the organization soliciting their support, especially if its fundraising goal is relatively modest. On the other hand, if the organization can point to more specific objectives, including the number of people it expects to help, its case may be more plausible (Rosso, 1991). Thus, while lofty goals may inspire, an organization's objectives need to be viewed as achievable, so that donors can make the connection between their gifts and some realistic anticipated outcome.

Let's see how the characteristics of a strong case might play out in a hypothetical example. Consider two versions of the case for support of the Downtown Performing Arts Center, presented in Box 5.2. Again, these statements are summaries of the *case for support*, not case statements, which are larger documents. Both statements reflect basically the same facts and describe the same organizational needs. But Downtown Performing Arts Center Case #1 is stated entirely in terms of the organization's own problems, with no reference to the broader needs of society. The fact that the center is losing money and talent

---

BOX 5.2 Downtown Performing Arts Center Case for Support

Downtown Performing Arts Center Case #1

Our performance space has deteriorated in recent years, since we have not had enough money to maintain it, and it is too small. The best artists will no longer perform here because of our poor acoustics. The neighborhood where we are located also has declined, making it less attractive to audiences. We have experienced high turnover on our staff. Newer performing arts centers have been developed in the suburbs. They have lower ticket prices and easier parking and have attracted larger audiences, further cutting into our revenue. We need to raise $10 million to renovate our aging facilities, build a parking garage, and increase salaries in order to retain our staff members. Without those investments, it is difficult to see how the Downtown Performing Arts Center can survive.

Downtown Performing Arts Center Case #2

The arts inspire the human spirit and are at the center of urban life. The Downtown Performing Arts Center always has been dedicated to advancing the vitality of our city and providing access to the performing arts for people of all economic backgrounds. Our continued excellence is essential to the future development of the city and its economy. For that reason, the board of trustees has established an exciting plan to make the Downtown Performing Arts Center one of the outstanding centers in the state, a force in revitalization of its neighborhood, and a source of enrichment in the lives of the people of the city and beyond. To achieve that goal, we must raise $10 million to renovate and expand our facility, attract the highest-quality artists to perform here, and build an excellent professional staff.

and its facility is deteriorating are reasons for concern but also may be seen as reasons not to give it money, lest the funds be wasted on a failing enterprise. Case #1 also does not offer any explanation for why the negative trends it cites may be occurring, leaving open the possibility that they may reflect mismanagement on the part of the center's leaders. In other words, Case #1 does nothing to establish the credibility of the Downtown Performing Arts Center as a worthy recipient of support. There is no reason to think that the center's goals are achievable and nothing in Case #1 that would warm the heart; indeed, it is a cold statement of an unfavorable business reality.

In contrast, Downtown Performing Arts Center Case #2 takes a positive approach, beginning with the importance of the performing arts to the human spirit and to urban communities. It places the center's needs in the context of its mission and values and connects it to human opportunity. It explains the financial goal in relationship to the board of trustees' strategy, suggesting that the financial needs are based on sound planning. And it uses emotionally laden words and phrases, such as *exciting, excellence,* and *vitality*.

A well-written case is constructed with an understanding of donors' perspectives (Seiler & Aldrich, 2011). Thinking back on the donor types discussed in Chapter 3, Case #2 offers something for several of them. Inspiring the human spirit is a purpose likely to resonate with idealists. Economic development of the city is a goal investors may see as important. Expanding opportunities for enrichment to people in the city and beyond may be a priority for repayers who experienced similar opportunities in their lives. The fact that the improved performing arts center will contribute to revitalization of a neighborhood may enhance the appeal to communitarians.

CREATING A CULTURE OF PHILANTHROPY

The term **culture of philanthropy** has been introduced into the fundraising literature in recent years and is used in various ways. For example, dissertations and research articles, and a number of practitioner articles, have examined how organizations create a culture among their constituents that promotes giving. Much of this literature relates to higher education and describes the efforts that colleges and universities undertake to develop such a culture among their students and alumni (e.g., Buckla, 2004; Hurvitz, 2010). Other scholars have examined culture among certain types of donors, for example, venture philanthropists (Moody, 2008), corporate donors (Genest, 2005), and the wealthy (Ostrower, 1995). Some have explored the relationship between national cultures and philanthropy (McDonald & Scaife, 2011).

Others use the term *culture of philanthropy* to refer to *organizational culture* that influences fundraising effectiveness, which more accurately might be called the organization's *culture of fundraising*. Bell and Cornelius (2013) explain:

> While familiar to fundraising professionals, the term culture of philanthropy is not yet well understood nor commonly used across the [nonprofit] sector. Not to be confused with institutional grant making or the act of giving money as a donor, a culture of philanthropy refers to a set of organizational values and practices that support and nurture development within a nonprofit organization. (p. 3)

The account of my experience at the University of Maryland, with which this chapter began, speaks to the absence of a culture of philanthropy at that institution in the late 1970s. So, too, do the examples in Chapter 2 of the research institution at which the development office was located in the basement, staffed by a director who did not have ready access to the organization's volunteer or senior staff leaders.

CompassPoint's 2013 study found that organizational culture is an obstacle to fundraising effectiveness in a wide range of nonprofit organizations (Bell & Cornelius, 2013). The researchers concluded that ineffectiveness in fundraising is attributable in part to problems related to the director of development position, including unqualified incumbents and high turnover. However, they also determined that the problem often goes beyond one person or position, reporting that "a surprising number of organizations lack the fundamental conditions for fund development success—basic tools such as a fundraising plan and database, essential board and executive leadership and development skills, and a *shared culture of philanthropy across the organization*" (p. 20, italics added). They conclude that

> creating the conditions for success—at both the organizational and sectoral levels— requires nonprofit staff, executives, boards, funders, and capacity builders to make small and large changes in belief and practice. Fundamentally, it requires all of us in the sector to adopt a profoundly different stance towards fundraising—moving away from an approach that is passive, apologetic, and siloed in nature, to an integrative approach that deeply values donors and constituents and puts them right in the center of our organizations and movements. (p. 22)

Understanding Organizational Culture

A few principles related to organizational culture are helpful to understanding fundraising's place in an organization and how it might be enhanced. *Culture* is a word frequently used in everyday conversation, and most people probably have a reasonably accurate understanding of what it means. But organizational scholars offer precise definitions. For example, Schein (2010) breaks culture down into three categories: (1) *artifacts and creations*—for example, logos, symbols, ceremonies, rituals, and words used in conversations; (2) *basic values*—the less observable understandings of "how things are done around here," for example, who communicates with whom within the organization and in what manner, what external relationships are important, and so forth; and (3) *basic assumptions*—for example, how people see things, their personal theories about human nature, and expectations about whether people in the organization should be entrepreneurial and aggressive or compliant and passive.

Among the artifacts and creations relevant to a culture of philanthropy are items and activities related to donor recognition, for example, plaques on walls, listings of members in giving societies, and stewardship events that honor donors. Think back on the point discussed in Chapter 4 that donor recognition is not only undertaken for the benefit of the donors; it also serves the interest of the organization by holding up examples that others may emulate. In addition, it has an impact on the internal culture of fundraising by signaling the importance of philanthropy in the life of the organization. In other words, it may shape values and assumptions held by staff and volunteer leaders.

The values of nonprofit organizations may present a challenge in building a culture of philanthropy. Nonprofits are values-based and mission-driven organizations. In a business, the end is to earn profit, and the products and services provided are means to that end. In a nonprofit, the reverse is true. Money is a means to delivering programs in order to achieve the mission. This difference may lead to a "service culture" (Letts et al., 1999) and one that encourages conflict avoidance rather than engagement (Anheier, 2005). That culture may guide some individuals who work in nonprofit organizations to view fundraising as, at best, a necessary evil, in which they prefer not to be too involved. Even program managers who accept the need to raise funds for their own programs may define fundraising as primarily proposal writing and may be less comfortable with the idea of raising funds from individual donors. Of course, there may also be members of the board who view their contributions to the organization as related to their own professional knowledge and expertise and who are also reluctant to become involved in fundraising, preferring that it be handled by the CEO and the development office. To use the old joke, most people enjoy the sausage, but many may prefer to remain ignorant about how it is made.

It is an oversimplification to speak of an organization's culture, as if it is coherent and uniform throughout. Most organizations, except perhaps the smallest, include various subcultures—that is, groups of individuals "who share strong values about basic beliefs with some, but not all, of the other members of the organization" (Clegg, Kornberger, & Pitsis, 2005, p. 277). The senior managers of most nonprofit organizations have professional backgrounds related to core programs. They may be social workers, psychologists, physicians, artists, or educators. Their values are derived from their professional cultures and may be quite different from the culture of fundraising.

Fundraising professionals have their own professional culture, too, which may not be shared or easily understood by others within their organizations. Fundraisers are focused on securing gifts from private sources and interact frequently with people of wealth. It is possible that over time, they may come to identify with the worldview and values of such people. They often spend considerable time out of the office, traveling and joining donors for meals or other social events. This reduces opportunities to develop relationships with program managers and other staff within the organization and may appear to some to be a lavish lifestyle that engenders resentment. There may even be differences in the personality types of fundraising professionals and those of other professionals in the organization, with many fundraisers being extroverts and others having more introverted personalities that prefer a different communication style (Hall, 2014a).

For these reasons, as the CompassPoint study found, fundraising as a management function sometimes exists on the periphery of the organization (Bell & Cornelius, 2013). The result may be unrealistic expectations placed on fundraising professionals who are expected to succeed with little support, leading to their frustration, turnover, and a loss of continuity in relationships with donors—what Bell and Cornelius (2013) describe as the "vicious cycle that threatens [organizations'] ability to raise the resources they need to succeed" (p. 2).

Strategies for Building a Culture of Philanthropy

The growing literature on the topic includes a number of recommendations for building a culture of philanthropy; let's consider a few of the most common.

The CEO's Example

As Herman and Heimovics (2005) discovered in their research, the nonprofit CEO holds a position of "psychological centrality" in the organization (p. 156). For that reason, his or her behavior signals others, including staff and volunteers, as to what is valued. Building a culture of philanthropy thus requires that the CEO accept his or her fundraising role and demonstrate the importance of the fundraising function within the organization (Bell & Cornelius, 2013). As Seiler (2011a) explains, "Acceptance of fundraising as a management function and as a management process requires the acceptance of the chief fundraising officer as an important member of the senior management team" (p. 47). The CEO indicates the importance of the chief fundraising officer not only by the placement of that position on the organizational chart but also by including that person in key meetings as a senior officer of the organization and by devoting his or her own time and interest to supporting that person's work.

Produce Short-Term Wins

One of the important steps in Kotter's (1996, 2012) model of organizational change is producing short-term wins, that is, achieving intermediate goals in order to reassure followers and produce momentum for long-term change. This is a strategy that nonprofit organizations can employ to advance a culture of philanthropy. It implies establishing fundraising goals that can be achieved; celebrating the success; giving generous credit to individuals who were in any way involved in cultivation, solicitation, or stewardship; and emphasizing the positive impact on the organization's program. This helps create positive feelings about the experience and may encourage more confidence and participation in larger fundraising efforts in the future.

A successful campaign—a topic discussed further in Chapter 11—can help to build an organization's culture of philanthropy. This result may occur in part because a campaign is often preceded by strategic planning, which helps to identify and reinforce shared vision and values and brings a disciplined approach to building culture. In a 2004 study, 90 percent of fundraisers at liberal arts colleges responded that a campaign is somewhat or very effective in encouraging a culture of philanthropy, and 60 percent responded that it is helpful in sustaining such a culture (Isaak, 2004). However, the researcher concluded that sustaining a culture of philanthropy also required a continued effort (Isaak, 2004).

Expand Fundraising Involvement

As Bell and Cornelius (2013) describe, in an organization that has a culture of philanthropy, "most people in the organization (across positions) act as ambassadors and engage in relationship building. Everyone promotes philanthropy and can articulate a case for giving" (p. 3). This argues for pushing down and spreading out responsibility for fundraising throughout the organization, rather than isolating it as an activity conducted only by the development office. This requires "identifying specific activities in which all can participate and [reinforcing] accountability [by including] development goals in the annual performance evaluation process for staff" (p. 27).

Such activities may include solicitation or relate to other steps in the fundraising process, such as identifying prospects, acknowledging gifts, and stewarding relationships with donors. For example, at the Maryland Food Bank, the communications manager and other staff participate in fundraising events and ask people who donate food to also give cash. Easter Seals of New Jersey asks staff to become involved in fundraising events, and participation is reflected in their personnel evaluations. Clinicians at some Planned Parenthood chapters solicit gifts from patients, and faculty at some colleges and universities solicit alumni who were their former students (Preston, 2010). As one consultant advises, "Everyone in the organization . . . from the janitor to the president of the board . . . [should] understand that philanthropy and fund development are critical to organizational health AND that each individual (both the janitor and board president) has a role in the process" (Joyaux, n.d.).

BUILDING THE FUNDRAISING TEAM

Fundraising will not succeed if it is the responsibility only of a development office that is siloed on the periphery of the organization. But even where a pervasive culture of philanthropy exists, effective fundraising is a team effort that involves three principal players: the governing board, the CEO, and the chief development officer.[2]

BoardSource (2010) describes the relationship among the three parties as a partnership and assigns to the board the responsibility for setting goals consistent with the mission, helping to develop the case for support, establishing fundraising policies, and evaluating fundraising performance. The board also has a role in giving and participating in fundraising, but as discussed further later, there are various approaches to how that role is defined. In BoardSource's formulation, the organization's staff, including the CEO and chief development officer, supports the board by providing fundraising infrastructure—such as prospect research and gift processing. But Burk (2013) reports that there is widespread confusion within many nonprofits about "who is responsible for what" (p. 18). This is especially true among board members, who may understand in general terms that they should be involved in fundraising but lack clear direction about how their roles actually should be played (Burk, 2013).

An Unusual Game

General descriptions of fundraising responsibilities are helpful, but they itemize the roles of each player without saying much about how they interact in practice. When it comes to execution—that is, working together in fundraising—it may be useful to think about another kind of team and how it functions when the game is being played. In three previous books (Worth, 2005, 2010, 2012) I describe the workings of the fundraising team through the metaphor of a football team. This section is adapted from those previous works.

Baseball, basketball, and soccer are great sports, but football's characteristics make it most like fundraising. Baseball and basketball emphasize individual performance; it is possible for an individual to put points on the board through heroic achievements. But in football, like in fundraising, scoring points usually requires the coordinated, simultaneous action of multiple players. There rarely is a fundraising equivalent to a three-point shot or a home run. The roles of the key players on the fundraising team also exist in football. Looking back at the responsibilities identified by BoardSource (2010), the board members are the team's owners. They are focused on the overall success and sustainability of the enterprise. They set the standards for team performance and monitor results. But what makes this football team unique is the expectation that on the day of the game the owners will come down from their sky boxes and engage in the game on the field; that is, they will become personally involved in the fundraising process. Indeed, fundraising is one of the only functions in which board members (owners) are asked to go beyond their policymaking role and become deeply involved in execution.

On the fundraising team, the CEO holds down three jobs at once. He or she may be a member of the board, and thus an owner, but the CEO is also the coach—leading, guiding, and sometimes pushing the board and other members of the team in their game performance. The CEO also is the team's star running back. That is, in addition to inspiring the team, training the other players, and developing the game plan, the CEO also must run the ball on many occasions and will be among the most visible players on the field—cheered by the fans on winning days and booed when the game goes south.

The CEO is often the person most able to advance the ball (that is, the organization's cause) and may be the most visible and applauded member of the team. But the whole game unfolds according to a plan, and each player respects and adheres to the game plan. This point is crucial: Successful fundraising requires a plan that pulls together the contributions of all the players in an organized, coordinated way. Some CEOs sometimes may be inclined to run the ball alone. But anyone who has played on a team with a player who hogs the ball will recognize that such a player often engenders resentment from teammates. Some CEOs may be drawn to the idea of single-handedly securing the largest gifts and achieving acclaim from the fans. But, it is important to remember, a ball hog may be a star when the team is winning but will also receive the blame in a loss.

The chief development officer is the quarterback. He or she calls the plays and may sometimes run the ball but often hands it off or passes it to other members of the team. The development officer's role is complicated, too, in that fellow players (that is, the board and the CEO) are also the owners and the coach. The chief development officer may work for the CEO and the board but also sometimes needs to push the CEO and the owners to high performance as members of the fundraising team.

Some chief development officers may be ball hogs, too. Indeed, most development officers do solicit gifts, and some large development offices have a staff of major-gifts officers who do so continuously, with or without the engagement of volunteer leaders. But there are advantages to sharing responsibility. When quarterbacks try to run alone without a team around them, they sometimes gain yardage but sometimes get sacked. In fundraising as in football, it is best to keep the focus on overall team performance, sharing both the celebrations of success and the responsibility for inevitable disappointment.

Board's Role in Fundraising

Many authors have addressed the fundraising roles of CEOs and fundraising professionals. They are the subject of numerous motivational and prescriptive writings by practitioners and consultants as well as academic studies, many focused on the fundraising roles of presidents in higher education (e.g., Miller, 2013; Pinchback, 2011; Stovall, 2004). There is also an extensive literature regarding the role of development officers, also including both practitioner writing and academic studies (e.g., Edwards, 2003; Johnsen, 2005; Meisenbach, 2004; Schiller, 2013). But discussion and debate is especially vigorous with regard to the fundraising role of the governing board.

As discussed in Chapter 2 of this book, the board has a wide range of responsibilities. In the view of many authors, securing resources is among the board's top responsibilities and includes both personal giving and participation in fundraising (Ingram, 2009). Some view the board's involvement in fundraising as interwoven with its broader responsibilities as fiduciaries and stewards of the organization. As Grossnickle (2011) writes,

> Fundraising [is] a key means by which the role of [the board] may be performed better and with more clarity and success. After all, fundraising concerns much more than money. In practice, fundraising constitutes one of the most effective arenas in which [board members] can practice the skills that make them better [board members] overall. This is because active involvement in fundraising necessarily calls for talking authentically about organizational purpose, reconciling where the organization has been with where the future lies, and harmonizing the philanthropic wishes of the individual donor with the organization's plans. (p. 276)

Board members' personal giving and their involvement in fundraising are linked. Think back on the discussion of sequential fundraising in Chapter 4. Gifts are solicited from the top down and the inside out. Larger early gifts help to raise the sights of others throughout the fundraising pyramid. Gifts committed by those closest to the organization, including the board, help to establish the importance of the purpose and demonstrate to others that it is worthy of their support. In other words, support from board members **authenticates** the organization's case for support.

The significance of these principles is easily understood if we consider their absence. Think about the example of proportionate giving offered in Chapter 4. You might be disinclined to give your support to an organization that has a member of the wealthiest family in town as a board member if you learned that the family had not given. Thus, the failure of the board to set an example may be devastating to the entire fundraising effort. Giving and soliciting are linked simply because a volunteer cannot be a credible solicitor without having given first. Thinking back on Chapter 3 and the discussion of social influences on giving, recall Seymour's (1966) classic prescription that "the solicitor should be a giver whose own giving standards and whose place in the scheme of things are commensurate with the goals [he or she] seeks and the people [he or she] sees" (p. 76). The point has shown continuing relevance; even fundraising on the Internet follows its logic, showing the names and amounts of those who have given, including the individual making the request.

Curiously, although it is a common tenet of practitioners and authors writing about fundraising, the view that fundraising is a central responsibility of boards is not emphasized by scholars whose focus is on governance. For example, Chait et al. (2005) state that "board members are often good at fundraising and community relations" (p. 22). However, ignoring the principles of sequential fundraising and social influences on donors discussed earlier, they argue that "board members are not uniquely qualified to do this work; managers often perform both functions alongside board members" (p. 22). Another widely read authority on governance, John Carver (2006), notes that "in many types of organizations, fundraising is not even remotely related to the board's job" (p. 323).

Carver's statement is correct. For example, the boards of private foundations do not engage in fundraising. Elected boards of membership associations often are not selected with concern about their fundraising interest and capability. Some nonprofits providing services to low-income communities that accept government funds are required, as a condition of that funding, to have a significant percentage of their boards composed of former or current clients. Most of those individuals are likely to have limited ability to give or assist with fundraising, so such boards usually do not play a large fundraising role. And at many larger institutions, such as universities, major-gifts officers on the development office staff solicit gifts without the involvement of volunteers. These are commonly known as **staff-driven programs**. However, in most situations, the involvement of a board leader is a very positive ingredient.

CEOs and development officers do solicit many gifts without including a volunteer leader and may be tempted to do so in the desire to move quickly. However, regardless of their passion, the CEO and development officer are asking as a part of their job responsibilities, a reality that may affect, even if subconsciously, the way in which they are perceived by the prospective donor. But the involvement of a respected volunteer board member who has already made his or her gift has a power that simply cannot be duplicated by a fundraiser or even a CEO. The volunteer brings credibility by virtue of his or her voluntary status, which reflects a commitment to the cause. Indeed, in a 2008 study, twenty-three out of thirty-three major donors reported that knowing someone on the board was a principal reason for their giving (Fredericks, 2010).

Board's Fundraising Performance

If the board's involvement in fundraising is so vital, what is the current state of affairs? Various studies suggest room for improvement. In a 2008 study of midsize nonprofits, 62 percent of nonprofit CEOs rated their boards "poor or fair" in their fundraising performance (Ostrower, 2008). A 2011 study undertaken by CompassPoint and the Meyer Foundation found a similarly dismal situation:

> Fewer than half of respondents reported strong board member participation in donor identification and prospecting (48%), asking for gifts (42%), and donor cultivation

(41 %)—activities frequently cited as areas in which board member participation is critical. The fact that less than half of executives report board member participation in those areas highlights a possible disconnect between the traditional view of the board's role in fundraising and the day-to-day realities experienced by executives working in partnership with boards. (Moyers, 2011, p. 3)

The reported ineffectiveness of boards with regard to fundraising is troubling, especially since many nonprofit organizations face growing financial pressures. Strengthening the board's fundraising performance has become a priority for many organizations. Three principal strategies have been adopted toward that end: recruiting more board members of affluence and influence, focusing the board's attention on fundraising, and establishing policies to set standards and expectations for board members' personal giving and involvement in fundraising.

Balancing Wealth and Wisdom

The need to increase gift revenue has increased competition among nonprofits for board members who have the capacity to give and raise funds. But this requires somewhat of a balancing act. Remember from Chapter 2 that the board must be Janus-like, promoting the organization but also providing oversight. In order to fulfill both roles, boards need members with various skills and perspectives. Some may bring a valuable understanding of the community served by the organization. Some may bring experience in management or financial matters. Others may have professional skills related to mission programs, for example, backgrounds in social work, medicine, or some other field that enable them to evaluate the organization's programs. But some may not have the ability to make significant gifts and may not be positioned to solicit such gifts from others.

On the other hand, a board composed entirely of wealthy people may bring financial benefits but be ill-equipped, or lack the time, to do an effective job of governing. Of course, there may be some board members who bring multiple characteristics to their work, including experience, a community perspective, and financial capacity. But many boards find they need to strike a balance between recruiting members who are prepared to govern and others whose primary contribution may be financial (Worth, 2005).

A strategy some nonprofits have adopted is to have two boards—a governing board that has fiduciary responsibility and an *advisory council* that does not.[3] The criteria for membership may be different; for example, the governing board may be broadly representative of the community, while the advisory board is composed primarily of individuals who can give and raise funds. Or the definition of the two boards may be exactly reversed; that is, the governing board may be composed of philanthropists, while an advisory council with specialized expertise provides community input and guidance on program matters (Worth, 2008). The challenges of managing two such boards, in either arrangement, can be complex, but a full discussion of that is beyond the scope of this text.

Focusing the Board's Attention

A second strategy many boards have adopted is to establish a committee of the board focused on fundraising, usually called a fundraising or **development committee**.

The development committee normally establishes fundraising policies and goals, monitors the performance of fundraising programs, reports and interprets results to the full board, and provides leadership in the board's participation in fundraising. Such a committee is helpful in keeping the board's attention focused on fundraising, but it is important to assure that the committee does not come to be perceived as the fundraising committee. In other words, participation in fundraising is a responsibility of the *full board* and should not be viewed as something delegated to a committee, thus relieving other board members of their own responsibility. In many cases, it may be better to create a fundraising committee or task force only as the need arises, for example, in a campaign, rather than as a standing committee of the board (BoardSource, 2010).

Establishing Policies

Some boards have established policies that set expectations for the board's own participation in giving and fundraising. Four common approaches are summarized in Table 5.1 (BoardSource, n.d.).

First, some boards establish a policy that all members of the board are exacted to make an annual gift and to support capital campaigns—that is, they require 100 percent participation—but do not specify a minimum amount, implying that each member will be expected to give commensurate with his or her ability (BoardSource, n.d.). Other boards establish a minimum annual gift that every board member is expected to provide

TABLE 5.1   Four Common Approaches to Board Participation in Giving and Fundraising

Board Policy Approach	Advantages	Disadvantages
Require 100 percent participation but do not specify a required gift from each board member	Assures 100 percent participation and permits each board member to give commensurate with his or her capacity	Does not establish a clear standard, and some board members may not give as much as they are capable of giving
Establish a minimum gift that every board member is required to make	Establishes a clear standard, assures 100 percent participation, and makes board giving predictable	May lead to a board that is not diverse and may discourage financially capable board members from giving more than the minimum
Establish a minimum amount that every board member is expected to give or get	Establishes a clear standard, makes gift revenue produced by the board predictable, provides flexibility for board members who are not personally wealthy	Requires careful management to assure that board members do not engage in uncoordinated fundraising activity
Develop an individualized fundraising plan for every member of the board	Assures that every board member will participate in giving and fundraising in a manner most appropriate to their individual capabilities	Requires investment of time by the board chair or development committee chair to meet individually with every board member

(BoardSource, n.d.). A third approach some boards adopt is known as a **give-or-get policy** (Bristol, 2012), requiring board members to give personally or secure gifts from others—or some combination—totaling a specified minimum amount. Sometimes the policy is stated harshly as "give, get, or get off," meaning that the board member should leave the board if he or she is not prepared to live up to the requirement (Bristol, 2012). A fourth alternative is to take an individualized approach. The chair of the board or the chair of the development committee meets annually with every member of the board to develop a plan for how that member will contribute to the organization's fundraising in the year ahead. That includes a personal gift at a level appropriate to each person's financial capacity and also further involvement, based on each person's particular abilities and skills. The goal of this approach is to maximize the contributions of the board to the fundraising effort, while recognizing that its members may do so in various ways (BoardSource, 2010). Each approach offers advantages and disadvantages, and the decision about how best to approach the topic depends on the characteristics of each organization and board.

IDENTIFYING AND RESEARCHING PROSPECTS

Not every person, company, and foundation in the world is a prospect for support of every nonprofit organization or institution. Before proceeding with fundraising, it is necessary to identify the organization's constituency, identify those within that constituency who are potential prospects, and obtain sufficient information about those prospects to be able to develop effective cultivation and solicitation strategies.

Defining a Constituency

An organization's constituency can be defined as its stakeholders (Sargeant, Shang, et al., 2010). Stakeholders are the individuals, companies, or foundations that have an interest—or stake—in the organization; in other words, it matters to them in some way. Thinking back to Lohmann's (1992) theory, discussed in Chapter 2, an organization's constituency also may be understood as the members of the commons that care about it.

A constituency is often depicted in a series of concentric circles, similar to those in Figure 5.2. In the center are those most directly involved with the organization, for example, members of the governing board, staff members, active volunteers, current major donors, and others. A circle beyond the core might include clients/customers, former clients, members, smaller donors, and others who are aware of the organization but not significantly involved. Outer circles would encompass those who have a general interest in the issues the organization addresses but who have no direct relationship with the organization in particular. Everyone else is essentially outside the universe with respect to the organization, uninvolved, unaware, and not really interested. These four categories generally correspond to what public relations scholars Grunig and Repper (1992) call the "active public," the "aware public," the "latent public," and the "nonpublic." The probability of obtaining financial support diminishes as the organization moves outward to circles more distant from the core. Remember from Chapter 4 that the principle of sequential

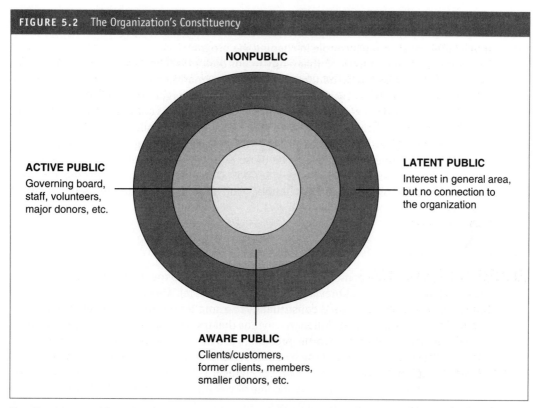

FIGURE 5.2 The Organization's Constituency

NONPUBLIC

ACTIVE PUBLIC
Governing board,
staff, volunteers,
major donors, etc.

LATENT PUBLIC
Interest in general area,
but no connection to
the organization

AWARE PUBLIC
Clients/customers,
former clients, members,
smaller donors, etc.

Note: Terms *aware public, active public, latent public,* and *nonpublic* from Grunig and Repper, 1992.

fundraising reflects this reality, requiring that solicitations proceed from the inside out, so that the commitments of those closest will establish authenticity and positive examples for those in more remote circles who are less motivated to give.

Every nonprofit organization has a core constituency, including at least its board and current major donors, however the latter may be defined (Seiler, 2011c). But when we move to the next circle, nonprofits face different situations. For example, former students of colleges and universities, who may have spent four years of their lives physically at the institution, are likely to have relatively strong connections. That may be true as well of former hospital patients whose lives were saved or improved through their experiences. But former clients of many organizations may have had a relatively fleeting experience, and their identification with the organization may be weak.

It is not efficient to dedicate too many resources to the outer circles of the constituency, but that is not to say that they should be ignored. Individuals in the periphery of the constituency may be solicited for annual gifts, using relatively low-cost methods such as mail and the Internet. Some may respond, self-identifying as potential prospects for larger gifts, in other words, by moving into a circle closer to the core. Some may indeed jump in at higher levels of the pyramid, without having an extensive history with the organization, if presented with an important opportunity consistent with their philanthropic interests. That is especially true of entrepreneurial donors, if they see the potential for significant impact and are able to play a role in shaping the program.

But it is not realistic to think that many major donors will be found in the outer circles initially. And in cases where donors appear to have emerged from the periphery to make a major gift, further investigation often reveals that the organization indeed established linkage and engaged in extensive cultivation before the gift was committed. In other words, in such cases, the individual may indeed have been systematically included within closer circles—that is, cultivated—before making the gift. For most organizations most of the time, the best prospects are likely to be those closer to the center of the organization's constituency. Heetland's (1993) advice is sound: "Don't look for wealthy people and hope that some will become your friends. Rather, look at your friends and hope that some of them are wealthy" (p. 10).

Defining Prospects

Rosso established the principal criteria that define a prospect: **linkage**, **ability**, and **interest**, sometimes just abbreviated as **LAI** (Seiler, 2011c). Applying these criteria helps to narrow the focus from the total constituency to a smaller number of prospective donors. Linkage—or what some call affiliation—means that the individuals have some connection to the organization; in other words, prospects are likely to be within the two innermost circles as depicted in Figure 5.2 (Hogan, 2008). Thinking back to the discussion in Chapter 4, these would be individuals in the top half of Figure 4.1. Ability refers to financial **capacity**. Those who do not have discretionary income or wealth may contribute to the organization in other ways but cannot participate in giving. As the term implies, *interest* refers to the extent to which the potential prospect cares about the organization and its work.

All three criteria must be met or the individual is not a **prospect**. A few examples help to make this obvious. Let's consider someone who is an active volunteer for the organization but is financially constrained. That person is not a prospect for a significant gift, no matter how much he or she might care about the organization's work. Now consider someone who has linkage, perhaps as a former client, and is also known to have wealth. It would be easy to think that the individual is a prospect, but suppose that when you meet with the person he or she expresses no interest or, indeed, has a negative view of the organization. Frustrating as such a conversation might be for a fundraiser, unfortunately, even two out of the three criteria are not enough to make someone a prospect.

Identifying and Developing Prospects

Figure 5.3 depicts a process for prospect development through which a nonprofit organization identifies and qualifies prospects following the criteria of LAI (Birkholz, 2008). The process begins with an analysis of the constituency to identify an initial list of potential prospects.[4] This analysis may employ various tools, some of which are discussed shortly. The next step, determining an individual's capacity to make a gift—also known as **qualifying the prospect**—is more complex and requires further research. Prospect

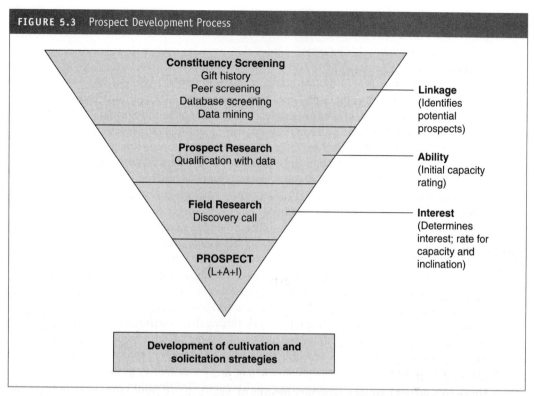

FIGURE 5.3 Prospect Development Process

Source: Adapted from Birkholz, J. M. (2008). *Fundraising analytics: Using data to guide strategy.* Hoboken, NJ: John Wiley and Sons, p. 39.

research professionals use a variety of resources to undercover signs of wealth in publicly available data, including, for example, real estate holdings, ownership in public companies, family relationships, and known philanthropic history.

Based on **prospect research**, an initial *rating* is established, that is, an estimate of what the individual *could* give. The next step, determining interest, requires a personal contact, what is called a *discovery call* or *discovery visit*. This may be undertaken by a fundraising professional, perhaps a major-gifts officer or, in a smaller organization, a volunteer or even the CEO. Again, the purpose of this contact is not to solicit a gift but rather to listen and determine the individual's interest and perhaps gain more insight on the individual's capacity.

The individual making the discovery call produces a **contact report**, summarizing what has been learned, and the rating of the prospect may be revised to include not only financial capacity but what is called **inclination** (Hogan, 2008) or **likelihood** (Birkholz, 2008), that is, the probability that the prospect will make a gift. The findings of research and information from contacts are used to develop a profile of the prospect and then to plan and manage cultivation and solicitation strategies. Chapter 7, which discusses major-gifts programs, provides more detail on how ratings are used to manage the major-gifts process, in order to allocate fundraising time and effort among those prospects likely to produce the greatest return.

Tools of Prospect Development

One of the simplest ways to identify potential prospects for major gifts is to analyze gift histories. An individual who has become a regular donor to the annual fund, especially if that person increases his or her gift every year, is self-identifying as someone who has an interest in the organization and at least some financial capacity. Some organizations use past giving as the primary or only indicator of a potential major-gift prospect and will undertake research on any donor whose annual gift reaches some defined level, say $1,000 (Birkholz, 2008).

Another traditional tool for identifying potential major-gift prospects is **peer screening**, which was the standard approach before the existence of sophisticated information systems and is still a low-cost and effective tool for many small nonprofits (Sprinkel-Grace, 2005). Board members, current donors, volunteers, and others are asked to review lists of names and provide what information they have regarding their interests and capacity. Obviously, this information may not always be accurate, but if various sources provide similar responses, confidence is increased. A useful by-product of peer screening is that it engages volunteers in the fundraising process, raising their awareness and perhaps causing them to consider their own gifts. However, for a large organization, with a database including thousands of names, peer screening is not an efficient way to proceed. Its usefulness also is greater for organizations that have a tight-knit constituency or that operate in a local community, where people are more likely to have more information about each other than they would in a large urban area or on a national basis.

Electronic database screening is a service provided by various companies. Names in the organization's database are matched against those in the service's database, which are collected from multiple public sources. The result is information about individuals' interests, assets, known philanthropic history, and other data. Some services also map individuals' relationships to other people, for example, through common board memberships (Wine, 2014). Some services also offer the ability to research specific names, at a lower cost than screening the organization's entire database. Although the cost can be considerable and some critics note inaccurate data resulting from electronic screening, it is a powerful tool that can help to narrow the number of potential prospects worthy of further investigation by the organization's own researchers (Wine, 2014).

A third research tool is **data mining** (Birkholz, 2008). Rather than matching its database against that of an outside company, the organization analyzes the data it already has regarding donors and prospects. The purpose is to identify patterns of donor behavior and then apply that insight to others in the constituency who might share characteristics associated with giving. Although data mining is used to identify potential major-gift prospects, it is also a useful tool in achieving efficiency in broad-based solicitation programs, by focusing on segments of the database deemed to have the highest likelihood of a positive response.

The field of **fundraising analytics**, which encompasses data mining, *pattern analysis*, and *predictive modeling*, has gained prominence as nonprofit organizations have worked to improve both the efficiency and effectiveness of their fundraising programs (Birkholz, 2008). This is essentially "moneyball" applied to fundraising. Various sophisticated tools are employed, including correlation and regression analysis. However, fundraising remains a combination of art and science. In assessing and developing a potential prospect's interest, there is no substitute for the judgment of an experienced fundraiser or a relationship cultivated over time.

So far this text has considered the unique characteristics of nonprofit organizations and their implications for fundraising, donor motivations, fundamental principles of fundraising, and actions an organization must undertake to prepare itself for successful fundraising. With this foundation in place, let's move on to look at the programs through which funds are solicited. The next chapter begins near the bottom of the pyramid, with annual giving. Subsequent chapters take us up the pyramid, to major and planned gifts.

CHAPTER SUMMARY

Fundraising begins with the organization itself. Before a nonprofit can successfully raise funds, it needs to clarify its mission and set program goals, determine its financial needs, develop a case for support, create a culture of fundraising, build a fundraising team, identify and research prospective donors, and develop a fundraising strategy and plan.

Some people criticize *strategic planning*, because it may not produce a strategy and may take considerable time and effort (La Piana, 2008). However, the process offers significant advantages to a nonprofit organization and provides a foundation for fundraising. It may help to develop internal consensus about goals, avoid *goal displacement* and *mission drift* due to *donor-driven* priorities, and reassure donors that the organization is well-managed.

The *case* is "the general argument for why a nonprofit deserves gift support" (Seiler & Aldrich, 2011, p. 27). It is also called the *case for support*. The *case statement* is a document that expresses the case. The *internal case statement* is a reference document that provides extensive information on the organization that is useful in developing proposals and other materials. The *external case statement* is a sales document that is usually produced as a brochure or electronically. A strong case for support starts with a purpose larger than the organization itself, establishes the organization's credibility and differentiates it from others, describes achievable program goals, justifies financial needs in terms of program goals and organizational strategy, and appeals to emotion as well as reason (Seiler & Aldrich, 2011).The term *culture of philanthropy* is used in this book to refer to organizational culture that influences fundraising effectiveness. Studies have found that many nonprofits lack such a culture (Bell & Cornelius, 2013). Strategies for changing the culture are derived from organizational theory and include creating artifacts that honor giving, the CEO's visible involvement and commitment to fundraising as a management function, producing short-term wins to build credibility and confidence, and involving people throughout the organization in fundraising.

Effective fundraising is a team effort, and the key players are the governing board, the CEO, and the chief development officer. Some authors view the board's involvement in fundraising as intrinsically linked to its broader governance responsibilities (Grossnickle,

2011), although fundraising is not a priority for boards at some types of organizations (Carver, 2006). The engagement of volunteers in solicitation helps to *authenticate* the organization's cause and mobilize the power of peer relationships. Various studies and surveys have revealed broad dissatisfaction with the fundraising performance of nonprofit boards (Moyers, 2011). Some actions taken to strengthen boards' performance include establishing a development committee and adopting policies that define board members' giving and participation in donor cultivation, solicitation, and stewardship (BoardSource, 2010).

An organization's constituency includes its stakeholders, who may be depicted in concentric circles around the core depending on their level of affiliation. Those who meet all three criteria of *linkage*, *ability*, and *interest* may be identified as *prospects* (Seiler, 2011a). Those who are determined to have ability, or financial capacity, are said to be *qualified*. Tools for identifying and researching potential prospects include *peer screening*, *electronic database screening*, and *fundraising analytics* or *data mining*. Prospect research is part of a process of prospect development, which includes the development of cultivation and solicitation strategies that reflect the *ratings* assigned to prospects based on capacity and *inclination* or *likelihood* (Birkholz, 2008).

A *fundraising strategy* defines the overall mix of solicitation programs, methods, techniques, and primary constituencies to be emphasized in order to meet an organization's financial needs. Two generic strategies include *ongoing programs* and *campaigns* (Dove, 2000). The organization's needs and characteristics of its constituency influence the fundraising strategy it adopts. For example, organizations whose prospects have income but limited assets may adopt a *high-volume/low-dollar* strategy while those with a smaller constituency that has wealth may adopt a *high-dollar/low-volume* major-gifts-focused strategy (Birkholz, 2008). A *fundraising plan* defines how the fundraising strategy will be implemented, including what activities will be undertaken, by whom, and on what schedule.

Key Terms and Concepts

Authenticates (case for support)	Development committee	High-dollar/ low-volume strategy
Campaigns	Electronic database screening	High-volume/ low-dollar strategy
Capacity		
Case/Case for support	External case statement	Inclination (or likelihood)
Case statement	Fundraising analytics	Internal case statement
Contact report		
Continuous programs	Fundraising plan	LAI (linkage, ability, interest)
Culture of philanthropy	Fundraising strategy	
Data mining	Give-or-get policy	

Ongoing major-gifts program	Qualifying the prospect	Strategic planning
Peer screening	Solicitation strategy	SWOT analysis
Prospect	Staff-driven	(strengths,
Prospect research	programs	weaknesses,
	Strategy	opportunities,
		threats)

Case 5.1: American Red Cross

The American Red Cross is one of the nation's largest nonprofit organizations, founded by Clara Barton in 1881 and chartered by the United States Congress in 1900. It "prevents and alleviates human suffering in the face of emergencies by mobilizing the power of volunteers and the generosity of donors" (American Red Cross website). The Red Cross is well known for its disaster relief services, which respond to major disasters, such as Hurricanes Katrina and Sandy, as well as local emergencies, such as house fires and floods. Equally well known are Red Cross blood services, which provide 40 percent of the nation's blood supply. Its programs also include support to military families and health and safety services, such as CPR training. The American Red Cross is also part of the global Red Cross and Red Crescent network that works to alleviate human suffering around the world. It has a unique responsibility to carry out the duties of the United States as a signatory to the Geneva Conventions (American Red Cross website).

The American Red Cross is headquartered in Washington, DC, and has about 600 chapters located in communities across the country, all of which operate under the same national charter. Total revenues were over $3.4 billion in 2013, including over $1 billion in gifts from corporations, foundations, and individual donors (American Red Cross, n.d.).

Although the Red Cross is a fundraising powerhouse, historically its fundraising program faced two challenges. First, there were sometimes tensions between the national office and local chapters regarding access to prospects and the allocation of gift revenue. Before 1998, the national office and chapters might both contact the same donors, a tactic a Red Cross fundraiser described as the "piranha approach" (Dickey, 1998). In order to reduce friction and achieve a more coordinated approach, new policies were established giving chapters the right to solicit donors in their area and requiring that the national office contact chapters in advance before doing so (Dickey, 1998). But tensions remained.

The second challenge was that donors would give in response to major disasters but then not continue their support in years when none occurred, making it difficult for the Red Cross to sustain ongoing programs and remain prepared for future disasters. For example, more than $1 billion was raised quickly after the terrorist attacks of 9/11 and $2 billion after Hurricane Katrina in 2006, but by 2008 the organization was facing deficits and the need to lay off one-third of its national headquarters staff. Although other forces were at work, including a national recession, some pointed to a need for the Red Cross to dramatically revise its fundraising strategy (Hall, 2009).

Gail McGovern became president of the Red Cross in 2008, with a background in business and finance. She reduced costs throughout the organization and eliminated the deficit by 2009 (American Red Cross website). And she worked with chapters to develop a new approach to fundraising.

In the past, chapters had raised money for their own needs and were also expected to raise money to meet the needs of major disasters elsewhere, but they did not get credit for gifts that people and companies in their area gave for the major disasters not in their community. So if they succeeded in raising funds for the larger effort, the result might be that they could not meet their own local needs. This was a source of friction and created competition between the national office and local chapters. Under a new arrangement that McGovern implemented, the chapters would raise money for their own needs as well as for major disasters in other areas and would get credit for all gifts. If gifts they raised toward national needs caused them to fall short on meeting local needs, national would make up the difference, thus eliminating competition (Hall, 2009).

A coordinated approach made it possible to develop more integrated relationships with donors. For example, as McGovern (n.d.) describes,

> Instead of different parts of the Red Cross approaching donors in different ways at various times, we are now working more collaboratively to connect donors with every part of our mission. One donor that has engaged with the Red Cross is Nationwide Insurance. The company supports our disaster response efforts, . . . has the only permanent corporate blood collection center in the country, and engages employees in the work of the Red Cross by offering CPR classes and involving them in our [other programs]. Our restructuring efforts will help us create more relationships like this in the future. (p. 2)

With increased expectations for their fundraising performance, chapters also would receive more help from the national Red Cross office. The national office assigned a fundraising professional to each of the regions to help chapters develop fundraising strategy and coach them on solicitations (West, 2012). New training programs were established to prepare chapter fundraisers, and such efforts showed quick results. For example, one local chapter sent its executive director and four board members to a two-day program and the board members each accepted responsibility for ten prospects whom they would solicit for a $1,000 gift (Hall, 2009). The allocation of functions between the national office and the chapters also was revised. As McGovern describes, back-office operations had been duplicated in the chapters. Moving those to the national office helped to gain efficiency while also freeing up the chapters' resources for fundraising.

A new annual giving program was implemented, with the goal of developing regular donors who would give every year even if there was no disaster (Hall, 2009; McGovern, n.d.). A new year-end solicitation included greeting cards for member of the military and veterans through a Holiday Mail for Heroes program and an appeal for blood donations. Annual Disaster Giving and Disaster Responder programs were established to develop regular corporate and foundation donors. The Tiffany Circle, composed of women donors, was expanded. New programs for recognition of annual-fund donors were established, including the Humanitarian Circle for donors of $10,000 to $24,999, the Leadership Society for donors of $25,000 to $99,000, and the President's Council for donors of $100,000 or more (American Red Cross website).

Not all problems were immediately solved, and change was not without controversy. Budget pressures required additional staff layoffs in 2011, and in 2013, the Red Cross received criticism for its fundraising in response to Hurricane Sandy. It responded to this criticism by clarifying the options offered to donors on its donation webpage (Caruso, 2013). To improve overall coordination and reduce costs throughout the organization, the number of chapters was reduced and local CEOs now report to nine regional division vice presidents. As one chapter executive described the change, "That was a cultural shift. . . . We have long been one 501(c)(3), but we were operating like multiple ones" (West, 2012). The overall reorganization met with some objections at the local level that had implications for fundraising. For example, board members at one chapter resigned in protest of what they saw as too much control by the national headquarters, and one local United Way refused to give, citing concern that the funds might leave the community (West, 2012).

Reflecting on her first five years as president in 2013, McGovern reported, "As we've increased teamwork and built new partnerships, both internally and externally, I have been awestruck by the unity shown by Red Crossers—from employees to volunteers to board members to donors. Because of their passion and commitment to our mission, we have made dramatic strides in strengthening the Red Cross" (McGovern, n.d., p. 2).

Questions for Discussion

1. How would you describe the Red Cross' culture of philanthropy before the changes discussed in the case? How do you think the changes undertaken will affect that culture?

2. In a few sentences, how would you summarize the case for an individual or company providing regular annual support to the American Red Cross, rather than just giving episodically when there is a disaster?

3. How would you briefly summarize the new fundraising strategy adopted by the American Red Cross starting in 2008?

4. Thinking back on the three pyramids discussed in Chapter 4, what was the shape of the Red Cross' pyramid before the changes described in the case, and how will it change if the new fundraising strategy is successful?

5. What is the Red Cross' constituency for fundraising? Which groups of individuals or organizational donors would be in each of the various concentric circles depicted in Figure 5.2?

Suggestions for Further Reading

Books

Birkholz, J. M. (2008). *Fundraising analytics: Using data to guide strategy.* Hoboken, NJ: Wiley.

Bryson, J. M. (2011). *Strategic planning for public and nonprofit organizations* (4th ed.). San Francisco: Jossey-Bass.

Hogan, C. (2008). *Prospect research: A primer for growing nonprofits.* Sudbury, MA: Jones and Bartlett.

Schein, E. H. (2010). *Organizational culture and leadership* (4th ed.). San Francisco: Jossey-Bass.

Walker, J. I. (2012). *A fundraising guide for nonprofit board members* (The AFP/Wiley Fund Development Series). Hoboken, NJ: Wiley.

Williams, K. A. (2013). *Leading the fundraising charge: The role of the nonprofit executive* (The AFP/Wiley Fund Development Series). Hoboken, NJ: Wiley.

Reports

Bell, J., & Cornelius, M. (2013). *UnderDeveloped: A national study of challenges facing nonprofit fundraising.* San Francisco: CompassPoint Nonprofit Services and the Evelyn and Walter Haas, Jr. Fund. http://www.compasspoint.org/sites/default/files/images/UnderDeveloped_CompassPoint_HaasJrFund_January%202013.pdf.

Moyers, R. (2011). *Daring to lead 2011 Brief #3: The board paradox.* San Francisco: CompassPoint Nonprofit Services and the Meyer Foundation. http://daringtolead.org/wp-content/uploads/Daring-Brief-3-080511.pdf.

Web Document

The operational plan: How to create a yearlong fundraising plan (2011/2012 ed.). Sioux City, IA: Stevenson. http://www.nonprofitalliance.org/system/res/135/original/tool_06.12.pdf.

Website

APRA (formerly Association of Professional Researchers for Advancement): http://www.aprahome.org.

Notes

1. Seiler and Aldrich (2011) use a somewhat different vocabulary than this text. What they call "the case for support" is referred to in this text as the internal case statement.

2. A more general statement would be that the three parties are the CEO, the chief development officer, and *volunteer leaders*. In some cases the primary volunteer leaders involved in fundraising might not be governing board members. For example, in a campaign, there might be a campaign leadership committee that plays that role. But members of the governing board are the organization's top volunteers so this discussion is focused on the board.

3. The terms *advisory council* and *advisory board* are both commonly used, often interchangeably. I prefer to use advisory *council* for a group that does not have governing responsibility, to distinguish it from a governing board that does (Worth, 2008).

4. Potential prospects who are "suspected" to have capacity and interest but who are not yet qualified are sometimes referred to as *suspects*. The prospect research community has made an effort to replace that term with the more respectful *potential prospects*. However, the term *suspects* is still frequently used in practice (Hogan, 2008).

CHAPTER 6

Annual-Giving Programs

Say *fundraising*, and many people think about receiving solicitations by snail mail or e-mail, likely in significant volumes at certain times of the year. Or they may have been invited to sponsor a friend's participation in a charity event, have attended a social event billed as a "fundraiser," or have been approached by a solicitor at their door or on the street. These perceptions of fundraising are understandable, since such broad-based programs reach the largest numbers of prospective donors and most people will never be engaged by a major-gifts program. The solicitations most people receive on a regular basis are sent in connection with an annual-giving program.

CLARIFICATION OF TERMS

It may be useful for us to understand some of the terms used with regard to annual-giving programs. Williams (2004) explains:

> The terms *annual fund* and *annual giving* have quite different meanings (a little like charity and philanthropy). The term annual fund . . . is generally used to refer to the kind of fund raising or the name of the fund itself. Traditionally, the annual fund was, and continues to be, a one-time volunteer assisted campaign effort, undertaken at the same time each year to generate annual contributions that are used to underwrite the annual operating budget of an organization. (p. 39)

Contrasting the annual fund with annual giving, Williams (2004) writes:

> Annual giving . . . better describes how many of the annual fund-raising efforts are designed today. Annual giving implies a broad range of activities that may be very different in size and scope, i.e., a personal solicitation campaign for board members or a special event to solicit parents of students. . . . These activities may be implemented throughout the year and raise funds for both general operating purposes and special needs. (p. 39)

Alexander and Carlson (2005) define the **annual campaign** similarly to Williams's annual fund, emphasizing the involvement of volunteers. As Williams notes, the terms *annual fund* and *annual campaign* are almost synonymous.

In common usage, many people simply refer to the larger concept that Williams describes as the **annual-giving program** and to the money that it produces as the **annual fund**, with the latter having different definitions in various organizations, some including only unrestricted gifts and others including all gifts available to support current programs, even if designated. That is generally how the terms are used in this text.

The term *annual fund* in its broader meaning has its origins in higher education (Williams, 2004). Indeed, the tradition in raising annual gifts for colleges and universities always has focused on the amount of the gift, usually with only one solicitation per year. This makes sense for educational institutions; alumni are the most important but also a relatively finite constituency, so the risk of alienation from oversolicitation could be high. Other types of nonprofit organizations often do solicit gifts more frequently than once per year, but Burk (2013) emphasizes the risks in that approach. In one health care institution she studied, some donors had become confused by the frequency of solicitations. Some forgot that they had made a gift recently and thus responded again to a subsequent mailing but felt they had been "duped" into giving on discovering the error.

Next to earned income, annual gifts are the largest source of unrestricted revenue and are for some nonprofit organizations a critical component of the operating budget. But, as mentioned previously, some organizations may define the annual fund to include some restricted gifts that support current programs. This might be the case, for example, for larger organizations, including universities, with diverse funding sources and budget flexibility. They may view restricted gifts that support budgeted activities to be as useful as unrestricted gifts, since they free up funds for reallocation; such gifts are said to be **budget-relieving** (Jarrell, 2013).

In addition to generating needed revenue, a broad-based annual-giving program provides a front door for first-time donors and a vehicle for establishing a pipeline of potential major-gift prospects. Annual giving is the bedrock of philanthropy for most nonprofit organizations.

APPLYING MARKETING PRINCIPLES

Think back on the discussion in Chapter 1 about whether fundraising is a specialty of marketing and Paton's (2007) argument that marketing is more relevant to some types of gifts than to others. Annual-giving programs are one component of fundraising that indeed draws substantially from the field of marketing. Such programs use the methods of **direct-response marketing**, including direct mail, phone solicitation, and e-mail. As the term implies, a characteristic of direct-response marketing is that it includes a means of *response*—a means of making a gift—for example, a reply envelope, a link to a website, or the opportunity to provide a credit card number to a caller (Sargeant, Shang, et al., 2010). Events also play an important role in raising current operating funds for many nonprofit organizations, and some annual-giving programs include personal solicitations, especially at the leadership gift level (Lowman, 2012). Advertising is a method of direct-response marketing used by some charities—generally large national organizations. The advertisement directs the listener to a webpage or points to some other way to make a gift (Sargeant, Shang, et al., 2010).

This chapter discusses the principal methods of direct-response solicitation, but discussion of personal solicitation is deferred to Chapter 7, where it is considered in the context of major-gifts programs. This text does not consider grassroots techniques such as personal solicitations undertaken door-to-door or on the street, which are used by some nonprofit organizations.

Direct-response fundraising is the most scientific component of an organization's fundraising program, making use of analytics and modeling techniques discussed in Chapter 5. As marketing scholars Sargeant, Shang, et al. (2010) explain,

> Direct-response activity has the advantage of being infinitely measurable. Whereas mass marketers can only make educated guesses about the impact of a traditional advertising campaign, the customer response to most forms of direct marketing can be measured to one, two, or even three decimal places. Opportunities for testing abound and direct-response marketers rolling out an expensive campaign are now in a position to predict with high accuracy the response that will ultimately be achieved. (pp. 240–241)

Fundraisers using direct-response methods can control which messages are sent to specific **segments** of the database, identified on the basis of common characteristics. They can test various messages, measure results, and adjust subsequent communications in order to develop an ongoing relationship with each donor.

ACQUISITION, RENEWAL, UPGRADE

The annual-giving program has three principal objectives: the **acquisition** of new, first-time donors; the **renewal** of support in subsequent years, that is, developing regular donors; and **upgrading** gifts, that is, increasing them from year to year, moving donors toward the major-gifts level (Ciconte & Jacob, 2009; Williams, 2004).

Acquisition

Acquiring a new donor, also called **converting** a nondonor into a donor, is a critical first step. First-time donors are most likely to be found within the organization's constituency, and the rate of response to a solicitation is likely to be higher in circles closer to the core rather than in those that are more remote (Seiler, 2011a). In other words, members, volunteers, current and former clients, and client family members usually can be converted to donors at lower cost than prospects who have only a general interest in the mission of the organization. However, nonprofit organizations do explore for new donors beyond their own constituencies.

Profiling and Targeting

An organization seeking new donors uses **profiling** and **targeting** to maximize the effectiveness of solicitations. It develops a profile of its typical donor and then solicits others who have similar characteristics. One relevant variable may be **geographic** location. For example, a nonprofit serving a particular community or neighborhood, and drawing most of its donors from that area, would be most likely to attract new donors from that same area. Lists also may be selected according to **demographic** criteria, for example, age, gender, or income, again depending on the characteristics of the organization's current donor database. Individuals also may be selected based on **psychographic** characteristics, such as "personality traits, values, lifestyles, or a combination of these elements" (Sargeant, Shang, et al., p. 160). In this context, *lifestyle* refers to an individual's overall patterns, including interests, activities, reading choices, opinions, and so forth.

Putting these characteristics together may help to identify individuals more likely to become donors to a particular nonprofit organization than others who have different profiles. For example, it should not be surprising that a young, single person who lives in a city, uses public transportation, likes hip-hop, and receives news from the Internet might tend to support different causes than an older couple who live in the suburbs, drive an SUV, listen to classical music, and watch the network evening news. Remember from our discussion in Chapter 3 that this type of analysis is based on donor behavior and does not necessarily include any insight on motivations. In other words, if a certain type of individual responds to a certain solicitation, it is statistically more probable that others who are similar will respond as well, but we may not know, or really care, for what reasons. Understanding motivation is less important than the numbers at this level of the pyramid and, of course, more important with regard to major gifts.

Acquisition by Mail

Donors may be acquired using various methods, including events, telephone solicitations, and online. Although online giving is growing rapidly, direct mail is still a principal method for acquiring donors for many organizations. In 2010, 16 percent of new donors gave online, while 76 percent used mail and 8 percent some other offline method. However, the percentage of new gifts made online increased from 9 percent to 16 percent just within the period from 2007 to 2010 (Flannery & Harris, 2011). In 2013 alone, online giving grew by 13.5 percent but still accounted for only 6.4 percent of philanthropy (Sharf, 2014). In a 2014 survey, most Millennials reported that they were most likely to give using a mobile phone, suggesting that online giving is likely to dominate in the future (Sharf, 2014). But, for now, direct mail remains important. As discussed later in this chapter, many organizations are pursuing **multichannel strategies** during this time of transition.

Some organizations share, or swap, mailing lists of donors, based on the assumption that donors who support one may support another in a similar field. The practice is, understandably, controversial. Others rent or purchase mailing lists, including individuals who fit the desired profile, from commercial **list brokers**. Donors acquired through a mailing to such a list are then incorporated into the organization's own database for resolicitation in the future.

One downside of acquiring new donors from **cold lists**—that is, lists of people not already a part of the organization's constituency—is high cost. Because the targeted individuals have no specific relationships to the organization, the **conversion rate** may be relatively low. First-time gifts may be relatively modest. Indeed, the cost of acquiring a new donor commonly exceeds the amount of the donor's first gift; in other words, solicitations aimed at acquiring new donors may be operated at a loss. So why engage in this activity at all? Because money spent to acquire a new donor should be viewed as an investment in the future of the organization's fundraising program. If the donor's giving is renewed and upgraded in future years, the relationship becomes, in essence, an income-producing asset of the organization. In other words, the appropriate measure of donor acquisition should not be the immediate return but the **lifetime value** of the relationship, that is, the total the donor may be expected to give over the entire length of his or her relationship with the organization (Lindahl, 2010; Sargeant & Jay, 2004). Various methodologies and formulas can be applied to estimating lifetime value in order to correctly evaluate the return on investment in acquisition activities (see, for example, Sargeant, Shang, et al., 2010).

Acquisition by E-Mail

E-mail is a less expensive method of acquiring donors than direct mail. However, e-mail and text messages, especially when sent to a mobile device, may be more intrusive than regular mail and may not be well received by the prospective donor if that individual does not have a previous relationship with the organization. In addition, sending cold e-mail requires some legal caution. Two laws, the Telephone Consumer Protection Act (TCPA) and the Controlling the Assault of Non-Solicited Pornography and Marketing Act (CAN-SPAM), make it illegal to send unwanted commercial e-mail and text messages. The laws apply to commercial messages and may not apply to much of the mail a nonprofit would send, but if the message includes a commercial offer it could be problematic, both legally and in terms of the negative impressive on the person who receives it (FCC, 2014).

Retention

It is generally more cost-effective to renew and upgrade a donor than to acquire a new one. For that reason, donor retention has received increased emphasis in many fundraising programs. As Burk (2003) explains, "Retained donors are increasingly cost-effective over time because they tend to give more while requiring less investment based on cost-per-dollar raised. Maximizing return on investment from a manageable number of donors within a portfolio of fundraising programs is the key to success" (p. 96).

There is a hierarchy of cost-effective groups available for solicitation. The highest priority might be given to resolicitation of current donors and to those who gave in the previous year but who have not yet done so in the current year, known as **LYBUNTS** (last year but unfortunately not this). Donors who have lapsed in their giving may be reactivated at lower cost than those who have never given. Annual giving professionals use a variety of acronyms to identify segments of their lists to be targeted. Among other groups commonly identified are those who have given in some past year but unfortunately not this year

(**SYBUNTS**) and those who gave at some time in the past five years but unfortunately not this year (**FYBUNTS**) (Warwick, 2011).

Lists of previous donors targeted for resolicitation also are sometimes segmented according to *recency* (date of last gift), *frequency* (how often they give), *giving level* (dollar amount of previous gifts), and *source of first gift* (for example, mail, phone, Internet) (Warwick, 2011). Additional criteria for identifying segments might include **cumulative giving**, **longevity** (number of years given), *giving designations* (if any), *linkage and affiliation* with the organization, and *ability* or capacity (Williams, 2004). Segmenting in this way can help to determine the most effective solicitation methods to be used and the messages to be delivered to donors demonstrating various characteristics.

While renewal is more cost-effective than acquisition, attrition rates are high. As Burk (2003) observes, "About 50 percent of donors do not renew their gifts after making a first contribution and, by the time of the fifth [subsequent solicitation], about 90 percent have stopped giving to the charities that once elicited their support" (p. 19). This attrition represents a significant loss of potential revenue for nonprofit organizations, and since it requires continuing expensive efforts to acquire new donors, it drives up the overall cost of fundraising. The reasons are reported to be a lack of stewardship and continuing communication with donors. As Burk (2003) reports from her study:

> 46 percent of donors surveyed indicated that they had stopped giving to an organization because they lacked information on how their gifts were used or felt unappreciated, while 93 percent said they would give again if they were provided sufficient information and 74 percent said they would continue giving indefinitely if the organization continued to provide the information they desired. (p. 23)

Pressures to increase the effectiveness of fundraising programs have led to an increased emphasis on **donor retention**, that is, the avoidance of donor attrition. This has included an expanding body of scholarly research on the topic (e.g., Aron, 2007; Shapiro, 2008) and the introduction of innovative techniques. For example, nonprofit For Love of Children (FLOC) trains every member of its staff to be able to tell the organization's story and monitors social media to identify individuals who can be recruited to serve as online ambassadors (Dixon & Keyes, 2013). Other organizations have implemented a program of **loyalty calls**, that is, phone calls to donors that do not include a solicitation but simply provide information (Holloway, 2013). The emphasis on retention has been reflected in the growth of development office staff positions and resources dedicated to donor relations, stewardship, and communications, which have become identifiable professional specialties.

Upgrading

In addition to retaining donors, annual-giving programs employ various techniques to encourage increased giving from current donors. As explained, increased giving over time from regular donors has a significant impact on the cost-effectiveness of an annual-giving program overall. Annual giving follows the principles of the giving pyramid discussed in

Chapter 4. That means that Pareto's principle applies. The smaller number of donors who have been upgraded to high levels will account for a larger percentage of total gifts than the larger number of smaller donors at lower levels (Williams, 2004). For that reason, upgrading is central to building a cost-effective program over time.

Asking for the Increase

The simplest strategy for upgrading is, of course, to ask explicitly for a larger gift. As Warwick (2013) describes with regard to direct-mail solicitations, "A true upgrade letter lays out a set of reasons why the donor should give more—and the argument to give more is a central theme in the copy, not an afterthought" (p. 207). Upgrade letters typically suggest a range of gifts, including some higher than the donor's **highest previous contribution (HPC)**.

Prospects deemed capable of giving at the leadership level of annual giving may be removed from regular direct-marketing solicitations and targeted for upgrading through personal solicitation, either by volunteers or specially assigned leadership annual-giving staff (Lowman, 2012).

Giving Clubs and Societies

Many upgrade solicitations emphasize the opportunity to be recognized as a member of a **giving club** or **giving society** (Warwick, 2013). *Giving clubs, giving societies, gift clubs, gift societies*—these terms are used interchangeably—are devices for recognizing donors in levels, according to the amount of their gifts. The use of giving societies is also sometimes known as a *graded recognition program* (Burk, 2003). In addition to gift amount, some organizations have clubs to recognize donors based on other characteristics of their giving history. For example, some organizations have societies to recognize donors by the number of consecutive years in which they have given, to recognize those who have subscribed to monthly giving, or to recognize donors according to the total of their cumulative lifetime giving. Others have clubs or societies to recognize donors who have bequest intentions or other planned-giving arrangements to benefit the organization. Many annual-giving clubs use common names, for example, Patrons, Sponsors, Friends, or are named for officers of the organization, for example, the Chairman's Club, the President's Club, the Director's Circle, and such.

The clubs provide a way to somewhat soften the solicitation of an increased gift. For example, rather than saying, "We hope you will increase your gift from $100 to $250 this year," a letter or an e-mail might be worded like an invitation: "We appreciate your membership in the President's Club and hope that you will be able to join others as a member of the Chairman's Club this year."

Membership in some clubs provides nothing more than listing in an annual report, on a website, or perhaps in a program; it is synonymous with recognition and provides no tangible benefit. These listings are sometimes identified as **honor roles**, perhaps invoking the lists on which our parents wanted us to appear as high school students. Box 6.1 provides an example of a typical array of gift societies, offered by the Meriter–UnityPoint Health System in Wisconsin, to recognize annual as well as other types of gifts.

> **BOX 6.1**   Meriter–UnityPoint Health
>
> ### Donor Recognition Societies
> #### Annual Giving
>
> Our annual giving contributors of $500 and more are recognized on a donor wall in the main lobby of Meriter Hospital.
>
> - Circle of Care: $500–$999
> - Circle of Health: $1,000–$2,499
> - Circle of Life: $2,500–$4,999
> - Meriter Society: $5,000–$9,999
> - Leaders of Vision: $10,000 and above
>
> #### Cumulative Giving
>
> Donors whose cumulative giving exceeds $25,000 may designate a room or area of the Hospital in their name or in honor of a loved one.
>
> ### Legacy Society
>
> We are grateful to individuals who include Meriter in their estate plans. Gifts such as these have been an instrumental source of support for capital projects, establishing educational initiatives and endowing programs.

Source: Meriter–UnityPoint Health website, http://foundation.meriter.com/our-donors/donor-recognition.

Other gift clubs offer an array of articulated benefits, including attendance at events, free admission or discounts, or access to senior officers of the organization. This approach is common at performing arts institutions. But it may not be the best approach for other types of nonprofits. Think back on our discussion in Chapter 3 about the risk of offering tangible benefits. Too much emphasis on benefits could convert a philanthropic action into a pure exchange in the perception of the donor, possibly undermining the effort to upgrade giving. If membership in a giving society provides only recognition, donors may see the various levels as a way of gauging their interest and also of determining an appropriate amount to give. If they see others whom they know listed at certain levels, social influences may encourage some donors to select a place among their peers. However, if membership brings tangible benefits, it could cause donors to make a different calculation, perhaps thinking about giving more like a quid pro quo transaction and evaluating the gift against the benefits received rather than the benefits provided to others (Bekkers & Wiepking, 2011). Providing tangible benefits to gift club members also may have tax implications. If a donor makes a payment that brings a benefit of substantial value, the fair market value of that benefit is not deductible. For example, if a donor gives $100 but receives a ticket to a concert that is worth $40, that is considered a **quid pro quo contribution**. The donor can only claim a charitable gift deduction for $60. Benefits of **insubstantial value** do not pose a problem (IRS, 2014b). Nonprofit organizations need to consult legal counsel concerning the implications of these rules in the context of their own programs.

Do gift societies work; is this an effective strategy for upgrading? In Burk's (2003) study, 71 percent of donors reported that having their names listed by gift level does not cause them to give more than they otherwise would have done, and 58 percent reported that the listing does not cause them to maintain their gift level if they had been considering a reduction. Of course, self-reports by donors may or may not reflect actual behavior. Burk concludes that the use of gift clubs and societies may have a positive influence on some donors and likely does no harm. But she urges fundraisers to be mindful of the time and resources devoted to such programs and notes one potential downside, the possibility that listing at a certain level may result in a donor being "locked into a giving ceiling, when [the donor] could have given much more" (p. 126). In that case, the gift club structure would negatively affect the effort to upgrade.

Matching Gifts

The use of **matching gifts** or **challenge gifts** is not strictly a strategy for upgrading, since it is sometimes employed in soliciting first-time gifts as well. But one purpose of a matching gift is to motivate donors to give *more*, based on the understanding that the impact of their gifts will be leveraged by a match from another donor.[1] Such an offer generally has a dollar limit and a time limit, for example, stating that Donor X will match gifts up to a total of $10,000 made this year.

Cialdini and Martin (2006) offer theoretical support for the challenge gift strategy. Among several principles of effective persuasion, they identify scarcity and social proof, arguing that people tend to want something that is available for only a limited time and tend to look to others as a guide to their own behavior. A challenge gift limited to a specific period of time and offered by a donor who brings an element of prestige would meet both tests. But does the strategy work in practice? Research suggests that the answer is yes, with some caveats.

The effectiveness of matching gifts has been studied by economists. Remember from the discussion in Chapter 3 that economists predict that changing the cost of a gift will affect how much donors give. In that discussion the cost was related to the income tax deduction, which lowers the out-of-pocket cost of giving a certain dollar amount, thus enabling a donor to give more in nominal terms. A matching gift would also affect the cost of a gift in a somewhat different way. If a donor can give $1 but have $2 of impact, because another donor is matching the gift dollar for dollar, that is like achieving $2 of impact for half the cost. It might thus seem logical that a larger match—say that every gift of $1 is now matched with an additional $2—would provide an even greater incentive, since $3 of impact now could be achieved for only $1 out of pocket; in other words, the cost of the impact has been further reduced.

Much of the practitioner literature asserts that a higher match will motivate more giving. But, in a field experiment using direct mail, economists Karlan and List (2007) reached a different conclusion. The researchers found that the offer of a matching gift does indeed increase the revenue per solicitation and the response rate. However, increasing the match ratio from 1-to-1 ($1 matches $1) to a higher ratio, for example, matching each $1 with $2 or $3, does not have any additional impact.

In order for a challenge gift to be an ethical strategy, the challenge needs to be real. In other words, just saying there is a challenge gift when there is not is a lie and never acceptable. Approaching a donor who has already given and asking that donor to retroactively designate his or her gift as a challenge is unethical, since the gift is really not conditional on what others give and telling others that it is would be a lie.

Sometimes organizations announce challenge gifts from anonymous donors or from groups of individuals (for example, the board). If there really is such a donor and the challenge gift is indeed conditional on what others give, then this is not unethical. But it may not have as much credibility as a challenge from a donor who is identified.

Designated Purposes

Some experts (e.g., Burk, 2003, 2013) argue that one way to increase the amount of gifts is to permit donors to designate specific purposes for their gifts, on the assumption that supporting something specific is more satisfying than making an unrestricted gift toward the organization's general needs. And designated gifts may be just as useful as unrestricted gifts if they are budget relieving, that is, designated to support activities the nonprofit was intending to undertake in any event. Some donors may find it difficult to relate an unrestricted gift to any tangible impact that they might find satisfying. Observing that reality, Burk (2013) argues that most nonprofits offer the opportunity to designate a gift only to larger donors when it should be offered to donors at all levels as a strategy for building loyalty. However, she notes that there may be resistance to designated giving on the part of many nonprofit managers, based on the commonly held view that it restricts the organization's flexibility and places too much power in the hands of donors. She disputes those assumptions and advises that the options offered to donors reflect the organization's needs and priorities as identified in its strategic plan.

One technique organizations employ is to identify specific needs that are *equivalent* to gifts at various levels. Donor gifts are not restricted to these specific purposes—they are made to an unrestricted annual fund—but using examples helps to convey the impact of gifts at each level. Box 6.2 is an example of this technique as employed by Food & Friends, a nonprofit that prepares and delivers specialized meals and groceries in conjunction with nutrition counseling to people living with HIV/AIDS, cancer, and other life-challenging illnesses. Food & Friends' listing of opportunities is related to *monthly giving*. Donors may find this approach attractive, and offering it can be a useful strategy for upgrading, since a donor may find a larger gift to be less onerous if it can be spread out in smaller monthly amounts.

In a variation of the same idea, Urban Ministries of Durham, in North Carolina, took a humorous approach in 2014, promoting "names for change" on its website. Some of the opportunities for naming included physical facilities and major equipment items (for example, a pantry, a garden, a room), but others were common, everyday items. The latter included light bulbs ($2 gift), washcloths ($5 gift), and brooms ($20 gift). The use of gifts was not restricted to the particular items, which were merely symbolic, but the donors

---

BOX 6.2 Food & Friends: Monthly Giving Opportunities

Illness is a Year-Round Battle. Join Our Bread & Butter Monthly Giver Club.

Bread & Butter Club monthly givers guarantee Food & Friends regular and predictable funds. These donations allow us to respond immediately and year-round to those living with HIV/AIDS, cancer and other life-challenging illnesses.

See how far your monthly gift can go for a person in need.

Become a Bread & Butter Monthly Giver TODAY!

$15 a Month
The food needed to make comforting soups and stews for 9 meals.

$30 a Month
2 First Day Deliveries - delivered by Food & Friends staff who can answer questions and be a friendly ear.

$60 a Month
One month of renal supplements for a client living with AIDS and undergoing dialysis for kidney failure.

$150 a Month
Groceries and freshly-prepared meals for a month for a child living with cancer and her grandmother, her primary caregiver.

Source: Adapted from http://www.foodandfriends.org/site/pp.asp?c=ckLSI8NNIdJ2G&b=7565877.

---

received certificates that could be shared on social media, recognizing for example, "the (name) fruit cocktail." The campaign was reported to have raised almost $50,000 ("The Twist," 2014).

SOLICITATION METHODS

In Chapter 4, we briefly considered the principal solicitation methods applied in the annual-giving program—direct mail, phone solicitation, events, and electronic communication—and some best practices that practitioners and researchers recommend. Now let's look at those methods in more detail. We also look briefly at some additional methods, including crowdfunding, social media, and text messaging, although most nonprofits have yet to fully adopt them in connection with soliciting regular gifts to the annual fund. Each of the principal methods has advantages and disadvantages, as summarized in Box 6.3.

Personal solicitation is the most effective method of soliciting a gift (Rosso, 2003). It is just more difficult to ignore or give fleeting attention to a human being who is sitting in your presence. A personal conversation is the most effective way to build a relationship and offers the opportunity to read nonverbal cues as well as words spoken, enabling the solicitor to adjust the message and tone of the discussion in real time. However, personal

	BOX 6.3 Common Methods: Advantages and Disadvantages	
Method	**Advantages**	**Disadvantages**
Personal solicitation	• Focused attention of prospect • Includes nonverbal cues • Builds relationship	• Expensive • Low volume
Direct mail	• Inexpensive • Creates a visual image • Long life (may be kept and read again later) • Can communicate complex message	• Easily ignored, lost in clutter • Requires donor initiative to make gift • Limited ability to personalize
Phone	• Two-way communication • Can negotiate gift • Can tailor message to individual • Immediate gift (credit/debit card)	• More expensive than mail • Barriers (caller ID, mobile phones) • Intrusive
Events	• Visibility/involvement • May provide first contact with potential new donors	• Often not cost-effective (hidden costs) • Often the event makes no connection to the case
Electronic communication (e-mail)	• Inexpensive • Can personalize/segment message • Interactive/relationship building • Immediate gift	• E-mail list maintenance • Barriers (e.g., spam filters, overload)

Source: Adapted from Worth (2014), pp. 275–276.

solicitations involve significant cost, especially if undertaken by paid staff, and can be completed only in relatively low volume. For that reason, they are appropriate only for major gifts or, in the annual-giving program, gifts at the leadership level.

Direct mail is less expensive than personal solicitation and provides a physical item—the package mailed—in the hands of a prospective donor. The recipient is forced to pay at least some fleeting attention—he or she must at least look at the outside envelope before discarding it. And the donor can put the mailing aside to be considered further at a later time; in other words, the solicitation can have a long life. This may be an advantage over e-mail, which is, perhaps, more readily deleted.

Direct mail also offers the opportunity to communicate a complex message and include visual features, such as photographs. And technology permits letters to be highly personalized, with salutations and the inserting of specific data, such as the individual's previous gift. However, mail provides a passive solicitation. The donor reads it alone; there is no opportunity for real-time dialogue or for a solicitor to address donor questions or concerns. The donor must take some initiative to make the gift, either writing and mailing a check or going to the organization's website. That creates the risk that even the intention to give may be overtaken by more pressing events and that the gift therefore is never completed.

Soliciting gifts by phone is more expensive than using the mail, since it requires lower volume, but it offers some of the advantages of personal solicitation at less cost. The solicitor can develop a relationship and tailor the message to the individual's reactions. And the gift can be obtained at the point of solicitation. But, as most people would agree, phone solicitation can be intrusive, and there are significant barriers posed by phone technology and the prevalence of mobile phones.

As discussed further later, events can be effective for prospect identification, cultivation, solicitation, and stewardship, if properly planned and executed. But events intended to raise funds from gifts or from the proceeds of ticket sales, entry fees, or other types of payments must be carefully evaluated. In many cases, the costs of producing the event may be high, especially when associated overhead costs are considered.

Electronic communications are often used to promote events. In addition, emerging techniques such as crowdfunding and peer-to-peer solicitation are growing. However, the most commonly used online solicitation method is e-mail, which combines some of the advantages of direct mail and phone solicitation, at lower cost than either of those methods. However, the volume of e-mail accumulating in in-boxes is so substantial that one message can easily be deleted, even unintentionally. Like a direct-mail package, an e-mail can be put aside for later consideration. However, once it slips off the current screen, it may become less of a reminder than an envelope that remains physically on the donor's desk or kitchen counter. In addition, spam filters are raising obstacles similar to those that voice-mail systems have presented to telemarketing.

Some organizations have been successful with solicitations sent using text messages to mobile phones. However, this method is intrusive and currently presents other limitations, including barriers to identifying donors for follow-up communication. However, it is a new technology that may be refined and improved in the future.

So, what is the best method or methods to use? There is obviously no one right answer; the decision requires balancing cost and effectiveness and understanding the communication preferences and behavior of the donor segments to be addressed. In today's environment, nonprofit organizations are being advised to communicate using multiple methods. That is a topic to which this chapter returns shortly. First, let's take a closer look at each of the principal methods in turn.

Direct Mail

Direct-mail solicitations still account for the largest number of annual gifts. And the creation of direct-mail packages remains at least partly an art. According to Mal Warwick (2013), one of the best-known practitioners of direct mail and a prolific writer,

> If fundraising by mail is a science (a dubious proposition at best), its fuzziest, most inexact, least scientific aspect is writing the letters. There are those in the field who claim fundraising letters can be written by formula, but I'm not one of them. Writing this stuff is tough work because what's effective for one organization may prove counterproductive for another. And what worked last year or last time may not work today. (p. 1)

A solicitation by direct mail typically includes a **package** of materials, all of which are strategically designed, including the outside envelope (also called the *carrier envelope*), a reply envelope and card (also called a *response device*), and the solicitation letter. Some also include a brochure or other inserts intended to gain involvement, offer an endorsement, provide further information, or create an incentive to respond (Warwick, 2013). The latter sometimes includes a gift, such as address labels or a bookmark, called a **front-end premium**. Other mail solicitations offer a gift to be sent to the donor after a gift has been made; this is known as a **back-end premium**.

The creation of a direct mail letter is about appearance as well as words. Such letters usually reflect rules recommended by Warwick (2013): indent every paragraph; avoid paragraphs more than seven lines long; vary the length of paragraphs; use bullets and indented paragraphs; in long letters, use subheads that are centered and underlined. The writing style effective in direct mail also has particular characteristics, including frequent use of the words *I* and *You*; simple, straightforward language; use of colloquialisms, clichés, and figures of speech; repetition of points; and conversational sentence structure and punctuation that many English teachers would likely correct (Warwick, 2013).

Despite Warwick's emphasis on the art of direct mail, his recommendations and those of other practitioners do have support in theory and research. In the classic book *Handbook of Direct Mail*, German marketing professor Sigfried Vögele (1992) described the pattern of a reader's eye movement over the pages of a letter and identified phases in the reader's process during which the solicitation might be rejected. Vögele emphasized the first twenty seconds of the reader's interaction with the package, during which he or she may proceed to open the envelope or discard it. His principles are reflected in the design of direct-mail packages, which include attention to all elements, including the carrier envelope and the letter. Numerous studies have built on Vögele's work, and recent scholars have extended it to the design of e-mail communications and webpages.

More recently, experiments undertaken by Goering, Connor, Nagelhout, and Steinberg (2011) confirmed that letters written in a highly readable style and that include bulleted items produce the highest level of gifts. Moreover, the researchers found that effective letters included the rhetorical elements of a strong case, as discussed in Chapter 5: "rational appeals (arguments based on logical reasoning through the presentation of facts and causal relationships), credibility appeals (arguments based on the authority of the writer) and affective appeals (arguments targeting the reader's emotions)" (Goering et al., 2011).

Although the principles about what makes an effective direct-mail letter are well-established, those who are not professional fundraisers may sometimes be hesitant to embrace the style. For example, some executives of educational institutions and nonprofit organizations may be uncomfortable with the emotional tone and unique style of a solicitation letter, particularly if it will bear their signatures. Some would prefer to write a more formal, thoughtful, reasoned letter, explaining the organization's achievements in a tone more suited to an annual report and, some may feel, more appropriate for the leader of an organization. The initial concern is understandable. One way to address such concerns might be to undertake a test in which the CEO's preferred letter is mailed to a sample of prospective donors, while a more typical direct-mail letter is mailed to another sample, with the results in gifts to be compared. In most instances, the results are likely to confirm the principles of effective direct-mail fundraising, possibly persuading the executives to agree to a different approach.

Characteristics of direct-mail content, many of which also apply to online fundraising, have been identified in multiple studies. Solicitations that feature individuals in need are more effective than those that describe groups in statistical terms (Cryder, Loewenstein, & Scheines, 2012). Andresen (2006) offers an example. A relief and development organization for which she worked sent out a direct-mail solicitation that featured the organization's food programs, including a photo of a girl holding an empty bowl. It was tested against an alternative, which "described the program department's passions—community-development projects, sustainability, and self-help." As she describes the results, "Guess what? 'Empty bowl' trounced the community-development appeal when the dollars were counted. Why? People gave to our organization because they wanted to feel they had made an immediate difference in response to a real person's acute need" (p. 142).

This book does not provide examples of direct-mail materials. Some are provided in Warwick's 2013 book, which is listed as suggested reading at the end of this chapter. Students also may find examples arriving in their mailboxes, especially near the end of the year; analyzing their design and content can be an informative and interesting pastime.

Phone Solicitation

Many nonprofit organizations solicit gifts by phone. In the commercial sector, this practice is called *telemarketing*; sometimes that term is commonly used in fundraising as well. A telephone campaign also is sometimes called a **phonathon**. Usually, a phonathon is a time-limited effort, undertaken at certain times of the year, rather than an ongoing program.

Phone campaigns are sometimes undertaken by volunteers and sometimes by paid callers, who may be employees of the organization or employees of a commercial telemarketing firm. There are advantages and disadvantages of both approaches. Professional callers are likely to be more efficient, completing more calls, and the content of their conversations can be controlled with scripting and careful management. However, some donors may find such calls to be impersonal and, in addition, the engagement of volunteers in phonathons also may help to increase their own awareness of the organization's fundraising needs.

Nonprofits use phone calls to acquire, renew, and upgrade donors. Broad-based phone solicitation for the purpose of acquiring new donors follows principles similar to those of direct mail using cold lists. The organization profiles its current donors and then targets phone calls to individuals with similar characteristics, using lists that may be rented or purchased. Of course, these campaigns are often the most costly element in an organization's fundraising program and often the subject of criticism, especially when a substantial portion of the funds raised is offset by fees charged by a commercial telemarketing firm.

A 2012 study by the New York attorney general's office found that the nonprofit organization involved had received less than one-half of the funds raised in 78 percent of phone campaigns conducted in the state (Perry, 2013). As discussed, it may be acceptable to break even or lose money on acquiring new donors if those donors then can be renewed and upgraded, keeping overall fundraising costs within reasonable limits over time.

On the other hand, there have been examples of inappropriate, even illegal practices that are not justifiable under any scenario. While high costs are not per se illegal, such cases have been the basis for several media stories exposing unethical telemarketing practices, which have tainted the field (Cohen, 2013). The DMA (Direct Marketing Association) has developed ethical principles that address the use of direct-marketing methods, including phone solicitation, and there are laws in most states that also govern the practice (DMA, 2013).

Like direct-mail fundraising, telephone solicitation combines science and art. Especially when callers are trained, conversations follow carefully crafted scripts that reflect principles of interpersonal communications theory. For example, research suggests that people will respond more favorably when first asked how they feel. Most will say that they feel "fine" or "OK," which then predisposes them to a positive attitude toward the conversation (Simmel & Berger, 2000). Asking this question first, which many phone solicitors do, is called the **foot-in-the-mouth technique**. The **foot-in-the-door** technique involves starting with small requests, then working up to something more substantial (Dillard & Knoblock, 2011). For example, the caller may ask the prospect to verify his or her name and address before moving on to ask for a gift. This technique is based on the theory that individuals are more likely to comply with a request if they already have complied with an earlier one. The **door-in-the-face** technique involves starting with a high request, which the individual is likely to deny, then asking for something less. The theory suggests that people may wish to please the caller with a positive answer, having initially given a negative response (Dillard & Knobloch, 2011.) Many of us may feel uncomfortable about these techniques, which sound disingenuous and manipulative, but there is evidence that they are effective and they are applied in many telephone solicitations (Simmel & Berger, 2000). With knowledge of these principles, students who receive such a call may find it entertaining to stay on the line to see if the solicitor seems to follow a script that reflects them.

Events

As stated earlier, events may be conducted with one of four objectives: **prospect identification**, **cultivation**, **solicitation**, or **stewardship**. It is critical to have a clear objective in mind when the event is planned and to evaluate its success against that objective. As shown in Table 6.1, the financial implications and evaluation criteria vary depending on the event's objective. If the primary objective of the event is to generate revenue, then the bottom line of profit (revenue minus cost) should be the principal criterion for evaluating its success, although there may be other, secondary benefits, including the identification and cultivation of prospects. But if the objective is to identify prospects, cultivate relationships in advance of a solicitation, or engage in stewardship with regard to current donors, then measures of effectiveness need to be more long-term, perhaps including the tracking of gifts from attendees at the event in subsequent solicitations.

An event can be the first step in donor development but will only be effective if the event itself is one component of a larger program. Perhaps an individual attends an event because of an invitation from a friend or because the event itself looked like it would be fun and offer opportunities for social contact. But if the event provides very little information about the organization's mission and programs or if there is no follow-up contact with the

TABLE 6.1 Evaluating Events

Event Objective	Event Revenue	Event Financial Result	Evaluation Criteria
Prospect identification	None or minimal	Break even or revenue less than cost	Were new prospects identified?
Cultivation	None or minimal	Break even or revenue less than cost	Were relationships with prospects enhanced?
Solicitation	High	Positive net revenue	Was the net revenue from the event substantial in comparison to costs; was it cost-effective?
Stewardship (including recognition)	None or minimal	Break even or revenue less than cost	Were relationships with donors enhanced, increasing the likelihood of continued and increased support?

Source: Based on Cox (2010), p. 523.

guests afterward, it is unlikely to result in a new donor who will subsequently develop an ongoing relationship with the organization. Even if an individual attending the event makes a gift on that occasion, it is unlikely that he or she will ever give again unless something more happens beyond social contact and unless there is systematic follow-up.

Some organizations design events as part of an overall plan for constituency building. For example, the consulting firm Benevon offers a model that, by its report, some 4,000 nonprofits have adopted. The model includes a series of events. The initial event is identified as a "point of entry" that introduces guests to the organization. That event is followed up with personal contact, and if the donor is receptive, a solicitation is conducted, either one-on-one or at an "ask event." Relationships with donors are enhanced through cultivation events, and at an appropriate point, they are asked to engage others in a point-of-entry event, continuing a cycle.

Online Fundraising

As mentioned previously, direct mail remains the primary source of gifts and new donors. But giving online is growing rapidly, representing 16 percent of giving in 2010, up from just 9 percent in 2009 (Flannery & Harris, 2011). In 2010, new donors acquired online exceeded those acquired through mail in every age group with the exception of people age sixty-five and above. In addition, new donors who make their first gift online tend to be younger and from higher-income households than donors who make their first gift through the mail. Donors who make their first gift online tend to give more than those who make a first gift through the mail. And the retention rate of donors who make a first gift online is lower than for donors who make a first gift through the mail (Flannery & Harris, 2011).

As mentioned previously, the most common method of online solicitation is e-mail. The purpose of the e-mail is to drive donors to the organization's donation page. This page may be maintained by the organization itself or operated by an outside vendor, such as Network for Good, which provides back-office support for processing online gifts.

Soliciting gifts through e-mail follows many principles similar to those for direct mail. It starts with list development and requires continuing attention to list maintenance. The list can be grown by including every contact with the organization. As in direct mail, e-mail lists can be segmented to deliver personalized messages.

Given the volume of e-mail most people receive, the construction of the message should follow certain principles. Although there is debate on the topic, a common rule of thumb is a subject line of forty characters or fewer (Network for Good, 2014). Various subject lines and message content can be tested and tracked and provide insights that can be reflected in subsequent mailings. Given the rapid growth in the use of mobile devices, best practices in design make it possible for the receiver to easily click on a link in the message with a finger. An effective donations page, accessible through PCs or mobile devices, should load quickly, minimize the amount of data the donor needs to enter, use short copy and calls to action, be formatted for simple viewing, keep content front and center, and make links and buttons easy to use (Network for Good, 2014).

Social Networks

A growing number of nonprofit organizations are using social media and networks as tools for communicating, building a constituency, and advocating a cause. Some are also benefitting from fundraising events organized on social networking sites. Social networking is especially effective in peer-to-peer fundraising, in which friends invite friends to participate in such activities as walks and runs (Held, 2014b). And as demonstrated through the success of the ice bucket challenge, which raised over $100 million for the ALS Association in 2014, one-time campaigns that go viral on social networks can raise substantial funds (Wolfman-Arent & Switzer, 2014). But for most nonprofits, social networking is more important for communication and building a constituency than for fundraising (Held, 2014b). And one-time promotions may not be replicable and thus not useful as a way to generate ongoing annual support. In 2011, only 1 percent of nonprofits reported raising $100,000 or more through social networks (MacLaughlin, 2011). In 2014, it was reported that only 1 percent of all funds raised online was attributable to social networks, including Facebook (Held, 2014b). But this is not to suggest that organizations can minimize the importance of having a presence on social networking sites, including Facebook, Twitter, and others. As Dixon and Keyes (2013) emphasize, and as the ice bucket challenge campaign illustrates, social networks enable individuals to become advocates or "cause champions" for organizations and causes, bringing value beyond their own giving.

Crowdfunding

Crowdfunding sites have received increasing attention. They include sites such as Kickstarter, which enables individuals to support creative projects, and Donors Choose, through which individuals can support specific needs of classroom teachers. Other well-known sites include CauseVox, Fundly, Razoo, and indiegogo; all have unique features. These sites have proven effective in raising funds for projects but may be less useful for developing ongoing support. For example, a campaign on indiegogo in 2012 raised almost $1.4 million to build a museum in honor of electricity pioneer Nikola Tesla (Bray, 2013). The use of crowdfunding in capital campaigns, which often focus on projects like the Tesla Museum, is discussed in Chapter 11.

Multichannel Communication

The view that nonprofits must adapt to new technologies by communicating with donors across multiple channels—mail, phone, Internet, advertising, and others—has received considerable discussion. The idea of **multichannel communication**, that is, that solicitation methods might be used in combination, is, of course, not a new one.[2] For example, nonprofits have long employed a technique in which a letter is sent in advance of a phone solicitation. The combination offers advantages over the use of mail or phone alone, since the subsequent call reinforces the letter and the letter helps to prepare the prospect for the call.

Anecdotes reporting the successful combination of traditional direct-response methods and online communication abound. For example, Wyoming Seminary, an independent school in Pennsylvania, converted its annual phonathon to a "connectathon," using e-mail, followed by a phone call, and outreach on social media (Berkshire, 2012). And, in another example, year-end fundraising for Oxfam America in 2013 used a variety of media, including advertising on billboards and bus shelters, direct mail, and a series of e-mails (Wallace, 2014).

But evidence of the effectiveness of multichannel strategies remains inconclusive. A study by Pentecost and Andrews (2010) concluded that it is necessary to use varied channels to communicate with various segments of the donor constituency, for example, using e-mail for younger prospects and mail for older prospects, but did not identify groups of individuals who indeed respond across channels. As Flannery and Harris (2011) clarify, there needs to be a distinction between multichannel *communication* by nonprofits and multichannel *giving* on the part of donors. As they report, "Multichannel donors are almost exclusively online-acquired donors who later start giving direct mail gifts. This is the only situation in which there are consistently significant numbers of cross-channel donors across all organizations" (p. 10).

PLANNING THE ANNUAL-GIVING CAMPAIGN

Think back to Chapter 4 and the discussion of the principle of proportionate giving. The exact ratios may vary, but the overriding principle—that a relatively small number of larger gifts will account for a disproportionate portion of total dollars—applies to annual giving as well as to other fundraising programs. As noted in Chapter 4's discussion, this is true because wealth and income are unevenly distributed across a donor constituency and because commitment to the organization varies among prospective donors. This abstract reality is given specific representation in a **gift table**, such as that shown in Table 6.2,

TABLE 6.2 Annual-Gift Table

Gift Range	Number of Gifts Now	Total in Range Now ($1,000,000)	Number of Gifts Needed ($2,000,000 goal)	Total Needed in Range ($2,000,000 goal)
$200,000	0	0	1	$200,000
150,000	0	0	1	150,000
100,000	1	$100,000	2	200,000
75,000	2	150,000	3	225,000
50,000	3	150,000	5	250,000
25,000	5	125,000	8	200,000
10,000	10	100,000	20	200,000
5,000	20	100,000	40	200,000
1,000	50	50,000	75	75,000
<1,000	1,125 (avg. $200)	225,000	1,500 (avg. $200)	300,000
Totals	1,216	$1,000,000	1,655	$2,000,000

which reflects a hypothetical situation.[3] The gift table is a device developed in capital campaigns, and our consideration of it is expanded in Chapter 11 in that context. But the same general patterns apply in annual giving, and the gift table is a useful tool in planning the annual-giving program.

In the hypothetical example portrayed in Table 6.2, the nonprofit organization raised $1,000,000 in its annual-giving program last year, derived from the gifts shown. As fundraising principles would predict, almost one-half of the total was produced by just the six largest gifts. Perhaps those gifts came from members of the governing board or from local foundations or companies that have long-standing relationships with the organization. The largest single amount, $225,000, came from 1,125 smaller gifts, but they accounted for less than one-fourth of the total raised in annual gifts last year. And, of course, if we were to analyze the costs associated with the annual-giving program, we would likely find that a disproportionate expenditure was required to raise those smaller gifts.

Now let's assume that the goal for next year's annual fund is $2,000,000. This is, of course, an unlikely scenario, since that would be a huge jump, but it makes the math somewhat simpler for the purposes of our discussion. It is likely that the same general patterns of giving will apply next year as last year. In other words, the gifts identified in the two columns to the right of the table will need to be obtained. It is not realistic to think that the larger goal can be achieved only through the acquisition of new donors at lower levels of the chart. There will need to be a strategy for upgrading current donors to produce the greater number of gifts shown at higher levels of the table. But there also will need to be a strategy for acquiring new donors to produce a larger number of gifts near the bottom.

Notice that the bottom level, gifts of less than $1,000, shows an increase in the number of gifts, from 1,125 to 1,500, but the same average gift of $200. That may or may not be realistic, depending on the size of the organization's constituency; further analysis may suggest that the average gift needs to be increased as well, calling for an emphasis on upgrading. The organization may need to consider not only its base of prospects but the methods it is employing in the annual-giving program. For example, increasing the number of donors at lower levels may require additional investment in direct mail and online fundraising efforts. Increasing the amount of top gifts may require expanding the number of personal solicitations at the leadership annual-gift level, either by expanding the staff or involving more volunteers. This may present a challenge to the board in terms of its own role.

In considering the top levels of the chart, it may be necessary for members of the board to increase their own personal commitments, in order to meet the requirements of the gift range chart based on the new, higher goal. Or perhaps the board needs to consider recruiting new members with giving capacity at those levels or with strong ties to corporate prospects that might provide such support.

With the gift table in front of them, fundraising staff and the organization's volunteer and executive leaders need to address the following questions:

- What is our current pattern of gifts?

- What gifts are needed to reach higher goals?

- Are these gifts available? (Do we have the prospects?)

- What are the most promising donor constituencies (individuals, corporate sponsors, foundations)?

- Which mix of alternative strategies may be most promising (larger base, new donors, upgrade current donors)?

- What are the best methods to use (mail, phone, Internet, events)?

- What will we need to spend and on what?

The gift table thus serves many purposes. It is a tool for planning but also provides a check on the reality of dollar goals that may be unrealistic. By breaking it down into specifics, the table helps to forestall the setting of fundraising goals based on unsupported optimism, reflected in statements such as "it's out there," or "we need the money and will just need to work harder." Unless there are names, constituencies, and strategies that can be identified at every level of the chart, the overall goal is likely to not be achievable. Alternatively, if the organization has committed to the goal, the gift table helps to clarify where increased effort must be applied and what additional budgetary resources will need to be invested.

Given the continued advance of communication technology and generational differences in the use of communication media, the methods used in annual solicitations can be expected to evolve. However, principles of donor motivation, characteristics of a strong case for support, the principle of proportionate giving, and other fundamentals discussed in this text are likely to remain more stable. Nonprofit organizations will need to adapt their strategies and methods to a new environment, but established principles of practice and the insights provided by theory and research will continue to provide useful guidance.

CHAPTER SUMMARY

The annual-giving program is the most visible component of most organizations' fundraising. Annual-giving programs generally emphasize unrestricted gifts (sometimes called the *annual fund*), although some also include designated gifts that are *budget-relieving* (Jarrell, 2013).

Annual-giving programs use the methods of *direct-response marketing*, including direct mail, telephone solicitation, e-mail, and text messaging. Some also use personal solicitation, especially for gifts at the leadership level (Sargeant, Shang, et al., 2010).

The annual-giving program has three principal objectives: the *acquisition* of new donors, *renewal* of donors' giving in subsequent years, and *upgrading* donor gifts from one year to the next. Since results can be readily measured, annual-giving programs use the science of fundraising as well as the art. Nonprofits that use direct mail to acquire donors develop a profile of donors who currently give and then target prospects who have similar characteristics, sometimes renting or purchasing lists from commercial list brokers. Criteria for profiling and targeting may be *geographic*, *demographic*, or *psychographic*.

Acquiring new donors through direct mail, from *cold lists*, can involve high costs, often exceeding the revenues obtained from mailings. But if new donors who are acquired subsequently become regular donors and, over time, increase their gifts toward the major-gifts level, the costs of the acquisition effort then should be evaluated against the *lifetime value* of the relationship to the organization (Sargeant & Jay, 2004). Some nonprofits with high fundraising costs are behaving unethically, but there is also misunderstanding about the concept of lifetime value. Events can also be a strategy for acquiring new donors, but it is important to keep their purpose in mind when planning.

It is more efficient to retain donors than to acquire new ones. For that reason, efforts to retain and renew previous donors have received increased attention, including enhanced programs of donor communication and stewardship (Burk, 2003). Strategies for upgrading donors' gifts include asking explicitly for the increase, recognition through *gift clubs* or *gift societies*, *matching (challenge) gifts*, and permitting donors to designate gifts for specific purposes (Warwick, 2011). Some nonprofits list specific impacts to which gifts at various levels are equivalent, even if the gifts are unrestricted.

Various solicitation methods have advantages and disadvantages, including effectiveness in obtaining a gift, cost, and possible scale. Direct-mail solicitations, which include a *package* of materials, remain the largest source of annual-fund gifts. Creating direct-mail letters is an art and involves both the physical characteristics of the letter as well as the words (Warwick, 2011). Telephone solicitations are used to acquire and renew donors and to upgrade giving. Phone programs intended to acquire donors are sometimes controversial because of their high cost (Perry, 2013). Criticism may reflect misunderstanding in some cases, but in other cases nonprofits and commercial telemarketing firms have behaved unethically. There are professional standards established by the Direct Marketing Association as well as state laws that relate to phone solicitation. Events can be used to identify new prospects, solicit gifts, cultivate donor relationships, or for stewardship. Events should be evaluated depending on their objectives. Only solicitation events should be expected to produce a significant net profit (Cox, 2010). Events may be an effective way of introducing new prospects to the organization, but there needs to be individual follow up to secure gifts.

While direct mail remains the largest source of annual gifts and of new donors, online giving is growing rapidly, especially among younger donors (Flannery &d Harris, 2011). The most common method of online solicitation is e-mail, which offers some of the advantages of direct mail, at lower cost.

Nonprofit organizations are using social networking to involve donors and volunteers, build a constituency, and develop advocates, but it is not a significant method of fundraising at this time (MacLaughlin, 2011). *Crowdfunding* sites have proven effective in raising funds for projects but not for obtaining continuing support. Nonprofits are using *multichannel strategies* to communicate with donors, although donors who use multiple channels generally are those who renew through direct mail after making a first gift online (Flannery & Harris, 2011).

The *gift table* is a tool for planning that reflects the principle of proportionate giving. It also is useful to provide a check on the reality of dollar goals and to define the resources required to achieve higher annual-giving totals.

Although annual-giving methods will change with the advance of communication technology, donor motivations, the characteristics of a strong case for support, the principle of proportionate giving, and other fundamentals discussed in this text will continue to apply.

Key Terms and Concepts

Acquisition
Annual fund
Annual-giving
   campaign
Annual-giving
   program
Back-end premium
Budget-relieving
   (gifts)
Cold list
Conversion rate
Converting (nondonor
   to donor)
Crowdfunding

Cultivation (event
   objective)
Cumulative giving
Demographic
   (profiling)
Direct-response
   marketing
Donor retention
Door-in-the-face
   technique
Foot-in-the-door
   technique
Foot-in-the-mouth
   technique

Front-end premium
FYBUNTS (some year
   in past five but
   unfortunately not
   this)
Geographic (profiling)
Gift table
Giving club/giving
   society
Highest previous
   contribution (HPC)
Honor role
Insubstantial value
Lifetime value

List broker	Package (of materials in direct mail)	Segments (of database)
Longevity	Phonathon	Solicitation (event objective)
Loyalty calls	Profiling	
LYBUNTS (last year but unfortunately not this)	Prospect identification (event objective)	Stewardship (event objective)
Matching gifts (challenge gifts)	Psychographic (profiling)	SYBUNTS (some year but unfortunately not this)
Multichannel strategies	Quid pro quo contribution	Targeting
	Renewal	Upgrading

Case 6.1: #GivingTuesday

In 2012, Harry Timms, deputy director of the 92nd Street Y in New York, was thinking about what had become known as Black Friday, the day after Thanksgiving when many people begin their holiday shopping, and what has become known as Cyber Monday, when holiday shopping online spikes. He wondered how the power of those brands might be connected with the fact that a third of all charitable gifts are made in the last three months of the year. Could a tradition similar to Black Friday and Cyber Monday be developed to create a national day of giving? Timms and the 92nd Street Y thought that might be possible and came up with the idea of #GivingTuesday (Gowen, 2012).

#GivingTuesday would not be one solicitation program but rather a movement in which nonprofit organizations and business partners would cooperate to bring visibility to giving, with each organization undertaking its own promotions, solicitations, and events on the same day (#GivingTuesday website).

The idea gained immediate support in 2012. The UN Foundation joined the 92nd Street Y as a partner, and a "Team of Influencers" was assembled, including prominent executives of technology companies. Dozens of websites that combine online giving and social media joined the effort, and prominent philanthropists, such as the Case Foundation, offered to match gifts (Gowen, 2012). Over 2,500 nonprofit partners joined the campaign, and giving on Tuesday, November 27, 2012, increased significantly over the year before on the same date (#GivingTuesday website).

Although most gifts were made online, some organizations leveraged the visibility of #GivingTuesday using traditional methods as well. For example, The Associated Jewish Community Federation of Baltimore conducted a phonathon and raised $1 million, including a $100,000 gift (Flandez, 2012a).

The second #GivingTuesday, conducted in 2013, brought significant growth. The company Blackbaud reported that gifts it processed increased by 90 percent from 2012, and Network for Good handled $1.8 million in online gifts, up from $1 million the year before (Flandez & Frostenson, 2013). Baltimore's The Associated was again the most successful organization, as part of a coordinated effort among Baltimore nonprofits called Bmore Gives More. The goal for Bmore Gives More was $5 million in total, which was exceeded by

$500,000 (Flandez & Frostenson, 2013). The 2013 effort achieved notable visibility. #Giving Tuesday was the number one trending topic on Twitter and was recognized by a display of lights in Times Square. More than 10,000 partners participated, in all fifty states and abroad (Ditcoff & Timms, 2013).

Despite success in its first two years, #GivingTuesday did attract some expressions of concern and caution. Some skeptics wondered if it would increase overall giving throughout the year or just on that one day. Another concern was that #GivingTuesday would reward digitally savvy nonprofits but that small organizations would perhaps be disadvantaged. Some expressed concern that concentrating giving on one day might preempt giving that would otherwise occur throughout the year or at year-end through traditional solicitation programs. However, others minimized the latter concern. For example, after the 2012 campaign, Marc Terrill, president of The Associated in Baltimore, was asked if he was worried that #GivingTuesday might preempt other year-end gifts. "Not at all," he replied, "because these people [#GivingTuesday donors] have now said, 'I'm here, I'm counted, I'm going to contribute'" (Flandez, 2012a).

Some cautioned that organizations should be careful to use #Giving Tuesday as the beginning of relationships with donors and not to see it as a one-time transaction (Watson, 2013a). As Watson (2013b) advised, "Organizations [should] view Giving Tuesday as another potential on-ramp for engagement—one of many throughout the year. It should be seen as a window of opportunity to appeal to more potential donors, and build support over time—rather than as a destination for most year-end giving. Perhaps the focus on philanthropy can encourage more involvement, even tied to the big holiday shopping push. But it should not evolve into the main giving day of the year. Given what's at stake in the U.S. nonprofit sector, engagement is a year-round goal."

Note: Students may wish to keep abreast of #GivingTuesday results in subsequent years. The movement is widely reported in the media and updates can be obtained from the #Giving Tuesday website (http://www.givingtuesday.org).

Questions for Discussion

1. Some critics note that total philanthropy in the United States has remained at about 2 percent of gross domestic product for many years. If that continues to be true, what might be the impact of efforts like #GivingTuesday on the nonprofit sector and on specific nonprofit organizations? In other words, if such efforts do not affect the overall total of philanthropy, how might they affect patterns of giving?

2. What might be some strategies a nonprofit could employ to assure that it develops continuing relationships with donors who make a first gift as a part of #GivingTuesday?

3. What are some ways in which a nonprofit organization might undertake a multichannel strategy in connection with its participation in #GivingTuesday and similar initiatives?

4. Think about a fundraising event you attended. Did it provide guests with information about the organization and its mission that might have encouraged them to become regular donors? If not, how might the event have been improved to accomplish that objective?

5. Review a direct-mail solicitation letter or the giving webpage of a nonprofit organization. How does it reflect the communication principles discussed in this chapter? How might it be improved?

Suggestions for Further Reading

Books

Andresen, K. (2006). *Robin Hood marketing: Stealing corporate savvy to sell just causes.* San Francisco: Jossey-Bass.

Burk, P. (2003). *Donor centered fundraising: How to hold on to your donors and raise much more money.* Chicago: Cygnus Applied Research.

Davis, E. (2012). *Fundraising and the next generation: Tools for engaging the next generation of philanthropists.* Hoboken, NJ: Wiley.

Warwick, M. (2013). *How to write successful fundraising appeals* (3rd ed.) San Francisco: Jossey-Bass.

Report

2011 Internet and multichannel giving benchmarking report. (2011, July). Charleston, SC: Target Analytics. https://www.blackbaud.com/files/resources/downloads/WhitePaper_MultiChannelGivingAnalysis.pdf.

Articles

Dixon, J., & Keyes, D. (2013, Winter). The permanent disruption of social media. *Stanford Social Innovation Review.* http://www.ssireview.org/articles/entry/the_permanent_disruption_of_social_media.

Websites

Blackbaud: https://www.blackbaud.com
Donors Choose: http://www.donorschoose.org
GivingTuesday: http://www.givingtuesday.org
Global Giving: http://www.globalgiving.org
Network for Good: http://www1.networkforgood.org

Notes

1. As mentioned at earlier points in this text, the vocabulary of fundraising is unsettled and terms are often used without precision. Such is the case for *challenge gifts* and *matching gifts*, terms some writers use

interchangeably. For example, the AFP Fundraising Dictionary defines a challenge gift as "a gift donated by a person made on *condition* that other gifts or grants will be obtained on some prescribed formula, usually within a specified period of time, with the objective of encouraging others to give" (AFP Fundraising Dictionary Online; italics added). That dictionary offers a definition of *matching gift* that is only slightly differentiated: "1a) a gift contributed on the *condition* that it be matched, often within a certain period of time, in accordance with a specified formula. 1b) a gift by a corporation matching a gift contributed by one or more of its employees" (italics added). In contrast, Rondeau and List (2008) define a challenge gift as "an *unconditional* commitment by a donor, or set of donors, to provide a given sum of money to the cause" (italics added). In the Rondeau and List definition, a challenge gift is similar to a *lead gift*, that is, a gift made by one donor at the outset of a campaign to encourage giving by others.

2. This book refers to mail, phone, and the Internet as solicitation *methods*. From a communications perspective, these are *channels* through which nonprofits send messages to donors and others, which may be solicitations or not.

3. Some people use the term *gift chart* or *gift range chart* to refer to what is called a *gift table* in this text.

CHAPTER 7

Major-Gifts Programs

$\mathbf{A}$ few years ago a major donor to a university was asked to speak to a group that included university officials and development office staff and to explain how he came to be involved. He explained that he had no previous relationship with the university when one day the president called him. He was a prominent builder in his state, and the president asked if he would participate along with several other leaders from his industry as a volunteer member of a task force that would advise on a planned new construction project for the campus. "I'm not an expert on construction," the president had explained, "and I really need input from objective outsiders like you regarding the various proposals that have been presented to me."

The speaker agreed and attended several meetings of the task force. "It was very interesting to me," he explained. "I had never known anything about this university or, for that matter, any university, since I never graduated from college. But the more I learned, the more interesting it became to me."

After the task force had completed its work, the president called again to ask if the man would serve as a member of a permanent advisory council, to help consider various strategic issues involving the entire university. The speaker agreed. And after participating on the advisory council for some time, he was invited to join the university's governing board. He again accepted.

"As I learned more and more, I realized that the university was facing serious financial challenges and the need for a number of new investments," he explained. "I began to worry about it on my own time. The university's problems had become my problems. One night I was telling my wife about how concerned I was. She said 'Well, maybe you need to do something about the problem so you can stop worrying.'" That led to his first major gift, which was followed by a series of additional gifts. He became one of the institution's leading donors.

How did this man progress from stranger to major donor? What principles does his experience illustrate? What mechanisms were at work? And what can an organization's volunteer leaders, executives, and fundraising professionals do to develop more donors like him? These are among questions considered in this chapter.

DEFINITION AND CHARACTERISTICS OF MAJOR GIFTS

A *major gift* is defined by the dollar amount, which may vary considerably among nonprofit organizations and institutions. Larger organizations commonly define $100,000 as the threshold for a major gift, usually with the assumption that it will be paid in installments over five years. Smaller nonprofits may, of course, consider a major gift to be something less, depending on their particular histories and constituencies. For some small nonprofits, a gift of $5,000 or $10,000 on an annual basis may be considered major. A major gift is sometimes also a **special gift**, since it is over and above the donor's regular, annual gift. Some major gifts are unrestricted, but most are designated to support some particular purpose. Some are intended to support a program, but many are designated to meet capital needs or for endowment. A **principal gift** is a large major gift, commonly defined as $1 million or more, although again, the exact definition varies among organizations (Schubert, 2002).

Major gifts may be pledged and paid in installments over time, especially if made from the donor's income. But many are made from the donor's assets. In this chapter, we are primarily concerned with outright major gifts, which of course, are also planned gifts if they involve complex assets or require integration with the donor's financial and estate plans.

MAJOR-GIFTS CYCLE

The process of fundraising for major gifts is a particular adaptation of the generic fundraising process described in Chapter 4, focused on the organization's relationship with the donor. It has been described in similar terms by multiple authors (e.g., Broce, 1986; Kelly, 1998; Knowles & Gomes, 2009; Lindahl, 2010; Scarpucci & Lange, 2007; Seiler, 2011a). Figure 7.1 illustrates a parsimonious version of the cycle showing five basic steps: identify, cultivate, solicit, thank, and steward. Some models depict additional steps, but again, most are similar in concept.

The cycle depicted here relates to a particular prospect or donor, so identification is depicted as occurring only once, although an existing donor could, of course, be identified again in terms of readiness for another gift. Once the prospect has been identified, a strategy for cultivation and solicitation is developed, including a timetable and specific initiatives that will be undertaken to advance the relationship. The cultivation plan is implemented and a gift is solicited when the timing is right. Of course, there may be a period of negotiation and gift planning that occurs at this point. A variety of people may be involved in this phase, including the fundraiser and the donor but also the donor's financial and legal advisors and the organization's own legal and financial officers. Among the questions to be addressed may be the timing of the gift, the specific assets and gift vehicles the donor will use to make the gift, and the terms and conditions attached to use of the gift. And, of course, the process does not end with the donor's commitment of the major gift. Rather, acknowledgment and stewardship continue the cycle, becoming cultivation that leads to future major gifts. Some authors articulate additional strategies and techniques within the cycle. For example, Knowles and Gomes (2009) discuss the solicitation of a **trial gift**

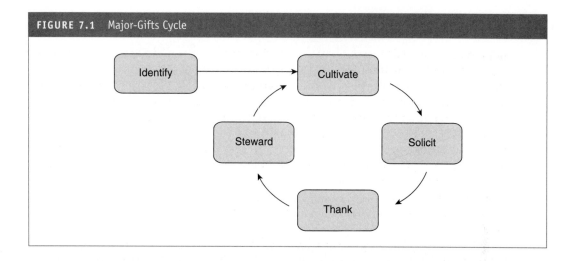

FIGURE 7.1 Major-Gifts Cycle

as a step that precedes moving on to a major-gift ask. And Fredericks (2010) emphasizes using a **pre-ask conversation** to test the waters by exploring the hypothetical of how a donor might respond to a future solicitation. For example, a development officer might ask an oblique question, something like "Bob, as you know, our campaign is focusing now on gifts of $100,000 and above. Should I bring the executive director to discuss something in that range with you, or would you advise me to wait until a later period of the campaign?" It's not quite a solicitation, but it plants a seed, paves the way, and elicits a response that may be helpful.

But, in general, again, the major-gifts cycle is described in similar terms by virtually all authors and includes a systematic and planned progression of interactions between the prospect and the fundraising organization, in which the relationship is nurtured on a continuing basis, in a cycle similar to that shown in Figure 7.1.

Major-gifts fundraising is distinguished by its emphasis on the cultivation phase of the process, on developing the relationship with the prospective donor. Thinking back on our discussion in Chapter 4, it is different from speculative fundraising, which emphasizes the volume of solicitations and relies on the probability that some percentage of those asked will give, even without much cultivation. In major-gifts fundraising, progress is measured not only by the end result, the gift, but by the progression of the relationship with the donor throughout the cultivation cycle.

CULTIVATING MAJOR-GIFTS PROSPECTS

Cultivation is itself a process, within the larger major-gifts cycle. Figure 7.2 depicts two versions of the cultivation cycle, developed by two prominent individuals in the history of major-gifts fundraising. This model is still the foundation of major-gifts programs. G. T. "Buck" Smith (1977) began his career as a fundraiser for his alma mater, Cornell University; became vice president at the College of Wooster for many years; and eventually served as

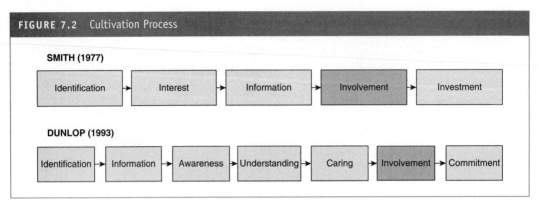

FIGURE 7.2   Cultivation Process

Sources: Based on Dunlop (1993); Smith (1977).

a college president. He retired in 2013 as president of Davis & Elkins College in West Virginia. David R. Dunlop (2002) also was an alumnus of Cornell, who served that university as a major-gifts and principal-gifts fundraiser for thirty-eight years. He retired in 1997 and became a well-known author and speaker on major-gifts fundraising across the country. Smith wrote earlier than Dunlop, who refined some of Smith's concepts and added his own; the two men defined many of the terms and practices used in major-gifts fundraising today.

Cultivation Cycle

Smith and Dunlop offer two similar versions of a model describing how an individual's relationship with an organization or institution develops over time. In some respects, it is consistent with theory from the behavioral and social sciences, but it also reflects some assumptions that may be unsupported or even contradicted by research.

Smith's (1977) model is perhaps the best known, probably because of its memorable nickname: the **Five I's**. It begins with *identification* of the prospect and determination of the prospect's *interest*—these are steps discussed in Chapter 5. With more *information* and then *involvement*, the prospect becomes ready for *investment*, in other words, giving. Dunlop's (1993) refinement of Smith's (1977) model includes somewhat different terminology and some additional steps—*identification, information, awareness, understanding, caring, involvement,* and *commitment*—but the two models share similar assumptions and have similar implications for the actions fundraisers should undertake.

Both models have some points consistent with the theories of donor motivation discussed in Chapter 3. For example, Schervish and Havens (2002) identified psychological identification with the needs of the organization's beneficiaries as an important phenomenon and stated that it arises from association, that is, interacting with those who have needs. This psychological identification is not to be confused with identification of the donor as a prospect, depicted as the first step in the process by both Smith and Dunlop; rather, it is more related to Smith's involvement stage and Dunlop's awareness, understanding, and caring. But both Smith's and Dunlop's models have shortcomings as well.

Smith's mixes *behavior* (e.g., investment) with psychological or emotional conditions the prospect might achieve (e.g., interest). In addition, as Kelly (1998) notes, both represent a type of **domino model**; that is, they seem to reflect the assumption that "communication increases knowledge, after which knowledge leads to a positive attitude, which results in a desired behavior—all in an inevitable progression" (p. 355). In other words, the models imply that one step in the process will automatically lead to the next, like a row of dominos causing others to fall in order. This is, however, inconsistent with communications theory and research, which suggests that the mechanisms through which individuals reach various emotional states are complex rather than linear. Moreover, theory does not support the idea that information by itself leads to changes in behavior (Kelly, 1998). However, despite their shortcomings, the Five I's model and Dunlop's refinement of it have intuitive appeal and are imbedded in fundraising jargon and practice. As illustrated by the example of the university donor with which this chapter began, they often seem consistent with experience.

Substantive Involvement

The common and pivotal stage in both Smith's and Dunlop's models, and thus highlighted in Figure 7.2, is involvement, which may lead to psychological identification with the organization's goals and problems (Schervish & Haven, 2002). As the university donor quoted at the beginning of this chapter explained, involvement with the organization and its cause may result in a situation in which the donor accepts its goals and problems as his or her own. In other words, the individual acquires a sense of ownership in the organization or institution. As Dunlop (1993) describes,

> When people first encounter an institution, they view its people and projects in the third person, in terms of "they," "them," and "those." Before they can become prospects for significant giving, that perspective must change to the first person: They must speak, think, and feel in terms of "we," "us," and "our." (p. 102)

Thus, a donor who spends time as a member of a committee, task force, or board may come to identify with the needs and goals of an organization as he or she comes to see first-hand the importance of its programs.

Another theoretical principle at work is the **rule of consistency**, identified by Cialdini (2003). As Cialdini explains, "[There is] a common tool of social influence that lies deep within people, directing their actions with quiet power. It is, quite simply, a desire to be (and to appear) consistent with what we have already done" (p. 25). Thus, an individual who agrees to serve as part of a group that identifies a problem, the solution to which is additional resources, is inclined to help provide those resources in order to exhibit behavior consistent with his or her position and role.

But involvement must be more than social; it must include what Seymour (1966) calls "involvement in program." As he explains, "Involvement . . . is more important than information, for information, alas, can be ignored" (p. 40). Involvement in program, or substantive involvement, may include asking an individual for advice, either as a member of a formal advisory body or individually. It may include inviting the individual to participate in program-related activities, serving as a volunteer or perhaps a speaker. It may include asking the individual to take *responsibility* for the organization in some way, perhaps by serving as a member of the governing board or by making a gift. Indeed, the rule of consistency may help to explain why past donors are the best prospects for future gifts; since they already have identified themselves with the organization's programs and needs, it is consistent to continue supporting them. Looking back to the example with which this chapter began, the university president engaged the future major donor in a way consistent with these principles. He asked for advice and then enlisted the individual as a member of an advisory council, a role that led to his election to the governing board and his emergence as a major donor to the institution.

CULTIVATION STRATEGIES

In well-managed major-gifts programs, cultivation of prospects is a systematic, planned activity. This suggests that every contact with the prospect is undertaken as part of a predetermined strategy, in order to maximize results. Some people may think that developing a human relationship with such rational intention is inherently manipulative and inconsistent with the noble purposes of nonprofit organizations and institutions. Some also may find the vocabulary of major-gifts fundraising, some of which is introduced here, to be more suited to selling commercial products than nonprofit programs. However, the alternative to a systematic and planned approach would be a random and disorganized approach, which would fail to meet the financial needs of organizations and their programs. That would ultimately harm the interests of those who benefit from those programs. The techniques and vocabulary of fundraising may seem uncomfortable to some, but most would agree with the higher purposes they advance.

Moreover, discomfort regarding the systematic methods of donor cultivation may be based on unrealistic assumptions about donors' interests and perceptions. Such methods do not reflect efforts to manipulate gullible donors, since most are more than sufficiently sophisticated to recognize and understand the process in which they are involved. Like a well-planned courtship, cultivation follows established principles in building a relationship that is mutually desired.

Major-Gifts Pipeline

From the perspective of the fundraiser, the Smith/Dunlop continuum is viewed as a **pipeline** (Scarpucci & Lange, 2007). Like a pipeline that carries water, the major-gifts pipeline contains a flow. Prospects enter the pipeline as they are identified and proceed through it during cultivation and solicitation. Maintaining a constant flow thus requires the continuing identification of new prospects and efforts to keep prospects moving through the pipeline. Experts suggest a variety of guidelines for the time and effort required to move an identified prospect through the pipeline to a major gift. One example is provided by Scarpucci and Lange (2007), who suggest that it requires eighteen to twenty-four months

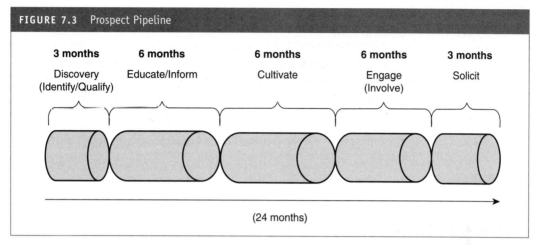

FIGURE 7.3 Prospect Pipeline

Source: Adapted from Scarpucci, P., & Lange, S. (2007, March). *Best practices in major gifts prospect management.* Presentation to the 44th annual AFP international conference. Retrieved April 10, 2014, from http://martsandlundy.com/reports-commentaries/ml-special-reports/2007/06/best-practices-in-major-gift-prospect-management.

from an initial contact with a prospect to securing a major gift of $100,000 or more. As shown in Figure 7.3, their conception of prospects' flow through the pipeline generally follows the Smith/Dunlop model.

Moves, Initiatives, Actions

The purpose of cultivation is to move prospective donors through the pipeline, from identification to solicitation (Lamb, 2012). The interactions undertaken to move prospects through that pipeline are commonly known as **moves**. The systematic implementation and **tracking** of those initiatives is known as **moves management**. The terms *moves* and *moves management* are generally credited to Smith and Dunlop, who introduced them at Cornell University (Weinstein, 2009). In more recent writing, Dunlop has substituted the term *initiative* for *move*, considering it a more respectful word (Dunlop, 2002). However, the terms *moves* and *moves management* are well-entrenched in the common vocabulary of major-gifts fundraising (Weinstein, 2009). Scarpucci and Lange (2007) offer a clarification on the terminology, defining the interaction a fundraiser initiates with a prospect as an *action*, and reserving the term *move* to describe the transition of the prospect from one stage to another, for example, from cultivation to being ready for solicitation. In other words, a contact with a donor that is just "keeping in touch" is not a move; the action must *move* the prospect one step closer to a gift (Lamb, 2012).

Dunlop (1993, 2002) identifies two basic types of initiatives (or moves): **background initiatives** and **foreground initiatives**. Background initiatives are those undertaken "for a group that includes one or more prospects" (Dunlop, 2002, p. 99). Such initiatives might include, for example, invitations to events, mailing of a newsletter or magazine, and other ongoing communications and contact. These activities have not been developed with regard to a particular individual; they are going on anyway. The major-gifts fundraiser simply includes them in the program of communication and interaction with the prospect. On the other hand, a foreground initiative is "conceived, planned, and executed with a specific prospect in mind" (Dunlop, 2002, p. 99). Such an initiative might include, for example, setting up a meeting with the nonprofit's CEO, sending the donor a report on the impact of his or her gift, or conducting an event at which the individual donor is recognized.

A cultivation strategy encompasses a series of background and foreground initiatives (or actions) intended to advance the organization's relationship with the donor prospect and to move that prospect through the pipeline toward readiness to make a gift, according to a specific timetable.

Cultivation Partners

Recall from Chapter 5 that fundraising is most effective as a team effort. Dunlop (2002) identifies and describes specific roles in the major-gifts cultivation process, including both volunteer leaders and fundraising professional staff.

Dunlop (2002) suggests identifying **natural partners**, individuals who have a close and influential relationship with the donor prospect and who are willing to be helpful in cultivation. Some are **primes**, people "in the best position to help guide and carry out the most appropriate foreground and background initiatives" (p. 101). Others who can help are identified as **secondaries**; as the term implies, they can help, but not as much as primes. A natural partner may be a volunteer who is involved with the organization, perhaps a board member, who has some relationship with the prospect. The natural partner may be a business associate, neighbor, a golf partner, or even the prospect's legal or financial advisor; usually, partners also will be friends of the organization, so they may be enlisted as allies in cultivation. The fundraiser may talk with such partners to gain advice on the prospect's interests and the best way to approach him or her. The partners also may play an active role, for example, inviting the prospect to an event at the organization or hosting a meeting with the CEO. Remember the discussion of cultivation events from Chapter 6. The model recommended by the consulting firm Benevon includes asking donors to reach out to others with invitations to point-of-entry events, in essence, to serve as partners in the cultivation of new prospects.

Figure 7.4 depicts a process similar to the Smith/Dunlop models. Developed by Tarnside Consulting, this version emphasizes the development of identified prospects into interested and engaged individuals, called "networking," and then "setting up situations where prospective donors can not only commit funds directly but can also become advocates and champions who bring in other donors through their own networks and influence," which is called "animation" (Tarnside, 2014). This conception is similar to the Benevon model, in which individuals are engaged first as prospects and donors and then as partners in the major-gifts process. Its depiction of "taking personal responsibility" as the ultimate stage in the relationship also is reminiscent of the story of the donor with which this chapter began.

Dunlop (2002) encourages a practical view in determining who may be effective partners—there are "reals" and "wannabees" (p. 102). Reals can actually help, while wannabees wish they could. There sometimes may be volunteers, board members or others, who offer to

FIGURE 7.4   Tarnside Curve of Involvement

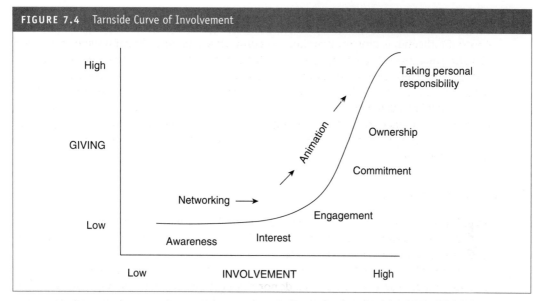

Source: Adapted from Tarnside Consulting, http://www.tarnside.co.uk/major_donor_development.php, retrieved July 28, 2014.

help with a prominent prospect at least in part because they seek an opportunity to advance their own association with that individual. But they may not be the best person to represent the organization to that prospect. This situation requires that the fundraising professional exercise judgment and diplomatically engage the reals rather than the wannabees.

Despite the importance of partners, Dunlop (2002) emphasizes the essential role of the fundraising professional, whom he calls the staff manager but who is usually called the **prospect manager** (Lamb, 2012). Some people who emphasize the importance of relationships in major-gifts fundraising use the term **relationship manager** for this role. The person who plays that role is often, by title, a **major-gifts officer**, sometimes called simply a **gift officer**. The staff professional is responsible for bringing discipline to the process, reviewing the relationship periodically, and coordinating the activities of the volunteer partners. In Dunlop's conception, the staff manager is primarily a facilitator and coordinator of initiatives—the quarterback from the football metaphor described in Chapter 5. Of course, in many development offices today, major-gifts officers are expected to facilitate and coordinate but also to engage in donor contacts, including solicitations, with specific goals for their activity.

MANAGING THE MAJOR-GIFTS PROGRAM

As discussed, effective major-gifts programs are not merely the sum of random activities that occur casually over some indeterminate period of time. The process of identifying, cultivating, soliciting, and stewarding donors is planned and managed. It is important to acknowledge that much of what is written about the management of major-gifts programs—and much of the discussion in this chapter—relates primarily to large and complex institutions. For a small nonprofit, the major-gifts program may encompass a small number of prospects, perhaps including members of the governing board and some leading local citizens. Setting priorities for cultivation may require little more than identifying a list of "Top 25" prospects and perhaps a list of the "Next 25" (Fredericks, 2010, p. 67). Major gifts may be a part of the overall responsibility of a development officer who also manages the annual fund, events, and other programs. In many nonprofits, the executive director, along with natural partners on the board, may in reality play the role of the major-gifts officer. But even on a small scale, the principles of the cultivation cycle apply and initiatives need to be carefully planned, executed, and tracked. It is possible for a small program to be overly managed, consumed with tracking and reporting to the detriment of time spent with prospects; however, there is nevertheless a need to take a disciplined approach. Larger organizations, especially those that have decentralized units or chapters, require more elaborate systems, policies, and protocols.

Setting Priorities

Chapter 5 discussed the identification and qualification of prospects and two basic variables by which prospects are rated—the financial *capacity* to make a gift and the *inclination* to do so, also sometimes called *likelihood* (Birkholz, 2008; Hogan, 2008). Some models define *interest*, *affinity*, or *connection* as rating criteria; they are essentially surrogates for inclination or likelihood. Some systems use **readiness** or **stage** as a rating variable, referring to the prospect's placement in the cultivation cycle. And some models rate prospects using more than two variables (Birkholz, 2008; Hogan, 2008). Whatever terms may be used, it is obvious that the only two relevant variables are the prospect's financial ability and some measure of the probability that he or she will make a gift to the organization.

Ratings may be developed through peer screening by volunteers, through contacts with the prospect by fundraising staff, through information obtained and analyzed by prospect researchers, through electronic database screening conducted by commercial vendors, or some combination of methods (Birkholz, 2008). Commercial vendors may have their own unique standards for rating prospects, but the two key variables remain capacity and inclination, by whatever term the latter may be identified.

One use of prospect ratings is to efficiently allocate time and attention among prospects in order to maximize gift revenue over time, that is, to establish priorities. Without a systematic approach, there can be a tendency to emphasize the short-term or to solicit the more readily available gifts while deemphasizing contacts with more capable prospects, who may not yet be ready to give but who may hold more substantial long-term potential. Table 7.1 illustrates a simple rating system that produces a priority ranking of prospects. This specific format is my creation, but the model is similar to what is used by a number of organizations. Let's walk through it.

The top portion of Table 7.1 displays the capacity ratings assigned to each identified prospect, while the middle box shows the ratings based on inclination. Both are expressed in numbers. Multiplying the two variables together yields an array of products (from 15 to 0), shown in the bottom box. This array provides a rough guide to the time and

TABLE 7.1	Prospect Ratings and Management
Capacity	
5 = $5,000,000	
4 = 1,000,000	
3 = 500,000	
2 = 250,000	
1 = 100,000	
0 = Less than $100,000	
Inclination	
3 = High inclination	
2 = Medium inclination	
1 = Low inclination	
0 = No inclination	
Priority Rankings (Multiply Capacity and Inclination)	
$5 \times 3 = 15$	$5 million capacity, high inclination
$4 \times 3 = 12$	$1 million capacity, high inclination
$5 \times 2 = 10$	$5 million capacity, medium inclination
$3 \times 3 = 9$	$500,000 capacity, high inclination
$4 \times 2 = 8$	$1 million capacity, medium inclination
$3 \times 2 = 6$	$500,000 capacity, medium inclination
$2 \times 3 = 6$	$250,000 capacity, high inclination
$5 \times 1 = 5$	$5,000,000 capacity, low inclination
$2 \times 2 = 4$	$250,000 capacity, medium inclination
$4 \times 1 = 4$	$1 million capacity, low inclination
$1 \times 3 = 3$	$100,000 capacity, high inclination
$3 \times 1 = 3$	$500,000 capacity, low inclination
$1 \times 2 = 2$	$100,000 capacity, medium inclination
$2 \times 1 = 2$	$250,000 capacity, low inclination
$1 \times 1 = 1$	$100,000 capacity, low inclination
$0 \times$ (anything) $= 0$ (inclination/interest but no capacity for major gift)	
(anything) $\times 0 = 0$ (capacity but no inclination, interest)	

attention that should be expended on prospects in various circumstances. Some of the results are entirely obvious. Surely a prospect who is capable of giving $5 million and who is highly inclined to do so, that is, who is ready, should be the highest priority. A $5 million prospect with a medium inclination should also receive a high level of attention, since we might think that some additional cultivation could result in completion of that gift within a reasonable time. Obviously, this prospect should receive somewhat lower priority than the $5 million prospect who is more inclined to make the gift now, but perhaps not much less.

It may seem counterintuitive that the $5 million prospect who is only moderately inclined should receive a somewhat higher priority than the $500,000 prospect who is highly inclined. Would it not be better to harvest that $500,000 gift than to spend time on the $5 million prospect, who is less likely to commit now? In practice, that is what might occur. But the two priorities would not be mutually exclusive; soliciting the ready-now $500,000 prospect could occur, even as the rankings remind us that continued cultivation of the not-quite-ready $5 million prospect is also a very high priority. One benefit of the priority ratings is that they remind the relationship manager to devote time and attention to the high-capacity prospect who is not quite ready and not simply harvest smaller gifts that are available right now.

Looking down through the balance of the table reveals some additional results that may initially seem to be counterintuitive but also some that make common sense. For example, prospects rated with relatively low capacity and/or who are less inclined should receive less time and effort now than those who are either more capable or more inclined. And, of course, those who lack the ability to make a major gift or who are disinclined to do so are just not relevant to the major-gifts program, although they may be fine people who are important to the organization in other ways.

The rankings are a rough guide. They are not intended to be followed blindly without further judgment. In practice, a gift officer may consider the rankings in clusters, perhaps defining just high, medium, and low priority. And there may be occasions when attention is directed to prospects of lower rank because of logistical realities; for example, a gift officer may be traveling and thus will focus on prospects in a certain location. It would make no sense to waste part of the trip by only visiting the top-rated prospects in the area, so the gift officer likely would spend some time as well with prospects of lesser immediate priority. But, again, establishing priorities helps to remind the fundraiser to focus on the long-term potential of prospects and not be distracted by more short-term opportunities.

Table 7.2 provides an interesting example of another priority-setting model, developed by the Corporation for Public Broadcasting as a resource for its member stations (Corporation for Public Broadcasting, 2012). In this model, prospects are rated on two criteria, called **affinity** and **life stage**. Again, the product of ratings on these two variables provides a priority ranking, the interpretation of which is included in Table 7.2. This model does reflect a donor-centered approach and a long-term perspective, especially as it relates to the donor's life stage, but it does not explicitly reflect financial capacity.

Reporting and Tracking Activity

Contact with a major-gift prospect is summarized in a *contact report* (or *call report*), which becomes a part of the organization's records (Lamb, 2012). Contact reports can be

TABLE 7.2   Prioritizing Prospects

Affinity or How Well Do They Like you?

Assign each prospect a ranking of 1, 2, or 3 indicating the strength of their commitment to you.

3 = They place your institution among the one or two most important in their life.

2 = They place you among the three to five most important.

1 = They know of you and support you.

Life Stage or Where Are They in Their Life?

Where are they in their life in terms of ability to make a major gift?

3 = Their children are grown and self-sufficient, or they have no children. Spouse is healthy or deceased. Wealth is certain; they are ready to dispose of wealth.

2 = They are at the peak of their career, their inheritance is expected. Children are beginning their own careers, starting their own families. Wealth is not yet certain; they are not yet disposing of their wealth.

1 = They are young, midway through their career, children are still at home.

Ranking: The Product of the Two

Multiply these two numbers together to get one of the following combinations, visualized in the moves management prioritizing grid:

9 = These are your best prospects. They are the most committed, have the greatest disposable wealth, and are most ready to give.

6 = These come next; either they need to become more committed to you (something you can influence), or they need to get older (nothing you can do here).

4 = Need both to like you better and to be in a better position to give to you. After addressing your 9s and 6s, turn to this group.

Source: Corporation for Public Broadcasting (2012). *Public broadcasting major gift initiative.* Retrieved April 9, 2014, from http://majorgivingnow.org/downloads/pdf/cultivation_system.pdf.

used by fundraising managers to track the movement of prospects through the pipeline, that is, for moves management, and also to evaluate the performance of major-gifts officers.

Various types of contacts are recorded, including personal visits, telephone and e-mail communications, and interactions at an event. The definition of a contact is sometimes a subject for discussion in development offices, with major-gifts officers often preferring a generous definition reflecting all of their activity and managers sometimes preferring a narrower definition that includes only personal visits and other substantive interactions.

Again, not every nonprofit organization has full-time professional staff members exclusively dedicated to major-gifts fundraising, although an increasing number of such positions are found in even medium-sized organizations. Where a fundraising professional holds such a position, his or her activity is tracked and evaluated.

Each gift officer carries a **portfolio**, that is, a list of prospect relationships for which he or she is responsible (Poust, 2012). The gift officer's portfolio is balanced, including prospects in various stages of the pipeline. Some are prospects in discovery; they have been recently identified, but their interest is still unknown. Others have been identified and qualified and are in the cultivation stage of the process. Some are ready for solicitation and others have made major gifts and are in the stewardship stage. The proportion of assignments in each stage may reflect the gift officer's time in the position. For example, someone in his or her first year in the job may be expected to engage primarily on qualifying new prospects, that is, making discovery calls or visits. In the second year, the gift officer will continue to qualify new prospects, but some who were qualified in the first year now will have moved into the cultivation stage. By the third year, if things are going well, more prospects will be ready for solicitations, which the gift officer will be expected to undertake or manage, although he or she will continue to contact prospects in earlier stages, maintaining the flow through the pipeline. Over time, the gift officer's responsibilities shift toward more solicitation, as more of his or her prospects reach that stage (Grabau, 2010). Of course, a gift officer's portfolio is not static. Discovery calls may determine that some individuals really are not major-gift prospects and they will be removed from the portfolio. New prospects will be continually added. And in some cases, it may be determined that the gift officer assigned is not the best person to be managing a particular relationship—for reason of personal chemistry or something else—and the prospect may be moved to another officer's portfolio.

The definition of gift officers' portfolios also may reflect the status of the organization's fundraising program. As Scarpucci and Lange (2007) suggest, the distribution of prospects by stage may vary depending on whether the organization's program is a start-up or mature and if it has recently completed a campaign. In a new program, most prospects have been recently identified and few are ready for solicitation. In a mature program, portfolios may be relatively balanced, with a constant flow of new prospects into the pipeline, others in cultivation or ready for solicitation, and others who are in stewardship after having made a recent major gift. At the conclusion of a campaign, there may be more donors than prospects, at least in the short term, as campaign pledges are fulfilled, so there may not be many individuals in the earlier stages of the pipeline, at least until the next turn of the cycle. Table 7.3 summarizes the proportions suggested by Scarpucci and Lange, although they are only illustrative and may or may not apply in a given situation.

TABLE 7.3 Prospect Portfolios

	Start-Up Effort	Balanced/Mature Program	Postcampaign
Discovery	75%	25%	15%
Cultivation	10%	25%	15%
Solicitation	10%	25%	20%
Stewardship	5%	25%	50%

Source: Adapted from Scarpucci, P., & Lange, S. (2007, March). *Best practices in major gifts prospect management.* Presentation to the 44th annual AFP international conference. Retrieved April 10, 2014, from http://martsandlundy.com/reports-commentaries/ml-special-reports/2007/06/best-practices-in-major-gift-prospect-management.

How many prospects should comprise a gift officer's portfolio? The answer depends, of course, on a variety of factors. If the gift officer has job responsibilities other than fundraising, for example, perhaps managing other staff members, then that person will be able to manage fewer prospects than one who has no such responsibilities. A gift officer whose portfolio includes prospects in various locations may be able to manage fewer relationships than a gift officer whose prospects are geographically concentrated, since some of his or her time will be used up in travel. A portfolio of highly rated prospects, for example, principal-gift prospects, may require that more time be spent with each and thus includes a smaller number of assignments. A range commonly recommended for a gift officer's portfolio is seventy-five to one hundred fifty prospects (see, e.g., Poust, 2012). That range was developed by fundraising practitioners and consultants, but it has some interesting theoretical support. Evolutionary psychologist Robin Dunbar studied social connections among groups of monkeys and then extended his research to various human situations. He determined that the capacity of the human brain permits us to maintain close relationships with no more than about 150 people. This has become known as Dunbar's number. Clans of ancient hunter-gatherers as well as military units have tended toward that limit. Although Dunbar does not specifically address major-gifts fundraising, his findings coincide with the conventional wisdom of practitioners. As an interesting aside, he does suggest that the number applies as well to social networking relationships, since the average number of friends on Facebook is about 130. As Dunbar notes, this is "just short enough of Dunbar's number to allow room for grandparents and babies" (Dunbar, 2010).

Prospect Management Policies

In large and complex organizations, there are often internal debates about who should be permitted to interact with donors and prospects. For example, this was an issue between the American Red Cross national headquarters and its local chapters as discussed in Case 5.1. It is also a common topic for discussion at universities, museums, and other large organizations with units that enjoy some degree of autonomy and have fundraising staff specifically dedicated to them. The absence of policies and procedures can lead to competition for access to prospects and multiple solicitations that may produce less revenue overall than a more coordinated approach. A fragmented approach may make the organization appear undisciplined to prospective donors, causing them to question its overall management. It also makes it difficult for the organization's senior leadership to develop comprehensive relationships with donors, like the Red Cross' partnership with Nationwide Insurance discussed in Case 5.1, or to obtain support for programs and projects that cut across departments, chapters, and other units.

Prospect management policies, commonly called **protocols**, define who is permitted to contact prospects and establish procedures for obtaining approval to do so. Such policies commonly permit anyone within the organization to interact with a prospect for purposes of cultivation but require explicit approval from the relationship manager assigned to that prospect before a solicitation can be undertaken. Contacts with prospects for principal gifts often are subject to more rigorous control, requiring approval from the relationship manager assigned and a development office official. For example, Box 7.1 includes policies

---

BOX 7.1   Prospect Activity and Contact Protocol

Contact report required fields in the . . . database include: Date of Contact, Contact Type, Purpose, Description (brief title) and Text or Attachment. This information must be entered in order for the contact report to be filed in the database. Prospect managers and team members who request administrative professionals to file contact reports on their behalf should provide administrative staff with data for all contact report required fields.

Prospect managers should update prospect stages with a contact report. Operations staff will change stages weekly based on the filing of a stage-change contact report.

Prospects with no record of activity within a 3-month period are subject to reassignment pending submission and review of proposed next steps in a strategy contact report to the research staff and the two AVPs of development.

Prospect managers should do a quarterly review of all prospects assigned and update ratings or request release. A contact report is required for release. (Suggest new assignment, if appropriate, through research staff.)

Cultivation efforts should begin immediately as part of a broader moves-management strategy for the prospect.

Initial solicitation is expected within 12 months of assignment at the minimum amount of $1,000 (President's Associates level).

A special gift or major gift solicitation ($10,000+) is expected within 23 months of assignment.

No one may contact an assigned prospect on matters related to a personal solicitation without the consent of the prospect manager.

Assigned prospects will not be automatically excluded from central or college-based direct mail solicitations.

Assigned prospects will not be automatically excluded from event mailings (golf tournaments, Front and Center, Vision and Visionaries, regional alumni gatherings, seminars, receptions, etc.).

Assigned prospects may be automatically excluded from central or college-based telemarketing programs by request.

The Alumni Association may mail membership material to assigned prospects.

Disagreements in strategy or assignments may be resolved through the appropriate AVP, dean, and/or the vice president for university advancement. The university president is the final arbiter in prospect assignment matters.

Senior university administrators are exempt from prospect management guidelines.

Source: Cal State Fullerton website (http://www.fullerton.edu/advancement/operations/research/contact-protocol.asp), retrieved July 28, 2014. (Policies in effect as of 11/20/12).

in effect at the California State University Fullerton in 2012. It articulates expectations of prospect managers for the movement of prospects through the pipeline, defines policies for contact with assigned prospects, and describes a process for the resolution of disagreement. Again, such formal policies would be overkill for small, centralized organizations with few major-gift prospects but are essential to maintain an organized approach in larger, decentralized institutions. Some examples of such policies can be found on the web.

Gift Officer Performance Evaluation

The standards by which major-gifts officers' performance is evaluated vary among organizations. Some may be judged entirely by how much money they secure. But that raises issues and concerns. Some of those are ethical concerns, which are discussed further in Chapter 14, but some are practical considerations. For example, if a gift officer is evaluated only by dollars raised, he or she may have an incentive to ignore priority rankings like those depicted in Table 7.1, focusing attention on those prospects most likely to give something this year and ignoring those who may not be ready to give until later, even though they may have greater financial capacity. That approach could maximize the gift officer's total this year, perhaps resulting in a raise, but it might be detrimental to the long-run interests of the organization. In complex organizations, especially with decentralized units, this method of evaluation also may create competition for the most promising prospects and discourage teamwork. And an exclusive focus on dollars could create an incentive for an unscrupulous fundraiser to pressure or mislead prospective donors, with obvious negative implications.

An alternative approach is to evaluate gift officers based on their productive activity, that is, on what they *do*, with thoughtfully designed objectives. Consider Table 7.4, which depicts a tool developed by Richard Dupree for the Corporation for Public Broadcasting (Dupree, n.d.). It is similar to models used by a variety of nonprofit organizations and institutions. In this model, the gift officer is evaluated based on a possible 100 points. An

TABLE 7.4 Major-Gifts Officer Evaluation

	Points
Dollar goal (cash and pledges)	25
Proposals submitted	25
Contacts	25
Quality of work	25
A. Success rate	5
B. Prospecting	5
C. Cultivations	5
D. Use of management/leadership	5
E. Budget management	5
Total possible points	100

Source: Adapted from Corporation for Public Broadcasting. (2012). *Public broadcasting major gift initiative.* Retrieved April 9, 2014, from http://majorgivingnow.org/downloads/pdf/cultivation_system.pdf

individual earning 75 points would meet expectations and likely remain employed. Fewer than 75 points might be grounds for probation and eventual dismissal. A total of 80 points or more could qualify the gift officer for an increase in compensation.[1]

Only 25 points can be earned based on dollars raised. To be successful the gift officer also needs to demonstrate a level of activity in submitting proposals, undertaking contacts with prospects, and measures related to quality of work. The criteria can, of course, be modified in order to alter the individual's anticipated behavior and to reflect the organization's priorities.

Again, if dollars raised was the only criterion of good performance, that could lead to a focus on short-term successes rather than long-term revenue or, in the case of a gift officer who closed a big gift in January, a disincentive to continue working hard the balance of the year. But neither situation is likely to occur if the gift total accounts for only 25 percent of the individual's overall performance. On the other hand, if performance were evaluated only on the basis of such metrics as contacts completed and proposals submitted, that could result in a gift officer who generates much activity but raises little money, so dollars need to be considered. A balanced approach to evaluation may result in an allocation of time and effort that is aligned with the organization's immediate and long-term goals and consistent with the priority ratings of prospects in the pipeline. In addition, the quality-of-work metrics included in the model can be varied to create incentives for cooperation and teamwork and to discourage destructive internal competition, often a concern in large and decentralized institutions (Dupree, n.d.).

DEVELOPING DONOR RELATIONSHIPS

Personal interaction with prospective donors is a hallmark of major-gifts fundraising. This section considers principles related to those interactions and common advice for developing relationships during the cultivation phase.

Donor Interaction Models

Schervish and Havens (2002) argue that "the prevailing strategies used by charity advocates" reflect a presumption that donors are disinclined to give. As they describe, in this view, "the demands of [donors'] needs are presumed to be so numerous and important, and the willingness of donors to be so meager and hesitant, as to warrant an attitude, if not an actual fund-raising practice, that enlists as it allies guilt, embarrassment, comparison shaming, and imposed obligation" (p. 223). These assumptions about donors lead to what Schervish and Havens (2002) label the **cajoling** (or **scolding) model** of fundraising, in which donors are presented, at least implicitly, with messages constructed in both negative and positive formulations, both unflattering:

Negative formulation

1. You are not giving enough

2. to the right causes

3. at the right time

4. in the right way.

Positive formulation

1. You ought to give this amount

2. to these causes

3. at this time

4. and in this manner. (pp. 223–224)

However, the authors argue, donors—especially wealthy donors—are *inclined* to be philanthropic. Thus, they recommend that fundraisers follow an **inclination** (or **discernment) model**, in which donor prospects are guided to be self-reflective in order to discover what gifts might be most fulfilling to them. Although the questions may not be asked explicitly in exactly this form, fundraisers who assume donors are positively inclined might lead a prospect to consider questions such as the following (Schervish & Havens, 2002):

1. Is there something that you want to do with your wealth

2. that fulfills the needs of others

3. that you can do more efficiently and more effectively than government or commercial enterprise

4. and that expands your personal happiness by enabling you to express your gratitude and actualize your identification with the fate of others? (p. 226)

Again, it would be awkward and unnatural for a fundraiser to ask a donor these four questions as written, and Schervish and Havens (2002) do not intend to provide a script. But a fundraiser following the discernment model would be advised to listen more than talk, ask the prospect open-ended questions that invite him or her to reveal values and priorities, and to be alert to how the latter may align with the values, priorities, and needs of the organization. In other words, the emphasis in cultivation should be on advancing the relationship with the prospect, from which gifts eventually will flow, rather than rushing to make the sale.

Appropriate Pace of Cultivation

In developing relationships with major-gift prospects, fundraisers are advised to proceed at an appropriate pace. As Dunlop (1993) suggests, "Let your friendships grow naturally. Don't assume familiarity that is not based on the experience of your relationship with the prospect. The best way I have found to judge the appropriateness of initiatives is to apply the same standards you use in your personal friendships" (p. 109). Maintaining an appropriate pace during the cultivation phase may at times conflict with the urgency of the organization's needs and the expectations placed on a gift officer to close the gift. That is one argument for establishing criteria for evaluation that are not exclusively focused on dollars raised, as discussed earlier. The right pace is one that proceeds deliberately and is mindful of the organization's goals but not so quickly as to offend or alienate the prospect. In addition to appropriate incentives, this requires sensitivity and judgment.

Appropriate Tone and Style

It is essential that a fundraiser maintain an appropriate tone and style in contacts with prospective donors. As Tempel (2013) observes, "The *organization* owns the relationship" (p. 410; italics added). That means that the fundraiser's relationship must remain professional and be focused on building the donor's relationship with the nonprofit, not personally with the development officer. Assuring that the relationship is between the donor and the organization is of particular importance in view of the high turnover among gift officers.

Kelly (1998) notes another reason for maintaining clarity about the nature of the relationship between the fundraiser and the prospect: it "guards against inappropriate behavior on both sides" (p. 495). The relationship between a gift officer and a prospect or donor can easily feel like personal friendship. As Kelly notes, multiple meetings may occur in personal homes or over meals, which may include alcohol. The focus is on building a relationship, and with increasing familiarity conversation can easily drift into personal matters. But the fundraiser is building a professional relationship with the donor as an agent of a nonprofit organization that he or she represents and it is essential that both parties understand and respect that distinction.

VISITS AND PURPOSES

Personal contacts are characteristic of major-gifts fundraising and, as discussed earlier, visits to the prospective donors occur in various stages of the cycle. Each type of visit has a different purpose and objective.[2]

Discovery Visits

Once a potential prospect has been identified, the first contact is a **discovery visit** (Birkholz, 2008), also commonly referred to as a *discovery call*. This visit is often undertaken by a fundraising professional, although sometimes a prospect may not be open to even an initial meeting with anyone who is not the CEO of the organization or a peer. The purpose of the discovery visit is to qualify the potential prospect with regard to the "I" of LAI, that is, to determine interest, and also to obtain additional information and insight that will add to the existing research regarding the individual's financial capacity (the "A").

The individual conducting the discovery visit listens more than talks and asks the prospect open-ended questions that may invite him or her to be forthcoming (Fredericks, 2010). For example, the fundraiser might ask biographical questions, such as, "Where did you grow up?" "How did you come to enter your current profession/business?" and "What are your volunteer interests in the community?" Such questions may put the donor at ease and encourage him or her to engage in conversation, perhaps providing clues as to his or her values and interests. For prospects who are already donors at some level, the questions might be even more specific. As Fredericks (2010) suggests, the discussion could provide especially useful insight if the prospect responds to questions such as "How did you come to be interested in our organization?" "Out of all the organizations . . . why did . . . you support us?" (p. 62). Responses to such questions reveal the prospect's attitudes about his or her experience with the organization and begin to explore the individual's interests and motivations. Thinking back to the seven faces of philanthropy discussed in Chapter 3, the discovery visit can be the first step toward identifying the prospect's donor type.

Cultivation Visits

Cultivation visits are undertaken with a qualified prospect to advance the relationship and pursue common interests. Such visits provide information to the prospect (one of the Five I's), including updates and reports on the organization's activities. A primary purpose of discussion on cultivation visits is to match the organization's programs and needs with the donor's interests. Some version of Schervish and Haven's (2002) questions may be useful but need to be asked naturally, not in a tone that suggests a scripted interrogation. Once a donor's interests have been determined, cultivation may include visits that introduce some new faces and begin to strengthen the prospect's relationship with the organization. For example, a program director might be invited to join a visit to discuss his or her work in more detail than a fundraising professional is able to do, or the prospect might be invited to visit the organization's facility to see its programs in action. Including others also helps to assure that the prospect develops relationships that go beyond one person, that is, that he or she builds a relationship with the organization itself and the various personalities who represent it.

Some authors have applied **coorientation theory** to the process of matching donor interests and organizational needs (e.g., Lindahl, 2010). Developed by Newcomb (1953) and expanded by McLeod and Chaffee (1973), coorientation theory explains how the relationship between two individuals interacts with an object, or an idea, about which they are communicating. If they see it differently, that causes a tension that is resolved either through deterioration in the relationship or through some evolution in their perceptions toward a more common view. The theory suggests the importance of maintaining a positive relationship and of ongoing communication to achieve understanding and consensus. In other words, it calls for developing a relationship, which may not unfold neatly or efficiently but requires give and take and mutual adjustment to the other person's viewpoint.

THE ASK

The cultivation process culminates in a solicitation—what is often called **the ask**—which some people may consider to be the essence of fundraising (Fredericks, 2010). If the objective is a major gift, the solicitation is almost always undertaken face-to-face. The ask involves a process of its own.

Getting in the Right Mind-Set

Before undertaking a solicitation, fundraisers are advised to be self-reflective and to get in the right mind-set to ask. That may include examining their own personal experiences, assumptions, and biases with regard to money.

Fredericks (2010) observes that money can be an emotional topic, with just the word bringing back memories of past struggles in one's own or family life. As she explains, "If money is viewed in negative terms, it becomes much more difficult during the [solicitation] because these negative feelings can sabotage [a solicitation] or make it extremely uncomfortable and unnatural when asking for money" (p. 4). Matheny (2010) likewise notes psychological barriers that may stand in the way of asking for a gift, including fear of failure, fear of rejection, and fear of losing control.

Most fundraising professionals and most nonprofit CEOs are not individuals who possess significant personal wealth. That reality may lead to an attitude toward money that stands as an obstacle to communication on the subject with individuals whose assets far exceed their needs. Of course, the potential for a problematic difference in perspective is reduced when a volunteer leader is involved in the discussion with a prospective donor. As discussed further soon in this chapter, that scenario is recommended as the most desirable, in part for this reason (Fredericks, 2010). For fundraising professionals and nonprofit CEOs, any psychological obstacle to asking may diminish with experience and, especially, with positive results.

Planning the Solicitation Meeting

The solicitation of a major gift is too important to proceed on the fly. In other words, it is essential that the individuals who will participate in the solicitation meeting are well-prepared with a plan for how they intend the meeting to unfold. If the solicitor is one individual, perhaps a major-gifts officer, that individual nevertheless needs to have a roadmap in mind for how the conversation with the donor will unfold and, indeed, may benefit from a rehearsal with a supervisor or colleagues (Gattle, 2011).

Questions to be considered in advance include the following:

- Who should be involved in the meeting, including both the individuals who will be part of the solicitation team and on the donor's side of the conversation?
- Where should the solicitation meeting be held?
- What gift amount should be solicited?
- What should be the purpose of the proposed gift?
- How should the meeting unfold; in other words, who should speak when?

- What are possible concerns or issues that the prospect might raise, known as *objections*, and what responses might be offered to each?
- How should the meeting end, under scenarios in which the donor's response is positive, negative, or ambiguous? (Fredericks, 2010)

Solicitation Team

The often-cited formula for a successful solicitation—sometimes called the **Five R's**—is "the right person asking the right person at the right time for the right amount for the right project" (Calhoun & Miller, 2004, p. 11). Most authors agree that the right "person" is often a team rather than one person, although major-gifts officers do solicit gifts alone. Fredericks (2010) argues that "the higher the Ask amount, the more imperative it is to have someone in a leadership role at the organization to do the Ask" (p. 84). She calls the combination of CEO and board chair the "dream team" and suggests it be used when soliciting the largest gifts" (p. 92).

A volunteer may bring special authenticity and credibility to the meeting. If a volunteer is part of the solicitation team, then it is common wisdom that the volunteer needs to have already made a gift at the level being solicited or above. Recall from Chapter 4 that this principle was articulated by Seymour in 1966; it has been endorsed by many others since (e.g., Fredericks, 2010; Gattle, 2011). However, some offer a modification, requiring that the volunteer solicitor be recognized as having made a **stretch gift**, which will be perceived as sacrificial in proportion to his or her means and not necessarily as much as is requested from a prospect known to have greater capacity (Fredericks, 2010). But if the volunteer solicitor is known to be capable of more than he or she has given and is soliciting another person for a larger gift, that volunteer is unlikely to bring much credibility to the ask.

How many members should be on the solicitation team? Fredericks (2010) recommends two, noting than "four eyes are better than two" in observing body language and the nuance of a prospect's words (p. 80). In addition, two solicitors give each other courage and assure that the report of what transpired in the meeting will reflect the consensus of two people, rather than the (perhaps) overly positive or negative perception of just one.

Sometimes the solicitation team can include more than two people; for example, it might include the CEO or a volunteer leader, the director of the program for which the gift is sought, and the chief development officer who has cultivated the relationship with the donor. But too many is a mistake and is likely to make the prospect feel overwhelmed.

Solicitation Location

There is something close to consensus in the literature regarding the ideal location for a major-gift solicitation. Fredericks (2010) recommends the prospect's home or office or an office or conference room at the organization's location, citing advantages of each setting. She advises against asking in a restaurant, due to the potential for interruptions and distractions. The choice between the prospect's office or home may depend on whether the individual is still working or retired and whether his or her spouse also should be included in the meeting.

Amount and Purpose

A major gift is most often designated to a specific purpose, in line with the prospect's interests as discovered and developed in the course of cultivation. Accordingly, the gift proposed in the solicitation relates to that purpose. But there are two questions on which opinions sometimes diverge: whether to ask for a specific amount or whether to take an alternative approach; and whether to present a written proposal at the solicitation meeting.

Fredericks (2010) is adamant: "If you don't ask the person for a specific amount, she may supply her idea of an appropriate sum, and it may be well below what you are anticipating or dreaming she will give" (p. 39). However, this approach assumes that prospect research and the cultivation process have resulted in assessments of the donor's financial capacity and inclination that are reasonably accurate. If they are not, it could result in an amount requested that is too low. The prospect may readily agree, but the organization may be leaving money on the table. An alternate approach, discussed in Chapter 6 in the context of telephone solicitation, is the door-in-the-face technique (Dillard & Knobloch, 2011). This involves asking for a high amount, while being prepared to negotiate to something lower if the donor provides a negative response to that initial request. Matheny (2010) suggests beginning with the *purpose* of the gift, for example, using phrasing such as "to establish a chair in dramatic arts would require $500,000." This might be followed by the statement, "We were wondering if you could consider a gift in the range of $500,000 to establish . . ." (p. 73). As Matheny observes, this phrasing immediately establishes the purpose of the gift, presents an exploratory amount, and leaves the door open to a wider range of responses than the simple statement "Please give $500,000" (p. 73).

The question of whether to prepare a written proposal that is delivered to the prospect at the solicitation meeting receives various answers. Broce (1986) expressed the classic view that the solicitor should "present the individually tailored written proposal . . . and review it quickly page by page" (p. 187). Kelly (1998) also describes a scene in which a prepared proposal, "clearly marked as a draft," is given to the prospect (p. 494). But Fredericks (2010) urges caution. Sending a proposal in advance may be a mistake, since it is equivalent to asking on paper rather than in person. Having a written proposal prepared for presentation to the prospect after the gift has been requested verbally may be an acceptable technique, but it is always possible that the discussion will go in unanticipated directions, perhaps inconsistent with the proposal that was written in advance. So the proposal had best be kept in the briefcase while the conversation unfolds. Fredericks (2010) suggests sending a written proposal (or letter) *following* the meeting. In that way, the proposal can refer to points discussed in the meeting and reflect the donor's responses. It also can provide an opening for a follow-up conversation with the donor, which is especially important if his or her response has been ambiguous.

Anticipating Objections

Not every solicitation results in an immediate positive response. Prospects may raise **objections**, although the term implies more negativity than is generally present

(Fredericks, 2010). Objections are issues or concerns that the donor may express and that need to be addressed before the gift can be made.

Matheny (2010) identifies common objections in categories, including the following:

- *Focus of the gift.* The donor may propose a use of the gift that is different from what the solicitor initially had in mind, requiring further discussion of alternative possibilities.

- *Timing of the gift.* The schedule for payment of the gift is a matter for discussion and negotiation. For example, a donor may offer a five-year pledge when the solicitor has requested three years.

- *Size of the gift.* As discussed earlier, the amount of the gift can be approached in various ways. If the solicitor requests a specific amount and the donor objects, that is, indicates that it is too much, then the solicitor needs to be prepared with alternatives.

- *Administration of the gift.* Administrative issues, such as the valuation of gifts of certain securities or the applicability of any overhead assessed against gifts by the organization, may require negotiation.

- *Stewardship.* Recognition of the donor, the donor's involvement in the use of the gift, and reporting may be topics that require discussion.

Matheny (2010) emphasizes that responding to objections may require flexibility on the part of the solicitor and the organization. If the prospect is generally favorable to the idea of making the gift but needs additional details in order to decide, objections may need to be addressed through follow-up communications, perhaps including a written proposal, additional information on planned giving, and other materials (Calhoun & Miller, 2004). As Matheny (2010) emphasizes, the priority throughout the process should be on maintaining the positive relationship with the donor.

ANATOMY OF THE SOLICITATION VISIT

Various authors have described in some detail the unfolding of a solicitation visit and the various turning points that occur in the dialogue (e.g., Broce, 1986; Fredericks, 2010; Gattle, 2010). Some (e.g., Fredericks, 2010) provide sample scripts. There is a high degree of consistency in the scenarios suggested; as a composite, the following phases of the solicitation visit are generally identified:

- Greeting and small talk

- Transition to the ask

- The ask

- Pause to hear response

- Listening and responding to concerns and objections

- Conclusion and plan for follow-up, if indicated

Critical points in the visit include the transition from introductory conversation to the business at hand, the ask, and then pausing to hear the donor's response before continuing (Gattle, 2010). Preparation for the visit should establish a clear plan for which member of the solicitation team will undertake the transition and which will make the ask (Fredericks, 2010). If the donor readily agrees to the gift, the solicitors move to a timely conclusion of the meeting. If the response is a flat negative, the solicitors remain gracious, thank the individual for taking the time to meet, and retreat to consider where their planning went awry. In many instances, however, prospects may provide an ambiguous response, perhaps including the expression of objections, a request for more information, or the need to consult with advisors and/or family members. In such instances, the solicitors suggest a specific next step, which may include a written proposal, another meeting, a visit to the organization's facility, or some other activity that will keep the discussion alive and move it toward an eventual conclusion.

FOLLOW UP, NEGOTIATION, AND GIFT AGREEMENTS

Major gifts represent a significant financial commitment by the donor, and it is common that full agreement cannot be reached in a single meeting. There may need to be a period of extended negotiation, involving numerous conversations and meetings, during which the terms of the gift are negotiated. This may be especially true if the donor's desire is to designate the gift for a program or purpose that is not exactly aligned with the organization's plans; for example, think back on Lindahl's case discussed in Chapter 1, in which a donor solicited for a health clinic offered to establish a dental clinic instead. In this scenario, and in others less complex, the organization may need to revisit its own goals and priorities and make decisions before returning for further discussion with the donor. Negotiation of the gift also may be prolonged and involve various financial and legal experts, especially if some component of the overall commitment is a planned gift, something we consider in detail in the next chapter.

Concern with **donor intent** has become heightened in recent years as a result of some high-profile cases in which an organization's use of a gift was challenged (Lewin, 2008). Some of these cases have resulted in negative publicity and even legal action, but all have reinforced the understanding that a major gift is a contractual relationship between the donor and the recipient organization. Carefully documenting the terms of the gift, both with regard to its payment and purposes, is of increasing importance the larger the amount and the more lasting the purpose. For example, a gift intended to create an endowment fund will be administered by people in the future, after the lifetimes of those who were involved in the conversations leading to the gift. Documenting understandings and agreements in writing is not only advisable from a legal perspective but consistent with an organization's moral obligation to remain faithful to the intentions of a donor who has provided a gift it has accepted. These understandings may be documented in a formal contract or in a **memorandum of understanding**, a hypothetical example of which is provided in Box 7.2.

BOX 7.2 Sample Memorandum of Understanding

Memorandum of Understanding Concerning the Jane and John Doe Endowment at the Center for American Understanding

Jane and John Doe ("the Donors") have expressed their desire to make a gift to the Center for American Understanding ("the Center"), to establish an endowed fund ("the Fund"), to be administered by the Center in perpetuity. This memorandum describes the terms and conditions of the gift and the mutual understandings of the Donors and the Center. It will be made a part of the Center's permanent file regarding the Fund, as a guide to those who will administer the Fund in the future.

About the Donors

Jane and John Doe are long-standing friends of the Center, and Mrs. Doe has served as a member of its board of trustees since 2010. Mrs. Doe is the chairman and chief executive officer of Jones International Trading Corporation, engaged in the management of relationships among governments and private firms throughout the Western Hemisphere. Mr. Doe is a retired foreign service officer, whose experience included service in several Latin American nations. Both Jane and John Doe believe that the future of prosperity throughout the hemisphere will require increased understanding among citizens of all nations, and their gift to the Center is intended to advance that goal.

Name and Purpose

The Fund will be known as "The Jane and John Doe Endowment." Its purpose will be to provide annual income in perpetuity to support activities of the Center described below.

Funding and Investment

The Fund will be established with gifts from Jane and John Doe totaling one million dollars ($1,000,000). These gifts will be paid with cash or negotiable securities in five equal installments of no less than two hundred thousand dollars ($200,000) each, payable annually on or before December 31 from 2016 to 2020.

These gifts will comprise the original corpus of the Fund, to be invested and reinvested in perpetuity under policies established by the Center's board of trustees. The Fund may be comingled with other endowments of the Center for purposes of investment, but a separate accounting of principal and income attributable to the Fund shall be maintained.

Investment earnings of the Fund may be expended for purposes described below. The amount of earnings available for spending in any given year will be determined according to policies established by the Center's board of trustees.

Uses of Income

Annual earnings of the Fund may be expended at the discretion of the Center's president to support any of the following activities. 1) Stipends for student interns working at the Center, with preference to be given to young men and women who express an intention to

(Continued)

(Continued)

pursue careers in international business related to the Americas. 2) Costs of bringing guest lecturers to the Center or for sponsoring seminars concerning relationships among nations of the Americas. Such costs supported by the Fund's income may include honoraria, travel and lodging for lecturers or seminar participants, costs of publicizing the lectures or seminars, related social activities, and the printing and distribution of proceedings. 3) Research related to economic cooperation among the nations of the Americas.

Recognition and Reporting

The Center will include the Fund in its listing of endowed funds in every annual report. The names of Jane and John Doe will be included as "Benefactors of the Center" on the donor wall in the president's suite. So long as one of them is living, the Center will provide an annual report to Jane and John Doe concerning the status of the Fund and activities undertaken with its support.

Changed Conditions

If at some future time it becomes impossible for the Fund to serve the purposes for which it was created, the Center's board of trustees shall direct that its principal and income be devoted to alternative purposes of the Center that it deems to be most consistent with the original intentions of the Donors.

Mutual Understanding

We agree that this memorandum accurately reflects our mutual understandings concerning the gift from Jane and John Doe to the Center and the Center's administration of the Fund.

BY THE DONORS:

———————

Jane Doe   Date

———————

John Doe   Date

FOR THE CENTER:

BY:

———————

I. M. Executive, President   Date

Note: This sample was developed by the author. It is hypothetical and illustrative only. It is not intended as a draft to be adopted for any legal purpose. Gift agreements or memoranda of understanding should be drafted and reviewed by legal counsel of the nonprofit organization and the donor.

MAINTAINING CLARITY OF PURPOSE

As mentioned previously, some people may find the vocabulary and methods of major-gifts fundraising to be uncomfortable or even offensive. It may imply the manipulation of people for the purpose of inducing them to part with their money. Surely it is important for fundraisers to avoid using the jargon of their field in the presence of prospective donors, who might experience such a reaction.

But it is also important to maintain clarity about the purpose of major-gifts fundraising. In the end, it is not about obtaining money but about advancing the programs and causes of nonprofit organizations and institutions, which are important and worthy of a professional, well-managed, and effective approach. And it is essential to remember that making a gift is not something onerous but rather an action that brings great satisfaction to those able to apply their wealth to noble ends. In the conclusion to his *Handbook for Educational Fund Raising*, Pray (1981) expressed a similar sentiment in words that continue to be true even decades later. He writes, "[This is] a world in which greed and need and misery are still all too dominant, but [it is also] a world in which some of the more decent of human . . . urges and needs can come together with some hope of making a significant impact on the future." He adds in a message to fellow fundraising professionals, "To be a part of the line of contact between the institution and the better impulses of humanity outside is a privilege we share with relatively few others" (p. 403).

CHAPTER SUMMARY

A major gift may be five to twenty times as much as a donor's annual gift (Dunlop, 2002), is usually made to meet a special need of the organization, and may be paid from the donor's income or assets. Many are pledged and are paid in installments over time.

The process for raising major gifts is a particular application of the generic fundraising cycle, including the identification and qualification of prospects, cultivation, solicitation, and stewardship. The cultivation phase is also a cycle that includes distinct stages. Smith (1977) identified the *Five I's* of identification, interest, information, involvement, and investment. Dunlop (2002) offers a similar model with different terms and additional phases: identification, information, awareness, understanding, caring, involvement, and commitment. Both models are in some respects consistent with theory regarding donor motivations (Schervish & Havens, 2002), but they are also *domino models* in that they imply one step automatically follows the other, which is contradicted by theory (Kelly, 1998). Both have intuitive appeal and seem to be consistent with some donor accounts of their experiences. A critical step in both models is the involvement of the prospective donors in program, that is, in substance, which leads to psychological identification with the organization and its cause (Schervish & Havens, 2002; Seymour, 1966). People involved in an organization also tend to give because of the *rule of consistency* (Cialdini, 2003), which suggests that individuals are motivated to behave in ways consistent with the commitments they have made in the past or that are reflected through their actions.

Relationships with prospective donors are cultivated in a planned and systematic manner. Staff members of the nonprofit are assigned as *relationship managers* or *prospect managers*. They are often *major-gifts officers* (or just *gift officers*). They maintain a *portfolio* of prospective donors and engage in actions intended to move prospects through the *pipeline*, from identification to a major gift, within about eighteen to twenty-four months (Scarpucci & Lange, 2007). The actions are commonly known as *moves* (or *initiatives*), and an organized approach to making them is *moves management*. Initiatives include *foreground initiatives* and *background initiatives* and often are undertaken with *natural partners*, people who know the prospect and can help (Dunlop, 1993, 2002).

Management of major-gifts fundraising may be relatively simple for small organizations, which may just maintain a list of their top twenty-five or so prospects. Larger organizations require more complex systems and policies governing contact with donors and prospects. Prospects are prioritized according to their financial *capacity* and *inclination* to give, with time and attention allocated accordingly in order to achieve maximum long-term support. Other variables, including some related to the donor's life stage, are used by some organizations to establish similar priority rankings (Dupree, n.d.).

Prospect managers' activity is planned and tracked. Assigned prospects may be in different *stages* of the *cultivation cycle*, including discovery, cultivation, solicitation, or stewardship. A typical portfolio includes seventy-five to one hundred fifty prospects, which is possibly the maximum number of relationships an individual can maintain (Dunbar, 2010; Scarpucci & Lange, 2007). In large and especially decentralized organizations, contact with prospects is regulated by formal policies, or *protocols*, that may require prior clearance and *contact reports* (Birkholz, 2008). Gift officer performance is evaluated by various criteria, which should include productive activity rather than just the amount of money raised, in order to assure that their time and effort are consistent with prospect priority rankings and the priorities of the organization (Dupree, n.d.).

Relationships with donors are developed through personal contacts. Since major donors are inclined to give, an *inclination* or *discernment* approach is recommended, rather than a *scolding* or *cajoling model* (Schervish & Havens, 2002). Relationships should be developed at an appropriate pace and with an appropriate tone (Dunlop, 2002; Kelly, 1998). Donor relationships should be with the organization, of which the fundraiser is an agent, and not be viewed as a personal relationship by either party (Temple, 2011).

Personal visits may be for the purpose of discovery, cultivation, solicitation, or stewardship. During cultivation, the fundraiser and the prospective donor mutually consider gift opportunities, and *coorientation theory* may explain the process through which a common perspective is achieved (McLeod & Chaffee, 1973; Newcomb, 1953). Solicitation visits are carefully planned with regard to who should be involved, the location, the amount and purpose of the gift to be requested, the assignment of speaking roles, appropriate endings under various conditions, and responses to anticipated donor concerns, called *objections* (Fredericks, 2010; Matheny, 2010). Most experts think that a solicitation team is most effective, with a combination of the CEO and a volunteer who has already given advanced as an ideal. A solicitation team of at least two people offers advantages, but too many people can be problematic. Most experts recommend that a solicitation occur at the prospect's home or office and that a specific amount be requested. There are differences of opinion regarding the use of written proposals (Fredericks, 2010).

Solicitation meetings follow a format that is commonly prescribed, including opening conversation, a transition to the ask, the ask, a period of silence while the prospect responds, responses to objections, and a conclusion that includes a specific plan for follow-up. The follow-up may include additional meetings, negotiation, and the drafting of a formal gift agreement or *memorandum of understanding*.

Some people may find the vocabulary and methods of major-gifts fundraising to be uncomfortable, but it is important to remember the noble purposes for which gifts are solicited and made.

Key Terms and Concepts

Affinity (of prospect)

The ask

Background initiative

Cajoling model (scolding model)

Coorientation theory

Cultivation visit

Discovery visit

Domino model

Donor intent

Five I's

Five R's

Foreground initiative

Inclination model (discernment model)

Life stage (of prospect)

Major-gifts officer (gift officer)

Memorandum of understanding

Moves

Moves management

Natural partners

Objections

Pipeline (of major-gifts prospects)

Portfolio

Pre-ask conversation

Primes

Principal gift

Prospect manager

Protocols

Readiness

Relationship manager

Rule of consistency

Secondaries

Special gift

Stage

Stretch gift

Tracking (of initiatives/moves)

Trial gift

Case 7.1:   Don R. N. Blitzer

SCENARIO

The executive director and director of development of College Opportunity, a nonprofit that assists high school students gain admission to college, plan to visit Don at his office to solicit his gift to a campaign for renovation and expansion of its headquarters building, where most programs are conducted. Given plans for the project, the gift could be paid over five years.

PROSPECT PROFILE

Age: 50

Family: married (wife Donna), two children in college

Business: independent home building contractor

Relationship: Don is a member of the College Opportunity board of directors, serving his first three-year term. He was recruited to the board by its chair, who knew him through a business relationship.

Gift history: The Blitzers have made annual-fund gifts for years, usually ranging from $1,000 to $2,500. Since Don was elected to the board of directors two years ago, their annual gift has been $5,000. The Blitzers, or Don's company, also are listed as annual donors to other organizations, with gifts ranging from $100 to $5,000. Donna has been a volunteer at College Opportunity, counseling young people about college admissions.

Assets/capacity: Don is a home builder. The business is a private company, so no information on revenues or profits is available, but most people say that Don has been very successful. The Blitzer home, located across town from the College Opportunity facility, is valued at $1 million. Don Blitzer is also the owner of a small office building where his company and other commercial tenants are located. The building has an appraised value of $2 million. The development office rates the Blitzers as capable of a $500,000 gift, payable over five years.

Previous contacts: The chair of the College Opportunity board knew Don Blitzer through business. He invited Don to join the board. Don was reluctant at first, saying he is overcommitted, but then accepted. He has attended most board meetings but has not participated on a committee. The executive director visited Don and his wife, Donna, at their home a year ago, shortly after Don had joined the board, and discussed the plan for the facility expansion. She did not solicit a gift. Donna did not seem interested and left the room to do other things several times during the meeting. The executive director gained the impression that she was not interested in the discussion and maybe was uncomfortable with it. Don showed considerable interest and mentioned that since he is a builder, he would be willing to provide advice on the project.

Project: College Opportunity is expanding its headquarters facility, which is also the site at which most of its programs are offered. The total project cost is $10 million, all to be funded through philanthropy. The project will include refurbishing of the existing building and construction of two new wings. The building currently has no name, and the level for a naming gift has been set at $5 million. Each of the new wings can be named for $1 million and each of several study rooms for $500,000 each. Donors of gifts below $500,000 will be listed on a plaque in the lobby.

Case 7.2:   Phillis N. Thropist

SCENARIO

The executive director and a trustee of an art gallery, now known as City Gallery, are planning to visit Phillis at home to solicit her gift to the gallery's campaign.

PROSPECT PROFILE

Age: 70

Family: widowed, no children

Business: Phillis's late husband, Sam, was a corporation executive and a trustee of the gallery. He passed away shortly after retiring at age sixty-five. Phillis is an artist who sells some of her work at regional art shows and fairs.

Relationship: When Sam was a trustee of the gallery, Phillis attended many events with him. She has not attended many events since his death.

Gift history: When Sam was alive, the Thropists regularly gave $10,000 to the annual fund. Since Sam's death, Phillis has continued to give but at the $5,000 level.

Assets/capacity: Phillis lives in the same house she and Sam occupied while he was alive, in the next town over from the where the gallery is located. It is a modest house, which includes her art studio. It is appraised at $250,000. We have little additional information about her assets but presume that she continues to receive income from Sam's retirement. Phillis is rated by the development office as a prospect for a $50,000 gift, payable over five years.

Previous contacts: Phillis's annual gift qualifies her as a member of the gallery's Director's Circle. She came to a few luncheons right after Sam passed away, but she has not been at the gallery lately. The curator of the gallery knows Phillis. She occasionally visits Phillis at her home to discuss art and says that Phillis is especially interested in opportunities for young artists and students pursuing careers in gallery administration. Phillis also has mentioned to the curator how much Sam enjoyed serving on the gallery's board and said she would like to "give something back" someday. The curator thinks that Phillis has "some money" but doesn't know anything more detailed. She says that Phillis should be solicited for a gift to the campaign but thinks the amount requested should not be "too ambitious."

Project: The overall campaign is for $2 million. Of that amount $1 million will be for renovation of the gallery. Since it is now known merely as City Gallery, it could be renamed to recognize a $500,000 gift toward the renovation. In addition, the campaign will raise $1 million to endow internships for students who work at the gallery, and a fund/internship can be named with a $50,000 gift.

Case 7.3: Martha and Fred Generous

SCENARIO

The president and a major-gifts officer from Siwash College are planning to visit Martha and Fred together at home to solicit a major gift toward the college's campaign.

PROSPECT PROFILE

Ages: 62, 60

Family: Married, two grown children.

Business: Martha and Fred own and operate a large local building supply company.

Relationship: Martha and Fred graduated from college in another state. But they have developed a relationship with Siwash over the past twenty years. Their daughter is an alumna. They live near the campus and see it as important to the local economy. They have provided part-time jobs to many students from the college. Martha serves on the board of trustees. Fred was active as an annual-fund volunteer when their daughter was a student at the college but has not been active since.

Gift history: Martha and Fred give $1,000 to the annual fund every year. In the college's last campaign, they gave $25,000, paid over five years. That was when their daughter was a student. It is known that they recently made $50,000 gifts to building projects at their church and at a local nonprofit.

Assets/capacity: Martha and Fred's home is appraised at $350,000, and it is known that Martha has investments inherited from her father, who was a stockbroker. The development office has rated Martha and Fred as prospects for a $100,000 gift.

Previous contacts: Martha is well aware of the college's campaign. As a member of the board of trustees, she was present in all the planning discussions and voted to approve the campaign. She belongs to the same private club as the chair of the college's board of trustees. On one occasion, she told the chair casually, "I know someone will be coming to see me about the campaign. Fred and I are discussing it now."

Project: The college is in a special capital campaign for a library renovation project. The total cost is $5 million; $2 million already has been committed by the chair of the board and another $1 million from a major bank serving the region.

Case 7.4: Ellen Entrepreneur

SCENARIO

The chief development officer and a board member of Brilliant Science Center (BSC) are visiting Ellen at her apartment in New York to solicit her gift to the center's campaign.

PROSPECT PROFILE

Age: 40

Family: Ellen is single

Business: Ellen is a technology entrepreneur. She started her own software business shortly after graduating from college and ten years later sold her company. She now is an investor who spends part of the year in New York and part of the year in California. She is involved in a variety of new start-up companies.

Relationship: Ellen had a postdoctoral research fellowship at the Brilliant Science Center after she finished graduate school but left after her first year to start her company.

Gift history: Ellen has made a few gifts to the annual fund in the $500 to $1,000 range but also misses some years. Three years ago, she gave the center a gift of $100,000, paid in cash, to provide scholarships for young people from urban backgrounds who would attend a new summer program aimed at increasing their interest in science and technology careers. She is on the board of a small nonprofit in New York that works with low-income children to help them go to college.

Assets/capacity: Ellen's apartment in New York is valued at $2.5 million. Her second home, in California, is valued at $1.5 million. We know that she received $20 million from the sale of her company, but we do not know the nature of private investments she now holds. The center's development office has Ellen rated as a prospect for a $1 million gift.

Previous contacts: Ellen stays in touch with some of the full-time researchers at the center, and a few were early investors in her company. Her $100,000 gift was solicited by one of them, who also was a donor to the special summer program. The center's director visited her once to thank her for her $100,000 gift and asked her if she would consider joining the center's board. She said she was too busy and declined. The chief development officer has tried to visit Ellen on several previous occasions, but she always has been traveling or unavailable, so he is pleased to have secured this appointment and thinks maybe having a board member involved made the difference.

Project: The center is in a comprehensive campaign for $50 million, including $40 million for endowment. This will provide support for ongoing research projects, reducing the center's reliance on annual grants, and will support more postdoctoral fellowships like the one Ellen held. Based on the amount of fellowship stipends that are provided and in light of the center's investment policies, a fellowship can be endowed and named with a gift of $750,000.

Questions for Discussion

Suppose you are a member of the major-gifts team for the nonprofit described in each of the previous cases and are asked to participate in a discussion to develop a strategy for each solicitation visit. For each case, consider the following questions. (Of course, each profile is quite brief, so your answers will require some speculation and perhaps imagination.)

1. Based on the history described in the profile, do you think the prospect is ready to be solicited? If not, why?

2. Do you think the planned scenario—that is, the time, place, and participants in the meeting—is the right one? Should other people have been involved? Are there obvious natural partners who should be consulted about the best way to proceed? Are there others who should be included in the meeting? Why?

3. What do you think motivates this prospect? What can you discern about this from his or her past giving and overall relationship with the organization? Do the theories of donor motivation discussed in Chapter 3 add to understanding of the donor's motivational type?

4. Assuming the solicitation visit goes forward as described, how should the discussion unfold—which member of the team should start the conversation, which should ask for the gift, which should decide when to close the meeting, and so forth? Why? What might be the pros and cons of various alternatives?

5. Considering what you know about each prospect, how should the solicitors make their case? What arguments might be most effective with each of these prospects? What points should be emphasized? How much emphasis should they give to naming opportunities?

6. What should be the ask amount? Should they ask the prospect for a specific amount? If so, based on the prospect's profile, what should that amount be? Should they ask for the amount suggested in the profile or suggest a larger gift first, then be prepared to negotiate to a lesser amount? Should they begin with a general range and be guided by the prospect's response? What might be the benefits and risks in each of these approaches?

7. Should the solicitors prepare a written proposal in advance of the solicitation meeting? Why or why not?

8. What questions or concerns (objections) might the donor raise, and how should the solicitors be prepared to respond to each?

9. Assume that the prospect does not make a decision during the solicitation visit. How should the solicitors finish the meeting, and what follow-up should they propose?

Suggestions for Further Reading

Books

Fredericks, L. (2010). *The ask: How to ask for support for your nonprofit cause, creative project, or business venture.* San Francisco: Jossey-Bass.

Matheny, R. E. (2010). *Major gifts: Solicitation strategies.* Washington, DC: Council for Advancement and Support of Education.

Walker, J. I. (2006). *Nonprofit essentials: Major gifts.* Hoboken, NJ: Wiley.

Book Chapter

Dunlop, D. R. (2002). Major gift programs. In Worth, M. J. (Ed.), *New strategies for educational fund raising* (pp. 89–104). Westport, CT: American Council on Education and Praeger. (Note: This work is dated but considered a classic, in which Dunlop defines many of the terms and concepts used in major-gifts fundraising today.)

Articles

Knowles, P., & Gomes, R. (2009). Building relationships with major-gift donors: A major-gift decision-making, relationship-building model. *Journal of Nonprofit & Public Sector Marketing, 21*(4), 384–406.

Schervish, P. G., & Havens, J. J. (2002, March). The new physics of philanthropy: The supply side vectors of charitable giving: Part II: The spiritual side of the supply side. *CASE International Journal of Educational Advancement*, 2(3), 221–241.

The delicate balance. (Winter, 2014). *Grenzebach-Glier Quarterly Review,* http://www .grenzebachglier.com/gga-quarterly-review.html.

Website

Public Broadcasting Major Giving Initiative: http://majorgivingnow.org

Notes

1. Dupree recommends that major-gifts officers who exceed 80 points receive an incentive bonus. The subject of incentive compensation for major-gifts officers is controversial. It is discussed further in Chapter 14, which discusses ethical issues.

2. The terms *visits* and *calls* are used interchangeably in the literature to describe a personal meeting with the prospect at the fundraiser's initiative. Of course, a call could be a contact made by phone, but sometimes a visit is also referred to as a "call," as in "calling upon" a person at home or the office.

CHAPTER 8

Planned Giving

In 1999, John J. Havens and Paul G. Schervish, scholars at Boston College, declared that "a golden age of philanthropy is dawning." Based on their research, they predicted that an intergenerational transfer of wealth totaling at least $41 trillion would occur by 2052, including $6 trillion that would go to charity (Havens & Schervish, 1999). Their findings were greeted as good news, except perhaps by some who contemplated the implications. Their projections anticipate the eventual demise of the baby boom generation, one of the largest segments of the current population.

Havens and Schervish's estimates of the amount to be transferred were much higher than previous estimates and have been challenged (Hall, 2006; James, 2009a). However, in 2014, these scholars released results of a new study that estimated a transfer of $59 trillion by 2061 (Havens & Scherish, 2014). Regardless of the specific amount to be transferred, the reality remains that the largest generation of Americans is aging and will eventually be deceased. Possessing six times the financial assets of their predecessors at the same age, baby boomers are clearly in a position to be philanthropic (Gist, 2005). The decades ahead may be a golden age for philanthropy. In anticipation of that possibility, a golden age for planned giving has already arrived.

Many forms of what we call planned giving have a long history. For example, charitable bequests and gift annuities have existed in Europe and the United States for centuries; the American Council on Gift Annuities was established in 1927. But two national laws are often mentioned as having given impetus to planned giving as we know it today—the Tax Reform Act of 1969, which changed the rules of gift planning, and the Tax Reform Act of 1986, which enhanced the attractiveness of some planned-giving vehicles.

Changes in tax policy and the demographic trends just mentioned have given impetus to the growth of planned giving as a recognized and important specialization within the fundraising profession. Once common only in large institutions, **planned-giving officers** or **gift planners** are now more common in various types of nonprofit organizations. There also has been growth in the numbers of planned-giving professionals employed in financial institutions, law firms, and wealth management firms, as well as independent gift planners and consultants. The Partnership for Philanthropic Planning, originally the National Committee on Planned Giving, was created in 1988 and is a federation of 108 local councils and 8,000 individual members. PPP publishes a journal and provides extensive training programs, as do local councils.

At least a basic understanding of planned giving has become essential for all fundraising professionals as well as chief executive officers and even volunteer leaders who interact with donors. This chapter is intended to provide that basic understanding. Students who wish to learn more are encouraged to explore further reading suggested at the end of this chapter.

DEFINITIONS AND KEY POINTS

The term *planned giving* does not imply that other gifts are necessarily spontaneous or made without forethought, that is, unplanned. But planned gifts involve coordination and integration with the donor's overall financial and estate planning and take maximum advantage of the incentives for charitable giving included in the tax law.

It is important to reiterate a point made earlier in this text. No person ever *gains* from making a charitable gift. He or she would always be better off by paying the taxes due and keeping the rest. Taking advantage of the incentives provided in the tax law is not tax evasion; it is not illegal or unethical. The tax incentives have been placed in the law intentionally in order to encourage people to make gifts and to make it possible for them to give more. That is because we have decided as a society that charity and philanthropy are important and have reflected that value in our public policy.

Remember from Chapter 4 that planned giving is viewed in this text as a strategy for major gifts, rather than as a core solicitation program. But most organizations do not limit the marketing of planned giving to individuals who have been identified as major-gift prospects. The criteria by which potential planned-giving prospects may be identified are discussed further shortly, but they often include regular donors to the annual fund, even if they are not rated with significant financial capacity. As Gerry Lenfest (2011), himself a major philanthropist, writes, "Planned gifts are the major gifts of the middle class and such gifts, cumulatively, have a significant impact" (p. xvi). On the other hand, planned gifts are a component of many major gifts and are the largest source of gifts to endowment.

Nor is planned giving to be viewed as something of interest only to large nonprofit organizations and institutions. To be sure, some planned gifts can be complex and require the involvement of professional specialists. But others, such as bequests, are quite simple and can be promoted by nonprofit organizations of all sizes, at little additional cost. Lenfest (2011) addresses this point as well, writing, "No organization is too small to benefit from having a planned giving endeavor as a critical component of its development program. It can be very tempting for charities to focus limited resources only on immediate annual giving or short term pledges, such as for capital campaigns. However, for any nonprofit organization to achieve long-term sustainability, it must incorporate, at the very least, the fundamentals of a planned giving program" (p. xvi).

OVERVIEW OF TAX LAW AND IMPLICATIONS FOR GIVING

Planned giving maximizes the incentives to philanthropy provided in the tax laws, so at least a basic understanding of tax law is important to determining which planned-giving vehicles may be most appropriate in various situations. Tax law is complex, and this text does not attempt to provide a thorough explanation. Many points are simplified. In addition, the discussion only applies to federal taxes and does not address state taxes, which also have an impact on charitable giving. Students are encouraged to look to other sources for a more complete understanding and not to rely on the brief presentations in this chapter in actual practice.

Impact of Taxes

The relevance of taxes for charitable giving was discussed briefly in Chapter 2, but let's review it. Individual donors are permitted to deduct charitable gifts from their income before calculating their tax due. There are certain limits, but they are ignored here in the interest of simplicity. The tax deduction produces a tax saving that, in effect, lowers the out-of-pocket cost of making the gift. In the example from Chapter 2, a donor is in the 25 percent tax bracket and makes a $100 gift to a charitable organization. He or she can deduct that $100 from his or her income before calculating the tax due. At 25 percent, that produces a tax saving of $25; in other words, the donor's tax bill will be $25 less than it would have been without the deduction. The effect of the deduction is to reduce the actual out-of-pocket cost of that gift from $100 to $75, since the additional $25 would otherwise have been paid in taxes.

This basic principle applies to three federal taxes an individual might pay: the **income tax**, the **capital gains tax**, and the **estate tax**. Of course, many of us pay other taxes, including, for example, payroll taxes, sales taxes, and property taxes. But these taxes do not provide for a charitable deduction, so they are not relevant to our discussion here. There is also a federal *gift tax*, but its workings are complex and it is ignored here, for the sake of simplicity.

Income Tax

We are all familiar with income taxes. Unless an individual's taxable income is below a minimum amount, he or she will pay federal income tax, on a graduated scale, as shown in Box 8.1. The higher a person's income, the higher the **marginal tax rate** he or she will pay on income *exceeding a certain level*. That does not mean that the person will pay that rate on all of his or her income, since some will be taxed at lower rates. For example, the top bracket in 2014 is 39.6 percent on income over $406,750. That does not mean that a person making just one dollar over that amount would pay 39.6 percent on all of his or her income, just on the extra dollar.

Capital Gains Tax

If someone buys an asset and then sells it for a higher price, that person has a *capital gain*. For example, if that individual buys a stock for $100 and sells it for $200, there is a capital gain of $100. That gain may be subject to the capital gains tax. Again, someone whose income is below a minimum level would not have to pay, but others would have to pay either a 15 percent or 20 percent tax on capital gains, depending on the level of total taxable income (2014 rates). These rates are less than the rates on ordinary income, which includes money earned as salary. Lower tax rates on capital gains are intended to encourage people to invest and help the economy to grow. The capital gains tax applies to stocks, real estate, and other assets, but special rules apply to a home that is a personal residence. As with the income tax, the law provides incentives to charitable giving by enabling individuals to reduce or avoid the capital gains tax.

Estate Tax

Most Americans will never need to worry about the federal estate tax. It applies to the assets left behind when a person dies, with some exceptions, but only to that portion of a taxable estate that exceeds $5,340,000 (in 2014).[1] In some circumstances a couple may have an exemption of double that amount. Again, the estate tax affects a very small percentage of people, but for the very wealthy it may be significant, since the top rate can be 40 percent. Making a gift to charity through a will removes the gifted assets from the person's taxable estate and thus reduces the amount that might be subject to the estate tax. Again, this provides an incentive to charitable giving.

As we will see as we work through some examples, all three taxes may be involved in some gift plans, and some planned-giving vehicles are particularly advantageous with regard to one or more of them. Remember that point, because it has an important implication: the gift plan best suited to a particular individual depends on what type of assets that person owns and about which of the three taxes he or she is most concerned.

BOX 8.1   U.S. Federal Taxes Rates Relevant to Philanthropy

U.S. Federal Income Tax

Progressive marginal rates: 10%–39.6%

U.S. Federal Capital Gains Tax

0%–20% (20% for taxpayers in highest bracket)
(Plus a 3.8% Medicare surtax on high-income taxpayers)

U.S. Federal Estate Tax

Up to 40% on estates over $5,340,000 (in 2014)
(Could be $10,680,000 for a couple, under certain assumptions)

Source: www.irs.gov.

Note: Data show 2014 rates. Tax laws and rates change, and readers should check other sources for the current situation.

TYPES OF PLANNED GIFTS

As discussed in Chapter 4, there are three types of planned gifts—*outright planned gifts*, *expectancies*, and *deferred gifts*. Some outright gifts are planned gifts because they involve complex assets, such as stocks or real estate, and may require the assistance of financial experts to complete. An expectancy is a promise a donor makes to provide a gift to the organization at some future time, generally at death, through a bequest, life insurance, or a retirement plan. These are also commonly known as **testamentary gifts**. Deferred gifts are gifts the donor makes now but are not available to the organization until some future time, generally after the death of the donor or some other individual (Regenovich, 2011).

Before we move on to consider these types of gifts, one term needs to be defined, a **trust**. Not all planned gifts involve trusts, but some do. A trust is "a relationship in which one person holds title to property, subject to an obligation to keep or use the property for the benefit of another" (IRS, 2014c). A trust is managed by a **trustee**, who controls but does not personally own the assets held in the trust. The trustee, which might be an individual or a company, has a legal responsibility as a *fiduciary* to serve the interests of the trust's beneficiaries, which could be an individual, more than one individual, or a charitable organization. There are various types of trusts, and we encounter a couple of different ones in this chapter.

OVERVIEW OF PLANNED-GIVING VEHICLES

Now let's look at some of the more common planned-giving vehicles, within the three types mentioned: outright planned gifts, expectancies, and deferred gifts. Box 8.2 provides a summary of the most common vehicles, which are discussed in the following sections.

Outright Planned Gifts

An **outright planned gift** occurs when the person gives the money *now* and the nonprofit organization benefits *now*. Of course, that is the case with most gifts people make. But an outright gift is also a planned gift if the method of making it is based on financial and tax considerations. This section reviews three such methods—gifts of *appreciated property*, *donor-advised funds*, and *charitable lead trusts*.

Gifts of Appreciated Property

When most people think about making a gift, they probably think about paying with cash or perhaps a check or credit card. But the tax law makes it attractive for individuals to give **appreciated property**, meaning assets they own that have gone up in value since they bought them. Among the most common are real estate holdings and stocks, also called *equities*. That is because there is no capital gains tax to be paid if the appreciated property is given directly to a nonprofit organization.

BOX 8.2 Summary of Common Planned-Giving Vehicles

Name	Description	Most Attractive To
OUTRIGHT GIFTS		
Gift of appreciated property	An individual gives an asset, for example, stock or real estate, that has a value greater than what was paid to acquire it (cost basis).	Individuals who wish to receive an income tax deduction for the full value of the asset and avoid paying a capital gains tax on its sale.
Donor-advised fund	An individual irrevocably transfers assets to a fund, maintained by a community foundation or other charitable entity. The donor (or other designated individual) retains the right to recommend recipients of gifts to be made from the fund but cannot direct or require the distributions.	Individuals who wish to earn an immediate income tax deduction for their gifts to the donor-advised fund but to have the funds paid to one or more nonprofit organizations in the future. This may be the case with individuals who have a year in which they receive unusually high income, for example, upon sale of an asset or a business.
Lead trust	An individual places assets in a trust, which is managed by a trustee. The trustee pays income earned by investments of the trust to a nonprofit organization for a specified period of years. At the end of that period, the trust ends and the assets are returned to the donor, the donor's heirs, or to other named beneficiaries.	Individuals who own income-producing assets, do not need the income they produce, and wish to make gifts to a nonprofit organization. There are also potential estate tax savings if the assets are ultimately returned to the donor's heirs.
EXPECTANCIES (TESTAMENTARY GIFTS)		
Bequest	A statement in an individual's will or revocable trust that designates a specific asset, amount, or percentage of the estate to be paid as a gift to a nonprofit organization upon the individual's death.	Individuals who wish to retain control of their assets during their lifetimes and who seek a simple method of making a charitable gift at death.
Retirement plan or IRA	An individual names a nonprofit organization as the beneficiary of assets remaining in a retirement plan or IRA at the individual's death.	Individuals who wish to retain access to their retirement funds while living and who seek a simple method of making a charitable gift at death.
Life insurance	A nonprofit organization is named as the owner and beneficiary of a life insurance policy that will pay a benefit to the organization upon the individual's death.	Individuals who can afford premium payments but wish to make a larger gift at death than their assets may permit.

DEFERRED GIFTS

Charitable gift annuity	A contract between an individual and a nonprofit organization in which the organization agrees to pay a fixed lifetime income to the individual (or to another designated individual) in exchange for the gift. The income payments are secured by the full faith and credit of the organization. Some charitable gift annuities are immediate (the income starts as soon as the gift is made) and others are deferred (the income begins at some designated future date). There are other variations.	Individuals who wish to receive an immediate income tax deduction (for a portion of the gift) and receive a relatively secure but fixed lifetime income. A fixed income may be more attractive to older donors, who are less concerned with the effects of inflation over their remaining lives.
Charitable remainder trust	An individual gives assets to a trust. The trustee manages the trust and pays income to the individual (or to one or more other designated individual) for life. Upon the death of the last surviving income recipient, the trustee pays the trust's principal to a designated nonprofit organization. There are two basic types. Charitable remainder annuity trusts pay a fixed income. Charitable remainder unitrusts pay a variable income that is a fixed percentage of the trust's assets each year. Income payments would cease if the trust's assets became depleted. There are other variations.	Individuals who own appreciated assets and wish to avoid or defer capital gains taxes that would be payable if the assets were sold outside of the trust. Individuals who seek an immediate income tax deduction (for a portion of the gift). The unitrust may be attractive to individuals who want the possibility of increasing income payments over their lifetimes and are willing to accept the risk of an income that may vary from year to year.
Life estate	An individual gives his or her personal residence to a nonprofit organization, retaining the right to continue living there for his or her lifetime.	Individuals who desire to use their homes as an asset to make a gift but also desire to continue living there.

Note: Compiled by the author from various sources.

Let's consider an example in which a person paid $2,000 for a stock that is now worth $10,000. The $2,000 original cost is also known as the **cost basis**. And let's assume that the person has a high income, so he or she is subject to a 20 percent capital gains tax rate. If he or she were to sell that stock, there would be a capital gain of $8,000, and a capital gains tax of $1,600 would be due (20 percent of the $8,000 capital gain). Now, that person could take the cash resulting from the sale of that stock after the tax, which would be $8,400, and give it to a charity, earning a tax deduction for that amount. If this person were in the top income tax bracket, with a marginal rate of 39.6 percent, that gift would produce a savings of $3,326 on income taxes ($8,400 × 39.6%).

But if the stock were to be given *directly* to the charity, the individual would pay *no capital gains tax* and receive a tax deduction for its full **fair market value**, that is, $10,000. In addition, the gift would provide the individual with an income tax savings of $3,960 ($10,000 × 39.6% tax rate). The charity can sell the stock and will not pay a capital gains tax either, because it is a tax-exempt organization. Consider the advantages of this approach to the individual taxpayer and the organization:

Market value of the stock =	$10,000
Minus original cost (cost basis)	− $2,000
Capital gain	$8,000
Income tax charitable deduction	$10,000
Income tax savings	
($10,000 × 39.6% tax bracket)	$3,960
Capital gains tax avoided	
($8,000 × 20% capital gains tax rate)	$1,600
Total tax savings	$5,560
Donor's out-of-pocket cost of the gift	
($10,000 − total tax saving of $5,560)	$4,440
Charity receives	$10,000

Thus, by giving the stock rather than selling it first, both the donor and the charity have benefitted. The charity has received $10,000, rather than $8,400. And the individual has saved a total of $5,560 on taxes, rather than $3,326. In general, it is advantageous for donors to give appreciated assets to charity rather than sell them first and give the resulting cash. On the other hand, if an asset has declined in value, the donor is often advised to sell it first, deduct the loss, and then give the proceeds to the charity, earning a charitable deduction.

Donor-Advised Funds

Donor-advised funds are offered by funding intermediaries, such as community foundations and charitable entities affiliated with commercial wealth management firms, including, for example, Fidelity Charitable, operated by Fidelity Investments. Although created in the 1930s, the use of such funds has grown dramatically since the 1990s. It was estimated that assets in donor-advised funds totaled $45 billion in 2013, more than the assets of the Bill and Melinda Gates Foundation (Neyfakh, 2013).

The donor-advised fund is a nonprofit entity—a public charity—so the donor receives an income tax deduction when he or she makes a gift to the fund. If the gift is made with appreciated securities, the donor also can avoid the capital gains tax. The funds are managed by a trustee, who has responsibility for the funds but does not own them. And the money in the donor-advised fund need not be paid out to operating nonprofits immediately. The donor can make *recommendations* to the trustee of what gifts to make, to which organizations, and when. This offers some obvious advantages. For example, think about a donor who has a windfall, perhaps from the sale of an investment or a business. He or she could give money to a donor-advised fund and earn an immediate income tax deduction, helping to reduce the tax on that windfall, but then spread out the grants to be made from the fund over a longer period of time. This offers an attractive way to manage an individual's tax liability from year to year while maintaining flexibility in the distribution of the gifts.

In some ways, establishing a donor-advised fund is similar to creating a foundation, but with two advantages. There is less administrative cost involved, and donor-advised funds are not required by law to pay out a minimum amount each year, as are private foundations. Some trustees do establish minimum distributions, but that is not a requirement of law. These and other reasons account for the growing popularity of such funds.

Some large nonprofit institutions, such as universities, offer donor-advised funds, competing with commercial firms and community foundations. For the majority of nonprofits that do not, donor-advised funds raise some complications. For one, many organizations would prefer to receive gifts directly rather than see them go to a donor-advised fund, which they may view as competing for the donor's dollars. Second, when the trustee of the donor-advised fund sends a gift to the nonprofit, the fund is legally the donor. The organization needs to assure that it identifies the original donor to the donor-advised fund and expresses thanks to that individual, while also sending the official gift receipt to the trustee. Third, an individual donor cannot make a pledge to a nonprofit and then have pledge payments come from a donor-advised fund. That is because the donor no longer controls the assets in the donor-advised fund and can only make recommendations of distributions to the trustee. In other words, the individual cannot legally commit the assets of the donor-advised fund, which he or she does not control.

Lead Trusts

Another planned giving vehicle that provides immediate support for a nonprofit organization is the **charitable lead trust**. The donor places an income-producing asset into the trust, which is managed by a trustee. The income the trust earns each year is given to a nonprofit organization or organizations, for the life of the trust, which may be the lifetime of the donor or a fixed term of years, commonly twenty. After the trust terminates, the assets it owns are returned to the donor or to his or her heirs. Perhaps the simplest way to think about a lead trust is in terms of a gift of income-producing real estate. The rents go to the charity for the lifetime of the trust and the property eventually returns to the donor or heirs.

The donor may receive a tax deduction for the value of the asset placed in the trust and may receive an income tax deduction for the stream of income paid to the nonprofit, depending on how the trust is structured. A significant advantage is potential savings on the estate tax if the trust is designed to eventually return assets to the donor's heirs. The way in which this works is complex, beyond the scope of the discussion here, but it may be an attractive feature to a very wealthy donor. Most nonprofits will never become involved with a lead trust but should be aware of it as a possible vehicle for a donor who owns income-producing assets, does not need the current income they produce, and may be concerned about estate taxes on a very substantial estate.

Expectancies

The term **expectancies** applies to promises that donors make with regard to gifts that will be paid at the time of their deaths. The term *testamentary gifts* is also commonly used. No assets change hands when the promise is made, so these are not outright gifts. And the arrangement generally can be changed during the donor's lifetime. The three most common vehicles are bequests, gifts from retirement plans and IRAs, and life insurance gifts.

Bequests

By a wide margin, a simple bequest is the most common vehicle for planned gifts, and many nonprofit organizations will never receive anything more complex. A bequest is a gift made from a person's estate following his or her death, based on an instruction to his or her executor written in a will.[2]

There are four basic types of bequests. A **general bequest** identifies an amount of money or a percentage of the estate to go to the charity (e.g., "$100,000" or "20 percent"). A **specific bequest** identifies a particular asset or item of property to be given to the nonprofit (e.g., "my vacation home in Florida" or "my Renoir"). A **residuary bequest** addresses what is left of a person's estate after other distributions have been made, for example, to friends and family members. And a **contingent bequest** states that money or an asset will be given to the charity only if another beneficiary does not survive. For example, someone might leave a portion of his or her estate to a nephew but say that the nephew's share should go to a charity in the unfortunate event that the nephew is no longer living when the individual dies.

It is important that the wording of a bequest be clear about the exact organization that is intended to benefit, since the donor will no longer be living to clarify if any confusion arises. So, for example, a will that instructs an executor of the estate to give money to "the cancer charity" could be problematic, since that could mean more than one organization. The following language, which describes a residuary bequest, is much more specific and, indeed, is recommended by the American Cancer Society for donors who wish to benefit that organization:

> I give, devise, and bequeath to the American Cancer Society, Inc., TAX I.D. #13-1788491, all [or state the fraction or percentage] of the rest, residue, and remainder of my estate, both real and personal. The American Cancer Society may be contacted

in care of its National Office of Probate and Trust Management Services, P.O. Box 720366, Oklahoma City, OK 73162, 1-800-ACS-2345. (American Cancer Society, 2015)

Since bequests are easy to understand, every nonprofit organization can encourage them and be prepared to provide recommended language to a donor or to his or her advisors.

Gifts From Retirement Plans and IRAs

A donor who has a retirement plan through his or her employer, or an individual retirement account (IRA), can name a beneficiary to receive the balance of assets remaining in the account at his or her death. This is even simpler than a bequest, since it often requires little more than filling out a form designating the charity as a beneficiary and does not require the involvement of an attorney to revise a will. Of course, the donor retains the right to change his or her mind and name a different beneficiary any time while he or she is living.

The tax advantage to this arrangement would be the avoidance of income taxes and possibly estate taxes that might be levied on the retirement funds when the donor dies; because the proceeds are passing to a charity, there would be no taxes to be paid. Donors old enough to qualify may withdraw funds from an IRA and then give that money to a nonprofit organization. That would be, of course, an outright gift. The law regarding the income tax implications of this type of transaction has changed over recent years. At the time of this writing in 2015, Congress was considering legislation that would affect the tax benefits associated with making charitable gifts directly from individual retirement accounts. It is not possible to predict what the law may be at the time this chapter is being read, and students are encouraged to check websites such as Independent Sector to learn what current law provides.

Life Insurance Gifts

As with a retirement account, an individual can name a charitable organization as the beneficiary of a life insurance policy, that is, as the entity to receive the death benefit paid when the individual dies. As with a bequest or other beneficiary designation, this can be changed at any time during the donor's lifetime.

It is also advantageous for a donor to give ownership of a life insurance policy to a nonprofit organization. If the policy has a cash value, that amount would be eligible for an income tax deduction. If the organization both owns the policy and is the beneficiary, the donor could pay the premiums on the life insurance policy and they would be tax deductible.

Deferred Gifts

Deferred gifts include transactions in which the donor gives money *now*, but the nonprofit organization does not receive the full benefit until after the donor's death. They are partially outright gifts, since the donor parts with the money or assets now. But they are also partially testamentary gifts, since the nonprofit does not receive the benefit until later. But, to be clear, there is a big difference between a testamentary gift and a deferred gift. In the former, the donor can change his or her mind at any time during his or her lifetime. A will can be revised and the beneficiaries of retirement fund and life insurance policies usually can be easily changed. With a deferred gift, the decision to give is **irrevocable**, meaning that it cannot be taken back. There are various types of deferred gifts; let's look in some detail at two of the most common—the *charitable gift annuity* and the *charitable remainder trust.*

Charitable Gift Annuity

A **charitable gift annuity** represents a simple contract between a nonprofit organization and one or two individuals. The donor agrees to pay a certain amount to the nonprofit, and the nonprofit agrees to pay to the donor (and/or another individual named by the donor) an income for life. The amount of the income is set as a percentage of the gift amount, but it remains *fixed* for the donor's entire life. Figure 8.1 illustrates the basic mechanism of a charitable gift annuity, which has the following features:

- The rate of income is negotiable, although most nonprofits follow rates recommended by the American Council on Gift Annuities (ACGA).

- Income payments can extend to two lives, so, for example, they could be made to the donor and a spouse or partner, then to the survivor.

- Income payments are backed by the full faith and credit of the nonprofit organization.

- The donor receives an income tax deduction for a *portion* of the payment made to the nonprofit (based on rate of income paid, the age of income beneficiary, and the **IRS discount rate** in effect at time of gift, also known as the **applicable federal rate**).

- A portion of annual income received by the donor is tax-exempt during the life expectancy of the income beneficiary. That is because it is assumed that some portion of the income paid is a return of the money used to purchase the annuity.

- If the annuity is purchased with appreciated property, any capital gains are spread out over the life expectancy of the income beneficiary, so some portion of the annual income is taxed at the capital gains rate.

Let's focus on the benefits of this type of gift to the donor and the nonprofit organization. The donor receives an income tax deduction for only a portion of the gift. That is because the IRS regards it as partly a gift and partly an investment, since the donor is expected to receive some of the money back. Obviously, the older the donor, the more this transaction is like a gift, since he or she will be receiving income for fewer years; a younger donor will receive more money back, so he or she gets a smaller deduction, all other things being equal. The ACGA rates reflect an assumption that the beneficiary will receive about 50 percent of the gift back and that about 50 percent of it will remain for the charity to use; the permissible deduction reflects that assumption. Of course, how things actually turn out

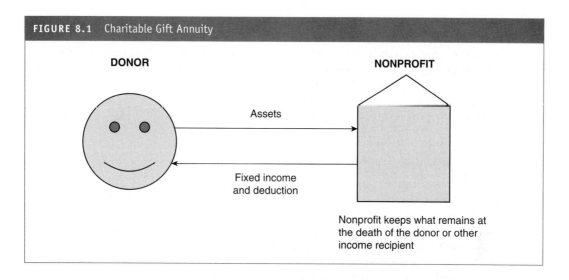

FIGURE 8.1 Charitable Gift Annuity

DONOR

NONPROFIT

Assets

Fixed income
and deduction

Nonprofit keeps what remains at
the death of the donor or other
income recipient

depends on how long the donor lives, but the IRS makes a projection based on tables that predict the donor's life expectancy when the annuity begins. Because some of the income is considered to be a return of the donor's original money, a portion of the annual payment is not subject to additional income tax. And, since the money used to purchase the annuity is removed from the donor's estate, there also could be savings on estate taxes.

For those who wish to look at the charitable gift annuity in more detail, Box 8.3 provides an illustration of how this type of gift might work for a hypothetical individual given certain assumptions.

BOX 8.3 Charitable Gift Annuity Example

Scenario

Susan, age seventy-five, wishes to make a major gift to a nonprofit where she works as a volunteer. But she has limited retirement income and needs to supplement it in order to maintain her lifestyle.

She purchases a charitable gift annuity from the nonprofit, using $100,000 in cash that she withdraws from a savings account. She is eligible to claim an income tax deduction for $45,028.* Her deduction is only for part of the amount she pays, since the IRS assumes that she will be receiving part of her money back as income.

Based on her age and income rates recommended by the American Council on Gift Annuities, Susan receives a fixed annual income equivalent to 5.8 percent of her gift, $5,800.**

Of the total $5,800 annual income, $4,433 is tax-exempt for the first 12.4 years, which is Susan's estimated life expectancy, based on actuarial tables. The balance of $1,366 is

(Continued)

(Continued)

taxable as ordinary income. After the 12.4 years, all of the income is taxable, for reasons that are complex.

Assumptions

Beneficiary Age: 75

Gift Amount: $100,000.00

Payment Rate: 5.8%**

Payment Schedule: Quarterly

Benefits to Donor

Income Tax Charitable Deduction: $45,028

Total Annual Income Payment: $5,800

Tax-Free Portion of Annual Payment: $4,433***

Portion of Annual Payment Taxed as Ordinary Income: $1,366***

*Calculated using IRS discount rate of 2.2%, as of April 18, 2014.

**Based on the rate recommended by the American Council on Gift Annuities for the assumptions depicted, as of April 18, 2014.

***After 12.4 years, the income payment is all taxable as ordinary income.

What type of donor would be interested in charitable gift annuities, and what type of organization should offer them? Since the income payment is fixed, it would be most attractive to donors who are older, since they would be less concerned with the impact of inflation on the purchasing power of their income. In addition, since the income payment is backed by the full faith and credit of the organization, the donor would need to have confidence in its financial sustainability, since the annuity payment could end if the nonprofit were unable to continue it. Gift annuities are regulated by states, and there can be a considerable administrative burden associated with maintaining a program. The nonprofit must be confident that it will have the resources to pay the annuity and that it can manage the administration of the program or contract the administration to an outside vendor.

Charitable Remainder Trust (CRT)

Another common vehicle for making a deferred gift, and one that also provides a lifetime income to the donor (and possibly other individuals), is the **charitable remainder trust** (CRT). There are various types of charitable remainder trusts. One is called a **charitable remainder annuity trust**, which pays a fixed income; it is not to be confused with the charitable gift annuity just discussed. Another is called a *unitrust*, and it pays the donor a *variable* income. For simplicity, our discussion here is limited to the **charitable remainder unitrust**.

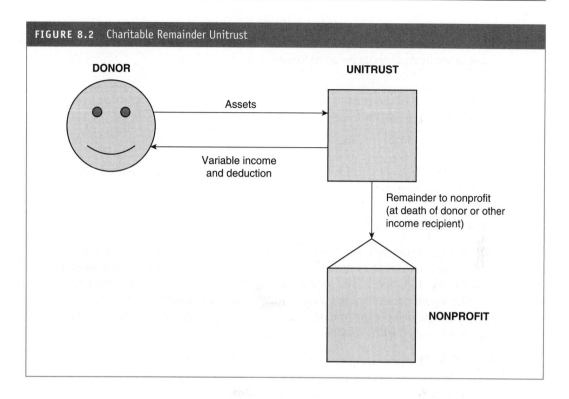

FIGURE 8.2   Charitable Remainder Unitrust

As illustrated in Figure 8.2, the charitable remainder unitrust is not a simple agreement between the donor and nonprofit like the charitable gift annuity we just reviewed. It involves a third party, a trustee. The trustee may be an individual or an institution, for example, a bank. The donor places assets in the unitrust. The trustee invests those assets and pays a lifetime income to the donor. When the donor dies, the trustee gives whatever assets remain in the trust to the designated nonprofit.

It is important to understand that with a charitable remainder trust, unlike the charitable gift annuity, the nonprofit is not a party to the transaction when a charitable remainder trust is created. The transaction is between the donor and the trustee. The nonprofit receives the balance of the trust when the donor dies but usually is not actively involved in management of the trust during the donor's life. Setting up a charitable remainder trust requires a legal agreement between the donor and trustee. Such a document always should be drafted by an attorney, but the IRS provides sample agreements on its website.

The charitable remainder unitrust has the following key features:

- Assets are *irrevocably* transferred to a trustee; the donor cannot take them back.

- The trustee pays a *variable income*, which is a *percentage* of the trust's value each year. That percentage, or rate, is established when the gift is made. It must be between 5 percent and 50 percent, with a projected remainder of at least 10 percent going to the charity.

- Because the income paid is based on a percentage of the trust's value, it varies with the market value of the trust and may fluctuate from year to year. This means the donor's income could go up or down.

- The income is not backed up by the assets of the nonprofit; it depends entirely on investments of the trust. If the trust were to be depleted through poor investments, the income could end.

- When the donor or last income recipient dies, the trustee pays the remaining principal of the trust to the nonprofit organization. Depending on how the trust's investments have performed, this could be more than the original gift made to establish the trust.

- The donor receives an income tax deduction for only a portion of the gift, at the time the trust is set up, since he or she will be receiving lifetime income.

- If the gift to the trust is made with appreciated property, for example, stock, there is *complete* avoidance of the capital gains tax at the time the property is placed in the trust. In other words, the trust could sell the asset, and since it is tax exempt, the trust would not need to pay a tax on the capital gain. However, if the trust distributes capital gains to the income beneficiaries, they are subject to capital gains tax on the amounts received.

For those who wish to look at a charitable remainder trust in more detail, Box 8.4 includes an example of how it might work in a hypothetical case.

BOX 8.4   Charitable Remainder Unitrust Example

Scenario

Mary, age seventy-five, wishes to make a gift to a local performing arts organization where she has been a season ticket holder for many years. She lives on income from her investments, including stocks she purchased years ago. Since she is in good health and expects to live a long time, she is concerned that her income has the potential to increase, in order to keep pace with inflation in the years ahead.

Mary meets with her attorney and a representative of a financial institution that could serve as the trustee of a charitable remainder trust. Mary and the trustee agree on a 5 percent payment rate, so her first year's income from the trust would be $5,000.* But, while the rate will stay the same, the income will vary with the value of the trust. If the trustee makes good investments and the trust doubles in value, say to $200,000, Mary's income will increase as well, to $10,000. Of course, Mary's attorney reminds her, this payment is not backed up by the nonprofit organization; it depends entirely on the investment performance of the trust. If the trust's investments go down, so too could Mary's income. Since she has other assets, Mary says she is comfortable with that risk.

Mary establishes the charitable remainder trust with a gift of $100,000. That entitles her to an income tax deduction of $60,140, based on a number of variables, including her age and the IRS discount rate in effect at the time the gift is made.** Since Mary is in the top income tax bracket with a 39.6 percent marginal rate, that creates an income tax savings of $23,815 ($60,140 × 39.6%).

In addition, Mary establishes the trust by giving stock valued at $100,000 but for which she paid only $50,000 a number of years ago. If she had sold the stock, that would have generated a capital gains tax of $10,000 based on the $50,000 gain, since she is in the 20 percent capital gains tax bracket. That tax is now avoided.

Taking into consideration both the income tax savings and the capital gains tax savings, the total amount of tax Mary saves by making this gift is $33,815 ($23,815 + $10,000). So this gift did not cost her $100,000; rather it cost $66,185 ($100,000 − tax saving of $33,815).

Mary's income in the first year is $5,000. Based on the actual cost of the gift, that is equivalent to a return of 7.6 percent ($5,000 / $66,185). In other words, if Mary had sold the stock, paid the capital gains tax, and invested it outside the trust, she would have had to find an investment that would return 7.6 percent to do as well. And income may go up in future years if the trust's investments grow. And the performing arts organization will receive a gift of $100,000, or perhaps even more, when Mary eventually passes away.

Assumptions

Beneficiary Age: 75

Gift Amount: $100,000.00

Cost Basis: $50,000.00

Payment Rate: 5%*

Donor's Marginal Income Tax Rate: 39.6%

Donor's Capital Gains Tax Rate: 20%

Benefits to Donor

Income Tax Deduction: $60,140**

First Year's Income: $5,000 (future income will vary with trust value)

Income Tax Savings: $23,815 ($60,140 × 39.6% income tax rate)

Capital Gains Tax Savings: $10,000 ($50,000 capital gain × 20% capital gains tax rate)

*The income rate is negotiable with the trustee and could be higher; 5% is assumed for this example.

**Calculated assuming IRS discount rate of 2.2%, in effect as of April 18, 2014.

Again let's focus on the benefits to the donor and the nonprofit. Thinking back on the three types of taxes described earlier, the charitable remainder trust offers advantages related to all three. The donor receives an income tax deduction, but for a portion rather than the whole amount of the gift, since he or she will be receiving something back in the form of lifetime income. One very attractive feature of the charitable remainder trust is that if the donor makes the gift with appreciated property, for example, stock, his or her deduction is based on the full market value and there is *no* payment of capital gains tax by the trust and any gains subsequently distributed to the income beneficiaries are likely to be spread out over an extended period of time. That can be a major advantage for a donor who owns stock, real estate, or some other property that is worth far more than he or she paid for it. And third, since the amount given to the trust is removed from the donor's estate, there is a potential saving on estate taxes.

The nonprofit will receive the balance of the trust when the donor dies. That could be more or less than the original gift, depending on how the trust's investments perform. If the trustee does a good job, it is possible that the nonprofit will receive more than the original gift the donor made to establish the trust.

What type of donor would be interested in a charitable remainder unitrust? He or she would tend to be older rather than young, since older people get a larger tax deduction, all other things being equal. The charitable remainder unitrust also is attractive to donors who own appreciated assets, as explained earlier. And the donor must be willing to accept some financial risk, since the income he or she will receive may fluctuate. Remembering that the nonprofit generally does not have responsibility for managing the trust, any organization could be the beneficiary of such a trust. Some larger organizations may provide information and assistance to donors, and some may serve as trustee, but again, the transaction is between the donor and the trustee.

Charitable Remainder Trust Variations

There are numerous variations on the basic charitable remainder trust, too many to discuss in this text, but let's look at two creative ideas as examples of what can be done to accommodate the needs of donors in various situations while also providing a gift to the nonprofit organization.

As mentioned, income can be paid for one lifetime or more. Thus, a couple could arrange to receive the income during their joint lives and then have the income continue for the lifetime of the survivor. What about a couple who wish to make a gift and receive income for their two lives but also have concerns about leaving an estate to help an heir, perhaps a child or other relative, and do not wish to make the charity wait until the child has died to receive the remainder of the trust? Figure 8.3 depicts a plan that can accomplish all of those goals.

Let's assume that the donors own stock worth $1 million that pays them a modest dividend, perhaps 1 percent ($10,000) per year. Maybe they purchased that stock many years ago for a fraction of its current value, so would need to pay a substantial capital gains tax if it were to be sold. In addition, they have an heir for whom they wish to provide. Also, let's assume that they are wealthy people and could face a top estate tax rate of 40 percent. A creative solution could be to establish a charitable remainder trust with a **wealth replacement feature**. Here's how it might work: the donors give the stock to the unitrust, paying no immediate capital gains tax, and the trustee pays them an annual income at a 5 percent rate. Based on the full $1 million value of the assets they gave to the trust, that would provide $50,000 per year in income, $40,000 more than they had been receiving before. What might they do with the extra $40,000? Depending, of course, on a variety of factors, it might be possible to use that extra income to purchase a life insurance policy that would pay a death benefit of $1 million to the heir after both of the donors are deceased. If the life insurance is placed in a separate trust, there also would be no estate tax to pay, so there are additional tax savings.

As Figure 8.3 portrays, without this plan, the heir might eventually have received as little as $600,000, since there could have been $400,000 to be paid in estate tax (if the donors were in that top bracket). The nonprofit would have received nothing. With this creative gift plan, the heir now will receive $1 million tax-free from the life insurance policy, while the charity will receive the assets of the charitable remainder trust, which may be $1 million or even more.

Let's look at one more variation that might be a good fit with the circumstances of some donors. Let's say a donor wants to contribute some asset to a charitable remainder trust that does not generate any current income, for example, undeveloped land. The trust can be designed to pay *either* the stipulated percentage (for example, 5 percent) *or* the actual income produced, whichever is less. As long as the trust owns the land, there would be no income so no income would be paid out to the donor. But when the land is sold and the money is reinvested in something that does produce income, the trust *flips* to operate like a standard unitrust. For this reason, this is known as a flip trust. The donor then receives his or her 5 percent every year. There are two variations, a **net income charitable remainder trust**, called a **NICRUT**, and a **net income with makeup charitable remainder trust**, also known as a **NIMCRUT**. The latter permits the trustee to pay the donor extra income, above the 5 percent, to make up for the years in which he or she did not receive any income or received something less than the full 5 percent to which he or she was entitled. This type of trust also can be used to shift income payments to the future,

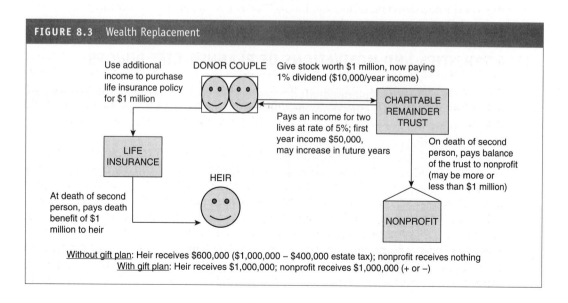

FIGURE 8.3 Wealth Replacement

Use additional income to purchase life insurance policy for $1 million

DONOR COUPLE

Give stock worth $1 million, now paying 1% dividend ($10,000/year income)

CHARITABLE REMAINDER TRUST

Pays an income for two lives at rate of 5%; first year income $50,000, may increase in future years

On death of second person, pays balance of the trust to nonprofit (may be more or less than $1 million)

LIFE INSURANCE

HEIR

At death of second person, pays death benefit of $1 million to heir

NONPROFIT

Without gift plan: Heir receives $600,000 ($1,000,000 – $400,000 estate tax); nonprofit receives nothing
With gift plan: Heir receives $1,000,000; nonprofit receives $1,000,000 (+ or −)

perhaps as part of retirement planning. And, as with all CRTs, the donor can avoid capital gains taxes if appreciated assets are contributed to the trust.

Obviously, developing such creative and complex gift plans requires the involvement of financial and legal experts. Most development officers do not need to understand the details but should be aware that such plans exist so that they can recognize circumstances in which they might help a donor to make a gift. Only the largest of institutions can afford to have gift planning experts on the development office staff. But there are many outside specialists—including attorneys, accountants, financial planners, and others—who can help. The experts then can be called in to put the plan together when the situation warrants.

Life Estate

One additional deferred gift that may be appropriate in some circumstances is called the **life estate**. This is available only for a gift involving the donor's personal residence, farm, or vacation home. The donor can give the home to the nonprofit now but retain the right to continue living in the home for the balance of his or her life. The donor would receive an income tax deduction for a portion of the home's market value, but not the full amount. That is because the right to live there has a monetary value; it is similar to receiving a lifetime income in the form of free rent. The home also is removed from the donor's estate, so it is possible that there would be an estate tax savings if the donor were a wealthy person. The nonprofit owns the home, so when the donor is no longer living, it can immediately sell it or perhaps covert it to its own use.

This could provide a good solution for a donor who wishes to make a gift, to continue living in his or her home, and perhaps wishes to simplify the eventual settlement of his or her estate by having ownership of the home already vested in the nonprofit organization. Of course, as with any gift of real estate, the nonprofit would need to engage professional advisors to assure that its ownership of the home would not involve liabilities, for example, if the property posed environmental issues that would be expensive to resolve.

CHARACTERISTICS AND MOTIVATIONS OF PLANNED-GIFT DONORS

Much of the research on planned-gift donors identifies characteristics and motivations related to all donors, including those discussed in Chapter 3 of this book. That is, planned-gift donors are motivated by altruism, self-interest, and mixed motives and are influenced by both individual needs and social relationships. But are there characteristics or motivations that apply specifically to planned-gift donors and that can help fundraisers identify those most likely to give in this way? Students will remember from previous chapters that research on donors falls into two categories: some looks at who gives, what, and to whom—this describes donor behavior—and some looks at why people give, which is donor motivation. Studies of planned-giving donors, most of which have focused specifically on bequest donors, are similarly divided.

James (2009b) studied over 18,000 individuals who had died and identified characteristics of those more likely to have left a charitable bequest. Among his findings, bequest donors are more likely to

- Have greater wealth.

- Have a higher level of education.

- Have a history of giving during their lifetimes.

- Attend religious services more frequently.

- Have no children or grandchildren.

James notes that while wealth is an indicator of a prospective bequest donor, the individual's perception of his or her own financial security may be as important as the actual numbers. This suggests that an individual's attitudes and perceptions about money and his or her financial security may be important in thinking about the type of planned gift that person might consider. For example, someone concerned about having access to resources during the balance of his or her life may be reluctant to make the irrevocable decision that a charitable gift annuity or charitable remainder trust would require; he or she may be more comfortable arranging for a testamentary gift. An individual who is risk adverse may find the variable income from a charitable remainder unitrust to be a concern but perhaps may find the fixed income from a charitable gift annuity, secured by the full faith and credit of an institution, to be more reassuring. Wealthy individuals may be prospects for planned gifts, but James (2009b) notes that those with estates greater than the estate exemption amount ($5,340,000 in 2014) may not be the best prospects for many nonprofit organizations, since they may be more inclined to create their own foundations or donor-advised funds.

The relationship between outright giving during a lifetime and planned giving is commonly mentioned by planned-giving practitioners. Regularity of annual giving is more important than the amount. For example, a 2012 study conducted by the Stelter Company, a firm that produces planned-giving materials and advises nonprofits on marketing of planned gifts, found that "the majority of planned givers (78 percent) have also made annual gifts to the charity they support. Gift amounts, however, cannot be used as a bellwether of planned giving. Nearly 40 percent of current planned givers with a history of giving make annual donations of less than $500" (Stelter Company, 2012). Stelter's report also notes that one in five planned gifts comes from a donor who has never given to the nonprofit before, perhaps suggesting that such gifts should be promoted broadly beyond an organization's immediate constituency (Stelter Company, 2012).

James (2009b) identifies the lack of children or grandchildren as the most significant variable distinguishing bequest donors. That seems intuitive, since people without children or grandchildren may have less need to provide for family members in their estate plans. But perceptions also may be important. Some who do have children and grandchildren may hold a philosophy that limits the amount they are likely to leave to them. They may believe, as Warren Buffet has said, that children who have an education and are healthy should be given "enough money so that they would feel they could do anything, but not so much that they could do nothing" (Loomis, 2012). And, as the review of various planned-giving vehicles reviewed in this chapter suggests, planned giving may offer creative ways for donors to provide financial security for family members while also making a charitable gift.

Stelter's 2012 research offers an insight that may be useful to nonprofits in identifying prospects to whom planned giving should be promoted. Those who already have a planned gift in place are distributed about evenly across various age categories, but those who report that they intend to establish one in the future tend to be younger; 72 percent of the latter are under age sixty. The implication is that nonprofits should not limit promotion of planned giving to older people but should also communicate with younger donors who have not yet established a planned-gift arrangement, although the payoff from such efforts will be further in the future.

While motivations may be inferred from some of the patterns discussed earlier, most of the data relate to donor behavior. It suggests that people with varying characteristics are more or less likely to engage in planned giving. What about their motivations?

Sargeant and Shang (2011) studied donors who support nonprofits with a bequest and focused on motivations. The authors found that many of the motivations expressed by donors are generic; that is, they relate to the motivation to give generally. But the authors identified four motivations they identified as "specific" to bequest donors: a lack of family needs; a desire to "manage" estate taxes; a desire to "live on" (that is, achieve some type of immortality and leave a legacy); and a desire to make a difference (Sargeant & Shang, 2011, p. 988). Stelter's (2012) study concluded that "affinity for a nonprofit's mission trumps everything . . . [with] 83 percent of current planned givers and best prospects saying they have a natural affinity to the cause the charity cares about and that was part of their decision to put a planned gift in place" (p. 10).

In other words, while data may be useful in identifying prospects with a higher propensity to planned giving, developing their support involves many of the principles discussed previously in this text, including cultivation to advance their commitment to the organization and its cause.

PLANNED-GIVING PROGRAM

As discussed earlier in this text, planned giving is regarded primarily as a strategy for securing major gifts, although planned-gift donors may not all be major-gift prospects, and some planned gifts may be modest. While planned giving is often managed in the context of the major-gifts program, some larger organizations do dedicate substantial resources to planned giving, which may be structured as a distinctive program.

Developing a Planned-Giving Program

Organizations that develop a planned-giving program often do so in phases. Many will never proceed beyond Phase 1, and those that do may advance one step at a time as the potential justifies and budgets permit (Partnership for Philanthropic Planning website).

Phase 1

A Phase 1 program is focused entirely on testamentary gifts, that is, on the promotion of bequests and beneficiary designations. The organization may do little more than mention bequests on its website and in existing regular publications, such as newsletters and annual-fund mailings. Many provide an opportunity for donors to indicate they have a bequest provision that provides for an eventual gift to the organization. Or donors may be provided the opportunity to request more information, the response to which may be the mailing of a general brochure on bequests and suggested language that clearly specifies the specific nonprofit. Implementing a Phase 1 program requires little expertise on the part of the development staff. To the extent that donors might pose technical questions, the organization can refer them to outside legal or financial advisors.

Phase 2

A nonprofit that decides to expand its planned-giving program may move to Phase 2, which introduces various life-income vehicles, including charitable gift annuities and charitable remainder trusts. The decision to offer charitable gift annuities may require additional resources, in order to comply with state laws and support the management of funds, including income payments. The alternatives include building such expertise in-house or contracting with an outside firm or financial institution.

Since charitable gift annuities do represent a financial obligation of the organization, offering them would be appropriate only for nonprofits that enjoy financial stability; indeed, many donors would be reluctant to undertake such a contract with an organization that did not.

A nonprofit may be able to purchase a commercial annuity from an insurance company to offset the risk, but this entails costs that reduce the eventual benefit to the nonprofit and thus would be inconsistent with the philanthropic goals of the donor.

Charitable remainder trusts do not require an extensive investment by the nonprofit organization, since in most cases the trustee is an independent financial institution or, perhaps, an accountant or attorney. The organization can provide basic information on how such trusts operate, provide illustrations to prospective donors, and even provide sample documents. All of these resources are readily available from commercial firms and, indeed, free from the IRS. Commercially available software packages that can be used to generate illustrations of planned gifts also include model documents. Several well-known firms offer printed literature that can be adapted to a specific organization and maintain websites that include calculators prospective donors can use to generate their own illustrations using various assumptions. Nonprofit websites often provide a link to such a site maintained by a commercial firm with which that organization has a contractual relationship.

Moving to Phase 2 does require some additional planned-giving expertise on the part of the organization's development officers, but it is generally sufficient to provide training to existing major-gifts officers and not necessary to employ a specialized gift planner on staff. Again, an organization can maintain a list of independent experts on whom it can call, or to whom it can refer donors, when more complex situations arise.

Phase 3

A Phase 3 program is more proactive and sophisticated. "This is the level at which organizations engage in professional gift planning and counseling with prospective donors. It involves well-trained third parties, such as attorneys, accountants, financial planners and other members of the planning team in the dialogue with prospective donors" (Partnership for Philanthropic Planning website). The nonprofit may engage a network of independent specialists or employ a gift planner on staff.

In this phase, the promotion of planned giving goes beyond passive techniques such as buttons on the website. The organization will send direct-mail promotions to priority prospects, using profiling and targeting selection methods similar to those used in the annual fund, discussed in Chapter 6, and applying some of the criteria believed to predict planned giving, as discussed earlier. Some maintain a program of estate planning seminars, offered to members of their constituency without charge. Such programs generally include general information on estate and financial planning as well as planned giving. In a Phase 3 program, gift officers are well-trained in planned giving and proactively identify, cultivate, and solicit prospects.

As mentioned, some large institutions, such as universities, may employ gift planners on the development office staff and offer a full range of services to donors. Some even serve as trustees of charitable trusts. But in most development offices, planned giving is handled by fundraising professionals who also have other responsibilities, including the solicitation of outright gifts. In many cases, the planned-giving program is managed by an individual who also has overall responsibility for the fundraising program, a director or vice president for development (Partnership for Philanthropic Planning, 2012).

For-profit gift planners also work with donors, who may choose to give to any nonprofit organization. Many consultants who advise nonprofit organizations on marketing of planned giving recommend maintaining relationships with outside advisors, including attorneys, financial planners, and trust officers at financial institutions, who may be sources both of professional guidance and referrals. Some nonprofits create advisory councils to engage such professionals in an organized and continuing way.

RECOGNIZING PLANNED-GIFT DONORS

Many nonprofit organizations and institutions establish giving societies to recognize planned-gift donors. Common names include variations on "heritage society" and "legacy society." Others are named for institutional historical figures, the founding date, or some other institution-specific theme. There are various rationales for this technique. One is the belief that the promise of recognition may attract some individuals to notify the organization of a planned-gift arrangement of which it might otherwise be unaware.

In the case of a charitable gift annuity, the organization would be a party to the contract so, of course, would know about it. But, for example, in the case with a bequest or a charitable remainder trust, the donor might work directly with an attorney or a trustee without any communication with the organization. In a majority of instances where a donor works with an independent gift planner, the nonprofit is not notified of the gift arrangement a donor makes (Partnership for Philanthropic Planning, 2012). It might be helpful for a nonprofit to know about such arrangements in order to inform its financial planning. Moreover, in the case of expectancies, the donor retains the right to change the charitable beneficiary, so the organization would prefer to be aware and have the opportunity to continue its stewardship with the individual.

A second rationale for a planned-giving recognition society is that by listing the names of members, and perhaps conducting events for them, the nonprofit can mobilize the impact of social influences on others. But the usefulness of planned-giving recognition societies has been challenged. In Stelter's 2012 study, most planned-giving donors, and those who said they were considering such a gift, expressed little interest in such recognition or in developing relationships with other donors, for example, through events. However, of those who had informed the organization of their plans, 62 percent rated the communication they received from the organization as excellent and 31 percent described it as good. Most preferred written to in-person communication, while 75 percent of those over the age of seventy preferred neither. A majority of potential planned-gift donors who were younger reported using social networking, and the authors of the report recommend that nonprofits communicate with planned-gift prospects through that channel. It must be noted that self-reported information from donors may not always be reliable and that the study was conducted by a commercial firm that provides publications and online communication services to nonprofit organizations.

WORKING WITH PLANNED-GIFT DONORS

In many respects, the principles of interaction with planned-gift donors are no different from those that apply to major-gifts fundraising generally, many of which were discussed in Chapter 7. However, planned-giving officers who are employed by an organization or institution must be especially vigilant to maintain clarity about where their responsibilities lie in their relationships with donors.

Independent gift planners serve individual clients and, like accountants, attorneys, or general financial planners, are responsible to those clients. Professionals employed by organizations and institutions may understand that ethical practice requires appropriate sensitivity to the interests of donors, and many do, indeed, see themselves as serving both their employers and the donors. Some may object to being identified as fundraisers at all (Sharpe, 1999). But they are compensated by their employers, who may have expectations with regard to their productivity. This requires that they be forthcoming with donors about their interests and loyalties and assure that donors receive independent advice from their own financial and legal counsel. Caution may be especially important when the planned-giving officer is indeed educated as an attorney or financial professional, whose recommendations may be viewed as authoritative by the donors with whom he or she meets. Such fundraising professionals can provide information and examples of how various planned-giving arrangements might work and communicate and coordinate with the individual's advisors. But they must always be clear that they are not providing legal or financial advice. The Partnership for Philanthropic Planning has established standards for best practice, which apply to both independent and organization-based gift planners, as shown in Box. 8.5.

BOX 8.5   Partnership for Philanthropic Planning: Model Standards
of Practice for the Charitable Gift Planner

Preamble

The purpose of this statement is to encourage responsible gift planning by urging the adoption of the following Standards of Practice by all individuals who work in the charitable gift planning process, gift planning officers, fund raising consultants, attorneys, accountants, financial planners, life insurance agents and other financial services professionals (collectively referred to hereafter as "Gift Planners"), and by the institutions that these persons represent. This statement recognizes that the solicitation, planning and administration of a charitable gift is a complex process involving philanthropic, personal, financial, and tax considerations, and as such often involves professionals from various disciplines whose goals should include working together to structure a gift that achieves a fair and proper balance between the interests of the donor and the purposes of the charitable institution.

I. Primacy of Philanthropic Motivation

The principal basis for making a charitable gift should be a desire on the part of the donor to support the work of charitable institutions.

II. Explanation of Tax Implications

Congress has provided tax incentives for charitable giving, and the emphasis in this statement on philanthropic motivation in no way minimizes the necessity and appropriateness of a full and accurate explanation by the Gift Planner of those incentives and their implications.

III. Full Disclosure

It is essential to the gift planning process that the role and relationships of all parties involved, including how and by whom each is compensated, be fully disclosed to the donor. A Gift Planner shall not act or purport to act as a representative of any charity without the express knowledge and approval of the charity, and shall not, while employed by the charity, act or purport to act as a representative of the donor, without the express consent of both the charity and the donor.

IV. Compensation

Compensation paid to Gift Planners shall be reasonable and proportionate to the services provided. Payment of finder's fees, commissions or other fees by a donee organization to an independent Gift Planner as a condition for the delivery of a gift are never appropriate. Such payments lead to abusive practices and may violate certain state and federal regulations. Likewise, commission-based compensation for Gift Planners who are employed by a charitable institution is never appropriate.

V. Competence and Professionalism

The Gift Planner should strive to achieve and maintain a high degree of competence in his or her chosen area, and shall advise donors only in areas in which he or she is professionally qualified. It is a hallmark of professionalism for Gift Planners that they realize when they have reached the limits of their knowledge and expertise, and as a result, should include other professionals in the process. Such relationships should be characterized by courtesy, tact and mutual respect.

VI. Consultation With Independent Advisors

A Gift Planner acting on behalf of a charity shall in all cases strongly encourage the donor to discuss the proposed gift with competent independent legal and tax advisors of the donor's choice.

VII. Consultation With Charities

Although Gift Planners frequently and properly counsel donors concerning specific charitable gifts without the prior knowledge or approval of the donee organization, the Gift Planners, in order to insure that the gift will accomplish the donor's objectives, should encourage the donor, early in the gift planning process, to discuss the proposed gift with the charity to whom the gift is to be made. In cases where the donor desires anonymity, the Gift Planners shall endeavor, on behalf of the undisclosed donor, to obtain the charity's input in the gift planning process.

VIII. Description and Representation of Gift

The Gift Planner shall make every effort to assure that the donor receives a full description and an accurate representation of all aspects of any proposed charitable gift plan. The consequences for the charity, the donor and, where applicable, the donor's family, should be apparent, and the assumptions underlying any financial illustrations should be realistic.

IX. Full Compliance

A Gift Planner shall fully comply with and shall encourage other parties in the gift planning process to fully comply with both the letter and spirit of all applicable federal and state laws and regulations.

X. Public Trust

Gift Planners shall, in all dealings with donors, institutions and other professionals, act with fairness, honesty, integrity and openness. Except for compensation received for services, the terms of which have been disclosed to the donor, they shall have no vested interest that could result in personal gain.

Adopted and subscribed to by the National Committee on Planned Giving [now the Partnership for Philanthropic Planning] and the American Council on Gift Annuities, May 7, 1991. Revised April 1999.

Source: Partnership for Philanthropic Planning website, http://www.pppnet.org/ethics/model_standards.html.

Concern with ethical practice goes beyond financial matters. Given the importance of family circumstances and life stage in planned-giving decisions, gift planners often become familiar with the intimate details of individuals' lives. They learn what they care about. They discuss with them what they wish to leave to their families, both in terms of financial assets and legacy. Inevitably, they lead them to contemplate the meaning of their lives and eventual deaths. The practice of planned giving today bridges two worlds. Commercial wealth management firms often promote it much as they do any investment, primarily in terms of the financial and tax benefits. But it is more than that; it is philanthropy. Planned giving offers intelligent strategies and vehicles to those motivated by a commitment to a cause and the desire to improve the lives of others. Those noble motivations always should remain paramount.

CHAPTER SUMMARY

A substantial amount will be transferred between generations in coming decades as the baby boom generation ages. Some portion of their assets will pass as gifts to nonprofit organizations. This demographic reality has resulted in more emphasis on planned giving. Planned giving is a strategy for raising major gifts, but many organizations also promote it to donors who are not wealthy.

Planned gifts are those that involve coordination and integration with the donor's overall financial and estate planning and take maximum advantage of the incentives for charitable giving included in the tax law. It is a specialty in the fundraising field, with experts known as *planned-giving officers* or *charitable gift planners*. But a basic understanding of planned giving is essential for all major-gifts fundraisers. Even small nonprofits can promote the simplest types of planned gifts and provide assistance to donors in arranging them.

Individuals may pay three principal taxes to the federal government: the *income tax*, the *capital gains tax*, and the *estate tax*. The law provides ways to minimize or avoid all of these through charitable giving, provisions that lawmakers have made intentionally to encourage giving. There are also additional benefits under many state tax laws.

There are three types of planned gifts: *outright planned gifts*, *expectancies*, and *deferred gifts*. Some outright gifts are planned gifts because they involve complex assets, such as stocks or real estate, and may require the assistance of financial experts to complete. An expectancy is a promise a donor makes to provide a gift to the organization at some future time, generally at death, through a bequest, life insurance, or a retirement plan. Such promises may be informal or documented in writing. Deferred gifts are gifts the donor makes now but are not available to the organization until some future time, generally after the death of the donor or some other individual (Regenovich, 2011).

Outright planned gifts are those a donor makes now and provide income to a nonprofit organization immediately. Common vehicles include gifts of *appreciated assets*, *donor-advised funds*, and *lead trusts*.

Expectancies, also called *testamentary gifts*, include bequests, which are the most common type of planned gift. Some donors also may designate a nonprofit to receive the remainder of a retirement fund or an IRA or as the beneficiary of a life insurance policy. In most cases, such arrangements are revocable by the donor during his or her lifetime; that is, the donor can change them.

Two common vehicles for *deferred gifts* include *charitable gift annuities and charitable reminder trusts.* Both provide a lifetime income to the donor or another designated individual. Income from a charitable gift annuity is fixed. Income from a *charitable remainder unitrust* varies with the value of assets held in the trust. A type of charitable remainder trust known as an *annuity trust* provides fixed income but is different in operation from a gift annuity.

Variations on the charitable remainder trust make it a useful tool in an individual's financial and estate planning. Such a trust can be used with life insurance to provide *wealth replacement* in order to benefit an heir. A variation known as a *flip trust* can be used to shift income to a later time.

A donor can give his or her personal residence to a nonprofit and reserve the right to live there for life; this is known as a *life estate.*

Planned-gift donors generally have the same motivations to give that apply to all donors, but some studies have identified unique characteristics and motivations. They generally have greater wealth than others, but their giving may be conditioned by their perception of their financial situation and their attitude toward money and risk. They often have been regular donors to the nonprofits they support with their planned gifts, but regularity is more important as an indicator than is the amount of annual gifts. Lack of children or grandchildren increases the likelihood of a planned gift, but some people believe they should not leave too much to heirs in any event (Stelter Company, 2012). Research suggests that planned-gift donors are motivated by a commitment to the nonprofit's cause, by the desire to "live on," and by the desire to have an impact on society (Sargeant & Shang, 2011).

A nonprofit organization might develop a planned-giving program in phases. Phase 1 emphasizes simple bequests and beneficiary designations. Phase 2 introduces life-income arrangements, such as charitable gift annuities and charitable remainder trusts. Phase 3 becomes more proactive and complex and provides donors with assistance in financial and estate planning.

Most fundraising professionals who work with planned giving and are employed by nonprofit organizations also have other responsibilities, for example, as major-gifts officers. There are also many independent advisors and consultants, including gift planners. All professionals who work with planned-giving donors should follow ethical best practices and be clear about their own interests and priorities.

Key Terms and Concepts

Appreciated property	Charitable remainder	Deferred gifts
Capital gains tax	trust	Donor-advised funds
Charitable gift annuity	Charitable remainder	Estate tax
Charitable lead trust	unitrust	Expectancies
Charitable remainder	Contingent bequest	Fair market value
annuity trust	Cost basis	General bequest

Gift planners
Income tax
Irrevocable
IRS discount rate
(applicable federal
rate)
Life estate
Marginal
tax rate

Net income charitable
remainder trust
(NICRUT)
Net income with
makeup charitable
remainder trust
(NIMCRUT)
Outright planned
gifts

Planned-giving
officers
Residuary bequest
Specific bequest
Testamentary gifts
Trust
Trustee
Wealth replacement
feature

Case 8.1: Mary

Mary is eighty-five and widowed. She still lives in a small apartment she occupied with her late husband, who died fifteen years ago. She has $5,000,000 in assets, inherited from her husband, all invested in U.S. Treasury bills and certificates of deposit. She spends little and worries that ill health eventually may require her to spend all of her money on assisted living. She would like to help your organization but feels she cannot take the risk of giving any money away.

Case 8.2: Tom and Barbara

Tom and Barbara are age sixty-four and sixty-two, respectively, and have been married for many years. They have two grown children who are financially successful in their own right. Tom has a small real estate business and has acquired a portfolio of rental properties over the years at very low cost, which represent most of their estate. Tom has been diagnosed with a treatable heart condition and feels that he now wants to retire and reduce his workload in managing the properties. He wants to make sure that he and Barbara will have a secure retirement and that Barbara will be secure should anything happen to him. Both have been active volunteers in your organization and wish to provide significant support.

Case 8.3: Mildred and Sue

Mildred and Sue have been partners for forty years and both are age seventy-five. Both had careers, and they are living on small pensions plus some investments and accumulated savings. Neither has children or close relatives, and both are concerned that the other will have secure income after the first one dies. They tell you they are skeptical about the stock market and were shaken by the financial crisis in the late 2000s. They have both been volunteers at your organization for many years and wish they could give more than their usual annual gifts.

Case 8.4: Harry and Beth

Harry and Beth are both age sixty-five and close to retirement. They have a substantial portfolio of growth stocks built up over the years. Most of the stocks pay little dividend. Harry has worked for the federal government and expects a secure retirement income. However, they have a granddaughter about whom they have some concern. They want to maintain enough in their estate to provide something to her after they are both deceased. They would like to make a major gift to your capital campaign but have been unable to reach a decision.

Case 8.5: Nick

Nick is fifty-five and single. He started his own real estate company and owns a substantial parcel of undeveloped land, now worth millions of dollars. His cost basis in the land is very low, and it comprises a substantial portion of his assets. He would like to diversify his investments and avoid paying tax on the substantial capital gain. He plans to start a new project and knows there are risks, so he would like to sock some away to produce income during his eventual retirement. He does not need to receive any additional income now. He is a new board member at your organization and knows he should make a substantial gift.

Case 8.6: Ann

Ann has lived in her house in Memphis for fifty years, and the mortgage has been paid off for decades. She is widowed and her only son lives in California. Her only income is Social Security and a pension earned by her late husband. She remains in good health and does not want to move from her home. But she is concerned about the burden on her son of having to deal with selling the house from California when she passes away. Ann has been a donor to your organization for many years and wishes to someday create an endowment to help support your programs in perpetuity.

Case 8.7: Eduardo

Eduardo has amassed a substantial portfolio of commercial properties. He is a member of your board and would like to make a long-term commitment to a substantial annual gift. In the course of your conversation, he mentions an office building he owns near the waterfront, saying, "I don't really need the income from it. I'm just holding on to it for the long run. Someday that area will be redeveloped, and it will be worth a lot more, but I'll never see it—maybe my grandchildren will."

Questions for Discussion

Consider the following questions with regard to each of the donors described in Cases 8.1 through 8.7:

1. Summarize the nature of their financial assets. In view of the type of assets they hold, might some planed-giving vehicles be more attractive than others?
2. How would you characterize each party's attitude toward money and risk? Why?
3. What are the most relevant points regarding the donor's family circumstances and life stage with regard to a possible planned gift?
4. What objections might each express with regard to an outright gift? In other words, are there facts related to each donor's assets, attitudes toward money, or life circumstances that might be perceived as obstacles to such a gift?
5. In view of each donor's assets, attitudes toward money, family circumstances, and life stage, which gift planning tools might you propose in each case and why?

Suggestions for Further Reading

Books

Jordan, R. R., & Quynn, K. L. (2009). *Planned giving: A guide to fundraising and philanthropy.* Hoboken, NJ: Wiley.

Rosen, M. J. (2011). *Donor-centered planned gift marketing.* Hoboken, NJ: Wiley.

Articles

James, R. N. III (2009a, December). The myth of the coming charitable estate windfall. *American Review of Public Administration, 39*(6), 661–674.

James, R. N. III (2009b). Health, wealth, and charitable estate planning: A longitudinal examination of testamentary charitable giving plans. *Nonprofit and Voluntary Sector Quarterly, 38*(6), 1026–1043.

Schervish, P. G., & Havens, J. J. (2002, March). The new physics of philanthropy: The supply side vectors of charitable giving: Part II: The spiritual side of the supply side. *CASE International Journal of Educational Advancement, 2*(3), 221–241.

Websites

American Council on Gift Annuities: http://www.acga-web.org
Partnership for Philanthropic Planning: http://www.pppnet.org

NOTE: Commercial firms offering planned-giving consulting and materials to nonprofit organizations maintain websites that include extensive resources. They are not included in this listing in the interest of impartiality, but students will easily find them through a search using keywords such as *planned giving*. In addition, many nonprofit institutions have planned-giving webpages, some including online calculators that can be used to generate examples.

Notes

1. Under 2014 law, the estate tax exemption amount is indexed to inflation and thus increases every year.

2. Some individuals establish *revocable trusts*, also called *living trusts*, to own their assets while they are living. These are not charitable trusts. Upon the person's death, the trust is controlled by a trustee, who then distributes the assets of the trust according to instructions stated in the trust agreement. That may include charitable bequests. The trust agreement thus functions much like a will, with certain legal advantages.

CHAPTER 9

Corporate Support

When I was vice president for development and alumni affairs at The George Washington University, I engaged in an annual ritual that involved taking Amtrak to a nearby city to meet with the contributions officer of a corporation headquartered there. He would always take me to lunch at the same restaurant and the conversation would be much the same. He was an older gentleman who had been with the company for many years and at some point had been rewarded for his dedicated service with this pleasant assignment, which consisted largely of having lunch with people like me who came to solicit the company's annual gift, most of which went regularly to the same organizations and institutions every year. We would chat, and at the end of lunch he would promise the same amount as last year and that was that. I never really needed to even ask. I would return home on the train and it was always a pleasant day.

The last time I saw him, which was sometime in the 1990s, he told me he was retiring. "Things have changed," he said. "Now they want me to come up with all sorts of explanations of how our giving is related to corporate strategic objectives, to measure the impact of our philanthropy, and to justify every grant. It's just not the way that I have done things, and I think it is time for me to start spending more time with my grandkids." He once again promised the same gift as the year before, but he offered a warning: "There will be a new guy here next year, and it will be a whole different ballgame." And, indeed, it was. The transition symbolized the changes in corporate relationships with nonprofit organizations and educational institutions that have occurred over the past few decades.

DEFINITIONS AND CONCEPTS

This chapter is titled "corporate support" rather than "corporate philanthropy" for a reason. Corporations do engage in philanthropy; that is, they give money to nonprofit organizations without any explicit quid pro quo. But financial resources that come to nonprofit organizations from corporations are not always gifts. Sometimes there is a quid pro quo that is explicit, indeed, contractual. In these cases, the transaction is not entirely, or even mostly, philanthropic. However, the responsibility for relationships with corporations is often assigned to professional staff members who work in the development office. Their interactions with corporations often involve a variety of commercial relationships as well as philanthropy, and all of their activity may be regarded as fundraising by their organizations.

For that reason, this chapter discusses corporate philanthropy but also a range of relationships that produce revenue to nonprofit organizations.

The emphasis in this chapter is on relationships between public corporations and nonprofit organizations and does not necessarily relate to fundraising from small, privately owned businesses, although some of the concepts apply to working with small businesses as well. Small businesses are often an important source of support for nonprofit organizations serving their communities. But in most cases, the decision to give is made by the owner or owners. They may decide based partly on business considerations—remember the communitarian-type donors discussed in Chapter 3—or their giving may entirely reflect their own values and priorities. Since they have no shareholders to whom they must answer, owners of private businesses can readily make such decisions. Approaching such businesses is usually less complex than securing support from a public company.

Again, thinking back to the discussion in previous chapters, corporations may be prospects for unrestricted gifts or sponsorships; some of the latter may produce unrestricted revenue; that is, it can be used to meet the organization's general operating needs. But larger corporate gifts and grants are likely to be designated for specific programs or projects. Corporations rarely give for building projects and almost never make gifts to endowment funds, although there may be exceptions when the corporation and the nonprofit have a particularly long and close relationship.

From the corporation's perspective, relationships with nonprofits, whether philanthropic or otherwise, are a part of **corporate social responsibility**, but they are not synonymous with it. Corporate social responsibility is a broader concept that also includes such additional considerations as the company's treatment of its employees, its environmental impact, and its overall ethical behavior (Andreasen, 2009).

Let's start by looking at various relationships between nonprofits and corporations and then return, later in this chapter, to a further discussion of each. Galaskiewicz and Colman (2006) define and describe four types of **alliances** between corporations and nonprofits, which are summarized in Box 9.1. They call them **collaborations**, but they are commonly called **partnerships**.

1. **Philanthropic collaborations**. As the term implies, these relationships involve *traditional* corporate philanthropy, that is, the giving of money to a nonprofit without any explicit quid pro quo. Although there may be benefits to the corporation, for example, goodwill, those benefits are not tangible.

2. **Strategic collaborations**, also called **strategic philanthropy**. These relationships represent philanthropy, since money is *given* to the nonprofit. But the corporation has an objective that goes beyond general goodwill; the giving is purposeful. The gift is made with specific objectives in mind, consistent with the corporation's business strategy. The objectives may include visibility or perhaps goodwill within a particular market.

One example is *sponsorships*, in which the company gives in exchange for the display of its name or logo, perhaps at an event. Another type of transaction that may fall into this category is gifts of company products, called *gifts-in-kind*. A typical example might be a software company that gives a nonprofit its product for free. That is surely of benefit to the nonprofit, and there is no explicit benefit to the company. But it may

BOX 9.1 Corporate–Nonprofit Collaborations

Type	Characteristics	Example
Traditional philanthropy	Gift with no quid pro quo	Corporation makes a gift to support the organization's programs
Strategic philanthropy	Gift with a specific benefit to the corporation	*Sponsorship* of an event that brings visibility to the corporation's logo
		Gift of products that will have the effect of introducing them to consumers
Commercial	Primary purpose is to increase sales of the corporation's product, while also producing revenue to the nonprofit	*Cause-related marketing:* The nonprofit receives a payment for each sale of the corporation's product.
		Licensing agreement: The nonprofit is paid a royalty for the use of its name or logo on the corporation's product.
Political	Primary purpose is to change the political climate or influence opinion	A corporation makes a gift to support a nonprofit that advocates for business interests or purposes that might increase demand for its products.

Source: Based on Galaskiewicz and Colman (2006).

result in people becoming accustomed to using the product, perhaps leading them to stick with it when they consider purchasing software for their own business or personal use, so the gift serves a strategic purpose. This type of collaboration is "quasi-charitable," since the payment by the corporation is generally tax-deductible as a gift but also "quasi-commercial," since the company is seeking a direct and specific benefit (Galaskiewicz & Colman, 2006).

3. **Commercial collaborations**. In these relationships, the payment that goes to the nonprofit is directly related to sales of the company's product. Two of the most common are called *cause-related marketing* and *licensing agreements* (Galaskiewicz & Colman, 2006). Cause-related marketing is discussed further shortly, but in its simplest form, it involves an arrangement in which the company gives the nonprofit a set amount of money, or a percentage of the sale, every time someone buys a product. For a simple example, every time you buy a cup of coffee, ten cents goes to charity.

Under the terms of a licensing agreement, the nonprofit permits the corporation to use its brand or logo to sell its products, either on the product itself or in its advertising. The corporation pays the nonprofit a royalty for the use of its name, but the payment is not explicitly related to the *volume* of sales. For example, you might buy a T-shirt with the logo of an environmental organization. The organization is paid to permit the display of that logo but does not get a percentage of your particular purchase. Some licensing agreements have been controversial; some examples are discussed later in this chapter.

Commercial collaborations are, as the term implies, not philanthropic exchanges. The nonprofit may benefit, but the corporation's primary motivation is to sell more products.

4. **Political collaborations**. Sometimes corporations give to nonprofits with the goal of affecting the political environment in ways beneficial to the company. A clear example might be supporting nonprofits that advocate for less regulation. But sometimes the goal is to improve the company's general business environment. An example could be bicycle manufacturers supporting nonprofits that advocate for more bike trails (Galaskiewicz & Colman, 2006).

This chapter focuses on philanthropy and the most common types of commercial partnerships between nonprofit organizations and corporations. But it is important to acknowledge that distinctions are often blurred. By definition, a *partnership* is a relationship that benefits *both* parties and that may be true even of those that represent traditional philanthropy, which may provide the company with some recognition and goodwill. Moreover, some nonprofit–corporate relationships are complex, including both philanthropic and commercial elements. Indeed, there has been a trend toward comprehensive relationships that cut across the types that have been described. It is important to note that nonprofits and corporations sometimes have operational relationships. For example, nonprofits may be suppliers to for-profit corporations, either of products or labor, and some nonprofits are engaged in joint business ventures with corporations. This chapter does not explore such relationships; although they may produce earned income for the nonprofit, the development and management of operational relationships between nonprofits and businesses is usually not regarded as fundraising.

As Andreasen (2009) notes, it is fair to argue, as many do, that the ultimate purpose of all corporate relationships with nonprofits is to increase sales. Corporations exist to create wealth for their owners, not to advance social goals. That is not to imply that the pursuit of profit is inconsistent with social benefit; indeed, the resources generated by business make possible the programs of nonprofits and government that address social needs. Subject to ethical and legal constraints, the pursuit of profit is an entirely honorable endeavor, consistent with the advancement of society. Certainly individuals who manage corporations are often personally altruistic, and some corporate philanthropy may reflect their values. As Galaskiewicz and Colman (2006) correctly observe, "Philanthropic partnerships are seldom purely altruistic and commercial partnerships often have an element of altruism" (p. 180).

HISTORICAL OVERVIEW

Although it is a familiar part of the landscape today, corporate support for nonprofit organizations actually has a relatively brief history—spanning less than one hundred years. Chapter 1 of this text discussed the philanthropy of business titans like John D. Rockefeller and Andrew Carnegie. But it is important to understand that their giving came from their personal fortunes and that, indeed, it would have been illegal for the corporations they founded to have made gifts from corporate funds except under limited circumstances. Before the 1920s, courts generally held that corporations could not make gifts unless they directly benefitted the company. This permitted, for example, gifts from railroads to benefit YMCAs, since the Y's provided temporary housing that was used by railroad workers (Burlingame, 2011). But corporations were prohibited from making gifts simply as good citizens for the general benefit of society. This was based on the philosophy that management's responsibility was to increase dividends to shareholders, which the shareholders could use to make gifts, if they chose to do so as individuals. The law changed in 1953 with the historic case of *A. P. Smith Manufacturing Co. v. Barlow*, in which the Supreme Court of New Jersey recognized the right of a corporation to make a gift that was not directly tied to the company's interests (Galaskiewicz & Colman, 2006).

Corporate philanthropy flourished in the 1950s and 1960s, in light of a generally favorable economic climate, and continued to grow even during the 1970s, a decade that brought difficult economic conditions (Galaskiewicz & Colman, 2006). In those decades, giving decisions often were made by the corporation's officers. It was not uncommon that the recipients were well-established institutions, including colleges and universities from which executives had graduated and those that had corporate executives or members of their families on the board. And corporate giving was local, generally confined to communities in which the company was headquartered or had a major presence. Recipients of corporate support during this period were often the same organizations most years, as exemplified in the anecdote with which this chapter began.

It is impossible to cite an exact starting date for the transition from traditional corporate philanthropy to strategic philanthropy. The 1970s and 1980s brought globalization and a more competitive business environment. Some people became critical of traditional corporate philanthropy at a time when jobs were being eliminated and companies were being forced to downsize and restructure. More people began to agree with the view of economist Milton Friedman, who favored individual philanthropy but argued that "the social responsibility of a business is to increase its profits" (Meyerson, 2006). During the 1980s, thinking shifted toward the opinion that corporate philanthropy should be driven by the company's business interests and strategies. The trend toward strategic philanthropy was identified and given impetus by an influential article in the *Harvard Business Review* by corporate social responsibility scholar Craig Smith (1994). By 2008, Reynold Levy, a former president of the AT&T Foundation, observed the shift and pronounced that "the age of pure corporate philanthropy is drawing to a close" (Levy, 2008, p. 66).

Meanwhile, in 1983, American Express had undertaken an experiment that captured the attention of the business community. It offered to make a payment toward the campaign to restore Ellis Island and the Statue of Liberty for every transaction made with one of its credit cards. The use of American Express cards increased by 28 percent during the promotion, and the success was widely noted. This is generally identified as the specific beginning of cause-related marketing (Andreasen, 2009).

Corporate relationships with nonprofit organizations today are becoming more integrated within the corporate structure and often include multiple goals and components, including traditional philanthropy, commercial partnerships, employee volunteer programs, and others. Some companies also are undertaking long-term relationships and are focusing on impact with regard to broad social causes, for example, education, hunger, the environment, and others. Some are defining corporate values in terms of causes the company supports; that is, they are identifying the corporation's commitment to a social cause as "the essence of what we stand for" (Center on Philanthropy, 2007). There also is an increasingly global perspective reflected in the philanthropic programs of some corporations. In a 2013 study, 60 percent of fifty-nine companies surveyed were giving outside the United States, and 86 percent of those expected to maintain or increase their global giving (Lilly Family School of Philanthropy, 2013).

For an individual nonprofit organization, especially one that is local in its impact and does not enjoy a prominent brand, these trends may increase the challenge of securing significant corporate support.

CORPORATE PHILANTHROPY

Again, it is not always possible to draw a clear distinction between philanthropy and partnerships, and some relationships between corporations and nonprofits encompass both. But philanthropy and partnerships are separated for purposes of clarity in our discussion in this chapter. This section focuses on corporate philanthropy—encompassing pure or traditional giving and strategic philanthropy—and the next section discusses commercial relationships. Corporate giving in 2012 totaled $18.15 billion, accounting for about 6 percent of total philanthropy. The total includes gifts of company products, that is, **gifts-in-kind**, as well as cash, but not payments made to nonprofits as part of commercial partnerships (Lilly School of Philanthropy website). The total also includes **matching-gift programs**, under which companies make gifts to match those made personally by employees. Some have restrictions on the types of organizations that can receive matching gifts, and most have limits on the amount that can be matched per employee (Pagnoni & Solomon, 2013). These programs are especially beneficial to colleges and universities, which have large numbers of alumni employed by corporations. Those institutions sometimes undertake focused solicitations of donors known to be employed by corporations that provide matching gifts, emphasizing the leverage the companies' programs provide.

Many national corporations have giving programs that operate on two levels—local and national. Some funds are allocated to local or regional managers, who can authorize relatively small gifts to nonprofits in their communities. These may include cash gifts as well as sponsorships, for example, buying a table at a dinner or providing T-shirts for an event. At the national level, corporations may give directly from corporate offices or through a **corporate foundation**.

Corporate Foundations

Companies that give directly from corporate accounts may do so through an office of community relations, public relations, marketing, or some other unit. Some have contributions committees that involve employees from various departments and levels of the organization. Gifts-in-kind of company products (and the negotiation of commercial part-nerships) are always handled directly by the company. But for cash gifts, some have estab-lished a corporate foundation; there were 2,700 corporate foundations in 2011, which gave an estimated $5.2 billion (Foundation Center, 2012a).

Establishing a foundation offers both advantages and disadvantages to a corporation. A corporate foundation is a private foundation under the tax law, and the company receives a tax deduction when it transfers funds to the foundation. Thus, the company can make contributions to the foundation in years when it has high profits, building up its resources for years when profit is lower. That enables it to maintain its giving in lean years and pro-vides a more even pattern of support to grant recipients. This approach also can be used to smooth out the company's tax obligations as its taxable profits fluctuate from year to year. In addition, a corporation can claim a tax deduction when it gives funds to its foundation, and the foundation then can make gifts to organizations outside the United States, which would not be deductible if made directly (McDowell, 2003). This is a major advantage to corporations that seek to establish a global philanthropic presence.

But there are complications with the use of a foundation to manage corporate philan-thropy. The foundation is an independent nonprofit entity. Its broad purposes usually align with the corporation's activities, but it is not legally permitted to make gifts that *directly* benefit the corporation. This may be an advantage that buffers corporate giving from internal politics and maintains a more thoughtful, planned approach (McDowell, 2003). But it also may cause tension between the foundation and corporate officers or sharehold-ers, who might prefer to see a more closely aligned strategic approach (Galaskiewicz & Colman, 2006).

Sponsorships

Galaskiewicz and Colman (2006) classify **sponsorships** as a form of strategic phi-lanthropy, although some authors subsume them under a broader definition of cause marketing. The payment is not tied to the sales volume of the company's product. In a sponsorship arrangement, the funds are given to the nonprofit with the requirement that the company's name or logo be displayed in connection with the activity sponsored. Think, for example, about the presence of corporate logos at the Olympic Games or at charity walks, rides, and runs. The visibility given to the company may be only slightly more than what traditional donor recognition programs would provide—the quid pro quo may not be substantially greater—so a sponsorship is philanthropy. But the recognition is explicitly described as a condition of the payment, so it is strategic philanthropy, not a pure gift.

It is important to distinguish sponsorship from advertising. Advertising features the company's products and usually includes information about the benefits of using them. Sponsorship is limited to exposure of the company's name or logo and is intended to enhance the company's overall visibility and image, not to promote the sale of specific products. Indeed, sponsorships and advertising are treated differently under the tax law. A nonprofit that receives a payment in connection with a sponsorship can consider it like a gift. But if it receives payment for an advertisement, there could be a question about whether it represents revenue unrelated to its charitable mission that is subject to the unrelated business income tax.

Corporations commonly sponsor events such as charity walks, runs, and rides and athletic competitions. Others sponsor facilities, such as athletic arenas and auditoriums, which may be named for the corporation. The facility may be named in perpetuity to recognize a corporate gift, but those named as part of a sponsorship arrangement carry the company's name only for the term of the contract. The company generally makes regular payments to the organization or institution operating the facility. But corporate sponsorship dollars are relatively concentrated in a few areas. For example, in 2014, it was projected that 70 percent would be related to sports events, 10 percent to entertainment, 9 percent to causes, 4 percent each to the arts and to festivals, fairs, and other annual events, and 3 percent to associations and other membership organizations (IEG, 2014).

Sponsorships may offer nonprofits the benefits of added revenue and possibly also increased visibility through the company's promotion of the relationship. But it is important to consider the consistency of the corporation and its products with the mission and values of the nonprofit organization. For example, it would be unlikely for an athletic event to accept sponsorship from a tobacco company or an organization serving children to be visibly associated with a company that sells alcohol.

Pursuing Corporate Philanthropy

The process for soliciting corporate philanthropy depends on how the corporation has organized its giving program. For a small nonprofit serving a single community, the most promising source may be the local or regional manager of a national corporation, who may have a budget for contributions. If the nonprofit is seeking a major grant, it more likely will need to go to the corporation's national headquarters.

If the corporation's philanthropy is managed through a foundation, the process for soliciting support is likely to be highly structured. The foundation is likely to have clearly articulated priorities, guidelines, and application procedures. In other words, large corporate foundations operate like any large private foundation.

Despite the professionalization of corporate giving programs, relationships with individuals within the company matter. For example, many corporations support nonprofits at which members of their management are engaged as board members, and others provide gifts to nonprofits at which their employees serve as volunteers. Indeed, some nonprofits engage volunteer groups from corporations as a strategy for cultivating such relationships. The companies value the volunteer opportunities for the contribution they make to employee morale and corporate culture and encourage them through their corporate giving programs.

Reynold Levy (2008), a former president of the AT&T Foundation and also a former nonprofit CEO, emphasizes the importance of relationships that provide access to corporate decision makers: "As with other prospects, the first challenge is securing favorable, if not privileged access. Ideally, a member of your board of directors is a senior officer of the company. Alternatively, someone on your board, or among your donors, friends, or colleagues, is a leading customer of the firm. In general, there is nothing to which a company is more responsive than a customer calling on behalf of its favored institution or cause" (pp. 73–74).

NONPROFIT–CORPORATE COMMERCIAL PARTNERSHIPS

Again, it may be correct to say, as some writers do, that all corporate support of nonprofit organizations ultimately is intended to advance the company's interests. But with philanthropic support, those interests may be broad and general, including goodwill and a positive overall image. The purpose of commercial partnerships is more specifically related to increasing sales of the company's products. Let's look at two of the most common relationships, *licensing agreements* and *cause-related marketing*.

Licensing Agreements

If students buy T-shirts or coffee mugs with the name and logo of their college on it, they probably do not think that the college manufactured the garment, but they may not know by what arrangement the school's logo is displayed. There is likely a licensing agreement between the college and the manufacturer of the shirt or mug.

A **licensing agreement** is a contract that permits a for-profit company to use the nonprofit's name or logo on its products in return for a royalty payment to the organization. The benefit to the nonprofit is the revenue it gains from the royalty and the increased visibility of its name. For the company, having the organization's logo on its products will presumably attract purchases from individuals who are affiliated with the nonprofit or who prefer the product over others because of the benefit to the cause. But there is also something more subtle at work. By using the nonprofit's name or logo on its product, the company gains some of the attributes of the organization's brand; that is, the company may come to be seen as more caring, more green, or perhaps more concerned about specific groups of people by virtue of its association with the positive qualities that people attribute to its nonprofit partner. In effect, when it enters a licensing agreement, a nonprofit organization leverages some of its **brand equity** into a stream of income in the form of royalties from the corporation.

Most licensing agreements bring few risks. For example, there is probably little that can go wrong by having a college's logo on a sweatshirt. But some licensing is more controversial. The appearance of a nonprofit's logo in connection with a product is especially sensitive when the product relates to food, health, or the environment. The concern is that the presence of the logo implies the nonprofit's endorsement of the product; that is, the appearance of the name or logo may suggest to consumers that the nonprofit is certifying the product's benefits, which may or may not be the case. In the American Heart Association's food certification program, for example, the products have been screened and found to comply with the association's criteria for saturated fat and cholesterol (American Heart Association, 2014). However, in other instances, the appearance of the logo means only that the company has provided a royalty payment to the nonprofit. It does not ensure that the nonprofit has investigated the product or guarantees its consistency with the organization's values. This could be easy for consumers to misunderstand. One well-known licensing fiasco occurred in 1997, when the American Medical Association (AMA) licensed its name to be used on home medical products manufactured by Sunbeam Corporation. The endorsement implied that the AMA had established the effectiveness of the products, but it had not done so. There was public criticism and an outcry by doctors, who are the association's members. The AMA was forced to end the relationship with Sunbeam, paying the company almost $10 million in a lawsuit settlement. Not surprisingly, some AMA employees also lost their jobs (Sagawa & Segal, 2000).

Cause-Related Marketing

Some writers use the term **cause-related marketing** (or just cause marketing) broadly to encompass virtually all relationships in which a nonprofit's and a corporation's identities are combined, including licensing and sponsorships. This text uses the term in a more specific way to mean an arrangement under which the company's support is tied to a transaction. In the simplest and most common form, the company contributes either a fixed amount for each sale of a product or a specified percentage of its sales of a product to the nonprofit, usually in connection with a short-term promotion. This is what Eikenberry (2009) calls **consumption philanthropy**.[1]

Cause-marketing relationships are governed by a contract between the nonprofit and the corporate partner. When the payment to the nonprofit is based on sales, the contract spells out how much is to be paid (e.g., a fixed amount per sale or a percentage); the length of time for which the promotion will be in effect; the maximum sum (if any) that the corporate partner will give; and rights of approval that each partner retains with regard to ad copy, use of its logo, and related concerns. One important question is whether and how the terms of the contract will be clearly disclosed to consumers. Promotions that include statements such as "a portion of your purchase will be given to charity" are inadequate, since they do not disclose what portion, whether the promotion covers only certain dates, or whether the total contribution by the company is capped at some maximum amount, as many are. In sum, such a statement does not assure an individual consumer that his or her own purchase will result in a payment to the nonprofit. Standard 19 of the Better Business Bureau (BBB) Wise Giving Alliance Standards for Charity Accountability addresses these potential issues, requiring that nonprofit organizations clearly disclose how the charity benefits from the sale of products or services and the terms and conditions of its agreement with the corporate partner. Standard 19 is shown in Box 9.2.

The Wise Giving Alliance standards apply to nonprofit organizations; the Better Business Bureau certifies that organizational practices either meet or do not meet their guidelines. In other words, Standard 19 applies to the conduct of the nonprofit organization that is partnering with a corporation, rather than to the corporation. It requires that when a nonprofit enters a cause-related marketing contract, the contract it negotiates with the corporation should include the disclosure requirements as a provision binding on both parties. In addition, however, laws in twenty-two states require registration by **commercial coventurers**, that is, corporations engaged in cause marketing. Some require specific provisions in the contract between the nonprofit and the corporation and disclosure of the agreement to the state (Copilevitz & Canter, 2014).

> **BOX 9.2** Better Business Bureau Wise Giving Alliance Standards
> for Charity Accountability
>
> ## Standard 19
>
> 19. Clearly disclose how the charity benefits from the sale of products or services (i.e., cause-related marketing) that state or imply that a charity will benefit from a consumer sale or transaction. Such promotions should disclose, at the point of solicitation:
>
>   a. the actual or anticipated portion of the purchase price that will benefit the charity (e.g., 5 cents will be contributed to abc charity for every xyz company product sold),
>
>   b. the duration of the campaign (e.g., the month of October),
>
>   c. any maximum or guaranteed minimum contribution amount (e.g., up to a maximum of $200,000).

Source: Better Business Bureau Wise Giving Alliance website, retrieved April 28, 2014, from http://www.bbb.org/us/standards-for-charity-accountability/.

While the traditional definition of cause-related marketing is transaction-based, as addressed in Standard 19, a number of variations have emerged, including the following identified by Cone Communications (2010), a public relations and marketing firm.

1. *The Proud Supporter Method.* The company makes a gift to a cause or nonprofit organization, and the gift is not tied to sales of a product or action by the consumer. This is similar to traditional philanthropy, except that the company's role as a "proud supporter" is mentioned on its product displays, with the expectation that consumers will be encouraged to buy them.

2. *Donation With Label or Coupon Redemption.* The company makes a gift when the consumer submits, online or in a store, a code or label that comes with the product. The gift is not triggered by the sale itself but by this additional action by the consumer.

3. *Donation With Consumer Action.* This method does not require a purchase. The company promises to make a gift when the consumer takes some action, for example, hosts an event. It is not directly tied to the sale of the product but may help to identify the product with the cause.

4. *Dual-Incentive Method.* With this method, the company asks the consumer to make a gift and offers an incentive to do so, for example, a discount coupon. It is "dual" because it both creates an incentive to make a gift and also to buy the product, with a discount. It helps to build consumer loyalty.

5. *Consumer Pledge Drives.* This is similar to the dual-incentive approach. The company encourages consumers to pledge a gift to a social issue or nonprofit partner, sometimes

offering a corporate match. One variation occurs when a customer at the supermarket checkout is asked if he or she wishes to make a gift, or round up the total of the bill, to support a nonprofit cause. Of course, in these programs, the individual is not recognized as a donor and cannot claim a tax deduction.

6. *Buy One, Give One (BOGO) Method.* With the **buy one, give one (*BOGO*)** approach, the company promises to give a product, or some equivalent, when a consumer purchases its product. For example, the shoe company Tom's promises to give a pair of shoes to a child in need for every pair of shoes that consumers purchase.

7. *Consumer-Directed Donation.* This is a variation of **crowdfunding**, which is discussed in more detail elsewhere in this text. The company permits consumers to vote on the organizations or causes that will receive a company gift. It is not tied directly to sales but may drive traffic to the company's website and help to develop interactive relationships between the corporation and consumers.

8. *Volunteerism Rally.* This type of promotion encourages consumers to volunteer in support of a social cause. Consumers are rewarded for their volunteerism with complimentary goods or services. It is not tied directly to the sale of a product but may help to generate consumer loyalty and drive traffic to the company's website.

All of these variations have advantages and disadvantages, from the perspective of the corporation and the nonprofit, including the extent to which they directly affect sales or simply provide a longer-term benefit through an enhanced relationship between the company and its customers (Cone Communications, 2010).

COMPREHENSIVE RELATIONSHIPS

Some nonprofit–corporate relationships are comprehensive and integrated. They may include sponsorship, cause marketing, corporate philanthropy, employee volunteering, and additional interactions. Some are also long-term relationships that result in a close identification of the corporate brand with the nonprofit organization or cause. For example, one well-known partnership is that between Timberland and City Year. The relationship began in 1989, when Timberland contributed fifty pairs of boots for City Year volunteers, who work in urban areas. In 1993, Timberland became the official supplier of clothing for all City Year volunteers, which enhanced the brand of both its products and City Year. By 1994, Timberland's CEO was chair of the City Year board and the company gave $5 million to support the program's expansion to more cities. That expansion was coordinated with events at Timberland stores in those communities. By 2010, City Year's headquarters was colocated in Timberland's offices (SR International, 2010).

Another trend has been the development of products branded with a cause. For example, Product Red is a brand licensed by the Global Fund to Fight AIDS, Tuberculosis, and Malaria to a variety of corporate partners, including American Express, Apple, Dell, Starbucks, and others. Pink products, intended to raise awareness of breast cancer and provide support for breast cancer research, also have become ubiquitous. Such programs have attracted numerous critics, who express concern about a lack of transparency regarding the use of funds generated (Raymond, 2009).

BENEFITS AND RISKS

Cause-related marketing, and its variations, may offer benefits to both corporations and nonprofits, but it may also entail risks for both parties.

Benefits to Corporations and Nonprofits

In a number of studies, consumers have indicated that they would be more inclined to buy products when they know that the sale benefits a charitable organization. For example, in a 2008 study conducted by Cone Communications (n.d.), 85 percent of consumers surveyed said that they have a more positive image of a product or corporation that supports a cause they care about. And 79 percent said they would switch from one product to another if the new one supports a good cause, assuming that price and quality were comparable. That suggests that corporations gain both tangible and intangible benefits from such relationships. Of course, Cone's findings are subject to positivity bias; in other words, people are inclined to give the "right" answer to questions about what their hypothetical behavior might be, and that does not assure that they will actually behave in that manner (Andreasen, 2009). And, as Andreasen also notes, other studies have produced findings with more ambiguous implications. For example, Morris, Bartkus, Glassman, and Rhiel (2013) found that consumers held more positive attitudes toward companies that engaged in traditional giving than toward those that supported nonprofits through purchase-based marketing programs.

For the nonprofit, the marketing relationship may generate not only additional revenue but *unrestricted* revenue, which may be challenging to raise through philanthropy. In addition, because it is usually tied to product sales, the revenue from marketing partnerships may be more substantial than the amounts typically provided through corporate gifts and grants. However, the financial benefits and costs may be difficult to assess. Some studies have suggested that in some partnerships, the corporate partner may receive a greater benefit than the nonprofit (Gourville & Rangan, 2004).

The nonprofit also may gain increased visibility through the marketing of the relationship; promotions often feature the logos of both the nonprofit and the corporate partner, and a comprehensive campaign may include advertising, in-store displays, and exposure in other media. The nonprofit may benefit from the expertise of company employees who volunteer, some possibly bringing professional skills the nonprofit would find expensive to purchase in the marketplace (Community Wealth Partners, 2009).

Risks to Corporations and Nonprofits

But partnerships have potential downsides for both companies and nonprofit organizations. One risk to the corporation is that its relationship with a nonprofit organization or cause might be viewed as a cynical attempt to improve its image or that it might even highlight issues with its business practices. Examples include General Motors' tree-planting program in the 1990s, which some critics attacked as "greenwashing," in view of the negative impact of automobile emissions on the environment (Andreasen, 2009). There is also the risk that the nonprofit partner will engage in some activity that generates negative publicity and that the company's identification with it will become a liability. Think, for example, about Nike's sponsorship of Livestrong, which became quite uncomfortable when Lance Armstrong, Livestrong's founder, acknowledged his use of performance-enhancing drugs.

Nonprofits run the risk that their relationships with for-profit companies will be characterized as greed or selling out or that corporate misbehavior will reflect negatively on their reputations. Some may be offended by nonprofit commercialism (Andreasen, 2009). And it is possible that people will come to think that nonprofits with visible corporate partnerships have all the funding they need and therefore refrain from making traditional gifts. Krishna's (2011) study found that cause marketing indeed reduces charitable giving by consumers, although others have not identified such crowding out as a phenomenon (Andreasen, 2009). Again, positivity bias, the tendency of people to give what they think are the right answers, obscures the evidence on this point.

The risks of harm to an organization's reputation may be most acute for highly visible nonprofits with well-established national brands. Although we may think about corporate partnerships as something nonprofits *seek out*—that is, we may think about them in terms of a typical fundraising posture—in reality many of the most visible organizations face the challenge of screening the many opportunities presented to them. Many have clearly defined guidelines on what type of relationships are acceptable and, especially, conditions under which their brand or logo may be used. As one example, Box 9.3 includes the policies established by Autism Speaks. The largest national nonprofits indeed face some threat from what is known as **ambush marketing**, the unauthorized use of their names in connection with sales, which may or may not produce any revenue to them. Think, for example, about small merchants who may display the Red Cross logo following a national disaster, representing that some portion of sales will go for disaster relief. Without policies and some vigilance by the organization, the potential for scams may be high.

BOX 9.3   Autism Speaks: Corporate Partnership Guidelines

Autism Speaks offers its corporate partners a unique, high-profile opportunity to engage on a national and local level with the fastest growing developmental disability health issue of our time. Our team will work with you to develop customized programs to help you reach your cause marketing and philanthropic goals while promoting a positive corporate image, building employee morale and engaging consumers in a cause that has become part of the national and global health agenda.

In turn, our Corporate Partners enable Autism Speaks to raise awareness of the fastest growing developmental disability around the globe and to fund research, community services and advocacy efforts.

Some of our national corporate partnership opportunities include: Walk Now for Autism, retail promotions, golf, galas, concerts, underwriting publications and educational programs, and direct investment in cutting edge research.

Our corporate relations team seeks partners with significant track records and a positive, family-oriented image who would like to help us achieve our mission.

Partnership Guidelines

Thank you for considering Autism Speaks. Please review the information below to determine if a partnership with Autism Speaks makes sense for your company.

- Autism Speaks requires a minimum of one year in business to become a partner.
- Autism Speaks requires full disclosure when funds are raised through a consumer purchase or promotion (e.g. 20% from the sale of each item) on all packaging, advertising and promotional materials in accordance with cause marketing best practices.
- Autism Speaks owns the registration for the Autism Speaks name, logo, web site and programs "Licensed Marks." A party that desires to obtain permission to use these Licensed Marks must execute a written contract with Autism Speaks that outlines how the Licensed Marks will be used. Until a fully executed Letter of Agreement is received by the organization, use of the Autism Speaks name, logo, or any of its licensed marks is strictly prohibited.
- Your organization may be required to register in certain states as a "commercial co-venturer." Autism Speaks recommends our partners obtain legal counsel to ensure that they comply with these registration requirements.
- Autism Speaks is unable to secure celebrities for promotional purposes.

Once you have reviewed the above guidelines and are interested in more information about partnering with Autism Speaks, please register at AutismSpeaks.org/Partnership Request. We welcome the opportunity to speak with you.

Source: Autism Speaks website, retrieved October 20, 2014, from http://www.autismspeaks.org/ways-give/corporate-sponsors-guidelines#sthash.hMLaYgnQ.dpuf.

Implications for the Nonprofit Sector and Society

Cause marketing may bring benefits and risks to the corporations and nonprofits that engage in such relationships. But what are the implications for the nonprofit sector and society overall? Proponents emphasize the potential to leverage the power of the market to address social problems on a global basis. But balance requires acknowledging critics who voice concerns.

While such partnerships bring short-term benefits to companies and nonprofits, some critics are concerned that the longer-term impact could be detrimental. One concern is that cause marketing "individualizes solutions to collective social problems" and distracts consumers from thinking about the underlying causes of social ills (Eikenberry, 2009). Others argue that the visibility of cause marketing, and other types of corporate–nonprofit partnerships, may distort philanthropic priorities. Corporations may be inclined to associate themselves with feel-good causes, not necessarily those that are the most urgent or important (Andreasen, 2009). In addition, the feel-good nature of marketing partnerships could obscure the role that some companies and products themselves may play in causing social ills; for example, people may see the company engaged in socially desirable activities and fail to question whether the product creates a negative environmental impact or is perhaps manufactured with exploited labor (Eikenberry, 2009).

Thinking back on the discussion of donor motivations in Chapter 3 of this text, recall that some research suggests the possibility that offering donors tangible benefits may undermine altruism and turn giving into a transaction. Some argue that cause marketing presents a similar threat, that consumers who buy products will think that "they have already donated their philanthropic share" and be less likely to give in response to more traditional, and emotionally based, methods (Eikenberry, 2009). If the satisfaction that comes from altruistic giving is sacrificed, the impact on philanthropy could be negative. Krishna's (2011) research raises this concern, finding that consumers "appear to realize that participating in cause marketing is inherently more selfish than direct charitable donation, and are less happy if they substitute cause marketing for charitable giving" (p. 338). In other words, a disconnect between altruism and commercial transactions and the ubiquitous nature of cause marketing may desensitize people to the real needs of society (Eikenberry, 2009).

DEVELOPING AND SUSTAINING SUCCESSFUL PARTNERSHIPS

Now that we understand the various relationships between corporations and nonprofit organizations and the benefits and risks involved, let's look at the pragmatic question of how successful partnerships may be developed. There is a considerable literature directed to for-profit companies seeking to develop relationships with nonprofit organizations or incorporate causes in their marketing strategies (e.g., Kotler, Hessekiel, & Lee, 2012). But this discussion takes the perspective of a nonprofit organization that desires to develop such relationships as a part of its overall fundraising strategy.

Obstacles to Partnerships

Partnerships with corporations may offer nonprofits an attractive option for expanding and diversifying sources of revenue. And collaborations may advance nonprofit missions in ways that go beyond financial. But they are not without pitfalls and do not offer a panacea. Sagawa and Segal (2000) identify some natural obstacles to the development of corporate–nonprofit alliances that need to be acknowledged, so that they can be anticipated and addressed at the outset:

- *Different language.* Communication may be difficult between entities that have their own jargon.

- *Different culture.* The stereotypical business with its "time is money" orientation may clash head-on with a slower moving, consensus-oriented and resource-poor nonprofit.

- *Different status.* Because of their greater resources, businesses may receive or expect greater deference than their nonprofit partners.

- *Different world view.* Nonprofits may consider business to be "part of the problem" and view a business partner only as a check writer; a business may believe social sector organizations foster dependency and fail to solve the problems they were created to address.

- *Different bottom lines.* Because each sector measures success differently, cross-sector partners may clash over goals for the alliance (p. 180).

Given the potential for these obstacles to arise, Sagawa and Segal (2000) advise nonprofit organizations to begin the process of considering business alliances by assessing themselves.

Nonprofit Self-Assessment

The self-assessment Sagawa and Segal (2000) recommend includes identification of the organization's needs and its assets that may be attractive to for-profit partners, including, for example, a well-known brand, a compelling cause, the ability to demonstrate impact, a well-known leader, connections to influential individuals, the ability to provide expertise needed by a business, volunteer opportunities for corporate employees, attractive events, facilities or equipment related to a potential partnership, and the ability to provide recognition.

But a successful collaboration requires not only matching the nonprofit's assets and capabilities against the needs of potential corporate partners but also compatibility with regard to intangibles. For that reason, the self-assessment also needs to include reflection on the nonprofit's internal culture, including consideration of the following questions: "Do staff and board members have positive attitudes toward business? Would a person with a business background feel comfortable working in the organization? How quickly does the group make decisions?" (p. 189). Various authors also emphasize the importance of matching *organizations* as well as programs, that is, the need for nonprofits to seek corporate partners with which they are compatible based on values and culture (e.g., Iyer, 2003; Thompson, 2012).

Identifying Potential Corporate Partners

The process for identifying potential corporate partners is parallel to that of identifying donor prospects, following something similar to the logic of LAI, as discussed in Chapter 5. Linkage may highlight companies already supporting the organization in some manner, perhaps with gifts or with company employees serving as board members or volunteers. As with all fundraising, personal relationships matter and can provide at least the access to initiate a conversation.

The identification of potential corporate partners requires matching of nonprofit needs with those of companies, that is, in the vernacular of LAI, determining a rationale for why the company might have an interest. This requires developing a "win-win" concept that brings both tangible (e.g., revenue, sales) and intangible (e.g., visibility, reputation) benefits to both partners (Thompson, 2012). But it is also essential that any nonprofit–corporate relationship be a good fit and that the corporation's participation be perceived as authenticate and appropriate. In other words, the partnership needs to make sense.

Let's look at a few examples of good and not-so-good fits. Ralston Purina, a manufacturer of pet food, joined the American Humane Association in a campaign to encourage pet adoptions and reduce euthanasia. That made sense, since both parties had an obvious interest in keeping more animals alive and in the hands of caring owners (Austin, 2003). In another case, Visa, the credit card issuer, partnered with Reading Is Fundamental, a literacy nonprofit. That may have made less obvious sense, but Visa had surveyed its cardholders and found that they had a high interest in literacy, so there was a logic to it (Austin, 2003). And use of a credit card is not inconsistent with the goal of promoting literacy. However, to consider a partnership that was not received as well, in 2012, the Nature Conservancy partnered with a website called the Gilt Groupe, which promotes special events. The specific project was Gilt's promotion of *Sports Illustrated*'s annual swimsuit issue. As the arrangement was described, "With the deal, the charity, America's wealthiest conservation group, gets all the money from the sales of goods and events Gilt produced to promote the swimsuit issue. One such offer gives members [of the Nature Conservancy] the opportunity to mix and mingle with the swimsuit models at the issue's launch in a posh New York nightclub. A $1,000 VIP ticket ensured up to 12 drinks, all to benefit 'the Nature Conservancy's beaches and oceans conservation work'" (Flandez, 2012b). Controversy ensued, including protests from members of the Nature Conservancy's board and staff. The Conservancy's purpose was reported to be strengthening its visibility among a younger audience, including readers of *Sports Illustrated*. But the partnership was perceived not only as inappropriate but contrived, since the connection between promoting swimsuit models and the goal of conserving beaches and oceans simply did not sound plausible.

Approaching the Potential Corporate Partner

Initial contact with a potential partner may begin with individuals inside the company who are already known to the nonprofit organization, including current donors and volunteers. But it is ultimately important to engage the attention and support of the chief executive officer. As Andresen (2006) notes, "The higher the level of the person involved in each organization, the better the chances of strong results" (p. 116).

Presenting a proposal to a potential corporate partner requires defining a **value proposition**. In other words, nonprofits must shift their thinking from their own needs to the mind-set of the company. It is fine to articulate the benefits of the proposed relationship to the nonprofit organization and the cause and to appeal to the altruism of corporate officers, but that is not sufficient. The nonprofit needs to understand the company's business goals and strategies and explain how the proposed collaboration can further them. Daw (2006) urges nonprofits to be realistic about the benefits they can deliver to a corporate partner. Noting than many nonprofits are accustomed to making "a little go a long way," she cautions that corporate partners may expect performance that could overwhelm a nonprofit's staff and systems, also leaving the partner disappointed.

Sustaining a Successful Partnership

A commercial partnership is different from a gift. A nonprofit may accept a gift from a company and provide little more than thanks and some level of recognition, whether that is simply a listing in an event program or something more explicit, like displaying the corporate logo in a prominent location. But when it enters into a commercial partnership with a nonprofit, a corporation is usually making a larger commitment. The commitment is not just for one event but involves a relationship that will continue, at least for some period of time. And there is more at stake than money, since the company's image and reputation will be exposed. Assuring success and sustaining the partnership thus requires that certain practices be followed. Expert advice includes the following recommendations:

- Develop a written plan and strategy agreed to by both parties. The plan needs to state explicitly the goals of the alliance and how success will be defined and measured. It should spell out the responsibilities of both parties, define a governance structure through which decisions will be made, describe legal structures, and establish the financial commitments to be made by both partners (Sagawa & Segal, 2000).

- Assign day-to-day responsibility for the partnership to a designated relationship manager, who may be an individual in a particular office, such as the development or communications office, but also build wide support for the relationship among senior executives, members of the board, and staff—at various levels and in both partner organizations (Andresen, 2006; Sagawa & Segal, 2000).

- Maintain open and candid communication, evaluate results, and be willing to undertake adjustments in the relationship as needed (Andresen, 2006; Sagawa & Segal, 2000).

REDEFINING VALUE

As recounted earlier in this chapter, corporate philanthropy as we know it has existed for less than a century and cause marketing as we define it today for only about three decades. But some observers see the engagement of corporations in social issues in a sweeping historical perspective. In an article in the *Harvard Business Review* in 2011, Michael Porter and Mark Kramer called for a new model, in which companies go beyond the conventional view of corporate social responsibility, which they call "a mind-set in which societal issues are at the periphery, not the core" (Porter & Kramer, 2011, p. 64).

Defining **shared value** as "policies and operating practices that enhance the competitiveness of a company while simultaneously advancing the economic and social conditions in the communities in which it operates," Porter and Kramer (2011) explain:

The concept rests on the premise that both economic and social progress must be addressed using value principles. Value is defined as benefits relative to costs, not just benefits alone. Value creation is an idea that has long been recognized in business, where profit is revenues earned from customers minus the costs incurred. However, businesses have rarely approached societal issues from a value perspective but have treated them as peripheral matters. This has obscured the connections between economic and social concerns. (p. 66)

The authors argue that nonprofits have not historically thought in terms of value, considering benefits but not costs. But they predict an evolving congruence between the perspectives of nonprofits and business and call for companies to adopt a "new conception of capitalism" that encompasses social values as well as profit (Porter & Kramer, 2011).

Whether a new model of capitalism takes hold, there is a vigorous dialogue occurring at the boundaries of the for-profit and nonprofit sectors. The discussion surrounds the social responsibilities of companies and their engagement in social change, in an environment of growing frustration regarding society's persistent ills. That suggests that relationships between nonprofit organizations and corporations are likely to increase and evolve in the years ahead, possibly requiring new definitions and conceptions of fundraising.

CHAPTER SUMMARY

Corporate support of nonprofit organizations includes giving, that is, philanthropy, but also a variety of other relationships. These relationships are a part of *corporate social responsibility* but are not synonymous with it. The emphasis in this chapter is on relationships between nonprofit organizations and public companies that are national or international in scope, although some principles may apply to nonprofits and privately owned local businesses.

Four types of relationships, also called *alliances*, *collaborations*, or *partnerships*, are those that are *philanthropic*, *strategic*, *commercial*, or *political* (Galaskiewicz & Colman, 2006). This chapter discusses philanthropic collaborations, including traditional giving programs and strategic philanthropy, and commercial relationships, the pursuit of which is defined as fundraising by many organizations. It does not discuss operational partnerships between nonprofits and corporations. The lines separating the four types are often blurred. Corporations may have altruistic motives but also usually seek some specific business benefit from their relationships with nonprofits or causes. Profit seeking is nevertheless an honorable goal that benefits society.

Corporate giving was restricted by law before 1953 but grew significantly in the decades that followed. A shift from traditional philanthropy to a strategic approach has occurred since about the 1980s. A promotion by American Express in the 1980s is credited as the beginning of *cause-related marketing* (Galaskiewicz & Colman, 2006).

Corporate philanthropy includes cash gifts, gifts of products, and *sponsorships*. It is sometimes managed both locally and nationally. Gifts of products and sponsorships are managed directly by the company, but cash gifts are made from corporate accounts or through a *corporate foundation*, which offers some advantages (McDowell, 2003). Sponsorships are philanthropy, but recognition of the corporation through display of its logo is a part of a contract, so it is a strategic approach. Nonprofits that seek corporate support need to consider how the giving program is organized and establish personal relationships with individuals in the company.

Commercial partnerships include *licensing agreements*, under which a nonprofit is paid a royalty for the use of its logo in selling corporate products, and *cause-related marketing* (*cause marketing*) collaborations. The basic cause-related marketing arrangement provides a fixed amount or a percentage of the sale of the company's product; it is transaction based. There are other variations, including the proud-supporter method; the donation-with-label-or-coupon-redemption method; the donation-with-consumer-action method; the dual-incentive method; consumer pledge drives; the buy one, give one (BOGO) method; consumer-directed corporate donations; and the volunteerism rally (Cone Communications, 2010). Some nonprofit–corporate relationships are comprehensive and long-term, encompassing many of the different types and methods described in this chapter.

The Better Business Bureau Wise Giving Alliance Standard 19 defines what information should be disclosed regarding the payments to the nonprofit in a cause-related marketing partnership; it applies to nonprofit organizations that seek to be compliant with the alliance's standards. Some state laws also require registration and disclosures by *commercial coventurers*.

For corporations, partnerships with nonprofits may increase sales and improve image, but some research findings are inconclusive. For the nonprofit, a relationship with a corporation may produce increased revenue, visibility, and other benefits. But there are risks to the reputations of both partners related to possible negative behavior of the other. Some research suggests that support given through commercial transactions may reduce traditional giving by individuals (Krishna, 2011), but other studies contradict that finding.

Some observers see a downside to nonprofit–corporate partnerships from the perspective of society as a whole, including the possibility that *consumption philanthropy* will undermine altruism, distort nonprofit priorities, and undermine giving (Eikenberry, 2009).

There are natural obstacles to nonprofit–corporate relationships, including different vocabularies, cultures, and worldviews. A nonprofit that seeks to develop partnerships with corporations should begin with an assessment of its own culture and values (Sagawa & Segal, 2000). The identification of potential corporate partners requires matching of nonprofit needs with those of companies. That requires developing a "win-win" concept that brings both tangible (e.g., revenue, sales) and intangible (e.g., visibility, reputation) benefits to both partners (Thompson, 2012). But it is also essential that any nonprofit–corporate relationship be a good fit and that the corporation's participation be perceived as authenticate and appropriate. In other words, the partnership needs to make sense. Presenting a proposal to a potential corporate partner requires defining a *value proposition*, that is, demonstrating how the relationship can further corporate goals. The need to match the prospect's interests to the needs of the organization is a principle in all fundraising, whether from individuals or corporations.

Building and sustaining successful partnerships requires that nonprofits follow best practices, which include developing a written plan and strategy agreed to by both parties, assigning specific staff responsibility for managing the partnership, building broad support at all levels of both partner organizations, and maintaining communications and a willingness to make changes as results may dictate (Andreasen, 2009; Sagawa & Segal, 2000).

Some authors call for a new model of capitalism, in which both businesses and nonprofits measure success in terms of *shared value*, which considers social benefits as well as profits. Future developments may require a new definition of fundraising (Porter & Kramer, 2011).

Key Terms and Concepts

Ambush marketing
Brand equity
Buy one, give one
  (BOGO)
Cause-related
  marketing (cause
  marketing)
Collaborations
  (alliances,
  partnerships)
Commercial
  collaborations

Commercial
  coventurers
Consumption
  philanthropy
Corporate foundation
Corporate social
  responsibility
Crowdfunding
Gifts-in-kind
Licensing agreements
Matching-gift
  programs

Philanthropic
  collaborations
Political
  collaborations
Shared value
Sponsorships
Strategic
  collaborations
  (strategic
  philanthropy)
Value
  proposition

Case 9.1: Susan G. Komen for the Cure and KFC

In 2010, Susan G. Komen for the Cure, a nonprofit organization that works to fight breast cancer through research, community health outreach, and advocacy, and restaurant chain KFC (formerly Kentucky Fried Chicken) initiated a promotion called "Buckets for the Cure." KFC agreed to give Komen fifty cents for every special pink bucket of chicken. The description of the relationship stated that "KFC restaurant operators have contributed 50 cents to the Susan G. Komen for the Cure for each Komen branded bucket purchased *by the operators* from April 5, 2010–May 9, 2010. . . . Customer purchases of KFC buckets during the promotion will not directly increase the total contribution." In other words, no purchase by the consumer was required; the contribution was based on KFC's sales of the product to its franchise operators. KFC guaranteed that the total contribution would be $1 million (Huget, 2010; italics added).

Case 9.2: No Kid Hungry and Denny's

Every September since 2008, over 9,000 restaurants, representing 373 brands, participate in Dine Out for No Kid Hungry, a program of nonprofit Share Our Strength (Hessekiel, 2013). As a part of this overall effort, Denny's, one of the nation's largest restaurant chains, and the America's Egg Farmers donated one egg to local food banks for every "Build Your Own Omelette" purchased at a Denny's restaurant from September 9 to September 15, 2013. The company also promoted "Denny's Dine Out for No Kid Hungry" with TV commercials and a social media campaign. In addition, Denny's asked customers to give $3 to No Kid Hungry, in exchange for coupons worth $9. As a result of Denny's efforts, more than $730,000 was given to the No Kid Hungry program.

Case 9.3: WWF and Avon

Tropical forests are being destroyed at an alarming rate. For example, since 1985, more than half of Sumatra's natural forests have been lost.

Avon Products, Inc. is the world's largest direct seller of beauty, fashion, and home products, with more than $11 billion in annual revenue. As a large brochure producer and consumer of paper products—distributing product brochures in more than 120 countries—Avon can influence the adoption of sustainable solutions throughout the pulp and paper supply chain.

WWF's (formerly the World Wildlife Fund) mission is to conserve nature and reduce the most pressing threats to the diversity of life on Earth. Forest conservation is a top priority in WWF's work.

Avon joined WWF's Global Forest & Trade Network (GFTN) in 2010, committing to purchase responsibly sourced paper. By participating in GFTN, Avon receives technical support from WWF to help meet its commitment that all papers used for the company's product brochures and other marketing papers are sourced responsibly.

Avon's Hello Green Tomorrow campaign is actively supporting WWF's reforestation efforts. In more than fifty countries the campaign is raising funds and building awareness to help end deforestation and restore critically endangered rainforests. As a company committed to empowering women, Avon knows that forests also provide a direct source of income for hundreds of millions of entrepreneurial women. In addition to traditional forest-related employment opportunities, Hello Green Tomorrow has funded WWF projects that provide well-paying jobs for women.

To fund these important projects, Avon has turned to its customer base for support. In the United States, 100 percent of the net proceeds from an exclusive Hello Green Tomorrow reusable water bottle and other products go to WWF and other conservation organizations for the restoration of critically endangered forests. Through this partnership, Avon has donated almost $2 million, providing critical funding for forest conservation.

SOURCE: Condensed and adapted by the author from WWF website, http://worldwildlife.org/partnerships/avon-products, retrieved May 1, 2014.

Case 9.4: Los Angeles Plaza de Cultura y Artes and PepsiCo Foundation

In partnership with the Los Angeles Plaza de Cultura y Artes, a PepsiCo Foundation $1 million grant has supported the development of an "Edible Teaching Garden" and Culinary Arts Program in the heart of Los Angeles.

The program seeks to teach Mexican and Mexican American children about the nutritional value of fruits and vegetables in an imaginative way, as they learn about Mexican American history and culture.

The 30,000-square-foot Edible Teaching Garden features a wide variety of vegetables and fruits. Daily food and nutrition classes are held to educate children living in the surrounding area, many of whom live below the poverty line. Tools are also provided that enable participating children to bring information home to their families. The program is fun and engaging and challenges children to assume personal ownership of their health through smart food choices.

Through the partnership, more than 7,000 students to date have received transportation to the center and cultural and educational experiences.

SOURCE: Condensed and edited by the author from PepsiCo Foundation website, http://www.pepsico.com/Purpose/Global-Citizenship/Strategic-Grants, retrieved May 1, 2014.

Case 9.5:   Nestlé and Reading Is Fundamental

Reading Is Fundamental is the largest children's literacy nonprofit in the United States. It delivers free books and literacy resources to children in need. In 2010, Nestlé, a food company, encouraged consumers to participate in a drawing for a $5,000 prize by entering a code found on specially marked bags of candy. Nestlé promised to give ten cents to Reading Is Fundamental for every submission and $2 for every instant winner, with a minimum donation of $100,000.

SOURCE: Reading Is Fundamental website, retrieved May 4, 2014, from http://www.rif.org/us/donate/supporters/nestle.htm

Case 9.6:   Dawn and the Gulf Oil Spill

In 2010, millions of gallons of oil were spilled into the Gulf of Mexico as a result of a catastrophic accident at a BP drilling rig. The spill took a high toll on the Gulf's wildlife, including many birds. Bird rescue organizations, led by the National Audubon Society, mobilized to save them.

Dawn is a dish detergent manufactured by Proctor & Gamble. It had been used for more than thirty years for cleaning birds and other animals affected by oil spills, and its effectiveness was well documented. As explained by the executive director of the International Bird Rescue Research Center in California, it is uniquely strong enough to remove oil but also mild enough not to damage skin or feathers.

Following the Gulf spill, Dawn contributed over 12,000 bottles to nonprofits working to rescue birds and animals in the area. The company also raised money for the rescue effort from consumers, totaling over $500,000, and it ran advertisements featuring its involvement in the cleanup. Comedian Stephen Colbert joked that maybe Dawn had caused the oil spill in order to gain such favorable publicity (Kaufman, 2010).

Dawn's involvement with animal rescue did not begin with the Gulf Oil spill or end after most of the cleanup had been completed. In 2014, it committed to donate over $1 million to its nonprofit partners, the Marine Mammal Center and International Bird Rescue. It promised consumers that "when you buy Dawn, you're using a brand that supports wildlife rescue efforts."

Questions for Discussion

1. Are you more inclined to buy a product when you know that a portion of the proceeds goes to a nonprofit cause or organization? If so, would you be willing to pay a higher price or go to a less convenient location to make your purchase? If so, is there a limit to what you would be willing to do?

2. Some people might say that nonprofits address social and human problems that result from the practices of business corporations and that partnerships with corporations are inherently inappropriate. Do you agree, disagree, or think that "it depends"? Explain.

3. Consider each of the following questions with regard to Cases 9.1 through 9.6:

   a. Is the nature of the relationship described philanthropy, a commercial partnership, or some combination?

   b. Why do you think the corporation found this relationship to be of interest, and what business objective might it further?

   c. In your opinion, is the relationship a good fit; in other words, does it seem logical, reasonable, and appropriate for the product and the cause to be connected in a marketing promotion? Why or why not?

   d. What might be the risks of the relationship to the nonprofit organization or cause?

   e. What might be the risks of the relationship to the corporation or business?

Suggestions for Further Reading

Books

Austin, J. E., & Seitanidi, M. M. (2014). *Creating value in nonprofit-business collaborations: New thinking and practice.* San Francisco: Jossey-Bass.

Cordes, J. J., & Steurle, C. E. (2009). *Nonprofits and business.* Washington, DC: Urban Institute.

Daw, J. (2006). *Cause marketing for nonprofits: Partner for purpose, passion, and profits.* Hoboken, NJ: Wiley.

Wymer, W. W., Jr., & Samu, S. (Eds.). (2003). *Nonprofit and business sector collaborations.* Binghamton, NY: Best Business Books.

Articles

Center on Philanthropy at Indiana University [now Lilly Family School of Philanthropy]. (2007, May). *Corporate philanthropy: The age of integration (A report from the Center on Philanthropy at Indiana University).* Indianapolis, IN: Center on Philanthropy at Indiana University.

Eikenberry, A. M. (2009, summer). The hidden costs of cause marketing. *Stanford Social Innovation Review,* http://www.ssireview.org/articles/entry/the_hidden_costs_of_cause_marketing/.

Galaskiewicz, J., & Colman, M. S. (2006). Collaboration between corporations and nonprofit organizations. In Powell, W. W., & Steinberg, R. (Eds.), *The non-profit sector: A research handbook*. New Haven, CT: Yale University Press.

Websites

Boston College Center for Corporate Citizenship: http://www.bcccc.net/corporate-philanthropy.html
Committee to Encourage Corporate Philanthropy (CECP): http://cecp.co
The Conference Board: https://www.conference-board.org/topics

Note

1. Cause-related marketing (or cause marketing) is not to be confused with *social marketing*. The purpose of cause marketing is to increase sales of a company's products while also generating revenue to a non-profit organization. The purpose of social marketing is to change people's behavior in a way favored by the marketer; for example, this might include campaigns to encourage people to stop smoking, use seatbelts, or recycle trash.

CHAPTER 10

Foundation Support

Let's take an imaginary walk to somewhere that has a lot of foot traffic—maybe Main Street, a shopping mall, or the student union on a large campus. And let's stop people at random and make a simple request: "Name an American philanthropist." What names do we think will be mentioned? I would guess that we will hear names like Rockefeller, Carnegie, Ford, and Gates. Then we might also ask each person to estimate how much of total philanthropy in the United States comes from foundations. You can offer your own speculation about what estimates we might hear, but I guess that most would be something higher than 15 percent, which was the actual percentage in 2013 (Giving USA, 2014b). Finally, we might ask how many foundations there are in the United States. I would speculate that few of our random respondents would come close to 81,777, the actual number (Foundation Center, 2013a).

If things unfolded as I am guessing, what might we have learned from our field research? I suggest a few possible conclusions. For many people, the best-known philanthropists are those for whom foundations are named. Philanthropy is almost synonymous with foundations in the minds of many people. And most people do not know much about them. As students of fundraising, we obviously need to know much more. This chapter discusses these highly visible institutions, their role in American philanthropy, issues that sometimes surround their programs, and strategies and methods nonprofit organizations and institutions employ to obtain their support.

OVERVIEW OF FOUNDATIONS

Chapter 2 of this text introduced some basic definitions and distinctions related to foundations. This section provides a review of those points and adds some further detail.

Public Charities and Private Foundations

Students will recall that there are two types of charitable nonprofits, both exempt from taxation under Section 501(c)(3) of the Internal Revenue Code—**public charities** and **private foundations**. Public charities and private foundations are distinguished in the law and face different requirements and limitations. In simplest terms, public charities receive public support, from various sources, while private foundations usually have one

	Public Charities (raise funds from multiple sources)	Private Foundations (receive funds from one or a few donors)
TABLE 10.1 Public Charities and Private Foundations		
Grant making (make grants to other nonprofits)	*Examples:* community foundations, Jewish federations, United Way, institutionally related foundations	*Examples:* Gates Foundation, Ford Foundation
Operating (maintain and fund their own programs)	*Examples:* Red Cross, Habitat for Humanity, colleges, hospitals	*Examples:* Colonial Williamsburg, Longwood Gardens

or a few donors. Public charities engage in active fundraising to obtain revenue, while most private foundations obtain their resources from gifts made by their founders or from earnings on their investments. Table 10.1 includes some examples that may help to clarify the distinctions. Let's look in more detail at the two types.

Public Charities

Within the category of public charities are two subtypes: **operating public charities** and **grant-making public charities**, which are sometimes called **public foundations**. Operating public charities include most of the organizations people think about when the term *nonprofit* is used, including colleges, hospitals, arts institutions, and nonprofits that provide human services. As the term implies, grant-making public charities raise money and then give it to other nonprofit organizations; most do not operate their own programs. Some well-known examples include community foundations, the United Way, and Jewish federations.

One source of confusion is that some grant-making public charities have the term *foundation* in their names, although they are not private foundations. These include community foundations and **supporting organizations** (some of which are called "foundations"). Community foundations receive gifts from various donors—so they are public charities— and give it to other nonprofits—so they are grant making. Some community foundations have discretionary funds from which the foundation can make grants at the discretion of its board, but most grants are made from donor-advised funds for which the community foundation serves as trustee, on the recommendation of the individual who established the fund. Supporting organizations are public charities that receive gifts from various donors and make gifts only to the one organization they were established to support. They are grant-making public charities. Among the best known are university-related foundations that function as the fundraising arms of public universities; for example, the University of Connecticut Foundation raises money only for the University of Connecticut.

Private Foundations

There are also two subtypes of private foundations—**private operating foundations** and **private grant-making foundations**. Most people think about foundations as grant-making entities and, indeed, most are. They include the familiar names we heard during our imaginary survey at the beginning of this chapter, including Rockefeller, Carnegie, Ford, and Gates. But some private foundations are also **operating foundations**. Some of them may make some grants, but most primarily support their own activities. Two well-known examples include Colonial Williamsburg, in Virginia, and Longwood Gardens, in Delaware. They have the legal status of private foundations but do not make grants. Again, there are some private operating foundations that make some grants, but operating foundations are not, for the most part, promising prospects for support of other nonprofits.

Although nonprofits may receive support from both private and public grant-making foundations, the discussion in the balance of this chapter emphasizes private grant-making foundations.

Legal Requirements

Both public charities and private foundations are tax exempt under section 501(c)(3). It may seem odd, since there are more public charities than private foundations, but the income tax law makes a *presumption* that every charitable nonprofit is a private foundation *unless* it can demonstrate that it is in fact a public charity. In order to demonstrate that it is *not* a private foundation, a nonprofit must meet the requirements of section 509(a) of the Internal Revenue Code, meaning it must be one of the following:

- Organizations described in Section 170 (b) (1)(A), which covers churches; schools, colleges, etc.; hospitals, medical research institutes, etc.; supporting organizations to educational institutions; governmental units; and publicly supported organizations (including community foundations)

- Organizations that normally receive more than one-third of their support from gifts, grants, fees, and gross receipts from admissions sales, etc., *and* normally receive *not more* than one-third of their support from investment income

- Supporting organizations which, although not publicly supported, are controlled by and operated in close association with a public charity

- Organizations operated exclusively for testing for public safety (Collins, 2008, p. 2)

Why does it matter whether an organization is a private foundation or a public charity, since both are tax-exempt? It is not necessary to go into all the technical details, but private foundations face some requirements and restrictions that do not apply to public charities.[1]

For one, a donor who makes a cash gift to a public charity generally can deduct that gift up to 50 percent of his or her income, with certain other limitations (Hopkins, 2009). But a donor to a private foundation can claim a deduction for only 30 percent of his or her income. Private foundations must pay an excise tax on their investment earnings, which public charities do not. Thus, the Gates Foundation pays tax on its investment earnings, but Harvard is not required to do so.

A big difference is that grant-making private foundations must make **qualifying distributions** equivalent to 5 percent of the fair market value of their assets in any fiscal year, known as the **payout requirement** (Collins, 2008). The qualifying distributions can be grants or operating expenses, but the definition of which operating expenses can be included has been a matter of policy debate. Public charities do not have a payout requirement; in other words, they could hold funds in an endowment and simply reinvest the investment earnings without expending any toward programs. Recall from the discussion of donor-advised funds in Chapter 8 that they are not required by law to pay out a minimum amount each year. That is because the entities that serve as trustees of those funds, including community foundations and commercial charitable gift funds, are public charities. This difference also has been a matter of debate, and it is important to note that some trustees of donor-advised funds do require a minimum payout as a matter of their own policy, although it is not required by law.

Private foundations also face additional restrictions that do not apply to public charities, including the requirement that they refrain from lobbying and not make grants to support lobbying activity, except under narrow conditions. Public charities can engage in lobbying, within some limits (Independent Sector, n.d.).

For these reasons, public charities take care to meet the criteria for classification as *not* a private foundation, so that they and their donors will not be subject to the greater limitations. That includes assuring they have sufficiently diverse sources of revenue in order to meet what the IRS calls the **public support test** (IRS, 2014d).

From the perspective of a nonprofit organization seeking foundation support, private grant-making foundations are likely to be the best prospects from among the various types discussed here. Some operating foundations also do make some grants, but most are not good prospects for grants to other organizations. Supporting organizations are not usually prospects either. They are intermediaries that transmit donor gifts to the one organization with which they are associated and usually not to any others. Public charities that are funding intermediaries, such as community foundations, may be prospects for grants. But the largest portion of grants made by community foundations is awarded on the recommendation of individuals who established donor-advised funds, and the pursuit of such gifts therefore requires relationships with those individuals.

It is possible that community foundations will increase the portion of discretionary funds they manage in coming years. But most funds they manage now are donor-advised. For example, the Silicon Valley Community Foundation is the nation's third largest and has gained visibility as a result of highly publicized gifts, such as those from Mark Zuckerberg and Priscilla Chan in 2013 ("Zuckerberg Commits," 2013). The foundation manages a general endowment fund, advised funds, and some that are quasi-discretionary; they permit the foundation to make grant decisions but are targeted to specific **fields of interest**, such as the arts or education. In 2012, grants from advised funds totaled over $200 million, while grants from the general endowment fund and fields-of-interest funds totaled $8.5 million (Report of Independent Auditors, 2012). Thus, the foundation has discretion only with regard to a small portion of the assets it manages.

Independent, Family, and Corporate Foundations

There are two basic subtypes of private grant-making foundations: corporate foundations and independent foundations. One was already discussed in Chapter 9—the *corporate foundation*, established with funds from a public corporation. Many corporations make gifts directly from corporate accounts, but there are some advantages to creating a foundation to manage at least a portion of corporate philanthropy. There also are some complications. A corporate foundation is a type of private foundation, a separate legal entity from the corporation itself, and must follow all of the requirements that apply to private grant-making foundations discussed already. One requirement is that the foundation must avoid engaging in what are defined as **self-dealing transactions**, except as narrowly permitted by IRS regulations. That means, for example, that it must be careful about providing direct benefits to employees of the company (Minnesota Council on Foundations, 2015).

A foundation that is not associated with a corporation is an **independent foundation**—they are independent in the sense that they are not affiliated with a corporation. The largest number of independent foundations are **family foundations**, which totaled over 40,000 in 2011 (Foundation Center, 2014). As the term implies, family foundations are established with gifts from members of a single family. In addition, although family foundations have no specific legal definition, the Council on Foundations (n.d.) defines family foundations as those that "have at least one family member serving as an officer or board member of the foundation and . . . that individual (or a relative) [plays] a significant role in governing and/or managing the foundation." Thus, a foundation might begin as a family foundation, but over a period of years there may be fewer members of the founding family involved. Eventually, there may be no members of the founding family involved, at which point the foundation is no longer a family foundation, just an independent foundation.

Independent foundations vary widely in their size and methods of operation. Some are **pass-through foundations**, merely vehicles through which a family channels its annual giving. Others have endowments and make grants from investment earnings. The majority do not have professional staff. This is true of most family foundations, which are managed by members of the family or perhaps by the family's accountant or attorney. Other independent foundations employ substantial numbers of professionals, including subject-area experts in fields in which the foundation makes grants.

Most family foundations start small, but some evolve. A family foundation may start as a pass-through foundation managed by family members, with grant decisions being made around the dinner table. Over time, the foundation may grow and the family engages a professional to direct it, often on a part-time basis. The foundation may grow considerably larger through additional gifts or when a member of the family dies, leaving a bequest to create an endowment. As years go by, the endowment and the foundation's grant making may grow, requiring the employment of a larger staff to manage investments and analyze grant applications. Eventually, the family's involvement may be reduced to nothing beyond representation on the board of the foundation. But it is important to emphasize that small size and status as a family foundation are not synonymous. For example, the Bill and Melinda Gates Foundation is a family foundation, since it is controlled by Bill and Melinda Gates and Mr. Gates's father, who are actively involved. But it is the world's largest foundation and employs many people on its staff.

The strategies and methods for soliciting foundation support vary according to the foundation's size and decision-making process. Raising funds from a small family foundation usually requires building relationships with individual members of the family. Raising funds from a larger independent foundation with a professional staff involves a more formal and structured approach. Let's get back to these points later in this chapter.

HISTORICAL BACKGROUND

The history of foundations closely parallels the history of philanthropy more generally. With origins in England's 1601 Statute of Charitable Uses, the law in Europe and the United States has long provided for charitable entities, but organizations operating on a large scale were a development of the early twentieth century in the United States. Most early foundations in the United States were focused on a single institution, for example, a school or hospital, but the early twentieth century saw the development of a new type of organization, the **general-purpose foundation**. New foundations created in that era, including the Rockefeller Foundation and the Carnegie Corporation of New York (a foundation, despite its name), were able to direct their support to multiple organizations and issues and change their priorities as society's needs evolved. That created the potential to have a more significant impact on society (Collins, 2008). Andrew Carnegie is identified as having defined a new role for foundations, one that goes beyond making grants to existing organizations to becoming a force for social change. That role includes promoting reforms in areas such as education and health and supporting the establishment of new organizations and institutions to further such change (Lenkowsky, 2011).

The number of foundations and the size of foundation assets have grown with the economy over decades but in cycles. For example, foundations grew during the 1950s and 1960s, with overall expansion of the economy. In the 1960s, foundations gained the attention of political leaders, some of whom were critical of what they viewed as a political orientation in some foundation activities. Following hearings and a study by the Treasury Department, Congress passed the Tax Reform Act of 1969. That law established the legal framework for private foundations described earlier in this chapter. Some observers thought the law would discourage the creation of new foundations, and, indeed, fewer were created in the 1970s, which also was a decade of economic challenges (Collins, 2008). But the birth rate of new foundations increased again in the 1980s and, especially, during the boom years of the 1990s. Inspired perhaps by the example of Bill Gates, many of that decade's entrepreneurs and investors created family foundations. That growth trend continued into the twenty-first century, and by 2009, one-half of existing foundations with assets of $1 million or more were no more than twenty years old (Lawrence & Mukai, 2011). Reflecting the growth in the number of family foundations in need of professional management, an industry of philanthropic advisory firms has developed, encompassing, for example, firms such as Arabella Advisors and Rockefeller Philanthropy Advisors.

ISSUES AND IMPACT

Given the flexibility general-purpose foundations enjoy and their growing resources, it is not surprising that they have at times been controversial. Debates have surrounded various issues, including the three discussed in this section.

Spend-Down Versus Perpetual

Although some foundations are of the pass-through type already mentioned, most have endowment assets, which generate annual investment earnings to support grants. Some foundations are designed to expend the principal of their endowments within some period of time; they are called **spend-down** or **limited-life foundations** (Ostrower, 2009). For example, in creating their foundation, Bill and Melinda Gates provided that the assets would all be spent within fifty years after their deaths (Thelin, 2013). Another example is the Atlantic Philanthropies, a foundation established in 1982 by retailing entrepreneur Charles "Chuck" Feeney, who espoused the philosophy of **giving while living**. The foundation had given $6.3 billion by 2014 and was scheduled to conclude all grant making by 2016 (Atlantic Philanthropies, n.d.). However, most foundations are intended to exist in perpetuity; in other words, like institutional endowments, the principal is to remain invested forever, in order to provide annual income for grants.

The decision on whether the foundation has a limited life or exists in perpetuity reflects the personal preferences of the individual who established it. Some prefer to see most of the benefits of their giving while they are alive, while others wish to create a legacy by establishing an institution that will survive them. Some wish to create a perpetual foundation so that future generations of their families will be engaged in philanthropy (Ostrower, 2009).Whether perpetual foundations are desirable from society's perspective is a different question, and it is a matter of debate. The arguments relate not only to foundations but to endowments in general, including those controlled by colleges and other institutions. One argument against perpetual foundations is that society changes over time, and the original intentions of donors may no longer be realistic or desirable (Madoff, 2010). Some argue that either of two conditions will occur. A foundation may remain faithful to the intent of its donor and become irrelevant as society's needs change; this is sometimes called the *dead-hand* argument. Or the foundation's activities may diverge from the intent of its donor, which is a violation of trust. For example, some point to activities of the Ford Foundation that they think would be anathema to Henry Ford were he alive (Ostrower, 2009). However, this may be an argument for keeping the purposes of foundations broadly stated, rather than narrowly defined, so that trustees in the future can adapt grant making to contemporary realities while remaining faithful to the donor's broad intent. It is not necessarily an argument against perpetual foundations per se.

Another angle of attack on the idea of perpetual foundations relates to impact and intergenerational equity. If a donor creates a perpetual foundation with a $1 million endowment, that means the foundation's grants will be about $50,000 per year every year forever, assuming a 5 percent payout requirement (and ignoring possible growth of the principal). Some argue that more impact would be achieved by spending the $1 million today and that preserving the principal in order to benefit future generations shortchanges current needs. For example, if the $1 million were spent to provide scholarships for young people today, their contributions to society would be enhanced, with ripple effects that could be significant over time. Deferring that impact to future generations both delays and diminishes it. Moreover, future generations are likely to live in a more prosperous society. So, some argue, creating an endowment in perpetuity deprives the current generation in favor of future ones, whose needs may not be as great; it is essentially taking resources from the relatively poor living today in order to preserve them for the relatively wealthy who will live in the future (Fried, 2011).

Of course, arguments can be made in favor of perpetual foundations. One rests on donor intent; if an individual wishes to use his or her wealth to create a lasting legacy using his or her private property, some would ask why society should prevent that. In addition, some philanthropy should perhaps support purposes that may not be popular or economical in the future; for example, the advocacy of a particular philosophy or the preservation of art and antiquities. In addition, endowed foundations may provide a counterweight to the power of government and the market and may be able to undertake risks for social change that other, less-independent institutions are unable to consider.

Foundation Policy Influence

Some people argue that foundations have too much influence on public policies that should be decided through the democratic process rather than by private wealth. For example, this was an issue in the case of New York City parks (see Case1.1). Some people argued that parks should be supported by public dollars rather than philanthropy because the latter could result in inequities.

The influence of foundations on public policy has a long history in the United States. As Hagerty (2012) describes, "From the earliest days of the American nation, philanthropy has had a defining role in leading change. Philanthropy has provided vision and voice for nascent social movements ranging from civil rights and the women's movement to AIDS research and environmentalism" (p. ii). And foundations long have engaged in partnerships with government on a variety of issues, generally performing one or more of several functions: (1) develop and invest in pilot programs in collaboration with government; (2) jointly fund established programs with government; (3) support capacity building within government and government grantees; (4) convene government officials, experts, and various stakeholders; (5) educate the public and members of the policy community; (6) fund research and policy analysis; and (7) evaluate policy implementation (Abramson, Soskis, & Toepler, 2012).

But concern about the role of private foundations has become more common as foundation resources have increased and is voiced by people of all political views, depending on the particular issue. As one harsh critic decries,

> They've [big foundations] developed a new style of philanthropy for exercising power: programmatically aggressive, publicity-seeking, and pushing against the remaining limits on political activity. They devote substantial resources to advocacy— selling their ideas to the media, to government at every level, and to the public. Many have preconceived notions about social problems and solutions, and they finance researchers likely to produce studies that support their ideas. They hire or create myriad nonprofits to run projects they've designed themselves. (Barkan, 2013)

The debate has been especially vigorous with regard to the role of foundations in public education. The most frequent target of criticism is the Bill and Melinda Gates Foundation, the nation's largest, although the Broad Foundation, the Walton Family Foundation, and others also have supported school reform initiatives. The Gates Foundation's influence and impact is especially substantial, since it gives about $3 billion every year and employs over 900 people. One of its priorities has been the use of student test scores to evaluate teacher performance, an approach that has attracted criticism from, among others, teachers' unions (Kaufman, 2011). But some research on the influence of foundations on schools has produced mixed findings, suggesting that it is often mitigated by the power of elected school boards (Carr, 2012).

Because reform in many areas invites diverse opinion, some individuals have charged that philanthropy has become politicized through the involvement of Gates and other large foundations in the shaping of public policy (Abramson et al., 2012). Ironically, however, another line of criticism against foundations is that they have not been effective enough in accomplishing social change.

Impact on Nonprofit Missions

Another criticism leveled at foundations is their emphasis on making grants related to priorities that they have identified, rather than general operating support to enable non-profit organizations to achieve their missions. Some critics charge that this pattern has led nonprofits to follow the money, shifting activities from one priority to another in response to changing foundation initiatives, at the expense of enhancing the impact of their own programs and building their own sustainability. Such critiques were especially prevalent during the economic recession of 2008–2009, when some observers called for founda-tions to readjust their giving to sustain nonprofit services in light of declining government support.

A related concern is that foundations do not provide sufficient support for nonprofits' overhead expenses, insisting that grants be used for programs and that overhead expenses be minimized. As Gregory and Howard (2009) observe, this approach may feed a "nonprofit starvation cycle":

> Our research reveals that a vicious cycle fuels the persistent underfunding of over-head. The first step in the cycle is funders' unrealistic expectations about how much it costs to run a nonprofit. At the second step, nonprofits feel pressure to conform to funders' unrealistic expectations. At the third step, nonprofits respond to this pressure in two ways: They spend too little on overhead, and they underreport their expenditures on tax forms and in fundraising materials. This underspending and underreporting in turn perpetuates funders' unrealistic expectations. Over time, funders expect grantees to do more and more with less and less—a cycle that slowly starves nonprofits. (p. 50)

An understanding of these issues is important to an organization or institution that seeks or receives the support of foundations, especially larger, independent foundations. Nonprofits must consider the tradeoffs that they are willing to make. There may be time and resources that must be dedicated to measurement and reporting that could distract from program activities. The organization may struggle to meet overhead costs associated with supported programs without adequate reimbursement from its foundation funders. There may be a tradeoff of the organization's autonomy in exchange for foundation support. Many foundations practice *strategic philanthropy*. They have predetermined goals and will support organizations willing to manage programs that advance those goals. If a nonprofit's goals coincide with those of the foundation, this may produce a useful partnership. But the leaders of nonprofits need to be clear-eyed in making decisions and recognize that their partnerships with foundations may not always be entirely on their own terms. Foundations that are strategic in their grant making often care little about an organization's perception of its own *need*. They are more concerned with the organization's *capability* to advance the goals the foundation has identified.

OVERVIEW OF FOUNDATION GIVING

Now that we have an understanding of what foundations are, the various types of foundations, and the role they play in society, let's focus on the questions that may be of particular interest to nonprofit organizations and to those who raise funds to support them: What do foundations give and where? What are some foundation practices that may have an impact on foundations that seek or receive their support? And what is the process for securing foundation funds? This section discusses the first two questions and the next section considers the third.

Before we get started, it may be useful to clarify some terminology. A payment a nonprofit receives from a foundation is, in common vocabulary, a **grant**, even if it is unrestricted and does not require significant reporting on its use and the result accomplished ("CASE reporting standards," 2009). In the latter case it is functionally a gift in terms of how the nonprofit uses and accounts for it, but it is likely to be called a grant since it came from a foundation. Of course, some grants do have more specific requirements, both for use and reporting.

Patterns of Support

Data on foundation giving are compiled annually by the Foundation Center and are made available on its website. In its 2011 survey of the largest 1,122 U.S. foundations, the Foundation Center found that grants totaled $49 billion. The top 1 percent of recipients received one-half of grant dollars, while the median grant amount was just $28,462 (Foundation Center, 2013b). Those figures illustrate a wide dispersion of grant amounts and suggest that large foundation grants are concentrated among a relatively small number of recipients, primarily universities and other large institutions.

Overall data may be of limited usefulness to a particular nonprofit organization seeking foundation support. For one thing, the Foundation Center's data only encompass the largest foundations, accounting for just 56 percent of total foundation giving. And the totals include Gates, which accounts for more in grant dollars ($3.2 billion) than the next six largest foundations combined! In addition, the data include corporate, independent, and community foundations and international as well as domestic giving. So these data paint a picture with a rather broad brush.

Of perhaps greater interest to a nonprofit seeking foundation funds is the distribution of grants by type of support, by fields of activity, and by geographic distribution. The latter is especially important, since many foundations have geographic restrictions, either because they are community foundations that serve only one region or because of requirements established by donors. Data on the purposes of support are complex, since the Foundation Center is not able to categorize one-fifth of the grants and many cut across more than one category. Fifty-five percent of the grants reported in 2011 went for program support and another 17 percent for research, suggesting that these are high priorities for many foundations. Of the total grants made, 29 percent were for general operating support and 21 percent for capital purposes, but some of the grants combined such support with other purposes (Foundation Center, 2013b). Community foundations are more likely than others to make grants for general operating support, most reflecting the recommendations of individuals who established donor-advised funds managed by the foundation and who have their own relationships with particular nonprofit organizations (Foundation Center, 2012b).

The top four fields in which grants were made in 2011 include health (28%), education (20%), arts and culture (14%), and human services (14%). The highest number of grants went to organizations in the human services subsector, suggesting that they were relatively small in amount compared with those made to educational and health institutions. The top recipient of grant dollars was an educational institution, the University of Southern California (Foundation Center, 2013b).

In the United States, grant distribution by region broke down like this in 2011: 33 percent to the South, 26 percent to the Northeast, 24 percent to the West, and 18 percent to the Midwest. California ranked first among the states; organizations and institutions located there received $2.7 billion in foundation support (Foundation Center, 2013b).

Foundation Practices

To emphasize again, private foundations vary greatly in size and methods of operation. Some may be little more than conduits for the personal philanthropy of individuals or families. In those cases, the foundation's operations may be quite informal. However, larger foundations, employing paid staff, reflect the professionalization of philanthropy and the growth of a philanthropic industry, with its own infrastructure of support organizations and established practices. Best practices of foundations have been the subject of numerous studies and are disseminated by associations of foundations, for example, Grantmakers for Effective Organizations, which includes larger foundations among its members. There are some identifiable characteristics and trends associated with that professionalization.

Emphasis on Grantee Results

Foundations' evaluation of grantee performance is not new, and there have been staff members in larger foundations with evaluation-related responsibilities since the 1970s (Coffman, Beer, Patrizi, & Heid Thompson, 2013). But evaluation has increased in the past decade with the rise of strategic philanthropy, the involvement of business-minded donors, and the development of new evaluation tools and methods (Coffman et al., 2013). Again, there are differences between small foundations and larger foundations, with formal evaluation more likely to be practiced by the latter.

In a 2012 study of thirty-one large foundations, Coffman et al. (2013) learned that the commitment of foundations to evaluation is increasing, the role and scope of evaluation staff within foundations is expanding, and 75 percent of foundations had an evaluation professional at a director level. Evaluation is moving beyond postgrant analysis toward more integration with the foundation's strategy, and evaluation is moving "up the grant-making chain to include evaluation of whole program areas" rather than individual grants (p. 48). However, the study also discovered that evaluation professionals working in foundations hold some frustration regarding their employer's use of evaluation data and that such data may not be fully integrated in foundation decision making. Nevertheless, the researchers conclude that "commitment to evaluation in philanthropy is now deeply rooted and no longer considered a trend that might fade" (Coffman et al., p. 50).

Evaluation by foundation funders is thus a reality prospective grantees must be prepared to address, even though some critics argue that it has gone too far, leading nonprofits to an obsession with measurement that may stifle risk taking and innovation (Beresford, 2010). In addition, especially since the financial crisis of the late 2000s, foundations have provided assistance to nonprofits engaged in finding ways to reduce costs, increase efficiency, and explore funding alternatives (López-Rivera & Preston, 2011). Given continued economic pressures, it seems likely that foundations' emphasis on evaluation and efficiency is likely to expand.

Emphasis on Foundation Effectiveness

Concomitant with foundations' greater emphasis on the performance of grantees has been an increased emphasis by the foundation community on measuring its own effectiveness. The two emphases are, of course, related. Foundation program officers must require grantees to be accountable, in part because those program officers must be accountable to their boards for the impact of foundation grants.

The methods foundations apply to self-evaluation vary. Ostrower (2006) studied foundation evaluation methods and found that they fit into various categories independent of foundations' legal status or the fields of interest they support. She developed a typology based on evaluation measures on four scales: the foundation's proactivity, its impact on grantees' capacity building, its influence on social policy, and opportunities for the professional development of its own staff.

Collaboration Among Foundations

Collaboration among foundation funders is not a new development. **Regional associations of grant makers** have long provided a forum for exchange of information and coordination of activities among foundations serving a particular community or region. The first was created in 1948; by 2014 over 4,000 grant-making organizations were members of a national network, the Forum of Regional Associations of Grantmakers. There are also networks of foundations that emphasize particular issue areas, for example, children, aging, energy, and the environment (Wei-Skillern, Silver, & Heitz, n.d.).

Foundations have collaborated successfully on a significant scale. For example, in 2007, the Edna McConnell Clark Foundation led an effort that raised $120 million from other foundations to support three nonprofits Clark favored, Citizen Schools, Nurse-Family Partnership, and Youth Villages. But there remain obstacles to such collaborations, including donor preferences, the small scale of some issues individual foundations address, and challenges in coordinating the operations of multiple funders (Seldon, 2013).

Collaboration Among Recipients

The growing number of nonprofit organizations has led some observers to advocate for more collaboration, even mergers, as a way to gain more efficiency in the sector. This view was especially prevalent during the economic downturn of the late 2000s. Foundation funders have often been prominent among those advancing it, and some have provided grants to support such activity. But some critics charge that foundations sometimes have responded to mergers by reducing their grants—using the merger as an "exit strategy"—rather than by continuing support to the new organization at the previous combined total (Gammal, 2007). That obviously provides a disincentive to the nonprofits involved.

Foundations remain favorable toward collaboration among grant recipients, and organizations seeking foundation support may find that such efforts with other nonprofits are attractive to funders (Preston, 2011). Reflecting this emphasis, the Foundation Center maintains a comprehensive database including examples of successful nonprofit restructuring and collaboration (Foundation Center, 2015).

In addition, some foundations have shifted their focus away from single causes or issues toward support for community groups that work together to solve local problems (Donovan, 2014). Others have joined coalitions that include government, businesses, schools, and various nonprofits in addressing community issues, such as schools or health, an approach known as **collective impact** (Gose, 2014b).

Professionalization of Grant Process

Professionalization of the grant process has become a hallmark of well-managed foundations. Larger foundations, especially those with professional staff, have established transparent grant criteria and procedures for requesting support, with comprehensive resources available on their websites. In addition, some have streamlined the proposal process by adopting **common grant application forms** developed by regional associations of grant makers. The process for soliciting foundation support is discussed further in the next section.

SEEKING FOUNDATION SUPPORT

This section provides an overview of the process for soliciting foundation support, but it is only an introduction. There are many sources of guidance available to nonprofit organizations in books, on websites, and through formal training programs on proposal writing and grant seeking. Some of those sources are mentioned in this section and listed as suggested additional reading at the end of this chapter.

General Rules

Some general rules apply to fundraising from foundations, suggested by multiple authors (e.g., Collins, 2008). First, it is essential to be professional in approaching foundations. Contacting a foundation that has priorities or limitations that exclude the nonprofit from consideration, or using a method other than what the foundation prescribes, is worse than a waste of time. It creates an impression of amateurism that can negatively affect the organization's reputation. As mentioned earlier in this chapter, foundations do communicate and, in some regions, may coordinate their grant making. Making a poor impression on one foundation could cause collateral damage with others if the nonprofit comes to be known as unprofessional or inconsiderate in its fundraising practices.

The second rule, closely related to the first, is that successful fundraising will be targeted to those foundations most likely to have an interest in the organization or its program. This is more than a matter of making a good impression; it is essential to using the non-profit's resources efficiently in the search for grants. Foundation fundraising is more like the major-gifts program than the annual-giving program. Sending out mass mailings to foundations is just never a sound practice.

Third, as discussed earlier, it is important that a nonprofit seeking support understand the foundation's point of view. Small foundations may have broad purposes, but larger foundations have well-defined goals and will evaluate proposals from nonprofits in terms of how they may advance those goals. A proposal that entirely reflects the nonprofit's emotionally based case is likely to receive no more than a routine rejection letter. A useful mind-set for the fundraiser is to consider how to help the foundation achieve its goals.

For example, consider the priorities of the Kellogg Foundation, as described in Box 10.1, drawn from the foundation's website. Unless an organization's mission and programs are related to children and families, it is highly unlikely that the Kellogg Foundation would be a promising source of support. Indeed, the limitations are even narrower than that, since the foundation focuses on children under the age of eight. The fact that the foundation concentrates its grants in relatively few locations also suggests that a nonprofit that does not operate at a large scale would probably not have a good chance of receiving a grant. On the other hand, an organization that has scale and programs that might be attractive to Kellogg would identify the foundation as one to be explored.

Fourth, even when a foundation's giving program and priorities are highly formalized and structured, personal contacts and relationships are important. For example, if a board member of the nonprofit has a relationship with a member of the foundation's board, that may provide access and perhaps a more careful consideration of the organization's request. If the foundation has professional staff, they should be cultivated like any prospective donor. That calls for open and honest communication, follow-up, and expressions of gratitude for any assistance they provide. That should be the case even if a grant request is denied, since there is often a next time, and, again, the nonprofit's positive reputation in the foundation community generally should be carefully nurtured (Collins, 2008).

Finally, fundraising from foundations follows many of the same rules that apply to fundraising more broadly and that have been discussed previously in this text. The process begins with the organization itself, including a clearly articulated mission and goals, an understanding of what makes the organization unique, and a clear definition of financial

---

BOX 10.1 Kellogg Foundation Priorities

The W.K. Kellogg Foundation (WKKF) places the optimal development of children at the center of all we do and calls for healing the profound racial gaps and inequities that exist in our communities. We believe in supporting and building upon the mindsets, methods and modes of change that hold promise to advance children's best interests generally, and those of vulnerable children in particular.

Concentrating our resources on early childhood (prenatal to age 8), within the context of families and communities, offers the best opportunity to dramatically reduce the vulnerability caused by poverty and racial inequity over time.

There is strong evidence that optimal child development means providing children with the stimulus, tools and support necessary for their emotional, intellectual, physical and cultural growth. To achieve this, we organize our work and investments toward attaining three strategic goals:

- *Educated Kids:* Increase the number of children who are reading-and-math proficient by third grade.
- *Healthy Kids:* Increase the number of children born at a healthy birth weight and who receive the care and healthy food they need for optimal development.
- *Secure Families:* Increase the number of children and families living at least 200 percent above the poverty level.

Within and around each goal are commitments to *Community & Civic Engagement* and *Racial Equity*—because both are necessary for communities to create the conditions under which all children can thrive.

We take a place-based approach to our work, concentrating as much as two-thirds of our grantmaking in a limited number of specific places where we believe we can have maximum impact.

Source: W.K. Kellogg Foundation website (http://www.wkkf.org/what-we-do/overview).

needs. Creating those conditions permits the organization to present its case, to prepare for questions likely to be posed by prospective funders, and to identify which foundations may be the most promising to approach (Collins, 2008).

Researching Foundation Prospects

The criteria for identifying foundation prospects can be conceived as a series of screens that narrow the search from the 82,000 foundations in existence to a manageable number. Students may see some similarity between the screens applied and the principle of LAI (linkage, ability, and interest) discussed earlier in this text with regard to individual donors. They include the following identified by Collins (2008):

- Does the foundation accept unsolicited applications? Foundations may have organizations they support on a regular basis and may prefer to spare themselves the burden of reviewing numerous proposals, so they are not open to unsolicited contacts. They are not likely worth much effort; *however*, if the nonprofit has a personal contact with the foundation, for example, through a board member, this restriction may not be insurmountable.

- What is the foundation's financial position? If the foundation has experienced a decline in its assets, it may be reluctant to consider new commitments. On the other hand, if it recently completed a major pledge or received an injection of funding from a donor, the timing may be right.

- Does the foundation make grants in your subject field? For example, if a foundation's mission is to preserve the environment *and if* its grant history demonstrates that it adheres to that focus, it is probably not a prospect for a nonprofit working in the field of early childhood education.

- Does the foundation have a geographic restriction? Most foundations focus their giving in certain areas, and it is obviously not useful to approach one that does not serve the community or region where the grant-seeking nonprofit operates.

- What has been the pattern of the foundation's recent grants? Perhaps even more useful than what a foundation states as its policies is the insight provided by what it actually *does*. In other words, much can be learned by analyzing its grants over recent years. Does it appear to support the same organizations every year, or is there variation? Does the grantee list include organizations like yours, or are they clearly in a different category? Are there obvious connections between the foundation and its grantees?

- What is the foundation's typical grant range? If the foundation's average grant is $10,000, then it is unlikely to be a prospect for a $100,000 project. On the other hand, if its grants are all substantial and support wide-ranging programs, it is unlikely to be attracted by a small project.

- Does the foundation cover full program costs or prefer to participate with other funders? It is not probable that a first-time funder will make a major commitment to support a nonprofit's entire program; it may prefer to join with other funders in a more limited way.

- Finally, does the nonprofit have a personal relationship or a historic relationship with the foundation? Personal relationships always matter. And, as discussed earlier in this text, past donors are always the best prospects for additional support.

Once the list of potential foundation prospects has been narrowed using these screens, more detailed research is required in order to refine the list further and to begin developing solicitation strategies. Sources of public information on small family foundations may be limited, but for larger, professionalized foundations they are readily available. The preeminent resource for information on foundations is the Foundation Center. Its database is available for searching at its regional libraries in several major cities or through the

Foundation Directory Online, which is available for a fee. A premium version also offers access to a database of potential corporate funders.

All foundations are required to file Form 990PF with the IRS annually, and these forms are available from various sources online, including Guidestar. They provide information on foundations' donors, assets, and boards, among other useful data. Many foundations also maintain extensive websites, including detailed information on their programs, grants, and grant application procedures.

When researching individual prospects, it might be inappropriate, and likely would be unproductive, to ask other organizations about their knowledge and experience with a donor. But that is not as much the case with foundations. While nonprofits may compete for foundation support, that competition is based on the merits of their proposals and therefore is not as personal or sensitive as it might be with regard to an individual. Moreover, since foundations are more transparent, there is less of an issue of confidentiality. And since foundations *exist* to give money away and are often seeking opportunities to advance their missions, persuasion is less a part of the process that it is with individuals. For those reasons, colleagues in other nonprofits that have received support from a foundation may be forthcoming and provide useful advice. Development professionals who work in foundation relations also share information on listservs and at conferences. Foundation executives often speak at such conferences and offer sound advice.

Approaching Foundations

As mentioned previously, methods of approaching a foundation for support vary widely. Contacting a small family foundation may involve developing a relationship with family members, but initiating a conversation with a large independent foundation may follow a more prescribed process. Many now provide detailed instructions on their websites and many accept online grant applications. For example, Box 10.2 includes instructions provided by the Charles Stewart Mott Foundation, which are quite specific.

Sometimes foundations issue a request-for-proposal (RFP) that prescribes a particular format and process for applying. Others outline a process on the foundation's website. Some require **online grant applications** and others accept a common grant application form.

Few, if any, will be impressed by receiving a full-blown proposal unsolicited. Some foundations that have professional staff may be receptive to an initial inquiry by telephone, but that can place considerable pressure on the caller. More common is the use of a **letter of inquiry** as the initial contact with a prospective foundation funder (Collins, 2008). The purpose of the letter is to briefly introduce the idea and inquire if the foundation might have an interest in receiving a full proposal. This method is preferred by many foundation officers for the obvious reason that it is less reading than a long proposal and provides sufficient initial information with which to weed out ideas that are just not a good fit. It is also a good method for the nonprofit, since preparing it does not require as much work as writing a full proposal.

The response to a letter of inquiry may be an invitation to meet or speak in order to discuss the idea, a request for a more detailed proposal, or a letter of rejection. A meeting with

---

BOX 10.2 Charles Stewart Mott Foundation

How to Apply

Letters of Inquiry

We strongly prefer that unsolicited requests be made through Letters of Inquiry. The letter should describe the purpose and objectives of the project, general methodology and total cost of the project. A letter of inquiry enables the Foundation program staff to determine the relevance of the proposed project to the Foundation's programs and to provide advice on whether to submit a full proposal.

Full, Formal Proposals

If your Letter of Inquiry receives a favorable response, please follow this checklist for what should be included in a solicited formal proposal:

- A cover letter, detailing the amount of money requested and the grant period, signed by the individual responsible for signing grant contracts on behalf of the grant applicant.
- A project description, including an explanation of why the project is needed, who will be served and what will be accomplished.
- A documented line-item expense budget and a revenue budget, showing all projected sources of funds for the project over the proposed grant period. (A budget template is available in our For Grantees section.)
- A plan for financial and programmatic sustainability of the project.
- A plan for evaluation and dissemination of the project's results.
- Information about the organization seeking funds, including names and titles for key staff, names and professional affiliations for members of the board of directors, legal classification, history and recent accomplishments. For U.S. organizations, proof of tax-exempt 501(c)(3) status by the IRS is required. Other financial and organizational information is required for non-U.S. organizations.

Applicants must submit copies of their organization's published annual report and audited financial statements before a grant is made. If these are not available, a U.S. organization will be required to submit a copy of its latest IRS Form 990 return. Videotapes should not be included with the application; they will not be returned.

Source: Excerpted from Charles Stewart Mott Foundation website (http://www.mott.org/grantsandguidelines/ForGrantseekers/appprocedures#section3).

a foundation officer to discuss the idea is especially valuable. It provides the opportunity to develop a personal relationship, to ask and answer questions, and to receive input and advice from that foundation executive. If things go well, the foundation officer becomes a partner in developing the proposal, which greatly enhances the odds of success. The invitation to submit a proposal is also a positive response and does not preclude the possibility of a meeting during the period when the proposal is under consideration. A rejection letter is, of course, always a disappointment.

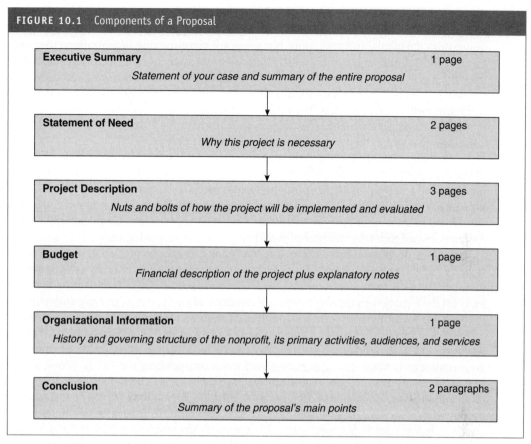

FIGURE 10.1   Components of a Proposal

Executive Summary	1 page
Statement of your case and summary of the entire proposal	

Statement of Need	2 pages
Why this project is necessary	

Project Description	3 pages
Nuts and bolts of how the project will be implemented and evaluated	

Budget	1 page
Financial description of the project plus explanatory notes	

Organizational Information	1 page
History and governing structure of the nonprofit, its primary activities, audiences, and services	

Conclusion	2 paragraphs
Summary of the proposal's main points	

Source: Adapted from Geever, J. C. (2012). *The Foundation Center's guide to proposal writing* (6th ed.). New York: The Foundation Center, p. 13. Used with permission.

Again, this book does not provide detailed instructions on writing a proposal, but standard formats are commonly used. Figure 10.1 provides an outline that includes the essential sections. There are examples in books and online, and proposal-writing courses and workshops are available at colleges, universities, and various other institutions. The Foundation Center offers an extensive program of training, at modest cost, with availability in cities across the country.

CHAPTER SUMMARY

Foundations are among the most visible sources of philanthropy and synonymous with giving in the minds of many people.

Charitable nonprofits, which are exempt from taxation under section 501(c)(3) of the Internal Revenue Code, are either *public charities or private foundations*. Within both categories, some are *operating* entities and some are *grant-making* entities. Most people may think of private foundations as grant making, but some are operating; they only support their own programs. Most people may think of public charities as operating, like universities, hospitals, and museums, but some are grant-making organizations that raise funds from the public and then redistribute them to other nonprofits. Confusion arises from the fact that some of the latter are sometimes called *public foundations*, although they are public charities, not private foundations. That includes community foundations and some supporting organizations. The former raise money from multiple donors and give it to multiple organizations. The latter raise money from multiple donors to support a single nonprofit with which they are affiliated, for example, a university.

Private foundations face greater requirements under the law than do public charities, including limitations on the tax deduction available to their donors, a minimum *payout requirement*, a tax on investment income, and greater restrictions on lobbying. The IRS presumes that charitable nonprofits are private foundations unless they can demonstrate they meet certain criteria, including the *public support test*. Grant-making private foundations are generally the best prospects for grants to operating public charities.

Two types of private foundations are *corporate foundations* and *independent foundations*. *Family foundations* are a subset of independent foundations that have the donors or members of their family actively involved. Some are *pass-through* foundations that give away all the money they receive from their donors every year, but most have endowments that provide investment income to support at least some of their grants (Collins, 2008).

Entities similar to foundations have existed for centuries, but *general-purpose* foundations arose in the United States in the early twentieth century (Collins, 2008). The number grew significantly again during periods of economic prosperity in the 1950s, 1960s, 1990s, and early twenty-first century. There always have been issues and debates about foundations and their role in society. Some prefer *limited-life foundations*, which spend all their money while the donor is alive, but there are also arguments for *perpetual foundations* that continue forever with earnings from their endowments (Ostrower, 2009). Some people say that foundations have too much influence on public policy, for example, in public education, and that decisions should be made through democratic processes rather than by private wealth (Abramson et al., 2012). And some argue that foundations contribute to nonprofit mission drift because they often support programs rather than general operations and are reluctant to support overhead expenses essential to capacity building and organizational sustainability (Gregory & Howard, 2009). Many foundations practice *strategic philanthropy* and have their own predetermined goals. Nonprofits must recognize that there may be tradeoffs in accepting support from such foundations.

Support from a foundation is commonly called a *grant*, although it may technically be a gift, which is usually less restrictive. Most data on foundation support include only the largest foundations and account for about half of all grants. Grants are concentrated on relatively few recipients but are distributed in all regions of the United States. The purposes of grants favor program support and research, but many cut across various categories. Health and educational institutions are the largest recipients.

Foundation practices today include an emphasis on the performance of grant recipients, formal evaluation of their own effectiveness, collaboration with other funders, the encouragement of collaboration among grant recipients, and professionalization of the grant application and grant-making processes (Coffman et al., 2013; Ostrower, 2006; Seldon, 2013). Nonprofits seeking foundation support need to understand these realities.

Nonprofits pursuing foundation support should first identify prospects using abundant research resources, including those from the Foundation Center. Foundations can be screened against various criteria to identify those most likely to support a particular organization or program. Personal relationships and contacts are important, however, so nonprofits should consider approaching foundations with which they have relationships through a board member or past support. Contacts should be selective and professional, so that they do not create an image that harms the organization's reputation in the foundation community (Collins, 2008).

Many foundations provide detailed grant applications on their websites and many accept online applications. Unless a foundation prescribes a different method, the initial approach is often by phone or through a brief *letter of inquiry*, to which the foundation may respond with an invitation to speak or meet, a request for a full written proposal, or a rejection. If a full proposal is invited, the nonprofit should follow the format recommended by the foundation or the standard outline provided in this chapter. Some foundations request *online grant applications* or *common grant application forms* developed by regional associations of grant makers and others.

Key Terms and Concepts

Collective impact

Common grant
   application form

Family foundation

Fields of interest

General-purpose
   foundation

Giving while living

Grant (versus gift)

Grant-making public
   charity

Independent
   foundation

Letter of inquiry

Online grant
   application

Operating
   foundations

Operating public
   charity

Pass-through
   foundation

Payout requirement

Private foundation

Private grant-making
   foundation

Private operating
   foundation

Public charities

Public foundations

Public support test

Qualifying
   distributions

Regional associations
   of grant makers

Self-dealing
   transactions

Spend-down
   (limited-life)
   foundation

Supporting
   organization

Case 10.1: Pew Charitable Trusts

Joseph Newton Pew was the founder of Sun Oil Company, based in Philadelphia. Over a period of years, from 1948 to 1979, his children established seven charitable trusts. The trusts reflected the varied interests of the family members who established them but also pursued some common interests collaboratively (Pew Charitable Trusts website). The seven trusts were legally separate and classified as private foundations, but they were managed as if combined. The management was provided by Glenmede Trust, a company established to administer all of the Pew family's resources (Blum, 2003; Strom, 2003). The seven were known collectively as the "Pew Charitable Trusts," but they had separate names, and this term was simply used informally as an umbrella to refer to them together; it had no legal meaning.

Early priorities of the Pew trusts included cancer research, the Red Cross, and assistance to historically black colleges. Over time, their grants evolved. By the 1970s, priorities had expanded to include preservation of the environment and support for conservation organizations. Beginning in the 1980s, the trusts began to support research on public policy at the federal level and in the 1990s began providing nonpartisan reporting and research, advocacy, and technical assistance to cities and states. In 1995, the trusts began engaging in public opinion research. Today, a subsidiary called the Pew Research Center provides polling data and other social science research, for which it is well known. By 2003, Pew was deeply engaged in policy research and advocacy and supported six separate policy research institutes based in Washington, DC.

In 2003, Pew announced it would create one umbrella organization, to be known as the Pew Charitable Trusts. The new legal entity would be classified as a public charity. The new Pew organization was able to qualify as a public charity because the separate trusts were viewed by the IRS as distinct donors, so that the umbrella entity could meet the public support test. With creation of the new organization, the seven separate trusts were reclassified under the law as supporting organizations (Blum, 2003). In other words, the Pew Charitable Trusts became a public charity that had at least seven different donors.

Among advantages of the new legal status would be the opportunity to improve communication and coordination among Pew staff working in various fields. Another plus would be more freedom for Pew and its grantees to "jump in on timely policy issues" (Blum, 2003). As a public charity, Pew would be able to raise funds from other donors toward projects it would support and, indeed, would be required to do so in order to sustain its status as a public charity. The new organization would file a Form 990, required of public charities, rather than a Form 990PF, required of private foundations. It would enjoy the other advantages of public charities discussed in this chapter.

Not all observers were enthusiastic about the change. Some critics charged that the Pew Charitable Trusts were not remaining faithful to the founders' intentions and views, although this criticism related more to the trusts' grant-making priorities than to the change in legal structure per se. The trusts responded by citing ongoing support to institutions favored by the elder Mr. Pew and the continued involvement of Pew family members ("The Contested Legacy," n.d.). Other observers expressed concern that the change in status could have an adverse impact on nonprofits and on society. Eisenberg (2003) called the change in status "legal gimmickry" and posed a hypothetical example to make the point:

> Consider the implications. What if a husband and wife, both individually wealthy, and one of their children with inherited money together contributed funds to a family foundation, then later decided to convert the foundation to a charity. Would it

have met the IRS's public-support test? Probably not. But had the family members established three trusts under a single umbrella foundation, would the foundation have been declared a charity under the IRS's reasoning? Probably. Would the money be more "public" under the latter setup than the former? Of course not. The money would have come from the same source. (Eisenberg, 2003)

In 2014, the change in status had been accomplished, and the Pew Charitable Trusts described itself as "a global research and public policy organization . . . operated as an independent, non-partisan, non-governmental organization dedicated to serving the public" (Pew Charitable Trusts website).

Case 10.2: Northwest Area Foundation

The territory that now comprises the states of Minnesota, Iowa, North Dakota, South Dakota, Montana, Idaho, Washington, and Oregon once was served by the Great Northern Railway. In 1934, Louis W. Hill, the son of the railway's founder, established the Northwest Area Foundation "for charitable, educational and scientific purposes which contribute to the public welfare" (Northwest Area Foundation website). The mission of the foundation was to promote economic revitalization and improve the standard of living for the people of the region. Today, the foundation is headquartered in St. Paul, Minnesota, and has assets exceeding $400 million.

For more than fifty years, the foundation was a traditional grant maker, providing short-term grants to nonprofits to support programs related to the arts, medical research, agriculture, and poverty reduction. Then, in 1998, the foundation board adopted an ambitious new strategic plan: "to focus on a single poverty-reduction mission, and to do so in a way that allocated a significant portion of the Foundation's resources directly to communities, often through newly created organizations" (Lenkowsky, 2011). The approach was similar to what today is called *collective impact*; the foundation would bring businesses, governments, and nonprofits together, under the foundation's leadership, to solve pressing problems. Rather than offering short-term grants, the foundation would enter ten-year partnerships with nonprofits (Boss, 2011). Over the next decade, the Northwest Area Foundation invested over $200 million according to this plan (Northwest Area Foundation website). By 2008, it became clear that the foundation's innovative efforts had produced some successes, but in other cases it had failed or possibly even caused harm ("Gaining Perspective," n.d.). The foundation commissioned a consulting group, FSG Social Impact Consultants, to analyze what had gone wrong. And it went public with the story of its failures (Boss, 2011).

Some of the failures were attributed to the foundation's own mistakes. The goal of reducing poverty was clear, but there was not much direction on how it would be accomplished. The strategy was fuzzy. In other words, the foundation lacked a theory of change, leading to disagreements among the foundation's board and staff about what should be done (Lenkowsky, 2011). As the consultants' report concluded, "Foundation board and staff agreed on a broad definition of the 'what' (the foundation's mission of reducing poverty), but did not come to agreement on the 'how.'" Unclear expectations left staff in a position of "shooting darts at a moving target" ("Gaining Perspective," n.d.).

The effort to work with new community groups also ran into problems. There was an imbalance of power between the foundation and poor communities. Some felt the foundation was trying to impose its own ideas on poor communities. Some said the foundation was creating a culture of dependency. Disputes arose within communities over which nonprofits best represented them (Lenkowsky, 2011). The foundation was accused of cultural ignorance in its dealing with some Native American communities (Boss, 2011).

Some people said the failures were due not only to the foundation's mistakes but also to more general realities in society. One observer cited the lack of readiness in some communities, saying, "Ten years is a very short time for communities to become ready and to reduce poverty. You can't buy readiness" (Boss, 2011). Another speculated that solving problems as big as poverty may simply be beyond the capability of foundations; in other words, they may be setting themselves up for failure by taking on too much (Lenkowsky, 2011). As Lenkowsky (2011) expressed it, "By seeing themselves as champions of big and bold goals, investors of wealth and expertise, and professionals in social change, they may have created circumstances that make many of their efforts more difficult and less likely to succeed."

In 2008, the foundation's new president acknowledged the failure of the previous strategy, explaining that "we embraced the upside of risk without thoroughly assessing and preparing for the downside." The foundation would return to its roots as a traditional grant maker, still focusing on the reduction of poverty but with grants to established nonprofits that had a track record of impact within their communities. It also pledged to work more collaboratively with others, to communicate more openly with grantees about expectations, and to conduct itself with "humility" regarding its own power to create change ("Gaining Perspective," n.d.).

Questions for Discussion

1. In addition to more flexibility with regard to advocacy, which is mentioned in Case 10.1, what other advantages would the Pew Charitable Trusts have gained by its classification as a public charity rather than a private foundation? In other words, what might have made that change attractive to its leaders?

2. If you had been a nonprofit grantee of the Pew Charitable Trusts prior to the change in its classification, what concerns might you have held about its transition from a private foundation to a public charity? In other words, what differences apply to these two classifications that you might have feared could work to your disadvantage?

3. Do you think the failure of the Northwest Area Foundation was most likely due to the foundation's own mistakes in implementation, or is it simply unrealistic to think that foundations can have a significant impact on major social problems like poverty?

4. As the case of the Northwest Area Foundation illustrates, foundations are sometimes accused of arrogance in their dealings with grant recipients and communities. What are some practices they might adopt in order to avoid creating that impression?

5. Think back on the features of donor-advised funds, discussed in Chapter 8, and the legal requirements of private foundations discussed in this chapter. If you were a wealthy individual considering how best to manage your philanthropy, would you create a donor-advised fund at a community foundation or your own foundation? What would be the advantages and disadvantages of either approach?

Suggestions for Further Reading

Books

Anheier, H. K., & Hammack, D. C. (2010). *American foundations: Roles and contributions.* Washington, DC: Brookings Institution.

Collins, S. (Ed.). (2008). *Foundation fundamentals* (8th ed.). New York: The Foundation Center.

Fleishman, J. L. (2007). *The foundation: A great American secret: How private wealth is changing the world.* New York: PublicAffairs.

Geever, J. C. (2012). *The Foundation Center's guide to proposal writing* (6th ed.). New York: The Foundation Center.

Articles

Hager, M. A., & Boris, E. T. (2012). Compensation for governance in grantmaking foundations. *Public Integrity*, 15(1), 51–70.

Twersky, F. (2014, Summer). The artful juggler. *Stanford Social Innovation Review.* http://www.ssireview.org/articles/entry/the_artful_juggler.

Websites

Bill & Melinda Gates Foundation: http://www.gatesfoundation.org

Council on Foundations: http://www.cof.org

Foundation Center: http://foundationcenter.org

Note

1. Private operating foundations are classified differently from private grant-making foundations by the IRS and face different requirements and restrictions than do grant-making foundations (Collins, 2008). Those differences are not discussed here.

CHAPTER 11

Campaigns

Columbia Thank You Day celebrates $6.1 billion capital campaign funding.

—*Columbia Spectator*, April 3, 2014

Fort Wayne Children's Zoo to announce $7 million capital campaign Tuesday.

—*News-Sentinel*, April 21, 2014

Scott County Y announces $4M capital campaign.

—*Quad-City News*, May 13, 2014

Community center launches $1.2 million capital campaign for expansion.

—*Conway Daily Sun*, May 13, 2014

Humane Society of Lebanon County Capital Campaign gets started.

—*Lebanon Valley News*, January 3, 2014

Central Indiana Girl Scouts council kicks off capital campaign.

—TribStar.com, April 16, 2014

The origins of today's fundraising strategies are identifiable in efforts undertaken centuries ago, including some that were discussed in Chapter 1 of this text. For example, the fundraising mission for Harvard that Hibbens, Peter, and Weld launched in 1641 included what is thought to be the first fundraising brochure. Mathew Carey and Benjamin Franklin planted the seeds of modern techniques in their fundraising in Philadelphia in the nineteenth century, including rated prospect lists and the concept of sequential solicitation. And, of course, Ward and Pierce, in their 1902 campaign for the YMCA in Washington, DC, established the essential principles and practices of organized campaigns that are still employed today.

Developed in YMCA fundraising and then applied to other nonprofit organizations and institutions by the consulting firms that dominated the field in the first half of the twentieth century, the campaign has evolved and adapted to changing circumstances. As the opening collection of headlines demonstrates, campaigns are the most visible of fundraising initiatives. And, while campaigns in higher education achieve the largest goals and receive the most attention, the headlines show that they are also important events in the lives of nonprofits of all types in communities across the nation.

A campaign is a fundraising *strategy*, not a program. It may be a strategy for raising major gifts toward a capital project, for example, a new building. Or it may be a strategy for increasing revenue in all of an organization's fundraising programs, including annual giving as well as major gifts. And in many campaigns today, fundraising goals of a campaign are accompanied by communication and marketing goals that are also important. But it is not synonymous with an organization's ongoing fundraising program; it is an extraordinary effort. The discussion in this chapter applies some concepts from Chapter 3, which concerned donor motivations, and from Chapter 4, which introduced fundamental fundraising principles. For example, social influences on donor motivation, discussed in Chapter 3, are reflected in the importance of campaign volunteer leadership. Research by Vesterlund (2003), discussed in Chapter 4, helps explain the importance of lead gifts in a campaign and thus, the critical role of sequential fundraising as a campaign solicitation strategy. Since relevant theories and research were presented in earlier chapters, they are not discussed in detail again in this chapter. But students may sometimes find it useful to go back and review those points again when proceeding through this chapter.[1]

TYPES OF CAMPAIGNS

There are three basic campaign types, as summarized in Box 11.1. For most of the twentieth century, most campaigns were **capital campaigns**. As the term implies, these efforts were focused on a capital project, usually a new building. The campaign generally consumed all of the organization's fundraising energies for a period of time (usually three to five years) and included solicitation of its entire constituency for one-time commitments toward the featured project (Dove, 2000). A shortcoming of this approach is that it may have a negative impact on the annual fund as well as fundraising for other priorities, such as the endowment. When donors' attention is focused entirely on a single capital project, they may be inclined to direct their gifts toward that purpose, perhaps reducing or suspending their support of the annual fund. If that occurs, the organization is, in effect, underwriting some of its own campaign, since funds are simply transferred from the annual fund to the capital budget.

In order to overcome the shortcomings of the capital campaign model, beginning in about the 1970s and continuing, campaigns in higher education came to be defined more broadly as **comprehensive campaigns** (Dove, 2000). Like the capital campaign, a comprehensive campaign effort seeks support from the entire constituency of the institution. But rather than focusing on a single capital project, the campaign encompasses all of the organization's financial needs, including one or more capital projects, the annual fund over the period of the campaign, often support for specific programs, and endowment. Comprehensive campaigns usually count *all* gifts received by the organization during the defined campaign period toward the overall campaign goal (Kihlstedt, 2010). Some

| | **BOX 11.1** Basic Types of Campaigns | | |

	Traditional Capital Campaign	**Comprehensive Campaign**	**Special Purpose/ Focused/ Special Project**
Objectives	Single capital project, e.g., a new building	Various priorities of the organization, including capital projects, endowment, programs, capacity-building initiatives, annual giving	Single purpose, which may be a building, an endowment fund, a project, a program
Constituency solicited	Total donor constituency. All donors and prospects are asked to give support to the priority project.	Total donor constituency. Donors are asked to support priorities of interest to them or to make combined gifts, including annual giving and a capital commitment.	Selected prospects who have a particular interest in the purpose.
Length of campaign	Typically three to five years	Typically five to eight years	Typically three years or less

Sources: Based on Dove (2000); Kihlstedt (2010).

organizations' campaigns encompass more than capital needs but are not comprehensive. For example, a campaign might include the annual fund and endowment but no building projects. Kihlstedt (2010) uses the term **combined campaign** to describe such efforts. There is a trend among campaigns for nonprofit organizations to include increased working capital and capacity-building initiatives as objectives in combined campaigns that also encompass annual giving (Barr, 2008).

In a comprehensive campaign, donors usually are offered choices and are solicited for support of campaign objectives of particular interest to them. In this approach, a donor's gift to the annual fund or to endowment counts as a gift to the campaign, so such gifts are not discouraged in the same way they might be in the traditional capital campaign model. Comprehensive campaigns are usually longer than traditional capital campaigns; college and university campaigns often continue for seven to eight years. The comprehensive campaign has become the norm in higher education and is a model many nonprofits in other sectors also have adopted, depending on their needs and circumstances. Indeed, since comprehensive campaigns have become so common, the older model is now sometimes called the **historical capital campaign** (Dove 2000). But many organizations still undertake capital campaigns (see the examples at the opening of this chapter). For that reason, this book uses the term **traditional capital campaign**, rather than historical, since the latter may imply that such campaigns are entirely of the past.

Many organizations also undertake short-term campaigns related to specific projects or programs. This type of campaign is called a **special-purpose campaign**, **focused campaign** (Dove, 2000), or **special-project campaign** (Kihlstedt, 2010). Such campaigns are different from traditional capital campaigns because solicitations are limited to those prospects who have a particular interest in that project, rather than presenting the project as the top priority to the entire donor constituency. For example, if a hospital is having a focused campaign for a new birthing center, it might only solicit former patients who had babies at the hospital. If a university is raising funds for scholarships, it might limit the solicitations to former scholarship recipients.

In common usage, many people just use the term *capital campaign* to refer to all three types. But it is obviously important to understand the distinctions.

CAMPAIGN DEFINING CHARACTERISTICS

Although dated, Dove's 2000 book on campaigns clarified much of the standard vocabulary and remains widely cited. In that book, he offers a succinct definition of the campaign that is still quoted or paraphrased in many works: "an organized, intensive fundraising effort . . . to secure extraordinary gifts and pledges . . . for a specific purpose or programs . . . during a specified period of time" (p. 5). That captures the essence of what distinguishes a campaign from ongoing fundraising. But let's look further at some principles that differentiate a campaign from other types of fundraising strategies.

Announced Goal and Deadline

Donors respond to needs that are urgent, and it is human nature to defer action until a deadline approaches. Campaigns are designed with an understanding of those realities. A fundraising effort that has no goal, for example, that is intended to "raise as much as we can" or that continues until a certain total has been achieved, is therefore not a campaign. A goal and deadline known only to those within the organization may bring discipline to their efforts, but it does not influence the thinking of prospective donors, so that approach is not a campaign either. A campaign has a *specific* dollar goal and a *deadline* for achieving it that are *announced* to the public, in order to capture attention and motivate timely action by all who need to be involved. That includes individuals within the organization's leadership. By committing the organization and themselves to a goal and deadline that is publicly known, the board and CEO raise the stakes for everyone (Dove, 2000; Kihlstedt, 2010).

Specific Purposes

The annual-giving program may include general appeals that are based on the overall case for the organization. But a campaign is undertaken for a specific purpose or purposes, not just to raise more money. It is centered on specific *objectives* that relate to strategic priorities of the organization. Those may include a new building project, a renovation, needed equipment, endowment, program support, increased annual giving, or some combination (Kihlstedt, 2010). The purposes are justified with a case that relates them to the organization's broader strategic goals.

Rated Prospect Lists and Specific Asks

Campaign fundraising is based on the principle of proportionate giving, discussed earlier in this text. In other words, prospects are asked to give in proportion to their capacity to do so, based on ratings the organization and its prospect researchers have developed. They are not asked simply to give what they can. The latter type of initiative might be called a **collection**, but it would not meet the definition of a campaign. In a campaign, the top prospects are asked for specific *amounts* for specific *purposes*, based on an assessment of their financial capabilities and interests.

Sequential Fundraising

The principle of *sequential fundraising* (Brakeley, 1980) is central to the success of a campaign. A fundraising effort that begins with a solicitation of the organization's entire constituency is not a campaign. It is an **appeal**. It is unlikely to maximize giving because it does not engage the power of standards and visible role models in order to guide donors as to what their own response should be. In other words, it does not activate the social influences on giving that are important to raising donor sights.

Campaign gifts are solicited "from top down and the inside out" (McGoldrick & Robell, 2002, p. 141). As *inside out* implies, the first groups to be solicited include members of the governing board, top prospects, past donors, and often the organization's staff. The campaign then gradually rolls out to prospects in more distant circles of the organization's constituency, as defined and discussed in Chapter 5. The top-down/inside-out process unfolds over the course of the campaign, and discipline in following it is important to maximize support, although sometimes difficult to sustain. Rolling out the campaign prematurely runs the risk of preemptive gifts that lower sights throughout the pyramid (Dove, 2000; Kihlstedt, 2010). Consistent with the principle of sequential fundraising, campaigns are conducted in phases, discussed soon.

Organized Volunteer Leadership

Organized volunteer leadership is characteristic of a campaign. As discussed earlier in this text, people tend to follow the example of others whom they admire or with whom they wish to be associated. This principle has been fundamental in the practitioner literature (e.g., Seymour, 1966) and is supported by theory discussed in Chapter 3 (e.g., Harbaugh, 1998). The visible engagement of prestigious volunteer leaders is thus a critical ingredient of a campaign strategy and authenticates the case for support. Such leaders are enlisted to serve in visible roles as campaign chairs or cochairs or as members of the campaign leadership committee. And, of course, the example of their own leadership gifts and active engagement in cultivation and solicitation also are helpful (Fredericks, 2010; Kihlstedt, 2010).

Emphasis on Major Gifts

Although comprehensive campaigns usually encompass all gifts to the organization during the campaign period, including annual gifts, all campaigns emphasize the solicitation of major gifts. Thinking back on the discussion in Chapter 4, this emphasis is essential in light of the *Pareto principle*, which suggests that 80 to 90 percent of the dollar total comes from just 10 to 20 percent of gifts to the campaign (Weinstein, 2009).

Another traditional campaign axiom is the **rule of thirds**, attributable to Harold J. Seymour (1966). It holds that about one-third of the campaign total comes from the top ten gifts, a second third comes from about the next one hundred gifts, and the final third of the total comes from all other gifts, in smaller amounts. The importance of major and principal gifts in today's campaigns may render Seymour's (1966) exact proportions obsolete, but the general point is still correct: a successful campaign relies disproportionately on major gifts.

PHASES OF THE CAMPAIGN

Consistent with the principles already described, a campaign is conducted in **phases**. Various authors define the phases somewhat differently and offer varied inventories of what tasks are to be completed in each phase (e.g., Dove, 2000; Kihlstedt, 2010; McGoldrick & Robell, 2002; Pierpont, 2003; Worth, 2010). But most descriptions include many commonalities. Figure 11.1 depicts phases of the campaign in a diagram I have devised but is generally consistent with what other authors describe.

There are two broad phases, a **quiet phase** and a **public phase**. The quiet phase encompasses a time when planning and preparation for the campaign are well-known among insiders, but the campaign has not yet been announced to the general public.

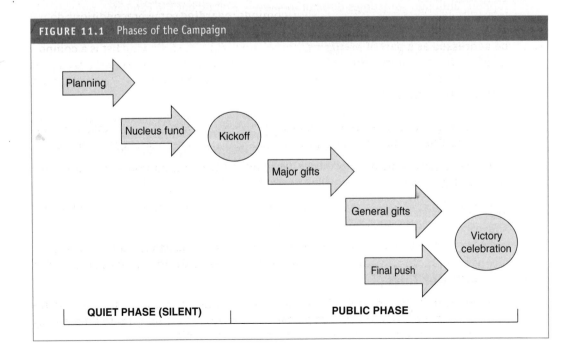

FIGURE 11.1   Phases of the Campaign

Some people refer to this as the *silent phase* of the campaign, but I prefer the term *quiet*, since some people—often many—are aware of what is happening. As the term suggests, the public phase occurs after the goal and deadline for completion of the campaign have been announced. Within each of these phases are several distinct stages and milestones, although, as depicted in Figure 11.1, they often overlap. Let's look at each in turn.

Campaign Planning

Planning for a campaign initially proceeds on two tracks. During this stage, the organization is engaged in strategic planning, which identifies its priorities and financial needs. As described in Chapter 5, the case for support and the case statement for the campaign will flow from this process. At the same time, in the development office, campaign-specific planning and preparation are occurring, with intensified efforts to identify and research prospects and to build development staff and systems necessary to support the campaign. These processes are interactive; that is, fundraisers need to be informed of what priorities may be emerging from strategic planning in order to guide and gauge their preparation for the campaign, and strategic planners need input from fundraisers on the potential for philanthropic support of various initiatives they may be considering.

Campaign Readiness

As a part of campaign planning, the organization assesses its readiness for a campaign. Various preconditions have been well-documented in the practitioner literature. Some (e.g., Dove, 2000; Pierpont, 2003) have created numerical rating scales to assess campaign readiness based on various criteria, although that may imply more precision than is realistic. In addition, shortcomings regarding some preconditions do not mean the organization should stop campaign planning in its tracks, since some can be addressed as a part of preparing for the campaign. The following list is a composite of readiness criteria generally consistent with what various other authors suggest (e.g., Dove, 2000; Kihlstedt, 2010; Pierpont, 2003). This specific list is adapted from my earlier work (Worth, 2010):

- The organization has a clear vision of its mission and unique qualities that set it apart from others in terms of its impact on society; that is, it has a strong case for support.

- The organization has a plan for its future growth and improvement based on a strategic plan.

- Specific fundraising goals and objectives have been identified, rooted in the institution's strategic priorities, as articulated in the plan.

- Major objectives of the proposed campaign are well-understood internally and enjoy a broad consensus among board members, professional staff, and other stakeholders at various levels.

- Members of the governing board are committed to the organization's plan and the goals of the campaign and are prepared to support the campaign with time, energy, and personal resources, commensurate with their ability.

- The CEO is well-regarded, is willing to commit a sufficient amount of time to the campaign, and is able to articulate the importance of the campaign's priorities.

- Other administrative leaders of the organization, for example, program or unit directors, are supportive of the campaign and willing to play appropriate roles, including participation in the cultivation and solicitation of prospects with interest in their units or activities.

- The organization has identified potential volunteer leaders of the campaign who are committed to its purposes, well-known and respected in its constituency, prepared to commit sufficient time to leading the campaign, and preferably experienced in fundraising.

- There are prospects who have the capacity to make leadership gifts totaling a significant portion of the anticipated campaign goal (and who have been cultivated to a point of readiness to make such commitments).

- There are a sufficient number of prospects who have linkage to the organization, a known or demonstrated commitment to its purposes, and the financial capacity to provide the gifts required to attain the balance of the proposed goal.

- The organization has adequate knowledge (including records, prospect research, and other information) regarding the interests, philanthropic priorities, and life and financial circumstances of its prospects, in order to formulate timely and appropriate solicitation strategies.

- The development office is led by a fundraising professional who serves as a senior officer of the organization, is well-regarded by the governing board, has access to the CEO and board members, and preferably has significant campaign experience.

- The development staff is sufficient in size, is properly configured, and has the experience and skills needed to execute a campaign.

- Fundraising information systems and services, including prospect research, are adequate to support a campaign.

- The development office has established relationships with such specialists, either internal or external, as may be needed during the campaign, for example, fundraising counsel, planned-giving counsel, and professionals in communications, publications, and event management.

- Adequate budgetary resources have been committed to the campaign.

- There are no conditions affecting the organization that will have a strong negative impact on the campaign, for example, recent controversies or internal political divisions.

- There are no conditions in the external environment that will have a strong negative impact on the campaign, for example, a poor economy or directly competing campaigns by other organizations in the same community.

Again, it is important to emphasize that the absence of one or more preconditions should not be reason to forgo a campaign. Rather, an assessment of the organization's readiness may help to define the tasks that need to be undertaken in preparation for a campaign. And, of course, not every precondition is equally relevant for a specific nonprofit at a particular time, facing a particular set of needs, which may be more or less compelling (Worth, 2010).

At some point in the planning process, the tracks of strategic planning and fundraising planning come together to provide a preliminary list of objectives and an estimate of philanthropic market potential with regard to those objectives. A tentative campaign goal is established and a brief preliminary case statement is drafted. At this point, it is common to undertake a feasibility study (Kihlstedt, 2010).

Feasibility Study

The **feasibility study** is a market test, often conducted by an independent outside consultant who specializes in campaign planning. Under some circumstances, the feasibility study can be undertaken by the organization's development staff, but an outside consultant brings the benefit of experience and objectivity (Pierpont, 2003). Preceded by a letter from an organizational leader explaining the nature of the study and the draft case statement, the consultant meets with prospective donors whom the organization has identified. They generally include top prospects and representatives of various donor constituencies.

The consultant conducts confidential, structured interviews with prospects identified by the organization. Since the interviews are confidential, the consultant receives frank feedback from interview participants regarding their general perceptions and attitudes toward the organization and its leadership, their view of the specific objectives of the proposed campaign, and the likely amount and purpose of their own gifts. In addition, the interviews often produce names of new donor prospects and insights on who might be the most effective volunteer leaders of the campaign. In addition to one-on-one interviews, some feasibility studies also include focus groups and/or online surveys, in order to sample the perspectives of a larger number of constituents.

A summary of responses, not identifying individual respondents, is shared with campaign planners. The findings often require adjustments in the goal and objectives of the campaign. Some consultants prefer to call a feasibility study a **campaign planning study**, since the recommendations may go beyond the feasibility of the proposed goal, including insights on other key questions, including the strength of the case for support, the number of prospects required at various levels, best prospects for campaign leadership, timing of the campaign, public relations and communications requirements of the campaign, staffing required, and the campaign budget (Pierpont, 2003).

With a positive study report, the organization now may be reasonably confident that the planned campaign is feasible, but it is still not time to make a public announcement. There is one more critical test to come, the solicitation of **lead gifts** (or **advance gifts**), which will comprise the **nucleus fund** of the campaign (Dove, 2000; Kihlstedt, 2010; Worth, 2010).

Nucleus Fund

Preparation for the campaign is now widely known to insiders, but it remains in its quiet phase. There may be rumors about the eventual goal, but the actual number under consideration is known to only a few. Solicitations begin, carefully following the *top-down, inside-out* sequence (Kihlstedt, 2010). Since the prospects being solicited are those who are top-rated, each solicitation needs to be carefully planned. A disappointment could have a negative ripple effect throughout the pyramid. Recall the hypothetical example from Chapter 4 in which the top donor prospect provides a disappointing response. If that occurs, the campaign may be doomed from the outset because of the effect on the motivations of other donor prospects.

Gifts solicited during the quiet period of the campaign comprise the nucleus fund. Expert recommendations on the ideal size of the nucleus fund vary, generally from 40 to 60 percent of the ultimate campaign goal (Lindahl, 2008). The exact number depends on many variables, including the size and capacity of the organization's constituency. Based on his study of campaigns, and applying economic and business theories to the question, Lindahl (2008) recommends a nucleus fund totaling a minimum of 40 percent of the goal. His findings also strongly support the desirability of deferring the campaign's public phase until that threshold has been achieved.

Kickoff

The vocabulary of campaigns includes an interesting mixture of metaphors from athletics and the military. The term *campaign* itself comes from the military. The public phase of a campaign begins with a **kickoff**, like a football game (Kihlstedt, 2010). The campaign ends with a *victory celebration*, which again implies the conclusion of something adversarial, either a game or war (McGoldrick & Robell, 2002).

The kickoff is usually an event, sometimes quite elaborate, at which the campaign is introduced and described, the nucleus fund is announced, and lead-gift donors are recognized. The kickoff event should be commensurate with the scale and purpose of the campaign. A campaign to raise money for a hospice should perhaps be somewhat more subdued and dignified than for a campaign to build a new sports arena. The campaign kickoff for a small nonprofit may be a relatively modest event that includes volunteer leaders, donors, and perhaps some community dignitaries. University kickoffs are often lavish events that include entertainment, fireworks, and live video feeds to groups gathered across the country or the globe. But the purposes are the same: to generate excitement, visibility, optimism, and momentum, inspiring the campaign's leaders as well as those yet to be solicited.

The campaign's goal often has been rumored for months before it is announced. Some campaign planners intentionally work to keep expectations on the low side to this point, preferring to surprise with a nucleus fund total and goal that are more than people expect. Announcing a goal that is below what has been rumored is a tactical error that can make the kickoff a disappointment rather than the exciting event intended.

Public Phase

Once the campaign has been announced, its public phase begins. Some experts warn of the possibility that the campaign will hit a **plateau of fatigue** right after the kickoff, since both volunteers and staff may have worked hard to bring the campaign to this key milestone and may be inclined to savor the moment (McGoldrick & Robell, 2002). Maintaining the momentum is often a critical challenge for campaign leaders. It can be equally challenging to maintain the discipline of top-down solicitation. Now that the campaign is public, some people may suggest just moving right to broad-based solicitations—the initiation of mailings, crowdfunding initiatives, and so forth. But the principle of sequential fundraising is to be respected, as early solicitations in this phase continue to be conducted top-down while the solicitation of smaller gifts from a broad base of donors—which in the context of a campaign are sometimes called **general gifts**—is deferred until a later stage.[2]

Final Push and Victory Celebration

In its closing months or years, the campaign rolls out to the organization's total donor constituency, as general gifts are solicited. Mailings, e-mails, events, and other methods are employed to increase participation. Because the campaign is nearing its conclusion and the goal is in sight, renewed urgency is common at this point. Based on a study that included a donor survey, Lindahl (2008) recommends that campaigns begin the final push when the campaign total reaches 95 percent of the goal. He also suggests that this stage of the campaign be identified as the **goal-line phase**, a distinct third phase of the campaign following the quiet and public phases. The final stages of the campaign also include what are called *cleanup* activities. That may involve going back to prospects visited earlier, who may have deferred their decisions, and sometimes to those who gave early in the campaign and are close to completing campaign pledges, with the hope that they may increase their commitments.

The campaign ends with a **victory celebration**, often another major event, at which volunteers and donors are recognized and everyone associated with the organization is invited to bask in the glow of success. The campaign is over, but work remains to be done. Postcampaign analysis begins the following day and, in many cases, so does planning for the next campaign.

GIFT TABLE

The *gift table* (or **gift-range chart**, as it is often called) is a fundamental tool for campaign planning, management, and analysis. It provides a numerical representation of many of the principles discussed in this book, including the fundraising pyramid, the principle of proportionate giving, the Pareto principle (Weinstein, 2009), and Seymour's (1966) rule of thirds.[3]

TABLE 11.1 Gift Table: Goal of $25 Million (following traditional "rule of thirds"; 4:1 conversion ratio)

Gift Range	No. Gifts Required	No. Prospects Required	Total at This Level	Cumulative Total	Cumulative Percentage of Goal
Top Ten Gifts					
$2,500,000	1	4	$2,500,000	$2,500,000	10%
1,000,000	3	12	3,000,000	5,500,000	22%
500,000	6	24	3,000,000	8,500,000	34%
Next 80–100 Gifts					
250,000	12	48	3,000,000	11,500,000	46%
100,000	27	108	2,700,000	14,200,000	57%
50,000	50	200	2,500,000	16,700,000	67%
Balance of Gifts					
25,000	100	400	2,500,000	19,200,000	77%
10,000	200	800	2,000,000	21,200,000	85%
5,000	300	1,200	1,500,000	22,700,000	91%
<5,000	Many	Many	2,300,000	25,000,000	100%
TOTALS	**681+**	**2,724+**	**$25,000,000**	**NA**	**NA**

The gift table reflects a pattern of gifts often observable after a successful campaign has been completed. Because that pattern is relatively consistent, the relationships reflected in the table have been adopted as predictive tools. Thus, an organization planning a campaign can compare the gifts *required* to reach a goal, as depicted in a gift table based on that amount, against its **prospect pool**, that is, its list of rated prospects. That helps to determine if its constituency has the financial capacity to produce the goal. If not, it may be necessary to reconsider the goal or to undertake more prospect development activity, along the lines discussed in Chapter 5, before launching the campaign.

Table 11.1 depicts a gift table based on a goal of $25 million, reflecting traditional assumptions. Whether these assumptions are realistic in today's environment is a matter of discussion, to which we will soon turn. But first let's look at what this table shows.

- A lead gift of at least 10 percent of the goal (Kihlstedt, 2010). This is the traditional standard, but there may be situations in which it does not apply.

- The amount of gift in each successively lower range is *about* one-half that in the range above, and the number of gifts required at that level is *about* double that of the range above. This is the standard way of constructing the table, although there may be deviations from the strict formula in some circumstances (Dove, 2000).

- The rule of thirds (Seymour, 1966). In Table 11.1, the top ten gifts account for about one-third of the campaign, the next 100 (or so) gifts account for about another third of the campaign, and the remaining gifts account for the last third. This is the traditional principle identified by Seymour (1966).

Data suggest that contemporary campaigns may need to obtain far more than one-third from the top ten gifts, although contemporary authors continue to emphasize the critical importance of those top ten gifts (Kihlstedt, 2010). This change in the pattern of giving to recent campaigns may reflect increasing wealth disparity among donors and/or economic uncertainty that inhibits major gifts below the top levels. The traditional rule-of-thirds principle may offer a starting point for developing a gift table, but the table may need to be adjusted to reflect current realities and the constituency of the particular organization.

Considering changing patterns in campaign giving, Pierpont (2003) suggests that Seymour's rule of thirds may need to be modified and proposes the following formulation: about 40 to 60 percent of the goal should come from the ten to fifteen largest gifts; about 33 to 50 percent should come from the next 100 to 150 gifts; about 10 to 20 percent of the goal should come from all other gifts.

- Table 11.1 implies that four prospects must be identified at each level to produce each gift required at that level. This assumes that not all solicitations will be successful, so there needs to be more identified prospects at each level than the number of gifts required. The ratio of prospects to gifts obtained is called the *conversion rate* or *ratio*. Some experts use a different ratio than is reflected in Table 11.1 or vary the ratio throughout the table, assuming that more or fewer prospects may be needed at higher or lower gift levels (Kihlstedt, 2010). For example, some might argue that prospects for the top-level gifts are individuals who are well-known to the organization. They have been cultivated for a long time, and the nonprofit's leaders therefore may have a relatively accurate estimation of their likely campaign gift; so fewer than four prospects may be needed to produce one gift. On the other hand, this argument might run, prospects at lower levels of the table are less well-known, so a higher ratio of prospects to gifts is required to assure success—in other words, solicitations in this range will be more speculative, so the conversion rate will be lower. But others might take just the opposite approach, arguing that the top gifts are more sacrificial for the individuals making them and thus the probability of completion is lower, calling for a higher number of prospects. In this view, gifts lower in the table are an easier decision for a donor to make, likely resulting in a higher conversion rate and a need for fewer prospects. Use of the 4:1 ratio at all levels of Table 11.1 is a relatively conservative approach. An organization that has a long history of fundraising, perhaps including previous campaigns, and has maintained close relationships with its prospective donors, may consider a different conversion rate to be realistic.

- In this chart, 90 percent of the goal is achieved through gifts of $5,000 or more. Gifts below that amount might be considered general gifts to be raised in what Lindahl (2008) calls the goal-line phase. Again, this is consistent with proportionate giving and roughly consistent with Pareto's principle and Seymour's (1966) rule of thirds.

Table 11.1 reflects the standard assumptions used to construct a gift table, but this is not an exact science. For one, it is easy to observe that the figures in the gift table presented here are approximate and rounded. There are gift table calculators available on the web (for example, from Blackbaud) that apply a strict mathematical model, in which the gift amount is reduced by half and the number of gifts is doubled at each level. But that approach leads to some numbers not consistent with the giving levels donors usually consider. For example, halving the gift level from $250,000 produces a range at $125,000, but donors would be more likely to think in terms of the round number $100,000. For this reason, in a mathematically developed table, the amounts and gift numbers in each range are usually adjusted in order to present a simpler picture.

The gift levels in the table also need to be adjusted to coincide with recognition opportunities. For example, let's say the campaign is for expansion of a building and there will be two identical new wings, each of which can be named to recognize a $250,000 gift. In order to maintain logical consistency, the ranges in the gift table should be adjusted to show the need for two gifts at that level, even if the standard formulas might not produce them.

There are other reasons why standard formulas might not be applied in a given case. For example, a nonprofit with a relatively small constituency but one major donor might need to obtain a lead gift of 20 percent or even more from that donor to have any chance of meeting its goal. The same organization may need several gifts near the top of the table, since it has few prospects in the lower ranges. The gift chart thus would be tailored to that particular scenario—it would be top-loaded. For example, Table 11.2 shows a simple gift table for a $2 million campaign, with a 20 percent lead gift.

When the organization is relatively confident that a lead gift is available and its amount is known, the gift table constructed for purposes of campaign planning and the feasibility study would reflect that reality. Thus, in the scenario depicted in Table 11.1, suppose that a board member already has informally said that he or she is considering a $5 million gift.

TABLE 11.2 Gift Table for $2 Million Campaign (20 percent lead gift)

Gift Range	No. Gifts Required	Total at This Level
$400,000	1	$400,000
250,000	1	250,000
150,000	1	150,000
100,000	2	200,000
50,000	2	100,000
25,000	10	250,000
10,000	15	150,000
5,000	25	125,000
<5,000	Many	375,000
Total		**$2,000,000**

Presenting the board with a gift table that shows a $2.5 million lead gift would be foolish. The gift table would show a lead gift of $5 million and the numbers in lower ranges would be adjusted accordingly.

There may be situations in which a lead gift of less than 10 percent may be acceptable. For example, consider a university comprehensive campaign that encompasses several years of ongoing annual giving, grants received for programs, and planned-gift commitments. The campaign will include thousands of gifts from alumni and other donors. In this scenario, it may not be necessary, or realistic, to secure a single gift that is 10 percent of the *overall* goal. For the portion of the campaign that relates to capital objectives, however, a lead gift in that range would still be the standard; but it might comprise less than 10 percent of the overall campaign.

The gift table has practical usefulness in campaign planning that is difficult to exaggerate. Imagine, for example, a nonprofit board that has limited understanding of fundraising but holds ambitious aspirations for the organization's future. Without fully understanding the implications, some board members may propose a campaign goal that the CEO or chief development officer believes to be unrealistic. For either of them to argue against it based on generalities, such as "our donors don't have that kind of money," could be perceived as defensive and negative. An alternative approach would be for the CEO or development officer to suggest developing a gift table and then returning for another discussion. At the next meeting, the board could be presented with a gift table that shows the specific gifts required to reach the goal proposed, the number of prospects needed to produce those gifts, and the number of prospects currently identified. With the gift table in front of the board, the discussion can be grounded in reality. In addition, the table makes evident the level of lead gifts required, which board members will understand may need to come from them. Thus, discussion of the proposed goal in terms of the table helps to test the commitment of the board to the number it has proposed. As Dove (2000) describes, the gift table can be a "sobering thing" (p. 72). Of course, the table also can help to make a realistic argument in the opposite scenario, in which a campaign goal is indeed realistic but a cautious board is unpersuaded. The data portrayed in the table help to ground the discussion in fact rather than perception, wishful thinking, or undue pessimism.

The gift table is also used in feasibility studies. It is often shown to interview participants, who are asked to judge whether the proposed goal is achievable. Their ability to do so is greater if they can conceptualize the goal in terms of the gift table than if they are asked to react to one big number. In addition, when asked to estimate his or her own likely gift to the campaign, reference to the gift table enables the individual to answer in the context of all the gifts required. Indeed, the consultant may sometimes phrase that question in terms similar to "Where do you see yourself participating on this table?" There is a subtle difference between that question and the more direct, "How much do you think you will give?" The former may lead the individual to consider the answer in terms of proportionate giving, that is, with regard to the whole range of gifts required, rather than just an isolated number.

The gift table also is useful as a management tool throughout the campaign. Comparing results against the table can identify areas of underperformance, perhaps requiring a reallocation of efforts and resources.

STRATEGIC DECISIONS

Planning and preparation for a campaign require making several strategic decisions, which include not only the dollar goal but how the purposes of the campaign will be defined and described, the structure of the campaign organization, the length of the campaign, policies regarding what gifts will be accepted and how gifts of various types will be counted toward the campaign goal, what solicitation strategies will be followed, what donor recognition opportunities will be offered, and how the costs of the campaign will be covered.

Setting Campaign Goals

In the vocabulary of a campaign, the term **goal** refers to the dollar total the campaign is expected to achieve. There may be an overall goal and then various subgoals, which could be broken down by project or subunit.

As discussed, the preliminary goal is based on the gift table and the organization's internal ratings of prospects. That preliminary goal then may be tested in a feasibility study and refined in light of study findings. This sounds relatively straightforward, but other variables make goal setting more complicated.

One variable is the type of campaign. If the campaign is a traditional capital campaign, for example, focused on a single building project, the preliminary goal may be the cost of the project. But the feasibility study may find that the full cost of the project cannot be raised through the campaign, so decisions need to be made about alternative financing and what role philanthropy realistically can play. And, of course, campaign planners need to decide over what time period donors may pay pledges and determine how that aligns with the cash flow requirements of the project.

If the campaign is comprehensive and will include annual giving over some number of years, then the goal depends in part on the *length* of the campaign; a campaign that includes eight years of annual giving obviously can have a larger overall goal than one that only includes three years of annual giving. A longer campaign also provides more time to cultivate prospects before soliciting their campaign gifts, and new prospects may be identified over the course of the campaign. So perhaps an achievable goal may be greater than the current prospect pool can support. But establishing a larger goal based on speculation about new prospects that may be identified in the future increases the risks. Another variable is the policies campaign planners adopt regarding how certain types of gifts will be counted. The topic is discussed in more detail later in this chapter, but two key decisions involve the pledge payment period and whether and how planned gifts will be counted.

It is realistic to acknowledge that in some instances, another consideration in setting a campaign goal is the impact of that number on the image of the organization or institution. This phenomenon is primarily relevant in higher education, where colleges and universities often feel compelled to announce a goal that is at least as large, and preferably larger, than their competitors. This is based on the belief that the campaign goal in relationship to others has an impact on the institution's positioning among its peers. Thus, setting the campaign goal is not quite a scientific exercise; judgment is required.

Defining Priorities and Objectives

The *purposes* for which the dollars are being raised have come to be described and presented in different ways over time. In earlier decades they were usually called *needs*, and a compilation of them was the **needs list**. Those terms are still used, but since about the 1990s, the purposes of campaigns have come to be called **objectives**, adopting the language and perspective of strategic planning (Kihlstedt, 2010). In comprehensive campaigns, some may be identified as **featured objectives**, that is, those that are the most critical. For example, in a campaign that includes funds for a new building but also encompasses the ongoing annual fund and endowment gifts, the building project may be presented as the featured objective. Objectives are similar to needs; that is, they are specific purposes, such as endowment or construction or renovation of a building. A study of comprehensive campaigns conducted in 2009 found that since the mid-2000s there has been a trend in comprehensive campaigns, especially in universities, toward describing the purposes supported by the campaign as **priorities** or **strategic priorities**. Terminology is not consistently applied (Worth, 2010).

Campaign Organization

Organized volunteer leadership is characteristic of a campaign and brings various benefits. As discussed in Chapter 4, volunteer leaders authenticate the case for support, provide role models and examples, and mobilize the power of social influences on donor motivations. This is consistent with theory describing social influences of giving. In addition, in a small nonprofit with limited development staff, execution of the campaign often relies on volunteer committees. In large institutions, volunteers play a less hands-on role in day-to-day management of the campaign, but their involvement in cultivation and solicitation is of great benefit, for reasons discussed earlier in this text.

Potential volunteer leaders are first involved during the campaign's planning stage. Members of the governing board, advisory councils, and possibly other volunteers often serve as members of task forces and other groups involved in strategic planning. This helps to develop their recognition of and identification with the objectives and goals that eventually will be adopted for the campaign. As the organization moves from strategic planning to campaign planning, it is common to establish a campaign planning committee that includes a combination of staff and volunteer leaders (Kihlstedt, 2010). The task of this committee is to finalize the goal and objectives for the campaign, adopt a campaign plan, and enlist the campaign's volunteer leadership. If a feasibility study is undertaken, the campaign planning committee generally provides oversight and guidance to the study and receives and evaluates the findings. The campaign planning committee typically makes a recommendation to the full governing board to approve the campaign goal, plan, and leadership.

Although some of the same individuals may continue into the next stage, the campaign planning committee typically disbands once the board approves the campaign and the quiet phase officially begins, to be succeeded by a campaign **leadership committee**. The latter may be called the campaign **steering committee**, the campaign **executive committee**, the **campaign cabinet**, or by some other term.

Traditionally, it was common to have a single **campaign chair**, who was a major donor and prominent leader, usually a member of the organization's governing board. In recent years, however, it has become common to enlist campaign cochairs, who share the responsibility of campaign leadership (Kihlstedt, 2010). This approach offers the advantages of sharing the workload and making it possible for the campaign to establish visible leadership that is diverse, perhaps better able than a single chair to represent the campaign to various constituencies.

One question often discussed is the amount of gift commitment that should be required of top campaign leaders. Historically, it was customary that the campaign chair also would be the top donor to the campaign. That assured he or she would be able to solicit any gift to the campaign, since all would be equal to or less than he or she had made. This approach still offers that advantage and is demonstrated in some campaigns. However, there are downsides. One is that the top donor may be someone not able to devote sufficient time to the campaign to offer the active leadership it requires. For example, if the top donor is an older person or a senior executive with a demanding schedule, he or she may be able to make a substantial gift but not provide hands-on leadership in the campaign. The other shortcoming in the traditional model is that the lead donor may not reflect the organization's overall constituency; that individual's gift may be valuable, but he or she may not offer a profile to which other donors will relate. A commonly expressed standard today is that the gift commitments of volunteer leaders of the campaign must be perceived as sacrificial in proportion to their financial capacity—that is, **stretch gifts**—but need not be the largest gifts to the campaign (Fredericks, 2010).

The chair or cochairs of the campaign are supported by committees that have responsibility for cultivation and solicitation. In the case of a relatively modest campaign, a single steering committee or executive committee may be all that is needed. In larger campaigns, especially for institutions with constituencies that are geographically dispersed, the volunteer structure is more complex. The campaign needs to engage enough volunteers to cultivate and solicit prospects and to provide a visible presence at campaign events. On the other hand, it is inadvisable to create a volunteer structure that is *more* than the campaign requires. The latter can create an administrative burden that will occupy the time and effort of development staff and require numerous meetings that become a diversion from direct fundraising activity.

A 2009 study of campaigns (Worth, 2010) identified four basic models for organizing campaign volunteer committees: by gift level or phase of the campaign; by sources of support; by unit, program, or project; and by geography.

In some campaigns, one committee is responsible for soliciting lead gifts (or advance gifts) during the quiet phase and then another takes the lead in soliciting major gifts in the early stages of the public phase. A general-gifts committee then may become activated as the campaign shifts to that stage. In other words, the committees are developed and activated sequentially with each phase of the campaign (Pierpont, 2003).

Sometimes committees are organized by source of support; for example, there may be a committee focused on soliciting corporate gifts and others on individual donor constituencies, for example, alumni of a college, local businesses, former patients, and so forth. In large, decentralized organizations, committees are often organized to focus on the objectives of individual administrative units, programs that are the focus of campaign objectives,

FIGURE 11.2   Campaign Volunteer Structure

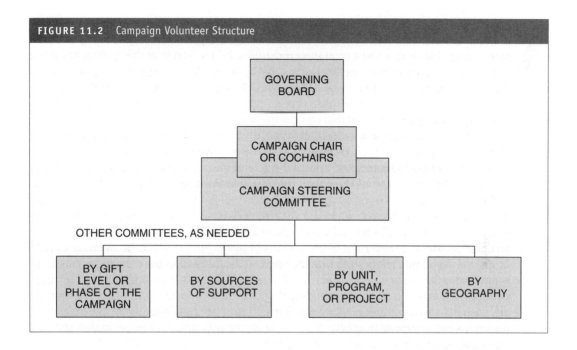

or projects encompassed by the campaign. This is common in universities, where a committee is focused on each of various colleges and schools. Finally, if the campaign is to be conducted in various communities or regions, it is typical to organize committees of volunteers to concentrate in each of those areas (McGoldrick & Robell, 2002).

Figure 11.2 depicts a typical volunteer organization for a campaign, but again, it is important to emphasize that the structure should be aligned with the constituencies of the particular organization and the fundraising tasks to be carried out (Pierpont, 2003). Enlisting volunteers without real need is counterproductive and can lead to excessive demands on campaign staff and the possibility of disillusioned volunteers (Weinstein, 2009).

Gift Acceptance and Crediting Policies

The dollar goal achievable in a comprehensive campaign is determined in part by what types of gifts will be accepted and how they will be credited toward the goal. Gift acceptance policies usually are developed with regard to a specific campaign, but well-managed organizations also have generic **gift acceptance policies** that also apply in noncampaign environments. (A fuller discussion of gift acceptance policies is thus deferred to Chapter 12 of this text.)

Policies describing how gifts will be valued and credited are most important in a campaign environment (Kihlstedt, 2010). For example, planners will need to decide if only outright gifts will be counted toward the campaign goal or whether deferred gifts and expectancies also will be counted in some manner. That decision has a significant influence on what overall goal may be attainable. An argument can be made for counting deferred gifts (e.g., charitable remainder trusts), since the donor gives the money now and that decision is irrevocable. But how should such gifts be counted toward the goal of the campaign—at their face value or at their remainder value? That is, at the amount expected to remain for the nonprofit after the last income beneficiary stops receiving payments? And what about bequests? There may be donors who, during the course of the campaign, inform the organization that they have made provision for an eventual bequest to its endowment or for some other purpose. But that commitment is revocable by the donor at any time. No cash has been received, and indeed, the date at which it might be received is impossible to predict; it likely will not be received during the official period of the campaign. Should the bequest intention be credited toward the goal of the campaign? If so, in what amount? Counting it may not make much sense if the objective of the campaign is a building, since it likely will be completed long before the gift is received. But what if the campaign includes a goal for endowment? Exactly when the gift is received may not be that critical. Some argue that bequest expectancies should usually be credited in some way, so that the donors will feel appreciated and keep their bequest plans in place. Not crediting the expectancy may be like saying to the donor, "Well, thanks, but you have not supported our campaign, which is our highest priority." On the other hand, if those funds really do not address the objectives of the campaign, then counting them could result in reaching the goal but without any cash in hand. For these reasons, the question may be answered one way in some campaigns and another way in others; it depends on the objectives of the campaign and also the organization's thinking about donor relations.

Campaign accounting questions have sometimes been a topic of debate. Various institutions may adopt different policies, making it impossible to compare campaigns on the top line, without digging into more detailed data on what has been counted (Light & Stratton, 2014). In an effort to offer uniformity and facilitate benchmarking across higher education institutions, the Council for Advancement and Support of Education developed voluntary reporting standards that recommend policies on the crediting of various types of gifts toward comprehensive campaign goals (CASE, 2009). With regard to the counting of planned gifts in campaign totals, the CASE standards suggest reporting revocable and irrevocable gifts in separate categories and offer the following guidance:

> Institutions may want to consider age requirements for inclusion of these types of gifts. For example, no inclusion if the intended donor is less than 50 years of age; inclusion at discounted value if individual is between 50 years of age and 69 years of age; inclusion at full face value if 70 years of age or older.
>
> In the case of externally managed irrevocable life income trusts that allow the donor to change the charitable beneficiary, because the designation is not irrevocably pledged to the institution, it should be counted as a revocable gift, at face value, and in the revocable gift category. (CASE, 2008)

Solicitation Strategies

Think back to the point made earlier in this chapter about the shortcomings of traditional capital campaigns. They may cause donors to focus their giving entirely on the capital project that is the objective of the campaign, possibly reducing or suspending their annual giving or giving to other purposes of the organization. That risk also exists in a comprehensive campaign in which various objectives are presented but some are identified as featured objectives. **Solicitation strategies** help avoid this risk.

One strategy is known as the **separate ask** (Dove, 2000) or the **dual ask** (Schroeder, 2003). The donor is solicited for a gift to a capital objective, such as a new building, but is told that annual-fund solicitations will continue as before. The donor is then solicited for an annual gift on the usual schedule, perhaps at the end of the year. This is a simple strategy, but it has some downsides. It is possible that the donor will become confused, or irritated, if the annual-fund solicitation arrives not long after he or she has made a capital pledge. And it is possible that the donor simply will not respond to the annual-fund solicitation, feeling that he or she already has given to the organization (Dove, 2000).

A strategy intended to overcome the shortcomings of the separate ask is called the **double ask** (Dove, 2000; Kihlstedt, 2010), also called the **combined ask** (Schroeder, 2003). Using this strategy, the donor is asked to make a pledge to the campaign, with some portion designated for a capital purpose and another portion identified as that person's annual-fund gift each year for the duration of the campaign. This strategy protects the annual fund and helps to communicate the message that annual giving is important, while also avoiding the necessity of soliciting the donor's annual gift every year during the campaign. But there is still the risk that the donor will not fully understand the distinction and will say something like, "I'll just give every year and you divide it up however you want" (Dove, 2000, p. 87). And by the time the pledge is completed, perhaps years from now, the donor may have forgotten the details of the arrangement, consider his or her commitment finished, and not resume regular annual giving.

A third strategy is the **triple ask** (Dove, 2000). The donor is asked to consider a commitment that encompasses a gift toward a capital project, an annual gift over the campaign period, and a planned gift. The disadvantages are similar to those of the double ask, and in addition, this is a sophisticated proposal some fundraisers and donors may find a little too complex. But it may be appropriate in a comprehensive campaign that includes a capital project, the annual fund, and an endowment. Again, if the overall commitment includes a planned gift toward the endowment component of the campaign, how to value and credit it is a relevant question.

Crowdfunding

Recall from Chapter 4 that crowdfunding is a method used to raise funds online. It is not an effective method for soliciting ongoing or regular support for an organization, which requires building an ongoing relationship that leads to renewal and upgrading, as discussed in Chapter 6. Crowdfunding also is likely to be a less effective method for soliciting major gifts. What about in a campaign, especially one focused on a discrete project, that is, a traditional capital campaign? Is there a role for crowdfunding in that situation?

In order to be successful, a crowdfunding appeal needs to go viral. That may only occur if it is something especially exciting or urgent. If the organization intends to raise the funds from its established constituency, then other strategies may be more effective in reaching them. According to Bray (2013), crowdfunding may be an effective strategy only under specific and limited circumstances, including the following:

- [The organization] has a particular, tangible goal in mind—such as a new piece of equipment; a trip to project site; medical care for an individual; production of a film; or a time-delineated concept around which to fundraise, such as a matching grant.

- [The organization] can confidently predict that the goal is sufficiently exciting, moving, or fun that [its] existing supporters and social media contacts will tell their friends about it and they, despite knowing little to nothing about [the] organization, will be moved to pitch in.

- [The organization] has the skills to present the idea in an attractive way, preferably complete with photos, graphics, and videos.

- [The organization] has supporters who will create tangential pages connected to [the] nonprofit's master page (as is allowed on some sites), on which they ask friends and connections to give. (pp. 104–105)

In sum, crowdfunding may be an appropriate solicitation strategy in connection with some specific projects in the context of a campaign, but it is not a substitute for the more complex methods of major-gifts fundraising and campaigns we have discussed.

Naming Opportunities

Campaigns often include specific **naming** (or **recognition**) **opportunities** related to major gifts that address campaign objectives. For example, these often include the naming of buildings, components of buildings (e.g., wings or rooms), endowment funds, and units of the larger organization (e.g., centers, institutes, schools, programs).

Some organizations have a generic donor recognition policy in place whether in a campaign or not, but such a policy is most essential when a campaign is underway. Naming opportunities relate to levels in the gift table and are presented to attract the interest of potential donors at those levels (Kihlstedt, 2010). But a clear policy, established as a part of campaign planning, is necessary to assure that recognition of donors is both appropriate and equitable.

For example, think about a situation in which a donor to a capital campaign has pledged $100,000, to be paid in five annual installments, and has been recognized with naming of a conference room in the organization's new building. Another donor sees the name on the door of the room and asks how much would be required to name the identical conference room across the hall. The reasonable answer would be $100,000. But what if the donor says that he or she can only give $50,000? Should the nonprofit accept the gift? Or, what if the donor says that he or she could give $100,000 but only if the pledge could be paid over ten years, instead of five? Absent a recognition policy, the decision whether to accept either offer would need to be made on an ad hoc basis and presents some obvious risks. Accepting either offer from the second donor could offend the first donor, who gave $100,000 over five years and might feel that he or she had been treated unfairly. But rejecting both offers could deny the organization either $50,000 or $100,000 that it might otherwise receive. Assuming there are no other donors lined up to name the second conference room, this additional gift revenue is available at no additional cost to the organization, and it may be tempted to accept it. There are often no simple answers to such dilemmas, which involve ethical as well as practical implications.

Absent a donor recognition policy, the risks of a decision are high because it may become personal. If the CEO or chief development officer is making the calls on a case-by-case basis, their relationships with the effected donors can be jeopardized. It is important for them to be able to rely on a clear policy that has been endorsed by the governing board and the campaign leadership committee in advance. Of course, there may be occasions when an exception should be made, but those decisions should be assigned to a committee rather than left to the discretion of individual administrative officers.

Financing the Campaign

A campaign usually requires resources beyond the normal fundraising budget, possibly including additional staff positions, funds for events and publications, travel, and other costs. There are various approaches to financing such additional expenditures (Matthews & Linett, 2009).

The most common method is to simply include the campaign, or some of it, as a line item in the organization's operating budget, with the assumption that an expanded fundraising effort will be continued even after the campaign ends (Matthews & Linett, 2009). Another approach is to use unrestricted gifts to finance the campaign; since those gifts are unrestricted, they can be used for this or any other purpose. In addition, some restricted gifts may be budget relieving, freeing up previously budgeted funds that can be reallocated to meet campaign expenses. In a traditional capital campaign, the costs of fundraising are sometimes identified explicitly as a component of the project budget.

Some public institutions face a challenge in financing a campaign if they are prevented from spending public dollars on fundraising. Institutions in that position use a variety of methods for generating campaign budget support. Some levy a charge against endowment income, an administrative services fee. Some charge what is commonly called a **gift tax**, that is, a percentage of gifts and/or bequests applied to operating expenses, including fundraising. Some use interest earned on the short-term investment of gift funds between the time of their receipt and transfer to an institutional account for expenditure (Holmes, 2010). If any such devices are used, they should be clearly disclosed in communications with donors.

CAMPAIGN PROS AND CONS

A campaign offers significant benefits and may be the most effective strategy for meeting the financial needs of a nonprofit organization or institution. Among those benefits may be the following:

- Preparing for a campaign may focus the organization on thinking about its future. Although a campaign is usually considered a strategy for implementing a strategic plan, in many cases the desire to have a campaign also brings discipline and urgency to the strategic planning process. Strategic planning can go on for a long time, but it may move more quickly when a campaign is known to be on the horizon.

- A campaign, with a specific goal and deadline, motivates donors to increase their giving and enables them to extend payments of a large pledge over a period of years (Association of Fundraising Professionals, 2009).

- A campaign builds and engages the organization's volunteer leadership (Association of Fundraising Professionals, 2009).

- A campaign changes the conversation with prospects and donors and provides an opportunity for discussing the organization's plans and goals (Lamberjack & Plourde, 2013). Rather than "we would like to come and talk with you about a gift," the campaign discussion begins with "we would like to come and talk with you about the future of our organization" (Worth, 2010).

- The visibility of the campaign also provides wider benefits in terms of marketing and communications, expanding the organization's standing in its community (Association of Fundraising Professionals, 2009).

- A campaign maximizes the impact of social influences on donor motivation.

- A campaign may have a positive impact on annual giving, with benefits extending beyond the period of the campaign itself (Association of Fundraising Professionals, 2009). In other words, it raises donor sights over the long haul.

The latter effect is illustrated in Figure 11.3, adapted from the work of John Cash (2007), a senior consultant with the consulting firm of Marts & Lundy.[4] The lower dashed line shows the trend of gift revenue that would be expected to occur without the campaign, gradually rising over the years. As the upper, solid line shows, gift revenue increases in the early years of the campaign, as new pledges are made and payments are completed. This campaign-responsive additional revenue, which Cash calls the **campaign premium**, eventually declines as pledges are completed and the campaign winds down. But ongoing gift revenue does not return to the precampaign trend line. Annual and capital giving continue to grow over future years, but at a higher level. The difference is what Cash (2007) identifies as **postcampaign value**.

But some people argue that campaigns also have disadvantages and are not always the best strategy. Arguments that ongoing programs for annual giving, major gifts, and planned giving may be more appropriate have a long history (Dove, 2000; Kelly, 1998; Smith, 1993). Some of the arguments were mentioned in Chapter 5 of this book, including the concern that a comprehensive campaign in which every gift is counted may produce some gifts that do not address the organization's greatest needs. A bottom-line goal may be achieved but include gifts that have limited utility to the nonprofit organization (Smith, 1993).

It also could be argued that campaigns are not well-aligned with the attitudes of donors in the twenty-first century. Many corporations and foundations are not responsive to

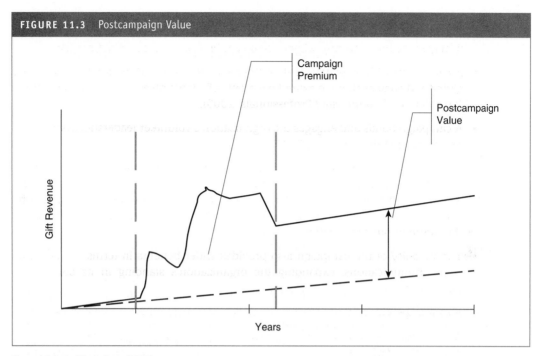

FIGURE 11.3   Postcampaign Value

Source: Adapted from Cash (2007).

campaigns and follow the concept of strategic philanthropy, supporting causes and organizations that align with their own goals and priorities. In addition, some individual donors—for example, the entrepreneurial donors we discussed earlier—are becoming more like corporations and foundations in their thinking. Many prefer to support programs with specific and observable impacts, rather than the traditional campaign objectives of annual giving, buildings, and endowment.

The demographic trends discussed in Chapter 8 suggest that planned gifts will become increasingly important, and the timing of such gifts may not coincide with the artificial timetable imposed by a campaign. It could be argued that trying to force giving into the deadlines and priorities of a campaign may be less productive over time than a more nurturing approach that emphasizes developing a relationship with the donor, identifying a donor's needs and priorities, thoughtfully matching donor needs and priorities with the organization's plans, and soliciting the gift only when the donor is ready—an approach that an ongoing program might accommodate better than a time-based campaign. Finally, our society has changed. People do not live in small communities; they are mobile and are influenced by social media and other forces. In this environment, it would be reasonable to argue that traditional ideas about proportionate giving, sequential fundraising, and impressive lead gifts are less relevant than in the past.

TWENTY-FIRST-CENTURY CAMPAIGNS

A campaign is not the right strategy for every organization facing every need. But the campaign strategy continues to be widely employed. In a 2011 survey, 53 percent of non-profit organizations with budgets exceeding $3 million were either engaged in or planning a campaign; the proportion of those with budgets between $1 million and $3 million was somewhat smaller, at 42 percent (Nonprofit Research Collaborative, 2011). And, of course, the nation's economy had not yet fully recovered from recession by 2011, possibly delaying the implementation of campaigns by some organizations.

Some of the potential downsides of campaigns do not relate to campaigns as a strategy per se but rather to their planning and execution. For example, concerns about the utility of gifts may arise when campaign objectives are not specific and gift-crediting policies are excessively broad. As discussed in Chapter 5 of this text, unless fundraising goals and objectives are rooted in the organization's mission and grounded in its strategic plan, there is the risk that campaigns may produce dollars on the bottom line but also lead to mission drift (Burk, 2003; Froelich, 1999).

Changing donor attitudes and methods are a reality. But campaigns also have evolved. Longer campaigns, especially common in higher education, provide the time needed to cultivate relationships. Comprehensive campaigns that encompass a range of objectives make it possible to propose gifts aligned with particular donor interests and circumstances, encompassing annual, capital, and endowment purposes and including outright as well as testamentary and deferred gifts. And for many nonprofit organizations and institutions, campaigns continue to offer nonfinancial benefits, including increased visibility, enhanced volunteer engagement, and opportunities to build a culture of philanthropy, all of which may have a long-run impact on philanthropic support.

CHAPTER SUMMARY

A campaign is a fundraising strategy, usually intended to increase major gifts.

Principles applied in campaigns had origins in earlier centuries, especially in the practices of consultants who dominated the field in the first half of the twentieth century. There are three basic types of campaign—*traditional capital campaigns*, *comprehensive campaigns*, and focused or *special-purpose campaigns*, defined by the scope of objectives encompassed and constituencies solicited (Dove, 2000).

A campaign is a fundraising initiative that has an announced goal and deadline, is undertaken to meet specific objectives, uses rated prospect lists and specific asks, follows the principle of sequential fundraising, engages organized volunteer leadership, and emphasizes major gifts.

Campaigns are conducted in phases, including a *quiet phase* and a *public phase* (Lindahl, 2008). The quiet phase encompasses the organization's strategic planning; an assessment of readiness for the campaign, applying established criteria; completion of a feasibility study (in many cases) to test preliminary goals and objectives established in planning; and the solicitation of *lead gifts* or *advance gifts* that comprise the *nucleus fund*. The nucleus fund comprises 40 to 60 percent of the final goal. The campaign is announced at an event known as the *kickoff*, which begins the public phase. Solicitations in the public phase remain focused on major gifts and follow the principle of *sequential fundraising*. Later in the public phase the emphasis shifts to *general gifts*, in what Lindahl (2008) calls the *goal-line phase*. The campaign concludes with a *victory celebration*, which is usually an event.

The *gift table* (or gift chart or gift-range chart) is a tool for campaign planning, management, and evaluation. The table depicts the amount and number of gifts required at various levels to achieve the campaign goal and is constructed following some established principles, generally including a lead gift of 10 percent of the goal, the *rule of thirds* (Seymour, 1966), and a *conversion rate* that dictates the number of prospects required to produce one gift at each level (Kihlstedt, 2010). Some say that traditional principles are less valid today, since campaigns are receiving higher proportions of their goals from fewer gifts in larger amounts. Organizations also depart from traditional gift table assumptions to address particular circumstances.

Planning and preparing for a campaign require that the organization make strategic decisions in several areas, including dollar goals; *objectives, featured objectives*, and *priorities* of the campaign; the structure of the volunteer organization; gift acceptance and counting policies specific to the campaign; solicitation strategies; recognition opportunities to be offered to donors at various gift levels; and sources of funds to meet campaign costs. In comprehensive campaigns, a decision needs to be made about whether and how to value and count deferred gifts and expectancies.

Three basic solicitation strategies are applied, in order to preserve annual giving and planned giving in the context of a campaign featuring capital projects. With the *separate ask* strategy, donors are solicited for a capital gift and then are solicited for a gift to the annual fund on a different occasion. The *double ask* strategy involves soliciting a donor for one commitment to the campaign that encompasses both a capital gift and an annual gift for each year during the campaign period. A *triple ask* includes a commitment encompassing an annual gift, a capital gift, and a planned gift (Dove, 2000; McGoldrick & Robell, 2002).

Campaigns offer multiple benefits to nonprofit organizations and institutions, including discipline and focus in planning; greater visibility of plans and goals, which may enhance overall marketing and communication efforts; effects on donor motivation that call forth larger and timely gifts; and a context in which solicitations can be discussions about plans and aspirations for the future. There also may be an impact on giving after conclusion of the campaign (Cash, 2007).

But the campaign strategy has pros and cons. Some critics express concern that campaigns may produce gifts that are not of high utility to the organization and argue that such a strategy is not well suited to the attitudes and giving methods of donors today. A campaign is not always the best strategy for an organization to pursue, and ongoing programs for annual giving, major gifts, and planned giving may be more appropriate in some circumstances. However, the campaign has evolved to address concerns and continues to be launched by nonprofit organizations in significant number, especially in periods of strength in the economy and financial markets.

Key Terms and Concepts

Appeal (in contrast to
campaign)
Campaign cabinet
Campaign chair
Campaign premium
Capital campaigns
(traditional or
historical)
Collection (in contrast
to campaign)
Combined campaign
Comprehensive
campaigns
Double ask
(combined ask)
Executive committee
Feasibility study
(campaign
planning study)

General gifts
Gift acceptance policy
Gift-range chart
Gift tax
Goal
Goal-line phase
Kickoff
Leadership
committee
Lead gifts (advance
gifts)
Naming (recognition)
opportunities
Needs list
Nucleus fund
Objectives (featured
objectives)
Phases (of campaign)
Plateau of fatigue

Postcampaign value
Priorities (strategic
priorities)
Prospect pool
Public phase
Quiet phase
Rule of thirds
Separate ask
(dual ask)
Solicitation
strategies
Special-purpose
(special-project,
focused)
campaign
Steering committee
Stretch gift
Triple ask
Victory celebration

Case 11.1: Keeping Our Promise: 40th Anniversary Capital Campaign for N Street Village

To secure the funds necessary to complete capital repairs and improvements . . . and to best equip us to continue on our path of strategic growth, we are launching a three-year capital campaign. With the help of committed volunteer leadership and financial support from the community, we intend to complete this $9 million campaign and open our newly renovated and expanded facilities by 2016.

Together [as a result of the campaign] we will:

- Expand our programs and increase our impact.

- Preserve affordable housing for 51 families and 63 women at our flagship site, and 20 women at Miriam's House.

- Expand our permanent supportive housing by 10%.

- Increase safety and hospitality by expanding our day center, creating secure entry points into our buildings, and creating new private meeting rooms.

- Build our Strategic Growth Fund and operating reserves to enable N Street Village to respond to emerging needs and to capitalize on new opportunities.

Gifts to the Keeping Our Promise capital campaign may be made in cash, stocks, bonds, and mutual funds. The gift of assets whose value and risk are not easily determinable (e.g., real estate, stock options) will be considered on a case-by-case basis. Gifts may be fulfilled over five years. All gifts made in support of the campaign will be tax-deductible to the fullest extent of the law.

SOURCE: http://www.nstreetvillage.org/capitalcampaign/, accessed May 21, 2014.

Case 11.2: Our Transformation: The Campaign for the North Carolina Museum of Art

In order to sustain our expanded facilities, support key areas, and build the endowment, the NCMA is in the process of a historic fund-raising campaign. The Campaign has four major goals to help secure future growth and sustainability.

1. *Endowment $20 million.* The importance of a strong institutional endowment cannot be overstated. Endowments at the North Carolina Museum of Art are no exception, as they enhance our ability to protect the institution from fluctuations in earned income sources and membership fees and sustain the Museum's collections and programs into the future.

2. *Museum Programs $10 million.* Every year the Museum provides countless programs for a variety of audiences, including teachers; college students; adults; preschoolers; families; museum professionals; and grade school, middle school, and high school students. For all audiences the Museum's exceptional art collection remains at the core of our programs.

3. *Museum Grounds $10 million.* The expanded Museum campus offers unparalleled opportunities to engage with art and nature. The courtyards and gardens intersecting the new gallery building, including the Rodin sculpture garden, bring the outdoors in. Dramatic sculptures abound in the landscape, and monumental contemporary works of art grace the 164-acre Museum Park.

4. *General Operating Support $10 million.* Unrestricted general operating support, critical to our long-term success, provides the Museum with the greatest flexibility to respond to its highest priorities.

SOURCE: http://www.ncartmuseum.org/campaign/, accessed May 22, 2014.

Case 11.3: White Plains Hospital: The Time Is Now Campaign

White Plains Hospital is engaged in the most important capital campaign in its almost 120-year history. The Time is Now Campaign is a $100 million dollar initiative that will help meet the region's demand for critical health services long into the future.

The campaign focuses on three areas that will have the greatest impact on our patients: infrastructure, technology and a superbly trained clinical staff. The projects will add 42,000 square feet of space, expand clinical space by 28% and include the following:

- Green buildings and sustainable construction

- A new six-story patient care building

- 24 new private patient rooms

- Five state-of-the-art operating rooms/surgical suites

- Expanded Outpatient Radiology Center

- New entrance and lobby

As a non-profit organization, White Plains Hospital depends on donations to maintain and improve our exceptional facilities and services. In fact, individuals, foundations and corporations have provided all of the funds for the Hospital's three prior capital campaigns. We are deeply proud and grateful for your community support and welcome your leadership and involvement as we embark on The Time is Now Campaign to transform your Hospital.

SOURCE: http://www.givetowphospital.org/The-Time-is-Now-Campaign.aspx, accessed May 22, 2014.

Case 11.4: Howard University: Bridging the Gap Student Aid Campaign

Since its founding in 1867, Howard University has answered the call to educate deserving young men and women, regardless of their financial circumstances. Unfortunately today, the nation's economic crisis has put a tremendous strain on many of our students. Pay cuts and unemployment continue to reduce or eliminate family contributions and federal student aid is limited; leaving many students to question . . . how will I pay for my Howard degree?

In response, President Sidney A. Ribeau launched the Bridging the Gap Student Aid Campaign in March 2012 to raise $25 million in current-use and endowed scholarship and fellowship assistance that will directly address the gaps in financial aid for deserving Howard students.

The campaign also addresses four related goals:

1. *Enhance Student Retention and Enrollment:* Nearly 10% of Howard's students have dropped classes for financial reasons, which delays and often prevents students from graduating. Last year, 600 students were unable to continue their enrollment as a direct result of their inability to meet financial obligations.

2. *Increase Overall Graduation Rates:* Howard's four-year graduation rate is less than 50%, with more students taking longer to obtain their degree and, in many cases, taking time off to pay for their educations.

3. *Reduce Student Indebtedness:* Last year, Howard awarded students more than $80 million in institutional aid. Only one third of the aid awarded was scholarships and grants, loans made up 64%.

4. *Increase Student Involvement in Enrichment Activities:* Students who must obtain employment to pay for their studies often work in excess of 25 hours a week. This tends to impede academic success and prevent full participation in enrichment activities, thwarting a well-rounded education.

Today, almost 90% of Howard students require some form of financial aid including scholarships. Yet, it is often not enough for them to achieve their dream of graduating from Howard and pursuing their careers without additional support.

In these challenging times, a successful campaign is essential to Howard's ability to remain true to its legacy and ensure that its students have access to an excellent education. Your generous support will significantly strengthen our ability to respond to the demonstrated needs of our students.

SOURCE: http://www.howard.edu/bridgingthegap/goals.htm, accessed May 22, 2014.

Questions for Discussion

Consider the following questions with regard to the campaigns described in Cases 11.1 through 11.4. (The cases are based on information obtained from the organizations' websites at the time of this writing.)

1. What type of campaign is each—capital, comprehensive, or special purpose?

2. What should the policy be regarding planned gifts that are expectancies or deferred? Would it be appropriate to count them toward the campaign goal in light of the campaign's objectives? Are there objectives of the campaign toward which such gifts could be counted and others toward which they should not? Describe the pros and cons of various approaches to counting bequests in the campaign.

3. In light of the campaign objectives in each case, what might be the advantages and disadvantages of a single-ask, double-ask, or triple-ask solicitation strategy?

4. Thinking back on the discussion in previous chapters and considering the objectives identified in each of the campaigns, which types of donors (individuals, corporations, foundations) may be the most promising constituencies in each case?

5. Thinking about the pros and cons of campaigns discussed in this chapter, is a campaign obviously the best strategy for obtaining the resources needed in each case? Or might an ongoing program also have been a successful strategy? Explain.

Suggestions for Further Reading

Books

Dove, K. E. (2000). *Conducting a successful capital campaign* (2nd ed.). San Francisco: Jossey-Bass.

Kihlstedt, A. (2010). *Capital campaign strategies that work*. Sudbury, MA: Jones and Bartlett.

Worth, M. J. (2010). *Leading the campaign*. Lanham, MD: Rowman & Littlefield and American Council on Education.

Articles

Lindahl, W. E. (2008). Three-phase capital campaigns. *Nonprofit Management and Leadership, 18*(3), 261–273.

Lysakowski, L. (2002, November). The importance of volunteers in a capital campaign. *International Journal of Nonprofit & Voluntary Sector Marketing, 7*(4), 325–334.

Nehls, K. (2012, April). Leadership transitions during fundraising campaigns. *Innovative Higher Education, 37*(2), 89–103.

Article Series

Note: On September 21, 2013, Harvard University announced a campaign for $6.5 billion, the largest undertaken in higher education to that date. The *Harvard Crimson* covered preparations for the campaign in a series of five articles, listed here, in order, which provide insights into the process and strategic decisions made.

Kansra, N., & Weinstock, S. Y. (2013, April 29). Centralizing through capital campaign priorities. *Harvard Crimson*, retrieved May 23, 2014, from http://www.thecrimson.com/article/2013/4/29/one-university-capital-campaign.

Ferreol, M. D. L., & Lucky, J. T. (2013, April 30). College looks to profit from capital campaign. *Harvard Crimson*, retrieved May 23, 2014, from http://www.thecrimson.com/article/2013/4/30/college-capital-campaign-priorities.

Fandos, N. P. (2013, May 1). Anticipating capital campaign, FAS sets priorities. *Harvard Crimson*, retrieved May 23, 2014, from http://www.thecrimson.com/article/2013/5/1/fas-capital-campaign-options.

Kansra, N., & Weinstock, S. Y. (2013, May 2). Administrators travel, schmooze donors as capital campaign approaches. *Harvard Crimson*, retrieved May 23, 2014, from http://www.thecrimson.com/article/2013/5/2/capital-campaign-donations.

Anasu, L., & Auritt, E. S. (2013, May 3). Harvard eyes internal, external models for capital campaign. *Harvard Crimson*, retrieved May 23, 2014, from http://www.thecrimson.com/article/2013/5/3/capital-campaign-2013.

Notes

1. Some content in this chapter includes concepts and ideas also expressed in earlier works of mine, including *Leading the Campaign* (Worth, 2010). Specific adaptations from such earlier works are cited as such.

2. Some authors identify major gifts, special gifts, and general gifts as three stages in the public phase. The term *special gifts* has become less common in this context.

3. The gift table is sometimes called a *gift-range chart* or a *standards-of-giving chart*. Its format is that of a table, and that term is used in this text.

4. Concepts in Cash's presentation were developed by Darrow Zeindenstein and Marts & Lundy. Used with permission of Marts & Lundy.

CHAPTER 12

Managing Fundraising Programs

$\mathbf{F}$or most of the twentieth century, fundraising was based on the accumulated wisdom of practitioners and was regarded mostly as an art, passed down from one generation of fundraisers to another at professional conferences and through occasional articles or books, most of which were filled with anecdotes. And most of the discussion involved interactions with donors rather than internal management. Few nonprofit organizations or institutions maintained full-time development staff positions prior to the 1960s, and when they did, the staff included one or a few people. Fundraising was undertaken primarily by CEOs and volunteers, so there was little need for management of the fundraising function. Larger staffs have been developed only in the past couple of decades, and some development offices now employ dozens or even hundreds of people.

Fundraising budgets have become larger, and philanthropic revenues have become more critical to the survival and growth of nonprofit organizations and institutions. In this environment, the effectiveness and efficiency of fundraising programs has gained the attention of researchers, governing boards, sophisticated donors, and sometimes the news media. Fundraising programs need to be managed in order to address both variables—revenues and costs. In sum, fundraising is no longer merely an art, practiced at the periphery of nonprofit organizations; it is an important and complex specialty of nonprofit management.

Topics related to the management of fundraising have been presented in earlier chapters of this text in specific contexts. For example, Chapters 4 and 5 both described tools for analyzing fundraising programs and focusing resources on the most promising constituencies. Tools for prospect development, including prospect research, data mining, and predictive modeling, were discussed in Chapter 5. Techniques of analysis intended to gain efficiency in programs, including profiling and targeting, were outlined in Chapter 6, which also mentioned issues related to the return on investment in fundraising. Chapter 7 addressed standards for evaluating the performance of major-gifts officers, and the discussion of campaigns in Chapter 11 included tools used to monitor and manage the progress of those efforts.

This chapter examines management topics from the perspective of the overall fundraising program, in four broad areas: managing costs, evaluating programs and allocating resources, managing information systems and development office operations, and establishing policies to guide fundraising and the acceptance of gifts. The following chapter considers the organization and management of fundraising staff.

INVESTING IN FUNDRAISING

Nonprofit organizations spend money to support various activities, including programs, general operations, capacity building, and fundraising. Fundraising is more than an expense, however; it can be viewed as an *investment* that produces revenue to support an organization's operations and programs.

One of the first studies to focus on the performance of fundraising programs was a pioneering effort undertaken by the American College Public Relations Association in 1966. The study examined programs in 105 colleges and universities and reached a conclusion that seems quaint by today's standards: "there are indicators which can be applied to evaluate [fundraising] performance, . . . certain quantitative measures can be made, and . . . the means (primarily electronic equipment) to obtain and analyze quantitative factors are readily available" (Heneman, 1969, p. x). Another landmark effort to measure and compare fundraising and other institutional advancement costs in higher education, known as the "Lilly Study" because of its sponsorship by the Lilly Endowment, was undertaken in 1990 by CASE (Kroll, 2012). From 1999 to 2004, the Urban Institute and the Indiana University Center on Philanthropy (now the Lilly Family School of Philanthropy) conducted an overhead cost project that looked across the nonprofit sector, resulting in numerous papers and reports (Wing, Hager, Rooney, & Pollak, 2004). In 2006, the Fundraising Effectiveness Project was initiated by the National Center for Charitable Statistics, part of the Urban Institute, and AFP. The project includes an annual survey of nonprofits and published reports. And in 2011, CASE expanded on the earlier Lilly study by initiating the Advancement Investment Metrics Study (Kroll, 2012). In addition, for-profit consulting firms and vendors of fundraising products have published related reports (e.g., Blackbaud, 2013; Wealth Engine, 2013). And there have been dissertations and peer-reviewed articles that offer sometimes highly complex methods for evaluating the performance of fundraising programs (e.g., Yi, 2010). Some of these sources will be cited again in the discussion below. But first, let's look at some fundamental terms and concepts.

Efficiency and Effectiveness

Two concepts need to be distinguished when evaluating fundraising programs: **efficiency** and **effectiveness**. Kelly (1998) offers succinct definitions: efficiency is "a measure of the proportion of resources used to produce outputs or attain inputs-cost ratios," whereas effectiveness "is measured by comparing the results achieved with the results sought" (p. 428). As Kelly further observes, "Although efficiency may help an organization be more effective, the two concepts are not interchangeable" (p. 428). Indeed, some argue that an emphasis on efficiency may in fact work against the effectiveness of organizations by discouraging investment in capacity. Unfortunately, efficiency (expressed in terms of low **overhead**) often has dominated the public dialogue about nonprofits (Pallotta, 2010).

Efficiency is a measure noted to some extent by two of the best-known charity watchdogs, the Better Business Bureau Wise Giving Alliance and Charity Navigator. The BBB Charity Accountability Standards mostly include recommended best practices; that is, they suggest what nonprofits should *do* with regard to how they govern, ways in which they spend money, the truthfulness of their representations, and disclosure of basic information to the public (Better Business Bureau Wise Giving Alliance, 2014). Notably, the BBB does not attempt to evaluate the effectiveness of nonprofits in achieving their missions; the standards require only that organizations measure results, according to their own methodologies. In two areas, however, the BBB standards do relate to efficiency, requiring that at least 65 percent of a nonprofit's expenditures be devoted to support of programs, rather than administration or fundraising, and that fundraising expenses be no more than 35 percent of contributions (BBB Wise Giving Alliance, 2014). The BBB does allow some flexibility, permitting organizations that do not meet these standards to provide reasonable explanation.

Charity Navigator's approach is different from that of the BBB and is evolving. Charity Navigator rates organizations using a four-star scale, based in part on financial ratios, obtained from Form 990s. Two of the ratios are the percentage of its total expenses that go for fundraising and how much it spends to generate one dollar in charitable contributions, the latter determined by dividing fundraising expenses by total gifts received. Charity Navigator defines the ratio as a measure of fundraising "efficiency."

Before 2011, financial ratios were the only data Charity Navigator used in its ratings of nonprofits. It subsequently incorporated measures of accountability and transparency, moving somewhat more in the direction of the BBB approach. In 2015, Charity Navigator was working to incorporate mission-related results in its ratings in future years. But financial ratios, including fundraising efficiency, will continue to be among the criteria on which its ratings will be based.

The emphasis on efficiency measures has come under increasing scrutiny in recent years. Some critics have charged that "the undue emphasis on financial ratios diverts attention and resources from the development of more meaningful measures that address performance against mission and program objectives" (Hager & Flack, 2004, p. 4). Leading thought in the nonprofit field has embraced such concerns, as reflected in a 2013 "letter to the donors of America," cosigned by the Better Business Bureau Wise Giving Alliance, Charity Navigator, and Guidestar. The letter urged donors to discard "the common misconception that the percentage of charity's expenses that go to administrative and fundraising costs—commonly referred to as 'overhead'—is, on its own, an appropriate metric to evaluate when assessing a charity's worthiness and efficiency" (Overhead Myth, n.d.). However, the importance of low overhead, especially including low fundraising cost ratios, is well-established in the thinking of the public, the news media, and some nonprofit board members. This reality defines the environment in which fundraising managers must monitor and manage costs.

Cost Per Dollar Raised and Return on Investment

Let's consider two ways of expressing the relationship between a nonprofit organization's expenditures on fundraising and the gift revenues that result. The relationship can be expressed in terms of the **cost per dollar raised** (also called the **cost to raise a dollar** or **fundraising cost ratio**) or in terms of the **return on investment (ROI)** in fundraising. Box 12.1 shows how these two measures are calculated and provides examples of how the

---

BOX 12.1   Cost Per Dollar Raised Versus Return on Investment (ROI)

Assumptions

Revenue: $200,000
Expenses: $100,000
Net: $100,000

Cost Per Dollar Raised (Cost to Raise a Dollar)

(expenses ÷ revenue) × 100 [expressed in cents]
$100,000 ÷ 200,000 = .50 (50 cents)

Return on Investment (ROI)

(revenue ÷ expenses) × 100 [expressed as percentage]
$200,000 ÷ 100,000 × 100 = 200 percent

---

calculations would play out in a hypothetical situation. It is important to note that ROI is *not* a useful way to look at fundraising in the aggregate, a point explained later in this chapter. But just to define the concept and distinguish it from cost per dollar raised, let's look at it that way for now.

The cost per dollar raised is calculated by dividing fundraising expenses by gift revenues and multiplying by 100. The result is usually expressed in cents; for example, in Box 12.1, an organization that spent $100,000 on its fundraising and received gifts totaling $200,000 spent 50 cents for each dollar raised. In other words, cost per dollar raised is a measure of *efficiency*. By most standards, including the BBB's 35 percent limit, the example in Box 12.1 would be viewed as a relatively inefficient program. Indeed, some donors might perceive the situation as "for every dollar I give, fifty cents goes to fundraising." But this might be too simplistic an interpretation.

The ROI, as it is commonly calculated for fundraising, is the inverse of the cost per dollar raised. To obtain the ROI, gift revenue is divided by fundraising expenditures; the result is multiplied by 100 and expressed as a percentage. Looking at the example in Box 12.1, the ROI is 200 percent, which most financial investors would think to be rather good. Thus, the same numbers may be perceived differently, depending on how they are expressed. Again, ROI is most useful as a tool for analyzing specific fundraising programs within an organization and for considering the allocation of resources among programs, as we will soon discuss.[1]

How much should a nonprofit spend on fundraising? That turns out not to be a simple question. Take a look at Figure 12.1, which summarizes three hypothetical scenarios for fundraising expenditures and revenues. The results are not intended to portray what might necessarily be realistic in terms of actual results; the examples are simplified to illustrate a point.

FIGURE 12.1 Three Scenarios

SCENARIO #1

Revenue: $1,000,000
Expenses: $100,000
Net: $900,000

Cost per dollar raised (expenses ÷ revenue) = 10 cents
Return on investment (revenue ÷ expenses) x 100 = 1,000%

SCENARIO #2

Revenue: $1,300,000
Expenses: $300,000
Net: $1,000,000

Cost per dollar raised (expenses ÷ revenue) = 23 cents
Return on investment (revenue ÷ expenses) x 100 = 433%

SCENARIO #3

Revenue: $2,000,000
Expenses: $900,000
Net: $1,100,000

Cost per dollar raised (expenses ÷ revenue) = 45 cents
Return on investment (revenue ÷ expenses) x 100 = 222%

In Scenario #1, the organization spends $100,000 on fundraising and receives $1 million in gifts, producing net revenue of $900,000. That produces a cost per dollar raised of 10 cents and an ROI of 1,000 percent. Either number likely would be viewed as quite favorable. The program probably would be judged to be highly efficient. Now, let's suppose the organization is so encouraged by its results that next year it increases its fundraising expenditures to $300,000, as shown in Scenario #2. It receives $1.3 million in gifts, producing a net of $1 million, which is higher than last year. Its cost per dollar raised has increased to 23 cents, which is still below the threshold at which the Wise Giving Alliance standards or most other guidelines would be a concern, and its ROI is still a very impressive 433 percent. This seems to be an outstanding result, since the organization now has an additional $100,000 available for its operating budget. It can expand its programs, and its fundraising ratios are still within an acceptable range.

Now let's look at Scenario #3. Very encouraged by its past success, next year the non-profit *triples* its fundraising budget to $900,000. Gift revenue surges to $2 million and net revenue from fundraising is now $1.1 million, making yet another $100,000 available for the organization's programs. It might think this is a great result. Sure, the ROI has dropped to 222 percent, but one can imagine the CEO saying to the board, "That's still a higher ROI than any individual could expect on their investments." But the cost per dollar raised now has increased to 45 cents, exceeding the limits of the Wise Giving Alliance and most other standards. The organization has more net revenue than ever before to apply to its programs, but it now might need to explain why its fundraising cost ratio is so high. A donor might say, "You mean almost half of my gift went to pay for fundraising?" There would be an explanation, of course, but the donor might not readily understand the fine points.

The nonprofit's board and managers might wonder on what number they should be focusing when they set the fundraising budget. Should they keep the cost per dollar raised low and the ROI high, or should they maximize the net revenue available to support mission-related programs? Which approach will be acceptable to their donors, the charity raters, and possibly the media? And which approach will be most beneficial to clients who benefit from the nonprofit's services?

Economists might argue that a rational approach would be to increase fundraising expenditures up to the point that the **marginal cost** is equal to the **marginal revenue** (Steinberg, 1994). In other words, if an extra dollar of spending produces more than a dollar in gifts, why not spend it? That approach would maximize net revenue. Obviously, it would make no sense to spend beyond that point, since the additional revenue generated would be less than the additional spending and thus would reduce the net. And spending below that point would always leave money on the table. But this approach might bring risks as well, for a couple of reasons. For one, it is not always possible to accurately calculate the marginal revenue attributable to a marginal increase in spending (Steinberg, 1994). For another reason, the high cost ratios might have a negative impact on the perceptions of the public and donors, whether justified or not. In today's environment, a nonprofit needs to balance the optimal economic approach with the realities of public perception and opinion.

Explaining Variations in Costs

Both cost per dollar raised and return on investment give us some insight on an organization's fundraising results. Those insights are useful if properly applied. As we will discuss further soon, ROI is a useful tool for analyzing an organization's fundraising programs and making decisions about the allocation of budget resources. And organizations can learn from comparing their programs against those of peers, that is, through *benchmarking*. But there is considerable risk in comparing *aggregate* ratios, that is, in looking at the fundraising cost ratios of organizations overall. That is just too simplistic and does not fully acknowledge the many variations among nonprofit organizations that influence their fundraising costs. Recognizing that some variations are beyond the control of the organization, Brooks (2004) developed a tool called **adjusted performance measures** (APMs), which try to adjust for such differences. Based on regression analysis, these tools may be useful to scholars studying fundraising performance but are likely to be too complex for application by most nonprofit organizations.

Among the differences that influence fundraising ratios are the following.

Size of Organization

In general, larger organizations have lower costs per dollar raised than do smaller organizations (Proper, Caboni, Hartley, & Willmer, 2009; Wealth Engine, 2013). There are fixed costs a nonprofit may incur just to maintain a fundraising program, for example, information systems, that may not increase substantially with scale. The costs of direct-mail programs may increase with volume but perhaps not in proportion to the gift revenue produced. Larger organizations thus may experience economies of scale that reduce the cost per dollar raised and increase the return on investment.

Age and Maturity of Program

Fundraising cost ratios are influenced by the age and maturity of the fundraising program (Kroll, 2012; Wealth Engine, 2013). Think back on the discussion in Chapter 6 of this text. The costs of donor acquisition are high, and the fundraising program of a young nonprofit organization may be largely directed toward that purpose. If things go as planned, the cost per dollar raised will come down as those donors are renewed and upgraded in future years. If the fundraising program is mature, that means there has been a long time for the cultivation of major-gift prospects. The major gifts they give will count as revenue in the current year, but the costs associated with the cultivation are in the past; in the vocabulary of economists, these are **sunk costs** not reflected in current-year accounting. An organization at this stage of its development thus may have a lower current cost ratio than one just starting out (Greenfield, 2011).

Mix of Fundraising Programs and Strategies

A nonprofit that relies on direct mail and events will have a higher cost per dollar raised than one that raises more in major and planned gifts. Of course, this mix may be related to the age and maturity of the program, but it also depends on the nature of the nonprofit's donor constituency; if it has few major-gift prospects in its constituency, its cost per dollar raised is likely to be higher than another organization that has, for example, a wealthy board or that serves a more affluent community (Greenfield, 2011; Wealth Engine, 2013). An organization that is in a campaign when the costs are measured is likely to demonstrate more efficiency than one that is not (Kroll, 2012).

Location

A nonprofit located in one community may face different fundraising realities than one located in a different community (Brooks, 2004). This may be true because of differences in the affluence of those communities and other variables. For example, if the nonprofit is surrounded by corporate headquarters and locally based foundations, its fundraising environment is more favorable than that of a nonprofit in a remote rural area. Differences in cost of living, including salaries, also are relevant, since they affect costs.

Nature of the Cause

Nonprofits with missions that address popular causes, or those that affect many people, usually have a lower fundraising cost ratio than those that address more obscure or controversial issues (Sargeant, Shang, et al., 2010; Wealth Engine, 2013). For example, almost everyone is willing to support research on cancer, because so many are stricken with it. But organizations that are pro-life or pro-choice have smaller constituencies, since each is limited to the portion of the public that shares its views.

Cost Accounting Policies

One challenge in comparing fundraising costs across organizations is that apples may not always be compared with apples. For example, one organization may allocate the expenses of a mailing entirely to fundraising, while another may consider some portion of the mailing to be public education and thus a program expense (Sargeant, Shang, et al., 2010). In addition, what overhead expenditures have been included in reported fundraising costs by different organizations? Does one organization include a portion of the electric bill and building maintenance and another not? And how do they allocate the time the CEO devotes to fundraising?

In addition to the complexity involved in identifying costs, determining the relevant revenue also involves more than just adding up numbers. Some gifts may be unrelated to expenditures in the current year; for example, perhaps the organization received a large bequest that was planned many years ago. Its revenue this year would be high and its cost ratios thus would be low, but that would tell us very little about the efficiency of its fundraising this year. For another example, maybe an organization is preparing for a campaign and has invested significantly in new staff. Its costs will be high this year in comparison to this year's revenues, but just making that comparison ignores the likely impact of the new staff on revenues in future years, once the campaign is underway.

For these reasons, and others, "organizations should be cautious about comparative analysis of fundraising performance between nonprofits, including between like organizations in the same community or geographic area. Such assessments can be counterproductive and lead to misinterpretations and incorrect assumptions" (Greenfield, 2011, p. 350). In other words, it is difficult to precisely answer the question some board members and CEOs may ask: "How much should we be spending on fundraising?" Sometimes, as Kroll (2012) correctly observes, "the only certainty is that a lack of investment will yield a lack of results" (p. 10). But, in reality, CEOs and boards may want more specific answers; they likely will want the organization's fundraising effectiveness to be evaluated in some manner.

EVALUATING PROGRAMS

Given the variations among nonprofits and the risk that comparing aggregate cost ratios may lead to erroneous interpretations, Greenfield (1996) argues against doing so. However, he explains, "what is . . . worth studying is how each solicitation activity performs measured against its own results from prior years. This comparison leads to an accurate understanding and appreciation of how existing solicitation activities are working to achieve their potential, what improvements can be made based on previous results and changing conditions, and what expectations can be made for higher levels of productivity and profitability with reliability" (p. 25).

The annual Fundraising Effectiveness Report developed by AFP and the Urban Institute, with a number of additional partners, reflects Greenfield's view, since it focuses on year-to-year growth rather than ratios calculated as a snapshot in one year. Survey data include gains and losses, in dollars and donors, from year to year, since "growth in giving is increased both by maximizing gains and minimizing losses" (Urban Institute & AFP, 2013, p. 4). The data relate to cost although do not express it directly. The 2013 survey report provides an example:

> [An] organization that has gains in annual giving of 65% from one year to the next but has annual giving losses of 55%, achieves a net growth-in-giving of only 10%. . . . [For that organization] increasing gains by 10 percentage points—from 65% to 75%—would double the net growth from 10% to 20%. Reducing losses by 10 percentage points—from 55% to 45%—would also double the net from 10% to 20%. And, a reduction of losses by 20 percentage points—to 35%—would triple the net to 30%. It usually costs less to retain and motivate an existing donor than to attract a new one. For most organizations—and especially those that are sustaining losses or achieving only modest net gains in gifts and donors—taking positive steps to reduce gift and donor losses is the least expensive strategy for increasing net fundraising gains. (Urban Institute & AFP, 2013, p. 4)

As the 2013 report further advises, "The [survey] data . . . make it possible for fundraisers, management, and boards of nonprofit organizations to not only compare the performance of their organization from one year to the next, but also to compare with the performance of other organizations in terms of total dollars raised and total number of donors in a variety of categories. With this information, they can make more informed, growth-oriented decisions about where to invest increased resources and effort to improve their fundraising effectiveness" (p. 4).

In addition to ratios, such as cost per dollar raised and return on investment, Greenfield (1996) proposes nine measures for evaluating programs, including the number of participants from each group solicited, income received, expenses, percent participation, average gift size, net income, average cost per gift, cost of fundraising (cost per dollar raised), and return (similar to ROI). In a 2013 survey of development offices, Wealth Engine (2013) identified similar varied metrics in use, including the number of gifts upgraded or downgraded, the number of gifts renewed or maintained, the number of new and recaptured donors, the increase/decrease in average size of gifts, the increase/decrease in number of gifts, the increase/decrease in average cultivation time, the increase/decrease in size of prospect pool, the number of contacts per prospect to secure a gift, and the number of prospects per major gift secured.

ALLOCATING RESOURCES TO EFFECTIVE PROGRAMS

By analyzing the ROI for each of its fundraising programs, an organization can gain insights to guide the allocation of fundraising investments. These data are more useful than aggregate ratios and can inform decisions to be made in developing the fundraising budget. In simplest terms, it would make sense to allocate more resources to activities that produce a high ROI instead of those that produce a low ROI. But, again, things are not always so simple.

For one thing, some solicitation programs inherently produce a lower ROI than others, although they are essential to undertake. For example, the annual-giving program has a lower ROI than the major-gifts program, but as discussed earlier in this text, the latter usually cannot exist over the long run without the former. It is cheaper to solicit gifts using e-mail, but it may still be necessary to maintain a direct-mail program, since donors may respond across channels. Some nonsolicitation activities also are important but produce no measureable return directly, for example, gift processing and stewardship. For this reason, Levis (1993) suggests dividing activities into two categories: **capacity-building activities** and **net income producing activities** and applying different standards to each. Activities like prospect research and stewardship are related to capacity building, as are communications programs and some events. Measuring their effectiveness requires different metrics than evaluating income-producing programs, such as annual giving, major gifts, corporate and foundation support, and planned giving. Even within solicitation programs, activities need to be disaggregated. For example, annual-fund mailings intended to acquire new donors are capacity-building activities and may be operated at a break-even point or even a loss, whereas renewal and upgrade mailings would be intended to produce net income.

Another complication is that measuring the ROI on some activities is difficult to accomplish. Our instinct might tell us that investing in more prospect research will result in more prospects and ultimately in more major gifts, but the connection is not always easy to demonstrate. For example, Wealth Engine (2013) argues that investments in wealth screening, analytics, and other related activities—services the company provides—have a "*potential impact on ROI*" (italics added). But exact numbers may be elusive, especially on a short-term basis. For this reason, it is important to use varied metrics and multiyear data to avoid shortchanging nonsolicitation activities that are important to building the program over the long haul. For this reason and others, various authors recommend that ROI be measured for each program over a three- to five-year time frame (Association of Fundraising Professionals, n.d.; Wealth Engine, 2013). Lindahl (1992) suggests that optimizing gift revenue over the long term requires balancing investments between high-potential, high-cost, long-term programs and low-cost, short-term programs.

The reality that some investments may produce returns only over a period of years has important implications for evaluating those investments up front. If an investment will be made this year and is expected to produce returns over a period of years, calculations need to incorporate the fact that inflation will erode the real value of those returns over that period. In other words, if the investment will be made in today's dollars, the future returns need to be expressed in today's dollars as well, not in inflated dollars years from now.

Techniques drawn from finance and economics can support an evaluation in such a scenario, including the concepts of **discounted cash flow** and **net present value** (Sargeant, Shang, et al., 2010). This text does not explore the details of these techniques, which are likely to be employed only by the most sophisticated of institutions. But a simple and handy way to think about the time value of money is the Rule of 72. If the number 72 is divided by an interest rate, say 10 percent, the result tells us roughly how many years it will take for money to double if invested at that rate, assuming compound interest. So, if a sum of money is invested at 10 percent compounded, it will double in 7.2 years. At

5 percent, it will double in 14.4 years, and so forth. But this principle also works in the other direction; in other words, it can tell us about how much real purchasing power a dollar amount will lose as a result of inflation. Let's say inflation is 10 percent a year—that would be very high, but it simplifies the example. Dividing 72 by 10 gives us 7.2, which would be the number of years it would take for the same amount of money to be worth *half as much* in real terms, that is, in terms of what it can buy. If inflation is 5 percent (still high, but not unprecedented), money loses half of its value in 14.4 years. Think about the implications of this in a comprehensive campaign that will extend for eight years, with pledge payments extending for as long as five years after that—in other words, a planning period totaling thirteen years. If inflation over that period is somewhere around 5 percent, the final pledge payment will have purchasing power equal to only about half of what the same dollar amount has today. The rate of return on an investment in the campaign today thus would need to be evaluated against the discounted present value of the cash flow from gifts over the entire length of the campaign, which may be significantly affected by inflation.

This is also relevant when considering naming opportunities offered to donors in a long campaign. For example, an endowment of $100,000 may be adequate to support a scholarship today. But if tuition continues to increase at the rate of inflation, the scholarship supported by that $100,000 will have much less impact after ten years have passed. So, the length of a campaign and the length of the pledge payment period determine the impact a gift may have on a program as well as the rate of return on investment in the fundraising program.

BENCHMARKING

Despite the need for caution in comparing different organizations, nonprofits commonly undertake comparisons with others, a process called **benchmarking**. Benchmarking involves collecting data from multiple organizations "in order to 'peg' the performance of a particular [organization] in relation to [those offering] comparable programs" (Poister, 2003, p. 238). For example, an organization might look at statistics on client outcomes across a group of organizations providing services to individuals with similar problems or compare its patterns of gift revenues with those of similar organizations. This macro approach, called **statistical benchmarking**, may be a useful technique for identifying strengths or weaknesses of the organization that require further analysis.

Another approach to benchmarking, what Poister (2003) calls **corporate benchmarking**, "compares the organization's practices with those of others doing similar things but who are deemed to be the best at doing it" (Murray, 2004, p. 361). A technique adopted from business, this type of benchmarking requires identifying best practices—that is, the most effective or efficient methods of performing specific functions—and seeing how the subject organization compares with the best.

Sargeant, Shang, et al. (2010) describe a nine-step process for benchmarking, including developing the rationale, selecting the measures to be compared, identifying the **cohort** (also called **peers** or **competitors**) to whom the comparison will be made, acquisition of data, standardization of data, setting an acceptable zone of tolerance, undertaking the comparison, identifying areas where performance differs, and undertaking corrective action, that is, changes to improve the practices of the organization that show less effective performance.

Among the most critical steps is the selection of peers or competitors, against whom the organization's data will be compared. If the purpose of the benchmarking is to identify best administrative practices, differences among organizations may be less important than if the goal is to compare fundraising ratios. The amount of time required to send a receipt for a cash gift may be more comparable across organizations than fundraising costs or gift revenues, which are effected by the range of variables discussed previously. No two organizations are exactly alike, but some analysis can be used to narrow down the most relevant for benchmarking purposes.

There always will be questions about the peer group selected. One problem is that when we refer to benchmarking against peers, people may have different perspectives on what that means. Some may think about an organization they know that seems similar to them, but they may not know enough to be fully aware of the differences. Some may think about peers in terms of the current time, and fewer may think about the differences in histories and cultures that may be less visible but have an influence on fundraising capacity today. For these reasons, fundraisers engaging in benchmarking need to dedicate sufficient thought and effort to identifying the peer group and also to explaining the basis for the selection to CEOs, board members, and others who may be consumers of the data the benchmarking provides. Useful questions to ask include "Which organizations are most like us?" "How are they similar?" and "How are they different?" The questions are helpful not only in identifying the appropriate peer group but in preparing the individuals who will receive and consider the benchmarking results to understand both their value and their limitations.

The data generated through benchmarking often reveal that the subject organization varies from its peers on at least some metrics. If the variations are within some **zone of tolerance**, that is, if they are not great, then no action may be required (Sargeant, Shang, et al., 2010). If the differences are significant, that suggests the need for further investigation to determine the implications and possible corrective actions to be undertaken to improve results. Benchmarking is best undertaken with the purpose of learning and improving but not for the purpose of evaluation, especially of the performance of individual fundraising staff members. If the latter purpose is foremost, individuals may resist the benchmarking exercise or try to game the system by selecting peer organizations with which they think they may have the most favorable comparisons.

Some of the initiatives mentioned previously, including the Fundraising Effectiveness Project and CASE's Advancement Investment Metrics Study, provide data that individual organizations and institutions can apply for benchmarking purposes. In addition to this published data, various consortia of organizations share detailed and confidential data among members. And the culture of the nonprofit sector always has supported relatively open communication among organizations and especially among fundraisers. With the obvious exception of donor information, most development professionals are forthcoming with colleagues, at conferences or in individual conversations, about practices that have worked and that may be adapted to enhance fundraising effectiveness throughout the sector.

BUILDING A FUNDRAISING PROGRAM

Concepts discussed in the preceding sections of this chapter are important to understand, not only for fundraising professionals but also for nonprofit CEOs and board members making judgments about the investment of budget resources in fundraising programs. Organizations may sometimes have a difficult time accepting the realities of the time and investment required to build a successful program. Such organizations, and their CEOs, CFOs, and boards, do face some hard choices, which include taking risks with the resources entrusted to them, not always easy decisions to make. But halfhearted efforts are not prudent either; in other words, investing too little may run the risk of being wasteful. There may be some minimum threshold investment required, below which the return on investment will always be low or negative. Trying to build a fundraising program in too-small increments thus may lock the organization into a cycle of continued failure.

Consider two hypothetical scenarios, depicted in Figure 12.2, in which a nonprofit is initiating a fundraising program from the ground up. Let's assume the organization's constituency has the capacity and inclination to give, so the principal variable affecting ROI is the level of investment in the fundraising program. In both scenarios, the organization begins in a break-even position; it is spending no money on fundraising and receiving no gift revenue. But the curves diverge in the two different approaches taken.

In Scenario #1, the board's approach is to start small by appointing a director of development and then waiting to see how much new revenue is produced before deciding

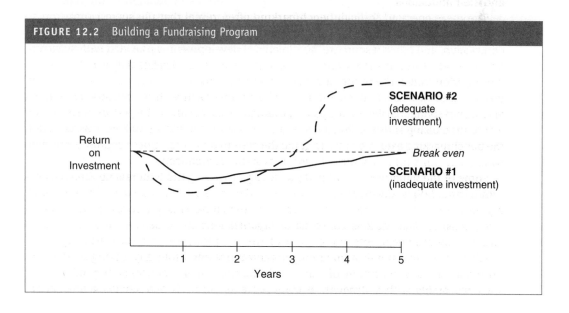

FIGURE 12.2   Building a Fundraising Program

whether to invest more. The position may be budgeted a year at a time, in order to minimize risk. The new director is hired and faces the need to build infrastructure, including an information system, some capacity for prospect research, a gift acceptance policy, and a capability for online fundraising, among other things. And there is a need for routine operations, including gift acknowledgment and processing, database maintenance, and budget. And, of course, there is the time absorbed by simply being an employee, attending staff meetings and so forth. She has little or no support staff, so much of the director's time is consumed by in-house responsibilities without much ability to engage in cultivation and solicitation. She has no budget for travel or entertainment, so it is impossible to complete many personal visits. The only solicitations going out the door may be a couple of mailings, but the mailings will be focused on donor acquisition and produce, at best, modest net revenue.

The return on this investment is understandably negative in the first year or so, since the director draws a salary and has other expenses, while devoting much of her time to capacity building and administration. There is little revenue attributable to her efforts, for the reasons described, so expenses exceed revenue and the return on the investment is negative. But even if the board continues to support the position for the next five years, which is doubtful, and even if the director of development stays, which is doubtful, the return on investment may take that long just to return to zero, that is, break even! Or it may indeed never be positive without further investments. The director of development always will be consumed with internal matters and have little time and resources to devote to solicitations. Since the returns continue to be negative or minimal, the board is never willing to add more resources that could make the enterprise successful. This is a cycle of failure.

In Scenario #2, the board establishes a new development office with a more substantial investment. The total package includes support positions in addition to the director of development position. Sufficient funds are provided to hire consultants or contractors to produce the needed infrastructure, including basic documents and policies, the information system, and other resources. The director of development is provided with sufficient funds to undertake cultivation, and solicitations and goals are established over a horizon of three or more years. The return on investment is still negative in early years, since the new expenditures will be compared with minimal revenue at first. However, since the director of development is able to engage in cultivation and solicitation, gift revenue increases and returns turn positive within a few years. As depicted in Figure 12.2, let's assume that by year three the board is encouraged and decides to add even more resources, including additional gift officers. The new gift officers have no administrative responsibilities and can devote all of their time to cultivation and solicitation. In addition, they are working with a pool of donors acquired in earlier years. The return on investment increases exponentially. Eventually, the return on investment increases more slowly or flattens out, as the potential of the organization's constituency is more fully realized.

Obviously, the two scenarios are hypothetical and may not be realistic in the real world. But they illustrate a point. Surely it would not be prudent for a nonprofit organization to try to jump-start its fundraising by hiring the equivalent of the Harvard development office at the outset. But investing *too little* makes failure inevitable. It would, indeed, be better to do nothing; that way, there is no investment and no return, but at least the organization is not losing money. Boards sometimes may think that growing the program in small increments, conditional on results, is a way to minimize risk. The irony is that investing too little may create a cycle in which the risk of failure is maximized. The entire investment is jeopardized from the beginning.

Many organizations have limited resources. Many are understandably risk averse. Many view resources invested in fundraising as detracting from those available for programs, as indeed may be the case in the short run. But application of some of the concepts and tools of analysis described in this chapter, including benchmarking against organizations that have successful programs, can reduce the risk and produce a long-term positive result. Fortunately, students who have proceeded to this point in this text are now prepared to bring such insights to the organizations they may serve, as CEOs, board members, or fundraising professionals.

DEVELOPMENT OPERATIONS/ADVANCEMENT SERVICES

As fundraising programs have grown in scope and complexity, the management infrastructure required to support them has expanded. The management of **development office operations**, **fundraising operations**, or **advancement services** (as it is commonly known in higher education institutions and some other organizations) has become an important specialty of the fundraising profession (Cannon, 2011). For simplicity, the term *development operations* is used in this chapter.

Although the specific core functions may vary among organizations, development operations generally include the maintenance of data; the application of technology, including information systems and online capabilities; reporting and analysis of information; gift processing; prospect development and management, including prospect research, data mining, and analytics; stewardship management; and other functions. In some organizations, the development operations unit may also have responsibility for managing the budget and HR functions of the development office (Cannon, 2011).

Prospect research was discussed in Chapter 5 of this book, and Chapter 7 discussed the management of major-gift prospects. This chapter focuses on general principles of development operations and, in somewhat more detail, fundraising information systems and uses of technology.

Operations General Principles

As Cannon (2011), a specialist in development operations, emphasizes, "Busy fundraising executives do not need to know *how* everything works in operations, but they do need to know *what works* and *what does not*" (p. 15, italics original). It is the chief development officer's responsibility to define what functions and capabilities are required to support the overall program and to establish standards for performance. But development operations is a technical area that employs highly trained professionals, on whom the chief development officer should rely for implementation (Cannon, 2011).

Cannon (2011) uses the metaphor of a "smoothly spinning top" to describe development operations, emphasizing the need for balance and tradeoffs (p. 16). For example, with regard to data processing and reporting, there may be tradeoffs among accuracy, speed, and volume. Accuracy is highly desirable, but if the expected standard is 100 percent, that may sacrifice speed and be inconsistent with handling large volumes. The chief development officer may need reports prepared quickly, at least on some occasions. As Cannon (2011) observes, "Speed should not typically trump accuracy, but sometimes the two priorities are dead even" (p. 21). Volume is a good thing, since it means that many gifts are being received, many solicitations are taking place, and so forth. But it is variable and often cyclical and can sometimes overwhelm capacity at peaks, for example, at the end of the year when many gifts are received. The capability to handle high volume with both speed and accuracy is desirable, but "it may be easier said than done" (Cannon, 2011, p. 24), requiring managers to set priorities. With regard to evaluating processes, Cannon urges managers to undertake objective analyses and rely on data rather than anecdotes.

Cannon (2011) emphasizes that data are not maintained for their own sake; rather, "a successful leader in fundraising operations maintains a constant drive toward leveraging available data and resources toward strategic action" (p. 45). In other words, the development operations unit needs to view itself—and be viewed by front-line fundraising staff—as partners in pursuing the overall goals and strategy of the fundraising program. Operations are not an end to themselves but rather one element of the overall effort, which is focused on the overriding goal of raising more money.

Fundraising Information Systems

Before the 1980s, the state-of-the-art in data storage was the paper file card. To paraphrase, in understatement, the ACPRA study of forty years ago quoted earlier in this chapter, "electronic equipment" now has become more "readily available" (Heneman, 1969, p. x). Systems for maintaining the donor database have grown in complexity and importance. Some nonprofits use home-grown systems, but most use a product from a commercial vendor, many of which offer similar features and capabilities. It is important to maintain a broad definition of an information system; it encompasses more than computer hardware and software and includes the entire set of processes through which data are obtained, stored, and used. As Luther (2005) notes, in its broadest conception, an information system may indeed still encompass some functions that use pencils and paper. But electronic systems are the foundation on which most fundraising programs are managed.

A full discussion of system capabilities and uses is beyond the scope of this chapter, but we might think about those in terms of how a nonprofit's needs might develop as its fundraising program grows. In other words, development of a nonprofit's information system is a progression as the organization's needs evolve (Luther, 2005).

The most basic need is for a system to store **core data elements**, including donor names, contact information, and gift history. A next step might be to maintain a **solicitation**

history for each donor, that is, a record of every solicitation he or she has received and the response. These data can be used to identify patterns and develop solicitation strategies. A third step might be to begin recording *interactions with donors*, including their attendance at events and one-on-one contacts by the organization's leaders and fundraising staff, including the **contact reports** written by gift officers. The eventual addition of more personal information on prospects, possibly including the results of **electronic wealth screening**, expands the usefulness of the system as a tool for prospect development and management (Lindauer, 2011). With such elements in place, information systems can provide the foundation for analyses and reports to inform fundraising strategies. Tools and techniques for that purpose are rapidly expanding (Cannon, 2011).

In large and decentralized organizations, one management issue is the distribution of access and authority concerning the donor database. This is especially relevant in universities, health care systems, and national nonprofits that have local branches, chapters, or affiliates.

In some instances, individual units or chapters may maintain separate databases, a situation that raises the risk of inaccurate data, presents an obstacle to developing coordinated relationships with donors, and complicates meaningful analysis. For example, this was an issue in the case of the American Red Cross, discussed in Chapter 5.

However, where such separate databases exist, there is often resistance to consolidation. Such resistance may be based on local pride and perhaps a visceral distrust of centralized management, but individual units may also have some pragmatic concerns, including access to data and to prospects. When donor data are consolidated on a central database, there need to be clear policies regarding access to information, to assure both confidentiality and coordinated activity. This need relates to both legal and ethical issues. In addition, the policies dictate who can make changes to data, in order to assure consistency and accuracy. But it is also essential to provide that individual units can obtain the data they need. As Cannon (2011) advises, "If information is maintained and overly controlled for its own sake . . . [if] access is denied [and] usage of the information is limited . . . program directors might . . . opt out of the formal system" (p. 44).

Development Operations Trends

Fundraising information systems are evolving into **customer relationship management (CRM)** systems like those used by businesses, with an emphasis on supporting relationships with donors (Cannon, 2011; Luther, 2005). CRM systems permit organizations "to integrate all of their data and electronic business processes into one central application" (Cannon, 2011, p. 137). Such systems are becoming more integrated with social networks and online communication and some permit donor access to individualized webpages.

Trends in development operations reflect broader advances in technology. They include the growth of mobile communication, the growing use of analytics (as mentioned earlier and discussed in Chapter 5), the shifting emphasis in software development from underlying technology to the user experience, the transition from in-house data infrastructure to the cloud, and increasing integration with social media (Cannon, 2011; Westmoreland, 2014).

FUNDRAISING POLICIES

Well-managed fundraising programs operate with established policies that guide key decisions and processes. Policies dictate internal procedures, including how gifts are to be acknowledged and processed, how access to major-gift prospects is to be cleared and how contacts are to be reported, and other matters. A fundamental policy describes the nature of gifts the organization accepts and the procedure for determining whether a specific gift may be acceptable, that is, a *gift acceptance policy*. There is a general gift acceptance policy and may also be subsidiary gift acceptance policies related specifically to planned gifts, corporate gifts, gifts in a campaign, and others as needed.

The purposes of a gift acceptance policy are to ensure that the organization does not accept gifts that may impose financial, legal, or administrative burdens or that may obligate the organization to additional expenditures not covered by the gift. The colloquial but common phrase used to describe the latter is **gifts that eat**.

Gift acceptance policies are especially important with regard to complex assets, such as real estate, closely held stock, partnership interests, art, boats, cars, and other tangible personal property. Some of the issues that need to be addressed include the usefulness of the gift (for example, works of art), the liquidity of the asset (for example, closely held stock), and potential liability (a particular concern with some gifts of real estate).

There are important reasons why a gift acceptance policy is essential, not only to provide legal and financial protection but also to avoid awkward situations and maintain relationships with donors. A CEO or a development officer who is confronted with the offer of a potentially inappropriate or risky gift, especially from an important donor or board member, should not be in a position of having to make the decision alone. He or she should be able to point to board policy and/or refer the matter to a higher authority. The absence of a policy puts the CEO or the development officer under unreasonable pressure and runs the risk of making the issue personal. In such situations, clear policies and a procedure that shares decision-making authority provide protection for both the institution and the individuals involved. Most gift acceptance policies designate a gift acceptance committee or the governing board as the ultimate authority for determining whether a specific gift meets the policy or warrants an exception. This provides some flexibility but also protects the CEO and development officer from having to offend a potential donor on a personal level. Indeed, the suggestion that the proposed gift might be discussed in a larger forum is often sufficient to dissuade a donor who may be trying to unload a useless asset, a circumstance that unfortunately sometime does arise.

Some gift acceptance policies are lengthy and include procedures for processing gifts as well as policies on acceptance. Others are brief but include references to other policies that expand on certain issues. Although most address common points, gift acceptance policies are unique to each organization. Box 12.2 provides one sample; additional samples are readily located on the web.

BOX 12.2 Sample Gift Acceptance Policy

[Organization Name] solicits and accepts gifts for purposes that will help the organization further and fulfill its mission. [Organization Name] urges all prospective donors to seek the assistance of personal legal and financial advisors in matters relating to their gifts, including the resulting tax and estate planning consequences. The following policies and guidelines govern acceptance of gifts made to [Organization Name] for the benefit of any of its operations, programs or services.

Use of Legal Counsel—[Organization Name] will seek the advice of legal counsel in matters relating to acceptance of gifts when appropriate. Review by counsel is recommended for:

A. Gifts of securities that are subject to restrictions or buy-sell agreements.

B. Documents naming [Organization Name] as trustee or requiring [Organization Name] to act in any fiduciary capacity.

C. Gifts requiring [Organization Name] to assume financial or other obligations.

D. Transactions with potential conflicts of interest.

E. Gifts of property which may be subject to environmental or other regulatory restrictions.

Restrictions on Gifts—[Organization Name] will not accept gifts that (a) would result in [Organization Name] violating its corporate charter, (b) would result in [Organization Name] losing its status as an IRC § 501(c)(3) not-for-profit organization, (c) are too difficult or too expensive to administer in relation to their value, (d) would result in any unacceptable consequences for [Organization Name], or (e) are for purposes outside [Organization Name]'s mission. Decisions on the restrictive nature of a gift, and its acceptance or refusal, shall be made by the Executive Committee, in consultation with the Executive Director.

Gifts Generally Accepted Without Review

- *Cash.* Cash gifts are acceptable in any form, including by check, money order, credit card, or on-line. Donors wishing to make a gift by credit card must provide the card type (e.g., Visa, MasterCard, American Express), card number, expiration date, and name of the card holder as it appears on the credit card.
- *Marketable Securities.* Marketable securities may be transferred electronically to an account maintained at one or more brokerage firms or delivered physically with the transferor's endorsement or signed stock power (with appropriate signature guarantees) attached. All marketable securities will be sold promptly upon receipt unless otherwise directed by [Name of Organization]'s Investment Committee. In some cases marketable securities may be restricted, for example, by applicable securities laws or the terms of the proposed gift; in such instances the decision whether to accept the restricted securities shall be made by the Executive Committee.

(Continued)

(Continued)

- *Bequests and Beneficiary Designations under Revocable Trusts, Life Insurance Policies, Commercial Annuities and Retirement Plans.* Donors are encouraged to make bequests to [Organization Name] under their wills, and to name [Organization Name] as the beneficiary under trusts, life insurance policies, commercial annuities and retirement plans.
- *Charitable Remainder Trusts.* [Organization Name] will accept designation as a remainder beneficiary of charitable remainder trusts.
- *Charitable Lead Trusts.* [Organization Name] will accept designation as an income beneficiary of charitable lead trusts.

Gifts Accepted Subject to Prior Review

Certain forms of gifts or donated properties may be subject to review prior to acceptance. Examples of gifts subject to prior review include, but are not limited to:

- *Tangible Personal Property.* The Executive Committee shall review and determine whether to accept any gifts of tangible personal property in light of the following considerations: does the property further the organization's mission? Is the property marketable? Are there any unacceptable restrictions imposed on the property? Are there any carrying costs for the property for which the organization may be responsible? Is the title/provenance of the property clear?
- *Life Insurance.* [Organization Name] will accept gifts of life insurance where [Organization Name] is named as both beneficiary and irrevocable owner of the insurance policy. The donor must agree to pay, before due, any future premium payments owing on the policy.
- *Real Estate.* All gifts of real estate are subject to review by the Executive Committee. Prior to acceptance of any gift of real estate other than a personal residence, [Organization Name] shall require an initial environmental review by a qualified environmental firm. In the event that the initial review reveals a potential problem, the organization may retain a qualified environmental firm to conduct an environmental audit. Criteria for acceptance of gifts of real estate include: Is the property useful for the organization's purposes? Is the property readily marketable? Are there covenants, conditions, restrictions, reservations, easements, encumbrances or other limitations associated with the property? Are there carrying costs (including insurance, property taxes, mortgages, notes, or the like) or maintenance expenses associated with the property? Does the environmental review or audit reflect that the property is damaged or otherwise requires remediation?

These sample policies are shared for educational purposes only and should not be considered legal advice for any specific situation. The Nonprofit Risk Management Center encourages all nonprofits to have governance policies reviewed by legal counsel. www.nonprofitrisk.org

Source: Reprinted with permission from the National Council of Nonprofits website, http://www.councilofnonprofits.org.

CHAPTER SUMMARY

In today's environment, fundraising is not merely an art, practiced at the periphery of nonprofit organizations; it is an important and complex specialty of nonprofit management. Fundraising budgets have become substantial, but fundraising should be viewed as an *investment* that produces revenue to support an organization's operations and programs.

The costs of fundraising have been studied since the 1960s, but an increasing volume of research has focused on the topic in recent years. It is important to distinguish *effectiveness* and *efficiency*, with the former related to results achieved and the latter related to the associated costs. Some argue that an emphasis on efficiency, or low *overhead*, may work against the effectiveness of organizations by discouraging investment in capacity (Hager & Flack, 2004).

Although their method and standards for evaluating nonprofit organizations differ, two leading charity watchdogs (the Better Business Bureau Wise Giving Alliance and Charity Navigator) consider organizations' *cost per dollar raised*, which is a measure of efficiency. The same data used to calculate cost per dollar raised also can be used to calculate its inverse, called *return on investment (ROI)*. Comparing either ratio between or among organizations at the aggregate level can lead to misleading conclusions.

Economists argue that fundraising expenditures should be increased until *marginal revenue* is barely greater than *marginal cost* (Steinberg, 1994). But this rational approach needs to be balanced against the realities of public and donor perceptions about fundraising costs.

Organizations often undertake *benchmarking* to compare their data with other organizations (Poister, 2003). But caution is required because fundraising ratios are significantly influenced by differences among organizations, including size, age, and maturity of the fundraising program; the mix of fundraising programs and strategies; location; the nature of the cause; cost accounting policies; and others (Greenfield, 2011; Kroll, 2012; Sargeant & Kahler, 1999; Wealth Engine, 2013). It is important to identify the appropriate *peers* for benchmarking studies. It can be expected that some data will differ from peers within a *zone of tolerance*, but if the differences exceed that zone it is worth investigating the reasons (Sargeant, Shang, et al., 2010). Benchmarking is more appropriate to identify best practices from other organizations that might be adopted than as a method for evaluating fundraising programs or staff.

Return on investment (ROI) is a useful tool for allocating budget resources among fundraising programs to maximize results. But it is important to distinguish between *capacity-building activities* and *net-income-producing activities*, which can be expected to have varied costs (Levis, 1993). It is also important to consider the time value of money, since current expenditures may produce revenues in future years, but those revenues will be worth less in real dollars, a concept called *net present value*.

Some nonprofits take a cautious and incremental approach to investing in fundraising programs. But investing too little can result in a negative or minimal return on investment because all expenditures are related to infrastructure and operations and there is little cultivation and solicitation activity. Too little investment may produce a cycle of failure, and the investment needs to be sufficient to move beyond supporting just overhead to enable revenue-producing activities to occur.

Development office operations are back-office functions, but the purpose is to contribute to the effectiveness of front-line fundraisers and the achievement of goals. Operations professionals are full partners with gift officers. In managing processes, there is a need to balance the goals of accuracy, speed, and volume in a realistic manner (Cannon, 2011).

Fundraising information systems have become complex. The donor database includes *core data elements*, but additional information is included as the fundraising program matures (Luther, 2005). Today's systems include sophisticated tools for analysis and reporting. Trends include a growing emphasis on integration with online fundraising and social networks and an evolution toward *customer relationship management (CRM)* systems like those used by businesses (Cannon, 2011; Luther, 2005).

A *gift acceptance policy* describes the nature of gifts the organization accepts and the procedure for determining whether a specific gift may be acceptable. It is essential to avoid inappropriate gifts or those that bring risks to the organization and to depersonalize decisions about gifts that may be unacceptable.

Key Terms and Concepts

Adjusted performance measures	Customer relationship management (CRM)	Marginal cost
Benchmarking		Marginal revenue
Capacity-building activities	Development office operations (fundraising operations, advancement services)	Net-income-producing activities
Cohort (peers, competitors) [for benchmarking]		Net present value
		Overhead
Contact reports		Return on investment (ROI)
Core data elements	Discounted cash flow	Solicitation history
Corporate benchmarking	Effectiveness	Statistical benchmarking
Cost per dollar raised (cost to raise a dollar, fundraising cost ratio)	Efficiency	Sunk costs
	Electronic wealth screening	Zone of tolerance
	Gifts that eat	

Case 12.1: Disabled Veterans National Foundation

The Disabled Veterans National Foundation (DVNF) was founded in 2007 with the mission of providing services to sick and wounded veterans. DVNF signed a seven-year contract with Brickmill Marketing Services, a subsidiary of direct-marketing firm Quadriga Art to conduct direct-mail solicitations. Under the terms of the contract, Quadriga would advance the money to cover the costs, to be paid back out of the gifts received (Perry, 2012a).

In 2008, Brickmill coordinated two mailings to about 3.6 million people. The mailings resulted in 528,000 gifts from 496,000 donors, about a 14 percent response rate, exceeding the usual returns for direct mail. Donors of $10 or more were subsequently resolicited and an additional 224,000 gifts were made (Perry, 2012a).

In 2010, the charity watchdog Charity Watch raised questions about DVNF, noting that it was accumulating considerable debt to its vendor, Quadriga, and charging that little of the funds raised had benefitted vendors. CNN ran a story about the accusation, and the Senate Finance Committee said it would investigate, but the investigation "went quiet after some initial inquiries" (Perry, 2014a).

Quadriga offered the explanation that it was trying to help a start-up nonprofit by advancing the costs of acquiring new donors, noting the high costs of acquisition. It argued that the program would eventually turn profitable through renewals. But one critic said the model was creating "dependency," since DVNF's indebtedness to Quadriga did not include "a plan to get weaned off this flow of seemingly free money." The same critic questioned the seven-year contact and said that DVNF had not engaged in competitive bidding (Perry, 2012b). Another critic noted that new fundraising programs may indeed require five years to become profitable but that the up-front costs are usually provided by a private donor rather than a commercial firm that stood to profit from the activity (Perry, 2012b).

In 2010, DVNF retained economist Richard Steinberg, a recognized expert on the economics of fundraising, to analyze its program and write a report. Steinberg noted a number of points related to fundraising costs that were discussed in this chapter, including the fact that new programs often operate at a loss in early years and that it is important to look at the lifetime value of a newly acquired donor rather than just the gifts total in one year (Perry, 2012a; Steinberg, 2010).

While DVNF's 2008 mailings had produced a loss of almost $7 million, its 2009 mailings to previous donors were profitable, bringing in $3.5 million compared with $3.2 million in costs. Steinberg calculated that the 2008 donors alone might provide a total of $6.6 million by 2033 as they made additional gifts. Indeed, he concluded that DVNF should have spent more on fundraising, since every dollar spent would have raised $1.58, providing an additional 58 cents toward its programs. He was quoted as saying that the results from the first two years of DVNF's contract with Quadriga were "highly encouraging," adding that "there is no evidence suggesting campaign expenditures are excessive" (Perry, 2012a).

In May 2012, CNN revisited the story with another program highly critical of DVNF and its relationship with Quadriga. According to CNN's report, DVNF had raised about $55.9 million from 2007 to 2012, but little had benefitted veterans (Fitzpatrick & Griffin, 2012). Based on CNN's review of DVNF's Form 990, it reported that by 2010 DVNF had run up a total of $61 million in fees due to Quadriga. It stated that few resources had been provided to veterans. DVNF stated that it had indeed made gifts-in-kind to benefit veterans, but CNN interviewed people who said the goods were not useful (Fitzpatrick & Griffin, 2012). According to CNN, DVNF had valued one shipment of goods at $838,000, but the network claimed its investigation had determined that the items were worth only $234,000 (Fitzpatrick & Griffin, 2012).

The CNN report generated controversy, resulting in an investigation of DVNF and Quadriga by the U.S. Senate Veterans Committee (Perry, 2012b). The Direct Marketing Association Nonprofit Federation, an industry association of which Quadriga was a member, launched its own inquiry (Perry, 2012b). And the New York attorney general began looking into the matter.

In 2014, the New York Attorney General's Office announced that its investigation of DVNF and Quadriga had led to a financial settlement. The settlement would cost Quadriga and Converge Direct Marketing, another firm that had advised DVNF on fundraising, a total of $25 million, including penalties and forgiveness of DVNF's debt to Quadriga (Perry, 2014a). The attorney general found that some solicitations were misleading; for example, one had featured an alleged veteran named "Arnie," who was fictitious. And almost 90 percent of all the funds raised had gone to Quadriga and other vendors (Perry, 2014a). In addition, the attorney general found conflicts of interest among officers of Quadriga and DVNF (Perry, 2014a). Professor Steinberg said that he had not known all of this information when he wrote his 2010 report, especially the conflicts of interest; however, he noted that settlement figures revealed that DVNF's fundraising was indeed starting to produce a surplus, as he had predicted (Perry, 2014a).

Following the settlement with New York State, Quadriga said it would tighten its rules for advancing money to charity clients to assure that they do not accumulate too much debt and that they report accurate information in their public documents. The CEO of DVNF stated that he welcomed the settlement and vowed to "improve the services we deliver and increase transparency with our loyal donors" (Perry, 2014a). Quadriga subsequently reorganized under the name Innovairre Communications (Perry, 2014b).

Questions for Discussion

1. Which concepts and terms discussed in this chapter are relevant in the case of the Disabled Veterans National Foundation?

2. Go back to Chapter 6 of this book. Are there concepts and principles from that chapter that apply to the case of DVNF? Explain the relevance.

3. Leaving aside issues such as conflicts of interest among officials of DVNF and its contractor Quadriga, and focusing on the fundraising results, were criticisms of DVNF by the media and other sources justified? Did they reflect a lack of understanding about direct-mail fundraising, or were there valid reasons to be concerned?

4. Donors may apply a different standard to nonprofit fundraising than to commercial transactions. For example, they may be concerned by high nonprofit overhead but be unconcerned about how much of their purchase price for a new iPhone goes to Apple's marketing and advertising. What explains why people think this way?

5. Why do you think the overhead costs of nonprofits, including fundraising, receives so much emphasis in the news media, to the relative exclusion of other measures?

Suggestions for Further Reading

Books

Cannon, C. M. (2011). *An executive's guide to fundraising operations: Principles, tools & trends.* Hoboken, NJ: Wiley.

Greenfield, J. M. (1996). *Fundraising cost effectiveness: A self-assessment workbook.* New York: Wiley. (Note: This book is dated but still widely cited.)

Pallotta, D. (2010). *Uncharitable: How restraints on nonprofits undermine their potential.* Lebanon, NH: Tufts University Press.

Taylor, J. H. (2007). *Advancement services: A foundation for fundraising* (2nd ed.). Washington, DC: Council for Advancement and Support of Education.

Reports

Association of Fundraising Professionals and Urban Institute. (2013). *2013 fundraising effectiveness survey report.* http://www.urban.org.

Wealth Engine. (2013). *Measuring fundraising return on investment and the impact of wealth intelligence* (white paper). https://www.wealthengine.com.

Website

Association of Advancement Services Professionals (AASP): http://www.advserv.org

Note

1. Return on investment (ROI) is defined and calculated in different ways. An argument can be made for various methods. In this chapter, ROI is defined as funds raised as a percentage of fundraising expenses; in other words, total gifts divided by the cost of raising them (multiplied by ten). This is the most common definition used by authors in works related to fundraising, including publications of AFP and CASE (e.g., Association of Fundraising Professionals, n.d.; Kroll, 2012; Sargeant, Shang, et al., 2010).

Organizing and Managing Fundraising Staff

Until the 1960s few fundraising professionals were employed by nonprofit organizations and institutions. When an organization initiated a campaign, it generally would retain a fundraising consulting firm to manage it. The organization's fundraising efforts often were scaled back or discontinued when the campaign was completed. Fifty years later, fundraising is a continuing priority for most nonprofit organizations and has become a profession that employs thousands of people. Some development offices employ hundreds of professionals, in various specialties. Many chief development officers are senior executives of their organizations, some earning substantial incomes.

This chapter considers topics related to the organization and management of fundraising professional staff. In a small nonprofit, such management may be a concern only to the CEO, who perhaps supervises one or a few fundraisers. In a large organization, the job of the chief development officer (CDO) may be substantially related to management, including the supervision of gift officers, development operations professionals, and others. Indeed, Schiller (2013) reports that CDOs spend as little as 10 percent of their time on direct fundraising, with the balance devoted to management responsibilities (p. xv).

The topic of managing staff is a large one, and this chapter is of necessity selective in the topics considered. It focuses on four: models for the organization of development office staff, some theories of motivation, the compensation of fundraising professionals, and tools for diagnosing and addressing performance issues. Some material in the section on motivation is based on my earlier work (Worth, 2014) but is used here with substantial editing.

ORGANIZING THE DEVELOPMENT OFFICE

In a small nonprofit organization, the development office staff may consist of only a single individual, commonly called the *director of development* or *chief development officer*. Depending on the custom of the organization regarding titles, that individual may hold the title of vice president for development or advancement, associate executive director, manager, or something else. To make things simple this chapter just uses the title chief development officer.

One essential principle, discussed earlier in this text, is that the chief development officer must report directly to the chief executive officer, have access to members of the board of directors and other top volunteers, and be positioned as a senior officer of the organization. As discussed in Chapter 4, that is essential to building a culture of philanthropy and to enabling the director to have credibility with donors, among other purposes.

The number of individuals supervised by the chief development officer varies, from zero to hundreds, depending on the size of the organization and the importance of philanthropy as a source of revenue. Remember from the discussion of resource dependency theory in Chapter 2 that even some large nonprofits do not emphasize fundraising, since their primary sources of revenue may be government, earned income, or some combination of which gifts are a relatively small component. So, the size of the organization is not the sole determinant of the scale of its development office.

As the development office grows beyond one individual, the subordinate positions added depend on the fundraising strategy adopted and the solicitation programs to be implemented. The left side of Figure 13.1, identified as "central development office," depicts typical second-line positions. Those include a professional dedicated to development operations/advancement services, each of the core solicitation programs, and possibly planned giving, although the latter is often subsumed under the major-gifts program. Of course, larger offices have additional professional positions, including specialists in prospect research, information systems, stewardship, and other functions. The solicitation programs may engage additional individuals at the associate or assistant director level and, in large programs, professionals focused on regions or special constituencies.

In larger and complex organizations, sources of funding for development positions follow various models, as do the channels through which development staff report. This is a significant consideration in universities that encompass various colleges, schools, institutes, and centers. It is also relevant in other types of nonprofit organizations, including health care systems and national or international nonprofits that have local branches, chapters, or affiliates.

There are three basic organizational models: **centralized**, **decentralized**, and **hybrid**. Each offers inherent advantages and disadvantages (Hall, 1992; Lindgren, 2002). The alternative relationships implied by these models are depicted on the right side of Figure 13.1.

In a purely centralized structure, all development positions report, through channels, to the chief development officer. Some may be assigned to work with the directors of specific units, for example, deans of schools in a university or program directors or chapter CEOs in a nonprofit, and their responsibility is to raise funds to meet priorities of that unit from prospects assigned to that unit. (Remember the discussion of prospect management from Chapter 7.) Development staff members may be physically housed in a central development office or in the individual units, which of course would be the case if those units are geographically dispersed. But their compensation is provided through a central development budget, and they are accountable to the chief development officer. The chief development officer may request input from the unit director on the performance of

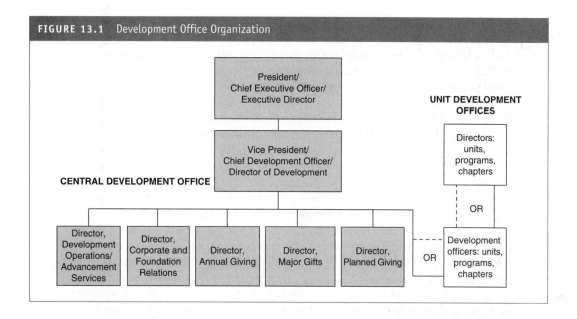

FIGURE 13.1   Development Office Organization

unit-assigned development staff, and unit-assigned development staff may take direction from the unit leader with regard to fundraising priorities of the unit; in other words, they may have an informal **dotted line** reporting relationship to that individual. But their **solid line**, or formal reporting relationship, is to the chief development officer, who is ultimately responsible for hiring and evaluating them.

In a purely decentralized model, development staff members serving a unit are employees of that unit. They are hired, compensated, and evaluated by the leader of that unit. As depicted on the right side of Figure 13.1, they may have an informal, dotted-line relationship to the chief development officer, and they are expected to follow organization-wide policies with regard to prospect management and other matters. And the unit head may consult with the chief development officer regarding the performance of development staff working in that unit, but he or she is ultimately responsible for their evaluation and compensation.

Centralization provides the chief development officer with greater power to set performance standards and hold staff throughout the organization accountable for meeting goals. And since unit heads are unlikely to be development professionals, the chief development officer may be better qualified to hire and evaluate fundraisers. On the other hand, unit-assigned staff who report centrally may be perceived as one of "them" in the unit, possibly hindering their ability to communicate and work with program directors and others in that unit. In addition, the centralized model may not provide a strong incentive to the unit director to take responsibility for fundraising, since the responsibility for achieving goals lies with the chief development officer.

Decentralization addresses some of centralization's problems but raises others. It provides the unit director with control and a stake in fundraising, but it also may result in fragmented, even competitive fundraising efforts across the organization, as well as uneven quality. There is also the risk that a unit director may assign the development professional other tasks unrelated to fundraising, such as managing events or writing a newsletter. This distracts from fundraising performance, often to the frustration of the chief development officer, who has little power to correct the situation.

A third model, the hybrid, is common in universities and some other complex organizations. It has variations but typically includes the development officer having a **joint reporting** relationship (in other words, two solid lines) to both the chief development officer and the unit director, who share responsibility for his or her evaluation and typically the costs of his or her compensation (Hall, 1992; Lindgren, 2002). This approach may avoid the disadvantages of the purely centralized and purely decentralized models, while also capturing some of the benefits of both. But it can be complex and relies on a positive relationship between the chief development officer and the unit director.

The hybrid model is sometimes described as requiring two to hire and one to fire, meaning that selection of the development officer serving a particular unit requires agreement between the chief development officer and the head of that unit but that dissatisfaction by either can lead to dismissal. That obviously presents a dilemma for the development officer, especially if his or her two bosses do not agree on priorities or methods. For that reason, making the model successful requires collaborative planning and clear performance objectives agreed on by the unit head and chief development officer.

Most importantly, however, the structure of the development function needs to be aligned with the organizational structure, budgeting model, and politics of the overall organization. For example, think about a nonprofit that has chapters spread out across the country, chapters with a high degree of autonomy in their operations. Trying to impose a centralized development structure might be inappropriate and ineffective. Unit-assigned staff either would be geographically remote from the units they are supporting or, if they are physically based in those units, remote from the centralized authority to which they report. Alternatively, think about an organization in one location that has various units, but the units are tightly controlled by the central administration. Budgets are centrally controlled and unit heads thus have little incentive to engage in fundraising. Most have no such experience; they are primarily program managers. In this situation, it is difficult to imagine how it would be useful to ask those unit directors to hire and supervise development officers to work on behalf of their units. That would be a responsibility of the chief development officer, who would assure that the needs of all units are addressed and that development officers meet performance standards.

UNDERSTANDING MOTIVATION

Theories about human motivation are of practical importance. Every manager holds some theory about motivation, even if only implicitly. What a manager may believe about human nature will dictate how he or she interacts with people, seeks to motivate them, and addresses disappointments with their performance. Many people have known great bosses, who inspired loyalty and created a pleasant, productive working environment, and perhaps also screamer bosses, whose demands, rants, and insults created a dysfunctional work-place. Such differences may in fact reflect the psychology of the manager and his or her own needs, but they likely also reflect the manager's theory of how other people operate.

For example, McGregor (1960) is well-known for his Theory X and Theory Y. **Theory X**, which McGregor saw reflected in management practices in most industrial organizations, is based on the assumption that workers are lazy, resistant to change, and not concerned with the organization's needs. It is basically a negative view of human nature. Someone who subscribes to **Theory Y**, on the other hand, views employees as capable of self-motivation and self-direction and sees his or her role as a manager as supporting the development of the people supervised. If the manager believes that people are basically lazy, he or she is likely to take a very directive approach. But if the manager believes that people are by nature capable and responsible, then he or she is likely to give individuals more autonomy, decentralize responsibility, and seek to unleash human potential. It is easy to imagine how a workplace shaped by the beliefs of one type of manager would differ from that of a manager of the other type. It is thus important for a manager to hold some explicit theory of human motivation, based on research, rather than just an implicit home-grown theory, perhaps developed through his or her own life experiences.

Now let's turn to some of the theories a manager might consider in trying to understand the motivations of his or her staff members. Organizational behavior is a large field and a full discussion is beyond the scope of this text; indeed, we will just scratch the surface with some well-known theories developed throughout the history of organizational behavior research. Students interested in knowing more will find additional suggested readings listed at the end of this chapter.

Needs Theories

Understanding human needs is essential to understanding how humans are motivated. Managers often think about how they can *motivate* their subordinates, but indeed, all people are motivated by their own needs, which arise outside the workplace and come with them to the office. Understanding those needs can help the manager understand how to direct individuals toward pursuing the organization's goals, in a way consistent with the needs they already have.

One of the most influential of all motivation theorists was Abraham Maslow. He developed his **hierarchy of needs** in the 1940s and 1950s. Although it has been challenged by some scholars, Maslow's (1954) theory had an important influence on later thinking and has been the foundation for much later work.

As the term *hierarchy* implies, Maslow's (1954) theory states that human needs progress from those at lower levels to those at higher levels as the lower-level needs are met. Human beings strive to meet their lower-level needs before addressing those in higher categories. In the lowest category—that is, at the bottom of the hierarchy—are basic physiological needs. Any student who has tried to study while hungry will readily recognize that it is difficult to focus on higher pursuits until more immediate needs are addressed. But once the basics such as food, drink, and shelter are met, people can turn their attention to meeting their higher-level needs. The next steps up the hierarchy include safety needs, social needs, self-esteem needs (also called ego), and, finally, self-actualization needs. Thus, once human beings have met their physiological needs, they may focus on safety. (A hungry person would take risks to obtain food or drink; in other words, those basic needs would outweigh the desire for safety.) Once individuals feel safe, they are then able to focus on meeting their needs for the camaraderie and affection of others and on meeting needs that satisfy their own egos and build their self-esteem. At the top of the hierarchy, self-actualization encompasses the need for self-fulfilment and achievement commensurate with one's ultimate capacity. People motivated at this level are the self-starters so often described as ideal candidates in fundraising job advertisements. They are in essence free to pursue their goals for fulfilment and achievement by having met lower-level needs.

Another way to understand Maslow's (1954) hierarchy is to think about how people might descend to lower-level needs under certain adverse circumstances. For example, someone engaged in fulfilling his or her ego and self-actualization needs might retreat to address lower-level needs if faced with a threat to safety or nourishment. For example, a person in fear of losing his or her job may not be thinking much about taking classes to expand his or her skills; that person's attention probably will be focused on the essential need to do the job at hand and remain employed. A person who feels psychologically unsafe at work—perhaps the manager has a quick temper and tends to scream at people— also may not be thinking much about how to bring innovation to his or her job. He or she will probably stick with the basics and try to remain as invisible as possible. But someone who feels safe in his or her employment and life may be able to reach further up the hierarchy to address higher-level needs, perhaps seeking greater personal and professional challenges or experimenting with new approaches to his or her work, in other words, to take risks in order to improve performance.

McClelland (1961) also focused on needs and on managers as well as their subordinates. Managers have their own psychological needs, which influence how they behave with regard to their subordinates. McClelland (1961) identified three principal needs of managers: the need for **achievement**, the need for **power** over others, and the need for **affiliation** or good relationships with others. Every person has a need for all three, in various proportions. For example, someone could be relatively high on the need for power and relatively high on the need for achievement but relatively low on the need for affiliation. Someone else might be motivated primarily by the need for affiliation and be relatively low on the needs for power and achievement. Although it might seem intuitive that staff members might prefer to work for a manager who has a high need for affiliation, that is, who will value relationships with them above other matters, it turns out that managers who balance a need for affiliation with a need for power (influence over others) are perceived as most effective.

Personality Styles

Katharine Cook Briggs and her daughter Isabel Briggs Myers made an important contribution to management by developing a tool known as the **Myers–Briggs-type indicator**, which is widely used in the workplace today. Myers-Briggs and other similar instruments are used to reveal **personality style**, which "refers to the manner in which individuals gather and process information" (Denhardt, Denhardt, & Aristigueta, 2013, pp. 30–31). Based on the theories of psychologist Carl Jung, personality tests like Myers-Briggs are used to provide individuals with insights about their natures, which may help them understand their own behavior and that of others with whom they work. Perhaps the best-known distinction made by Myers-Briggs is that between **introverts** and **extroverts**, although it measures personality in additional dimensions.

Motivators and Dissatisfiers

Like most theories, those of Frederick Herzberg, first described in the late 1960s, have been challenged by other researchers. However, his findings are still widely cited and have implications for the management of nonprofit staff. Herzberg conducted studies in which he claimed to identify two sets of factors that influence motivation. He called them **motivators** and **hygiene factors**, but they are also sometimes called **satisfiers** and **dissatisfiers**. Motivators relate to the job itself. Hygiene factors do not relate to personal hygiene but rather to conditions in the work environment. Table 13.1 shows both sets of factors. According to Herzberg (1968), there is a big difference between them. Reducing or removing negative hygiene factors from the work environment may reduce dissatisfaction, but doing so does not necessarily increase motivation. In order to increase the motivation of workers, the manager must turn to the motivators shown on the left side of Table 13.1.

To understand Herzberg's (1968) theory, students may find it useful to think about their own work or volunteer experience and what they find satisfying or intolerable in specific cases. Looking at the right-hand column of Table 13.1, dissatisfaction with a job can be caused by the frustrations that derive from company policy or administration—for example, the mindless bureaucracy reflected in Dilbert cartoons. Dissatisfaction may arise from poor interpersonal relationships with a supervisor or peer or from physical working conditions that do not provide safety and security. (Remember Maslow's hierarchy!) A tyrannical or incompetent boss, petty colleagues, or an unclean and unsafe work environment are reasons that might cause most people to go home discouraged and start looking for alternative employment.

TABLE 13.1 Herzberg's Motivators (Satisfiers) and Hygiene Factors (Dissatisfiers)	
Motivators (related to the job)	**Hygiene Factors (related to the work environment)**
Achievement	Company policies and administration
Recognition	Relations with supervisor
The work itself	Interpersonal relations with coworkers
Advancement	Working conditions
Growth	Compensation
Responsibility	Status and security

Source: Adapted from Herzberg (1968).

Take a look at the left-hand side of Table 13.1, a list of Herzberg's (1968) motivators. People who participated in his studies described the factors that motivated them at work as including achievement and recognition, opportunities for advancement, opportunities for greater responsibility and personal growth, and the inherent rewards of certain types of work. For example, soliciting gifts from interesting and generous people might be an inherently rewarding activity, as opposed to, let's say, collecting trash. If the work provides the motivators, the job may prove very satisfying, unless some dissatisfiers from the right-hand column get in the way. If dissatisfiers are present at significant levels, even rewarding work may not be enough to compensate for the aggravation, and people may become unmotivated and perhaps inclined to look for other places to spend their working hours.

What about money? Students will note that compensation—that is, salary, benefits, and other financial rewards—appears on the list of *dissatisfiers* and *not* as a motivator. In other words, according to Herzberg, salary may become a source of dissatisfaction—and that would need to be addressed—but it cannot be used to create motivation. That may seem counterintuitive. After all, do not many companies, and an increasing number of nonprofits, offer financial incentives to encourage higher performance? Let's hold on to this point and return to it shortly in a longer discussion of fundraiser compensation.

Generational Differences in Motivations

In Chapter 3, we discussed how people of different generations may bring different motivations to their philanthropic giving. If that is true, then they are likely to also bring comparable differences to the workplace. The time period in which an individual was born and the significant events that marked the emergence of a generational cohort also may create differences that managers need to understand.

Three generations predominate among nonprofit staff today. The values and worldviews of each generation have been shaped in part by the economic conditions that prevailed during their formative years and by critical events that occurred in their lifetimes. The baby boomers (born between 1946 and the mid-1960s) were shaped by the pressures of the Cold War and events such as Watergate and the Vietnam War. Many members of Generation X (born in the 1970s and early 1980s) were the first to grow up in families with both parents employed outside the home and witnessed such powerful events as the Challenger disaster and the fall of the Berlin Wall. Millennials (born after 1980) came of age with the development of the Internet, and some were shaped by events that included the terrorist attacks of September 11, 2001.

Although generalizations about individuals based on their generation can be as insidious as those based on age, gender, or other characteristics, a number of scholars have found some commonalities among members of these generations. For example, some argue that baby boomers are committed to institutions and organizations and are most likely to be motivated by praise, money, and position. Members of Generation X may be distrustful of large organizations and are motivated by independence and involvement. Millennials (also called Generation Y) seek work that provides meaning and makes a difference. Focused on meaning and purpose, "they want to know why before what" (Denhardt et al., 2013,

p. 177). As Denhardt et al. explain, "[Millennials] arrive at the workplace at the top levels of Maslow's hierarchy of needs" (p. 177).

Again, it is essential to recognize that individual differences may outweigh these generational stereotypes. But it also may be useful for development managers to recognize that individuals who are of generations different from their own may be motivated in different ways and that it may be a mistake to assume that one's own values and worldview are fully shared by others.

APPLYING THEORY TO FUNDRAISING MANAGEMENT

Now that we have reviewed, however briefly, some theories that relate to human motivation, how can they be applied in the management of fundraising staff?

Managers' Self-Knowledge

An important first point is that managers need to know themselves, that is, to understand their own motivations (Denhardt et al., 2013). Whether a manager holds McGregor's (1960) Theory X or Theory Y may determine how he or she interacts with the staff members he or she supervises. The manager's balance of needs for achievement, power, and affiliation (McClelland, 1961) also may influence how he or she approaches the job and how well he or she performs as a manager.

Some people who are excellent front-line fundraisers may not be effective when promoted to a position in which they are to manage others doing the same work. For example, a gift officer often works alone, undertaking cultivation and solicitation visits. Many take great pride in their own achievements and, indeed, can be quite competitive with colleagues in that regard. Although fundraising requires teamwork, it may be that those drawn to the specific work of developing productive relationships with donors have a particular pattern of needs. They may be high both on McClelland's achievement and affiliation needs but relatively low on the need for influence over others. Someone with that set of needs, well met through direct fundraising activity, may not find his or her needs met as well from a job in which the management of others displaces the ability to interact with donors directly. And, yet, it is common for management positions in fundraising to be filled by people who have been successful in direct fundraising. As Burk (2013) observes, this seems logical, since the person who can raise money might be expected to show others how to do it. But just because someone is good at a specific activity does not mean that person will be an effective manager of others who do the same work. For example, a great doctor might not necessarily have the skills to be a hospital CEO (Burk, 2013). Some who make the transition from fundraiser to manager may try to continue handling a substantial portfolio of prospects, something that meets their own needs. But it also may leave their subordinates poorly supervised and feeling unsupported. It would be better if such individuals could develop insight into their own needs and select their positions accordingly.

Recognizing Others' Needs

A second lesson for managers drawn from motivation theories is that the people who report to them come to work with preexisting needs, which may not match their own and which the manager may not be able to influence (Denhardt et al., 2013).

As Maslow's (1954) theory explains, whether an individual is the self-actualized, self-starting gift officer we might desire depends on whether his or her other needs have been met. And that will, of course, relate not just to the job but to other aspects of life outside the office. The staff member's behavior at work also may reflect his or her unmet needs; insight into that can sometimes pave the way to making an individual more productive.

Various authors and consultants have asserted that personality styles are relevant when selecting and managing fundraisers. For example, Kihlstedt (2013) describes four types, based on whether the individuals are introverts or extroverts and how they process information. She defines the following qualities:

> *Introverts* like to think before they speak. They're private people who are energized by their *inner lives*.
>
> *Extroverts* are energized by their *social lives*, and often need to talk to understand what they're thinking.
>
> *Analytics* prefer to focus on specific data from the past and the present.
>
> *Intuitives* prefer to focus on future possibilities and big ideas. (Kihlstedt, 2013, p. 9; italics original)

Putting introvert/extrovert on one axis and analytic/intuitive on the other, she defines four types:

> Analytical extroverts are *Rainmakers*—outgoing, objective people who work hard, plan well, and like to be in charge.
>
> Intuitive extroverts are *Go-Getters*—gregarious, big-picture thinkers who exude charm and energy.
>
> Intuitive introverts are *Kindred Spirits*—people who lead with their hearts and are inspired by stories of individual success.
>
> Analytic introverts are *Mission Controllers*—detail-oriented planners who guard against things that might go wrong. (Kihlstedt, 2013, p. 11; italics original)

Kihlstedt argues that it is more important for a fundraiser to understand his or her own style than the personality of the prospective donor for three reasons. The fundraiser is likely to revert to his or her own style under pressure, so trying to adapt to each prospect's personality is unrealistic. Self-understanding is most likely to build the fundraiser's own confidence. And self-knowledge is the foundation for understanding someone else. She proposes specific approaches each type of fundraiser she has identified should follow in selecting prospects, preparing the ask, setting up a visit, asking for the gift, and following through. While Kihlstedt provides self-help advice to individual fundraisers, such insights on those individuals also are of obvious value to their managers.

Clear, Achievable, and Challenging Goals

The need for clear and challenging goals is not specific to fundraising staff—it is a requirement of sound management of others in any environment (Denhardt et al., 2013). But in an activity evaluated ultimately in terms of dollars raised, the definition and determination of goals is obviously central.

As Herzberg (1968) discovered, the opportunity for achievement is a motivator for most individuals. But achievement requires clear goals by which it is defined. Otherwise, effort yields no emotional reward, the staff member may mistake activity for progress, or a situation may evolve in which individuals who feel they are achieving good results find that those results are still not sufficient to meet the expectations of their supervisors. Whetten and Cameron (2011) make the point with an example from *Alice's Adventures in Wonderland*:

> Discussions of goal setting often make reference to a conversation between Alice . . . and the Cheshire Cat. When confronted with a choice between crossing routes, Alice asked the Cat which one she should choose. In response, the Cat asked Alice where she was heading. Discovering Alice had no real destination in mind, the Cat appropriately advised her any choice would do. (p. 332)

Goals need to be achievable but also "appropriately challenging" in order to be motivating (Whetten & Cameron, 2011, p. 334). Staff members evaluate both the probability of success in achieving goals and the "significance of the anticipated achievement" (p. 334). In other words, in order for goals to motivate, achieving them must be something that brings a sense of achievement; reaching an easy goal just does not bring much satisfaction.

Salience and Probability of Rewards

Managers should think about the salience of various rewards in terms of individuals' needs (Denhardt et al., 2013; Whetten & Cameron, 2011). Again, individuals are motivated differently. They have different values. They may be in different places on Maslow's hierarchy. Generational and other differences also may play a role. What individuals find rewarding may be different in each case. A manager needs to listen, determine what each member of the staff finds important, and provide rewards consistent with that insight.

Some may thrive on recognition, for example, being named "gift officer of the week." Others may value the opportunity for flexible hours or to earn additional free time through outstanding performance. Some may need to have a clear understanding of the mission impact of their efforts. As Denhardt et al. (2013) emphasize, the interest and attention of the manager may itself be a reward that will reinforce high performance for some members of the staff.

But managers should be honest with people about what rewards are possible and what rewards are not (Denhardt et al., 2013) As Vroom (1964) discovered in his research, individuals may be motivated not only by the value of rewards but also by the probability that they can be obtained. We all may possess some intuition that enables us to distinguish between promises that sound realistic and those that do not. A manager who is unrealistic in promising increased compensation, increased responsibility, community recognition, or some other reward for achievement of goals may buy some short-term motivation. But over time, such a manager will lose credibility and the power to influence the behavior of his or her staff.

In order for promised rewards to be realistic, the achievements to be rewarded must be within the *control* of the staff member. This is particularly relevant in managing gift officers and is one argument why the amount of dollars raised is not appropriate as the sole basis for evaluation. Think back to Chapter 7 and the discussion of Dupree's model for evaluating gift officer performance. Performance was based on various measures, most of which the gift officer could control, including the number of contacts, proposal submitted, and so forth. Gifts resulting from the gift officer's efforts were but one variable determining his or her performance score.

The problem in measuring performance based only on gifts is that the ultimate decision to give is that of the donor, not the fundraiser. It may reflect the donor's emotions, economic and family circumstances, the state of the economy, and other variables over which the fundraiser has no influence. For that reason, establishing performance metrics based only on gifts is not a realistic or fair approach. The fundraiser might recognize, even if intuitively, that his or her own efforts may not fully determine what rewards he or she will receive. It is difficult for rewards to have impact when they seem to be based partly on the circumstances and decisions of others—or just on luck.

Treating People Fairly

A situation in which compensation is perceived as unfair, that is, in which staff members are paid differentially for doing the same work, is most certain to lead to dissatisfaction. Indeed, differential treatment of staff members in any regard is wrong, especially when such differences coincide with the characteristics of individuals, such as race, gender, national origin, religion, political perspective, sexual orientation, or other personal characteristics. Such an environment would include several of Herzberg's (1968) dissatisfiers.

An effective manager will assure that such unfairness is not permitted. Moreover, many nonprofit organizations have embraced diversity as an organizational value, seeking to draw the strength that comes from bringing together people of different perspectives, experiences, cultures, and backgrounds. Achieving greater diversity in the fundraising profession is a priority for both AFP and CASE, which have initiated programs toward that end.

Regrettably, however, various studies have revealed a continuing differential in compensation paid to male and female fundraising professionals. Whereas the majority of individuals in the fundraising profession are women, Mesch and Rooney found in 2008 that female chief development officers were paid 11 percent less than men. However, they did not find a differential when comparing bonuses paid to men and women, suggesting that when pay is related to *performance*, it is likely to be equal.

Maximizing Motivators and Minimizing Dissatisfiers

Looking back at Herzberg's findings, a good manager will work to minimize or eliminate the factors that cause dissatisfaction and to maximize the presence of motivators. Fostering good relationships among members of the team, simplifying bureaucratic policies and procedures, and providing good working conditions can help to avoid dissatisfaction. Opportunities for achievement, recognition, growth, advancement, and responsibility can be powerful motivators. Some useful techniques include recognizing high performers in front of their peers, promoting from within, and providing opportunities for career advancement by permitting time to participate in AFP, AHP, PPP, CASE, and other professional associations. Providing assignments that are inherently interesting, and perhaps varying assignments from time to time to keep things fresh, also can keep staff members interested and motivated.

COMPENSATING FUNDRAISERS

Now let's return to a point from Herzberg's findings—the role of compensation. Herzberg's (1968) research found that salary, or compensation, is a dissatisfier rather than a motivator. In other words, if compensation is too low or perceived to be unfair, that may lead people to be dissatisfied. But compensation in itself cannot make up for the presence of other dissatisfiers or for the absence of motivators. In other words, compensation in itself is not a motivator.

Again, it is important to recognize that many scholars have challenged Herzberg's (1968) findings. But his theory does seem consistent with what has been observed in many nonprofit organizations. Even though staff often are paid less than their counterparts in the for-profit world, many find their work very rewarding if Herzberg's motivators are present. Since they do not expect to receive the same salaries paid in some for-profit companies, they are not dissatisfied by their nonprofit incomes so long as they are at least adequate and perceived as fair. Indeed, one study of nonprofit workers conducted by the Princeton Survey Research Associates and supervised by the Brookings Institution (Light, 2002) provides insights on the motivations of nonprofit staff members consistent with Herzberg's (1968) theory.

The study found that nonprofit workers are indeed driven by mission rather than money. Only 16 percent of nonprofit staff surveyed said that they come to work for their pay, compared with 31 percent of federal employees and 47 percent of for-profit employees. More than 70 percent of nonprofit workers reported that they were satisfied with their pay. Other sources of satisfaction reported were flexibility, collaborative decision making, and being treated as well-rounded human beings rather than just workers. Most sources of dissatisfaction reported were related to ineffective supervision, overwork and burnout, or inadequate resources with which to work. The positives and negatives sound much like Herzberg's two sets of factors (Light, 2002). But what about fundraisers specifically? Are they motivated in the same way as other nonprofit staff members, or is their motivation more related to their compensation? The answer is unsettled.

Performance and Compensation Related

In her 2013 study, Burk found that incentives do not seem to be effective with fundraising professionals, nor are they a source of satisfaction to them in their jobs. However, a study by Mesch and Rooney (2008) focused on the relationship between fundraiser performance and compensation and provided some provocative findings and conclusions. Mesch and Rooney acknowledge other research suggesting that nonprofit staff members generally may be motivated more by the mission than money, but they also note that fundraisers are somewhat different. It may be challenging to measure the results of nonprofit programs or to attribute outcomes to the efforts of specific individuals. But "in comparison to other types of positions in nonprofit organizations, fundraising . . . is results oriented, and outcomes can be measured" (Mesch & Rooney, 2008, p.439).

The authors' study, using compensation data collected by AFP, found "a statistically significant relationship between pay and performance for most fundraising positions" (p. 450). They conclude that fundraisers are indeed different:

> There may be several explanations for our findings. First, for fundraisers, where a financial measure of performance relates directly to job responsibilities, pay and performance are more likely to be related—unlike most managerial positions in nonprofits, where pay and performance have not found much support in the empirical literature. Second, individuals who self-select into fundraising roles may behave more like those in the private sector—less risk averse in terms of linking their pay to performance. Fundraisers may be acting more like workers in the for-profit sector due to the nature of their job responsibilities and not sorting in the ways that typically have been found in nonprofits. These findings suggest the importance of examining the roles that individuals play in the nonprofit sector in terms of self-selection. (Mesch & Rooney, 2008, p. 458)

Of course, correlation does not prove causation. If there is a relationship between pay and performance, that may be because organizations reward performance with higher compensation, but it does not establish that the promise of higher compensation is what *motivated* the fundraisers to perform. Perhaps fundraisers are different from other nonprofit employees. Or it may be that nonprofit boards and CEOs regard fundraisers differently and have different expectations of them. If the latter, that has implications for the place of fundraising professionals within their organizations. If they are indeed—or are viewed to be—outsiders, motivated primarily by money in a mission-driven sector, it seems to define a tension that needs to be addressed. This is a question worthy of continued examination.

Incentive Compensation

Fundraising professionals are compensated for their work and sometimes substantially. Indeed, in a 2014 survey, the *Chronicle of Philanthropy* identified thirty nonprofit fundraisers earning salaries of more than $500,000 and a few over $1 million per year (Daniels, Hall, & Narayanswamy, 2014). Most are paid a salary; by definition, it is paid on a regular basis and its amount is not directly affected by the individual's performance in the short run. Of course, salary increases may be given to those who perform well, but the penalty for poor performance is usually the lack of a raise or, in the extreme case, dismissal.

Payment of **incentive compensation**, however, is contingent on the individual meeting certain goals. Although there are no comprehensive data available, it is an approach that has become more common as well as controversial, with reports of incentives comprising one-half of some fundraising executives' total compensation (Hall, 2014b).

There are various ways in which a fundraiser's pay could be tied to the amount of funds raised. One would be to pay a **commission**, that is, a percentage of gifts received. But that approach is contrary to the ethical standards of the leading professional associations in the field. For example, AFP's Code of Ethical Standards and Principles (Principle 21) states that "Members *shall not* accept compensation or enter into a contract that is based on a percentage of contributions" (AFP, 2007; italics added). CASE's statements on commission-based compensation also address the issue and provide a rationale:

> CASE discourages commission-based compensation for all fundraising employees of member institutions. It is recommended that all fundraising staff work for a salary, retainer, or fee, not a commission. Compensation should be predetermined and not based on a percentage of funds raised. This recommendation is based on the following beliefs:

> 1. Commissions will encourage inappropriate conduct by fundraisers anxious to secure gifts at any cost, whether or not those gifts meet the objectives of the institution they serve.

> 2. Commission-driven fundraisers could potentially draw compensation well above an equitable level in relation to services rendered when, in the final analysis, it is the institution and not the fundraiser that both attracts and merits charitable support.

> 3. Major gifts, which often require long-term cultivation, could be jeopardized by fundraisers seeking a swift donor response to benefit their own personal compensation goals.

> 4. Gift support might be lost if potential major donors realize that a percentage of their donation will go directly to the fundraiser.

> 5. Commission fundraising discourages the use of volunteers.

> 6. Since charities do not know exactly what motivates a donor to make a gift, it is difficult to determine the amount of compensation to which a fundraiser might be entitled under a commission/salary arrangement. (CASE, 2014)

But what about performance-based payments that are not a percentage of funds raised? Both AFP and CASE permit the payment of **bonuses** but with some caveats. AFP's Principle 22 states that "members may accept performance-based compensation, such as bonuses, provided such bonuses are in accord with prevailing practices within the members' own organizations and are not based on a percentage of contributions" (AFP, 2007). CASE's statements similarly permit bonuses, with some conditions:

Supplemental compensation programs should:

1. Not be expressed as a percentage of individual gifts or aggregate giving, since doing so would constitute a commission

2. Be based on pre-set goals that have been clearly stated and agreed-upon in advance by the employee and the institution (note that this guideline is not intended to preclude bonuses for exceptional individual or team achievement that may be allowable under an institution's compensation policies)

3. Relate goals to the fundraising context, given that potential to raise funds and associated effort required may vary widely across positions and operating units

4. Not serve as a replacement for base salary or result in under-compensation of employees who meet their job expectations. (CASE, 2014)

Assuming that incentive compensation for fundraisers is consistent with the standards articulated by AFP, CASE, and other organizations, questions remain about their effectiveness and appropriateness in the nonprofit sector, as applied to fundraisers and others. What motivates people to work in the nonprofit sector—is it primarily money or commitment to the mission? Was Herzberg right that compensation can be a dissatisfier but not a motivator, or can financial incentives lead to greater motivation and performance? And what are the implications of incentive compensation for fundraisers for the nonprofit sector as a whole?

A full discussion of the latter question is beyond the scope of this text, but Speckbacher (2013) provides an interesting analysis. He notes three presumed advantages of incentive compensation, including motivation for increased effort, signals that lead to self-selection of high-performing people to the workplace, and channeling employee attention to desired outcomes. But, he finds, incentive compensation for fundraisers may have an impact on the nonprofit sector overall and on organizations' relationships with their other staff members. Introducing explicit incentives (i.e., money) changes the relationship from social to contractual; in other words, it becomes a market relationship. "Trust and the feeling of obligation may disappear" (Speckbacher, 2013, p. 1021). Moreover, it is difficult to mix social incentives with financial incentives; the entire relationship is likely to become based on the latter. And if such incentives are introduced for some staff members (for example, fundraisers), it is likely there will be "spillover effects" on other staff members of the organization, who may come to see their relationship with their employer more in market terms (p. 1021). Speckbacher's analysis suggests that the debate about fundraiser compensation therefore may have significant implications for the nonprofit sector.

IMPROVING STAFF PERFORMANCE

Previous sections of this chapter discussed theories of motivation and behaviors managers can exhibit to provide an environment in which staff members may achieve high performance. Now let's consider performance in a little more detail and look at some tools that development office managers might apply to maximize the performance of staff members.

Whetten and Cameron (2011) provide three useful formulas:

Performance $=$ Ability $\times$ Motivation

Ability $=$ Aptitude $\times$ Training $\times$ Resources

Motivation $=$ Desire $\times$ Commitment

As these formulas suggest, an individual's performance is a result of ability and motivation, both of which are themselves complex variables. Motivation involves both desire and commitment, the former meaning that the person would like to succeed and the latter meaning that the person is willing to put in the effort to do so. Motivation is the product of these two variables, so a person the authors would define as highly motivated is one who both wants to do well and is willing to work hard to do so. All of us, perhaps, have known some people who would like to succeed—at least in theory—but simply never muster the commitment; they are slackers. We can also think of examples of people who are committed and work hard but care little about being especially successful; they are the plodders, who just are not especially inspired. Motivation refers to the *effort* someone puts forth, including both desire and commitment.

Motivation Problems

What can a manager do if a staff member appears to lack motivation? There are a couple of possibilities to examine. Perhaps the manager's goals and expectations are unclear. Perhaps there is a lack of Herzberg's motivators in the work environment, at least those that are salient for this staff member. Maybe the individual's motivation could be increased through more opportunities for achievement, recognition, growth, and advancement. Are current rewards salient to this individual, in terms of his or her needs? Perhaps he or she would respond more favorably to opportunities to have more days off in exchange for improved performance, rather than an increase in financial compensation. Alternatively, maybe this staff member would respond to a different structure of financial incentives. And, of course, it may be possible that the individual just finds fundraising inherently unrewarding and would be better suited to another line of work. If so, counseling him or her to find another line of work might be the manager's best and most humane course of action.

Problems Related to Ability

Some managers think about the performance of staff members primarily in terms of motivation. They assume people will do better if they just *try harder*. That would probably be the case, for example, with a manager who holds McGregor's Theory X about human nature. If a gift officer is not producing results, the solution offered by such a manager might be that he or she simply make more visits and work longer hours. But as Whetten and Cameron (2011) explain, motivation is only a part of the formula that produces performance; **ability** is essential, too.

But ability is complex; it has three components: **aptitude**, **training**, and **resources**. Aptitude refers to innate abilities and qualities a person brings to the job, for example, intelligence, communication skills, and personality styles. Training may be able to alter some of those qualities but probably within limits. It is unlikely that an introvert can be turned into an extrovert, even though he or she may learn better social skills. A person with poor communication skills may be able to enhance them, but in all likelihood they reflect training or the lack thereof at an earlier point in life and may be relatively difficult to improve significantly in the context of a job. Intelligence, unfortunately, is not subject to change, but it is important to remember that not every job is that of a rocket scientist, and people of varying aptitudes can make important contributions in the right positions.

But if poor performance is due to a lack of training or resources, rather than aptitude, there is a lot a manager might be able to do. For example, if a gift officer does not know the basics of gift solicitation but has the aptitude to succeed, there are many opportunities for training available. His or her manager might recommend the individual take a course that uses this textbook or consider various conferences and workshops available. If the lack of performance is due to resource issues, the manager can address those and remove obstacles to the individual's success (Whetten & Cameron, 2011). Think about the discussion in Chapter 12 about the hypothetical nonprofit that has invested so little in the development office that the director of development is simply unable to produce a positive return on investment; that example describes failure most likely attributable to the lack of adequate resources. Providing that director with some support staff and systems likely would improve his or her performance against fundraising goals.

Whetten and Cameron (2011) identify five responses a manager might make to a performance problem due to a lack of ability: **resupply**, **retrain**, **refit**, **reassign**, and **release**. Resupply means to provide more resources, and retrain means what it implies; some examples of both were just mentioned. And release is probably quite clear; it is the same as termination or dismissal. But what are refit and reassign?

Refitting involves leaving the individual in his or her position but *redesigning* the job to be a better fit with his or her abilities. For example, suppose the annual-giving program has recently expanded. The director was quite effective when the job just involved writing letters and managing mailings, but the budget has grown, as have the volume and methods of solicitation employed. The needs for analysis and administration have multiplied. Perhaps the previous director has great creative skills but is simply not equipped to manage these expanded activities. One solution might be to bring in someone else to manage the logistics of the program, while permitting the director to continue focusing on the creative side. Or perhaps it might be possible to reorganize in a way that has the director of annual giving report to an assistant vice president who has overall responsibility for individual giving and who can relieve him or her of the administrative and analytical burdens.

Reassigning also means that the individual remains employed but is moved to a position more compatible with his or her abilities. In the previous example, maybe the director of annual giving simply is unable to handle the increased responsibilities that have come with growth and there is no realistic way to redesign the position so that he or she can. But the person might be well-suited to a position in the organization's department of communications and marketing, where creative skills might be put to good use and where perhaps the demands of management might be reduced.

The concepts discussed in this section and principles of motivation discussed earlier in this chapter provide useful tools managers might employ in diagnosing and addressing performance issues on the part of development office staff.

RECRUITING AND DEVELOPING FUNDRAISING PROFESSIONALS

People are the most important asset in any organization, and that is especially so in the development office. And, except for periods of economic recession, the demand for individuals with development skills often has exceeded the supply. Smith (2010) observes this market reality and addresses the implications, asking "Should organizations recruit from the small pool of individuals with multiple years of specific educational fundraising experience, or should they focus on competent performers and those with transferable skills? Furthermore, what types of people should they hire, how should they assess fit, and what steps should be taken to ensure optimal productivity?" (p. 87). Smith (2010) concludes that organizations need to identify the aptitudes required for success as fundraisers, hire individuals with those aptitudes regardless of previous experience in the field, and provide sufficient training.

The challenge of recruitment is, of course, linked to the importance of retaining high-performing staff members and providing the management necessary to maximize the contribution of every member of the staff. The insights and models provided by theory and research can be applied by development managers to accomplish those goals.

CHAPTER SUMMARY

The organization and management of fundraising staff has become more important as development offices have grown.

There are three basic models for organizing development staff. In a *centralized* model, all staff report ultimately to the chief development officer and are compensated through a central development budget. In a *decentralized* model, staff are employed by individual units of the larger organization, report to the heads of those units, and are compensated through unit budgets. As the term implies, *hybrid* models include elements of the previous two. In this model, staff members usually are compensated in part through the central budget and in part through the unit budget and have *joint reporting* relationships. This model requires clear goals agreed upon by unit heads and the chief development officer. All models have advantages and disadvantages, and the one adopted should be a good fit with the overall structure, culture, and political environment of the organization (Hall, 1992; Lindgren, 2002).

Managers often hold theories about the motivations of their subordinates, for example, Theory X (people are lazy) or Theory Y (people are self-motivated) (McGregor, 1960). People are motivated to meet their psychological needs, and managers need to understand what those are. Maslow (1954) described a *hierarchy of needs*, ascending from basic physiological needs to the need for self-actualization. McClelland (1961) described the need for *achievement, affiliation, and power*, which influence the behavior of managers as well as subordinates. Myers and Briggs identified how *personality styles* affect how people process information and communicate (Denhardt et al., 2013). A theory developed by Herzberg (1968) holds that there are *motivators* that relate to the job (including achievement, recognition, advancement, growth, and inherently satisfying work) but that the work environment may include *hygiene factors* that are *dissatisfiers*. Herzberg identified salary as a potential dissatisfier but not as a motivator. Other variables may influence the motivations and behaviors of individuals at work, including generational patterns.

Applying the insights from research to the supervision of fundraising staff requires that managers know themselves; recognize the needs of others; establish clear, achievable, and challenging goals; consider the salience (or relevance) of various rewards to each individual; treat people fairly; maximize the motivators; and minimize the dissatisfiers present in the work environment.

Many fundraising professionals receive attractive salaries and some also receive *incentive compensation*, which is contingent on achieving certain goals. For various sound reasons, the ethical codes of AFP, CASE, and other organizations prohibit paying fundraisers *commissions*, that is, money based on a percentage of gifts. It is considered ethical to provide fundraisers with *bonuses*, provided they meet certain standards and are not based on a percentage of funds raised (AFP, 2007). Some research suggests that fundraisers may be motivated differently from other nonprofit staff members (Mesch & Rooney, 2008). If so, that has implications for the nonprofit sector.

When a performance problem occurs with a staff member, managers should explore whether it is attributable to a problem of motivation or ability. The problem may lie with motivation, which includes the person's desire to do well and commitment to work hard enough to achieve success. If the problem is due to motivation, possible issues to consider are unclear goals, a lack of incentives (motivators), or the failure of the incentives to be salient (relevant) to the staff member's needs (Whetten & Cameron, 2011).

Ability includes *aptitude*, *training*, and *resources*. If the performance problem relates to one of these components, the manager may address it in one of five ways: *resupply*, *retrain*, *refit*, *reassign*, or *release* (Whetten & Cameron, 2011).

The demand for effective development professionals often exceeds supply, requiring that organizations focus on recruitment of individuals with the right qualities and providing them with training. Market realities also require working with current staff members to retain them and maximize their performance (Smith, 2010).

Key Terms and Concepts

Ability (aptitude, training, resources)

Achievement (need for)

Affiliation (need for)

Bonuses

Centralized

Commission

Decentralized

Dotted line (reporting relationship)

Extroverts

Hierarchy of needs

Hybrid

Hygiene factors (dissatisfiers)

Incentive compensation

Introverts

Joint reporting
  (relationship)

Motivators (satisfiers)

Myers–Briggs-type
  indicator

Personality style

Power (need for)

Reassign

Refit

Release
  (dismiss)

Resupply

Retrain

Solid line (reporting
  relationship)

Theory X

Theory Y

Case 13.1: Getta Grant

Getta Grant is director of development at a medium-sized nonprofit that provides a range of services to adolescents from disadvantaged urban communities. She reports to the executive director. The organization receives some government funding but is also reliant on foundations and individual donors. Getta's responsibilities include staying informed about foundation interests and giving patterns and working with the organization's three program directors to identify foundations that may be prospects for support of their programs and projects. She drafts letters of inquiry and, where appropriate, meets with foundation officers and writes proposals. Getta has been with the organization for five years and was hired by the previous executive director, who always gave her "excellent" (the highest rating) on her annual performance reviews.

The current executive director has been in her job less than a year. She inherited Getta from her predecessor. When she had just arrived, it was already time for Getta's annual evaluation. The new executive director read a couple of proposals Getta had written, thought they were good, and continued her "excellent" rating without much further thought. Getta seemed pleased to have her high rating continued.

When Getta writes something, it is generally of high quality. But over the past year, the executive director has become unhappy with the amount of work Getta produces and with her inability to meet deadlines. Since her last review, Getta has produced only a handful of letters and two proposals. The executive director gave her positive feedback on that work, which was indeed good, thinking that would motivate her to work harder and faster. But Getta has continued to produce relatively few proposals, and in some cases, they have taken so long that she missed foundation deadlines. She is coming up soon for her second evaluation with the executive director, who is now quite frustrated with her performance.

The executive director met with Getta recently and explained that she is unhappy. She warned Getta that her next performance evaluation may not be as positive this year. Getta seemed shocked. "But you said my proposals are good," she protested, "and you gave me an 'excellent' rating last year! I work hard, and it takes time to write those proposals. I have to do all the research myself, meet with the program directors myself, write them myself, and even sometimes take them to the UPS store by myself to make sure they get in on time." Since that meeting, Getta has missed several days of work, calling in sick or saying she was "working at home." And the executive director has seen almost no additional work. (Adapted from Worth, 2014, p. 234)

Case 13.2: Sue Social

Sue Social is an executive assistant working in the development office of a performing arts center. Her responsibilities are to support the work of the director of special events by entering data, maintaining lists of RSVPs for various events, answering the phone, and handling other administrative tasks.

But the director of special events is dissatisfied with her work and comes to discuss the matter with the chief development officer, who manages the overall operation. The director says that Sue is often away from her desk, talking with colleagues, and takes long lunch hours to spend with her friends, leaving too much work undone. When there are social events for donors, which often follow performances, Sue always attends and manages to talk with all the guests. "She has excellent social skills," the director says, "and people really like her. But she just doesn't do the job she is supposed to do." Sue is supposed to be at the door issuing nametags as guest arrive, but she often misses people because she is talking with others. She is supposed to be coordinating with the caterers throughout the event to be sure things are running smoothly, but she is more often found talking and laughing with guests as if she were a guest herself. As a result, things have fallen through the cracks at a few events, and the director was unhappy about it.

The director reports she has met with Sue to try to resolve her concerns. Sue acknowledged that she finds it hard to focus on administrative tasks, saying, "It just wears me down to sit at the desk all day." But, she adds, "I think all the donors like me and I do enjoy talking to them." The director says she has told Sue that she is likely to receive a poor evaluation on her annual review and will not receive a raise in salary. She told Sue that she needs to try harder to do her job well, but Sue's behavior has not changed. The director asks the chief development officer what she should do as the next step.

Case 13.3: Movin' Bill

Bill is a major-gifts officer who works in the Graduate School of Mysticism at a major university. He reports jointly to the dean of the school and an associate vice president for advancement in the central development office. He has been in his position about a year. Bill is a personable and articulate young man, whom many people describe as "charming."

Prior to coming to the university, Bill was a staff member of the development office of the Wildlife Out West Association. Being an outdoors enthusiast himself, Bill connected well with the men and women in the association who shared his love of wildlife and the West. As a result, he had established a superb track record as director of annual giving for the association. Unfortunately for Bill, when the association merged with another nonprofit, the development office was downsized. Because Bill had the least seniority of all development staff, he was let go.

Since joining the university's staff, Bill has consistently completed more moves than any other major-gifts officer; indeed, his colleagues have nicknamed him "Movin' Bill." Bill diligently files his contact reports and they appear to reveal good conversations with prospects. But he has yet to close any major gifts. One time, Bill told the associate vice president that he was going to Ireland for a week, where he would be staying with the family of one of his prospects who owns a vacation home there. The associate vice president questioned whether that was a good use of his time, but Bill said he thought the prospect was getting close to making a major gift and that he thought he could close it during this extended contact. He returned from the trip and wrote a long report, with a lot of details about the prospect, his business, and his family, but it did not indicate that a gift was any closer than before.

The associate vice president became concerned while reading it and called the dean, who said she was enthusiastic about Bill's work. "He's really out there," the dean said. "We hardly ever see him. And our alumni tell me they really like him. He's terrific." The dean added, "We pay him a salary to build relationships with people and that's what he does. Frankly, I don't see the problem."

The associate vice president met with Bill and expressed his concern about his failure to close gifts. Bill seemed taken by surprise. Bill said he thought it was important to build relationships with prospects, and that's what he thought he was doing. He expressed confidence that some major gifts were about to come to fruition. The associate vice president felt somewhat reassured by what Bill said in the meeting. But that was three months ago. Bill continues to be the "move king" of the office and recently returned from a three-week trip to California and Hawaii, where he was visiting prospects. He has yet to close a gift, but he continues to draw a good salary. The associate vice president thinks he needs to identify the problem and decide what action to take.

Questions for Discussion

1. Suppose you are a candidate for a development officer position at a hospital that is part of a larger health care system, encompassing various hospitals, clinics, and other facilities. You are told that you will have a joint reporting relationship. You will report to the chief development officer in the organization's corporate office and also to the CEO of the hospital, where you will be physically based. These two individuals will collaborate in setting your goals and evaluating your performance. What questions do you need to have answered before deciding whether or not to accept this position?

2. If you were (or if you are) a fundraising professional, would receiving incentive compensation (for example, a bonus) make you more productive? If your answer is yes, does that imply that you were not as productive as you might have been before? Why?

3. Consider each of the following questions with regard to Cases 13.1 through 13.3:

    a. Does the problem seem to be due to motivation or ability?

    b. If the poor performance is due to motivation, what theories might explain it, and what might be some actions the manager could take to address the problem? Are Herzberg's motivators or dissatisfiers reflected in the case?

    c. If the poor performance is due to ability, is it a resources problem, a training problem, or an aptitude problem?

    d. What new approaches or strategies might the manager consider to address the ability problem, including the options of resupply, retrain, refit, reassign, or release?

Suggestions for Further Reading

Books

Denhardt, R. B., Denhardt, J. V., & Aristigueta, M. P. (2013). *Managing human behavior in public and nonprofit organizations.* Thousand Oaks, CA: Sage.

Kihlstedt, A. (2013). *Asking styles.* Rancho Santa Margarita, CA: CharityChannel.

Articles

Mesch, D. J., & Rooney, P. M. (2008, Summer). Determinants of compensation: A study of pay, performance, and gender differences for fundraising professionals. *Nonprofit Management and Leadership, 18*(4), 435–463.

Speckbacher, G. (2013, October). The use of incentives in nonprofit organizations. *Nonprofit and Voluntary Sector Quarterly, 42*(5), 1006–1025.

CHAPTER 14

Legal and Ethical Considerations

This chapter provides a brief overview of some legal requirements that relate to fundraising practice and of some ethical issues fundraisers commonly encounter. It is important to make some distinctions and define some limitations at the outset of the discussion.

First, law and ethical principles are related but distinguishable. It is always unethical to disobey the law, except perhaps in acts of nonviolent civil disobedience. Indeed, the AFP Code of Ethical Principles and Standards (Principle 5) requires compliance with the law, as do Independent Sector's Principles for Good Governance and Ethical Practice. But the fact that something is legal does not mean it is necessarily ethical. Many practices do not violate the law yet would nevertheless be inconsistent with formal fundraising ethical codes (discussed later) and/or common understandings of ethical behavior. Thus, the discussion in this chapter is divided into two broad sections—legal considerations and ethical issues.

The law is very complex, and many facets of it may impact fundraising and philanthropy. For that reason, this discussion of law is limited to a few selected principles, and in addition, nothing in this book should be relied on or taken as legal advice. The law is dynamic, and anything written today may become out of date at any time. That is another reason why this chapter discusses only broad points and students should check the web for any updates on points of particular interest.

Laws that affect nonprofits are primarily those related to the tax exemption and governance of *organizations* and to the tax deductibility of charitable *gifts*; some of those have been discussed at previous points in this book. This chapter focuses on legal requirements related specifically to the practice of *fundraising*, in the areas of *solicitation* and *gift acknowledgment*.

STATE REGISTRATION REQUIREMENTS

Laws related to the solicitation of charitable gifts exist at the federal, state, and local levels, but states have undertaken the most extensive regulation of fundraising. About forty states have laws requiring that nonprofits register before soliciting their residents for gifts. Many exempt certain types of organizations, notably religious institutions. State laws concerning registration by nonprofits vary, although the National Association of Attorneys General developed a model law in 1986.

Registration procedures differ across states, but most states accept a **unified registration statement (URS)**. In 2014, the National Association of State Charity Officials (NASCO) retained the Urban Institute to develop a single portal that would eventually permit nonprofits to register in multiple states electronically (NASCO, 2014).

In addition to the requirement that nonprofit organizations register, many states also require registration by **professional fundraisers** (some including consultants, who do not raise money) and **paid solicitors**, who, as the term implies, do solicit gifts. Many require that contracts between nonprofits and such external individuals or companies be filed with the state. Many also require the filing of contracts with **commercial coventurers**, that is, businesses that engage in marketing relationships with nonprofits such as those discussed in Chapter 9. Fundraising that involves games of chance, such as bingo and raffles, usually requires an additional license from the local or state government.

One important point is that registration with a state does not imply endorsement or approval of the organization by the state government. Another important point is that nonprofits are expected to register not only in the states in which they are located but in *all* states in which they solicit funds (Hopkins, 2009). So, if an organization is located in one state but sends solicitations to prospects in other states, it is expected to register in all of those states. That raises, of course, the question of what constitutes a "solicitation," particularly with regard to the use of the Internet.

Sending e-mails to residents of a state is the same as sending direct-mail solicitations to them, so the registration requirements are the same. But does merely having a website that can accept online gifts constitute soliciting gifts in all the states from which it can be accessed, which would be essentially all? In general, the answer is yes. But in 1999 NASCO recognized that this interpretation could be burdensome on small nonprofit organizations as well as the agencies charged with enforcing the solicitation laws. NASCO developed guidelines, known as the **Charleston principles**, intended to narrow somewhat the impact of registration requirements in this regard (NASCO, 2001). It is important to understand that the principles are recommendations to NASCO members but not laws.

The Charleston principles distinguish between a nonprofit that is **domiciled** in a state and one that is not. Domiciled means that the organization does its principal business there—usually it is headquartered there as well. If an organization is domiciled in a state and uses the Internet to solicit gifts in that state, it must, according to the principles, register in that state. This is true whether the solicitations are interactive, for example e-mail, or passive, that is, just maintaining a website with a donate button (Hopkins, 2009).

Things are somewhat different for an organization that is *not* domiciled in the state in which it is using the Internet for fundraising. The organization is required to register in that state if any of the following conditions apply:

- Its non-Internet activities alone would be sufficient to require registration.

- The entity solicits contributions through an interactive Website and either

  o specifically targets persons physically located in the state for solicitation,

  o receives contributions from the state on a repeated and ongoing basis or a substantial basis through its Website, or

  ○ solicits contributions through a site that is not interactive, but either specifically invites further offline activity to complete a contribution, or establishes other contacts with that state, such as sending email messages or other communications that promote the Website, and the entity engages in one of the foregoing two activities. (Hopkins, 2009, p. 87)

Applying the Charleston principles can be complicated. For example, a website is considered interactive if it has the capacity to accept a gift regardless of whether donors actually use it. And an organization may be considered to be soliciting residents of the state if it makes reference to them on its website or sends messages to people it knows or reasonably should know are residents of the state. The registration requirement does not, however, apply to organizations that provide technical support to nonprofits for online fundraising, for example, Internet service providers or companies that just process gifts (Hopkins, 2009). This is an area in which nonprofits should seek legal advice.

The cost of complying with state registration requirements is a substantial one for many nonprofit organizations, both in terms of time and money. Some large organizations that solicit gifts nationally have staff members assigned to the task of maintaining active registrations, while others use the services of law firms and other vendors to file the various registrations and pay the fees. The justifications for state registration laws include protecting donors, protecting beneficiaries of nonprofit programs, and helping scrupulous nonprofits by maintaining public trust. Although her study was focused on only a handful of states that did not require registration, Irvin (2005) found no significant difference with regard to levels of fundraising fraud or public trust of nonprofits between those jurisdictions and the states that do require registration. And, of course, the broad movement to state registration predated the growth of charity watchdog organizations, which collect and disseminate information on nonprofit organizations that is readily accessible to the donor public.

STATE DISCLOSURE REQUIREMENTS

Some states require that certain information be disclosed in materials provided to prospective donors at the point of solicitation (**point-of-solicitation disclosure**) or on request (**disclosure on demand**). Many states also require that registered organizations send a financial report to the state annually (Hopkins, 2009).

While state requirements vary, the information required at the point of solicitation is usually limited to such items as the name and purpose of the organization and the intended use of funds. The disclosure requirements are generally greater when a professional fundraiser is involved. Some state laws require that if a professional fundraiser is soliciting funds, the percentage of funds paid to the solicitor and the percentage going to the nonprofit be disclosed at the point of solicitation. Although such requirements remain in some state laws, in the 1988 case of *Riley v. National Federation of the Blind of North Carolina* (1988), the Supreme Court ruled that such provisions were unconstitutional restrictions of the First Amendment right of free speech. If a prospective donor asks the solicitor questions, however, it would be illegal to provide fraudulent answers.

GIFT SUBSTANTIATION REQUIREMENTS

In order to claim a federal income tax deduction for a charitable gift, a donor must have **substantiation** of the gift, meaning proof. In past years, a canceled check or some other document was sufficient, but that is no longer true for gifts of $250 or more. It is the donor's responsibility to have a formal and **contemporaneous acknowledgment** for any gift of $250 or more; that means a receipt from the organization sent shortly after the gift has been made. There is no legal penalty for the organization if it fails to send a receipt for a cash gift, but it obviously would not be good for donor relations to fail to do so, disqualifying the donor's tax deduction. The law does require specific action by the nonprofit organization in two instances: gifts that involve a quid pro quo, that is, a benefit provided to the donor, and gifts made with tangible property, that is, gifts-in-kind.

Quid Pro Quo Contributions

If a donor receives something in return for making a gift, then the transaction is partly a gift and partly a payment for goods and services. This type of transaction is typical in connection with many special events, for example, in which the donor receives a theater performance and/or a dinner. If the donor has paid more than the benefit is worth, the excess is deductible as a charitable gift. For example, if the donor makes a gift of $500 for the right to attend a theater performance that has a normal ticket price of $100, that produces a charitable deduction for only the difference of $400.

If an organization solicits a quid pro quo contribution, it is *required* to inform the donor of the law and provide a **good faith estimate** of the value of the goods and services the donor has received. Coming up with this value can sometimes be easy; for example, the value of a dinner may be determined by what nearby restaurants charge for something similar. But other cases can be more complex. For example, if a celebrity attends a charity event and does nothing, or does something different from that for which he or she is famous, other guests may not have received any commercial benefit. However, if the celebrity performs, it is possible that the value of that performance must be deducted from donors' total payment for the event in order to determine the deductible portion (Hopkins, 2009). Arriving at that value may not always be clear-cut.

Gifts of Property

When an individual makes a gift using property, other than money or publicly traded securities, he or she is entitled to an income tax charitable deduction for the fair market value of that property. Establishing a value that will pass muster with the IRS is the responsibility of the donor. If a gift is valued at $500 or more, the donor must complete and submit Form 8283 with his or her tax return. If the donor makes one gift or multiple gifts of *similar items of property*, with a total value of $5,000 or more, he or she is required to obtain a **qualified appraisal** of the property's value and attach an **appraisal summary** to Form 8283 in order to claim the deduction. In order to be qualified, the appraisal must be completed no more than sixty days before the gift, be signed by a **qualified appraiser**, and meet various

IRS requirements (Hopkins, 2009). A qualified appraiser is someone who has appropriate credentials and is independent of the donor. In some types of gifts, establishing the fair market value may be simple. But when the gift involves complex assets, there can be differences of method and opinion about what the property is really worth. There also are additional IRS requirements related to certain types of gifts, for example, vehicles and works of art (Hopkins, 2009).

Again, it is the donor's responsibility to establish the fair market value for purposes of his or her tax deduction. That is not the responsibility of the nonprofit organization. However, the nonprofit that receives the gift of property does have some obligations to the IRS. Form 8283 must be signed by the nonprofit as well as the donor and the appraiser when the gift is accepted. By signing Form 8283, the organization is not indicating that the claimed value is accurate, only that the gift has been received (Hopkins, 2009). Under some circumstances, the nonprofit also is required to report to the IRS, on Form 8282, if it sells the donated property within three years. The purpose of this requirement is to enable the IRS to compare the actual sale price against the appraisal on which the donor's tax deduction was based. Situations could arise in which a donor requests that the organization not sell property within that three-year limit, perhaps in order to avoid the possibility of this comparison. Formally agreeing to such an arrangement would be a legal violation by the nonprofit organization; an informal understanding would be unethical as well as bringing legal risk.

OTHER GOVERNMENTAL INFLUENCES

In addition to the requirements already discussed, specific fundraising methods must be compliant with laws and regulations of a variety of state and federal government agencies. For example, solicitations sent by mail that include untruthful information could constitute mail fraud. The Federal Trade Commission enforces laws regarding telephone solicitation. That includes the do-not-call law that applies to commercial sales calls. Nonprofits are exempt from that law but should maintain an internal do-not-call list to honor requests from individuals who are called, excluding them from future solicitations.

ETHICAL CODES, STANDARDS, AND GUIDELINES

Codes, standards, and guidelines have been established by various organizations, and a violation can have a significant impact on the reputation of a nonprofit, whether the standard is a matter of law or simply good practice. Although they do not carry the force of law, nonprofit charity watchdogs, including the Better Business Bureau Wise Giving Alliance and Charity Navigator, have sway because they may influence the perceptions of donors and because publicized violations may catch the attention of lawmakers, potentially leading to new regulation.

Principles of ethical practice for fundraising also have been developed and endorsed by nonprofit sector and professional organizations, including Independent Sector, AFP, AHP,

CASE, PPP, and others. They include **Independent Sector's Principles for Good Governance and Ethical Practice**, Principles 27 through 33, related to responsible fundraising (see Box 14.1); the **AFP Code of Ethical Principles and Standards** (see Box 14.2); and the **Donor Bill of Rights**, developed by AFP, AHP, CASE, and the Giving Institute and endorsed by various other organizations (see Box 14.3). Again, these principles do not have the force of law, but violations of them may bring unwanted and unhelpful scrutiny to an organization.

BOX 14.1   Independent Sector: Principles for Good Governance and Ethical Practice

Principles 27–33: Responsible Fundraising (2015 Edition)

27. Solicitation materials and other communications addressed to donors and the public must clearly identify the organization and be accurate and truthful.

A donor has the right to know the name of anyone soliciting contributions, the name and location of the organization that will receive the contribution, a clear description of its activities, the intended use of the funds to be raised, contacts for obtaining additional information, and whether the individual requesting the contribution is acting as a volunteer, employee of the organization, or hired solicitor. Descriptions of program activities and the financial condition of the organization must be current and accurate, and any references to past activities or events should be dated appropriately. Charitable organizations should be sure that all of their online, mobile, and print communications and any online or mobile fundraising platforms they use to process contributions include current, correct information on how anyone can contact the organization directly for more information. (A Donor Bill of Rights, created by the Association of Fundraising Professionals and endorsed by many organizations, is available at http://www.afpnet.org.)

If an organization is not eligible to receive tax-deductible contributions, it must disclose this limitation at the time of solicitation. Similarly, a charitable organization that the IRS has recognized as eligible to receive tax-deductible contributions should clearly indicate in its solicitations how donors may obtain proof of that status. The organization is required to provide a copy of the IRS letter awarding or confirming its tax-exempt status to anyone who requests it, or it may choose to post its determination letter on its website. If the solicitation promises any goods or services to the donor in exchange for contributions, the materials should also clearly indicate the portion of the contribution (that is, the value of any goods or services provided) that is not tax-deductible.

Social media and online fundraising channels offer many opportunities for charitable organizations to raise funds and generate support for their work. These channels also provide easy opportunities for inappropriate or fraudulent solicitations in the name of a charitable organization. Charitable organizations should counter attempts by others to use their name and reputation, or a similar name and purpose to misdirect donors, by providing warnings on their solicitation materials and encouraging donors to email, call or visit the organization if they have any question about either the charity or a fundraising solicitation. For more information about supervision and oversight recommended for online and mobile fundraising campaigns and platforms, see Principle 31.

28. Contributions must be used for purposes consistent with the donor's intent, whether as described in the relevant solicitation materials or as specifically directed by the donor.

When a donor responds to a charitable solicitation with a contribution, he or she has a right to expect that the funds will be used as promised. Solicitations should therefore indicate whether the funds they generate will be used to further the general programs and operations of the organization or to support specific programs or initiatives. A donor may also indicate through a letter, a written note on the solicitation, or a personal conversation with the solicitor or another official of the charitable organization how he or she expects the contribution to be used.

Before accepting a gift, the organization should review whether the gift is consistent with the organization's gift acceptance policy (see Principle #30) and should ascertain whether the donor has stipulated any specific terms for the use of the gift. If the organization will be unable or unwilling to comply with any of the terms requested by a donor, it should negotiate any necessary changes prior to concluding the transaction. Particularly in the case of substantial contributions, the recipient should develop an agreement that specifies any rights it may have to modify the terms of the gift if circumstances warrant. Some charitable organizations include provisions in their governing documents or board resolutions indicating that the organization retains "variance powers," the right to modify conditions on the use of assets. Such powers should be clearly communicated to donors through a written agreement.

If the organization accepts a gift that the donor expects will be maintained in a separate account or fund over which the donor expects to have advisory privileges as to the distribution or investment of those funds, it may be defined as a sponsoring organization of a donor advised fund. In such cases, organizations should consult with legal advisors regarding specific Form 990 and other reporting requirements and rules applicable to sponsoring organizations that hold donor advised funds particularly with regard to transactions with donors, either directly or by organizations receiving gifts from a donor-advised fund.

In some cases, an organization may not receive sufficient contributions to proceed with a given project or it may receive more donations than it requires to carry out that project. If the organization is unable or unwilling to use the contribution as stated in its appeal or in the donor's communication, it has an obligation to contact the donor and request permission to apply the gift to another purpose or offer to return the gift. Charitable organizations should strive

(Continued)

(Continued)

to make clear in materials that solicit contributions for a specific program how they will handle such circumstances.

29. A charitable organization must provide donors with specific acknowledgments of charitable contributions, in accordance with IRS requirements, as well as information to facilitate donors' compliance with tax law requirements.

Acknowledging donors' contributions is much more than a tax requirement, it is a critical part of building donors' confidence in and support for the activities they help to fund. Organizations should establish procedures for acknowledging all contributions in a timely manner, whether by mail or electronically. Donors must have written documentation to claim a tax deduction for charitable contributions on their annual income tax returns, and that documentation must come from the charitable organization for gifts of $250 or more. Charitable organizations are required to make a good faith estimate of the value of any goods and services (such as a meal at a fundraising banquet) the donor received in exchange for a contribution of more than $75. IRS publication 526 provides more information on the requirements for charitable organizations, including exceptions for benefits considered to be insubstantial, certain membership benefits, and intangible religious benefits.

In addition to thanking donors for their contributions, such acknowledgments should indicate how the donor can find more information on the activities they support through a website, print publications or visits to an organizational office. It is often helpful to provide regular email or newsletter updates so that donors can receive ongoing information about how their contributions made a difference through the organization's work. Many organizations also choose to include in the acknowledgment an easy way for donors to indicate that they do not wish their names or contact information to be shared outside the organization and how they can "opt out" of receiving communications from the organization going forward.

Acknowledgments of other gifts of property and other non-cash contributions should include a description, but not the value, of the item or items contributed. Specific rules apply to the deductions taxpayers are permitted to claim for various types of non-cash gifts, such as donations of motor vehicles, appreciated art, or non-publicly held stock. Organizations that accept such gifts should consult with qualified legal and accounting professionals regarding their obligations. They are also advised to alert donors to the IRS rules for substantiating such claims and encourage them to seek appropriate tax or legal counsel when making significant non-cash contributions.

30. A charitable organization should adopt clear policies, based on its specific exempt purpose, to determine whether accepting a gift would compromise its ethics, financial circumstances, program focus, or other interests.

Some charitable contributions have the potential to create significant problems for an organization or a donor. Knowingly or not, contributors may ask a charity to disburse funds for illegal or unethical purposes, and other gifts may subject the organization to liability under environmental protection laws or other rules.

Donors may also face adverse tax consequences if a charity is unable to use a gift of property in fulfilling its mission and must instead sell or otherwise dispose of the property soon after its receipt.

The policy should address how the organization will address relationships and sponsorship offers from businesses and other organizations to ensure that all communications with customers and prospective donors are clear and accurate, and that the terms of any payment to the charitable organization and any related tax consequences (such as payment of unrelated business income tax for advertising provided to the business sponsor) are clearly understood by both parties. The policy should discuss how contributions will be disclosed to the public and should stipulate that the organization will retain complete control over use of its name and logo and of all content related to a sponsored event or program activity. The board and staff leaders should also consider how affiliation with a particular business or product might affect the organization's reputation with donors and the public.

A gift-acceptance policy provides some protection for the board and staff, as well as for potential donors, by outlining the rules and procedures by which an organization will evaluate whether it can accept a contribution even before an offer is actually made. The policy should make clear that the organization generally will not accept any non-cash gifts that are counter to or outside the scope of its mission and purpose, unless the item is intended for resale or would otherwise produce needed revenue. It should list any funding sources, types of contributions, or conditions that would prevent the organization from accepting a gift. Charities should also consider establishing rules and procedures for determining whether a gift is acceptable and should identify circumstances under which a review by legal counsel or other experts would be required before accepting a gift.

31. A charitable organization should provide appropriate training and supervision of the people soliciting funds on its behalf to ensure that they understand their responsibilities and applicable federal, state and local laws, and do not employ techniques that are coercive, intimidating, or intended to harass potential donors.

Staff, volunteers, donors, and other stakeholders can be valuable allies in raising funds to support the charitable organization's work, but without proper training and oversight support, they can also mislead or misdirect donors and put the organization's reputation at risk. A charitable organization should provide careful

(Continued)

(Continued)

training and supervision of all those who solicit donations on its behalf to make sure they understand their legal and ethical obligations, as well as procedures to follow in representing the organization and working with donors. Training courses and materials are often available through local nonprofit education programs and associations of professional fundraisers. It is particularly important that fundraisers are respectful of a donor's concerns and do not use coercive or abusive language or strategies to secure contributions, misuse personal information about potential donors, pursue personal relationships that are subject to misinterpretation by potential donors, or mislead potential donors in other ways. All those who solicit contributions on the organization's behalf, including volunteers, should be provided with clear materials and instructions on what information to provide to prospective donors, including the organization's name and address, how the donor can learn more about the organization, the purposes for which donations will be used, whether all or part of the donation may be tax-deductible, and who the donor can contact for further information.

If a charitable organization decides to use an outside professional fundraising firm or consultant, it should have a clear contract—as required by law and guided by good practice—that outlines the responsibilities of the organization receiving the funds and of the firm or consultant. The contract should stipulate that donor lists will be treated as the proprietary information of the organization and should specify how information about donors will be handled and protected, and how funds will be transmitted to the organization. The fundraiser must agree to abide by any registration and reporting requirements of the jurisdictions in which fundraising will be conducted, as well as federal restrictions on telephone, email, or fax solicitations. The charitable organization should verify that the outside solicitor is registered as required in any state in which the solicitor will be seeking contributions.

Many charitable organizations contract with third party fundraising platforms to accept and process donations online or through mobile technologies. Just as with any outside fundraiser, the charitable organization should have a written contract with such entities that details any fees that will be charged to the donor or the charitable organization, how the site will protect donors' information, how contributions will be transmitted to the charitable organization, and whether the site has a privacy policy and process for preventing solicitation fraud.

Because some individuals may launch online and peer-to-peer ("crowdsourcing") fundraising campaigns without the beneficiary organization's knowledge, many charitable organizations have established written policies regarding who is permitted to raise funds on their behalf and the process for requesting and receiving authorization to do so from the charity. Charitable organizations that regularly solicit funds from the general public should routinely conduct website searches to identify whether and how their names are being used. If a charitable organization finds that others are soliciting contributions on its behalf, it should contact the soliciting individual or organization to determine whether the donors' information and contributions are being appropriately transferred to the charitable organization. If the charitable organization does not choose to be listed on a site or included in a campaign for any reason, it should send a written request that its name be removed and notify relevant charitable solicitation regulators of any problems.

In general, those soliciting funds on behalf of charities should refrain from giving specific legal, financial, and tax advice to individual donors. Rather, when such questions arise, fundraisers should encourage donors to consult their own legal counsel or other professional advisors before finalizing a contribution.

32. A charitable organization should not compensate internal or external fundraisers based on a commission or a percentage of the amount raised.

Compensation for fundraising activities should reflect the skill, effort, and time expended by the individual or firm on behalf of the charitable organization. Many professional associations of fundraisers prohibit their members from accepting payment for fundraising activities based on a percentage of the amount of charitable income raised or expected to be raised. Basing compensation on a percentage of the money raised can encourage fundraisers to put their own interests ahead of those of the organization or the donor and may lead to inappropriate techniques that jeopardize the organization's values and reputation and the donor's trust in the organization. Percentage-based compensation may also lead to payments that could be regarded by legal authorities or perceived by the public as "excessive compensation" compared to the actual work conducted. Percentage-based compensation may also be skewed by unexpected or unsolicited gifts received by the charitable organization through no effort of the fundraiser.

A similar logic applies to employees. Some charitable organizations choose to provide bonuses to employees for exceptional work in fundraising, administrative, or program activities. If so, the criteria for such bonuses should be clearly based on the quality of the work performed, rather than on a percentage of the funds raised.

Some online and mobile fundraising platforms and credit card providers charge charitable organizations transaction fees for processing donations that is often based on a percentage of the donation or transaction, but these fees should not be viewed or treated as fundraising compensation. Charitable organizations should ensure that the fees are reasonable and comparable to those charged similar organizations and businesses, whether they are applied to contributions or payments for services.

33. A charitable organization should respect the privacy of individual donors and, except where disclosure is required by law, should not sell or otherwise make available the

(Continued)

(Continued)

names and contact information of its donors without providing them an opportunity at least once a year to opt out of the use of their names.

Preserving the trust and support of donors requires that donor information be handled with respect and confidentiality to the maximum extent permitted by law. Charitable organizations should disclose to donors whether and how their names may be used, and provide all donors, at the time a contribution is made and in any future solicitations, an easy way to indicate that they do not wish their names or contact information to be shared outside the organization. In all solicitation and other promotional materials, organizations should also provide a means, such as a check-off box or other "opt-out" procedure, for donors and others who receive such materials to request that their names be deleted from similar mailings, faxes or electronic communications in the future. The organization should immediately remove a donor's name from any lists upon request and should ensure that at least once a year all donors are provided information about how they may request that their names and contact information not be shared outside the organization.

Organizations that gather personal information from donors and other visitors to their websites should have a privacy policy, easily accessible from those websites, that informs visitors to the site what information, if any, is being collected about them, how the information will be used, how to inform the organization if the visitor does not wish personal information shared, and what security measures the charity has in place to protect personal information.

In addition, the board of directors should adopt and enforce a policy stipulating that all information about donors is to be treated as the proprietary information of the organization, and not of internal or external fundraisers. The policy should further stipulate that such information cannot be sold, shared, or otherwise transferred to another organization without clear written permission of both the donor and the organization.

Source: Independent Sector (2015).

Independent Sector's Principles for Good Governance were developed in response to controversies that arose in the mid-2000s, leading to proposals in Congress to increase federal oversight of the nonprofit sector. That included proposals to extend application of provisions from the Sarbanes-Oxley Act, which regulates public corporations, to encompass nonprofit organizations. Such legislation was forestalled by Independent Sector's action in assembling the Panel on the Nonprofit Sector, which devised the principles with the promise that the sector could self-regulate without the need for additional legislation. The principles were issued in 2007 and a revised version was released by Independent Sector in 2015. Several of the principles that relate to governance are indeed similar to requirements of the Sarbanes-Oxley Act. However, Box 14.1 includes only those principles related specifically to responsible fundraising.

BOX 14.2   AFP Code of Ethical Principles and Standards (Ethical Principles Adopted 1964; Amended September 2007)

The Association of Fundraising Professionals (AFP) . . . exists to foster the development and growth of fund-raising professionals and the profession, to promote high ethical behavior in the fund-raising profession and to preserve and enhance philanthropy and volunteerism. Members of AFP are motivated by an inner drive to improve the quality of life through the causes they serve. They serve the ideal of philanthropy, are committed to the preservation and enhancement of volunteerism, and hold stewardship of these concepts as the overriding direction of their professional life. They recognize their responsibility to ensure that needed resources are vigorously and ethically sought and that the intent of the donor is honestly fulfilled. To these ends, AFP members, both individual and business, embrace certain values that they strive to uphold in performing their responsibilities for generating philanthropic support. AFP business members strive to promote and protect the work and mission of their client organizations.

AFP members [both individual and business] aspire to:

- practice their profession with integrity, honesty, truthfulness and adherence to the absolute obligation to safeguard the public trust;
- act according to the highest goals and visions of their organizations, professions, clients and consciences;
- put philanthropic mission above personal gain;
- inspire others through their own sense of dedication and high purpose;
- improve their professional knowledge and skills, so that their performance will better serve others;
- demonstrate concern for the interests and well-being of individuals affected by their actions;
- value the privacy, freedom of choice and interests of all those affected by their actions;
- foster cultural diversity and pluralistic values and treat all people with dignity and respect;
- affirm, through personal giving, a commitment to philanthropy and its role in society;
- adhere to the spirit as well as the letter of all applicable laws and regulations;
- advocate within their organizations adherence to all applicable laws and regulations;
- avoid even the appearance of any criminal offense or professional misconduct;
- bring credit to the fund-raising profession by their public demeanor;
- encourage colleagues to embrace and practice these ethical principles and standards;
- be aware of the codes of ethics promulgated by other professional organizations that serve philanthropy.

Ethical Standards

Furthermore, while striving to act according to the above values, AFP members, both individual and business, agree to abide (and to ensure, to the best of their ability, that all

(Continued)

(Continued)

members of their staff abide) by the AFP standards. Violation of the standards may subject the member to disciplinary sanctions, including expulsion, as provided in the AFP Ethics Enforcement Procedures.

Member Obligations

1. Members shall not engage in activities that harm the members' organizations, clients or profession.

2. Members shall not engage in activities that conflict with their fiduciary, ethical and legal obligations to their organizations, clients or profession.

3. Members shall effectively disclose all potential and actual conflicts of interest; such disclosure does not preclude or imply ethical impropriety.

4. Members shall not exploit any relationship with a donor, prospect, volunteer, client or employee for the benefit of the members or the members' organizations.

5. Members shall comply with all applicable local, state, provincial and federal civil and criminal laws.

6. Members recognize their individual boundaries of competence and are forthcoming and truthful about their professional experience and qualifications and will represent their achievements accurately and without exaggeration.

7. Members shall present and supply products and/or services honestly and without misrepresentation and will clearly identify the details of those products, such as availability of the products and/or services and other factors that may affect the suitability of the products and/or services for donors, clients, or nonprofit organizations.

8. Members shall establish the nature and purpose of any contractual relationship at the outset and will be responsive and available to organizations and their employing organizations before, during, and after any sale of materials and/or services. Members will comply with all fair and reasonable obligations created by the contract.

9. Members shall refrain from knowingly infringing [on] the intellectual property rights of other parties at all times. Members shall address and rectify any inadvertent infringement that may occur.

10. Members shall protect the confidentiality of all privileged information relating to the provider/client relationships.

11. Members shall refrain from any activity designed to disparage competitors untruthfully.

Solicitation and Use of Philanthropic Funds

12. Members shall take care to ensure that all solicitation and communication materials are accurate and correctly reflect their organizations' mission and use of solicited funds.

13. Members shall take care to ensure that donors receive informed, accurate, and ethical advice about the value and tax implications of contributions.

14. Members shall take care to ensure that contributions are used in accordance with donors' intentions.

15. Members shall take care to ensure proper stewardship of all revenue sources, including timely reports on the use and management of such funds.

16. Members shall obtain explicit consent by donors before altering the conditions of financial transactions.

Presentation of Information

17. Members shall not disclose privileged or confidential information to unauthorized parties.

18. Members shall adhere to the principle that all donor and prospect information created by, or on behalf of, an organization or a client is the property of that organization or client and shall not be transferred or utilized except on behalf of that organization or client.

19. Members shall give donors and clients the opportunity to have their names removed from lists that are sold to, rented to, or exchanged with other organizations.

20. Members shall, when stating fund-raising results, use accurate and consistent accounting methods that conform to the appropriate guidelines adopted by the American Institute of Certified Public Accountants (AICPA)* for the type of organization involved. (*In countries outside of the United States, comparable authority should be utilized.)

Compensation and Contracts

21. Members shall not accept compensation or enter into a contract that is based on a percentage of contributions; nor shall members accept finder's fees or contingent fees. Business members must refrain from receiving compensation from third parties derived from products or services for a client without disclosing that third-party compensation to the client (for example, volume rebates from vendors to business members).

22. Members may accept performance-based compensation, such as bonuses, provided such bonuses are in accord with prevailing practices within the members' own organizations and are not based on a percentage of contributions.

23. Members shall neither offer nor accept payments or special considerations for the purpose of influencing the selection of products or services.

24. Members shall not pay finder's fees, commissions, or percentage compensation based on contributions, and shall take care to discourage their organizations from making such payments.

25. Any member receiving funds on behalf of a donor or client must meet the legal requirements for the disbursement of those funds. Any interest or income earned on the funds should be fully disclosed.

Source: Association of Fundraising Professionals website (http://www.afpnet.org).

> **BOX 14.3**   Donor Bill of Rights
>
> Philanthropy is based on voluntary action for the common good. It is a tradition of giving and sharing that is primary to the quality of life. To ensure that philanthropy merits the respect and trust of the general public, and that donors and prospective donors can have full confidence in the nonprofit organizations and causes they are asked to support, we declare that all donors have these rights:
>
> I. To be informed of the organization's mission, of the way the organization intends to use donated resources, and of its capacity to use donations effectively for their intended purposes.
>
> II. To be informed of the identity of those serving on the organization's governing board, and to expect the board to exercise prudent judgment in its stewardship responsibilities.
>
> III. To have access to the organization's most recent financial statements.
>
> IV. To be assured their gifts will be used for the purposes for which they were given.
>
> V. To receive appropriate acknowledgement and recognition.
>
> VI. To be assured that information about their donation is handled with respect and with confidentiality to the extent provided by law.
>
> VII. To expect that all relationships with individuals representing organizations of interest to the donor will be professional in nature.
>
> VIII. To be informed whether those seeking donations are volunteers, employees of the organization or hired solicitors.
>
> IX. To have the opportunity for their names to be deleted from mailing lists that an organization may intend to share.
>
> X. To feel free to ask questions when making a donation and to receive prompt, truthful and forthright answers.

Source: Association of Fundraising Professionals website (http://www.afpnet.org).

The AFP Code addresses fundraising professionals, including both nonprofit staff members and fundraising consultants. A violation can bring sanctions, including expulsion from AFP membership. In 2011, AFP launched its Ethics Assessment Inventory, an online tool that permits members to develop a snapshot of their ethical performance, compare themselves with peers, and assess and strengthen ethical dimensions of their practice.

The Donor Bill of Rights addresses both the behavior of organizations and of individual fundraisers; as the title suggests, it focuses on the treatment of donors with respect to their gifts and relationships with nonprofit organizations.

CONSIDERING ETHICAL DILEMMAS IN FUNDRAISING

As stated earlier in this chapter, the requirements of ethical practice go beyond the requirements of law and, indeed, beyond the requirements of specific ethical codes. Although legal and ethical issues are often intertwined, it may be possible to be compliant with all relevant laws and even formal ethical guidelines and yet be in violation of common understandings of ethical behavior. Moreover, while questions of legality may be relatively easy to answer, at least by those with legal training and experience, ethical issues may not always have simple yes-or-no answers. They may pose dilemmas, which by their nature offer choices that may include tradeoffs and alternative outcomes that may be less than ideal.

For purposes of discussion in this chapter, ethical issues are considered in five broad categories: issues related to the behavior of the fundraiser; issues related to the donor, including disreputable donors and tainted money; issues concerning the impact of gifts on organizational mission, autonomy, or priorities—including those that raise the possibility of inappropriate donor influence and control; issues about privacy and the use of donor information; and issues concerning organizations' faithfulness to donor intent.

Fundraiser Behavior

Some issues involve the behavior of the staff person interacting with the donor. As formal ethical codes provide, they would include making misleading or dishonest representations, for example, exaggerating the organization's effectiveness, lying about how the gift will be used, or making unreasonable or unrealistic promises to the donor about recognition or the financial benefits of giving. It is also unethical for a nonprofit staff member managing a relationship with a donor to attempt to use that relationship for his or her personal benefit or gain or to engage in behavior toward the donor that would be morally repugnant, for example, sexual harassment.

But some dilemmas are more subtle. Tempel (2011) raises the question of who the fundraiser's client is, the donor or the organization by which he or she is employed? In a formal sense, the fundraiser is usually employed by a nonprofit organization, which pays his or her compensation and to which the fundraiser is accountable. That fundraiser's responsibility is to advance the interests of his or her employer. But to what extent does ethical behavior require that the fundraiser balance the interests of the donor and the nonprofit? This is especially relevant when working with planned-gift donors, who are often older and whose decisions about giving may have significant implications for their financial security now and in the future. The question is also of obvious relevance to the issue of fundraiser compensation. A fundraiser whose personal compensation is directly tied to the amount of a gift may have an incentive, however subtle, to perceive the donor's interests and the organization's interests as consistent. For this good reason and others, recognized ethical codes and principles are unanimous in prohibiting compensation based on a commission or percentage of funds raised.

Tempel (2011) asks, "Who owns the relationship?" (p. 410). His answer? The organization. In other words, the fundraiser should always be clear that he or she is engaging with the donor as the organization's agent and never exploit the relationship for personal benefit. But the lines can become blurred. Sometimes a donor may misperceive the relationship as one of personal friendship. Depending on their personal circumstances, some may welcome the attention and company of a fundraiser who comes to visit. Some may offer small favors—perhaps lunch at a restaurant or tickets to a game? Perhaps these are *de minimis*, meaning too small to worry about. Indeed, refusing some may seem unduly cautious—for example, there is no reason why a donor cannot pay for lunch with a fundraiser for a nonprofit organization and often will do so to save the organization money. But suppose favors progress to more substantial benefits, for example, use of a vacation home, a vehicle, or even a cash gift. The fundraiser may decide to accept small benefits rather than risk hurting the donor's feelings, but at some point things may descend a slippery slope to a point of serious ethical concern.

A related question sometimes raised is whether a fundraiser who has moved to a new employer should contact donors to his or her previous employer on behalf of the new organization. Consistent with Tempel's point that the relationship belongs to the organization rather than the fundraiser as an individual, this might generally seem to be unethical. In addition, in the case of individual donors, the scenario is usually impractical as well, since the donor is likely to have loyalty to the first organization and unlikely to transfer it somewhere else simply because the fundraiser has moved on. But what if the donor has existing relationships with both organizations or programmatic interests that suggest the second organization would be of particular interest? For example, foundations or corporations might indeed wish to know about additional giving opportunities aligned with their giving priorities, and support given to a new organization would not necessarily be at the expense of existing grant recipients. If the fundraiser has an established relationship with the grants officer at the company from his or her previous employment, is there an ethical concern about contacting that individual to discuss the new organization for which the fundraiser is now working? Answers to such questions often require judgment beyond the provisions of formal codes.

Disreputable Donors and Tainted Money

A second category of ethical issues that may confront nonprofit organizations relates to the donor rather than the staff member. These issues can be divided into three principle subcategories: tainted money, controversial donors, and inconsistency between the donor's values and those of the organization.

In some cases, the organization may have reason to suspect that the funds being used to make a gift were illegally or unethically obtained; that is, they represent **tainted money**. Knowingly accepting a gift of such funds would be obviously unethical and illegal.

A second type of situation would involve a donor who is controversial, even though the funds may have been legally obtained. For example, maybe the individual is a convicted criminal, perhaps even one who has paid his or her penalty, but has earned wealth through legal means. Accepting a gift from such a donor would not violate the law but could raise ethical concerns and questions about the impact on an organization's reputation.

In this type of scenario, the passage of time and the donor's subsequent behavior may make a difference. Tempel (2013) offers the example of Michael Milken, who was convicted of securities fraud in the 1980s and served jail time. Subsequently, he dedicated his life to philanthropy and has been recognized for his important contributions to medical research and public health. Milken is generally viewed today as having earned his renewed respectability. Indeed, as Tempel (2013) observes, "Today it is almost a badge of honor to have a grant from the Milken Foundation" (p. 101).

A distinct but related issue might arise when a donor is convicted of a crime after making a gift; this may be especially problematic if the gift has been recognized through some naming opportunity that visibly associates the individual's name with the organization. Should the gift be returned or the name removed? In 2001, Seton Hall University removed the name of Richard Brennan from its recreation center after he was convicted of white-collar crimes and sentenced to jail (Hrywna, 2006). However, a chair in economics named for the late Kenneth Lay, convicted in 2004 after the collapse of Enron Corporation, continues at the University of Missouri. In 2006, Lay requested that the gift be redirected to charities in Houston, but the university refused. The university general counsel argued that the law did not permit the return of public funds, which the gift became once the gift was completed. While some questioned whether the name should continue to be recognized through naming of the chair, others justified continuing it since the gift predated Lay's legal problems (Booth & Dallas, 2006). Indeed, it continues today.

A third type of issue is more subtle. What if the donor is not a criminal and the funds to be used for the gift were legally obtained, but the donor's values seem at odds with those of the organization? For example, an organization dedicated to supporting people in recovery from alcohol or substance abuse likely would be disinclined to accept support from a company that produces alcohol, although alcohol is a legal product and is used responsibly by many people. The Salvation Army refused a gift from a lottery winner on the basis that its principles do not condone gambling, although lotteries are legal and promoted by many states. Should an environmental organization accept a gift from an oil company? Some might say no, but then what about a donor who drives a gas-guzzling SUV? (Temple, 2013). Answers may not be clear-cut, and there may be disagreement on the part of the organization's leaders.

Tempel (2013) recounts the dilemma posed by a gift from Percy "Master P" Miller to St. Monica's School, a Catholic school in Louisiana. Master P had made money as an artist in gangsta rap, which often includes song lyrics disrespectful of women and some think glorify violence. This struck many as inconsistent with the values of the school. On the other hand, Miller was an alumnus of the school, which served many poor children and was scheduled to close for lack of resources. Following a long and deliberative process, the school accepted the gift, after leaders of the Catholic Church determined that the value of the mission outweighed concerns about the donor and after the donor provided reassurance regarding his intended future behavior that they found persuasive.

The more subtle cases—when the money is legal and the donor not a criminal—can be more difficult to resolve than those in which the facts are more clear-cut. They involve matters of judgment. Should the decision be based on concern about appearances, or should a gift be refused only in the face of a glaring inconsistency between the mission and the activities of the donor? Who should judge that inconsistency? How should the good to be accomplished be weighed against the donor's shortcomings? And to what extent can or should an organization investigate and judge the legal behavior of donors whose funds have been legally obtained?

Impact on Mission, Autonomy, Priorities

Another ethical question is presented by some restricted gifts: Under what circumstances should an organization refuse to accept a gift that may require it to undertake new programs and perhaps incur additional expenses it had not anticipated? What if the new program is not entirely consistent with the organization's mission or would require a redefinition of its mission? The responsibility of a nonprofit governing board is to serve as fiduciary for the organization's financial assets and also to protect its mission. By what standards should the offer of a gift lead the board to consider taking on additional risk or altering or expanding the mission?

For example, if an organization concerned with young children were offered a gift to begin a new program to help prevent high school students from dropping out, it would need to consider whether expanding its mission in that way would jeopardize its focus on its primary mission, what additional costs the new efforts might create in the future, and whether such expansion might endanger the organization's overall health and other sources of support. It might not be an easy decision to make, since the needs of high school students are also important and possibly unmet in the community the organization serves. The decision might be further complicated if the offered gift were substantial and, especially, if the donor were an important local businessperson or even a member of the organization's board. The risk to the relationship in turning down the gift also would need to be weighed against the potential risk to the organization if it were accepted with the conditions that accompany it.

Another subcategory of questions arises with gifts that come with conditions that might give the donor inappropriate control. For example, most colleges will accept scholarship gifts that require recipients to be enrolled in certain academic programs; that raises few problems unless, for example, the college thinks it unlikely it will be able to recruit many students meeting the conditions. But there are limits to how much influence a donor can be allowed in the process of selecting specific scholarship recipients. Allowing the donor to select the recipients of the scholarships would not only present an ethical concern, but, indeed, it could also invalidate the tax deductibility of the donor's gift, making it legally a gift to the scholarship recipients individually rather than to the college, university, or school. Similar questions sometimes arise with gifts of art when the donor requires that a collection be kept intact or that it be displayed in a certain manner, implying some continuing costs to the organization and perhaps some personal benefit to the individual in the form of continued enjoyment of the works.

If a donor offers a gift with a condition that might advantage that person economically, then the transaction may run afoul of the law. For example, a gift tied to obtaining a business contract from the nonprofit that is disadvantageous to the organization could provoke **intermediate sanctions**, penalties imposed by the IRS (Tempel, 2013).

Privacy

A fourth category of ethical concern involves the privacy of individuals, specifically donors. The AFP Code (Obligations 10, 17, 18, 19), the Donor Bill of Rights (Item VI), and Independent

Sector's principles (Principle 33) address the issue. But, again, the interpretation and application of these principles can encounter some dilemmas.

The growing sophistication of prospect research requires maintaining appropriate safeguards to protect the privacy of donors and prospects. The development offices of many organizations may possess information obtained from public sources about individuals' financial wealth and income, real estate holdings, and even family situations. It is legal to obtain such data. But some might argue that when assembled to create a donor profile, its wide distribution in that format may be an inappropriate invasion of privacy.

In addition to data obtained from public sources, development office files may include information gained from reports written by staff members who have visited the donor over the years or heard secondhand from others who know the donor. Maintaining such information in the files of the development office may run the risk that the donor, and the organization, could be embarrassed if it were inappropriately or inadvertently disclosed to another person. Scanlan (2013) cites the example of information derived from prospect screenings, provided by volunteers with reference to peers. The purpose of such a process is to uncover information that may be useful in rating prospects and developing solicitation strategies, but it is possible that volunteers will provide information that is sensitive. For example, what if a lawyer reveals that he recently prepared a person's will and that he or she is wealthy; or if a neighbor says that he has seen expensive art in the person's home; or a friend reveals that a prospect recently inherited money from her late mother? Those individuals may have ethical issues of their own to consider, but once the information has been revealed, it is the organization that needs to decide how to record and use it, if at all.

Information obtained informally by gift officers, from a donor or a donor's friends and associates—basically gossip—can present a particular problem. This is related to a question discussed earlier in this chapter about the nature of the relationship between a donor and a fundraiser. If the fundraiser does not maintain a keen awareness of the professional nature of that relationship, perhaps coming to view it as a personal friendship, then the risk that inappropriate information will be transmitted is increased. Relationships with donors sometimes feel like friendships. But they are not, and the point needs to be kept prominently in mind.

There also can be concerns about the manner in which gift officers record their observations about major-gift prospects following visits. Appropriate language is essential. For example, it might be reasonable to state in a contact report that "Mr. Smith expresses no interest in philanthropy," but it would be totally inappropriate to write that "Mr. Smith doesn't have a charitable bone in his body." One criterion for judgment is the possibility that Mr. Smith would someday read his record at the nonprofit; the manner in which impressions are expressed should not be offensive in that event.

Who within the organization can or should have access to information is a question that needs to be considered as a matter of policy as well as procedure. The law has some relevant provisions. For example, in the case of educational institutions, access to student records is limited by law, and health care institutions are required to comply with the **Health Insurance Portability and Accountability Act of 1996 (HIPPA)**, which protects the confidentiality of patient records. Distributing such information even within the walls of the institution that controls it could be illegal as well as ethically unsound.

But, again, the law does not address all circumstances. Scanlan (2013) proposes a general standard that information be shared internally on a "need to know" basis.

Honoring Donor Intent

The first point articulated in the Donor Bill of Rights states that the donor has the right "to be informed of the organization's mission, of the way the organization intends to use donated resources, and of its capacity to use donations effectively for their intended purposes." The obligation of the organization to use gifts as intended is therefore of the highest ethical importance. In addition, some court cases have established that donors may have the right to bring legal action if their intentions are not observed. Let's look at a few celebrated examples, from different nonprofit subsectors.

American Red Cross

Following the terrorist attacks of September 11, 2001, Americans responded with generous gifts, many directed to the American Red Cross. Bernadine Healey, then president of the Red Cross, announced the establishment of the Liberty Fund, stating that it would be used to provide aid to victims of the attacks. This was a departure from previous practice, by which the Red Cross had received gifts to a general disaster relief fund to support victims of future emergencies such as hurricanes and floods. Healey also was on television requesting additional gifts of funds and blood, without specifically saying how they would be used. Critics charged that the Red Cross was intending to use resources from the Liberty Fund to prepare for future emergencies and that not all of the gifts would go to 9/11 victims, which most donors believed would be the case. Others questioned why the Red Cross continued to solicit blood donations with the implication that they would benefit 9/11 victims, when indeed most victims had perished.

By November 2001, Healey had resigned. Under mounting public pressure, the Red Cross announced that it would indeed use all of the Liberty Fund dollars to assist victims of the terrorist attacks and that a former United States senator had been engaged to guide the distribution of funds (Williams, 2002). Like the terrorists attacks themselves, the Red Cross' response marked a watershed moment. The issue of donor intent was thrust into the national spotlight. The issue was not only about specific promises made to specific donors but also about the implications of messages directed to the public and what reasonable people would infer from those communications about how their gifts would be used. Trust in nonprofits was at least temporarily diminished, and the events gave impetus to the growing movement for greater nonprofit transparency (Rhode & Packel, 2009).

Integris Health

In 2011, country music singer Garth Brooks sued Integris Health, a hospital system in Oklahoma, claiming that the organization had failed to honor an oral agreement he had made with a hospital executive to name a center after his mother, who had died of cancer. The hospital stated that nothing had been established in writing and that Brooks's understanding was based only on verbal conversations with a hospital president. But the jury agreed with Brooks, ordering that his $500,000 gift be returned and that, in addition, Integris Health pay him $500,000 in damages (Blum, 2013). The implication is that promises made to donors should be honored, even when they are not memorialized in written contracts.

Robertson Versus Princeton University

In 1961, Charles and Marie Robertson made an anonymous $35 million gift to Princeton University to expand the program at the Woodrow Wilson School. In 2002, their son William S. Robertson and other family members filed suit claiming that Princeton had not adhered to the terms of the written gift agreement with their parents. Specifically, they charged that the purpose of the gift was to prepare young men and women for careers in the federal government, especially in foreign affairs. Among other facts, the Robertson family noted that by 2002, most Wilson School graduates were not pursuing such careers. The legal case continued for years and was highly visible, with both sides issuing public statements and a debate raging in the media. In 2008, Princeton agreed to settle the case by paying the family's legal fees and contributing $50 million from its endowment to establish a new foundation that would support students at other public affairs schools (Gose, 2014c).

The Robertson case had significant implications for nonprofit organizations in all subsectors, possibly encouraging other suits from dissatisfied donors. Some observers had hoped that the court would use the occasion to articulate legal principles regarding donor intent, but that did not occur. As a result, the law surrounding the issue remains somewhat ambiguous. But the case and surrounding publicity further increased the focus on issues of donor intent and the steps organizations of all types should take to assure that the intentions of donors be both clear and strictly followed (Lewin, 2008).

ASSURING LEGAL AND ETHICAL ORGANIZATIONS

Nonprofit organizations and institutions can best address both the legal and ethical aspects of fundraising by establishing policies and practices in advance of events to which they may apply rather than responding to crises (Tempel, 2013). In addition, policies and prescribed practices must exist in a culture of awareness and support for strict standards of conduct.

First, the ethical standards included in this chapter—and others established by other associations serving specific types of nonprofit institutions—should be adopted and communicated as a part of orientation for members of the board and for new professional staff joining the development office. Both board and staff meetings should include periodic discussion related to such principles.

Although many people prefer not to create a daunting bureaucracy that will distract attention from fundraising, the current environment requires that a variety of formal policies be in place. As discussed earlier in this text, gift acceptance policies are essential both to avoid unethical decisions and to depersonalize difficult decisions that involve refusing offered gifts. Gift acceptance policies also can encompass guiding principles that explain organizational values that guide gift decisions, for example, a prohibition against accepting gifts from companies in certain industries or from donors in specific circumstances.

Policies regarding naming gifts also are important and may prevent issues in that regard. Policies on donor privacy and the security of information provide important safeguards.

The Robertson case has resulted in increased diligence with regard to gift agreements with donors of major gifts. Although they may be awkward to present to a potential donor, some organizations include **ethics clauses** in gift agreements, spelling out under what circumstances a donor's gift might be returned or recognition might be removed (Blum, 2013).

Most importantly, fundraisers need to communicate openly and clearly with donors, both in the process of soliciting the gift and as a part of stewardship after the gift has been completed. And, of course, transparency is essential to achieve and retain public trust.

CHAPTER SUMMARY

It is generally always unethical to disobey the law, but some legal actions may not be compatible with either formal codes of ethics or common understanding of ethical behavior.

There are laws regulating fundraising at the federal, state, and local levels, but most relevant law has been established by states. Most federal law relates to nonprofit governance and tax exemption and to the deductibility of gifts rather than to fundraising practice.

Most states require nonprofit organizations that solicit residents to register with the state, although registration does not imply the state's approval. The definition of a solicitation includes the Internet, but the *Charleston principles* recommend applications of the law to minimize burdens on nonprofits and regulators. Many states also require that nonprofits disclose certain information to donors either at the *point of solicitation* or *on demand* (Hopkins, 2009).

Federal law requires that donors have *contemporaneous acknowledgment*, essentially a receipt, for any gift of $250 or more. Nonprofit organizations are required to inform donors if any amount of their gift is not deductible because of a quid pro quo and to provide a *good faith estimate* of the deductible portion. When gifts are made with tangible property, donors must obtain a *qualified appraisal* if the value exceeds a certain amount and to attach an appraisal summary to Form 8283. The nonprofit must sign the form and report to the IRS if it sells the property within three years (Hopkins, 2009). Various governmental agencies regulate some aspects of fundraising practice, for example, using the mail or phone.

Although they do not have the force of law, standards of charity watchdogs have an impact on nonprofits' reputations. Various codes of ethical behavior and best practices have been adopted by associations, including *Independent Sector's Principles for Good Governance and Ethical Practice*, Principles 27 through 33, which relate to responsible fundraising (see Box 14.1); the *AFP Code of Ethical Principles and Standards* (see Box 14.2); and the *Donor Bill of Rights*, developed by AFP, AHP, CASE, and the Giving Institute and endorsed by various other organizations (see Box 14.3).

Ethical issues may not always have simple yes-or-no answers. They may pose dilemmas, which by their nature offer choices that may include tradeoffs and alternative outcomes that may be less than ideal. Most ethical issues fall into one of five categories: issues related to the behavior of the fundraiser; issues related to the donor, including disreputable donors and tainted money; issues concerning the impact of gifts on organizational mission, autonomy, or priorities or that raise the possibility of inappropriate donor influence and control; issues about privacy and the use of donor information; and issues concerning organizations' faithfulness to donor intent.

Fundraisers' interactions with donors should follow ethical principles and reflect the fact that the relationship is with the organization, not personally with the fundraiser (Tempel, 2011). Organizations should never accept a gift made with money obtained illegally, but the situation can be more complicated if legal money is offered by a controversial donor. The decision can be difficult in the case of donors who may have atoned for past mistakes or who are perhaps simply unpopular, although not criminal. Decisions often reflect a balancing of potential controversy with the needs of the organization and its mission. A nonprofit's board is a fiduciary and must carefully consider the implications of donor-restricted gifts for both the mission and future financial stability. Both organizations and individual fundraisers must exercise care with regard to what information about donors is recorded and with whom it is shared; there are requirements or law as well as ethical behavior in that regard. Recent cases have increased the public awareness of *donor intent* and the obligation of nonprofits to not mislead donors about how their gifts will be used.

Nonprofit organizations and institutions can best address both the legal and ethical aspects of fundraising by establishing policies and practices in advance of events to which they may apply rather than responding to crises (Tempel, 2013). Ethical standards should be adopted and communicated throughout the organization in a culture of integrity. A variety of formal policies are needed, including those on gift acceptance, naming gifts, and donor privacy and the security of information. Recent cases have resulted in an increased emphasis on gift agreements with major donors, some of which include *ethics clauses* (Blum, 2013). A most important practice is open and honest communication with donors during both solicitation and stewardship.

Key Terms and Concepts

AFP Code of Ethical
  Principles and
  Standards
Appraisal summary
Charleston principles
Commercial
  coventurers
Contemporaneous
  acknowledgment
Disclosure on demand
Domiciled (in a state)
Donor Bill of Rights

Ethics clauses
Good faith estimate
Health Insurance
  Portability and
  Accountability Act
  of 1996 (HIPPA)
Independent Sector's
  Principles for Good
  Governance and
  Ethical Practice
Intermediate
  sanctions

Paid solicitors
Point-of-solicitation
  disclosure
Professional
  fundraisers
Qualified appraisal/
  appraiser
Substantiation
Tainted money
Unified
  registration
  statement (URS)

Scenarios 1–12

Scenario #1

A generous gift is offered by a donor convicted of a white-collar crime. This individual was convicted of insider trading, because she bought and sold stock based on tips from a family member, who was a corporate executive. She paid a fine and served a brief jail term. Except for this incident, she has been a successful businessperson and has made smaller gifts to a variety of other nonprofit organizations. Will you accept it? What if it is intended to establish a free medical clinic for children in a disadvantaged neighborhood? What if it is intended to support cancer research and the donor's name will be displayed on the exterior of a hospital pavilion? What if it is to endow a chair in business ethics at a business school?

Scenario #2

A generous gift is offered by a donor who has committed no crime but who just does not enjoy a good reputation. Some members of the governing board say that he is an unpleasant person who is widely disliked by the local business community. Others say that there have been widespread rumors of personal weaknesses, including alcohol abuse and marital infidelities. Do you accept the person's gift? If not, what justification could be given? As in Scenario #1, does the purpose or amount of the gift make a difference?

Scenario #3

A board member who is a contractor offers to do the planning for a new building without charge. He says, "This will be a gift-in-kind from my company to the organization." And he adds, "Of course, I understand that you will need to get other bids for the eventual construction and there is no guarantee that we will win it." But you consult with others who say that doing the planning may give this contractor an advantage over other bidders in getting the construction contract itself and that they think this is why he is making the offer of free planning. Do you accept his offer? If not, how do you explain the decision to this board member?

Scenario #4

A college donor announces she will match her classmates' gifts to a reunion fund in connection with the class' twenty-fifth anniversary. You announce this to the class and they give generously. She then cancels her matching commitment, saying she is unhappy with something the college's president recently said in an article she wrote. Do you tell her classmates or keep quiet? Alternatively, how would you handle this situation if she says her reason for canceling the pledge is personal financial difficulty? Or serious health problems that she does not wish to become known to others? In the latter two instances, if you honor her request and do not inform her classmates, would you keep their gifts? If not, how would you explain refunding them?

Scenario #5

A board member who is a major donor wants to give an art collection. Her requirement is that the gallery be set up just like her home and that she be able to use it for private social events upon request. Do you accept? What would be the risks—to the organization and to the donor?

Scenario #6

In private conversation, a fundraiser is told a prospect's husband is seriously ill and the family has financial problems, despite appearances. Do you record that in the database? A volunteer is about to solicit that prospect for a major gift. Do you reveal this information to the volunteer?

Scenario #7

You are the chief development officer of a nonprofit organization. A donor you had cultivated dies. To your surprise, in her will she leaves a watch you had once admired, worth perhaps a couple of hundred dollars, as a personal gift to you. Do you accept it? What if she leaves you $5,000? What if it's $5 million?

Scenario #8

A donor calls you on January 15. She says she was ill on December 31 and just realized she didn't mail her annual gift on that date as she had intended. She will drop it off today. The check is dated December 31 and she wants a receipt dated last year. Do you do it? Does the amount matter? What if it is only $5? Or $100? Or $50,000? Does it matter that she is a regular donor who always has made her gift on December 31 and has never done this before?

Scenario #9

An elderly donor says she wants to change her will, leaving everything to your organization. You know that this decision will cut out her daughter, from whom she is estranged. The daughter, whom you know, is seriously disabled. Do you encourage or discourage the donor? Do you tell the daughter what is going on? Do you tell anyone else about this? If so, who?

Scenario #10

You are the chief development officer of a nonprofit performing arts center. A donor, with whom you worked closely, made a substantial gift to endow a program that would permit children from low-income neighborhoods to attend performances and educational programs at the center. The program has been going for several years. But the donor now has retired out of town and is no longer in close communication with the organization.

The executive director tells you that the center is facing serious financial problems. He says he needs to cut the children's program this year and use income from the endowment to meet the general operating budget. You express your concern that this is not what the donor intended. The executive director becomes testy and says, "Look, if the center closes then there will be no children's program, so immediate needs must take precedent." He says that maybe the program can be reinstituted if and when the center regains financial health. What do you say? Do you discuss this with others? If so, who?

Scenario #11

A foundation makes a challenge grant to support a specific building project at your organization, where you are director of development. The challenge grant is to be matched by new gifts. A trustee who recently made an unrestricted gift says she will send you a new letter, redesignating his previous gift for the building project so it can be counted toward the matching requirement. Do you accept her offer? If not, what do you say to this trustee? By the way, she is chair of the development committee and a close friend of your CEO. And the campaign is behind schedule and the CEO has said your salary next year depends on successfully completing the capital campaign for the building.

Scenario #12

You are the CEO of a local nonprofit involved in conservation. A local chemical company approaches you with an idea. The company would sponsor an annual conference at your organization related to the environment. The grant would cover the costs of the conference but also provide additional unrestricted funds to meet general needs of the organization. The corporate affairs officer tells you that they sincerely want to work as a partner to create more environmental awareness and that the company is working to improve its own environmental practices. Would you accept this sponsorship? If yes, what are the potential risks to your organization? If no, how do you explain that decision to the company? What if you call your colleague at a similar organization and learn that his organization regularly accepts gifts from the same company? Would that influence your decision?

Questions for Discussion

Consider the following questions with regard to Scenarios 1–12:

1. Does the scenario hold the potential for a violation of the law?

2. Does the scenario hold the potential for a violation of one of the ethical codes discussed in this chapter (Independent Sector, AFP, Donor Bill of Rights)? If so, which code and which principles?

3. Does the scenario hold the potential for damage to the organization's reputation, despite whether or not it raises issues with the law or formal ethical codes?

4. Does the ethical issue presented in the scenario relate primarily to: a) the behavior of the fundraiser, b) the character or reputation of the donor or the source of gift funds, c) the impact of the gift on the organization and its mission or donor influence and control, d) privacy and confidentiality, or e) faithfulness to donor intent?

5. How would you respond to the questions raised in each scenario? In some scenarios, alternatives regarding the amount and purpose of the gift are identified. Do they make a difference in what decisions you would make? Explain.

Suggestions for Further Reading

Books

Fishman, S. (2013). *Nonprofit fundraising registration: The 50-state guide* (2nd ed.). Berkeley, CA: NOLO. (Note: Students should check for more recent editions since the time of publication of this text.)

Hopkins, B. R. (2009). *Fundraising law made easy.* Hoboken, NJ: Wiley.

Pettey, J. G. (2013). *Nonprofit fundraising strategy: A guide to ethical decision making and regulation for nonprofit organizations.* Hoboken, NJ: Wiley.

Websites

Bruce R. Hopkins Nonprofit Law Center: http://www.nonprofitlawcenter.com/resources.php

National Association of State Charity Officials: http://www.nasconet.org

CHAPTER 15

International Fundraising and Philanthropy

Previous chapters of this book have focused on fundraising and philanthropy in the United States. Organized philanthropy and fundraising exist in the United States on a scale unmatched anywhere in the world. But the late twentieth century and early decades of the twenty-first have seen the expansion of these traditions across the globe, driven by dramatic political, economic, and technological changes and by the increasing wealth in nations undergoing rapid economic development. Those who will live their lives—and manage nonprofit organizations—in the balance of the twenty-first century will need to understand and be prepared to apply their skills in a global environment. This chapter provides an introduction to special considerations related to fundraising and philanthropy in the international arena.[1]

A SHRINKING PLANET

A century ago, when the fundraising pioneers discussed earlier in this book were beginning to develop new methods, an increasing number of people were becoming employed in industrial settings, including factories and mines, but many still lived and worked on farms or in small communities. Travel was expensive, and communication was slow. The Wright brothers' first flight had just occurred in 1903, and the majority of American homes would not have electricity until 1930. Television, the Internet, and space travel were almost beyond imagination.

World War I began in 1914 and ended in 1918. It was a watershed event and made Americans more aware of events abroad, but their lives were still primarily focused on the communities in which they lived and worked. Philanthropy included giving to one's church and an occasional campaign to build a new firehouse, hospital, or school. The greatest threats to human health included common diseases for which there were yet no cures.

Over the past one hundred years, the pace and magnitude of change have been staggering. Today, the greatest threats facing humanity, including disease, terrorism, climate change, and natural disasters, cannot be confined within national boundaries nor isolated by the oceans that separate the continents. Instant communications and frequent travel transmit ideas, images, news, and even diseases across the globe as rapidly as people a century ago could cross the town squares of their small communities. At the same time, the greatest opportunities for technological and economic advancement lie in cooperative efforts that engage people, and minds, across the planet. The fact that people in Western societies live in affluence while millions around the globe live in poverty has come to be viewed as increasingly anachronistic and unacceptable in an interconnected world. These changing realities have prompted an increasing flow of philanthropic funds from the developed countries of the West to organizations addressing global issues. And while the nonprofit sector in the United States remains the largest, and philanthropy on a large scale remains predominantly an American phenomenon, similar patterns are increasing in number and importance in many nations.

Why has the world become smaller? And why have nonprofit organizations come to play an important role on the world stage? The answer lies in advances in communication technology as well as changes in political, cultural, and economic realities. One reason is the end of the Cold War and the spread of a democratic and capitalist philosophy across the globe. This change removed political barriers to economic interaction and to nonprofit organizations, which had often been viewed as threats by repressive governments. The establishment of free-trade areas and organizations in the 1990s, including the World Trade Organization (WTO), the European Union (EU), and the North American Free Trade Agreement (NAFTA), led to greater economic integration across national boundaries (Thomas, 2002). At the same time, the movement toward devolution of government services and outsourcing to the private sector that has occurred in the United States has also been seen in other nations. As in the United States, private organizations have been called on to replace services previously provided through government programs and to seek financial support from the private sector, leading to the growth of fundraising as a worldwide profession. This new philosophy also has been reflected in the management of international aid programs, with governments preferring to deliver assistance through private organizations rather than directly (Anheier & Themudo, 2005).

Among the most powerful forces for change has been technology. In the twentieth century, development of satellites, the Internet, the World Wide Web, and fiber optic cable made global communication instantaneous. In the twenty-first century, the growth of social media and networks has led to the emergence of communities based on shared interests and concerns that easily span national boundaries. These advances have driven political movements and international economic competition in a "flat" world, in which national borders prevent no barrier to entry into the mainstream of business life (Friedman, 2006). They have increased the awareness of people in developed nations about the needs of others on the planet, stimulating unprecedented global responses to humanitarian needs. And they have introduced new techniques for fundraising and giving that have erased the limitations of geography.

DEFINITIONS AND SCOPE OF ORGANIZATIONS

Before we look at fundraising and philanthropy specifically, let's consider some basic terminology and the types of organizations that operate on the world stage. The term *nonprofit organization* is not widely used in the international environment, although organizations in many countries fit the definition of nonprofit used in the United States. Although the term has different meanings in different parts of the world, what we call a nonprofit in the United States is elsewhere most commonly referred to as a **nongovernmental organization (NGO)**. The term has its origins in the founding documents of the United Nations after World War II ("NGOs: A Long and Turbulent History," 2013). Another term often used is **civil society organizations (CSOs)** (Cagney & Ross, 2013).

Some NGOs operating in a single country are similar to U.S. nonprofits in their essential characteristics, although they vary widely in the legal frameworks within which they exist, the sources of their funding, and especially their relationships with government. Some organizations are operated by the governments of their countries and are known as **government-operated nongovernmental organizations (GONGOs)**. There is no concept quite like the U.S. nonprofit sector in most parts of the world. In the international context, some scholars refer to the collection of organizations that reside between government and the private sector as the **civil society sector** (Salamon, Sokolowski, & Associates, 2004).

International NGOs

The best-known NGOs are **international nongovernmental organizations (INGOs)**. These are organizations whose activities are not confined to a single country. They "make significant operating expenditures across national borders and do not identify themselves as domestic actors [within one nation]" (Anheier & Themudo, 2005, p. 102). In addition, they are sometimes said to be transnational because, as the term implies, they "organize . . . in pursuit of goals and purposes that transcend the boundaries of national territories and state jurisdictions" (Boli, 2006, p. 333). Until recent decades, most INGOs were based in the United States or Western Europe but are now more diffused around the world (Anheier & Themudo, 2005). INGOs include the large brand-name organizations that most people know. Cagney and Ross (2013) observe that a small number—for example, Save the Children, UNICEF, World Vision—have become so large and dominant that they are a "super league" of INGOs that are "able to fundraise and operate almost anywhere in the world" (p. 5).

The World Bank divides INGOs into two basic types: **advocacy INGOs** and **operational NGOs**. Advocacy INGOs are organizations that promote a cause or issue on a multinational basis, for example Amnesty International, which protects human rights. In the World Bank's definition, operational INGOs are those whose primary purpose is to design and implement economic development projects. However, the mission of other INGOs, for example, the Red Cross, is to provide immediate and short-term relief from human suffering, rather than support economic or infrastructure development over the long run. The latter distinction is analogous to the difference between charity and philanthropy discussed earlier in this book.

Many development INGOs, working in partnership with the UN and the World Bank, are focused on accomplishment of the UN Millennium Development Goals, adopted by world leaders in 2000. They include specific targets for the reduction of poverty, disease, illiteracy, environmental degradation, and discrimination against women to be achieved by 2015 (United Nations, 2012). Most efforts in pursuit of these goals are funded by governments, although philanthropy has begun to play a larger role.

Global Organizations

It is useful to clarify a distinction between international organizations and global organizations, especially since the terms are sometimes used interchangeably. An **international organization** may have some programs in other countries, but it is governed within and maintains a focus on its home country. A **global organization** is one that has activities throughout the world and probably has a governance structure that places decision making in the hands of individuals from multiple countries.

Koenig (2004) describes a continuum along which some nonprofits have evolved. They start as local organizations with local interests. Then they begin to develop an international awareness, perhaps including international topics in their conferences and published materials. They may then move along to develop some international programs, possibly hosting conferences attended by people from around the world or publishing materials in various languages. At this point along the continuum, they have started to become international organizations. At a later point in their evolution, such organizations may begin to admit international members, open offices or form chapters in other countries, and enter alliances or partnerships with organizations in other nations. Finally, some ultimately may evolve into global organizations "with members, programs, or operations in many different regions around the world and having a multinational board of directors or other decision-making group" (Koenig, 2004, p. 5).

Today, most American national nonprofits are at least international. Some large brand-name INGOs are global organizations. And some INGOs were created as global organizations from the beginning. For example, CIVICUS, an international alliance that works to strengthen civil society around the world, was founded in 1993 with a multinational board—it was global from the beginning, both in its purposes and governance (Koenig, 2004). Other INGOs started out in one country and then over time developed into international or global organizations, following one of various paths. Some grew by opening offices or branches in other countries—that is, they internationalized—while others are federations or alliances of nationally based nonprofits that have banded together to pursue a common mission or cause.

Indigenous NGOs

INGOs are often large and visible, but it is a more complex challenge to track NGOs operating *within* various countries around the world. There is no single source of comprehensive data, although research interest has increased in recent years. One of the most ambitious efforts, begun in 1991, is the Johns Hopkins Comparative Nonprofit Sector Project, a collaborative investigation led by Lester Salamon at The Johns Hopkins University. The project began with teams of local researchers in thirteen countries. Now working in forty-five countries, the project has developed extensive comparative data on civil society organizations, philanthropy, and voluntarism and has produced several books, more than sixty published papers, and the Johns Hopkins Global Civil Society Index. The index makes it possible to access more than three hundred research products, including many focused on global civil society and others related to the U.S. nonprofit sector.

Like nonprofits in the United States, NGOs in other nations engage in a variety of activities. According to the Johns Hopkins project research, the largest number or organizations provide services, including education and social services. Another significant percentage are engaged in what Salamon and Sokolowski (2004) call "expressive functions," including arts, culture, recreation, and professional associations. Others are advocacy organizations that bring social and human problems to public attention and work for change—for example, to protect human rights, preserve the environment, and other goals.

GOVERNING AND MANAGING INTERNATIONAL AND GLOBAL ORGANIZATIONS

Earlier in this text, fundraising was discussed as a function rooted in the larger context of organizations, closely tied to broader issues of governance and management. Governing and managing international and global organizations involves unique considerations, which encompass but also go beyond the generic challenges of nonprofit governance and management as practiced in the United States. Those considerations affect fundraising as well as other operations.

Unique Challenges and Pressures

Many of the pressures facing nonprofit organizations in the United States—including growing needs for services in the face of declining government support, calls for strengthened governance and accountability, and the need to balance commitment to mission with competition for resources—are present in the international environment as well. But there are also unique challenges that come from working across the globe.

NGO managers must accommodate national and regional differences in legal systems, languages, political environments, and culture. Among these, Thomas (2002) argues, culture is uniquely important for three reasons. First, "the economic, legal, and political characteristics of a country are a manifestation of a nation's culture" (p. 19). Second, while the legal and political characteristics of nations are explicit and observable, culture is often invisible, especially to those who have grown up in different environments. "The influence of culture is difficult to detect and managers therefore often overlook it" (p. 19). Finally, the practice of management often focuses on interpersonal relationships—with staff, volunteers, donors, and others—and it is in such interactions that cultural differences may be most manifest. It affects such ordinary events as how individuals greet each other, how directions are communicated, and other everyday interactions. It involves both language and customs regarding physical space, body language, and other subtle differences. And, as discussed further later in this chapter, it affects attitudes toward money and the practice of fundraising. An understanding of culture and its implications is essential to any manager expecting to work in the international environment.

Governing Models

In most nonprofit organizations in the United States, the governing board plays an important role in fundraising and its members are selected at least in part for their ability to contribute to the organization's advancement in that way. For an international or global organization, the development and management of the board presents unique considerations.

For example, as a U.S.-based nonprofit begins to internationalize and seek board members from other countries, it will be adding members who may not fully understand the fiduciary responsibilities of governing boards under U.S. law or the expectations of board members in American nonprofits, which may be quite different from those in their home countries (Koenig, 2004).

As the organization moves along the continuum described earlier in this chapter, evolving from an international to a global organization, its governance structure will need to reflect its evolving nature. One way to achieve international representation is to adopt bylaws that provide for a seat on the governing board for individuals representing each of the regions served by the organization. This might be an approach taken by an organization that is internationalizing: For example, a European seat might be created when it opens a European chapter of affiliates with a Europe-based partner, then a seat for a Latin American representative might be created as its programs expand into that region, and so forth. But as the organization continues to expand around the world, two problems may arise. First, the regional representatives may see their role as advocating for the interests of the region they represent, rather than focusing on the overall welfare of the entire organization. It could become a forum in which regional representatives vie for favorable treatment of their regions, with a diminishing portion of the board focused on building an integrated organization. Second, as programs expand and seats for a larger number of regional representatives are added, the board may become unmanageably large. And, of course, board members from various regions may not share the same understanding of fundraising or philanthropy.

In another model, an internationalizing organization might decide to add some number of international members to its board, for example, identifying three seats on an eleven-person board to be held by individuals from other countries but without specifying particular regions to be represented (Koenig, 2004). This approach keeps the board at a manageable size and does provide for an international perspective. In addition, since the international members are elected or appointed at-large, they may not be as inclined to view their role as advocating for regional interests. However, as the organization's programs expand around the world, this approach does not ensure that the perspectives and views of all its constituencies will be represented at the board table.

A third approach is one Koenig (2004) describes as the "most common" in organizations that have adopted "a greater global mindset throughout the organization . . . because it puts a premium on an integrated organization" (p. 102). In this model, board members are enlisted from around the world, based on the organization's needs for various skills, perspectives, and experiences—*including fundraising*. The board membership can be crafted to meet the organization's leadership needs at various times. In this approach, the organization's needs would be paramount, and the board's goal would be to enlist the best members from wherever they may be around the world. Gaining representation of various regions would also be a consideration, of course, but the nominating committee and the board would not be constrained by such requirements in selecting people who bring desired qualities. The downside of this approach is that it does not ensure that the perspectives of all regions will be reflected on the board.

Structuring International NGOs

Some issues related to the organizational structure of nonprofits in the United States—for example, relationships between national offices and chapters and the trade-offs between centralized and decentralized management—may become exacerbated as the organization expands internationally. This may affect fundraising strategy as well as other management decisions.

As mentioned, some NGOs have come into existence as global organizations. But others have evolved from local to international organizations by establishing chapters or clubs abroad, maintaining a close relationship with headquarters (Koenig, 2004). Another approach is to maintain relatively autonomous national organizations that are affiliated with but do not receive direction from headquarters. For example, Médecins Sans Frontières (MSF), known as Doctors Without Borders in the United States and some other countries, is made up of nineteen "associations," also called "sections," in Australia, Austria, Belgium, Canada, Denmark, France, Germany, Greece, Holland, Hong Kong, Italy, Japan, Luxembourg, Norway, Spain, Sweden, Switzerland, the United Kingdom, and the United States. The U.S. section, MSF-USA (known in English as Doctors Without Borders or DWB), was founded in New York in 1990 to raise funds and to advocate regarding humanitarian concerns within the United Nations and the U.S. government. Each national association is responsible to a board of directors elected by its own members, which include former and current field staff, at an annual assembly. The president of each section is a member of the MSF International Council, which meets twice a year at the international headquarters in Geneva, Switzerland. Among other responsibilities, the International Council promotes accountability and transparency within the MSF movement and publishes combined financial statements that are an aggregation of the financial statements of the nineteen sections (Médecins Sans Frontières, 2008).

Some organizations have evolved a hybrid model, combining chapters linked to headquarters and affiliations with other independent organizations abroad that share similar purposes. For example, when AFP began to expand internationally, there were already some existing organizations in other countries. In nations where no such organization existed, new AFP chapters were established with a close relationship to headquarters in the United States. However, wishing to preserve its good relationships with existing organizations and not be viewed as a competitor, AFP chose to develop strategic alliances with them.

The first three alliances were formed in 2002 and 2003 with the Institute of Fundraising in the United Kingdom, the Fundraising Institute of Australia, and the Fundraising Institute of New Zealand. Members of these national organizations can elect to join AFP and vice versa. Linked through the web, members of both partners can access each other's members, databases, publications, and other information resources.

As in nonprofits within the United States, achieving the proper balance between centralized control and local autonomy in an international organization requires careful calibration. Historically, many NGOs had centralized structures that were pushed out to chapters as they were established, but as growth extends into more geographically remote regions and diverse national and cultural settings, there is a trend toward greater autonomy for regional chapters or affiliates. The challenge is to determine what policies and functions need to be retained centrally in order to maintain ethical standards, quality of programs, and adherence to a common mission and which decisions can be left to local organizations. As the potential for fundraising increases with the expansion of wealth across the globe, there may indeed be a greater need for decentralization, so that local entities can tap the philanthropic markets in their own nations with an individualized approach.

Questions about centralization and decentralization are, of course, familiar ones even in national nonprofits within the United States. But working across legal, cultural, and language differences and considerable geographic distances makes them even more complex and delicate in the international environment, placing a premium on communication, flexibility, and a tolerance for ambiguity. In the nonprofit world, as in business, "conventional organizational forms are giving way to networks of less hierarchical relationships and cooperative strategic alliances with other [organizations]" (Thomas, 2002, p. 5). This changing environment requires that those intending to pursue positions of leadership in fundraising or general nonprofit/NGO management develop skills, qualities, and understanding that go beyond their own countries and societies.

INGO FUNDRAISING STRATEGIES

As Stroup (2012) observes, international NGOs pursue different revenue strategies, reflecting their missions as well as the realities of their home countries. For example, CARE USA relies mostly on grants from the U.S. government and receives only 17 percent of its revenue from American individual donors. Oxfam in Great Britain receives most of its revenue from private gifts, and MSF, based in France, receives only private support—about half from French donors and half from other parts of the world, including the United States. This reflects in part the sources of support available in their home countries as well as differences in the causes the organizations address. Individual donors may be drawn to giving to MSF in disasters and emergencies but perhaps not to the long-term programs of CARE, for which government support is more appropriate. But there are also issues related to resource dependency. (Remember the discussion back in Chapter 2 of this book.) Some are critical of CARE's dependence on government, charging that it limits the organization's independence. MSF's sections hold different views on whether to accept government funds, for reason of similar concern. But MSF is limited in its ability to raise funds in France, where individual giving in not substantial, and relies on its U.S. section for about a third of its revenue.

INTERNATIONAL PHILANTHROPY

Now let's narrow our focus from the overall international environment to take a closer look at philanthropy and fundraising in that arena. We'll start by considering philanthropy flowing from the United States and other Western countries to the rest of the world and then examine the growth of philanthropy and fundraising within various regions.

As reported by Giving USA, American philanthropy directed to international affairs totaled $14.93 billion in 2013, accounting for 4 percent of total giving (Giving USA, 2014a). That total was a decline from 2012 and included $199 million dedicated to disaster relief efforts. But the estimates are likely understated. For example, they do not include funds spent on international activities by U.S.-based nonprofits in fields such as education, health care, arts and culture, youth development, and religion, which are reported in other categories; they do not capture all foundation and corporate giving; and they do not include gifts that U.S. donors made to organizations based in other countries that are not chartered in the United States. Unless the recipient organization is registered in the United States, the donor cannot claim a tax deduction for the gift. Some organizations headquartered abroad establish U.S.-based nonprofits, often called a "foundation" or "friends of" in order to qualify to receive deductible gifts from U.S. citizens. Gifts to those organizations could be captured in the Giving USA totals, but gifts that Americans make directly to organizations abroad could not be, since the estimates are based on tax data. Giving USA data also do not include the substantial private payments made by recent immigrants to the United States who send funds, called **remittances**, directly to their home countries to support either families or projects.

One trend that leads to an underreporting of gifts flowing from the United States to purposes in other countries is the increasing tendency of corporations to give directly to organizations in those countries rather than those based in the United States that provide programs abroad. A study by the Lilly Family School of Philanthropy in 2013 found growth in corporate international giving, with 60 percent of surveyed companies reporting foreign gifts (Lilly Family, 2013).

Global poverty and health have become the focus of substantial gifts and priorities for foundation grant programs. The largest U.S. foundation, the Bill and Melinda Gates Foundation, is primarily concerned with global health and global economic development and accounts for about two out of every five dollars in international giving from the United States (Foundation Center, 2012c).

The Internet has greatly facilitated the ability of individual donors to support global causes. For example, GlobalGiving, a 501(c)(3) U.S. nonprofit, operates a website through which donors can make gifts to support specific projects listed by organizations throughout the world. Projects can be selected by country, theme (e.g., children, women, the environment), and other criteria. According to GlobalGiving's website, 390,941 donors had given $114,224,348 to 10,231 projects between 2002 and 2014.

While the United States remains the largest source of international giving, other nations are an increasing source. They include the developed nations of Western Europe and Japan but also the emerging economies of Brazil, China, India, and South Africa, which provided an estimated $366 million in philanthropic gifts to international causes in 2011 (Hudson Institute, 2013).

GLOBAL FUNDRAISING

At the same time that international giving from the United States and other nations has increased, NGOs in many parts of the world have been required to pursue new sources of revenue, including social enterprise and philanthropic fundraising.

Obstacles to Fundraising and Philanthropy

Fundraising and philanthropy face obstacles in many nations. First, philanthropy requires the presence of surplus income or wealth. While wealth is growing worldwide, it is highly concentrated. Not all nations have a sizable middle class, making it difficult to generate a broad base of giving, and not all wealthy people are philanthropic. Indeed, the Giving Pledge movement led by Bill Gates and Warren Buffet has met with mixed responses (Cagney & Ross, 2013).

Second, while most religions and cultures include expectations of altruistic behavior beyond one's family, not all cultures support organized fundraising or voluntarism on the U.S. model (Wagner, 2004). For example, in some cultures, it would be deemed inappropriate to ask another for funds to support an organization on whose board the solicitor served. In other countries, for example, states of the former Soviet Union, the idea of prospect research might find a negative reaction, seeming too reminiscent of the files the government maintained on its citizens in the Soviet era. In Japan, there historically has been no tradition of charitable bequests, with estates going only to families. Only 10 percent of individuals make a will, and inheritance is distributed among family members according to the law (Cagney & Ross, 2013).

There are legal obstacles in some nations, which have inhibited the growth of independent nongovernmental organizations. For example, until recently, China required organizations to work through a dual registration and management system, which made it difficult to become registered. Organizations were required to obtain a government agency to sponsor them and then also a second government agency to monitor and audit them (Cagney & Ross, 2013).

Even the desirability of philanthropy is a subject of debate in many nations. Some people are concerned about the potential for philanthropy to undermine the responsibility of the state to meet social needs. Others view philanthropy as extending control by wealthy elites, and some governments view NGOs as threats to their authority. For example, anti-NGO legislation was passed or proposed in 2013 in Russia, Ethiopia, and Rwanda, and some pro-democracy organizations were shut down after the Arab Spring uprisings in Egypt. In addition to cultural barriers, few national tax systems include benefits for giving as generous as those available to donors in the United States, although some have increased incentives in recent years (Cagney & Ross, 2013).

Fundraising Methods and Innovation

There are technical obstacles to the implementation of U.S.-style fundraising techniques in some countries; for example, telephone and mail systems may not support sophisticated telemarketing or direct-mail solicitation, and some countries have low rates of connectivity to the Internet. Despite these obstacles, fundraising has grown in nations around the world. Some have adopted U.S.-style methods and strategies, including direct mail, phone solicitation, and campaigns, but others have developed methods more suited to their unique traditions and environments. A comprehensive overview is beyond the scope of this chapter, but a few selected highlights provide a rich tasting of the varied methods in use:

- Argentina has a poor postal system but high levels of online giving (Cagney & Ross, 2013).

- Ethiopia has mounted some of the largest mass-participation events (Cagney & Ross, 2013).

- In Japan, most individual donors use giving boxes or respond to face-to-face solicitations on the street (Uo, 2013).

- Although Latin America is a diverse region encompassing diverse cultures, historically fundraising from individuals has surrounded events, including galas and sporting events (Galafassi, 2013).

- Western Europe also is a diverse region, each with different traditions. In some regions, many of the fundraising methods developed in the United States also are common; for example, direct mail is used in continental Europe. Raffles are popular in the United Kingdom, and individuals in Spain and Italy can make gifts via their tax returns (Carnie, 2013).

- In Australia and New Zealand, fundraisers use a method known as the **two-step**. Street canvassers collect information from individuals that is then used for a follow-up contact by phone, Internet, or mail (Triner, 2013)

- A technique used in India is, in essence, the opposite of the two-step. Called **telefacing**, it involves a phone call that sets up an appointment for a face-to-face solicitation (Menon & Tiwari, 2013).

- In Kenya, fundraising follows the tradition of Harambee, which means "all pull together." Harambee events are both small and large and are often advertised on social media (Muchilwa, 2013)

There have been examples of successful U.S.-style campaigns in other countries, especially in higher education. For example, the Universidad de Monterrey in Mexico launched the first capital campaign in Latin American higher education in 1995 and raised

$27 million (Cagney & Ross, 2013). Campaigns have become standard practice at universities in the United Kingdom. The University of Oxford announced a £1.25 billion campaign in 2008, with £575 million already having been committed, and in 2013 increased its goal to £3 billion.

FUNDRAISING AS A GLOBAL PROFESSION

As discussed in previous chapters, fundraising as a professional field has emerged in the United States primarily over the past fifty years and more recently internationally. Fundraising professional associations, like the Association of Fundraising Professionals (AFP) in the United States, have developed in a number of countries, and some have relationships with AFP and the Fund Raising School, part of the Lilly School of Philanthropy at Indiana University. By 2012, AFP had established eleven chapters outside of the United States and Canada, including those in Mexico, Southeast Asia, Puerto Rico, and Egypt. AFP also maintains alliances with other fundraising associations around the world and established international growth as one of the priorities of its 2011–2013 strategic plan. In 2006, in cooperation with its partner organizations, AFP developed an **International Statement of Ethical Principles in Fundraising**, which includes many points in common with U.S. standards. And in 2014, AFP initiated an "international advanced diploma," in cooperation with the Institute of Fundraising and the European Fundraising Association, to prepare senior fundraisers for international work. For Americans with fundraising experience, career opportunities abroad are plentiful, especially in higher education and in Britain and Australia (Hall, 2014c).

CHAPTER SUMMARY

Organized fundraising began in the United States at a time when most people were focused on local communities rather than events abroad. But changes in political, cultural, and economic realities and the spread of communication technologies have resulted in more philanthropy being directed from the United States and other developed nations to other parts of the world. In addition, wealth has expanded across the world, making fundraising a global activity. In many nations, governments are reducing services and relying on nonprofits to raise private funds to meet social needs.

In the international environment, nonprofits are usually called *nongovernmental* or *civil society* organizations. Some are government operated and are known as *government-operated nongovernmental organizations* (*GONGOs*). The best known are *international nongovernmental organizations* (*INGOs*). These are organizations whose activities are not confined to a single country. Some are *advocacy INGOs* and some are *operational INGOs*. Some of the latter are focused on economic development, but others provide sort-term relief in disasters and other circumstances.

A *global organization* is one that has activities throughout the world and has a governance structure that places decision making in the hands of individuals from multiple countries. There are various models for governing such organizations, and it is important to balance regional representation with the need to engage board members with particular skills, including fundraising. In addition to international and global organizations, there are nonprofit organizations (usually called NGOs) indigenous to a specific country that serve needs only in that country.

The management of international and global organizations is complex. It involves many of the same challenges of nonprofit management in the United States and, in addition, others that arise from national and regional differences in legal systems, languages, political environments, and culture. Organizations that operate internationally face many of the same questions about centralization, decentralization, coordination, and accountability that are common for U.S. nonprofits with branches or chapters. Regional divisions may have a close relationship with headquarters or be relatively autonomous. The structure has implications for the management of fundraising and other activities.

American philanthropy directed to international affairs totaled $14.93 billion in 2013 (Giving USA, 2014a). But this total does not capture gifts made by Americans to organizations based overseas and other transfers. U.S.-headquartered foundations and corporations have increased giving to issues related to poverty and health, and web platforms such as Global Giving facilitate international giving by individuals.

Fundraising by organizations in other parts of the world often faces barriers, including the lack of a middle class, cultural differences regarding philanthropy, legal obstacles, and the view that social services should be provided by government rather than private organizations. There are also barriers in some countries to the use of traditional fundraising methods. Organizations have developed some innovative methods and techniques suited to the traditions and technology of their own countries. Expansion of the Internet and mobile communication has provided ways for nonprofits worldwide to reach donors in their own areas and across the world.

Fundraising has become a global profession. AFP has established chapters in various nations and has partnered with existing professional associations in others. AFP and partners developed an *International Statement of Ethical Principles in Fundraising*. There is an increasing number of job opportunities for Americans with fundraising experience who also have the skills and understanding to work in other parts of the world.

Key Terms and Concepts

Advocacy INGO

Civil society organization (CSO)

Civil society sector

Global organization

Government-operated nongovernmental organization (GONGO)

International nongovernmental organization (INGO)

International organization

International Statement of Ethical Principles in Fundraising

Nongovernmental organization (NGO)

Operational NGO

Remittances

Telefacing

Two-step

Case 15.1: Haitian Earthquake Relief

On January 12, 2010, a 7.0 earthquake struck Haiti, leveling thousands of homes, cutting off electricity and telephone service, killing thousands, and leaving thousands more homeless and destitute in what had already been the poorest country in the Western Hemisphere (Romero & Lacey, 2010).

The philanthropic response to the catastrophe was immediate. Within twenty-four hours of the earthquake, people began responding with online gifts. Within three days, the Red Cross had received more than $1 million on its website and by phone and another $1 million in $10 gifts sent through text messages. Within a few months, gifts made by text totaled $50 million, compared with just $1 million given by text in all previous times (Charity Navigator, 2015). Social media played a significant role. Within days of the disaster, Oxfam received more than $800,000 in gifts, including $10,000 through a Facebook cause. Haiti quickly became a trending topic on Twitter, and users began posting advice on which organizations to support, warning against some and recommending others (Preston, 2010).

Celebrities mobilized for Haitian relief. Actor Sean Penn created a new organization dedicated to helping Haiti, and many performers began opening their concerts with appeals for gifts to Penn's and other Haiti-related nonprofits. A telethon hosted by actor George Clooney and many other celebrities raised over $57 million through phone, text, and the web, and iTunes contributed the proceeds of sales of the concert ("Haiti Telethon Haul," 2010). Former president Bill Clinton visited Haiti and announced a new initiative of the Clinton Foundation. He joined with former president George W. Bush in creating the Clinton-Bush Fund for Haitian relief and rebuilding, which raised over $36 million from U.S. citizens and businesses (Charity Navigator, 2015). President Obama gave $200,000 of his Nobel Peace Prize money to Haitian relief (Charity Navigator, 2015). One year after the disaster, Americans had given a total of $1.4 billion in philanthropy, and billions in additional aid had been committed from around the world, including support from individuals, governments, and intergovernmental agencies (Charity Navigator, 2015).

Progress on the ground was slow. It was not possible for organizations to quickly and effectively spend the funds given. The biggest problem was the extensive devastation, inaccessible roads, and the fact that the earthquake had occurred near Haiti's capital city, incapacitating many government agencies. But observers also cited other issues. Some NGOs were criticized for not working more closely with local organizations and grassroots leaders. One NGO executive described "a swarm of well-meaning but in some cases inexperienced aid organizations and individuals" who came to Haiti, claiming that "their money [was] disproportionately spent . . . on isolated, random activities [and] could have been better used by groups already working in Haiti" (Letson, 2010). Local realities also hampered efforts to rebuild. For example, many Haitian schools are run by individuals, and some were not willing to have a school rebuilt on their land. Some community meetings were held in English, rather than Creole, the language spoken by most Haitians (Preston & Wallace, 2011).

A year after the earthquake, conditions remained difficult. The dialogue began to shift from immediate disaster relief to longer-term economic development in Haiti, and debates about the best way to accomplish it continued. The U.S State Department's representative for Haiti explained the importance of making rebuilding "a Haitian-led effort, not a donor-led effort" (McCambridge, 2012). An official of Convoy of Hope, an NGO working in Haiti, emphasized the importance of coordination and working with the Haitian government: "The majority of all earthquake recovery funds are not directed to the Haitian government but are being routed through a variety of NGOs in Haiti, some of which work in parallel rather than in cooperation with the public sector, solidifying the system that ensures that Haiti will never develop or decrease its reliance on foreign aid" (Charity Navigator, 2015).

Two years after the disaster, Haiti remained among the poorest nations in the world. Over 800,000 had no electricity; 500,000 were illiterate; only 200,000 had regular jobs; and 80 percent survived on less than $2 a day (Charity Navigator, 2015).

SOURCE: Reprinted with editing from Worth (2014), pp. 392–393.

Case 15.2: The One Foundation and China's Social Sector

Philanthropy has a long tradition in China and is rooted in the traditions of the country's three principal religions, Confucianism, Buddhism, and Taoism. But with the founding of the People's Republic of China in 1949, the government either closed down existing charitable organizations or brought them under government control. Even the Red Cross Society of China lost its independent status and came under the control of the government, a status that continues. Along with economic reforms in the 1980s and 1990s came new laws to encourage giving, and new organizations were established but were still under government control (i.e., they were GONGOs). A new law in 2004, the Foundation Management Ordinance, changed the environment by permitting the establishment of private fundraising foundations. Combined with growing economic prosperity, the new legal environment opened the door to growing philanthropy in the first decades of the twenty-first century (Bo & Fang, 2013).

Until recently, the growth in giving was hampered by the cumbersome procedures organizations needed to follow to become registered, a requirement of tax deductibility. However, in 2014 the registration requirements were simplified and other legislation was under consideration to encourage the growth of the civil society sector (Simon, 2014). Individuals in China are entitled to a tax deduction for charitable gifts up to 30 percent of income, and nonprofit organizations are tax exempt on certain types of income (Bo & Fang, 2013). Most contributions still go to organizations controlled by or affiliated with the government, with poverty alleviation, education, and disaster relief among the three purposes attracting the most support (Bo & Fang, 2013).

The One Foundation was founded in 2007 by movie star Jet Li. Li and his family had barely survived the tsunami in the Indian Ocean in 2004, an experience that motivated him to create the new organization with the motto of "one person, one yuan, one world," emphasizing the power of many small gifts (Simon, 2014). The initial focus of the One Foundation was disaster relief, although it has since broadened its programs. During earthquakes and mudslides in 2008, 2009, and 2010, it won praise for its efforts and gained visibility (Yu, 2010).

Given the barriers to obtaining approval as an independent organization, the One Foundation was originally created as a part of the China Red Cross Foundation, which is a public, state-run foundation, under the name Red Cross Society of China Jet Li One Foundation Project (Simon, 2014). But this arrangement provided little freedom of action and was not secure, since the Red Cross held the power to terminate the project after a three-year term. Some who distrusted the Red Cross (as a government-controlled entity) were concerned that the Red Cross would just terminate the One Foundation and use its funds for other purposes. Understandably, this concern inhibited fundraising by the foundation. A public debate arose concerning the need to provide more freedom for private foundations in China (Yu, 2010).

On December 3, 2010, the One Foundation became the first independent, nongovernmental foundation to gain registration with the Civil Affairs Bureau without the requirement of a government sponsoring agency (Bo & Fang, 2013). Governed by a board of eleven people, the foundation stated as its mission "to promote philanthropic culture, to provide humanitarian aid in natural disasters, and to build a philanthropic platform by which everyone can join us in the philanthropic causes in every possible way" (Global Giving, n.d.). Its mission expanded to encompass the three areas of disaster relief, children's welfare, and philanthropy development.

But even with its new status, the One Foundation was not without problems. It was criticized after the Yushu earthquake in 2010 for not spending donated funds quickly enough. Chinese law requires that foundations pay out 70 percent of funds in the year after they are received, but One Foundation lacked accounting personnel sufficient to meet that standard, causing some to accuse the foundation of fraud. Jet Li and other members of the foundation staff acknowledged management problems (Simon, 2014). A new national Charity Law was under consideration in early 2014 that would establish the legal standards of care and loyalty for nonprofit boards, similar to the standards of governance in effect in the United States (Simon, 2014).

In 2011, an employee of the Chinese Red Cross (again, a government-operated organization) was accused of corruption in a widely publicized scandal. This generated considerable public skepticism regarding nonprofit organizations, which also affected the One Foundation. The foundation quickly clarified its independence from the Red Cross and removed a link to the Red Cross from its website. The One Foundation became an alternative to the Red Cross for some donors following an earthquake in 2013, although it is careful not to openly compete (Buterin, 2013). It was reported that earthquake relief raised by the One Foundation totaled at least 46 million yuan through online platforms and an additional 44 million yuan through bank transfers, from 610,000 gifts (Lijing, 2013).

The One Foundation undertakes programs to secure a broad base of support, consistent with its mission to expand philanthropy. This has included traditional methods such as collection boxes and also more contemporary approaches, including online giving, mobile phones, electronic payments, and partnerships with online shopping sites (Bo & Fang, 2013). In 2013, the foundation became one of the first to accept payments using Bitcoin (Buterin, 2013).

Nonprofits in China continue to face strict government supervision and periodic clampdowns of their activity. Although the government has encouraged more organizations to register under newly relaxed requirements, some remain suspicious that offering that option is just a way for the government "to co-opt the energy and resources of civil society" (Chinese Civil Society, 2014). Suspicion about the relationship between the government and nonprofits continues to inhibit giving by the public. Despite such tensions, China's growing middle class holds the potential for significantly increased philanthropy. In addition, there are now additional private foundations. Infrastructure organizations, including the China Foundation Center, are working to increase the transparency and professionalism of the social sector and to increase its impact on Chinese society (Spegele, 2010).

Questions for Discussion

1. Did the philanthropic response to the Haiti earthquake provide lessons that may apply to nonprofit organizations in nondisaster fundraising, or was it a unique situation?

2. How does the case of Haitian earthquake relief illustrate the complexities of management in the international environment discussed in this chapter?

3. Thinking about the One Foundation and other developments in Chinese philanthropy, how important do you think it is to have a democratic society in order to encourage philanthropy? Or will people give in any society if effective fundraising methods are followed?

4. If you had the financial capacity to be a significant philanthropist, would you focus your giving on reducing world poverty or on addressing social problems in the United States? Explain your answer.

5. Should governments be the principal sources of assistance for economic development and poverty reduction, or should philanthropy play the leading role? What are the advantages and disadvantages of each type of action? What should be the relationship between private and government efforts? Explain.

Suggestions for Further Reading

Books

Brinkerhoff, J. M., Smith, S. C., & Teegan, H. (Eds.). (2007). *NGOs and the millennium development goals: Citizen action to reduce poverty.* New York: Palgrave Macmillan.

Cagney, P., & Ross, B. (2013). *Global fundraising: How the world is changing the rules of philanthropy.* Hoboken, NJ: Wiley.

Simon, K. (2013). *Civil society in China: The legal framework from ancient times to the "new reform era."* New York: Oxford University.

Stroup, S. S. (2012). *Borders among activists: International NGOs in the United States, Britain, and France.* Ithaca, NY: Cornell University Press.

Websites

Global Fundraising wiki: http://globalfundraising.wikispaces.com/wiki/changes

Global Giving: http://www.globalgiving.org

Idealist.org: http://www.idealist.org

InterAction (American Council for Voluntary International Action): http://www.interaction.org

International Society for Third-Sector Research (ISTR): http://www.istr.org

The Johns Hopkins Center for Civil Society Studies: http://ccss.jhu.edu

Union of International Associations: http://www.uia.be

Note

1. Some material in this chapter has been adapted from my earlier work (Worth, 2014).

Conclusion

From Technician to Leader: Reflections
on the Development Officer's Role

In the Introduction to this book, I recounted my personal experience in beginning a fundraising career some years ago. I observed that most people then entered the field by chance, rather than as the result of an affirmative career choice. But things have changed, and many young people are planning—and preparing for—a career in fundraising.

Surely not every student reading this text is intending to pursue a career as a fundraising professional. Some may plan to pursue careers as nonprofit managers in other roles, recognizing that fundraising likely will be required as one aspect of their jobs. Others may be interested in fundraising more tangentially, perhaps thinking they may serve on a nonprofit board and should have some understanding of this important function. But this Conclusion explores the role of development officers in nonprofit organizations and institutions, with the hope that some students who have completed this text may decide to proceed in that career direction and may find some reflections on the topic to be at least interesting to consider in terms of their own future work.

ROLES OF THE DEVELOPMENT OFFICER

Let's begin with the question of exactly what a development officer does. In the simplest understanding, of course, a development officer raises money. But to stop there would be like saying that a manager runs an organization; it does not provide sufficient information about exactly what the role entails. If we were to interview some random sample of people—even those working in the nonprofit sector—and asked each what a development officer does, we might discover that there is not a common understanding. Indeed, Burk (2013) conducted such a study and found widespread confusion about the development officer's role, as well as that of nonprofit boards and CEOs.

Discussion about the role of the development officer has a long history and has been the subject of various academic studies. In the mid-1990s, a colleague and I (Worth & Asp, 1994) reviewed the fundraising literature to identify the roles various authors were attributing to development professionals. Most were not explicit about the role; rather, we inferred their perceptions of it from how they described it, and we placed those perceptions into four categories.

We found that some authors describe the development officer as a *salesperson*, essentially someone who solicits gifts, perhaps a common perception among the general public. Others describe the role as that of a *catalyst*, someone who makes things happen but does not necessarily solicit gifts. For example, that may include providing solicitation materials, research, and strategy to the CEO and volunteers (something like the quarterback role discussed in Chapter 5) or perhaps serving as a campaign director who clears assignments for others but does not raise funds directly (perhaps something like an air traffic controller). A third category of authors describe the development officer primarily as a *manager*, focused on internal operations of the development office. And, finally, some portray the development officer as a *leader* who helps to shape the organization's direction and policies as well as the acquisition of resources.

We (Worth & Asp, 1994) theorized that an individual might evolve through the various roles in the course of his or her career. That person might begin as a technician, focused on specific tasks, either internal (such as gift entry) or external (perhaps as a telemarketing caller). Eventually, the individual might achieve a position of leadership within his or her organization, requiring advanced knowledge and expertise on both internal and external matters. In 2006, Ryan conducted a study that applied the four Worth and Asp (1994) roles in a survey of development officers in higher education. He found that all four roles existed but did not observe or predict a progression as Worth and Asp (2004) had predicted. Rather, he concluded that development officers may be required to play any and all of the four roles, as the circumstances may require.

Various other scholars have studied development officer roles, using different models and looking at practitioners in various settings, for example, higher education and health care institutions (e.g., Waters, Kelly, & Walker, 2012; Williams, 2004). They use somewhat different terminology and arrive at somewhat different conclusions, but all agree that development officers may be viewed either as *technical specialists* or in a broader role as *leaders* of their organizations. And all agree that fundraising professionals can be most effective when able and permitted to play the larger role. As expressed by Burlingame and Hulse (1991), "All fundraisers should have the requisite technical knowledge, but the most effective are those working from a base of knowledge and wisdom. . . . They have a sense of who they are as professionals, appreciate the role of fund raising in their organization[s], and understand what they do is important to the philanthropic sector and to society as a whole" (p. xxii).

So what is the reality today? In their 2012 study, Waters et al. found, to their dismay, that most development officers are still perceived as what they called "expert prescribers." That is, they are seen as technical experts who are totally responsible for their organization's fundraising. The authors noted that fundraisers cast in this role face the serious risks of isolation, unrealistic expectations, and burnout.

The situation Waters et al. (2012) describe sounds much like what CompassPoint and the Evelyn and Walter Haas, Jr. Fund found in the UnderDeveloped study in 2013, discussed earlier in this text. They found that too many nonprofit organizations hire men and women to be development officers without a full understanding or definition of what that role should involve and then expect those individuals to somehow produce exceptional results—often with little help or support from their CEOs or boards. It should not be surprising that such an approach usually leads to unrealistic fundraising goals, burnout, and a high rate of turnover in fundraising positions (Bell & Cornelius,

2013). But recognition of the circumstances and the need for change also offers a unique opportunity for development professionals to become agents of an important transformation.

CALLS FOR LEADERSHIP

Among the recommendations of the UnderDeveloped study is that development professionals exercise greater *leadership* within their organizations. In other words, fundraising professionals can and should be more than salespeople, catalysts, or even managers—to use the Worth and Asp (1994) vocabulary. They should function as and be seen as *leaders* in their organizations. As Bell and Cornelius (2013) explain,

> Development directors should embrace the challenges outlined in this report by stepping-up their leadership and driving the change that is required within their organizations. While it is often impossible for one person to change an organization, the development director is in a key position to identify the organizational changes needed and then lead a process to realize them. This should include a plan for building the necessary fund development capacity within the organization. It will also require that the development director enthusiastically educates staff and board about what a culture of philanthropy entails, and just as importantly, what it promises for organizations and communities. It also includes taking responsibility for their own professional development by seeking out leadership development opportunities and identifying management skills-building needs. . . . Capacity builders and funders can support these efforts by offering and supporting relevant technical assistance and *leadership programs specifically for fund development professionals*. (p. 27; italics added)

In her book *Donor Centered Leadership*, Burk (2013) also calls for leadership. As she correctly notes, "Development professionals cannot be expected to address the deficiencies of the [fundraising] industry alone." She adds, "The power to effect meaningful change and, in doing so, unleash philanthropy at a whole new level, lies in the hands of those who bear the ultimate responsibility for the welfare of nonprofit organizations: Boards, Chief Executive Officers, and Chief Development Officers" (p. 330). The UnderDeveloped report authors agree, recommending substantial change that includes the elevation of fundraising as a central function of nonprofit organizations; greater investment by foundations and other funders in the fundraising capacity of organizations; and shared responsibility for fundraising results among development professionals, CEOs, and boards (Bell & Cornelius, 2013). Pursuing this agenda is essential, not only to the future of the fundraising profession and those who pursue it as their life's work but also to the future of the nonprofit sector.[1]

A FULFILLING CAREER

Those who choose a career in fundraising today will indeed face significant challenges and demands. Society's needs are not diminishing, and pervasive communication media have expanded awareness of those needs on a global basis. Across the planet, nonprofit and nongovernmental organizations and institutions are being called on to take ever greater responsibility for meeting current human needs and also for lifting up their societies. There will be pressures and disappointments and days when success seems elusive. But the trend is clear. Because financial resources are essential to sustaining and strengthening nonprofit organizations and institutions, fundraising professionals will play an increasingly central role in their organizations and in society. That provides enormous opportunities for a fulfilling career.

It is important that those preparing for fundraising careers acquire technical knowledge and appropriate credentials through formal educational and training programs. But maximizing their personal satisfaction and their contributions to society requires something more. Without a sense of purpose, work becomes just a way to spend the day. Those who approach fundraising as just a job—or even as a profession—may find it interesting and even well-compensated. But they will miss meaning and purpose in their lives. Those who view a fundraising career as an opportunity for leadership in the pursuit of noble ends, who see their role as improving society and the lives of people, and who take satisfaction in sharing the opportunity for service with others, will find few careers that can provide greater satisfaction.

Suggestions for Further Reading

Books

Croteau, J. D., & Smith, Z. A. (2012). *Making the case for leadership: Profiles of chief advancement officers in higher education.* Lanham, MD: Rowman & Littlefield.

Schiller, R. J. (2013). *The chief development officer: Beyond fundraising.* Lanham, MD: Rowman & Littlefield.

Wagner, L. (2005). *Leading up: Transformational leadership for fundraisers.* Hoboken, NJ: Wiley.

Articles

Ryan, L. J. (2006, September 15). Behavioral characteristics of higher education fund-raisers. *International Journal of Educational Advancement, 6*(4), 282–288.

Waters, R. D., Kelly, K. S., & Walker, M. L. (2012). Organizational roles enacted by healthcare fundraisers. *Communication Management, 16*(3), 244–263.

Website

UnderDeveloped: http://www.compasspoint.org/underdeveloped

Note

1. At the time of this writing, CompassPoint was developing an action guide for the implementation of the *UnderDeveloped* report recommendations, and students are advised to check on its progress at http://www.compasspoint.org/underdeveloped.

References

$100 million gift will create center to study human stem cells. (2013, November 4). *Chronicle of Philanthropy*. Retrieved January 4, 2014, from http://philanthropy.com/blogs/philanthropytoday/100-million-gift-will-create-center-to-study-human-stem-cells/77359.

AASP (Association of Advancement Services Professionals) website. http://www.advserv.org/?page = Definition.

Abramson, A., Soskis, B., & Toepler, S. (2012). *Public-philanthropic partnerships in the U.S.: A literature review of recent experiences*. Arlington, VA: Council on Foundations.

AFP (Association of Fundraising Professionals). (2007). *Code of ethical principles and standards*. Retrieved June 8, 2014, from http://www.afpnet.org.

AFP (Association of Fundraising Professionals). (2012). *Annual report*. Retrieved November 12, 2013, from http://www.afpnet.org/About/content.cfm?ItemNumber = 20777&navItemNumber = 4584.

AFP (Association of Fundraising Professionals) fundraising dictionary online. Retrieved November 11, 2013, from http://www.afpnet.org/files/ContentDocuments/AFP_Dictionary_A-Z_final_6-9-03.pdf.

AFP (Association of Fundraising Professionals) website. http://www.afpnet.org.

AHP (Association for Healthcare Philanthropy) website. http://www.ahp.org.

Alexander, C. D.. & Carlson, K. J. (2005). *Essential principles for fundraising success*. San Francisco: Jossey-Bass.

Allison, M., & Kaye, J. (2005). *Strategic planning for nonprofit organizations*. Hoboken, NJ: Wiley.

American Cancer Society. (2015). *Sample bequest language and declaration of support letter*. https://www.cancer.org/involved/donate/otherwaystogive/plannedgiving/sample-bequest-language.

American Heart Association. (2014). *Heart-Check food certification program*. Retrieved April 29, 2014, from https://www.heart.org/HEARTORG/GettingHealthy/NutritionCenter/HeartSmartShopping/Heart-Check-Food-Certification-Program_UCM_300133_Article.jsp.

American Red Cross website. http://www.redcross.org.

American Red Cross. (n.d.). *2013 Annual Report*. Washington, DC: American Red Cross.

Amos, O. M. (1982). Empirical analysis of motives underlying individual contributions to charity. *Atlantic Economic Journal, 10*(4), 45–52.

Anderson, D. M. (2010, September). Does information matter: The effect of the Meth Project on meth use among youths. *Journal of Health Economics, 29*(5), 732–742.

Andreasen, A. R. (2009). Cross-sector marketing alliances: Partnerships, sponsorships, and cause-related marketing. In J. J. Cordes & C. E. Steuerle (Eds.), *Nonprofits & business* (pp. 155–192). Washington, DC: Urban Institute.

Andreasen, A. R., & Kotler, P. (2008). *Strategic marketing for nonprofit organizations* (7th ed.). Upper Saddle River, NJ: Prentice Hall.

Andreoni, J. (1989). Giving with impure altruism: Applications to charity and Ricardian equivalence. *Journal of Political Economy, 97*(6), 1447–1458.

Andreoni, J., Brown, E., & Rischall, I. (2003). Charitable giving by married couples: Who decides and why does it matter? *The Journal of Human Resources, 38*(1), 111–133.

Andresen, K. (2006). *Robin Hood marketing: Stealing corporate savvy to sell just causes.* San Francisco: Jossey-Bass.

Anheier, H. K. (2005). *Nonprofit organizations: Theory, management, policy.* New York: Routledge.

Anheier, H. K., & Salamon, L. (2006). The nonprofit sector in comparative perspective. In W. W. Powell & R. Steinberg (Eds.), *The nonprofit sector: A research handbook* (2nd ed., pp. 89–114). New Haven, CT: Yale University Press.

Anheier, H. K., & Themudo, N. (2005). The internationalization of the nonprofit sector. In R. Herman & Associates (Eds.), *The Jossey-Bass handbook of nonprofit leadership and management* (2nd ed., pp. 102–127). San Francisco: Jossey-Bass.

APRA website. http://www.aprahome.org/p/cm/ld/fid = 37.

Aron, S. S. (2007). *The lapsed donor syndrome: The journey to donor disengagement.* Doctoral dissertation, Union Institute and University (UMI Number 3251486).

Association of Fundraising Professionals. (2009). *Hot topic: Capital campaigns.* Retrieved July 11, 2014, from http://www.afpnet.org/bbtdetail.cfm?itemnumber = 4018#2.

Association of Fundraising Professionals (n.d.). *Measuring and reporting fundraising costs: Guidelines for board members.* Retrieved May 29, 2014, from http://www.afpnet.org.

Atlantic Philanthropies. (n.d.). *About Atlantic.* http://www.atlanticphilanthropies.org/about-atlantic.

Austin, J. E. (2003). Marketing's role in cross-sector collaboration. In W. W. Wymer & S. Samu (Eds.), *Nonprofit and business sector collaboration* (pp. 23–40). Binghamton, NY: Best Business Books.

Barkan, J. (2013, October 20). As government funds dwindle, giant foundations gain too much power. *Chronicle of Philanthropy.* Retrieved May 12, 2014, from http://philanthropy.com/article/As-Government-Funds-Dwindle/142389.

Barr, K. (2008, May 21). *Reality check for capital campaigns.* Retrieved July 21, 2014, from https://nonprofitsassistancefund.org/blog/2008/05/reality-check-for-capital-campaigns.

Bekkers, R., & Wiepking, P. (2011, October). A literature review of empirical studies of philanthropy: Eight mechanisms that drive charitable giving. *Nonprofit and Voluntary Sector Quarterly, 40*(5), 924–973.

Bell, J., & Cornelius, M. (2013). *UnderDeveloped: A national study of challenges facing non-profit fundraising.* San Francisco: CompassPoint Nonprofit Services and the Evelyn and Walter Haas, Jr. Fund.

Beresford, S. (2010, October 3). What's the problem with strategic philanthropy? *Chronicle of Philanthropy.* Retrieved May 12, 2014, from http://philanthropy.com/article/What-s-the-Problem-With/124671.

Berkshire, J. C. (2012, September 30). Charities pick up new ways of reaching elusive donors by phone. *Chronicle of Philanthropy.* http://philanthropy.com/article/Charities-Find-New-Ways-to/134704.

Besson, C. (2013). *Meth awareness week kicks off November 30.* Retrieved December 16, 2013, from http://www.drugfree.org/newsroom/meth-awareness-week-kicks-off-november-30.

Better Business Bureau Wise Giving Alliance. (2014). *Standards for charity accountability*. Retrieved May 28, 2014, from http://www.bbb.org/us/standards-for-charity-accountability.

Birkholz, J. M. (2008). *Fundraising analytics: Using data to guide strategy*. Hoboken, NJ: Wiley.

Blackbaud. (2010). *The giving score*. Retrieved October 22, 2014, from https://www.blackbaud.com/files/resources/downloads/Datasheet_BlackbaudGivingScore.pdf.

Blackbaud. (2013). *Charitable giving report: How nonprofit fundraising performed in 2013*. Retrieved May 31, 2014, from https://www.blackbaud.com/files/resources/downloads/2014/2013.CharitableGivingReport.pdf.

Blackbaud. (n.d.). *Wearing the development and marketing hats at the same time: A bad fit and a headache*. Retrieved October 19, 2014, from http://www.resources.blackbaud.com/general-fundraising.

Blackwood, A. S., Roeger, K. L., & Pettijohn, S. L. (2012). *The nonprofit sector in brief: Public charities, giving, and volunteering, 2012*. Washington, DC: Urban Institute.

Blum, D. E. (2003, November 13). Big change afoot at Pew Trusts. *Chronicle of Philanthropy*. Retrieved May 8, 2014, from http://philanthropy.com/article/Big-Change-Afoot-at-Pew-Trusts/62535.

Blum, D. E. (2013, April 21). Charities deal with a stream of lawsuits from disenchanted donors. *Chronicle of Philanthropy*. Retrieved June 17, 2014, from http://philanthropy.com/article/Charities-Deal-With-a-Stream/138597.

Blum, D. E. (2014, February 9). Two brothers' bond with a leader of university brings $50 million. *Chronicle of Philanthropy*. Retrieved February 20, 2014, from http://philanthropy.com/article/How-the-University-of-South/144593.

Bo, L., & Fang, N. (2013). China. In P. Cagney & B. Ross (Eds.), *Global fundraising: How the world is changing the rules of philanthropy* (pp. 17–41). Hoboken, NJ: Wiley.

BoardSource. (2010). Fundraising. In *Handbook of nonprofit governance* (pp. 167–188). San Francisco: Jossey-Bass.

BoardSource. (n.d.). *Board members and personal contributions*. Retrieved July 19, 2014, from http://www.bridgespan.org/Publications-and-Tools/Nonprofit-Boards/Resources-for-Board-Members/Board-Members-Personal-Contributions.aspx#.U8rcM7FI680.

Boli, J. (2006). International nongovernmental organizations. In W. W. Powell & R. Steinberg (Eds.), *The non-profit sector: A research handbook* (2nd ed., pp. 333–354). New Haven, CT: Yale University Press.

Booth, C., & Dallas, T. (2006, May 24). Why Ken Lay wants a refund. *Time*. Retrieved June 17, 2014, from http://content.time.com/time/nation/article/0,8599,1197912,00.html.

Boss, S. (2011, Fall). When the big bet fails. *Stanford Social Innovation Review*. Retrieved May 13, 2014, from http://www.ssireview.org/articles/entry/when_the_big_bet_fails.

Bowman, W. (2011). *Finance fundamentals for nonprofits: Building capacity and sustainability*. Hoboken, NJ: Wiley.

Bragg, R. (1995, August 13). All she has, $150,000, is going to a university. *New York Times*. Retrieved January 15, 2014, from http://www.nytimes.com/1995/08/13/us/all-she-has-150000-is-going-to-a-university.html.

Brakeley, G. A., Jr. (1980). *Tested ways to successful fund raising*. New York: Amacom.

Bray, I. (2013). *Effective fundraising for nonprofits* (4th ed.). Berkeley, CA: Nolo.

Brest, P. (2012, Spring). A decade of outcome-oriented philanthropy. *Stanford Social Innovation Review, 10*(2), 42–47.

Bristol, E. (2012). *Getting your board members to give, get or get off: A best practices report from Bristol Strategy Group*. Retrieved July 19, 2014, from http://www.afpnet.org/files/ContentDocuments/AIE_Bristol_BoardGiveorGet.pdf.

Broce, T. E. (1986). *Fund raising: The guide to raising money from private sources* (2nd ed.). Norman: University of Oklahoma Press.

Brooks, A. C. (2004, August). Evaluating the effectiveness of nonprofit fundraising. *Policy Studies Journal, 32*(3), 363–374.

Brown, E. (2006). Married couples' charitable giving: Who and why. In M. A. Taylor & S. Shaw-Hardy (Eds.), *The transformative power of women's philanthropy* (pp. 69–80). San Francisco: Jossey-Bass.

Bryson, J. M. (2011). *Strategic planning for public and nonprofit organizations* (4th ed.). San Francisco: Jossey-Bass.

Buckla, R. J. (2004, May). *Organizational culture and alumni annual giving at private colleges and universities*. Doctoral dissertation, Peabody College of Vanderbilt University (UMI Number 3134710).

Burk, P. (2003). *Donor centered fundraising: How to hold on to your donors and raise much more money*. Chicago: Cygnus Applied Research.

Burk, P. (2013). *Donor centered leadership: What it takes to build a high performance fundraising team*. Chicago: Cygnus Applied Research.

Burlingame, D. F. (2011). Corporate giving and fundraising. In E. R. Tempel, T. L. Seiler, & E. E. Aldrich (Eds.), *Achieving excellence in fundraising* (3rd ed., pp. 138–149). San Francisco: Jossey-Bass.

Burlingame, D. F., & Hulse, L. J. (1991). *Taking fund raising seriously: Advancing the profession and practice of raising money*. San Francisco: Jossey-Bass.

Buterin, V. (2013, April 26). Chinese "One Foundation" first to accept bitcoin, receives $30,000. *Bitcoin Magazine*. Retrieved June 27, 2014, from http://bitcoinmagazine.com/4351/chinese-one-foundation-first-to-accept-bitcoin-receives-30000.

Cagney, P., & Ross, B. (2013). *Global fundraising: How the world is changing the rules of philanthropy*. Hoboken, NJ: Wiley.

Calhoun, P., & Miller, R. G. (2004). *Asking for major gifts: Steps to a successful solicitation*. Alexandria, VA: Association of Fundraising Professionals.

Cannon, C. M. (2011). *An executive's guide to fundraising operations: Principles, tools & trends*. Hoboken, NJ: Wiley.

Carnegie, A. (1889, June). The gospel of wealth. *North American Review, 148*(391), 653–665.

Carnegie Institution for Science website. https://carnegiescience.edu.

Carnie, C. (2013). Western Europe. In P. Cagney & B. Ross (Eds.), *Global fundraising: How the world is changing the rules of philanthropy* (pp. 89–107). Hoboken, NJ: Wiley.

Carr, P. J. (2012). *Private voices, public forces: Agenda setting and the power of foundations in the NCLB era*. Doctoral dissertation, Georgetown University (UMI Number 3504150).

Caruso, D. B. (2013, October 24). Red Cross to be more transparent in disaster fundraising. *Huffington Post*. Retrieved February 25, 2014, from http://www.huffingtonpost.com/2013/10/25/red-cross_n_4162962.html.

Carver, J. (2006). *Boards that make a difference* (3rd ed.). San Francisco: Jossey-Bass.

CASE. (2008). *Revisions to the CASE standards, March 2008*. http://www.case.org/Samples_Research_and_Tools/CASE_Reporting_Standards_and_Management_Guidelines/FAQ_RSMG/Revisions_to_Campaign_Standards.html.

CASE. (2009). *CASE reporting standards and management guidelines for educational institutions* (4th ed.) Washington, DC: Council for Advancement and Support of Education.

CASE. (2014). *CASE statements on compensation for fundraising performance.* Retrieved June 8, 2014, from http://www.case.org/Samples_Research_and_Tools/Principles_of_Practice/CASE_Statements_on_Compensation_for_Fundraising_Performance.html#commission-based.

CASE (Council for Advancement and Support of Education) website. http://www.case.org.

Cash, J. M. (2007, January 29). *A future of opportunity for San Jose State: A pre-campaign assessment.* (Presentation to the San Jose State University Academic Senate.) Retrieved May 22, 2014, from www.sjsu.edu/senate/docs/Najjarcc.pdf.

Cash, S. (2002, April). Smithsonian $35m gift. *Art in America, 90*(4), 33.

Center on Philanthropy at Indiana University. (2007). *Corporate philanthropy: The age of integration.* Indianapolis, IN: Center on Philanthropy at Indiana University.

Center on Philanthropy at Indiana University. (2008, May). *Generational differences in charitable giving and in motivations for giving.* Indianapolis, IN: Center on Philanthropy at Indiana University. Retrieved January 19, 2014, from http://www.campbellcompany.com/Portals/22807/docs/Generational%20Giving%20Study%20Executive%20Summary.pdf.

Center on Philanthropy at Indiana University. (2010a). *Women give 2010: New research about women and giving.* Indianapolis, IN: Center on Philanthropy at Indiana University.

Center on Philanthropy at Indiana University. (2010b). *Women give 2012 Part II: Causes women support: New research about women and giving.* Indianapolis, IN: Center on Philanthropy at Indiana University.

Center on Philanthropy at Indiana University. (2012, November). *The 2012 Bank of America Study of High Net Worth Philanthropy.* Indianapolis, IN: Center on Philanthropy at Indiana University.

Central Park website. http://www.centralparknyc.org.

Chait, R. P., Holland, T. P., & Taylor, B. E. (2005). *Governance as leadership: Reframing the work of nonprofit boards.* Hoboken, NJ: Boardsource/Wiley.

Charity Navigator. (2015). *Haiti earthquake: One year later.* Retrieved December 23, 2014, from http://www.charitynavigator.org/index.cfm?bay = content.view&cpid = 1194.

Chinese civil society. (2014, April 12). *Economist.* Retrieved June 27, 2014, from http://www.economist.com/news/china/21600747-spite-political-clampdown-flourishing-civil-society-taking-hold-beneath-glacier.

Cialdini, R. P. (2003, Summer). The power of persuasion: Putting the science of influence to work in fundraising. *Stanford Social Innovation Review, 1*(2), 8–27.

Cialdini, R. P., & Martin, S. (2006, December). The power of persuasion. *Training Journal, 12*(3), 40–44.

Ciconte, B. L., & Jacob, J. (2009). *Fundraising basics: A complete guide* (3rd ed.). Sudbury, MA: Jones and Bartlett.

Clegg, S., Kornberger, M., & Pitsis, T. (2005). *Managing and organizations: An introduction to theory and practice.* Thousand Oaks, CA: Sage.

Clemens, E. S. (2006). The constitution of citizens: Political theories of nonprofit organizations. In W. W. Powell & R. Steinberg (Eds.), *The nonprofit sector: A research handbook* (2nd ed., pp. 207–220). New Haven, CT: Yale University Press.

Cnaan, R. A., Jones, K., Dickin, A., & Salomon, M. (2011). Nonprofit watchdogs: Do they serve the average donor? *Nonprofit Management and Leadership, 23*(4), 381–397.

Coffman, J., Beer, T., Patrizi, P., & Heid Thompson, E. (2013, January). Benchmarking evaluation in foundations: Do we know what we are doing? *Foundation Review, 5*(2), Article 5.

Cohen, R. (2013, December 18). Some fundraising for veterans programs mainly enriches telemarketers. *Nonprofit Quarterly.* https://nonprofitquarterly.org/philanthropy/23408-some-fundraising-for-veterans-programs-mainly-enriches-telemarketers.html.

Collins, J. C. (2005). *Good to great and the social sectors: A monograph to accompany Good to Great.* Boulder, CO: Author.

Collins, J. C., & Porras, J. L. (1994). *Built to last: Successful habits of visionary companies.* New York: Harper Business.

Collins, S. (Ed.). (2008). *Foundation fundamentals* (8th ed.). New York: The Foundation Center.

Community Wealth Partners. (2009, October 1). *The recession: A good time for cause marketing?* Retrieved May 4, 2014, from http://communitywealth.com/the-recession-good-time-cause-marketing.

Cone Communications. (2010, March 19). *Top ten types of cause promotions.* Retrieved May 2, 2014, from http://www.conecomm.com/top-10-types-of-cause-promotions.

Cone Communications. (n.d.). *Past. Present. Future: The 25th anniversary of cause marketing.* Retrieved May 4, 2014, from http://www.conecomm.com/stuff/contentmgr/files/0/8ac1ce2f758c08eb226580a3b67d5617/files/cone25thcause.pdf.

The contested legacy of J. Howard Pew. (n.d.). Philanthropy Roundtable. Retrieved May 8, 2014, from http://www.philanthropyroundtable.org/topic/donor_intent/the_contested_legacy_of_j._howard_pew.

Cooper, M. (2012, December 12). Census officials, citing increasing diversity, say U.S. will be a "plurality" nation. *New York Times.* Retrieved January 16, 2014, from http://www.nytimes.com/2012/12/13/us/us-will-have-no-ethnic-majority-census-finds.html?_r = 0.

Copilevitz & Canter. (2014). *Working with commercial co-venturers & charitable promotions.* Retrieved April 29, 2014, from http://www.copilevitz-canter.com/practice-areas/nonprofits-charities/working-with-commercial-co-venturers.

Corporation for Public Broadcasting. (2012). *Public broadcasting major gift initiative.* Retrieved April 9, 2014, from http://majorgivingnow.org/downloads/pdf/cultivation_system.pdf.

Council for Aid to Education. (2014). *2013 voluntary support of education.* New York: Author.

Council on Foundations. (n.d.). *Family foundations.* http://www.cof.org/foundation-type/family-foundations.

Cox, K. (2010). Fundraising events. In A. Sargeant, J. Shang, & Associates (Eds.), *Fundraising: Principles and practice* (pp. 519–539). San Francisco: Jossey-Bass.

Cryder, C. E., Loewenstein, G., & Scheines, R. (2012). The donor is in the details. *Organizational Behavior and Human Decision Processes, 120*(2013), 15–23.

Cutlip, S. M. (1990). *Fund raising in the United States: Its role in America's philanthropy.* New Brunswick, NJ: Transaction. (Original work published 1965)

Daniels, A., Hall, H., & Narayanswamy, A. (2014, April 20). Fundraising "arms race" triggers big pay deals. *Chronicle of Philanthropy.* Retrieved July 31, 2014, from http://philanthropy.com/article/Fundraising-Arms-Race-Triggers/146009.

Daniels, D. (2014, February 9). As Ted Turner's $1-billion pledge ends, U.N. fund seeks new donors. *Chronicle of Philanthropy.* Retrieved February 20. 2014, from http://philanthropy.com/article/As-Ted-Turner-s-1-Billion/144591.

Davis, E. (2012). *Fundraising and the next generation: Tools for engaging the next generation of philanthropists*. San Francisco: Jossey-Bass.

Daw, J. (2006). *Cause marketing for nonprofits: Partner for purpose, passion, and profits*. Hoboken, NJ: Wiley.

Denhardt, R. B., Denhardt, J. V., & Aristigueta, M. P. (2013). *Managing human behavior in public and nonprofit organizations*. Thousand Oaks, CA: Sage.

Dickey, M. (1998, October 8). Fund-raising friction. *Chronicle of Philanthropy*. Retrieved February 25, 2014, from http://philanthropy.com/article/Fund-Raising-Friction/52732.

Dillard, J. P., & Knoblock, L. K. (2011). Interpersonal influence. In M. L. Knapp & J. A. Daly (Eds.), *The Sage handbook of interpersonal communication* (4th ed., pp. 389–422). Thousand Oaks, CA: Sage.

Di Mento, M. (2011, May 6). Giving pledge signers meet for first in-person meeting. *Chronicle of Philanthropy*. Retrieved November 19, 2014, from http://philanthropy.com/article/Giving-Pledge-Signers/127438.

Direct Marketing Association. (2013). *The DMA nonprofit federation announces new fundraising principles*. https://thedma.org/news/the-dma-nonprofit-federation-announces-new-fundraising-principles.

Ditcoff, S. W., & Timms, H. (2013, December 11). Giving that gets engagement. *Stanford Social Innovation Review*. Retrieved March 19, 2014, from http://www.ssireview.org/effective_philanthropy/entry/giving_that_gets_engagement.

Dixon, J., & Keyes, D. (2013, Winter). The permanent disruption of social media. *Stanford Social Innovation Review*. Retrieved March 19, 2014, from http://www.ssireview.org/articles/entry/the_permanent_disruption_of_social_media.

Donor acknowledgement and the rule of sevens. (2014). Supporting Advancement. Retrieved October 11, 2014, from www.supportingadvancement.

Donovan, D. (2014, March 23). Foundations are supporting more local groups working in tandem. *Chronicle of Philanthropy*. Retrieved May 12, 2014, from http://philanthropy.com/article/Foundations-Support-More-Local/145423.

Dove, K. E. (2000). *Conducting a successful capital campaign* (2nd ed.). San Francisco: Jossey-Bass.

Dove, K. E. (2001). *Conducting a successful fundraising program*. San Francisco: Jossey-Bass.

Dunbar, R. (2010, December 25). You've got to have (150) friends. *New York Times*. Retrieved April 14, 2014, from http://www.nytimes.com/2010/12/26/opinion/26dunbar.html?_r = 0.

Dunlop, D. R. (1993). Major gift programs. In M. J. Worth (Ed.), *Educational fund-raising: Principles and practice* (pp. 97–116). Phoenix, AZ: Oryx Press and American Council on Education.

Dunlop, D. R. (2002). Major gift programs. In M. J. Worth (Gen. Ed.), *New strategies for educational fund raising* (pp. 89–104). Westport, CT: American Council on Education and Praeger.

Dupree, R. K. (n.d.). *Measuring performance: A station manager's guide to evaluating major gift officers*. Retrieved April 10, 2014, from majorgivingnow.org/downloads/pdf/dupree.pdf.

Editorial: A farmer's great legacy. (2009, August 21). *StarTribune*. Retrieved February 17, 2015, from http://www.startribune.com/opinion/editorials/53857507.html.

Edwards, C. C. (2003). *Higher education development officers' use of affinity-seeking strategies in soliciting contributions.* Doctoral dissertation, Texas Tech University (UMI Number 3108695).

Eikenberry, A. M. (2009, Summer). The hidden costs of cause marketing. *Stanford Social Innovation Review.* http://www.ssireview.org/articles/entry/the_hidden_costs_of_cause_marketing.

Eisenberg, P. (2003, December 11). Pew's shift to charity status goes against what is best for the public. *Chronicle of Philanthropy.* Retrieved May 8, 2014, from http://philanthropy.com/article/Pews-Shift-to-Charity-Status/62527.

Eisenberg, P. (2014, July 10). Donors who lavish money on elite institutions only exacerbate the wealth gap. *Chronicle of Philanthropy.* Retrieved July 12, 2014, from http://philanthropy.com/article/Donors-Who-Lavish-Money-on/147583.

Facebook's Mark Zuckerberg gives $500-million. (2012, December 19). *Chronicle of Philanthropy.* Retrieved January 13, 2014, from http://www.philanthropy.com/blogs/philanthropytoday/facebooks-zuckerberg-gives-500-million.

Facts and figures: Endowments. (2013). *Chronicle of Philanthropy.* Retrieved December 27, 2013, from http://philanthropy.com/factfile/endowment.

Federal Communications Commission. (2014). *Spam: Unwanted text messages and email.* http://www.fcc.gov/guides/spam-unwanted-text-messages-and-email.

Fishman, S. (2012). *Nonprofit fundraising registration: The 50-state guide* (2nd ed.). Berkeley, CA: Nolo.

Fitzpatrick, D., & Griffin, D. (2012, May 8). *IRS forms show charity's money isn't going to disabled vets.* Retrieved June 3, 2014, from http://www.cnn.com/2012/05/07/us/veterans-charity-fraud.

Flandez, R. (2012a, December 3). #GivingTuesday's most successful charity raised $1 million. *Chronicle of Philanthropy.* http://philanthropy.com/blogs/prospecting/givingtuesday-most-successful-charity-raised-1-million/36631.

Flandez, R. (2012b, March 6). Nature Conservancy faces flap over fundraising deal to promote swimsuit issue. *Chronicle of Philanthropy.* Retrieved April 29, 2014 from http://philanthropy.com/article/Swimsuit-Deal-Causes-Flap-at/131084.

Flandez, R., & Frostenson, S. (2013, December 4). Giving Tuesday shows robust results. *Chronicle of Philanthropy.* http://philanthropy.com/article/Giving-Tuesday-Shows-Robust/143375.

Flannery, H., & Harris, R. (2011). *2011 donorCentrics Internet and Multichannel Giving Benchmarking Report.* Retrieved March 19, 2014, from https://www.blackbaud.com/analytics/multichannel-giving.aspx.

Foderaro, L. W. (2012, October 23). A $100 million thank-you for a lifetime's Central Park memories. *New York Times.* Retrieved July 28, 2014, from http://www.nytimes.com/2012/10/24/nyregion/billionaire-donates-100-million-to-central-park.html?_r=1&.

Foundation Center. (2012a). *Key facts on corporate foundations.* Retrieved April 28, 2014, from http://foundationcenter.org/gainknowledge/research/nationaltrends.html.

Foundation Center. (2012b). *Key facts on community foundations.* http://foundationcenter.org/gainknowledge/research/pdf/keyfacts_comm2012.pdf.

Foundation Center. (2012c). *International grantmaking update: A snapshot of U.S. foundation trends.* Retrieved June 24, 2014, from http://foundationcenter.org/gainknowledge/research/internationaltrends.html.

Foundation Center. (2013a). *U.S. foundation giving reaches an estimated $50.9 billion in 2012.* http://foundationcenter.org/media/news/20131001.html.

Foundation Center. (2013b). *Key facts on U.S. foundations.* http://foundationcenter.org/gainknowledge/research/keyfacts2013/grant-focus-priorities.html.

Foundation Center. (2014). *Foundation stats.* http://data.foundationcenter.org/#/foundations/family/nationwide/total/list/2011.

Foundation Center. (2015). *Nonprofit collaboration resources.* http://foundationcenter.org/gainknowledge/collaboration.

Fredericks, L. (2010). *The ask: How to ask for support for your nonprofit cause, creative project, or business venture.* San Francisco: Jossey-Bass.

Fried, V. (2011). *The endowment trap.* Retrieved May 9, 2014, from http://www.popecenter.org/about/index.html.

Friedman, T. L. (2006). *The world is flat: The globalized world in the twenty-first century.* London: Penguin Books.

Froelich, K. A. (1999, September). Diversification of revenue strategies: Evolving resource dependence in nonprofit organizations. *Nonprofit and Voluntary Sector Quarterly*, 28(3), 246–268.

Frumkin, P. (2006). *Strategic giving.* Chicago: University of Chicago Press.

Gaining perspective: Lessons learned from one foundation's exploratory decade (A report commissioned by the Northwest Area Foundation). (n.d.). Retrieved May 13, 2014, from http://www.nwaf.org/about/resources/lessons-evaluations.

Galafassi, N. (2013). Latin America. In P. Cagney & B. Ross (Eds.), *Global fundraising: How the world is changing the rules of philanthropy* (pp. 59–87). Hoboken, NJ: Wiley.

Galaskiewicz, J., & Colman, M. S. (2006). Collaboration between corporations and nonprofit organizations. In W. W. Powell & R. Steinberg (Eds.), *The non-profit sector: A research handbook* (pp. 180–206). New Haven, CT: Yale University Press.

Gammal, D. L. (2007, Summer). Before you say "I do." *Stanford Social Innovation Review,* 5(3), 47–51.

Gattle, K. (2011). Personal solicitation. In E. R. Tempel, T. L. Seiler, & E. E. Aldrich (Eds.), *Achieving excellence in fundraising* (3rd ed., pp. 213–222). San Francisco: Jossey-Bass.

Genest, C. M. (2005). Cultures, organizations, and philanthropy. *Corporate Communications,* 10(4), 315–327.

Gifts that can warp a museum. (2001, May 31). *New York Times*, p. A1.

Gist, J. (2005). *Comparing boomers' and their elders' wealth at midlife.* Washington, DC: AARP Public Policy Institute.

Giving Institute website. http://givinginstitute.org.

#GivingTuesday website. http://community.givingtuesday.org/Page/FAQ.

Giving USA. (2014a): *The Annual Report on Philanthropy for the Year 2013.* Chicago: Giving USA Foundation.

Giving USA. (2014b): *Highlights.* Chicago: Giving USA Foundation.

Global Giving. (n.d.). *One Foundation.* http://www.globalgiving.org/donate/15390/one-foundation/info.

Goering, E., Connor, U. M., Nagelhout, E., & Steinberg, R. (2011). Persuasion in fundraising letters: An interdisciplinary study. *Nonprofit and Voluntary Sector Quarterly, 40*(2), 228–246.

Goldberg, C. (2013). *Meth Project joins the Partnership at Drugfree.org.* Retrieved December 16, 2013, from http://www.drugfree.org/newsroom/meth-project-joins-the-partnership-at-drugfree-org.

Gordon, T. P., Knock, C. L., & Neely, D. G. (2009, November–December). The role of rating agencies in the market for charitable contributions: An empirical test. *Journal of Accounting and Public Policy, 28*(6), 469–484.

Gose, B. (2007a, February 8). Great Plains generosity. *Chronicle of Philanthropy*. Retrieved January 4, 2014, from http://philanthropy.com/article/Great-Plains-Generosity/54830.

Gose, B. (2007b, February 8). Executive embraces challenge of creating top-tier pediatric clinics. *Chronicle of Philanthropy*. Retrieved January 4, 2014, from http://philanthropy .com/article/Executive-Embraces-Challenge/54831.

Gose, B. (2014a, June 26). Master's programs in fundraising are helping students meet job demands. *Chronicle of Philanthropy*. Retrieved June 18, 2014, from http://philanthropy .com/article/Master-s-Programs-in/147145.

Gose, B. (2014b, March 23). "Collective impact" to solve problems gets more attention from grant makers. *Chronicle of Philanthropy*. Retrieved May 12, 2014, from http:// philanthropy.com/article/Collective-Impact-to-Solve/145441.

Gose, B. (2014c, May 18). Hard lessons from Princeton's $900-million donor-intent lawsuit. *Chronicle of Philanthropy*. Retrieved June 17, 2014, from http://philanthropy.com/ article/Hard-Lessons-From/146605.

Gouldner, A. W. (1960). The norm of reciprocity: A preliminary statement. *American Sociological Review, 25*(2), 161–178.

Gourville, J. T., & Rangan, V. K. (2004). Valuing the cause marketing relationship. *California Management Review, 47*(1), 38–56.

Gowen, A. (2012, November 27). Organizers launch "Giving Tuesday" to help charities. *Washington Post*. http://www.washingtonpost.com/local/giving-tuesday-launched-to-help-charities/2012/11/27/1c44092a-38af-11e2-a263-f0ebffed2f15_story.html.

Grabau, T. W. (2010, July 19). *Major gift metrics that matter*. http://www.bwf.com/ wp-content/uploads/2014/04/00090978.pdf.

Greenfeld, K. T. (2000, July 24). A new way of giving. *Time, 156*(4), 38–41.

Greenfield, J. M. (1996). *Fund-raising cost effectiveness: A self-assessment workbook*. New York: John Wiley & Sons.

Greenfield, J. M. (2011). Budgeting for fundraising and evaluating performance. In E. R. Tempel, T. L. Seiler, & E. E. Aldrich (Eds.), *Achieving excellence in fundraising* (3rd ed., pp. 349–361). San Francisco: Jossey-Bass.

Gregory, A. G., & Howard, D. (2009, Fall). The nonprofit starvation cycle. *Stanford Social Innovation Review, 7*(4), 49–53.

Grønbjerg, K. A. (1993). *Understanding nonprofit funding: Managing revenues in social services and community development organizations*. San Francisco: Jossey-Bass.

Grossnickle, T. R. (2011). The trustee's role in fundraising. In E. R. Tempel, T. L. Seiler, & E. E. Aldrich (Eds.), *Achieving excellence in fundraising* (3rd ed., pp. 275–284). San Francisco: Jossey-Bass.

Grunig, J. E., & Repper, F. C. (1992). Strategic management, publics, and issues. In J. E. Grunig (Ed.), *Excellence in public relations and communications management: Contributions to effective organizations* (pp. 31–64). Hillsdale, NJ: Lawrence Erlbaum Associates.

Hager, M. A., & Flack, T. (2004, August). *The pros and cons of financial efficiency standards* (Brief No. 5). Washington, DC/Indianapolis: Urban Institute/Indiana University Center on Philanthropy.

Hagerty, R. (2012). *The role of foundations in the changing world of philanthropy: A Houston perspective*. Doctoral dissertation, Antioch University (UMI Number 3510782).

Haiti telethon haul put at $57 million so far. (2010, January 23). Retrieved December 26, 2014, from http://today.msnbc.msn.com/id/35023278/ns/today-entertainment/t/ haiti-telethon-haul-put-million-so-far.

Hall, H. (2005, January 6). Fund-raising association clarifies stance on fees. *Chronicle of Philanthropy, 17*(6), 47.

Hall, H. (2006, April 6). Much-anticipated transfer of wealth has yet to materialize, nonprofit experts say. *Chronicle of Philanthropy.* Retrieved April 17, 2014, from http://philanthropy.com/article/Much-Anticipated-Transfer-of/58116.

Hall, H. (2009, October 29). Red Cross retools its fund raising to overcome a troubled financial picture. *Chronicle of Philanthropy.* https://philanthropy.com/article/Red-Cross-Retools-Its-Fund/173405#!/subscriptions/offers/?PK = M1224&cid = MP2WPW1.

Hall, H. (2014a). Analyzing fundraisers' personalities can help them click with donors. *Chronicle of Philanthropy, 26*(7), 1, 7.

Hall, H. (2014b, April 20). Critics slam bonuses—some larger than base pay—but charities say they are needed. *Chronicle of Philanthropy.* Retrieved June 8, 2014, from https://philanthropy.com/article/Bonuses-Sometimes-Are-Larger/153269.

Hall, H. (2014c, May 2). Job opportunities abound overseas for fundraisers. *Chronicle of Philanthropy.* Retrieved June 27, 2014, from http://philanthropy.com/article/Job-Opportunities-Abound/146359.

Hall, M. R. (1992). The decentralization of development: Impact on power, priorities, faculty perceptions. *Teachers College Record, 93*(3), 569–582.

Hall, P. D. (2006). A historical overview of philanthropy, voluntary associations, and non-profit organizations in the United States, 1600–2000. In W. E. Powell & R. Steinberg (Eds.), *The non-profit sector: A research handbook* (pp. 32–65). New Haven, CT: Yale University Press.

Hannon, K. (2013, November 7). Giving circles: More impact to go around. *New York Times.* Retrieved January 16, 2014, from http://www.nytimes.com/2013/11/08/giving/giving-circles-more-impact-to-go-around.html?_r = 1&.

Hansmann, H. (1987). Economic theory of nonprofit organization. In W. W. Powell (Ed.), *The nonprofit sector: A research handbook* (pp. 27–42). New Haven, CT: Yale University Press.

Harbaugh, W. T. (1998, May). The prestige motive for making charitable transfer. *The American Economic Review, 88*(2), 277–282.

Havens, J. J., O'Herlihy, M. A., & Schervish, P. G. (2006). Charitable giving: How much, by whom, to what, and how. In W. W. Powel & R. Steinberg (Eds.), *The nonprofit sector: A research handbook* (2nd ed., pp. 542–567). New Haven, CT: Yale University Press.

Havens, J. J., & Schervish, P. G. (1999). *Millionaires and the millennium: New estimates of the forthcoming wealth transfer and the prospects for a golden age of philanthropy.* Boston: Boston College Social Welfare Research Institute.

Havens, J. J., & Schervish, P. G. (2014). *A golden age of philanthropy still beckons: National wealth transfer and potential for philanthropy technical report.* Boston: Boston College Social Welfare Research Institute.

Heath, T. (2013, June 30). Carlyle Group's David Rubenstein practices "patriotic philanthropy." *Washington Post.* Retrieved December 16, 2013, from http://articles.washingtonpost.com/2013-06-30/business/40292844_1_david-rubenstein-carlyle-group-philanthropy.

Heetland, D. L. (1993, January). Identifying, evaluating, and cultivating prospective donors. *NSFRE Journal,* 10–13.

Held, T. (2014a). Giving circles popular with minorities and younger donors, says study. *Chronicle of Philanthropy.* Retrieved July 10, 2014, from https://philanthropy.com/article/Giving-Circles-Popular-With/150525.

Held, T. (2014b). Charities like Facebook for rallying support but not much for fundraising. *Chronicle of Philanthropy.* Retrieved July 21, 2014, from https://philanthropy.com/article/Charities-Like-Facebook-for/150511.

Heneman, H. J. (1969). Foreword. In J. W. Leslie, *Focus on understanding and support: A study in college management* (pp. ix–xii). Washington, DC: American College Public Relations Association.

Herman, R. D., & Heimovics, D. (2005). Executive leadership. In R. D. Herman & Associates (Eds.), *The Jossey-Bass handbook of nonprofit leadership and management* (2nd ed., pp. 731–736). San Francisco: Jossey-Bass.

Herzberg, F. (1968). One more time: How do you motivate employees? *Harvard Business Review, 46,* 36–44.

Hessekiel, D. (2013, September 17). Cause marketing competition on the rise. *Forbes.* Retrieved April 25, 2014, from http://www.forbes.com/sites/davidhessekiel/2013/09/17/cause-marketing-coopetition-on-the-rise.

Hogan, C. (2008). *Prospect research: A primer for growing nonprofits.* Sudbury, MA: Jones and Bartlett.

Holloway, B. (2013, February). Using the phone to reduce donor attrition and drive loyalty. *International Journal of Nonprofit & Voluntary Sector Marketing, 18*(1), 31–35.

Holmes, R. J., Jr. (2010, Spring). The challenge of funding fundraising. *New Directions for Higher Education, 149,* 27–37.

Hopkins, B. R. (2009). *Fundraising law made easy.* Hoboken, NJ: Wiley.

Hrywna, M. (2006, July 1). Even in death, Lay's gift stirs controversy. *Nonprofit Times.* Retrieved June 17, 2014, from http://www.thenonprofittimes.com/news-articles/even-in-death-lay-s-gift-stirs-controversy.

Hudson Institute. (2013). *Index of global philanthropy and remittances 2013.* Retrieved June 24, 2014, from http://www.hudson.org/research/9914-2013-index-of-global-philanthropy-and-remittances-with-a-special-report-on-emerging-economies.

Huget, J. J. (2010, May 4). Is buying KFC by the bucket a good way to fight breast cancer? *Washington Post.* Retrieved April 24, 2014, from http://www.washingtonpost.com/wp-dyn/content/article/2010/04/30/AR2010043001971.html.

Hurvitz, L. A. (2010). *Building a culture of student philanthropy: A study of the ivy-plus institutions' philanthropy education initiatives.* Doctoral dissertation, University of Pennsylvania Graduate School of Education (UMI Number 3410478).

IEG. (2014, January 7). Sponsorship spending growth slows in North America as marketers eye newer media and marketing options. *IEG Sponsorship Report.* Retrieved May 1, 2014, from http://www.sponsorship.com/iegsr/2014/01/07/Sponsorship-Spending-Growth-Slows-In-North-America.aspx.

Independent Sector. (2015). *Principles for good governance and ethical practice: A guide for charities and foundations.* Washington, DC: Author.

Independent Sector. (n.d.). *Lobbying guidelines for private foundations.* https://www.independentsector.org/lobbying_guidelines_private_foundations.

Ingram, R. T. (2009). *Ten basic responsibilities of nonprofit boards* (2nd ed.). Washington, DC: BoardSource.

Internal Revenue Service. (2014a). *Exempt purposes.* http://www.irs.gov/Charities-&-Non-Profits/Charitable-Organizations/Exempt-Purposes-Internal-Revenue-Code-Section-501(c)(3).

Internal Revenue Service. (2014b). *Charitable contributions—Quid pro quo contributions.* http://www.irs.gov/Charities-&-Non-Profits/Charitable-Organizations/Charitable-Contributions-Quid-Pro-Quo-Contributions.

Internal Revenue Service. (2014c). *Definition of a trust*. http://www.irs.gov/Charities-&-Non-Profits/Definition-of-a-Trust.

Internal Revenue Service. (2014d). *Exempt organizations annual reporting requirements - form 990, schedules A and B: Public charity support test*. http://www.irs.gov/Charities-&-Non-Profits/Exempt-Organizations-Annual-Reporting-Requirements-Form-990,-Schedules-A-and-B:-Public-Charity-Support-Test.

Internal Revenue Service. (2015). *Exemption requirements*. http://www.irs.gov/Charities-&-Non-Profits/Charitable-Organizations/Exemption-Requirements-Section-501(c)(3)-Organizations.

Irvin, R. A. (2005, June). State regulation of nonprofit organizations: Accountability regardless of outcome. *Nonprofit and Voluntary Sector Quarterly, 34*(2), 161–178.

Isaak, J. (2004). *Capital campaigns and the development of a culture of philanthropy in higher education*. Master's thesis, Saint Mary's University of Minnesota.

Iyer, E. (2003). Theory of alliances: Partnership and partner characteristics. In W. W. Wymer & S. Samu (Eds.), *Nonprofit and business sector collaboration* (pp. 41–58). Binghamton, NY: Best Business Books.

James, E. (1987). The nonprofit sector in comparative perspective. In W. W. Powell (Ed.), *The nonprofit sector: A research handbook* (pp. 397–415). New Haven, CT: Yale University Press.

James, R. N. III. (2009a, December). The myth of the coming charitable estate windfall. *American Review of Public Administration, 39*(6), 661–674.

James, R. N. III. (2009b). Health, wealth, and charitable estate planning: A longitudinal examination of testamentary charitable giving plans. *Nonprofit and Voluntary Sector Quarterly, 38*(6), 1026–1043.

James, R. N. III, & Sharpe, D. J. (2007, June). The nature and causes of the U-shaped charitable giving profile. *Nonprofit and Voluntary Sector Quarterly, 36*(2), 218–238.

Jarrell, A. (2013, May/June). Crowd around. *Currents*. Retrieved July 7, 2014, from www.case.org.

Johnsen, L. L. (2005). *Understanding deliberative conflicts that confront academic fund raisers: A grounded theory study*. Doctoral dissertation, Arizona State University (UMI Number 3166117).

Joyaux, S. P. (n.d.). *Building a culture of philanthropy in your organization*. Retrieved February 26, 2014, from http://www.simonejoyaux.com/learning-center/free-download-library/fund-development.

Karlan, D., & List, J. A. (2007, December). Does price matter in charitable giving? Evidence from a large-scale natural field experiment. *The American Economic Review, 97*(5), 1774–1793.

Katz, D., & Kahn, R. L. (1966). *The social psychology of organizations*. New York: Wiley.

Kaufman, L. (2010, June 15). Ad for a dish detergent becomes part of a story. *New York Times*. Retrieved May 4, 2014, from http://www.nytimes.com/2010/06/16/science/earth/16dawn.html?_r = 0.

Kaufman, L. (2011, June 3). *As Gates Foundation grows, critics question methods*. Retrieved May 9, 2014, from http://www.npr.org/2011/06/03/136920664/gates-foundation-shows-off-new-headquarters.

Kelly, K. S. (1998). *Effective fund-raising management*. Mahwah, NJ: Lawrence Erlbaum Associates.

Kihlstedt, A. (2010). *Capital campaigns: Strategies that work* (3rd ed.). Sudbury, MA: Jones & Bartlett.

Kihlstedt, A. (2013). *Asking styles: Harnessing your personal fundraising power*. Santa Margarita, CA: CharityChannel Press.

Knowles, P., & Gomes, R. (2009). Building relationships with major-gift donors: A major-gift decision-making, relationship-building model. *Journal of Nonprofit & Public Sector Marketing, 21*(4), 384–406.

Koenig, B. L. (2004). *Going global for the greater good: Succeeding as a nonprofit in the international community*. San Francisco: Jossey-Bass.

Koten, J. (2013, December 13). Giving: The unusual tale of Osceola McCarty. *Wall Street Journal*. Retrieved January 15, 2014, from http://online.wsj.com/news/articles/SB1000142405270230485480457923660306901679

Kotler, P., Hessekiel, D., & Lee, N. R. (2012). *Good works: Marketing and corporate initiatives that build a better world . . . and the bottom line*. Hoboken, NJ: Wiley.

Kotter, J. P. (1996). *Leading change*. Boston: Harvard Business School Press.

Kotter, J. P. (2012). *The 8-step process for leading change*. Retrieved July 10, 2014, from http://www.kotterinternational.com.

Krabbenhoft, K. (2008, Summer). Philanthropy: A priceless lesson in healthcare leadership—The Sanford Health story. *Frontiers of Health Service Management, 24*(4), 3–10.

Kramer, M. R. (2009, Fall). Catalytic philanthropy. *Stanford Social Innovation Review*. Retrieved December 16, 2013, from http://www.ssireview.org/articles/entry/catalytic_philanthropy.

Krishna, A. (2011, July). Can supporting a cause decrease donations and happiness? The cause marketing paradox. *Journal of Consumer Psychology, 21*(3), 338–345.

Kristoff, N. D. (2012, December 26). How giving became cool. *New York Times*. Retrieved February 21, 2014, from http://www.nytimes.com/2012/12/27/opinion/kristof-how-giving-became-cool.html?ref = tedturner&_r = 1&.

Kroll, J. A. (2012). *Benchmarking investments in advancement: Results of the inaugural CASE advancement investment metrics study (AIMS)*. Retrieved May 29, 2014, from http://www.case.org.

Kumru, C. S., & Vesterlund, L. (2010, August). The effect of status on charitable giving. *Journal of Public Economic Theory, 12*(4), 709–735.

Lamb, D. F. (2012). *The basics of prospect management*. Retrieved July 18, 2014, from https://www.blackbaud.com/files/resources/downloads/WhitePaper_TheBasicsOfProspectManagment.pdf.

Lamberjack, N., & Plourde, J. (2013, July 16). *The comprehensive campaign primer*. Retrieved July 11, 2014, from http://collinsgroup.com/wp-content/uploads/Comprehensive-campaigns-webinar-7-16-13.pdf.

La Piana, D. (2008). *The nonprofit strategy revolution: Real-time strategic planning in a rapid-response world*. St. Paul, MN: Fieldstone Alliance.

Lawrence, S., & Mukai, R. (2011). *Foundation growth and giving estimates: Current outlook*. New York: The Foundation Center.

Lenfest, G. (2011). Foreword. In M. J. Rosen, *Donor-centered planned gift marketing* (pp. xv–xxvi). Hoboken, NJ: Wiley.

Lenkowsky, L. (2011, March 6). Foundation's report on its failings should spur reflection among grant makers. *Chronicle of Philanthropy*. Retrieved May 12, 2014, from http://philanthropy.com/article/Do-Foundations-Recognize-Their/126576.

Letson, P. (2010, July 11). After helping Haiti at its worst, a need for economic development grows clearer. *Chronicle of Philanthropy*. Retrieved December 26, 2014, from http://www.acdivoca.org/site/ID/news-Haiti-six-months-later-Chronicle-of-Philanthropy.

Letts, C. W., Ryan, W. P., & Grossman, A. (1999). Virtuous capital: What foundations can learn from venture capitalists. In *Harvard Business Review on nonprofits* (pp. 91–110).

Boston: Harvard Business School Press. (Reprinted from *Harvard Business Review*, March/April, 1997)

Lewin, T. (2008, December 10). Princeton settles money battle over gift. *New York Times*. Retrieved June 17, 2014, from http://www.nytimes.com/2008/12/11/education/11princeton.html?_r = 0.

Lewis, N. (2002, February 21). Controversy over donor's role causes Smithsonian to lose $36.5 million. *Chronicle of Philanthropy, 14*(9), 16.

Levis, W. (1993, March). ROI analysis. *Philanthropy Monthly*. Retrieved June 2, 2014, from http://nccsdataweb.urban.org/PubApps/levis/roi.html.

Levy, R. (2008). *Yours for the asking*. Hoboken, NJ: Wiley.

Light, J., & Stratton, K. (2014, May 29). *Demystifying the finances of your development department*. Retrieved July 30, 2014, from http://www.advisory.com/research/financial-leadership-council/at-the-margins/2014/05/demystifying-development-department-finances.

Light, P. C. (2002, September 21). The content of their character: The state of the nonprofit workforce. *Nonprofit Quarterly*. Retrieved June 8, 2014, from https://nonprofitquarterly.org.

Lijing, P. (2013, April 23). Jet Li's One Foundation raises over 90 million yuan for Ya'an earthquake. *Economic Observer*. Retrieved June 27, 2014, from http://eeo.com.cn/ens/2013/0423/243076.shtml.

Lilly Family School of Philanthropy at Indiana University. (2013, October). *Giving beyond borders: A study of global giving by U.S. corporations*. Indianapolis, IN: Lilly Family School of Philanthropy.

Lilly Family School of Philanthropy at Indiana University website. http://www.philanthropy.iupui.edu.

Lindahl, W. E. (1992). *Strategic planning for fund raising: How to bring in more money using strategic resource allocation*. San Francisco: Jossey-Bass.

Lindahl, W. E. (2008). Three-phase capital campaigns. *Nonprofit Management and Leadership, 18*(3), 261–273.

Lindahl, W. E. (2010). *Principles of fundraising: Theory and practice*. Sudbury, MA: Jones and Bartlett.

Lindauer, J. A. (2011). Donor database management and segmentation. In E. R. Tempel, T. L. Seiler, & E. E. Aldrich (Eds.), *Achieving excellence in fundraising* (3rd ed., pp. 340–348). San Francisco: Jossey-Bass.

Lindgren, R. R. (2002). Structuring and managing the development office. In M. J. Worth (Ed.), *New strategies for educational fund raising* (pp. 267–283). Westport, CT: Praeger and American Council on Education.

Lohmann, R. A. (1992). *The commons: New perspectives on nonprofit organizations and voluntary action*. San Francisco: Jossey-Bass.

Loomis, C. J. (2012, November 21). *Should you leave it all to the children?* Retrieved April 21, 2014, from http://fortune.com/2012/11/21/should-you-leave-it-all-to-the-children.

López-Rivera, M., & Preston, C. (2011, March 6). As assets slowly recover, foundations grapple with how to help cash-strapped charities. *Chronicle of Philanthropy*. Retrieved May 12, 2014, from https://philanthropy.com/article/Foundations-Rethink-Priorities/158855.

Lowman, D. (2012). *Leadership annual giving: A case study in increasing revenue and participation*. Retrieved July 25, 2014, from http://www.grenzebachglier.com/assets/files/documents/Leadership%20Annual%20Giving%20Session%20-%20Lowman.pdf.

Luther, E. (2005). *How nonprofits use information systems for fundraising: A comparative case study*. Doctoral dissertation, Robert Morris University (UMI Number 3217249).

MacLaughlin, S. (2011, December 31). How much money is raised through online giving? *Nonprofit Trends*. Retrieved May 29, 2012, from http://www.nptrends.com/nonprofit-trends/how-much-money-is-raised-through-online-giving.htm.

Madoff, R. D. (2010, October 31). Opinion: Immortality for foundations can pose big challenges in shifting times. *Chronicle of Philanthropy*. Retrieved May 9, 2014, from https://philanthropy.com/article/An-Argument-Against-Permanent/125142.

Maslow, A. H. (1954). *Motivation and personality.* New York: Harper.

Matheny, R. E. (2010). *Major gifts: Solicitation strategies* (3rd ed.) Washington, DC: Council for Advancement and Support of Education.

Matthews, B. R., & Linett, C. S. (2009, April 21). *New research: Campaign funding methods and levels*. Retrieved July 10, 2014, from http://slaudienceresearch.com/files/Conference%20 Presentation%20-%20AFP%20Capital%20Campaign%20Financing.pdf.

McCambridge, R. (2012, January 11). Two years after Haiti's earthquake, the U.S. has delivered on only 30% of its pledge. *Nonprofit Quarterly*. Retrieved December 26, 2014, from http://www.nonprofitquarterly.org/philanthropy/19041-two-years-after-haitis-earthquake-the-us-has-delivered-on-only-30-of-its-pledge.html.

McClelland, D. C. (1961). *The achieving society.* New York: Free Press.

McCorvey, J. J. (2013, February 11). The United Nations of entrepreneurs. *Fast Company*. Retrieved February 20, 2014, from http://www.fastcompany.com/3005683/the-united-nations-of-entrepreneurs.

McDonald, K., & Scaife, W. (2011). Print media portrayals of giving: Exploring national "cultures of philanthropy." *International Journal of Nonprofit and Voluntary Sector Marketing, 16*, 311–324.

McDowell, S. R. (2003). *Private foundations: What the tax department should know*. Retrieved April 28, 2014, from www.steptoe.com/assets/attachments/2655.pdf.

McGoldrick, W. P., & Robell, P. A. (2002). Campaigning in the new century. In M. J. Worth (Ed.), *New strategies for educational fund raising* (pp. 135–152). Westport, CT: American Council on Education and Praeger.

McGovern, G. (n.d.). *Transforming for the future: A 2013 update from Gail McGovern, president and CEO*. Washington, DC: American Red Cross.

McGregor, D. (1960). *The human side of enterprise.* New York: McGraw-Hill.

McLeod, J. M., & Chaffee, S. H. (1973). Interpersonal approaches to communication research. *American Behavioral Scientist, 16*(4), 469–500.

Médecins Sans Frontières. (2008, July 21). *President's report/financial report for the year ending 2007*. Retrieved June 27, 2014, from http://www.msf.org/source/financial/2007/MSF_Financial_Report_2007.pdf.

Meisenbach, R. J. (2004). *Framing fund raising: A poststructuralist analysis of higher education fund raisers' work and identities*. Doctoral dissertation, Purdue University (UMI Number 3154694).

Menon, U., & Tiwari, A. (2013). India. In P. Cagney & B. Ross (Eds.), *Global fundraising: How the world is changing the rules of philanthropy* (pp. 267–289). Hoboken, NJ: Wiley.

Mesch, D. J., Brown, M. S., Moore, Z. I., & Hayat, A. D. (2011, November). Gender differences in charitable giving. *International Journal of Nonprofit and Voluntary Sector Marketing, 16*, 342–355.

Mesch, D. J., & Pactor, A. (2011). Women as donors. In E. R. Tempel, T. L. Seiler, & E. E. Aldrich (Eds.), *Achieving excellence in fundraising* (3rd ed., pp. 162–171). San Francisco: Jossey-Bass.

Mesch, D. J., & Rooney, P. M. (2008, Summer). Determinants of compensation: A study of pay, performance, and gender differences for fundraising professionals. *Nonprofit Management and Leadership, 18*(4), 435–463.

Meyerson, A. (2006, December). Milton Friedman on philanthropy. *Philanthropy*. Retrieved April 28, 2014, from http://www.philanthropyroundtable.org/topic/excellence_in_ philanthropy/milton_friedman_on_philanthropy.

Miller, M. W. (2013). *The role of the community college president in fundraising: Perceptions of selected Michigan community college presidents.* Doctoral dissertation, University of Nebraska–Lincoln (UMI Number 3558622).

Minnesota Council on Foundations. (2015). *Private foundation self-dealing.* http://www.mcf .org/publictrust/faq_private.

Moody, M. (2008). Building a culture: The construction and evolution of venture philanthropy as a new organizational field. *Nonprofit and Voluntary Sector Quarterly, 37*(2), 324–352.

More clues emerge about mystery donor. (2009, May 8). *Chronicle of Philanthropy*. Retrieved December 30, 2013, from http://philanthropy.com/blogs/philanthropytoday/ more-clues-emerge-about-mystery-donor/17272.

Morris, S. A., Bartkus, B. R., Glassman, M., & Rhiel, G. S. (2013, Winter). Philanthropy and corporate reputation: An empirical investigation. *Corporate Reputation Review, 16*(4), 285–299.

Moyers, R. (2011). *Daring to lead 2011 Brief #3: The board paradox.* San Francisco: CompassPoint Nonprofit Services and the Meyer Foundation.

Muchilwa, M. (2013). Africa. In P. Cagney & B. Ross (Eds.), *Global fundraising: How the world is changing the rules of philanthropy* (pp. 179–222). Hoboken, NJ: Wiley.

Murray, V. (2004). Evaluating the effectiveness of nonprofit organizations. In R. D. Herman & Associates (Eds.), *The Jossey-Bass handbook of nonprofit leadership and management* (2nd ed., pp. 345–370). San Francisco: Jossey-Bass.

Museums and money. (2001, May 31). *The Washington Post,* p. A24.

National Association of State Charity Officials (NASCO). (2001). *The Charleston principles: Guidelines on charitable solicitations using the Internet.* Retrieved June 10, 2014, from http://www.nasconet.org/wp-content/uploads/2011/05/Charleston-Principles-Final.pdf.

National Association of State Charity Officials (NASCO). (2014). *Urban Institute selected to build single portal website.* Retrieved June 10, 2014, from http://www.nasconet.org/ urban-institute-selected-to-build-single-portal-website.

Network for Good. (2014). *The 2014 online survival guide.* Retrieved July 3, 2014, from http://www.networkfor good.org/OnlineFundraisingSurvivalGuide.html.

Newcomb, T. M. (1953). An approach to the study of communicative acts. *Psychological Review, 60*(6), 393–404.

Newman, D. S. (2005). *Nonprofit essentials: Endowment building.* Hoboken, NJ: Wiley.

Neyfakh, L. (2013, December 1). Donor-advised funds: Where charity goes to wait. *The Boston Globe*. http://www.bostonglobe.com/ideas/2013/12/01/donor-advised-funds-where-charity-goes-wait/tYa8P5trm6av9BnXPhyQTM/story.html.

NGOs: A long and turbulent history. (2013, January 24). *Global: The Global Journal*. Retrieved June 24, 2014, from http://theglobaljournal.net/group/digital-news/article/981.

No. 3: T. Denny Sanford. (2011, February 6). *Chronicle of Philanthropy*. Retrieved January 4, 2014, from http://philanthropy.com/article/No-3-T-Denny-Sanford.

Nonprofit Research Collaborative. (2011, September). Untitled report. Retrieved May 27, 2014, from www.guidestar.org/ViewCmsFile.aspx?ContentID = 3916.

Northwest Area Foundation website. http://www.nwaf.org.

O'Neill, M. (2002). *Nonprofit nation: A new look at the third America.* San Francisco: Jossey-Bass.

Osili, U. O., & Du, D. (2005). Immigrant assimilation and charitable giving. *New directions for philanthropic fundraising, 48,* 89–104.

Ostrower, F. (1995). *Why the wealthy give: The culture of elite philanthropy.* Princeton, NJ: Princeton University Press.

Ostrower, F. (2006, September). Foundation approaches to effectiveness: A typology. *Nonprofit and Voluntary Sector Quarterly, 35*(3), 510–516.

Ostrower, F. (2008). *Boards of midsize nonprofits: Their needs and challenges.* Washington, DC: Urban Institute.

Ostrower, F. (2009). *Limited life foundations: Motivations, experiences, and strategies.* Washington, DC: Urban Institute.

Overhead Myth. (n.d.). *Moving toward an overhead solution.* http://overheadmyth.com.

Pagnoni, L., & Solomon, M. (2013, November 12). Challenge gift drives and corporate matching gifts. *Nonprofit Quarterly.* Retrieved April 28, 2014, from https://nonprofitquarterly.org/philanthropy/23223-challenge-gift-drives-and-corporate-matching-gifts.html.

Pallotta, D. (2010). *Uncharitable: How restraints on nonprofits undermine their potential.* Lebanon, NH: Tufts University Press.

Panas, J. (1984). *Mega gifts: Who gives them, who gets them.* Chicago: Pluribus Press.

Partnership for Philanthropic Planning. (2011). *Gift planner profile 6.* Retrieved April 22, 2014, from http://www.pppnet.org/resource/gift-planner.html.

Partnership for Philanthropic Planning. (2012). *Are you ready for planned giving?* Retrieved July 7, 2014, from www.pppnet.org.

Partnership for Philanthropic Planning (PPP) website. http://www.pppnet.org.

Paton, R. (2007). Fundraising as marketing: Half a truth is better than nothing. In J. Mordaunt & R. Paton (Eds.), *Thoughtful fundraising: Concepts, issues, and perspectives* (pp. 29–37). New York: Routledge.

Payton, R. L. (1988). *Philanthropy: Voluntary action for the public good.* New York: Macmillan.

Peloza, J., & Steel, P. (2005). The price elasticity of charitable contributions: A meta-analysis. *Journal of Public Policy & Marketing, 24,* 260–272.

Pentecost, R., & Andrews, L. (2010). Differences between students and non-students' willingness to donate. *International Journal of Nonprofit and Voluntary Sector Marketing, 15,* 122–136.

Perry, S. (2012a, August 16). An economist's projections for how a new charity's fundraising would fare in the long run. *Chronicle of Philanthropy.* Retrieved June 3, 2014, from https://philanthropy.com/article/An-Economist-s-Projections/156213.

Perry, S. (2012b, August 16). Tough questions raised about a fundraising company's approach. *Chronicle of Philanthropy.* Retrieved June 3, 2014, from https://philanthropy.com/article/Tough-Questions-Raised-About-a/156211.

Perry, S. (2013, March 10). Former fundraiser now crusades against telemarketing firms. *Chronicle of Philanthropy.* http://philanthropy.com/article/Former-Fundraiser-Now-Crusades/137753.

Perry, S. (2014a, July 13). $25-Million settlement puts spotlight on veterans charity fundraising. *Chronicle of Philanthropy.* Retrieved October 14, 2014, from https://philanthropy.com/article/25-Million-Settlement-Puts/152885.

Perry, S. (2014b, December 17). Quadriga, accused of misleading donors, reorganizes under new name. *Chronicle of Philanthropy.* Retrieved January 28, 2015, from https://philanthropy.com/article/Quadriga-Accused-of/152059.

Pew Charitable Trusts website. http://www.pewtrusts.org/about_us_history.aspx.

Pfeffer, J. (2003). Introduction. In *External control of organizations: A resource dependence perspective* (Classic ed., pp. xi–xx). Palo Alto, CA: Stanford University Press.

Pfeffer, J., & Salancik, G. R. (1978). *The external control of organizations: A resource dependence perspective.* New York: Harper & Row.

Phills, J. A., Jr. (2005). *Integrating mission and strategy for nonprofit organizations.* New York: Oxford University Press.

Pierpont, R. (2003). Capital campaigns. In H. A. Rosso & Associates (E. A. Tempel, Ed.), *Achieving excellence in fund raising* (2nd ed., pp. 117–138). San Francisco: Jossey-Bass.

Pinchback, G. K. (2011). *Fundraising and community college chief executives: A study of development in the Southern Regional Education Board states.* Doctoral dissertation, Arkansas State University (UMI Number 3449291).

Poister, T. H. (2003). *Measuring performance in public and nonprofit organizations.* San Francisco: Jossey-Bass.

Porter, M. E., & Kramer, M. R. (2011, January/February). *Harvard Business Review, 89*(1/2), 62–77.

Poust, J. (2012, Spring). Prospect portfolios: Getting donors in the major gifts pipeline. *Considering Philanthropy.* Retrieved April 14, 2014, from http://www.brakeley briscoe.com/images/uploads/2012%20Spring%20Considering%20Philanthropy%20 Newsletter_1.pdf.

Pray, F. G. (Ed.). (1981). *Handbook for educational fund raising.* San Francisco: Jossey-Bass.

Preston, C. (2010, April 4). More charities enlist staff members to pitch in with fund raising. *Chronicle of Philanthropy.* Retrieved February 24, 2014, from http://philanthropy.com/ article/More-Charities-Enlist-Staff/64910.

Preston, C. (2011, March 6). A focus on signature programs can help charities gain grant makers' support. *Chronicle of Philanthropy.* Retrieved May 12, 2014, from https:// philanthropy.com/article/Seeking-Foundation-Grants-in/126573.

Preston, C., & Wallace, N. (2011, January 6). Charities report slow progress in Haiti, despite $1.4 billion raised in a year. *Chronicle of Philanthropy.* Retrieved January 29, 2015, from http://philanthropy.com/article/Charities-Face-Struggles-to/125847.

Prince, R. A., & File, K. M. (1994). *The seven faces of philanthropy: A new approach to cultivating major donors.* San Francisco: Jossey-Bass.

Program on NonProfit Organizations at Yale website. http://ponpo.som.yale.edu/hist .html.

Proper, E., Caboni, T. C., Hartley, H. V. III, & Willmer, W. K. (2009, July 9). More bang for the buck: Examining influencers of fundraising efficiency and total dollars raised. *International Journal of Educational Advancement, 9*(1), 35–41.

Rainey, H. G. (2003). *Understanding and managing public organizations* (3rd ed.). San Francisco: Jossey-Bass.

Raymond, J. (2009, October 13). Seeing red in pink products: One woman's fight against breast cancer consumerism. *Newsweek.* Retrieved April 29, 2014, from http://www .newsweek.com/seeing-red-pink-products-one-womans-fight-against-breast-cancer-consumerism-222566.

Regenovich, D. (2011). Establishing a planned giving program. In E. R. Tempel, T. L. Seiler, & E. E. Aldrich (Eds.), *Achieving excellence in fundraising* (3rd ed., pp. 139– 158). San Francisco: Jossey-Bass.

Report of Independent Auditors, Silicon Valley Community Foundation. (2012). Retrieved May 12, 2014, from http://www.siliconvalleycf.org/content/financial-data.

Rhode, D. L., & Packel, A. K. (2009, Summer). Ethics and nonprofits. *Stanford Social Innovation Review*. Retrieved June 17, 2014, from http://www.ssireview.org/articles/entry/ethics_and_nonprofits.

Ribar, D. C., & Wilhelm, M. O. (2002). Altruistic and joy-of-giving motivations in charitable behavior. *Journal of Political Economy, 110*(2), 425–457.

Riley v. National Federation of the Blind of North Carolina, Inc., 487 U.S. 781 (1988).

Robbins, K. C. (2006). The nonprofit sector in historical perspective: Traditions of philanthropy in the West. In W. W. Powell & R. Steinberg (Eds.), *The non-profit sector: A research handbook* (pp. 13–31). New Haven, CT: Yale University Press.

Roeger, K. L., Blackwood, A. S., & Pettijohn, S. J. (2012). *The nonprofit almanac, 2012.* Washington, DC: Urban Institute Press.

Rohde, D. (1997, September 19). Ted Turner plans a $1 billion gift for U.N. agencies. *New York Times*. Retrieved February 21, 2014, from http://www.nytimes.com/1997/09/19/world/ted-turner-plans-a-1-billion-gift-for-un-agencies.html.

Romero, S., & Lacey, M. (2010, January 12). Fierce quake devastates Haitian capital. *New York Times*. Retrieved December 26, 2014, from http://www.nytimes.com/2010/01/13/world/americas/13haiti.html?_r = 1.

Rondeau, D., & List, J. A. (2008, September). Matching and challenge gifts to charity: Evidence from laboratory and natural field experiments. *Experimental Economics, 11*(3), 253–267.

Rose-Ackerman, S. (1996). Altruism, nonprofits and economic theory. *Journal of Economic Literature, 34,* 701–728.

Rosso, H. A. (1991). Understanding the fund raising cycle. In H. A. Ross & Associates (Eds.), *Achieving excellence in fund raising* (pp. 8–16). San Francisco: Jossey-Bass.

Rosso, H. A. (2003). The annual fund. In H. A. Rosso & Associates (E. R. Tempel, Ed.), *Achieving excellence in fund raising* (2nd ed., pp. 71–88). San Francisco: Jossey-Bass.

Rosso, H. A. (2011a). A philosophy of fundraising. In E. R. Tempel, T. L. Seiler, & E. E. Aldrich (Eds.), *Achieving excellence in fundraising* (3rd ed., pp. 3–9). San Francisco: Jossey-Bass.

Rosso, H. A. (2011b). The annual fund. In E. R. Tempel, T. L. Seiler, & E. E. Aldrich (Eds.), *Achieving excellence in fundraising* (3rd ed., pp. 51–63). San Francisco: Jossey-Bass.

Rosso, H. A., & Associates. (Eds.). (1991). *Achieving excellence in fund raising.* San Francisco: Jossey-Bass.

Ryan, L. J. (2006, September 15). Behavioral characteristics of higher education fund-raisers. *International Journal of Educational Advancement, 6*(4), 282–288.

Sagawa, S., & Segal, E. (2000). *Common interest, common good: Creating value through business and social sector partnerships.* Cambridge, MA: Harvard Business School Press.

Sagrestano, B. M., & Wahlers, R. E. (2012). *The philanthropic planning companion: The fundraisers' and professional advisors' guide to charitable gift planning.* Hoboken, NJ: Wiley.

Salamon, L. M. (1999). *America's nonprofit sector: A primer* (2nd ed.) New York: Foundation Center.

Salamon, L. M., Sokolowski, S. W., & Associates. (2004). *Global civil society: Dimensions of the nonprofit sector* (Vol. 2). Bloomfield, CT: Kumarian Press.

Sargeant, A., & Jay, E. (2004). *Building donor loyalty*. San Francisco: Jossey-Bass.

Sargeant, A., & Kahler, J. (1999). Returns on fundraising expenditures in the voluntary sector. *Nonprofit Management and Leadership, 10*(1), 5–19.

Sargeant, A., & Shang, J. (2011, October). Bequest giving: Revisiting donor motivation with dimensional qualitative research. *Psychology & Marketing, 28*(10), 980–997.

Sargeant, A., Shang, J., & Associates. (2010). *Fundraising: Principles and practice*. San Francisco: Jossey-Bass.

Sauvé-Rodd, J. (2007, July–September). Donor profitability measurement. *Journal of Direct, Data, and Digital Marketing Practice, 9*(1), 47–67.

Scanlan, E. A. (2013). Public privacy: An exploration of issues of privacy and fundraising. In J. G. Pettey (Ed.), *Nonprofit fundraising strategy: A guide to ethical decision making and regulation for nonprofit organizations* (pp. 53–76). Hoboken, NJ: Wiley.

Scarpucci, P., & Lange, S. (2007, March). *Best practices in major gifts prospect management*. Presentation to the 44th annual AFP international conference. Retrieved April 10, 2014, from http://martsandlundy.com/reports-commentaries/ml-special-reports/2007/06/best-practices-in-major-gift-prospect-management.

Schein, E. H. (2010). *Organizational culture and leadership* (4th ed.). San Francisco: Jossey-Bass.

Schervish, P. G. (2006, September). The moral biography of wealth: Philosophical reflections on the foundation of philanthropy. *Nonprofit and Voluntary Sector Quarterly, 35*(3), 477–492.

Schervish, P. G. (2008). Why the wealthy give. In A. Sargeant & W. Wymer (Eds.), *The Routledge companion to nonprofit marketing* (pp. 165–181). New York: Routledge.

Schervish, P. G. (2009). *Beyond self-interest and altruism: Care as mutual nourishment*. Retrieved January 3, 2014, from http://www.conversationsonphilanthropy.org/wp-content/uploads/2009_entire_journal.pdf.

Schervish, P. G., & Havens, J. J. (2002, March). The new physics of philanthropy: The supply side vectors of charitable giving: Part II: The spiritual side of the supply side. *CASE International Journal of Educational Advancement, 2*(3), 221–241.

Schiller, R. J. (2013). *The chief development officer: Beyond fundraising*. Lanham, MD: Rowman and Littlefield.

Schroeder, F. W. (2003). The annual giving program. In M. J. Worth (Ed.), *New strategies for educational fund raising* (pp. 75–88). Westport, CT: Praeger and American Council on Education.

Schubert, F. D. (2002). Principal gifts. In M. J. Worth (Ed.), *New strategies for educational fund raising* (pp. 105–111). Westport, CT: Praeger and American Council on Education.

Sciolino, E. (2001a, May 26). Smithsonian group criticizes official on donor contract. *New York Times*, p. A8.

Sciolino, E. (2001b, May 30). Citing differences, director of a Smithsonian museum resigns. *New York Times*, p. A20.

Sciolino, E. (2001c, May 10). Smithsonian is promised $38 million, with strings. *New York Times*, p. A20.

Seiler, T. L. (2011a). The total development plan. In E. R. Tempel, T. L. Seiler, & E. E. Aldrich (Eds.), *Achieving excellence in fundraising* (3rd ed., pp. 41–50). San Francisco: Jossey-Bass.

Seiler, T. L. (2011b). Plan to succeeed. In E. R. Tempel, T. L. Seiler, & E. E. Aldrich (Eds.), *Achieving excellence in fundraising* (3rd ed., pp. 10–17). San Francisco: Jossey-Bass.

Seiler, T. L. (2011c). Developing a constituency for fundraising. In E. R. Tempel, T. L. Seiler, & E. E. Aldrich (Eds.), *Achieving excellence in fundraising* (3rd ed., pp. 18–26). San Francisco: Jossey-Bass.

Seiler, T. L., & Aldrich, E. E. (2011). Developing and articulating a case for support. In E. R. Tempel, T. L. Seiler, & E. E. Aldrich (Eds.), *Achieving excellence in fundraising* (3rd ed., pp. 27–40). San Francisco: Jossey-Bass.

Seldon, W. (2013, March 10). Donor collaboration can bring big results, but most philanthropists prefer to go solo. *Chronicle of Philanthropy.* Retrieved May 14, 2014, from http://philanthropy.com/article/How-Donors-Can-Learn-to/137781.

Seymour, H. J. (1966). *Designs for fund-raising.* New York: McGraw-Hill.

Shapiro, S. L. (2008). *Donor loyalty in college athletics: An analysis of relationship fundraising and service quality effects on donor retention.* Doctoral dissertation, University of Northern Colorado (UMI Number 3318413).

Sharf, S. (2014, February 5). Charitable giving grew 4.9% in 2013 as online donations picked up. *Forbes.* Retrieved July 18, 2014, from http://www.forbes.com/sites/samanthasharf/2014/02/05/charitable-giving-grew-in-2013-as-online-giving-picked-up.

Sharpe, R. F., Sr. (1999). *Planned giving simplified: The gift, the giver, and the gift planner.* New York: Wiley.

Sievers, B. R. (2010). Philanthropy's role in liberal democracy. *Journal of Speculative Philosophy, 24*(4), 380–398.

Silverman, W. K., Robertson, S. J., Middlebrook, J. L., & Drabman, R. S. (1984). An investigation of pledging behavior to a national charitable telethon. *Behavior Therapy, 15,* 304–311.

Simmel, L. L., & Berger, P. D. (2000, Summer). The art of the ask: Maximizing verbal compliance in telefundraising. *Journal of Interactive Marketing, 14*(3), 12–40.

Simon, K. (2014, May 24). Charity and social enterprise in China. *Alliance Magazine.* Retrieved June 27, 2014, from http://philanthropynews.alliancemagazine.org/2014/05/24/charity-and-social-enterprise-in-china.

Sloan, M. F. (2009, March 6). The effects of nonprofit accountability ratings on donor behavior. *Nonprofit and Voluntary Sector Quarterly, 38*(2), 220–236.

Small, L. M. (2001, May 31). Mr. Smithson's was the first. *Washington Post,* p. A25.

Smith, C. (1994, May/June). The new corporate philanthropy. *Harvard Business Review, 72,* 105–116.

Smith, G. T. (1977). The development program. In A. W. Rowland (Gen. Ed.), *Handbook of institutional advancement.* San Francisco: Jossey-Bass.

Smith, J. P. (1993). Rethinking the traditional capital campaign. In M. J. Worth (Ed.), *Educational fund raising: Principles and practice* (pp. 167–177). Phoenix, AZ: Oryx Press and American Council on Education.

Smith, Z. (2010, September). Assessing educational fundraisers for competence and fit rather than experience: A challenge to conventional hiring practice [Special issue, human capital management]. *International Journal of Educational Advancement, 10*(2), 87–97.

Soskis, B. (2013, November 21). Parks and accumulation. *The New Yorker.* Retrieved July 28, 2014, from http://www.newyorker.com/news/news-desk/parks-and-accumulation.

Sparks, E. (2012, Fall). Philanthropy on the green. *Philanthropy.* Retrieved July 28, 2014, from http://www.philanthropyroundtable.org/topic/excellence_in_philanthropy/philanthropy_on_the_green.

Speckbacher, G. (2013, October). The use of incentives in nonprofit organizations. *Nonprofit and Voluntary Sector Quarterly, 42*(5), 1006–1025.

Spegele, B. (2010, July 12). Group aims to add transparency to China's charities. *Wall Street Journal China.* Retrieved June 27, 2014, from http://blogs.wsj.com/chinarealtime/2010/07/12/group-aims-to-add-transparency-to-chinas-charities.

Sprinkel-Grace, K. (2005). *Beyond fundraising:New strategies for nonprofit innovation and investment* (2nd ed.). Hoboken, NJ: Wiley.

Squadron, D. L. (2013, May 24). Can a tree grow in the Bronx? *New York Times*. Retrieved July 28, 2014, from http://www.nytimes.com/2013/05/25/opinion/can-a-tree-grow-in-brooklyn.html?_r = 0.

SR International. (2010). *Integrated partnership: City Year and Timberland*. Retrieved May 4, 2014, from http://srint.org/2010/11/01/integrated-partnership-cityyear-and-timberland.

Stannard-Stockton, S. (2011, March 29). The three core approaches to effective philanthropy. *Stanford Social Innovation Review*. Retrieved July 16, 2014, from http://www.ssireview.org/blog/entry/the_three_core_approaches_to_effective_philanthropy.

Steinberg, R. (1994). Economics and philanthropy: A marriage of necessity for nonprofit organizations. In J. M. Greenfield (Ed.), *Financial practices for effective fundraising (New directions for philanthropic fundraising, no. 3)* (pp. 7–25). San Francisco: Jossey-Bass.

Steinberg, R. (2010, September). *The lifetime value of donors to DVNF (Final report)*. Retrieved June 8, 2014, from http://img.2dialog.com/dvnf/custom/studio_main/doc/lifetime_value.dvnf.9.10.10.pdf.

Stelter Company. (2012). *2012 Stelter donor insight report: What makes them give?* Retrieved April 19, 2014, from http://www.stelter.com/research-whitepapers/WhatMakesThemGive-2012Research.pdf.

Stovall, W. M. (2004). *A case study of presidents' approaches to fundraising at four private and public historically black colleges and universities*. Doctoral dissertation, University of Missouri-Columbia (UMI Number 3144461).

Strom, S. (2003, November 7). Pew Charitable Trusts will become public charity. *New York Times*. Retrieved May 8, 2014, from http://www.nytimes.com/2003/11/07/us/pew-charitable-trusts-will-become-public-charity.html.

Stroup, S. S. (2012). *Borders among activists: International NGOs in the United States, Britain, and France*. Ithaca, NY: Cornell University Press.

Strout, E. (2007, February 2). What's the big idea? *Chronicle of Higher Education, 53*(22), A21.

Sullivan, P. (2013, October 14). Marketing vs. fundraising: Which is it? *The NonProfit Times*. Retrieved October 14, 2014, from http://www.thenonprofittimes.com/news-articles/marketing-vs-fundraising-which-is-it.

Tarnside. (2014). *Major donor development*. http://www.tarnside.co.uk/major_donor_development.php.

Tempel, E. R. (2011). Ethical frameworks for fundraising. In E. R. Tempel, T. L. Seiler, & E. E. Aldrich (Eds.), *Achieving excellence in fundraising* (3rd ed., pp. 395–412). San Francisco: Jossey-Bass.

Tempel, E. R. (2013). Tainted money. In J. G. Pettey (Ed.), *Nonprofit fundraising strategy: A guide to ethical decision making and regulation for nonprofit organizations* (pp. 79–107). Hoboken, NJ: Wiley.

Tempel, E. R., Seiler, T. L., & Aldrich, E. E. (Eds.). (2011). *Achieving excellence in fundraising* (3rd ed.). San Francisco: Jossey-Bass.

Thelin, J. R. (2013). The Gates Foundation's uncertain legacy. *Chronicle of Higher Education*. Retrieved May 9, 2014, from http://chronicle.com/article/The-Gates-Foundations/140293.

The twist to this pro-bono campaign? The rights are priced. (2014, January 21) *New York Times*. Retrieved July 17, 2014, from http://www.nytimes.com/2014/01/21/business/media/the-twist-to-this-pro-bono-campaign-the-rights-are-priced.html?ref = philanthropy&_r = 2.

Thomas, D. C. (2002). *Essentials of international management.* Thousand Oaks, CA: Sage.

Thompson, B. (2002, January 20). History for sale. *Washington Post,* pp. 14–22, 25–29.

Thompson, F. G. (2012, March/April). Corporate partnerships for nonprofits: A match made in heaven? *Nonprofit World, 30*(2), 6–9.

Triner, S. (2013). Australia and New Zealand. In P. Cagney & B. Ross (Eds.), *Global fundraising: How the world is changing the rules of philanthropy* (pp. 135–152). Hoboken, NJ: Wiley.

UMD Right Now. (2013). *University of Maryland hits $1 billion fundraising goal.* http://www.umdrightnow.umd.edu/news/university-maryland-hits-1-billion-fundraising-goal.

United Nations. (2012). *The millenium development goals report, 2012.* Retrieved July 10, 2012, from http://www.un.org/millenniumgoals/pdf/MDG%20Report%202012.pdf.

United Nations Foundation. (2012). *Global reach, global connections, global change, 2011–2012.* Retrieved February 21, 2014, from http://globalproblems-globalsolutions-files.org/gpgs_files/unf_website/pdf/globalreach12_UNF.pdf.

University of South Alabama press release (2013, May 3). Retrieved February 20, 2014, from http://www.southalabama.edu/publicrelations/pressreleases/2013pr/050313.html.

University of South Alabama website. http://www.southalabama.edu.

Uo, M. T. (2013). Japan. In P. Cagney & B. Ross (Eds.), *Global fundraising: How the world is changing the rules of philanthropy* (pp. 43–58). Hoboken, NJ: Wiley.

Urban Institute and Association of Fundraising Professionals. (2013). *2013 fundraising effectiveness survey report.* Retrieved June 2, 2014, from http://www.urban.org/publications/412906.html.

Varian, H. R. (1994). Sequential provision of public goods. *Journal of Public Economics, 53,* 165–186.

Verini, J. (2009, May). What meth made this billionaire do. *Fast Company, 135,* 84–89.

Vesterlund, L. (2003, March). The informational value of sequential fundraising. *Journal of Public Economics, 87*(3–4), 627–657.

Vögele, S. (1992). *Handbook of direct mail: The dialogue method of direct written sales communication.* New York: Prentice Hall.

Vroom, V. H. (1964). *Work and motivation.* New York: Wiley.

Wagner, L. (2004). Fundraising, culture, and the U.S. perspective. In L. Wagner & J. A. Galindo (Eds.), *Global perspectives on fundraising* (New Directions for Philanthropic Fundraising, No. 46, pp. 5–12). Hoboken, NJ: Wiley.

Wagner, L. (2011). Ethnicity and giving. In E. R. Tempel, T. L. Seiler, & E. E. Aldrich (Eds.), *Achieving excellence in fundraising* (3rd ed., pp. 183–198). San Francisco: Jossey-Bass.

Wallace, N. (2014, March 23). From billboards to bus shelters to email, charities try one message. *Chronicle of Philanthropy.* http://philanthropy.com/article/From-Billboards-to-Bus/145415.

Warwick, M. (2011). Direct mail marketing. In E. R. Tempel, T. L. Seiler, & E. E. Aldrich (Eds.), *Achieving excellence in fundraising* (3rd ed., pp. 223–234). San Francisco: Jossey-Bass.

Warwick, M. (2013). *How to write successful fundraising appeals* (3rd ed.) San Francisco: Jossey-Bass.

Waters, R. D., Kelly, K. S., & Walker, M. L. (2012). Organizational roles enacted by healthcare fundraisers. *Communication Management, 16*(3), 244–263.

Watson, T. (2013a, December 4). Inside the #GivingTuesday numbers: Will American philanthropy grow? *Forbes.* http://www.forbes.com/fdc/welcome_mjx.shtml.

Watson, T. (2013b, November 29). Five days for programmed consumers: Eat, shop, shop small, shop online . . . oh yeah, then give. *Forbes.* http://www.forbes.com/sites/tomwatson/2013/11/29/five-days-for-programmed-consumers-eat-shop-shop-small-shop-online-oh-yeah-then-give.

Wealth Engine. (2013). *Measuring fundraising return on investment and the impact of wealth intelligence.* Retrieved June 2, 2014, from info.wealthengine.com/measuring-fundraising-roi-apra.html.

Weinstein, S. (2009). *The complete guide to fundraising management.* Hoboken, NJ: Wiley.

Weisbrod, B. A. (1975). Toward a theory of the voluntary non-profit sector in a three-sector economy. In E. S. Phelps (Ed.), *Altruism, morality, and economic theory* (pp. 171–195). New York: Russell Sage Foundation.

Weisbrod, B. A. (1988). *The nonprofit economy.* Cambridge, MA: Harvard University Press.

Wei-Skillern, J., Silver, N., & Heitz, E. (n.d.). *Cracking the network code: Four principles for grantmakers.* Washington, DC: Grantmakers for Effective Organizations.

West, M. (2012, April 15). Red Cross makes a shift to stabilize revenue and give local leaders a bigger voice. *Chronicle of Philanthropy.* https://philanthropy.com/article/Red-Cross-Gives-Local-Leaders/156719.

Westmoreland, M. B. (2014). *Five ways technology will shape the nonprofit sector in 2014.* Retrieved June 4, 2014, from https://www.blackbaud.com/files/resources/downloads/2014/01.14.NonprofitTechTrends.tipsheet.pdf.

Whelan, D. (2007, September 22). Dying broke. *Forbes.* Retrieved January 4, 2014, from http://www.forbes.com/forbes/2007/1008/232.html.

Whetten, D. A., & Cameron, K. S. (2011). *Developing management skills* (8th ed.). Upper Saddle River, NJ: Prentice Hall.

Williams, G. (2002, January 10). Former senator chosen to direct Red Cross fund. *Chronicle of Philanthropy.* Retrieved June 17, 2014, from http://philanthropy.com/article/Former-Senator-Chosen-to/51951.

Williams, K. (2004). *Donor focused strategies for annual giving.* Sudbury, MA: Jones and Bartlett.

Wine, E. (2014, January). The massive potential and frustrating pitfalls of big data: Are prospect research services worth the cost? *Currents.* Retrieved March 6, 2014, from http://www.case.org.

Wing, K., Hager, M. A., Rooney, P. M., & Pollak, T. (2004). *Lessons for boards from the nonprofit overhead cost project.* Retrieved May 30, 2014, from http://www.urban.org/UploadedPDF/411119_NOCP_Guide_2.pdf.

Wolfman-Arent, A., & Switzer, C. (2014, August 29). Chart: Gifts from ice bucket challenge exceed $100 million. *Chronicle of Philanthropy.* Retrieved October 19, 2014, from https://philanthropy.com/article/Chart-Gifts-From-Ice-Bucket/152721.

Worth, M. J. (2002). *New strategies for educational fund raising.* Westport, CT: Praeger and American Council on Education.

Worth, M. J. (2005). *Securing the future.* Washington, DC: Association of Governing Boards of Universities and Colleges.

Worth, M. J. (2008). *Sounding boards: Advisory councils in higher education.* Washington, DC: Association of Governing Boards of Universities and Colleges.

Worth, M. J. (2010). *Leading the campaign.* Lanham, MD: Rowman & Littlefield and American Council on Education.

Worth, M. J. (2012). *Foundations for the future.* Washington, DC: Association of Governing Boards of Universities and Colleges.

Worth, M. J. (2014). *Nonprofit management: Principles and practice* (3rd ed.). Thousand Oaks, CA: Sage.

Worth, M. J., & Asp, J. (1994). *The development officer in higher education: Toward an understanding of the role. ASHE-ERIC Higher Education Report No. 4.* Washington, DC: The George Washington University Graduate School of Education and Human Development.

Yi, D. T. (2010). Determinants of fundraising efficiency of nonprofit organizations: Evidence from US public charitable organizations. *Managerial and Decision Economics, 31*(7), 465–475.

Young, D. R. (1983). *If not for profit, for what? A behavioral theory of the nonprofit sector based on entrepreneurship.* Lanham, MD: Lexington Books.

Yu, Y. (2010, September 30). *The dilemmas facing one foundation.* University of Nottingham China Policy Institute. Retrieved June 27, 2014, from http://www.nottingham.ac.uk/cpi/china-analysis/china-policy-institute-blog/2010-entries/charity-30-09-2010.aspx.

Zinsmeister, K. (n.d.). *Osceola McCarty (Philanthropy Roundtable Hall of Fame).* Retrieved December 30, 2013, from http://www.philanthropyroundtable.org/almanac/great_men_and_women/hall_of_fame/oseola_mccarty.

Zuckerberg commits $1-billion more to Silicon Valley community fund. (2013, December 19). *Chronicle of Philanthropy.* Retrieved January 13, 2014, from http://www.philanthropy.com/article/Zuckerberg-Gives-1-Billion/143691.

Zunz, O. (2012). *Philanthropy in America: A history.* Princeton, NJ: Princeton University Press.

Index